The Destruction of Flight CY284

Other books by Simon Hepworth

Late Shift (a paranormal crime novel)

The Dark Part of the Sky (an anthology of Bomber Command ghost stories)

Striking Through Clouds (with Andrew Porrelli)

Nothing Can Stop Us (with Andrew Porrelli and Harry Dison)

514 Squadron Profile (with Chris Ward)

The Beach Boys (with Andrew Porrelli and Roger Guernon)

*All are published by Mention the War Ltd.
Visit www.bombercommand books.com for full details.*

The Destruction of Flight CY284

Simon Hepworth

With Greek Translation by Fanoulla Argyrou

www.bombercommandbooks.com

First Published in the UK 2022 by Mention the War Limited, 25 Cromwell Street, Merthyr Tydfil, Wales, CF47 8RY.

This is an abridged version of the original book in English, Bealine Charlie Oscar – Flight CY284: The Real Story Behind a Forgotten Atrocity with Greek translation by Fanoulla Argyrou.

Copyright © 2018 - 2022 Simon Hepworth.

The right of Simon Hepworth to be identified as the Author of this work is asserted by him in accordance with the Copyright, Designs and Patents Act 1988.

The publisher and author acknowledge the role of the National Archives in Kew, London, in preserving and making available documents relating to the investigation into the loss of flight CY284. Access to the material, and reproduction thereof in this book, is under the National Archives Open Licence V2.0. All documentation and images reproduced in this book are accessed under Open Licence V2.0 unless otherwise stated.

The author and publisher have used their best endeavours to present information passed to them in the correct context, and in good faith. Wherever possible, all such information is directly attributed, except where the original source cannot be ascertained, or wishes to remain anonymous. In the latter case, it is presented as such where it is believed to be directly relevant to the account. Any person objecting to such information being attributed to them is invited to contact the publisher at mtwpublications@gmail.com.

All rights reserved. No part of this publication may be reproduced or transmitted, in any form or by any means, without permission of the publishers or author, except for brief quotes used in reviews. To contact the publisher, please write to the address above or email mtwpublications@gmail.com

A copy of this work is available through the British Library.

Cover design: Topics – The Creative Partnership Ltd.

ISBN: 978-1915335050

This book is dedicated to the 66 passengers and crew

of Cyprus Airways flight CY284,

lost when Comet 4B G-ARCO crashed in the Mediterranean

at about 0325hrs GMT on 12th October 1967,

and to their families and friends,

who have never forgotten them.

Crew

Captain Gordon Blackwood, BEA
Senior First Officer Dennis Palmer, BEA
Senior First Officer Michael Thomas, BEA

Senior Steward John Loizou, Cyprus Airways
Stewardess Thelma Efremi, Cyprus Airways
Stewardess Popi Fottou, Cyprus Airways
Steward Nicos Hasapopoulos, Cyprus Airways

Passengers

Mr. Achilleas Afatitis
Mrs. Reveka Afatitis
Mrs. Constantina Christaki
Police Sergeant Rodosthenis Christou
Miss Josephine Coldicott, BEA
Miss Mary Dalton
Mr. Constantinos Efstathiou
Mr. Elias Evgeros
Miss Areti Exarcheas
Miss Jean Falconer
Mr. Sotiris Georgiou
Mr. Hugh Griffiths
Mrs. Lily Griffiths
Mrs. Anastasia Harbstreet
Dr. George Ioannides
Mr. John Jakouris
Mrs. Margaret Joyce
Mrs. Iphigenia Kalogeropoulou
Miss Despina Karakosta
Mr. Charalambos Kontominas

Mrs. Stavroula Kontominas
Mrs. Eleni Koutroubinis
Mr. Georgios Koutroubinis
Mrs. Katerina Liassides
Miss Eleni Markidou
Mr. Vasilios Markidis
Mrs. Lily Marlborough
Mrs. Elaine McComb
Infant Roydon George McComb
Mr. Roydon John McComb
Master Andreas Nicolaides
Mrs. Irinoula Nicolaides
Mr. Loizos Nicolaides
Mrs. Maureen O'Brien
Mr. Michael O'Brien
Mr. Konstantinos Paleologos
Mrs. Theognosia Paleologos
Mrs. Melanie Papaioannou
Mrs. Eirini Papanicolaou
Mr. Nicos Papapetrou

Miss Maria Parzopoulou
Mr. Nicolas Peters
Mr. David Powell
Miss Dorothea Rachovidou
Mr. Ioannis Rigou
Miss Elpiniki Rodosthenous
Mr. William Sheris
Miss Hilary Smith, BEA
Mr. Avraam Solomou
Mrs. Anna Stewart
Mrs. Rosalie Stone
Master Guy Tasker
Mrs. Jan Tasker
Mr. Gerasimos Thiakou
Mrs. Polixeni Thiakou
Mr. Michael Thomaides
Miss Irini Voliotou
Mrs. Paraskevi Vougioukas
Miss Joyce White, BEA

Contents

Forewords 9
Author's Note 11
'An Uneventful Flight' 13
66 Souls on Board 17
Into the Night 27
'The Most Amazing Type of Accident' 30
In Deep Water 42
Bodies of Evidence 44
'The Answer Lies Somewhere Amongst This List' 51
The Bomb Theory 55
Probable Cause Established 64
The Final Report is Produced 78
Scotland Yard Investigates 82
Lines of Enquiry 98
Persons of Interest 103
Watching the Detectives 117
Analysis 124
Who Bombed Charlie Oscar? 133
Conclusion 151
Acknowledgements 155
CY284 Passengers and Crew List - Κατάλογος πληρώματος και επιβατών CY284 213
Correspondence between Police and Foreign Office – Αλληλογραφία μεταξύ Αστυνομίας και Υπουργείου Εξωτερικών 217

Πρόλογοι 225

Σε Προσωπικό Σημείωμα 228

«Μια πτήση χωρίς προβλήματα» 230

66 Ψυχές στο Αεροπλάνο 235

Μέσα στην νύχτα 246

Στα Βαθιά Νερά 250

Πτώματα Αποδείξεων 253

«Η απάντηση βρίσκεται κάπου ανάμεσα σε αυτήν τη λίστα» 261

Η θεωρία της βόμβας 265

Διαπιστώθηκε η πιθανή αιτία 275

Εκδόθηκε η Τελική Έκθεση 289

Η Scotland Yard ερευνά 293

Γραμμές έρευνας 311

Πρόσωπα Ενδιαφέροντος 317

Παρακολουθώντας τους Ντετέκτιβ 333

Αναλύσεις και Συμπεράσματα 340

Ποιος βομβάρδισε το Charlie Oscar; 350

Συμπέρασμα 371

Ευχαριστίες 376

About the Author - Σχετικά με τον Συγγραφέα 382

Forewords

It was a great pleasure to meet Simon Hepworth and his son William at the National Archives of the United Kingdom at Kew Gardens in Surrey. It was also a privilege to join forces with Simon with the difficult aim of digging deeper in pursuit of a 'daunting task': trying to find some equitable answers to the unanswered questions which, for more than 50 years, have confronted the relatives of the deceased victims of the bombing resulting in the crash of Bealine Charlie Oscar, otherwise known Cyprus Airways Flight CY 284, on 12 October 1967.

What exactly happened to Flight CY284 on 12 October 1967? Why was it bombed? And who was responsible?

My research into this immense tragedy had originally been prompted by Michael Thomaides whose father was one of the 66 persons killed by the bombing. As a result, and having studied all the files available at the time at the National Archives of the United Kingdom in Kew Gardens in Surrey, we published our findings in a joint article in 2011 in London-based Greek community weekly *Eleftheria*, i.e. *Freedom*, at www.eleftheria.co.uk.

As events were to unfold, Simon joined our efforts. He did so quite by chance having contacted Michael Thomaides following a posting on the *Pprune* forum (The Professional Pilots Rumour Network). Michael put me in touch with Simon and, thus, our cooperation over this matter began in the Reading Rooms of the National Archives in Kew, this unique 'store of knowledge and official documentation' as I call this magnificent institution which I first visited back in the mid-1980s and have never stopped visiting ever since.

I take this opportunity to thank the staff at the National Archives for their role in helping to facilitate the research behind this book.

Simon Hepworth's experience in policing and aviation was heaven sent for me, as well as for Michael and for the other relatives of the victims of this tragedy. The involvement of Simon enhanced our search to uncover the truth behind the bombing of Bealine Charline Oscar, who was responsible and why. Simon knew more than I did about aircraft accident investigations, methodology and procedures. He also has ties to the police and experience of police investigations and criminal intelligence. Simon's background not only proved to be an important tool for us. It also became the key to explaining complex methods which Michael and I were not familiar with.

Vivid proof of Simon's experience and knowledge is to be found in his composition – in a relatively short time – of this remarkable book. It draws upon almost all of the official documents in the released files at Kew plus many more from other sources.

In a sensitive and serious way, the book addresses the questions identified above. It comes close to providing proper answers and, in so doing, is richly illustrated in ways which brings to life the turbulent period of history when the bombing took place. The book ends with a fair set of conclusions based on the information available in the public domain at the time of writing.

I pray that the book prompts anybody 'in the know' to come forward and fill the remaining gaps. I also hope that the book spurs those in power to disclose the outstanding official documentation which remains classified. By such means, justice may be served, even if belatedly.

The book is humbly dedicated to the 66 passengers and crew who perished on Cyprus Airways Flight CY284 and to their families and friends who have never forgotten them. The book is also dedicated to Cyprus Airways, the much-loved airline of my native country which I had the most memorable pleasure to serve for almost six years from 1965 until 1971, the year in which I settled permanently in London.

Simon Hepworth, thank you.

Fanoulla Argyrou
Researcher/journalist/author, London 22 September 2018

***

At the age of 36 my father, Michalakis Thomaides, was a successful businessman in Cyprus when he so unfairly lost his life along with other 65 passengers and crew on Cyprus Airways flight CY 284 on 12th October 1967 at Kastellorizo, Greece.

May they always Rest in Peace!

We, the wives, husbands, children and grandchildren, will remember them with love and we will never stop to fight for justice for the killing of 66 innocent people by someone we believe must have been a cowardly fanatic.

Thanks to Simon Hepworth and Fanoulla Argyrou for the whole research and investigation they have done through the British National Archives and for publishing this book!

Maria-Niki M Thomaides
Daughter of deceased passenger Michalakis Thomaides

Author's Note

I remember the day of the crash very clearly. Eight years old at the time, I had been at school where teacher had focussed on what we were told was the discovery of America by Christopher Columbus on that day, in 1492. When my sisters and I got home, Gordon Blackwood's car, a steel blue Singer saloon, was parked in the lane at the end of our drive.

My mother was sitting by the kitchen window waiting for us. Walking into the house, I asked her what was wrong, and she told us that Gordon had been killed. He had been a close friend and a near neighbour of our family, as well as a colleague of my father, at that time a First Officer with BEA on the Trident fleet. My mother, under questioning from us as to what had happened, told us simply that his aircraft had crashed, and it would be on the television news. It all seemed so unfair, as it did to the many other people affected by the tragedy.

Over the next few months, the disaster was mentioned sporadically, then infrequently, eventually fading from the news and, for the most part, from public awareness. My parents spoke warmly of Gordon for the rest of their lives and kept in contact with Joyce Blackwood for the rest of hers.

In 1981, by then working for British Aerospace, I found a copy of the Accidents Investigation Branch report in the technical library. At least it told me what had happened, though not why. The advent of the internet, and my growing interest in writing aviation books, led me to start looking into the *Charlie Oscar* incident in greater depth. I had used the resources of the National Archives in London when researching the disappearance of my great uncle and his crew in their Lancaster in 1944. In the intervening half century, access to documents and other information had made it possible to lift the veil of secrecy which seemed, to my mind, to have settled over the whole affair.

I therefore admit to a wholly personal motive in writing this book. There was never any true closure for the family and friends of the 66 people who lost their lives in the Mediterranean just before dawn on 12th October 1967. As a child, the loss of someone close to our family circle made a very significant impact. My sense of loss, though, is nothing compared to that of the spouses, children and siblings of the victims. The half-century of silence has made this all the harder to bear. I dedicate this book to the 66 and their families.

Simon Hepworth

'An Uneventful Flight'

"Good morning Nicky, Bealine Golf Alpha Romeo Charlie Osc…[1]"

Senior First Officer Mike Thomas, co-pilot of a British European Airways Comet 4B airliner, did not get the chance to finish his opening message to Nicosia Air Traffic Control. Exactly why he was cut off in mid-sentence will never be known, but between two and seven minutes later his life was tragically ended.

The weather had been the usual autumnal low cloud and drizzle as Captain Blackwood and his fellow flight deck crew, along with their 38 passengers, plus one cat resting in splendid solitude in its pet carrier in the rear hold, had started their journey from London's Heathrow airport at 10.45pm UK time the previous evening. The first leg of the flight, operating as British European Airways flight BE284, was to Ellinikon airport, Athens. The aircraft would then fly on to Nicosia, Cyprus, on behalf of Cyprus Airways, operating as CY284[2]. BE/CY284 was a routine scheduled service, flying the route four times a week. As well as the passengers, their luggage and the cat, small, high-value items of freight were conveyed in the hold. On this flight, as a national carrier, BEA was also entrusted with the Royal Mail.

As the Comet climbed through the cloud to clearer air above, the passengers settled back to relax during the flight to Athens, whilst the cabin staff prepared to offer coffee, tea and refreshments. The flight was

---

[1] *'Bealine' was the airline callsign used by British European Airways. 'Golf Alpha Rome Charlie Oscar' was the phonetic form of the registration letters of the aircraft, G-ARCO. This registration was in sequence on the British Civil Aircraft Register rather than having any special significance. The crew having introduced themselves to each Air Traffic Control service en route with the full call-sign and ensuring that there was no other aircraft with a similar callsign that might cause confusion, subsequent transmissions were abbreviated, variously, to 'Golf Charlie Oscar', 'Bealine Charlie Oscar' or simply 'Charlie Oscar'.*

[2] *Cyprus Airways, the Cypriot flag carrier, was a fledgling airline as indeed Cyprus was a newly-independent nation. As a legacy of Britain's long association with the Mediterranean island, BEA owned a 22.7% shareholding in Cyprus Airways and was supporting it by operating jets on a number of major routes on its behalf, including the that between Nicosia and Athens. This route was politically the most significant for the majority of Cypriots, who were of Greek ethnicity. Enosis, union with the Hellenic motherland, was still the ultimate goal of many Cypriot politicians, though there were others on the island, especially amongst the second largest ethnic group, of Turkish heritage, who most certainly did not share that dream.*

scheduled to take just under three and a half hours. BEA ran the service as a Night Tourist flight, the prestige first class cabin remaining unoccupied. The service was aimed at people for whom the inconvenience of flying in the middle of the night was compensated for by the reduced fares.[3]

Charlie Oscar completed the first leg of the trip and landed at Athens at 0111hrs, GMT, 0311hrs local time and four minutes ahead of schedule. While Charlie Oscar was prepared for her flight to Nicosia, a further 31 passengers had joined the flight at Athens.

On this second sector, SFO Thomas would act as co-pilot, handling the throttles, radio communications and navigation whilst Captain Blackwood flew the aircraft. SFO Palmer sat behind the two other pilots, his role on this flight being to manage the aircraft's complex systems and monitor the two pilots flying the aircraft.

The 75-minute turnround gave the passengers and crew chance to stretch their legs in the terminal. With the exception of three passengers and the captain, all those traveling onwards to Nicosia took advantage of the opportunity. For security and safety reasons, the passengers could not be left alone on the aircraft. So that he could monitor the activity of the cleaners and caterers, as well as deal with the paperwork for the next sector, Captain Blackwood sat in the first-class cabin during the turnround.

During the first sector, which was later to be described in the press simply as 'an uneventful flight', the only technical issue to bother Captain Blackwood was a fault with one of the aircraft's compass sets. This was part of the Comet's instrument landing system but was duplicated so had not presented any serious problems. He had made an entry in the aircraft technical log and reported it to the duty engineer, Mr. N. Karaindros, at Athens. In turn, Mr. Karaindros, who was employed by Olympic Airways and was in charge of the servicing crew, directed Mr. A. Kalesidis, an instrument specialist, to deal with the defective instrument.

Mr. Kalesidis carried out a check and minor adjustment and the instrument now appeared to work. He made an appropriate entry in the tech log and explained to Captain Blackwood that the instrument now appeared to be serviceable.

Meanwhile, the rest of the ground staff continued with the routine tasks involved in preparing Charlie Oscar for the onward flight to Nicosia. Mr.

---

[3] *The Tourist Excursion return fare on flight 284 was £76 8s to Athens and £85 to Nicosia. The single fares were £56 4s and £65 respectively, so for passengers intending to travel two ways, the night flight represented something of a bargain. £85 in 1967 prices equates to an impressive £1,500 in 2018. The average UK wage at the time was £891 p.a. or £74 5s (£74.25) a month so flying was not yet an affordable means of travel for most people. Source: BEA.*

D Argymou oversaw pre-departure checks, including the refuelling. He was assisted in the checks by Mr. A. Anagousto, an aircraft mechanic; both men were satisfied that there were no outstanding defects.

Mr. George Diamandaras, BEA's Traffic and Administration officer, was responsible for looking after passenger handling.

Several other BEA staff were involved in servicing Charlie Oscar on the ground at Athens. Mr. Sabellarion serviced the toilets and loaded suitcases into the no. 2 hold; Mr. Pagonis, a Traffic Clerk, ensured that cargo, including newspapers, mail and a consignment of shoes, was correctly loaded, the weight amounting to 328kg. The cargo also included four packages of handbags, merchandise believed to belong to a Cyprus Airways Senior Steward, Frixos Michael. In Hold 2 were 24 pieces of baggage and twenty bags of mail. The mail loaded at Athens had originated at various locations across Europe, as well as New York. Part of the mail consignment was for the United Nations mission in Cyprus. Hold 3 contained eight pieces of baggage, uplifted at Heathrow and belonging to last minute passengers, including three BEA staff traveling off duty. A further eighteen or nineteen bags, belonging to London-originating passengers were in Hold 4. Finally, in Hold 5, were the remainder of the London bags, totalling sixteen or seventeen, along with some 500 kilogrammes of freight. There was nothing unremarkable or sinister about any of the cargo, which now joined the cat on its journey.

Mr. Morsetakis, Traffic Officer, prepared the ship's papers, which he handed to Captain Blackwood, then left the aircraft once the loadsheet was signed. Michael Zographos, Operations Officer, obtained the weather folder and put in a flight plan, which had been prepared by Olympic Airways. He had a conversation with Captain Blackwood, who was sitting near the galley entrance to the cabin. The captain signed the flight plan and fuel load.

Captain Blackwood checked the details of the en-route weather, which gave generally fine and clear conditions, with some scattered cloud well below the planned cruising altitude of 29,000 feet, with a small probability of cumulonimbus clouds from 3,000 to 30,000 feet. There was no expectation of icing or turbulence. At Nicosia, there would be scattered cloud at about 5,000 feet with visibility up to 40 kilometres. Overall, the weather did not look like it would cause any problems.

Mr. Televantos was the loader and tractor driver. From Customs, he took the bags belonging to the Athens-Nicosia passengers to the aircraft, though he did not carry out any loading himself.

Mr. Kalaitzis, Catering Loader, brought trays from the Catering Section and collected from the airport restaurant flasks containing the breakfasts that would be served on the Nicosia sector. Assisted by Mr. Chiladakis, he loaded the trays and flasks on to Charlie Oscar.

Cleaning the aircraft cabin was carried out by Mr. Lemneon, who noted that some passengers remained on board, almost certainly the three referred to by other staff.

Checking the cabin staff and loading the passengers was the responsibility of Mr. Carnemidas, Tarmac Controller. He was aware that the three passengers and Captain Blackwood were still onboard, therefore a guard was left on the aircraft during refuelling in case of a safety incident requiring their evacuation.

BEA's Duty Officer, Mr. C. Coliandris, did not meet Captain Blackwood. In his report he noted he had overheard Mr. Karaindros, the Olympic Airways engineer, comment something to the effect that "…some sheets were missing from the Technical Log." He had taken this up with Mr. Karaindros, who clarified the matter, explaining that there had been a minor error in adding up the flying hours on the paperwork, which he had corrected.

Mr. Coliandris went on to note that the Charlie Oscar departed for Nicosia at 0425hrs local time, five minutes earlier than scheduled.

66 Souls on Board

Captain Gordon Blackwood, 45, from Bracknell, Berkshire, was in command of the aircraft, with SFO Mike Thomas, from Farnborough, Hampshire as co-pilot. Also on the flight deck was a third fully-qualified pilot, SFO Dennis Palmer.

All three men were highly experienced, and all had served in the Royal Air Force prior to joining BEA. Captain Blackwood had joined the RAF in 1942, at the age of twenty. Sent to Canada to train as a pilot, his grades were sufficiently high that he was kept on as an instructor, rather than being posted straight back to Britain. This would almost certainly have saved his life; at that time most new RAF pilots were moved straight into Bomber Command, where the level of fatalities was very high. When he eventually left his training role, it was to be posted to the Mediterranean theatre of operations. 33-year-old Mike Thomas, who had joined BEA ten years earlier, was married with a son and daughter. Dennis Palmer, 35, had been a member of the Royal Auxiliary Air Force before joining BEA in 1957 and had been an industrial chemist with a firm of paper manufacturers in Aberdeen. He now lived with his wife, their son and daughter, in Goring-on-Thames, near Reading.

The three crew knew each other well, the Comet 4B fleet in BEA comprising only thirteen aircraft at that time. Over the preceding seven days, Dennis Palmer and Mike Thomas had flown together twice. Mike Thomas had not originally been rostered for BE/CY284. A colleague, John Weldon, had just found out that his wife had been diagnosed with cancer, so Mike volunteered to swap duties with him.

The cabin staff for the first sector, Senior Steward Tony Talaska, Stewards Clive Hummerstone and Alan Heard, and Stewardess Wendy Gibbs, were also British. They would leave the flight at Athens and operate a return flight to London on another BEA Comet service, arriving back at Heathrow the following day. After reaching Nicosia, Charlie Oscar would spend just over four hours on the tarmac before starting the return trip to Athens and London Heathrow as CY/BE265. The three pilots would operate CY/BE265 the following day.

The layout of the de Havilland DH106 Comet 4B was slightly different from most airliners, at the time and today. The forward entrance and exit was to the starboard[4] side of the aircraft, rather than the port. However, as

---

[4] *The author has used conventional aviation terminology throughout this book, to be consistent with the language used in the investigation reports. Port refers to the left-hand side of the aircraft looking forward, starboard to the right. The terms 'forward' and 'aft' refer to the front and back of the aircraft respectively.*

modern airbridge gantries were far from commonplace, most people had to enter and leave by portable steps wheeled to the aircraft door, so this was not an impediment to the boarding and disembarkation process. Equally unfamiliar would be the seat numbering on the Comet; row 1, which usually is the first row of passenger seats, was at the back, with subsequent rows of seats numbering to the front. In BEA's configuration, the Tourist (Economy) Class cabin contained 79 seats, in fifteen rows of five and one of four. Three seats, lettered A, B and C, were in a single unit on the port side of the cabin, with a unit of two seats, D and E, on the starboard.

In seat 1A, businessman Michael Costa Thomaides was a regular traveller on the London to Nicosia service. The son of an orange grove owner, in late 1950s he had started off as a sales commission agent, studying at nights to get his Pitman college diploma. He then set up a fruit and vegetable packing business, specialising in potatoes, carrots, grapes and citrus fruit. The venture soon proved to be successful, growing in to one of the largest agricultural produce traders in Cyprus. By 1967 the company was exporting to the UK, with offices in Long Acre Street, Covent Garden in London, as well as in Rotterdam. Amongst his customers, Michael's company exported potatoes to the Smith family, famed for the "Smith's Crisps" line of snacks, with whom he became close friends.

Because of the volume of work, which expanded to Egypt, Greece and even Turkey, before the 1963 troubles, Michael decided to move into shipping instead of chartering vessels. By 1965, along with his brother and his UK partners, Anthony and Robert Beeson, he was one of the first Cypriot ship-owners, with a refrigerated vessel, the *Cyprian Trader* and a bulk carrier, the *Cyprian Producer*. He found he still had to charter additional capacity to cope with the volume of work. Michael had signed a sales agreement with Smith's Potato Crisps, covering 25 countries in the Middle East and Eastern Mediterranean. This included Michael's company building the most advanced snack food factory in Europe. He purchased the land, near Famagusta in Cyprus, in the summer of 1967[5]. Michael had good reason to look forward to his return home from another few weeks

---

[5] *Michael's wife and brother continued with the project after his death, finishing the factory in 1969. Later, students would visit from Reading University for training purposes. The factory was lost in 1974 to the Turkish invading forces but continued to be used under the enforced new ownership. The Thomaides Group continues to thrive in Cyprus, under the leadership of Michael's first son, Artemis, his daughter Maria and Michael, born in November 1967, who bears the name of the father he never had the opportunity to meet.*

away on a successful business trip; his wife was expecting their third child within the next month.

Immediately in front of Michael Thomaides, in seats 2A and B, sat a Welsh couple, Hugh Seymour Griffiths and his wife, Lily, who were from the village of Cosheston, a couple of miles from Pembroke Dock. Hugh was a pharmacist, running a local chemist shop. They were taking their first flight to Cyprus, where they would be visiting Hugh's brother, a civil servant, who was due to leave the island. This would be their only opportunity to undertake the visit, so Lily was prepared to overcome her reluctance to fly in order that they could enjoy the holiday.

Mrs. Margaret Joyce sat across the aisle from the Griffiths, in seat 2D. Despite being some ten years younger than the couple opposite, she would have found them amenable company on the trip. The wife of the Rev. Henry Joyce, vicar of Hathersage in Derbyshire, Margaret was originally from much further north, having been born in Cumberland. She was on the way to visit her daughter who was in hospital in Cyprus at the time.

A 23-year-old American passenger of Cypriot heritage, Sotiris Georgiou, had the port side window seat, 4A. He had arrived in London from New York, where two cars of friends and family had accompanied him to Kennedy airport to see him off. He has stayed overnight in London with the family of his sister-in-law before transferring to BE284 for his onward journey to Cyprus. He was returning to Neokhorio Kythrea, a town just north east of Nicosia, to visit the family had left four years earlier when he moved to the USA. Sotiris worked as a car mechanic, specialising in Mercedes vehicles. Also in row 4, across the aisle in 4D, was 54-year old widow, Mrs. Lily Mailborough, from Stockton-on-Tees. The diminutive lady, only 5 feet 1 inch tall, with auburn and grey hair, was on her way to visit her 20-year-old daughter, Christine, who had moved to Cyprus with her 18-month-old son, Graham, and husband, Bob, who was serving with the Royal Signals on a three-year posting. On 11th October, Christine was surprised though delighted to receive a letter from Lily, saying that she would be arriving at 6 am the following day. Lily was another first-time flier with, according to her son in press reports, a terrible fear of flying which she overcame in order to visit her daughter. Her son's wife and child had planned to accompany Lily but cancelled their plans due to the four-year-old son being unwell.

68-year-old Anna Stewart was accompanying her long-time friend, Miss Jean Falconer, who was a retired schoolteacher. The two ladies, sitting in seats 7D and E, were from Edinburgh, where Anna's husband practised as an advocate. Jean had moved to Balloch, Inverness-shire, but still kept in touch with her friend. They were on their way to a holiday in Cyprus.

The McComb family, occupying seats 8A, B and C, were returning to Cyprus after an extended five-week holiday. 24-year-old Roy was serving with the RAF in Cyprus and was flying with his wife Elaine and their eighteen-month-old son,

Roydon George. They had been staying with Elaine's family in Mexborough, near Doncaster. Roy's family were originally from Osmotherly, North Yorkshire, where they had lived at The Lady Chapel. Roy went to school in Northallerton and, at the age of 16, joined the RAF as an Aircraft Apprentice. In 1965, he married Elaine and their son, Roydon George, was born the following year.

Across the aisle from the McCombs, in seat 8E, was Costas Efstathiou, described as a stocky man, 5 feet 7 inches tall. Aged 34, he was a hairdresser living in Alkrington, Middleton, on the northern edge of what is now the Manchester conurbation, and had lived in England for many years.

Doctor George Ioannides, 48, in seat 9A, was the son of the Head Master of the prestigious Pancyprian Gymnasium in Nicosia Cyprus, and Athena Ioannidou, a very well-known and respected woman in Cyprus, who directed the Nicosia Pancyprian Academy for Girls. George attended elementary school in the 1920s in Germany, where his father was studying at Leipzig University for his Doctorate degree. George's younger brother Christos became a lawyer and later on a judge in Cyprus, whilst George gained his medical degree from Athens University and, in the 1950s, practised in the Victoria Hospital, Accrington, Lancashire. Going on to practice medicine for several years in London, he was appointed as a consultant in charge for the North Paddington area hospitals. He was also in charge of the Pathology Department at the National Temperance Hospital in London. When he returned permanently to Cyprus, he married Ioanna Callimachou. Dr. Ioannides was therefore familiar with the medical system in London, having many contacts. On this trip he had escorted to London a seriously injured child of a close friend who had a road accident in Nicosia. He was returning in time for the annual memorial service for his father, who had died on October 13th, and for his daughter's second birthday on October 14th.

In seat 9D sat Police Sergeant Rodosthenis Christou, who had been born in the village of Arminou in Paphos, Cyprus on 17th of September 1927, the son of Athena Saloumi and Christos Mesariti. After his birth, his parents moved to another village, Mantria in Limassol, where he studied at the school of Mitsi Lemithou. He was one of four children.

After finishing school Rodosthenis went to the Police Academy, where he graduated and was later described as a model police officer. Some years later he was transferred to the police force in Famagusta. On one occasion, due to sickness, he was admitted to Famagusta hospital where he was particularly taken with one of the nurses caring for him, Eleni Kakouri Petrou. He asked her for a date, they fell in love and got married. They had four children, Sotos, Athina, Petros and Vasso. As a prosecutor for the police force, he wanted to further his studies and become a solicitor. He was well-educated and could speak four languages. With this intention in mind, he decided to travel to England to find ways to further his education through long-distance learning.

Rodosthenis booked a direct flight to London where he was greeted by family and stayed for a month. On his return home he also wanted to book a direct flight but had to settle for BE/CY284 which, despite the stop in Athens where additional passengers boarded, was a through flight so he could at least complete the journey on the same aircraft. From Athens, Rodosthenis would be joined by his goddaughter, 24-year-old Niki Rodosthenous, a beautician. Back home in Cyprus, his family were eagerly awaiting his arrival and had planned a family celebration to celebrate his return.

Sitting in seats 10A and B were Mrs. Katerina Liassides, 52, who lived in Muswell Hill, London, and 74-year-old Mrs. Melanie Papaioannou, whose son lived in Kingston Hill, Surrey. 53-year-old Mrs. Liassides had received a telegram earlier that day urging her to travel to Cyprus as soon as possible, as her brother was critically ill[6]. Notwithstanding the advice of her family to wait for the weekend, she insisted on booking her ticket for the next available flight. Mrs. Liassides was initially told that the flight was full, so made to leave the travel agent. However, they called her back to the desk and told her that there was, in fact, a spare seat on the flight. Melanie Papaioannou lived in the village of Pareklishia, thirteen miles east of Limassol, where her husband was the priest. The couple had six sons and a daughter. Melanie Papaioannou was described to the author as a very dynamic person with a strong personality. Once or twice a year, she would travel to London to visit her two sons, who were in the restaurant business. She was quite happy travelling alone, on one occasion visiting New York to see her eldest son. On this occasion, Melanie had been in Surrey for a month, and decided to return home without notifying her family there, in order to surprise them. Melanie's daughter and family received the news a few days later, without realising that Melanie had been on the flight.

US Marine Sergeant Michael O'Brien, was travelling with his 22-year-old British wife, Maureen. The couple were serving in Cyprus for their respective units, Maureen being a member of the Women's Royal Army Corps. Michael was from New Jersey whilst Maureen was from Warrington. Though originally due to travel on the following day, they had switched to the earlier flight to avoid a stopover in London. The couple, who occupied seats 10D and E, had only been married for thirteen days.

---

[6] *Ironically, her brother lived for a further six months.*

In seats 12A and B sat Mr. Loizos Nicolaides, 30, and his 23-year-old wife Irinoula, from the village of Pera Pedio. Their son Andreas, whose age was not recorded but whom a press photograph suggests was about four years old, was in the row in front of them. Mr. Nicolaides worked for the General Insurance Company of Cyprus, part of the Bank of Cyprus. The family was returning from London, where they had taken Andreas for a medical examination.

Another family with military connections were the Taskers, in seats 14A and B. Mrs. Jan Tasker was returning with her 3-year-old son Guy to Cyprus, where her husband was an NCO in the British armed services.

In seats 15A and B, 25-year-old Anne Harbstreet, and her father Nicolas Peters, were travelling together from Elizabeth, New Jersey, USA. Anne's husband had recently been posted to Vietnam, where the war was raging, and Nicolas thought it would help his daughter cope if they went to visit relatives in Cyprus.

22-yr-old Mary Dalton was travelling to visit her father, serving with the Royal Signals on the island. She had not seen him for over a year so was understandably

excited by the prospect of the reunion. She intended to stay in Cyprus for six weeks.

Hilary Smith, 32, and Joyce White, 29, were colleagues and great friends who frequently socialised together and made the most of BEA's staff travel concessions to travel abroad. They would often plan holidays together, and this was the third time the duo had visited Cyprus. Both women worked for BEA as cashiers at the West London Air Terminal. Hilary's father was a Baptist minister at a church in Richmond, Surrey. Joyce lived in Twickenham, not too far from her friend and equally convenient for their mutual workplace. They had completed their shifts that day before heading to Heathrow airport to catch their flight. In accordance with the staff travel scheme, they could only fly at the 90% discount rate if there were empty seats on the flight. They had considered themselves fortunate that neither sector was full, so both were accepted for the flight. Their good fortune increased even further when they were offered seats in the otherwise-empty first-class compartment by their cabin staff colleagues.

Also travelling from London were a retired forestry worker from Strovoli, Mr. Ioannis Tsiakouris, who had taken his son to school in London; Mr. David Powell, 27, who lived in Eltham Park Gardens, south east London, and Mrs. Rosalie Stone, aged 72, who had booked her flight in London and was visiting her son who lived in Nicosia.

As well as the BEA cabin crew, six passengers from London left the flight at Athens. Miss P. Downie, who lived in Battersea, was another BEA staff passenger, working in Ground Communication at West London Air Terminal. Mr. P.C. Bulgarides, who worked for Greek Line, was travelling on from Athens to Rome and Genoa before returning to London while a Greek seaman, Mr. Tsolakakis, having bought his ticket in Londonderry, Northern Ireland, was finishing his journey in Athens. Miss Petroboulou, who worked at Pembridge Gardens Hotel in the West End, had bought a return ticket from London to Athens earlier that day. Two tickets had been issued by Olympic Airways, the Greek national carrier. Mr. Papadopoulos had started his journey in Athens, flying to Zurich, Geneva, Paris and London. This was the final leg of his trip. Mr. Tsopourides, from Saloniki in Greece, had flown to Athens and thence to Frankfurt, Dusseldorf and London. From Athens he would take another flight home to Saloniki. All six collected their belongings when Charlie Oscar came to a stop on the apron at Ellinikon airport and went their separate ways to get on with the rest of their lives.

Twenty of the 31 passengers boarding at Athens comprised a group of Jehovah's' Witnesses, who were travelling to an international convention in Cyprus of members of their faith. They had made a block booking; the names of those travelling had been amended but the overall number in the group remained unaltered. The eventual members of the group on the flight were: Mr. Archilleas Afatitis, 28, a painting contractor from Neon Iraklion and his new wife, Reveka, 20, who had originally booked under her maiden name, Sifneou. They had decided to combine their honeymoon with a trip to the Jehovahs Witnesses convention. The group also comprised Miss Areti Exarcheas, 21 from Egalso; Mrs. Constantinas Christaki from Polikatikia; Mrs. Iphigenia Kalogeropoulou from Old Psychicon; Miss Despina Karakosta, 60 from Ionia; Mr. Charalabos Kontominas and his wife Stavoulas, from Piraeus; Mr. Georgios Koutroubinis and his 54-year-old wife, Eleni, aged 31 from Ionia; Mr. Gerasimo Thiakou, 48 and his wife Polixeni, 22, from Athens, Mr. Vasilios Markidou and his 22-year-old daughter Eleni, also from Athens; Mrs. Eirini Papanicolaou, 61, and Mr. Ioannis Rigou, 60, were both from Heraklion; Miss Maria Parzopoulou, also aged in her sixties came from Ahia Paraskavi. Miss Arini Voliotou, 25 was from Athens; 31-year-old Mrs. Paraskevis Vougioukas, was also from Ionia. The final member of the group is believed to have been Mr. Elias Evgeros, 28, from Petras.

The other Athens passengers were a mixture of individuals and couples. As expected, Niki Rodosthenou had joined Rodosthenis Christou. William Sheris, an American, was travelling from Fairfax, Virginia. 64-year-old Mrs. Dorothea Rachovidou was returning to Limassol from a visit to her daughter, who lived in the Greek capital. Mr. Nicos Papapetrou was a shoe salesman from Larnaca. He was returning from his fifth trip to Greece in the past twelve months. He supplemented his income of £80 a month with the money he gained as a professional gambler, whilst he developed a sideline in importing leather goods and watches. Mr. Konstantinos Paleologous and his wife Theognosia, from Piraeus, were visiting their daughter in Cyprus.

One passenger wanting to join the flight at the last minute found that he had to work very hard to make it happen. Avraam Solomou worked directly for the Cypriot Foreign Minister, Spyros Kyprianou. His duties were officially those of chauffeur and personal assistant. However, Mr. Solomou had been an active member of the EOKA[7] organisation, which had undertaken paramilitary activity in the 1950s during the Cypriot struggle for independence from the UK. He had permanent scars from bullet wounds to verify his credentials as a freedom fighter[8].

Mr. Solomou needed to return to Nicosia for an important appointment the following day but he had been issued with an incorrect ticket and could not get on to the flight. He had become quite assertive, according to check-in staff, insisting that it was essential that he was on CY284, and refusing to wait for the flight later that morning. Eventually, the matter was resolved and Mr. Solomou was allowed to take one of the empty seats, believed to be 16C.

Senior Steward Ioannis Loizou managed the cabin crew and in-flight service from the forward galley. He was assisted in this by Stewardess Calliopi Fottou. Ioannis was known by the anglicised version of his forename, John, whilst Calliopi was known to her friends and colleagues as Popi. Working from the aft galley were Steward Nicos Hasapopoulos and Stewardess Thelma Efremi.

Cyprus Airways was an even closer-knit community than BEA. John Loizou and Nicos Hasapopoulos had been in the same school class for twelve years before joining the airline. John's brother, Louis, also a steward with Cyprus Airways, was a class mate of Nicos' brother. Louis frequently worked on the Comet services and was due to operate the Athens to Nicosia flight, CY264, later that day. As the Loizou brothers were both staying in Athens before their flights, they had shared a meal with colleagues and friends in the evening before John reported for duty at Athens airport. This included Nicos Hasapopoulos as well as two stewardesses from Louis' flight. As they enjoyed their evening out, John told Louis that he was expecting a VIP passenger, General Georgios Grivas, to travel on the flight. The brothers discussed this at some length as they had previously had what Louis later described as raucous

---

[7] *EOKA [Ethniki Organosis Kyprion Agoniston - National Organization of Cypriot Fighters]*

[8] *Spyros Kyprianou was a prominent Cypriot politician and went on to serve as President of Cyprus from 1977 to 1988.*

encounters with members of the General's entourage. Grivas had led the EOKA organisation during the country's struggle for independence from Britain and was now the leader of the Cypriot National Guard. Cyprus was still going through a period of upheaval, in which Grivas was a prominent figure.

Senior Steward Frixos Michael had offered to swap flights with John Loizou, as he was shipping an expensive consignment of handbags to Nicosia. Whilst he would usually have obliged, on this occasion John had declined, for a very special reason. He had been in a long-distance relationship with a BEA stewardess who lived in London. According to Louis, his brother was very much in love with Josephine Coldicott, who was based in London. John and Josephine had limited opportunities to spend time together, and when she wrote saying that she had ten days leave to spend with him in Cyprus, he could not have been more delighted. Louis remembers his brother confiding in him that he wanted to propose to Josephine, as she was, for him, 'the one'. Josephine, who was entitled to use BEA's concessionary travel scheme, had written to John a few days earlier, to tell him that she planned to be on the London to Nicosia flight on the night of 11th October, the service that would depart Athens as CY284:

7/10/67

Dear John,,

Just a very quick note to say thank you for your wonderful letter. It was so good to hear from you as always. Unless I hear from you otherwise, I shall arrive at Nicosia at 0550 on CY284. As it is very early in the morning, you may also be working etc. I shall understand if you are not at the airport John and perhaps you could leave a message for me with Cyprus Airways at the airport, letting me know the exact place where to go and I can get a taxi.

I'm so looking forward to seeing you again and as I haven't been too well and been working hard, I really need a holiday. The only thing I must say is that I'm feeling nervous at meeting you again after so long. I've been looking in the shops to buy you a present, but I couldn't make up my mind so will wait and ask you and I can send it on to you when I come back here.

I will bring the cigs and drink off for you though as I did before.

Take care of yourself John and I hope to see you some time next Thursday.

God Bless.

Lots of love from

Josephine xxxxx

John had every intention of being on that flight, though he hadn't mentioned the fact to her, and was determined to surprise Josephine when he took over at Athens as senior steward for the flight to Nicosia.

The passengers, both joining and transit, were welcomed on board. Josephine Coldicott was absolutely delighted to be greeted by John Loizou so much earlier than she had anticipated. There was no sign of General Grivas, so the BEA staff passengers, now including Josephine, were ushered into the otherwise-unused first-class cabin, a regular perk for those who were flying among friends. John and Josephine, especially, wanted this to be a trip to remember.

Into the Night

Doors closed, and the aircraft secured by the cabin staff, the three pilots methodically went through the procedures that brought Charlie Oscar back into life. Ground power was used to feed the electrical systems, until the four Rolls-Royce Avon turbo jets were running. The Ground Power Unit, a massive towable generator, was moved out of the way, no longer required. The checklists confirmed that everything was in order and Charlie Oscar was ready to depart for Nicosia. As soon as Captain Blackwood was satisfied, SFO Thomas asked Air Traffic Control (ATC) for permission to start his engines. All four Avon engines running smoothly, the crew completed their pre-taxi checks, and then asked for permission to leave their parking bay on the apron.

SFO Thomas eased the throttles forward sufficiently to allow the aircraft to start moving, manoeuvring Charlie Oscar carefully across the apron, and onto the taxiway. Away from the floodlit stands, the pilots were guided by the lights either side of the tarmac path which led to Runway 33. SFO Thomas then contacted the tower, obtaining permission to transit the airways that would be their route to Nicosia.

Taking off to the north north west, due to the northerly wind blowing at ten knots, the aircraft would climb straight ahead whilst the undercarriage retracted, flap settings were adjusted, and the airspeed increased to the point where a steady climb could be initiated. As soon as he could do so safely, and usually before reaching 500 feet, Captain Blackwood would commence a turn to the left. This would take the aircraft away from the built-up areas in Athens and the port of Piraeus, in order to reduce the disturbance to the local population generated by a Comet at climbing power. As Charlie Oscar reversed her course she would head to the south of the airport till reaching four thousand feet, when she would head straight for another air navigation beacon, at Cape Sounion.

The taxiway, at that time, did not extend to the southern end of Runway 33, so the Comet had to use the runway itself to reach the turning area at its extremity. Despite being well sort of the maximum take-off weight, common sense and best practice meant starting the take-off roll with as much of the runway ahead of the aircraft as possible.

Charlie Oscar had reached the end of Runway 33 and had turned to line up with the runway centreline. The cabin crew had conducted their safety checks and taken their own seats. The final pre-take-off checks were correct. At Mike Thomas' request, Athens ATC gave the go-ahead for him to advance the throttles to take-off power, release the brakes and accelerate until they lifted off the ground. The instruction to turn to the left was emphasised once more. Somewhere between thirty-five and forty seconds later, Charlie Oscar was airborne.

ATC confirmed the time of departure as 0231hrs. Safely established in the climb, Mike Thomas retuned the aircraft's VHF radio to 119.1 MHz, the frequency for Athens Approach, responsible for coordinating aircraft movements in the vicinity of Athens airport.

The Comet climbed quickly; there was not a full load, either of passengers or fuel, so there was plenty of power to spare. Charlie Oscar had reached 4,000 feet as previously cleared.

Three minutes later, Mike Thomas gave Athens Approach a further update, with Charlie Oscar having reached the Sounion beacon at an altitude of 10,500 feet. As previously cleared, Captain Blackwood was continuing their climb to the assigned en-route altitude of 29,000 feet. He expected to join the high-altitude airway, R19, and pass the next reporting point, R19B, at 0246hrs. As they were now leaving the vicinity of Athens airport, they were passed over to the Athens Control Centre (ACC), who coordinated high-altitude flights in the region. SFO Thomas duly obliged, changing frequency once more, to 124.4MHz.

SFO Thomas confirmed that they had passed Sounion beacon at 0236hrs, and was passing overhead Ioulis, about ten miles to the south east of Cape Sounion. The crew confirmed that they expected to reach R19B at 0246hrs.

In the cabin, John Loizou and his cabin team were heating the meal boxes which contained the hot breakfasts for the passengers. On such a short flight, preparing and serving the meals had to be accomplished without delay. Tea and coffee would also be offered, along with bar sales. With the seatbelt signs off and the aircraft climbing through calm air, passengers were now free to stand up and move around the cabin, which complicated the meal service, but the crew coped admirably.

Charlie Oscar then received a transmission from the BEA Comet[9] flying the reciprocal service from Nicosia to Athens. However, at this point, it is apparent that they were not able to make themselves heard in return and brought this to the attention of Athens Control Centre.

Charlie Oscar was now at 21,500 feet, and still climbing. Aware of the approach of Bealine Mike Foxtrot, Athens instructed Charlie Oscar to climb as quickly as possible, to get above the other aircraft before their paths crossed.

It was fewer than fifteen minutes since they had taken off from Athens. They had climbed to 28,000 feet as quickly as possible, which was

---

[9] *The return service, operating as CY285 to Athens, then BE285 onwards to London Heathrow, was being operated on this night by Captain L. Emmerson, in Comet 4B G-APMF, phonetically Golf Alpha Papa Mike Foxtrot. The flight had been delayed at Nicosia due to technical problems.*

acknowledged by the controller. One minute later, Charlie Oscar passed the reporting point at Red 19B, and advised Athens of this, as was required. Thomas added that they were at their cruising altitude of 29,000 feet and expected to pass Rhodes at 0303hrs. Athens ATC acknowledged the message, instructing the crew to maintain that altitude and report overhead Rhodes.

Apart from the stars a few minutes of total darkness, remained before the eastern sky would begin to brighten[10]. Captain Emmerson, in Bealine Mike Foxtrot, saw the landing lights of Charlie Oscar approaching from the west, a thousand feet above him, which was the minimum legal separation by height. The greeting, 'Good morning,' came over the VHF radio, to which he responded in kind, flashing his own aircraft's landing lights. The exchange was picked up at Athens Control Centre. Such courtesies were not unusual in the small hours at an otherwise deserted location.

SFO Thomas advised Athens that Charlie Oscar was passing Rhodes at 0304hrs, still at 29,000 feet, and that they estimated the reporting point at R19C at 0316hrs. There was no mention of anything untoward onboard the aircraft. In the cabin, John Loizou and his team had cleared away the remnants of the passengers' hot breakfasts and were in the rear galley, preparing to count and seal the bars. Louis Loizou recalls that, at this point in the relatively short flight, the aisle would be occupied by many passengers standing up to stretch their legs for a few minutes before the aircraft began its descent into Nicosia.

At 0316hrs, twelve minutes after his last call to Athens, SFO Thomas had tried to contact the controller to confirm that Charlie Oscar was passing the second en route reporting point, R19C. They were now out of range of the radio, so Captain Emmerson in Mike Foxtrot, hearing the message, relayed it to Athens. Once again, this was routine practice at the time.

Two minutes later, at 0318hrs, SFO Mike Thomas keyed his microphone and started his initial contact call to Nicosia ATC, *'Good morning, Nicky, Bealine Golf Alpha Romeo Charlie Osc...'*

As he spoke, in the passenger cabin, all hell broke loose...

---

[10] *Sunrise in Antalya on 12th October is 0705LT / 0505Z. Sun rises six minutes earlier at 29,000 feet; therefore sunrise would have been 0659LT/ 0459Z. Twilight (astronomical) was 0635LT on the ground and 0529LT/0229Z at 29,000 feet.*

'The Most Amazing Type of Accident'

On hearing the transmission at 0318Z from SFO Thomas in Charlie Oscar, Nicosia Air Traffic Control Centre acknowledged the call and asked him to go ahead. There was only silence. Despite repeated attempts to contact Charlie Oscar, nothing further was heard.

SFO Thomas had previously told Athens that Charlie Oscar was estimated abeam the Myrtou beacon at 0340Z. The standard approach procedure would have given an arrival time at Nicosia airport ten minutes afterwards.

0350Z came and went with neither sight nor sound of Charlie Oscar. At 0404Z a Royal Air Force aircraft flying from Akrotiri to Luqa, Malta, was asked to divert to the last reported position of CY284, and commence a search. At 0405Z, the Duty Officer at Athens airport received a telephone call from the Flight Information Centre (FIC), Ellinikon, that Nicosia had had no contact with Charlie Oscar. Nicosia asked that Captain Emmerson, in the second BEA Comet, Mike Foxtrot, who had arrived in Athens at 0335Z, be asked for any information he might have about Charlie Oscar. Captain Emmerson replied that everything had seemed to be OK, confirmed that he had passed on the instruction to switch to the Nicosia frequency, and added that the last words from Charlie Oscar were *"OK, thank you."*

At 0420Z, Michael Zographos, the Operations Officer who had spoken to Captain Blackwood on board Charlie Oscar during the turnround at Athens, called FIC Ellinikon for a further update but there was nothing to report.

At 0443Z, Nicosia formally notified Athens that Charlie Oscar was overdue. The airport ATC called back to for details of the radio frequencies in use, and the survival equipment carried on board Charlie Oscar. They were informed that this consisted of lifejackets only. The Deputy Commanding Officer of the airport ensured that the ship's papers were preserved and retained, along with details of all the ground staff who had been involved in the turnround, just two and a half hours earlier.

Flight Lieutenant Dennis King was stationed with 70 Squadron at RAF Akrotiri. On the morning of 12th October, he was in charge of the duty Search and Rescue (SAR) crew, callsign Playmate 36. At 0420Z, F/L King received instructions to take off and search for the missing Comet. Airborne from Akrotiri at 0440Z, the crew flew along the line of airway to the R19C reporting point, at an altitude of one thousand feet. With the dedicated SAR aircraft on its way, the aircraft that had originally been deployed was stood down and allowed to continue its journey to Malta. When they reached R19C, the crew started flying a search pattern. This would gradually progress eastwards, back towards the Cypriot coast. On the second leg, at 0615Z, the crew sighted small white paper-like objects floating on the surface of the sea, and then larger pieces of wreckage coloured white and orange. They then spotted empty lifejackets, followed by bodies. Three miles east and slightly to the south of R19C, they had found what remained of Charlie Oscar.

Playmate 36 reported the find[11] and spent the next half hour making low passes over the crash site, which was marked with smoke flares. There was no sign of life. A ship, the Hungarian SS *Balaton*, was identified, steaming to the south east of the wreckage field, so Playmate 36 diverted to attract its attention. After two or three low passes, the captain's attention was caught, and the *Balaton* altered course to the direction indicated by Playmate 36.

At about 0715Z, with the *Balaton* making her way to the scene, Playmate 36 returned to the crash site, and called in a second SAR Hastings, Playmate 37. Having noted all there was to see at that stage, Playmate 36 carried out a more general search, and continued to shepherd the *Balaton* to the location. F/L King's report went on to give more specific details:

There were two main areas of wreckage, the southerly being more dense than the northerly.

There was a general area of light wreckage surrounded by a kerosene slick – disposition as shown on Sketch sheet. Most bodies were seen floating face downward, naked or partially naked, on the whole mainly intact. Clothing when seen attached was either around the head or the feet, or items of tight clothing – i.e. corsets or brassieres.

The general impression was gained that some bodies in the southerly area were wearing life jackets – about ten in all. Several life jackets and one baby life cot were seen floating around inflated. The main debris floating on the surface was fabric and broken pieces of plywood and drifting to the south were boxes and containers.

To the north of the slick was a circular silver object, approximately 6-10 feet in diameter, floating beneath the surface. We did not see any baggage – suitcases etc, or any major airframe components, or recognisable aircraft structure.

---

[11] When the message was received from Playmate 36 that the wreckage had been sighted, Mr. Papapetros, the Commander of Nicosia Airport, made a private call to Mr. Colliandris at Ellinikon airport, asking if the 'Mr. Papapetros' named on the passenger list was his brother. He then confirmed to Mr. Colliandris that aircraft wreckage had been found 70 miles south of the island of Kastellorizo.

The main wreckage field was pinpointed at 35° 55' N, 30° 01' E. Most bodies now appeared to be in the northern area and the crew of 37 had a strong impression that some were wearing life jackets.

In total, 24 bodies were recovered directly by the *Balaton's* crew, these being nine males and fifteen females, all of whom were adults. None of these were wearing lifejackets. Five were noted as fully clothed, five totally naked and fourteen partially clothed. The exact nature of individual injuries varied but overall, they were described as '...*generally frightful.*' As with other factors, the differences in appearance between bodies were considered to be significant as the investigation progressed. The captain noted that '*On the backs of female bodies could be seen slight burnings, around a redder centre were whitened skins.*' The sea surface was covered with a film of oil and some of the bodies smelled of '*petroleum*[12]'. Two wrist watches were recovered, the captain noting that these had stopped 5.27 and 5.30. There was also general wreckage; seats and cushions, lifejackets, clothing, newspapers and medicines, none of which the *Balaton* collected. Having completed her grim task, the *Balaton* delivered the 24 bodies to the *Navarinon*.

Playmate 36 left to guide in a Turkish patrol vessel, P127 *Bozcaada*[13], which commenced recovering bodies in the northern areaA third Hastings, TG533, Playmate 38, also attended the scene. Flight Lieutenant Mercer and his crew noted a group of some fifteen to twenty bodies along with wreckage, some four miles from the *Balaton*.

F/L King in Playmate 36 noted that the oil slick had thickened and, in an area previously considered clear of bodies, were some five bodies without life jackets; the crew's impression was that they had just 'popped up', along with some wreckage. The bodies were noted as being close together in groups, including two together, still strapped into their seats. The wreckage consisted of sound-proofing, flooring, seat cushions and clothing, along with a black 5-gallon drum, seemingly empty as it was floating high in the water. There was also a four-foot-long yellow drum, a white horseshoe-shaped object, thought to be a window frame or toilet seat, and two light blue objects which the crew thought might be child's flotation cots, inverted. As more wreckage continued to appear into the

---

[12] *The captain probably meant aviation fuel; his report concluded, 'I beg pardon about my English, I know not a perfect one.'*

[13] *Bozcaada was originally built in Canada in 1941, as a Bangor-class minesweeper of 672 tons. Commissioned into the Royal Canadian Navy on 11th November 1941 as HMCS Swift Current, she was active for the rest of the war. Sold to the Turkish Navy in 1958, she remained in service until 1971.*

afternoon, it was considered likely that the fuselage was disintegrating under the water, which was some 9,000 feet deep at this point.

At 1130Z, a large German merchant vessel, the MV *Astrid*, belonging to Transmarin of Hamburg and commanded by Captain H. Rohde, arrived to assist. She took up station to the south east of the main wreckage area and her crew started to recover bodies from the sea. On arrival, the crew had noted parts of the wreckage but no bodies. The wreckage comprised interior doors, many lifejackets, seat stuffing, carpets, overcoats, parts of suits, travel bags, children's shoes and two pilots' caps along with two uniform jackets, with gold buttons but no stripes on the sleeves[14]. fter searching the area for two hours, the crew of the *Astrid* learnt by radio that the *Balaton* had already found 24 bodies so, presuming that the other ship was at the main crash site, some three-and-a-half to four miles distant, the Astrid went to join her. En route to the second location, many pieces of wreckage were noted, but could not be recovered as the ship's boat was hoisted. When the *Astrid* reached the vicinity of the *Balaton*, she deployed her lifeboat and recovered a female body along with lifejackets, ladies' handbags and passports. The *Astrid* remained on station until about 1710Z, when the body, wreckage and other recovered items were passed to the Greek warship, *Navarinon*. At the end of his report, Captain Rohde observed,

> 'Out of this direction and the distance and the concentration of wreckage material on two positions might be concluded, that the Comet broke into two pieces in a certain height, so that one part with higher aerodynamic resistance came down in the second position and the other part with less resistance came down 3.75 sea-miles further on in the first position as mentioned above. And also, it might be concluded that the last course of the Comet was nearly southeast[15].'

with various other personal effects and a Marconi radio or electrical instrument in a box. They also saw the body of the cat, which was still in its carrier but was not recovered.

RHMS Navarinon, of the Royal Hellenic Navy, was commanded by Captain D.P. Alexandrou. Travelling east, the ship arrived on scene at 1315hrs local time, 1115Z. On sighting the wreckage, Captain Alexandrou

---

[14] *The uniform jackets probably belonged to the cabin staff as the pilots' jackets had gold braid stripes on the sleeves. It is possible that the caps, similar in design to those worn by pilots, also belonged to the stewards (see photo of BEA crew on p. 28).*

[15] *The phraseology is exactly as used by Captain Rohde.*

altered course to the south to establish the southern end of the area. The RAF had continued to mark the site which Captain Alexandrou estimated to be three to five miles long by two to three miles wide. The *Navarinon* zig-zagged carefully northwards, Captain Alexandrou directing his ship's boats towards bodies and wreckage. As a Greek warship, however, it was imperative that the *Navarinon* did not trespass into Turkish territorial waters, which imposed a northern boundary for the ship's effective search area.

The first body received by the *Navarinon* was from the Kastellorizo Harbour boat, skippered by the Harbour Master himself. The actual recovery location was not noted. Captain Alexandrou had a conversation with the Harbour Master, who was accompanied by the Customs Officer of the island. The Harbour Master related that he had been out fishing north-west of the island of Kastellorizo and had seen an aircraft descend at a steep angle (indicated as 45 degrees), leaving a trail of smoke or flames. The Harbour Master did not see the aircraft hit the water as it had disappeared behind the island's mountain[16]. One of the fishermen from Kastellorizo was Nikos Misomikes who, understandably, recalled the events of the day half a century later. In particular, he remembers that the bodies he and his colleagues recovered were definitely not wearing life jackets[17].

This truly international recovery effort was made possible by ships and aircraft from Hungary, Greece, Turkey, West Germany, the United Kingdom and USA. Israel also offered assistance. Turkey's not inconsiderable contribution included five warships and two helicopters. However, the records held on file in the National Archives in London, whilst comprehensive in all other regards, do not appear to contain any reports from Turkish recovery crews.

The day was spent scouring the area for bodies which, it was established, lay mainly in two clusters, one north and one south. Those found in the northern wreckage had been gathered by Turkish ships and were taken initially to the port of Finike. The bodies recovered in Greek waters, to the south, were transferred to the *Navarinon* and, when the work was done, the Greek warship conveyed them to Rhodes. After being unloaded at Finike, the bodies in what became known as 'the Turkish group' were flown to

---

[16] *Attempts were made by the investigation team to interview the Harbour Master; however, he retracted his eyewitness account of the crash itself. Captain Alexandrou commented that the Harbour Master may have been trying to impress him with his story.*

[17] *Told to Roger Aves who was researching the incident in Kastellorizo, on behalf of the author, July 2018.*

Rhodes for the complex and demanding, but absolutely crucial, process of post-mortem examination.

On his return to Heathrow that morning, Captain Emmerson submitted a full report in relation to his encounter with Charlie Oscar shortly before the latter went missing.

'I was in command of this flight (CY/BE285) which departed late from Nicosia due to hydraulics snag. After leaving the island we were climbing through FL250 when we saw another aircraft approaching above us. This was F-LTAC, an Air France Caravelle, I think. The night was very dark, no visible horizon, sky clear, stars visible. There was no cloud, no icing, no turbulence. Met had forecast thunderstorms in the Nicosia area, but we never saw any at all after take-off. After passing Rhodes I noticed an aircraft coming towards us and above me with landing lights on and a voice called out "Good morning." I replied, "Good morning" and flashed my landing lights on and off. Later I heard CO give his position over Rhodes and Athens control acknowledged and requested him to report UR 19C. Later on, I heard CO calling Athens control, but Athens did not hear him, so I asked Athens if he could read CO. Athens replied he could not, so I relayed CO's position (UR 19C) and ETA Nicosia to Athens. Athens said, "Thank you" and would I tell CO to change to Nicosia control. This I did, CO said "Goodnight" and I replied "Goodnight". After which I heard no more. I cannot think of any reason either weather-wise or control wise which would have any bearing on this tragic business.

Captain L. Emmerson.

BEA's Ops Control Centre, under the supervision of the Duty Operations Superintendent (DOS) was the communications, command and control centre of the airline.

David Nicholas was an Operations Officer in the BEA OCC on the night of 11th / 12th October 1967. He recalls;

'It was a normal night in every respect, to the best of my recollection. The outbound flight to Athens and Nicosia, BE/CY284 had departed before we started work and the reciprocal flight (CY/BE285, operated by G-APMF) was preparing to leave Nicosia.

'The first message that we received was by telephone to the DOS, probably, though I cannot confirm it, from Cyprus Airways in Nicosia, who as well as being partially owned by BEA were our Ground Handling Agents. The message was that G-ARCO had lost contact with Nicosia Area Control Centre (ACC) immediately following its first call after crossing the boundary into Cypriot airspace. From recollection the aircraft had

transmitted on the Nicosia ATC VHF frequency "Nicky, Bealine Golf Alpha Romeo Charlie Osc..." and had not made any further transmission when Nicosia replied, "Go ahead...."

'Although the ATC controller had not detected the truncation of "Oscar", this became apparent when the tape recording was replayed and was assumed to be the moment when disaster overtook the aircraft. Nicosia ATC advised that the aircraft had not entered radar cover and that they had initiated the Alert Phase (ALERFA). They then rang off with the promise to keep us advised.

'A further call after the ETA of the flight had elapsed indicated that no radar or radio contact had been made since the initial message, and the DOS announced to the OCC staff that he was initiating the company's Accident Procedure as the aircraft had now passed its fuel endurance without contact.

'Subdued, we all worked on, mechanically continuing the normal procedures required to prepare the company's operations for the new day, while a sense of numbness remained below the surface. Although the shift staff were of men and women of varying ages, from close-to-retirement to teenagers like me, nobody wept, nobody lost their composure and the normal procedure of cancelling the inbound flight[18] and publishing across the company the reason as 'Operational' was put in motion. The Comet Fleet assistant rearranged the fleet operating pattern for the day to ensure that subsequent services assigned to Charlie Oscar were covered by other aircraft, and Crew Control were advised that the aircraft crew was, pending confirmation, to be assumed to be lost. The human tragedy aside, the loss of staff also had future ramifications for the crew rosters for the Comet fleet.

'Behind the scenes, though it didn't cross my mind at that moment, someone – probably the Comet Fleet Manager – was preparing to advise the next of kin of the crew that their loved ones were missing, while a similar process took place in the Cabin Crew Centre. The ripples were starting to spread even before the fate of the aircraft was known for certain.

'I ended my duty at 0730, and as the early shift arrived most of the staff were unaware of the night's events and received the news with grim

---

[18] *The return flight in this case was CY/BE265, scheduled to be operated by G-ARCO, departing Nicosia at 0755Z.*

acceptance. The discovery by search aircraft of a fuel slick, floating wreckage and bodies in the sea in the early hours of daylight confirmed the worst fears and raised uncomfortable recollections of the earlier Comet 1 disasters (to which it was later found to have no relevance once the evidence of an explosion was found). In contrast to recent years, the 1960s were a period when fatal accidents were much more frequent than now. Many of the staff had experienced the Vanguard (G-APEE) crash at LHR in 1964, and the earlier BEA Comet accident (G-ARJM) at Ankara in 1961. Other British aircraft had crashed in that decade, often flying into high ground in the years before terrain avoidance systems were introduced. Older staff had experienced the war only 20-odd years previously and had in many cases directly experienced the loss of friends and colleagues in action. The entire culture was considerably different; nobody was offered any counselling and certainly would not be sent home in the aftermath of an accident. The important thing was to protect the integrity of the company's operation regardless of the challenges that occurred. A considerable esprit de corps had evolved over those years.'

Joyce Blackwood had driven up to Lincolnshire the previous day to spend a few days with their elder daughter. At about 9.30 am two women were sitting in a bedroom chatting when the telephone rang. Robert answered it in his office and called Joyce downstairs, saying that it was the BEA duty officer asking for her. She took the call and, after a pause while she listened to the message he was passing, Jill heard her mother say, *"Is there no hope at all, then?"* After another pause for the answer, Joyce put the phone down in silence.

Gordon had spoken on the phone the previous day to his father, mentioning that he had a night flight to Athens and Nicosia. His father, habitually an early riser, was at home with his wife when he heard the initial announcement on the radio that a BEA Comet had crashed whilst on a flight between the two airports. He turned to his wife and said, simply, *"I'm afraid we've lost Gordon."*

SFO Mike Thomas' wife Sally was on her way to drop off their daughter Alison at nursery when she heard on the radio that Charlie Oscar was missing. When she got home, she found various officials from BEA on her doorstep.

In Cyprus the family of Rodosthenis Christou were eagerly awaiting his return but, instead of celebrating his arrival, they were informed of the terrible tragedy with the plane exploding in mid-air. The authorities informed the family that there was a bomb on the aircraft and there were no survivors. The welcoming party became a solemn event. His children later recalled the day they heard the dreadful news[19]. His elder son Sotos, fifteen years old at the time, remembered, '*I found out about my dad's death when I went home and saw my mum crying and saying, "Your dad is dead, he is not coming back."*'

Athina, Rodosthenis' elder daughter, was twelve at the time: '

When I finished school and I was on my way to get the bus, a man who was acquainted with our family who also owned the kiosk near the bus stop, told me the plane in which my dad was travelling in, crashed and my dad was dead. I was feeling so alone and scared. When I got off the bus, I took my shoes and my socks off and I started to run to get home quickly so that I could be told all was a lie and my dad would be waiting there for me. When I finally got home to my dismay it was all true.'

As well as Sotos and Athina, Rodosthenis left two younger children, Petros, seven years old and Vasso, who was aged sixteen months at the time. The body of Rodosthenis Christou was found in the main group and picked up by a Greek ship. Due to the extremely severe injuries he had received, his family were not allowed to view him. His death affected all the family socially, physically and emotionally. His grand-daughter, Helen Kyriakou, told the author,

'*His youngest daughter Vasso was never given the opportunity to know her father or even to say the word "Dad". All was stolen from her. His widow Eleni was forced to become the father and mother of his children. In his memory all his children along with his wife changed their surname from Christou to Rodosthenous. Since his death, his wife was continuously asking "Why?" and she took that to her grave after 50 years of being apart. Rodosthenis was a loved person, outgoing, philanthropist, family oriented and he loved helping people without expecting anything in return. People who had the privilege to know him spoke very highly of him with passion and great affection. He was a very special and unique man.*'

Nick Georgiou, a brother of Sotiris, was awaiting the arrival of CY284 at Nicosia airport. When the dreadful news was broken to the friends and relatives that Charlie Oscar was overdue, Nick telephoned another brother, Renos, who also lived in New York. Sotiris had four brothers living in the US, Renos, Constantinos, Polyvios and Andrew. They immediately made arrangements to cross the Atlantic to Athens together. Andrew and Renos continued to Cyprus to support their family whilst Constantinos and Polyvios made their way to Rhodes in the hope of recovering Sotiris' body.

---

[19] *In a letter to the author via Helen Kyriakou.*

After John Loizou and Nicos Hasapopoulos had left the group to go to work, Louis had returned to his hotel in the expectation that they would meet up soon afterwards in Cyprus. John would, they hoped, have Josephine in tow. Louis told the author:

'I went to bed and woke up around dawn, with a feeling I had never experienced before or since. It was a definite feeling of the presence of someone close. My head was, for some reason, filled with thoughts of what I would do if I knew that a flight I was due to work on was going to crash. I knew I would refuse to fly on it even if I lost my job as a result. I went back to sleep for a bit, then got up quite early and went to a local market. When I returned to the hotel to get ready for work, the news was on the radio and everybody was talking about it. Even though I was very shocked and upset at losing John, I still had to work the flight. What made it really difficult was that some of our passengers were regular travellers and knew John and me. They asked me if John was on the flight, and I was not able to bring myself to answer them. It all affected my family and I greatly. He is still my brother and not for one moment has been out of my thoughts.'

Adding its own notification was Hawker Siddeley Aviation (HSA), a company that included de Havilland, the original manufacturer of the Comet type, amongst its constituent firms.

Mr. T. Burrell, from HSA's head office at Hatfield, sent the following cable to all operators of the DH106 Comet and their respective airworthiness authorities at 1515hrs the following day:

Comet 4B G-ARCO was lost on a flight from Athens to Nicosia on 12th October 1967 with 66 persons on board.

It has been reported that some wreckage was signed on surface of sea. There are no known survivors.

Investigation is proceeding.

To date there are no indications of the cause of the accident.

Operators and Airworthiness Authorities will be kept informed.

As a British-registered aircraft had crashed in international waters, responsibility for leading the investigation fell to the Air Accident Branch (AIB) of the Board of Trade. The Chief Investigator of Accidents was Group Captain John Veal, CBE, AFC and he took personal control of the matter. Working with him were Eric Newton, Chief Investigating Officer, and Norman Head, Principal Inspector. These three men would spearhead what was expected to be a complex and difficult operation to establish why Charlie Oscar crashed. Norman Head was immediately despatched to Athens to get the investigation underway.

BEA's own internal investigation was led by Captain William Baillie, the airline's General Manager, who travelled to Rhodes to await the landing of bodies and wreckage from the *Navarinon*. Captain Baillie was joined there by Mr. Head. Before leaving Heathrow, Captain Baillie told the press, "It is the most amazing type of accident in this day and age because it happened from a cruising altitude of 29,000 feet."

With so little wreckage recovered, and almost nothing from the airframe itself, hopes were pinned on a pathological examination of the bodies. This appallingly unpleasant task fell to Group Captain Ken Mason, MD, DMJ, a Consultant Pathologist with the RAF Institute of Pathology and Tropical Medicine.

After the post-mortem examinations, the bodies of the victims were released for burial. On Monday 16th October, a BEA Argosy cargo aircraft conveyed to Nicosia the coffins containing the bodies of fifteen of the Cypriot passengers, including cabin attendants Thelma Efremi and John Loizou, Dr. George Ioannides, Loizos and Irinoula Nicolaides, Michael Thomaides, Rodosthenis Christou and Niki Rodosthenous, Costas Efstathiou, Avraam Solomou, Nicolas Peters and Anne Harbstreet.

Popi Fottou's body was taken to Athens, where her fiancé lived. The British passengers were mostly returned to their homeland. Twelve of the Greek passengers were buried together on Rhodes. Still unaccounted for, and now presumed dead, were the three flight crew, Captain Gordon Blackwood, SFO Mike Thomas and SFO Dennis Palmer, along with steward Nicos Hasapopoulos, Andreas, the young son of Loizos and Irinoula Nicolaides, Vasilios Markidis, Konstantinos and Theognosia Paleologos, Nicos Papatreou, William Sheris, Mary Dalton, Sotiris Georgiou, Mrs Katerina Liassides, Elaine McComb, and Michael O'Brien. Their bodies have never been recovered.

For Joyce Blackwood this was to be something of a comfort; Gordon had long held the view that he hated the thought of being buried or cremated and had an enduring love of the sea. In a press interview some months after the tragedy, Joyce said she believed that a resting place in the sea was something of which he would have approved.

The funerals of most of the Cypriot victims were noted in *Cyprus Mail*. Th newspaper reported that Cyprus Airways staff had acted as pallbearers for John Loizou and Thelma Efremi. The service was held at Ayii Omoloyitades church, the same location as the funerals in 1961 for a further three Cyprus Airways cabin crew, killed when their Comet 4B had crashed on take-off from Ankara. The funeral was attended, noted the paper, by the Minister of Communications and Works, Mr. Titos Phanos, Cyprus Airways manager, Mr. Evdokios Savvas, Civil Aviation Director, Mr. L. Xenopoulos and BEA's Eastern Mediterranean Traffic Superintendent, Mr. Woodruffe. As a mark of respect to all victims, Cyprus radio had played quiet classical music all morning.

Dr. George Ioannides was accorded the honour of the Cypriot President, Archbishop Makarios, conducting his funeral service at the Phaneromeni Church. John Jakouris' funeral was held at Strovoli whilst that of Avraam Solomou was held at Tymbou, attended by Mrs. Kyprianou, wife of the Foreign Minister. Several funerals took place in Limassol, including the Nicolaides couple, whose pallbearers were drawn from their colleagues at the Bank of Cyprus, the others were for beautician Niki Rodosthenous and Dorothea Rachovidou.

Businessman Michael Thomaides was honoured in Famagusta in the presence of the mayor and leading citizens. His coffin was borne by staff and colleagues from his company. The funeral of Sergeant Rodosthenis Christou was attended by a police guard of honour.

The formalities completed, the families were now left to grieve, and to ask how and why their loved ones were killed. For the investigators, the hard work to provide the answers was only just beginning.

In Deep Water

From the outset, it was recognised that the paucity of wreckage, especially parts of the airframe and engines, and the absence of the flight data recorder, was likely to hinder or prevent the investigation determining the cause of the crash. However, Charlie Oscar had crashed into the Mediterranean at a place where its depth was between nine and fifteen thousand feet. This was likely to be a massive problem, if not insurmountable. The uneven sea bed made it very difficult to assess exactly how deep the wreckage of Charlie Oscar might lie, On 16th October, Mr. Riddoch and Eric Newton, along with John Veal, attended a meeting with Mr. Peter Flett, Marine Salvage Officer with the Ministry of Defence. Also attending was Commander Sims-Ross, of the United States Navy. Mr. Flett explained that the Royal Navy's equipment was inadequate for the task, especially considering the depth of water in which Charlie Oscar now lay. The MoD considered that the US Navy was much better equipped, and indeed the latter had useful experience in very deep-water salvage[20]. Commander Sims-Ross told the meeting, following enquiries he had made with Washington over the weekend, that two vessels, the *Aluminaut* and the *Alvin*, might be considered if the decision was taken to try to locate and recover the wreckage.

Aluminaut, an aluminium submersible vessel, had been used to search for a missing American hydrogen bomb off Palomares in 1966. The Reynolds Aluminium Company, who had constructed and operated *Aluminaut*, were keen to get involved. A cost estimate had been provided, the monthly sum of US $200,000 per month including the crew. However it transpired that *Aluminaut* was an observation rather than recovery vessel, and it would not be able to salvage any wreckage from Charlie Oscar.

Alvin, in contrast, was equipped for salvage operations, and could also operate down to 6,000 feet of water. In essence, the two vessels could work in tandem, *Aluminaut* searching and the *Alvin* retrieving any wreckage it could reach. There was a challenge in terms of plotting position to the degree of accuracy required.

The transfer of the two vessels to and from the United States would take an estimated one month in each direction, and the time on station for the

---

[20] *In January 1966, a B-52 bomber, carrying three hydrogen bombs, had collided with a KC-135 aerial tanker during an attempted mid-air refuelling operation over Palomares, Spain. Two of the bombs fell onto land but the third dropped into the Mediterranean Sea. The US Navy had managed to locate the two sites and recover the missing H-bomb, to the relief of the local populace at least.*

search was estimated to be a further month, taking the estimated cost, if all went well, to around US $2,000,000. This would cover a search area of some 15 square miles, assuming that operations were possible every day. It was noted that the crash position was, at that time, believed to be no more accurate than plus or minus five miles, meaning that the potential search area would therefore be of the order of one hundred square miles. Given the time of year, plus the time for the equipment to reach the scene, the Eastern Mediterranean would almost certainly experience spells of bad weather, increasing the overall cost even further, but still with what was considered to be no more than a 10% chance of success.

The meeting also considered the possibility of using television cameras to explore the seabed. Suitable equipment in the US was rigged to operate at depths of up to 4,700 feet, though it could be extended to 6,000 with additional cable. Such equipment was offered at no cost other than incurred expenses.

On 9th November, John Veal met with Bill Mallalieu, the Minister of State at the Board of Trade in London. They were joined by Mr. Riddoch, Mr. Flett, Commander Sims-Ross and Captain Searle, Supervisor of Salvage for the US Navy. Mr. Mallalieu explained to the Americans that he was grateful for their cooperation over recent weeks and that he was most anxious that the wreckage of G-ARCO should be recovered with a view to discovering the cause of the tragedy. However, he pointed out, the Government needed some idea of the chances of success should it go down the vastly expensive road of hiring the *Aluminaut*.

Captain Searle explained that the *Aluminaut* could work for fairly long periods at considerable depths. It was not, however, insured to work at depths greater than 8,000 feet and greater depths would be even more risky.

In the end, Mallalieu decided that it was time to draw a line under the consideration of salvage. Taking heed of the advice from various quarters, he appeared before the House of Commons on 22nd November to say:

> *The possibility of salvage has been carefully examined with Ministry of Defence and United States Navy experts and I have personally discussed the matter with the United States Navy Supervisor of Salvage. It is clear that salvage of the wreckage would be impracticable and that an attempt at recovery of the flight recorder alone would be an extremely difficult, lengthy and perhaps hazardous operation with little prospect of success. In view of this, and evidence which indicates detonation of a high explosive in the aircraft cabin, (it has been) decided that the question of salvage should not be pursued.*

Bodies of Evidence

The task of conducting post-mortems on the recovered victims fell to Group Captain Ken Mason, of the RAF Aviation and Forensic Pathology Department. Born in 1920, Mason was to spend thirty years working as an RAF pathologist, having been described by his colleagues in his later career at the University of Edinburgh[21] as '...*very much a pioneer of aviation pathology.*'

The work of Mason and his colleague, Squadron Leader Stan Tarlton, was to be arduous in the extreme. The department having been informed of the crash on the morning of 12th October, the duo travelled to Greece, leaving Heathrow at 2245hrs that evening and arriving in Athens at 0215hrs on 13th October, precisely 24 hours after Charlie Oscar had undertaken the same trip. They were informed when they got to Athens that the majority of bodies were being transported to Rhodes, where they were expected early that same morning. They therefore travelled on to Rhodes, arriving at 0930hrs.

Mason and Tarlton held a meeting at 1130hrs with Captain Baillie and Dr. Preston, Chief Medical Officer of BEA, along with two Greek representatives, Mr. P. Apostolides of the Foreign Office and K. Christopoulos, Health Council of Civil Aviation. Also present were unnamed representatives of Cyprus Airways and Mr. Canyon, from the British Association of Embalmers. Mr. Christopoulos outlined the official position regarding health aspects of identification, embalming and burial of the bodies. Mason and Tarlton were opposed to the idea of inviting relatives of the victims to identify the bodies as this would, they felt, interfere with their work. Mr. Christopoulos over-ruled their protestations, explaining that the presence of relatives was essential to the identification process.

Mason and Tarlton then made their way to Rhodes Hospital to organise the post-mortem examinations. Whilst attempting to do so, they were constantly interrupted by supposedly-urgent telephone calls, most of which

---

[21] *John Kenyon ('Ken') French Mason CBE served for three decades as a forensic pathologist in the Royal Air Force. Focusing on aviation medicine, he rose through the ranks to become group captain and director of the RAF's Aviation and Forensic Pathology Department and was regularly summoned to investigate aviation accidents. In recognition of his contributions to the forensic pathology of aircraft accidents, in 1973 he was awarded a Commander of the Order of the British Empire (Military Division). He subsequently held the post of Professor of Forensic Medicine at the University of Edinburgh. Afterwards he developed a third career in medical law. His career eventually spanned 74 years. He passed away on 26th January 2017 at the age of 97. Stan Tarlton passed away in 2014.*

turned out to be from the press. As a result, they did not manage to start the post-mortems until 1500 hrs, by which time they had gone thirty hours without sleep.

Mason considered that conditions were not ideal. The mortuary actually consisted of a single table with no drain. There was a wash basin which quickly became clogged up. The location of the mortuary also meant that it was impossible to work without children and adults looking through the window. By now, of course, Mason and Tarlton were extremely fatigued and managed to complete on six examinations before having to call a halt at 1900hrs in order to attend a conference with Captain Baillie.

The Greek authorities were unhappy, according to Mason in his later report[22] and the team felt itself under great pressure which affected their work. The following day the pressure grew further when the local Health Officer expressed his concerns about the general risk to health engendered by the investigation. Mason felt a degree of sympathy with that view; there was no facility for refrigerating the bodies which had been in the sea and then in transit for some 24 hours before they even reached Rhodes. However, the Health Officer understood the pathologists' plight and agreed to let them carry on. However, the arrival of the nineteen bodies from Turkey, delivered to the mortuary on the afternoon of 13th October, resulted in the Public Prosecutor directing that all bodies were to be sealed in coffins by the end of the following day, Saturday 14th October.

In the course of the 13th, Mason and Tarlton performed heroically and completed a total of 21 further autopsies; their work was further interrupted by the visit of a plane-load of relatives who were legally entitled to inspect each body. Christopoulos later reported that '*Identification of the bodies was rendered easier by the reliable evidence and declarations of the relatives who had arrived and in one difficult case by other elements of medical jurisprudence (operation scars, personal effects, etc.)*'[23] To Mason's considerable chagrin, the visitors also included, at the insistence of the Public Prosecutor, a number of Italian press photographers[24]. To add to the team's problems, the only deep freeze available to preserve blood samples and similar specimens was in a hotel, and Mason considered that

---

[22] *Aviation Pathology Report No. 15 1967, RAF Institute of Pathology and Tropical Medicine; AVIA101/225 The National Archives, London.*

[23] *Christopoulos' report (as translated), AVIA101 210 Chief Investigating Officer's Report – TNA.*

[24] *Photographs of a number of the dead, including a young child, appeared in the international press. The British press was, and remains, restrained in this regard. These photographs, although made available to the author, do not appear in this book.*

it was unreasonable to press on the management more than one day's batch.

Mason and Tarlton completed the remainder of the autopsies, bar four, in what they considered to be somewhat unsatisfactorily conditions. The other four bodies were removed by their families before post-mortem examinations could take place.

The Public Prosecutor was keeping up the pressure for a swift completion of the autopsies before dusk, with any remaining unidentified bodies being sealed in coffins and buried locally. However, he took a reasonable approach when it became apparent at the appointed hour that only six bodies were yet to be named.

There was more work for the pair the following day, 15th October, as they met up with Norman Head of the AIB to examine lifejackets and the small amount of wreckage that had been recovered. After this, Mason and Tarlton finished the identification procedure for the remaining six bodies[25], before holding a press conference with Norman Head that evening.

In his report, Mason acknowledged the assistance given to them by BEA, Cyprus Airways and the local authorities. They were particularly grateful for the presence of a photographer and interpreter.

In the immediate absence of a conclusive cause of loss, the possibility of a bomb could still not be definitely ruled out. On 13th October Norman Head had issued an urgent request to Ken Mason that all pieces of metal recovered from bodies be returned to the AIB by the quickest means and also suggested that all the bodies be X-rayed. There had been previous cases, mostly in North and South America, in which airliners had been brought down by the detonation of explosives in the passenger cabin or cargo hold. Investigation of the wreckage had revealed noticeable fragments of metal. In the case of suicide, the predominant characteristic had been the use of hand grenades, which dispersed large pieces of metal, and it was considered highly likely that a similar occurrence in Charlie Oscar would have left such evidence in the remains of the victims.

Mason and Tarlton having completed as best they could their incomprehensively difficult task over the weekend, went home to prepare their interim report[26]. There had initially been statements, by the RAF crew and others, that some of the bodies had been wearing lifejackets. It was only after the post mortems that the team was able to clarify that no one

---

[25] Christopoulos noted, 'Of the 51 bodies undergoing necrotomy, on two of them complete identification was not established, except nationality. These were taken to London for further collection of medico-jurisprudence elements of identification.'

[26] AVIA13 1383 Accident Investigation – National Archives.

had been doing. Mason and Tarlton noted that, by the time of the interim report, the seating positions of 28 passengers boarding in London were known, this information coming from the London – Athens cabin crew. They also recognised a potential significance in the distribution of the bodies, in terms of their recovery in either the 'Greek' (southern) or the 'Turkish' (northern) group.

Mason and Tarlton commented on the differences in the ratio of extreme to slight external injuries between the northern and southern groups; the southern group had a significant number of 'extreme injury' cases and fewer with slight visible injuries. Whilst not in itself conclusive, the difference was marked.

The uniformity of injury among those showing extreme injury was striking. Basically, the picture was one of massive head injury combined with severe injury to the thoracic spine (usually amounting to transection) and full fracture of the sternum; atrioventricular rupture was common and abdominal laceration invariable. This might be a result of being thrown violently around the cabin as the Comet descended.

Most of the 'slightly injured[27]' group had died from single injuries in the cardio-vascular system, but that the frequency of abdominal laceration even in this group was noteworthy.

The interim report considered similarities between the victims recovered from Charlie Oscar, and those from the Elba and Naples Comet crashes thirteen years earlier. Whilst there was no suggestion that the various injuries and clothing retention or loss were specific to accidents involving that particular aircraft type, they had all occurred in the Mediterranean and involved British aircraft. The results of the previous investigations were, therefore, readily available for comparison. Mason and Tarlton noted the common high frequency of head injuries, severe thoracic injuries and internal injury with an absence of severe external damage to many of the bodies. This suggested that there had been a degree of similarity in the process of descent following a catastrophic failure, and the destruction of the various aircraft when hitting the sea.

According to the rudimentary seating plan[28] reconstructed with the help of the London-Athens cabin crew and passengers, all the 'slightly injured'

---

[27] *Whilst it might appear anomalous to refer to victims who had suffered fatal injuries as 'slightly injured', this was the wording adopted by Mason and Tarlton so is used in that context.*

[28] *The assumptions made about the final seating pattern rely on no one having changed seats after the turnround at Athens. With the Tourist Class cabins being one-third empty, there is no guarantee that this was actually the case. However, it is unlikely that a*

passengers, whose seating could be placed, were located between rows 6 and 12, on the port side of the aircraft. The report considered that the twenty-strong group of Jehovah's Witnesses, mostly elderly, would probably have been sitting together in the rear portion of the cabin.

Mason and Tarlton stressed that any explanation of the mechanism by which the injuries were sustained must at the same time explain the presence of the 'slightly injured' group. They felt it was inevitable that the findings could only be satisfied on the basis of the 'slightly injured' group being thrown clear of the aircraft either before, or at the same time as, the other victims had been thrown around inside the fuselage. They went on to consider a number of possible scenarios based on the assumption that all the passengers gad been seated according to the seating plan provided to them after the interviews of the passengers and crew who disembarked at Athens.

Following the earlier Comet Mk1 tragedies, the first cause of loss considered by Mason and Tarlton was cabin pressurisation failure. It was also apparent to them that the head injuries in the earlier crashes were similar to those found in Charlie Oscar. However, they noted that no similar string of mishaps had occurred in any other major aircraft type, so cautioned against conclusions being drawn too hastily. They also pointed out that the Comet 4B was vastly different to the earlier model, and that it had probably been tested more thoroughly than any other aircraft in service. Had a cabin failure similar in scale to the earlier Comets occurred, it was seemingly impossible to explain why many passengers in the centre of the cabin had been spared the effects of turbulence. If it was on a markedly smaller scale it might still have been sufficient to destroy the side of the aircraft, allowing the ejection of the 'slightly injured' group. The second possibility, however, implied that the occupants might have fallen from different heights, with the 'slightly injured' group have fallen the greatest distance[29]. The evidence from the body recovery, with two distinct groups about half a mile apart, suggested that any ejection of the victims had occurred at a height significantly lower than Charlie Oscar's cruising

---

significant number of passengers would have changed seats unless there was some reason to do so.

[29] *Previous work had concluded that occupants falling from height were spared the 'cement mixer' effect of being flung around the cabin, and that impact with the sea would have caused fatal internal injuries, but without the external trauma of those inside the tumbling fuselage. Similarly, experiments after the Comet Mk 1 crashes suggested that a fall into the sea from a height greater than a few hundred feet would have so torn the clothing that it would be dislodged either on contact with the sea, or by the action of waves before the body was recovered.*

altitude of 29,000 feet. In particular, a number of the 'slightly injured' group retained some of their clothing, which was at variance with the experiments conducted after the Comet Mk 1 disasters.

The second possibility was loss of control of the aircraft, which might have been caused by one or more of a number of factors. These could have included, the pathologists suggested, pilot incapacitation, engine disintegration, sabotage, collision or lightning strike. As all three pilots were amongst the missing victims, there was no evidence to show or disprove incapacitation. A collision in the area of the passenger cabin would have produced a less uniform pattern of injuries, although they accepted that the point of impact might have been in the vicinity of the flight deck or outside the pressure cabin itself. Lightning strike could not be wholly excluded, but the pathologists noted that no steel possessions of the passengers, such as had been recovered, were found to be magnetised. Consideration of engine break up or sabotage, they stated, should be discussed in relation to Case No. 6, 28-year-old Mr. Achillea Afatitis, who was traveling with his new wife as part of the group of twenty, mostly older, Jehovah's Witnesses.

Mr. Afatitis' body was distinctive for several reasons:
    a. He had arm injuries, sustained before death, suggestive of flailing.
    b. His upper body was peppered with minute dark specks.
    c. His trachea strongly appeared to be affected by heat.
    d. His shirt also had minute holes similar to those in his chest.

The skin lesions appeared to be very superficial puncture wounds which showed marked heat coagulation. The minor lesions, along with the heat coagulation in the throat, showed vascular reaction, inflammation caused by minute blood vessels, suggesting that Mr. Afatitis had still been alive at the time the damage was caused. This was to prove a very significant development. Whilst nothing was found in the lesion examined, Mason and Tarlton noted that any such foreign body would have disappeared if it was liquid and would have been lost during the recovery and examination process, if it was a minute metallic object.

In their consideration of sabotage as the cause of the disaster, Mason and Tarlton considered reported American experience that large metallic fragments would be present, and none of these were found, either physically or by X-ray, in Mr. Afatitis' body, or any other victim.

If the cause had been a bomb or similar event, the pathologists reported, the medical evidence suggested three subsequent sequences in the destruction of Charlie Oscar:
    1. That a massive defect was produced in the aircraft at 29,000 feet.
    2. That the aircraft was put out of control and broke up under increasing stress at a much lower height.

3. That, being out of control, the aircraft struck the water, possibly port wing first, and disintegrated as it sped over the water, spilling victims as it went.

They considered it was probable that the engineering evidence would strongly support a massive defect having occurred at altitude, and that the available medical difference would provide little to help distinguishing between possibilities 2 and 3. Whilst the lung appearances in the 'slightly injured' group were comparable to those ascribed to free-fall water impact in the earlier Comet crashes, there was no reason they could not equally have been sustained by victims being thrown clear when Charlie Oscar hit the surface of the sea. Similarly, the more severe external injuries sustained by other victims were sufficiently uniform for them to have been caused in a non-survivable ditching, which was, to all intents and purposes, a crash into the sea rather than a controlled landing on water. In a pre-meditated water landing, however unsuccessful, it would have been expected that passengers would be wearing life jackets. Mason and Tarlton were able to examine a few life jackets but could find no evidence that any had been fastened to passengers, corroborating the observation of Nikos Misomikes. They did express some surprise that so many life jackets appeared to have come free from their stowage under the seats without some effort by the passengers, but the AIB investigators convinced them that no particular conclusions should be drawn from that.

Amongst the relatives in Rhodes was Polyvios Georgiou, who now faced the further distress of finding out that his brother Sotiris was amongst the eleven passengers and four crew whose bodies had not been recovered. Amongst the more bizarre incidents in what was an unremittingly horrendous experience was what Polyvios later described to the author as *'...a relentless attempt by some of the Jehovah Witnesses to convert my brother and I from being Greek Orthodox to becoming Jehovahs Witness disciples.'*

'The Answer Lies Somewhere Amongst This List'

At the beginning of the investigation, determining the cause beyond any reasonable doubt appeared to be a very tall order. Almost no substantial wreckage had been recovered, and there was no sign of the 'black box' flight data recorder. Charlie Oscar had crashed into the Mediterranean at precisely the point where there was an abyss, the water being an estimated 9,000 feet deep.

Speculation on the cause of the loss of Charlie Oscar was rife from the outset. By the standards of the time, in an age before social media and instant communication, the news-gathering operation was stunningly effective. The press lost no time in supplementing the scant facts of the crash and the names of the victims with personal details, interpretation and speculation. British newspapers carried the story from 13th October, initial reports such as that in the Daily Telegraph setting the tone. *'The cause of the crash remains a complete mystery,'* its readers were informed, though barely 24 hours had elapsed since Charlie Oscar was lost. In spite of the absence thus far of any evidence whatsoever, a number of causes were being mooted.

The investigators had very little to go on at the outset. Apart from the 51 recovered bodies, the evidence consisted of debris, almost all of which was identified as being fragments of the cabin fixtures. There was, of course, the data gathered right at the outset; the ATC recordings and weather records had been promptly and correctly seized and preserved for detailed scrutiny.

In the words of Sherlock Holmes, "When you have eliminated the impossible, whatever remains, however improbable, must be the truth[30]."

A number of specific lines of investigation were now started, working in parallel, in order to confirm or eliminate various possible causes of the disaster.

Amongst the debris recovered from the crash site was a triple-headed Graviner type 71A automatic fire extinguisher, part of the aircraft's installed equipment. It was identified as having come from the starboard side of the centre section of Charlie Oscar. After recovery and return to England, the bottle had been sent to the manufacturer for examination. It was concluded that the fire extinguisher had been fired electrically by an inertia (crash) switch, and that all parts of the operating mechanism appeared to have functioned correctly.

---

[30] *The Sign of the Four*, by Sir Arthur Conan Doyle.

The inertia switch was mounted in the nose of the aircraft with the recovered bottle being, as mentioned, in the centre section. The electrical wiring passes from the nose along the bottom of the forward fuselage to the aircraft centre section. Discharge of the bottle can only be activated by positive electrical energising, a short circuit not being sufficient. This led to the conclusion that the electrical circuit was complete at the time of discharge.

Significantly, the bottle had been recovered from the northern area, away from other flotsam and the bodies associated with the centre section of Charlie Oscar. It was considered highly unlikely that it would have separated on impact with the sea, and the examiners concluded that it probably detached due to the aircraft breaking up in the air. HSA calculated that, if the forward fuselage became detached suddenly, for example due to downward inertial loading on it, the load would be sufficient to trigger the crash switch, causing the bottle to discharge. A downward rotation of the forward fuselage, effectively causing it to 'snap off', would preserve the electrical wiring long enough for the bottle to discharge fully. The single fire extinguisher recovered had therefore provided very strong evidence that Charlie Oscar had broken up in mid-air.

A total of ten wrist watches had been recovered from the bodies of the victims during the post mortem examinations. A prominent watchmaker examined all the watches and established that most had stopped suddenly although three had, despite the catastrophic impact, stopped only when they wound down. It was noted with interest that these tended to be the cheaper watches. Seven of the watches had stopped at between twenty and twenty-five past either four or five o'clock [31]. Overall, the balance of evidence was that the watches had stopped at about 0325hrs GMT. Eight watches were contaminated by kerosene; where these could be linked to individual passengers, it was noted that they came from the southern group of bodies. The investigators were able to conclude that the earliest time of impact indicated by the watches was, therefore, at most two minutes after the last radio transmission, with the majority suggesting that the impact occurred some seven minutes after the final words of SFO Thomas.

Meanwhile, the direction of the investigation took a sudden turn on 5th November when the investigation team became aware that a metal object, apparently from an aircraft, had been recovered from the sea near the island

---

[31] *The hour's difference could be explained by the difference in local time between London and both Athens and Nicosia.*

of Symi, ten to fifteen miles west of Rhodes, a few days previously. It was identified as a fuel drop tank, intended for use with a North American F100D/F Super Sabre fighter-bomber, an aircraft used by the USAF and the air forces of a number of other nations. A report on 2nd November in the Greek newspaper Ethnos, linked the finding with Charlie Oscar, despite the not inconsiderable distance from the crash site, by pointing out that a police identity card belonging to a 'Miss Exeshea[32]' had also been found on a beach on Rhodes, having drifted some 100 miles from the crash site.

Significantly, the drop-tank bore a small trace of red paint. The drop-tank had been forwarded to the Greek authorities where it was examined by the Greek Civil Aviation Administration, Royal Hellenic Air Force and Olympic Airways. Whilst it was quickly identified as being military in origin, and not part of Charlie Oscar, the trace of red suggested that it might have been in collision with an aircraft bearing paint of that colour. BEA's aircraft had red-painted wings and the airline's logo was, in fact, a red square. The intriguing possibility arose: had Charlie Oscar collided with another aircraft?

A mid-air collision could certainly have accounted for the sudden interruption to SFO Thomas's last radio message. It was also a solution that would have removed any suspicion that there had been security flaws at Ellinikon Airport; for that reason, the Greek authorities were quite keen that the possibility of a collision should be explored to the greatest extent possible.

The investigation team had, understandably, asked for the drop tank to be brought to England for examination. The drop tank duly arrived on 20th November. The smear of red paint was considered to be the clue most likely to prove or negate physical contact with Charlie Oscar, so Government's Chemical Inspectorate at the Royal Arsenal, Woolwich, was tasked with carrying out a detailed examination. On 29th November, the eagerly-awaited results of the paint examination were fed back to Eric Newton, in a report by Mr. H Wells. Once again, the details provided show the extremely thorough and methodical way in which the examination was carried out. Mr. Wells noted that the paint smear on the drop tank had been examined and compared with some BEA Comet red paint applied to a test panel.

Mr. Wells was quite clear in his conclusion:

'The above observations, measurements of physical characteristics and chemical analysis show clearly that the smear of red paint on the piece of

---

[32] *Probably 21-year-old Miss Areti Exarcheas who was part of the group of Jehovah's Witnesses on board Charlie Oscar.*

drop-tank differs significantly in composition from the BEA Comet paint, and that the smear is not the result of violent impact with a red painted object.'

Two days after Mr. Well's report, word was received from a Mr. van Cott of the US Embassy. He had been informed that the drop tank was one of a pair dropped by a USAF F100, tail number 50-3970, on 14th July 1967 in clear conditions at a position 15 miles south of Incirlik Airbase, Turkey, from where the tanks had been obtained. The aircraft had been towing a target drogue sleeve and the tanks had been jettisoned to ensure that when the drogue was released the cable would not foul one of the tanks. The pilot had watched the tanks until they hit the water. Jettisoning had been in accordance with international procedure.

Charlie Oscar had definitely not had a mid-air collision with the aircraft carrying the drop-tank, and no aircraft was missing or had damage to suggest contact with the Comet.

The Bomb Theory

Some 27 seat cushions, recovered from the sea were submitted to RARDE by Eric Newton, where the investigation was conducted by Mr. V.J. Clancey, Principal Scientific Officer, with the assistance of other specialists[33]. They used sophisticated techniques, for that time, such as stereo-scan electron microscope, X-ray diffraction and fluorescence, electron microprobe analysis and micro-chemical analysis.

RARDE had been asked to become involved because of its facilities and experience in explosives technology. It also had specialised experience of forensic work in connection with explosives, and of investigating accidental explosions as well as bombs.

Evidence of an explosion of a high explosive, determined as being of a military or similar type, rather than ordinary gelignite, came primarily from the detailed examination of one particular cushion, identified as having come from Charlie Oscar's tourist cabin. This was supported by slight damage to another cushion, part of a torn shirt and also pathological examination of certain of the bodies, one of which had injuries believed to stem from an explosion.

The details of the evidence[34] were, firstly, superficial damage to the cushion, which consisted of a fan-shaped piece cut out of the cushion and surface-blackening, of a kind typical of an explosion. Straight cuts radiated from a common origin and must have been produced by a number of individual objects moving at very high speed, in the manner of fragments of material from an explosion. There were perforations in the cushion, through which wires were pushed. These defined the trajectories of the fragments that caused the perforations as emanating from the same origin as the cuts. X-rays showed the presence in the cushion of a large number of microscopic particles of metal. Their very small size, from 10 milligrams in weight down to microscopic, was consistent with having been produced in an explosion. The presence and distribution of such tiny

---

[33] *These are named in the above RARDE report as: Mr. Alfred Nichol-Smith, Chief Experimental Officer (in charge of metallurgical studies), Dr. George Todd, Principal Scientific Officer (analytical studies), Mr. R.L. Durant, Principal Scientific Officer (X-ray), Mr. J. Markham, Experimental Officer ((Stereo-scan electron microscope), Mr. D.F.T Winter and Mr. K.J. Jarvis (fragment velocity measurements) and Mr. H.J. Yallop and Mr. D.P. Lidstone (explosive trials). All are worthy of mention for their work.*

[34] *Accident to Comet 4B, G-ARCO – Interim report on examination of a seat cushion. D.F. Runnicles, Principal Superintendent, Explosives Division, RARDE, 1ˢᵗ January 1968, via The National Archives.*

particles of metal was also produced in laboratory trials with an explosive in a light metal case.

The examiners then carried out trials firing small particles at a similar cushion, whilst measuring the velocities. The penetration in the suspect cushion was caused by particles travelling at between 5,000 and 10,000 feet per second (3,000 to 6,000 miles per hour). Such velocities could only be produced by an explosion. When the team examined the particles recovered from the cushion from Charlie Oscar under an electron microscope, they found many surface features characteristic of explosive effects[35]. They then compared the particles produced in their test explosion and found markings so similar that this was deemed conclusive evidence. Further corroboration came from metallographic examination of the recovered fragments, which showed crystal structure features characteristic of explosive effects. Finally, laboratory trials showed that similar metal fragments could only be produced using a military or similar high explosive. Notably, they could not be produced from the bursting of an aerosol can or other 'innocent' source.

Having determined beyond any doubt that the damage to the cushion had been caused by a high explosive device, sometimes referred to as an 'infernal machine', the examiners then set out to establish the precise location of the device when it exploded. They were assisted by the bespoke shape of the cushions produced for each of the five seats across the Comet's tourist cabin.

The geometry of the damage to the cushion, location of fragments and the trajectories indicated a position where some parts of the cushion were screened by the seat structure. Because the two sides of the seat assembly were different, one bordered by the curved fuselage wall and the other by the aisle, and the two sides of the cabin required the designs to be mirrored, the only possible position for that particular cushion was on the port side of the aircraft i.e. under a seat numbered 'A', with the device being sited between the seat support and the cabin wall. The precise location was *'...an origin in a limited volume some 12 inches below the seat, roughly in the vertical plane of the rear edge of the cushion and about 3 inches from the line of the port edge of the cushion'*. This suggests that the location would therefore be consistent with the device being in the passenger footwell of the seat immediately behind that from which the cushion originated, and where it would have been clearly visible to any occupants in adjacent seats.

---

[35] *'The particles have been produced mainly by spalling and have in the main a cupped shape with rolled edges. On their surfaces they show diagnostic features, such as cracking, the effects of hot gas washing and bombardment by high speed micro-particles. In some cases, they have caused the cushion material to melt and adhere to their surfaces.'* -

The electron probe and X-ray analysis of the metal fragments showed that some were steel and some aluminium alloy. These were shown, with one exception, to be quite different from the few small steel fittings and the more widespread alloys used in the aircraft structure and seat. They were also different from the metals used in British detonators, and the team wished to continue with examination which would include comparison with detonators of foreign origin. The sole exception was a fragment of metal with a speck of brown paint; the alloy matched one used in a Comet passenger seat. Significantly, no fragments of alloy used in the flooring were found; this proved that the device was not placed beneath the cabin floor, such as in the baggage hold. This was corroborated by the absence of any fibres from the carpet. Many fibres were recovered from the damaged seat cushion, having been driven in by the force of the explosion. These were subjected to chemical, microscopic and X-ray examination, which showed their origin to have been the fabric covering the seats.

There was also damage, blackening and tears to the bottom surface of the cushion which showed that the explosion took place while the cushion was in its normal position on the seat frame, and that it was weighed down in a way typical of there being a passenger sitting on it at the time.

A second seat cushion had minor damage which appeared consistent with the first. The perforations in the second cushion suggested, though not conclusively, that the seat had been behind a little to the starboard of the explosion. Once again, there was blackening to the under surface, except where it had been masked by the seat webbing.

Veal's minutes note that he held a meeting on 13th November, those present with him being Harper, Gordon-Burge, Head and Newton. The group discussed the position regarding the examination of the seat cushion, with Harper being tasked to attain a positive identification of the cushion. This was subsequently followed back through the aircraft manufacturers, via the companies in the supply chain, to Dunlopillo in Aberdare, South Wales, who had produced the foam material for the damaged item. As an evidential chain it was exemplary.

Veal then noted:

'...The possible effect on the structure of an explosion of the size postulated was examined. It was felt that as an alternative to causing cabin failure, damage causing local collapse of the floor could occur with resultant damage to the aircraft controls which could set up a catastrophic situation. Mr. Harper was given the explosive pressure characteristics and agreed to examine the implications towards cabin and floor structure.'

Part of a white nylon shirt had a few small perforations in the region of the right-side front which could, the investigators thought, have been produced by high velocity particles. However, they could not be certain of this.

The investigators considered the amount of explosive required to cause the precise damage recorded; from previous experience and laboratory trials, they estimated that the damage could have been produced by 'about a pound of high explosive' which had possibly been inside a mild steel tube or similar container.

On the basis of the evidence derived from the seat cushions, Ken Mason was asked to re-evaluate the finding from Case No. 6, Mr. Afatitis. The X-rays taken during the post mortem were examined again, and minute opaque particles were noted, these being very similar to those found in the cushions. Further supporting evidence, not conclusive in itself but considered likely to occur in cases of blast, was found in the presence of isolated cases of amputation of the legs of three passengers, a number of burst abdomens, the lung damage of the passenger initially thought to have drowned, and injury to the buttocks of an elderly female passenger, Miss Parzopoulou[36].

Mason did note, however, that it was impossible to say that these injuries were not compatible with those to be expected in a severe aircraft accident due to a cause other than blast. In particular, he urged caution in ascribing sabotage as a definite cause, considering:

i. Mr. Afatitis was the only case to show such injuries; his wife's body provided no such evidence, though she was one of the last victims to be examined and her use of her maiden name meant that the relationship was not realised until weeks later.

ii. The skin lesions were very superficial. However, the explosives experts consulted considered that was not incompatible with the blast theory.

Mason and Tarlton could not state that the injuries sustained by Mr. Afatitis provided prima facie evidence of an explosive device causing the catastrophe. However, they did believe that such medical evidence could corroborate any such conclusion based on engineering evidence. Furthermore, they believed this would be of a device comprising plastic explosive rather than a grenade, and that this had made a difference to their ability to consider the injuries to the bodies to be prima facie evidence. At the time of Charlie Oscar's loss, previous bomb attacks on aircraft had been undertaken with what were considered at the time to be conventional explosives, including the deliberate detonation of hand grenades or

---

[36] *The passengers so described were all amongst the group of Jehovah's Witnesses who boarded at Athens and are believed to have been sitting together in the rear Tourist Class cabin..*

packages of dynamite or gelignite by suicidal passengers, and the use of a 'plastic bomb' was unique[37].

In light of the damage to the seat cushions, however, what might have been circumstantial evidence seen in the bodies was now sufficient to corroborate what the experts now collectively believed: an explosive device had been the root cause of the disaster.

The AIB now engaged with the Structures Department of the Royal Aircraft Establishment (RAE) at Farnborough, in the hope that they could put the explosion of a device into the context of a Comet 4B fuselage in flight at 29,000 feet. The work was supervised by Fred Jones, a 47-year-old structural expert, who had established a reputation as an air safety expert not least because of his involvement in the examination of the wreckage from the earlier BOAC Comet crashes. Fred Jones ultimately received an OBE[38].

Jones was a thorough man, with an excellent track record of deducing the cause of aircraft losses from the scantest of available evidence. In the case of Charlie Oscar, however, he had to fill in the gaps due to the absence of any significant airframe wreckage, and work on the recollection of ground staff and disembarked passengers and crew as to who was probably sitting where. He was not helped by the fact that fifteen passengers were missing and four had not been subjected to post-mortem examination. Jones certainly had his work cut out with Charlie Oscar.

Jones' report[39] started with an overview of the flight, the material recovered from the crash scene and what was known of the passengers. He noted:

Surface craft, engaged on recovery, were deployed in the two areas 'Northern' and 'Southern', and all bodies and flotsam were identified in the first instance, by these areas. It became apparent to the pathologists examining the bodies, that these could be divided into two general groups

---

[37] *Some consideration had also been given to a notorious 1943 murder in Rayleigh, Essex, in which a man in a bath chair had been killed by a device placed underneath the conveyance. On that occasion, the explosive had been an anti-tank mine.*

[38] *https://moretimespace.wordpress.com/2009/02/21/fred-jones-obe-mraes-ceng. Fred Jones was the author of 'Air Crash: The Clues in the Wreckage'. He passed away in 2003 at the age of 82.*

[39] *Accident Note No. Structures 337: Note on the Loss of BEA Comet G-ARCO over the Mediterranean Sea on 12th October 1967 by F.H. Jones C.Eng., AFRAeS., Royal Aircraft Establishment, March 1968.*

– extremely injured, and others. Furthermore, with a few exceptions, those in the extreme injury group were contaminated with kerosene whereas those only lightly injured were 'clean'. Investigators also noted that some flotsam was heavily contaminated by kerosene. <u>The contaminated bodies and flotsam were all recovered from the Southern area.</u> (Jones' emphasis).

Jones went on to consider what was known about the passengers and cabin crew, as discussed in Chapter 2. Jones considered that it was unlikely that the passengers originating in London had moved seats to any significant extent when re-boarding in Athens after the stopover. He commented that one group of passengers, now identified as the party of Jehovah's Witnesses who joined the flight at Athens, were block-booked in the rear tourist cabin. However, although the part of the cabin occupied by members of the group had been ascertained, it was impossible to determine which individuals sat in specific seats. The body of one member of the group, he commented, had not been recovered.

Jones noted the weather data at the approximate time of the accident, adding that the wind strengths and directions at various heights were specifically relevant to his calculations of the trajectories of falling items.

RARDE had supplied Jones with certain information derived from their examination of the cushions, pathological evidence and their experiments attempting to reproduce the explosion in the cabin. He was advised:

a) The explosion had occurred just above the floor of the aircraft.
b) The explosion had occurred under the rear of a tourist type seat.
c) That seat was occupied at the time of the explosion.
d) That seat was on the extreme port side of the aircraft.
e) One body, that of Mr. Afatitis, was injured in a manner to suggest that he had been in a seat one row to the rear, and one seat to the right, of that under which the explosion had occurred.
f) No other body recovered contained evidence of a comparable nature to suggest close proximity to the explosion[40]

As was his practice, whenever possible, when conducting examinations of wreckage, Jones arranged for the flotsam to be laid out on a full-scale layout of the Comet on the laboratory floor at Farnborough. Jones found that all the flotsam originated in the Comet's fuselage, and he noted that all the materials aft of the front wing spar were contaminated by kerosene, and all those forward were not. Clothing associated with individual

---

[40] *These points are as summarised in Jones' report. They are somewhat more concise than the more cautious Mason and Tarlton, who noted some other injuries that might have been caused by the bomb and also stated that there were a number of bodies who might have had shrapnel fragments which was not identified in their forcibly-expedited post mortem examinations.*

passengers, whose seating was known, could also be classified in this way. Jones also concluded, from the examination of the ten wristwatches, that Charlie Oscar had struck the sea at about 0325hrs GMT, 0525 local time, some seven minutes after SFO Thomas's last radio call. His report summarised his analysis and conclusions, which subsequently represented a significant conclusion to the final Accident Report.

The investigations by the AIB established the times and positions of the aircraft along its flight path... the flotsam and bodies were found nearly twenty miles back along the track from the estimated position of the last message.

Although no airframe wreckage was recovered from the sea sufficient material was found in the form of carpets, furnishings, seat cushions, passengers, etc., to give guidance as to the likely locations of the major parts of the fuselage in the sea. The natural division of all this material, by state, recovery area and identity, into two groups strongly indicated that the forward fuselage had landed in the sea in the northern area and the rear fuselage, and associated wings containing fuel tanks, in the southern area. Some seat cushions were found to the south between 1 to 1½ miles from the southern area. It is considered that separation of the fuselage into at least two major portions must have occurred before the aircraft struck the sea, to account for the distribution and state of the flotsam and bodies.

The examination of the flotsam suggested that the division of the fuselage, in the fore and aft sense, could have occurred at about the transverse datum position (centre-section front spar). Consideration of the general passenger injury pattern supported this finding. In general, those passengers forward of the transverse datum position had sustained relatively slight or intermediate injuries, whereas those to the rear had sustained intermediate or extreme injuries. It is apparent that such a division could only arise from the passengers experiencing very different circumstances, as in the case of breakage of a fuselage in the air.

Therefore, trajectory calculations were made on the premise that a fuselage separation occurred in the air at the front spar position. The design firm indicated that this would be a likely separation point under an ultimate loading condition.

Plots were first made from a specific point at 29,000 feet altitude, and the resulting scatter of debris and bodies at sea level noted. This distribution was too large to be reconciled with that seen by the search aircraft. Trajectories were then plotted from sea level upwards, from the general positions for items, as suggested by charts and maps from the search aircraft. A very close interception area of plots was found at about 15,000 feet altitude. It was concluded that the aircraft had not broken up at its cruise altitude, but at the lower altitude, to produce the general pattern in the sea of flotsam and bodies, and the damage and injury pattern to bodies. This conclusion was supported by the pathologists' report that there was no evidence of explosive decompression in any of the bodies, although this would have been expected if major disruption of the aircraft had occurred at a higher altitude.

A further indication that a fuselage separation had probably occurred in the air was given by the evidence of the discharged fire bottle. It was concluded from the recovery point of the bottle that it had discharged in the air due to operation of the inertia crash switch, located in the nosewheel bay, in the nose of the fuselage, and that this operation could be associated with inertia loadings brought about during a breakage of the fuselage at the front spar position.

If the aircraft had broken up at about 15,000 feet, then the heavier pieces of wreckage, containing passengers, or the falling bodies of the passengers, would have taken about two minutes to have fallen to the sea. If, therefore, the time of the final impact deduced from the watches (i.e. 0325 GMT) is correct, then break-up of the aircraft would have occurred at about 0323 GMT. This is five minutes after the last recorded message from the aircraft and would allow ample time for the aircraft to have passed its last estimated position on track at 29,000 feet and returned to the position of the break-up at 15,000 feet. No evidence was found by the RAE to give any indication of the flight path of the aircraft during the descent from 29,000 feet to 15,000 feet, or to explain the final break-up.

An attempt was made to locate the likely site of an explosion, which other investigations have shown to have occurred before the aircraft struck the sea. To recapitulate it appears that the explosion occurred under a tourist seat on the left had side of a row of three, that the seat was occupied, that the body of the occupant was not recovered and that the only body recovered with injuries of the type expected from an explosion, (i.e. no.6), was that of the occupant of the middle seat in the row behind. Unfortunately, passenger no. 6 was one of a group with a 'block-seating', so that his precise location in the cabin was not known, although it would have been in line B in one of the rows 3,4,5,6,7. The port side seats in this area would also have been occupied by members of the group, but none of these were injured in a manner to suggest they had been in close proximity to an explosion. However, one of the group was not recovered.

The nature of the damage to the seat, over the explosion, and to body no. 6 in line B, suggests that the effect of the explosion was not unidirectional. It is likely then that a person seated immediately to the rear of the explosion would also be injured by it. Since no such person has been recovered, it is possible that this was the person sitting in Seat 4A (known but not recovered) or was the missing group member, who may have been sitting in either seats 3A or 7A, i.e. behind either of two known but not recovered passengers. It would seem then that the explosion could have occurred under seat 4A, 5A or 8A, and that passenger no.6 was in seat 3B, 4B or 7B.

The aircraft itself was not at fault. The results of the ancillary lines of enquiry supported the view that the cause was the detonation of a bomb, and not to have been anything else. Scarcely six weeks had passed since Charlie Oscar had been lost, but the investigators had made the most of what little they had to work with. It was now established that she had not been lost in a mid-air collision with another aircraft, been brought down by a disintegrating engine or failure of the airframe. On 20th November, with relatively little fanfare, the Comet fleet was cleared once more to fly at normal cruising altitudes. All that remained was to find out who had planted the bomb, and why.

Probable Cause Established

Following the work carried out by the team at RARDE, and the associated investigatory activity, Veal now believed that he had found the probable cause of Charlie Oscar's demise. His pronouncements were restricted to facts, and contained caveats that allowed for the possibility of further developments. On Friday November 10th, 1967, the following press release was telephoned to the Press:

A number of lines of investigation are being followed up by the Accidents Investigation Branch of the Board of Trade, based on the Comet debris recovered from the Mediterranean and on other evidence.

One of the seat cushions, which is believed to be from the tourist cabin, has been found to have sustained damage which is consistent with that which would be caused by an explosive device within the cabin at floor level. There is other evidence, which is consistent with this having occurred, but which it would be premature to suggest confirms such an eventuality. Further experimental work and other investigations will be necessary before any definite conclusion can be reached regarding the relationship of this evidence to the cause of the Comet accident and before any further statement can be made.

Veal's rationale was probably that it was unlikely that any other, and more likely, cause would be established, and so it was in the public interest to make it known that the destruction of the aircraft was deliberate, rather than due to an inherent fault with the Comet.

The media has never been slow to speculate on activities behind the scenes, and on 26th November *The Sunday Telegraph* published a short and unattributed article, headed *MI6 in Comet Crash Inquiry*, in which it linked the Prime Minister at the time, Harold Wilson, with the matter:

Mr. Wilson is taking a personal interest in an investigation by British Intelligence into the destruction by a plastic bomb of the BEA Comet between Athens and Cyprus last month.

Following reports from MI6 it is almost certain that 66 people lost their lives because of an attempt to assassinate Gen. Grivas, commander of the Cyprus armed forces. Mr. Wilson is forced to play this down because of the Cyprus crisis.

Despite reports to the contrary, the whole investigation has been kept out of the hands of the British police. Normally Scotland Yard would be called in to discover who planted the bomb, and where.

This is invariably the case when a British plane and a Commonwealth country are involved.

Instead the criminal aspect of the inquiry has been handled entirely by Government intelligence acting in conjunction with the Foreign Office and the Board of Trade.

Gen. Grivas flew from Athens to Cyprus in another Comet on the day of the crash. His bodyguard, Mr. A Solomou[41] was on board the lost aircraft and it is almost certain that those who planted the bomb thought the General was on the same plane.

There is little doubt that the bomb was planted at Athens airport. Political extremists owing allegiance outside Greece may well have been responsible.

If the assassination attempt had succeeded it would have touched off the crisis between Greece and Turkey a month ago.

The Sunday Telegraph article, along with Veal's succinct press release identifying a bomb as the most likely cause, caused ructions in Greece. The same day, the Civil Aviation Administration in Athens put out its own release in rebuttal[42]:

Following a BBC broadcast and comments in the domestic and foreign press...we again state that according to detailed proof received by us up to 20th November the above comments by the press and BBC have no relation with the true causes of the accident. We advise who are in a hurry to jump to irresponsible conclusions to wait until the appropriate legal authority submits its official report. This legal authority...is the Board of Trade, Great Britain. They should also wait for the concurring opinion of the appropriate Greek authorities.

The press release by the Greeks caused some consternation in the British Embassy, who telexed Veal the following day:

You will no doubt have seen the column in yesterday's Sunday Telegraph...In our opinion such speculation can only irritate the Greek Civil Aviation Administration by implying criticism of the security

---

[41] *There is no evidence that Avraam Solomou was acting as bodyguard for General Grivas.*

[42] *Source is a telex from the British Embassy in Athens, the text being a translation by the Embassy from the Greek.*

arrangements at Ellinikon airport. We should be grateful therefore if you could let us have your comment on the ST column and any further evidence on the "explosive device" mentioned in your own statements.

Veal immediately replied, in an attempt to provide reassurance:

If Sunday Telegraph article is other than complete speculation or kite flying, we are unaware of sources of information. The only information put out by us on explosion aspect is press release you have already have and answer to a parliamentary question on 22 November on Comet salvage in terms "In view of this (impracticability of general salvage and difficulties and improbability of successful salvage of flight recorder) and evidence which indicates detonation of a high explosive in the aircraft cabin my Right Hon Friend[43] has decided that the question of salvage should not be pursued". Letter indicating present position in respect of investigation is on its way. Expect investigation of explosive aspect to be completed shortly confirming occurrence of explosion.

Veal wrote to JWG James, BEA's Operations Director, on 12th December, stating:

I have been in correspondence with General Skarmaliorakis, the Civil Aviation Administrator in Athens, and with Forbes-Johnson about evidence found during the investigation. I first wrote to the Administrator on 15th November telling him, amongst other things, about the cushion picked up with the cabin debris which showed damage consistent with what could be caused by an explosive device at cabin floor level. I followed this up with a further letter on 28th November in which I said that further investigation of the cushion, the damage to it and the particles it contained, indicated the detonation of a high explosive device within the cabin at floor level. I also told him that the medical evidence provided confirmation of the detonation of an explosive device.

We of course have no evidence that the infernal machine[44] responsible was introduced into the aircraft at Athens. Although some people might regard this as a reasonable assumption, I suppose the Greeks could argue that somebody took it on board in London and left it there when disembarking at Athens. Personally, I do not see that we are likely ever to get any evidence to resolve this aspect. This may indicate that your people

---

[43] Parliamentary term used when referring to a senior member of the same political party as the speaker.

[44] 'Infernal machine' is an archaic term for an explosive device.

will need to be very careful how they handle the matter with the Greek authorities but subject to this I would have thought I had already told General Skarmaliorakis sufficient for you to take some action in respect of preventative measures.

The work of the accident inspectors continued and on 12th December, Veal convened a meeting to bring together the various strands of the investigation, with the usual representatives from RARDE, RAE, Hawker Siddeley and the AIB. Mr. Clancey of RARDE gave a resume of the work of his colleagues, showing photographs of the fragments of metal retrieved from the cushion. The very high speed of the various particles detected, between 2,000 and 5,000 feet per second for the larger fragments and perhaps up to 15,000 feet per second for the smallest ones, had helped Mr. Clancey to form the opinion that there was 'a complete certainty of the detonation of a high explosive'.

Mr. Clancey continued, explaining that, although originally it had been thought that the evidence suggested that one ounce of explosive had detonated, it now seemed possible that the device had contained at least four ounces. As stated previously, it was believed that the locus had been at the left-hand end of a left-hand row of seats.

Mr. Clancey's RARDE colleague, Mr. Jarvis, added that the pressures associated with one ounce of explosive would be 200 psi at a distance of one foot from the point of the explosion, reducing to 30 psi at two feet and 13 psi at 3 feet. However, these pressures would be quadrupled if the device had comprised four ounces of explosive. It was clear that the detonation of an explosive device could potentially cause catastrophic damage and the almost-immediate break-up of the fuselage structure.

On 18th December, Veal was finally ready to submit his formal interim report:

Owing to the non-availability of the main aircraft wreckage the investigation of the accident has been concentrated upon examination of the cabin debris recovered from the Mediterranean, the results of the pathological examination of the bodies of the victims, the general circumstances of the flight and a F.100 drop tank subsequently recovered near Rhodes. In parallel with this the defect and repair history and the previous flight recorder data of G-ARCO have been studied and a detailed engineering investigation of other Comet aircraft has been made. Present conclusions on the matter are that: -

> *(i) None of the victims of the accident were wearing life jackets and no wreckage, other than cabin debris and a fire extinguisher bottle, was seen in the crash area, with*

the possible exception of a circular object which may have been a cabin pressure dome.

(ii) Examination of a fire extinguisher bottle, which had been installed in the right wing of the aircraft, shows it to have discharged as a result of action of the inertia switches, and that impact damage was sustained during the discharge process. It appears from investigation of the probable break-up sequence that the discharge of the bottle and the impact damage it sustained were associated with the break-up of the aircraft at a height. There is a clear demarcation between kerosene contaminated and non-contaminated cabin debris and bodies of victims which indicates at least a partial break-up of the cabin at a not inconsiderable height. Owing to the imprecise information on the points at which the various pieces of cabin debris were recovered it is not possible to construct an accurate trajectory plot from which the probable height of the break--up might be determined. However, the work done in this connection and the amount of scatter suggests that the break-up was well below the original cruising altitude and might have been between 10,000 and 20,000 feet.

(iii) The injury pattern of the victims, 80% of whom suffered head and other body injuries and 20% of whom had little external injury, has been investigated against the limited information available on seat positions and taking account of injuries sustained by the victims of other accidents in which a structural break-up has occurred at altitude. The pathologist, in considering whether sabotage might have occurred, had in mind that this would require the presence of large metallic fragments in the bodies. No such fragments were found by X-ray although three pieces of aircraft material were found as a result of visual examination. As a result of evidence obtained from a seat cushion further investigation of the X-ray photographs was made and this is dealt with below together with the implications of the pathological findings.

(iv) One cushion picked up with the cabin debris, which was positively identified as a Comet tourist cabin cushion, showed damage which, as a result of exhaustive investigation and experimental work at the Royal Armament Research and Development Establishment had been caused by detonation of a high explosive device. The primary evidence for this is the gross damage at the rear of the cushion, penetration holes through the cushion and the inclusion in the cushion of a number of ferrous material and aluminium alloy particles. Examination of the particles has been carried out using electron microscopy and other methods which show that the pieces of ferrous and aluminium alloy recovered possess the characteristics of damage due to high explosive detonation and has enabled the origins of the particles to be ascertained. Investigation of the penetration grooves using a probe technique indicates that the origin of the explosion was approximately at cabin floor level and between two rows of seats. There is evidence that the cushion was in the left-hand seat of a left-hand row, i.e. adjacent to the side of the fuselage. Another of the cushions recovered has also been found to have sustained a number of penetrations which indicate that this cushion was in the row behind that in which the other cushion was located. Cushion damage due to blast and carbon deposits within the penetration grooves of both cushions provide supporting evidence of the occurrence of an explosion. It has been calculated that the velocity of the larger particles found was between 2,000 and 5,000 feet per second and up to 15,000 feet per second in respect of the really small ones.

(v) It was originally suggested that a F.100 fuel drop tank recovered from the sea, which had suffered gross impact damage and bore traces of red paint, might be related to the circumstances of the Comet accident. On visual examination the red paint was seen to be substantially different in colour from the paint on BEA Comets and chemical analysis has established that it is essentially different. The paint appeared under examination to have been in a wet condition when it came in contact with the fuel tank and it appears that its origin was something on which the tank was resting or which had been brushed against the tank. The damage to the tank is consistent with water impact damage and checking through

> *American sources given reason to believe this was one of a pair of tanks dropped from a United States aircraft in July.*

> *(vi) Examination of the meteorological evidence indicates there was no reason to consider the weather was a factor in the cause of the accident.*

> *...When evidence of an explosion on board had been found from the cabin debris, the evidence available from the pathological examinations of the bodies was reinvestigated in an attempt to discover whether this showed any damage consistent with involvement in an explosion. This was complicated by the fact that only 51 bodies were recovered although 66 persons were killed in the accident and it was impossible to carry out complete pathological examination of all the bodies available. In addition the extent of the pathological examination was limited by the facilities available. This reinvestigation has shown in respect of one of the bodies sufficient medical evidence to provide confirmation of the occurrence of the detonation of an explosive device. In addition this medical confirmation is that the device was of the plastic explosive type and not of a grenade type.*

> *This note is essentially an interim account of the present position of the investigation but it is intended to make clear that detonation of a high explosive device was associated with the loss of the aircraft.*

> *As an adjunct, a note from Veal to Riddoch on 21st December adds:*

> *'RARDE...have now reached a position of certainty that there was detonation of a high explosive device and that this was larger than originally estimated, being probably of the order of 4 ounces[45].' A handwritten addendum to Veal's copy of this note states: Thank you. The President has commented: 'A v. first class and thorough interim account.'*

Veal also took the opportunity to inform Riddoch that his final report was dependent on the completion of subsidiary investigations, and that it was unlikely to be available until about the end of March. Veal had noted, in a message to Ken Mason, also on 21st December, that he had prepared the report as a resume of the investigation. He was still awaiting the final RARDE report, which he anticipated would follow by the end of January. He also noted:

---

[45] *4 ounces is approximately 113 grams.*

'I am being pressed to submit my official report as soon as I can, and I have intimated that I would hope to do this within two or three months. This is, of course, dependent upon my receiving your final report and that of RARDE by the end of January.'

Mason replied on 5th January:

Thank you very much for your (report) of 19th December 1967 and the photostat of the report by Mr. Christopoules. As I told you on the telephone, I am a little worried about what is to happen to this report. In the interests of international cooperation, I do not want to argue with it publicly and I hope that you will be able just to ignore it.

It is apparent from this that Veal was aware of the pressure from various parties, not least BEA and the press, to state unequivocally what he considered to be the cause. There were also queries from the Greek and Cypriot authorities who were equally eager to see the matter cleared up. To this end, Veal sent a copy of his interim report to General Skarmaliorakis of the Greek Civil Aviation Administration and awaited his response.

John Veal had included the Attorney General in the limited circulation list for the interim report. The Attorney General, having read this, clearly deemed the matter of importance as, on 3rd January, a message was passed to Veal asking that he might see any further reports, including the final report, when available.

Meanwhile, back on 19th December, Hugh Gordon-Burge had issued a provisional report of the BEA Air Safety Branch (ASB). Inevitably the ASB report mirrored that of Veal, though it did add the following provisional conclusions:

1. *The documentation of the aircraft was in order.*

2. *The pilots were properly licensed.*

3. *Whilst the aircraft was at cruising level between Rhodes and Cyprus, an explosive device detonated at floor level in some part of the tourist cabin.*

4. *The explosion within the cabin probably caused damage to the aircraft such as to render it effectively uncontrollable. Thereafter, and in the subsequent enforced descent, the aircraft broke up.*

The original draft also included a line stating the first presumed cause: 'The accident probably resulted from the detonation of an explosive device within the cabin.'

There can be little doubt that BEA breathed a corporate sigh of relief when it appeared most likely that neither the Comet as an aircraft nor itself as an operator of the aircraft, would be found blameworthy in the tragedy. It was clearly to the airline's benefit that the cause, a malevolent act of mass murder though it was, might have happened in any aircraft and to any operator. The travelling public would have no particular reason to shun BEA or avoid booking a flight on a Comet. Dependent as it was on revenue from passengers, BEA needed to make sure that this information was shared as soon as possible.

Sir Anthony Milward, BEA Chairman, certainly appeared to feel the need to reassure the public when he spoke to a correspondent for The Times newspaper during a visit to the Cardiff Business Club on 8th January. The unnamed reporter appears to have had something of a scoop when their paper broke the news the following day, under the headline *'Comet was sabotaged, BEA says.'* Attributing the information to Sir Anthony, the article continued:

'Scotland Yard detectives have been called in by the airline to investigate. A separate investigation by the Board of Trade accidents inspector is still being carried out. Tonight an official said that no comment could be made.

(Sir Anthony) told me: "Our tests have proved it was sabotage. We made our own inquiry into the crash and a seat cushion showed that an explosive device appeared to have been on board."

He had no positive theory why the aircraft...was sabotaged. "It appears that someone thought the former EOKA leader General Grivas or one of his henchmen might have been on the aircraft, although I have no evidence that this was so", he said.

"Our own inquiries are now at an end and we have handed everything over to Scotland Yard. The official Ministry inquiry is still being carried out. I do not know whether that will agree with our findings."

Meanwhile, the Londoners Diary section of the *Evening Standard* reiterated some of Sir Anthony's assertions the following day in a short piece titled *'Comet Delay':*

Yesterday's statement by the BEA Chairman Sir Anthony Milward that the Comet crash off Turkey last October was definitely caused by sabotage does not indicate that the Board of Trade is ready to make any announcement about the result of its investigations.

In November they made a cautious statement that "*one of the seat cushions thought to be from the tourist cabin is believed to have sustained damage consistent with that which would be caused by an explosive device*" but they hedged this with remarks like: "*Further experimental work and other investigations will be necessary before any definite conclusions can be reached.*"

And many months must still elapse before the final report is made public.

The paper then twisted the knife further by reporting that Captain William Baillie had expressed:

'*...some dissatisfaction today with the length of time taken over a report such as this. He said: "John Veal told me about two months ago that there was clear evidence that a bomb had exploded under the seat – ballistic and chemical evidence.*

"*Whether it was put there with the express purpose of blowing the aircraft up or not, we don't know. BEA must have been carrying many passengers into Nicosia with warlike devices in their luggage.*"

Captain Baillie is inclined to think the bomb was not aimed at General Grivas.

It is fair to say that John Veal was not best pleased with the comments from the BEA men to the press. On 10th January, he sent a somewhat terse letter to Henry Marking, the airline's Chief Executive.

'*The Times' of 9th January contained a report of an interview with Sir Anthony Milward in which he spoke about tests carried out by BEA in its investigation of the Comet accident.*

As BEA have not provided me with evidence on your 'tests which proved it was sabotage' or your 'inquiry into the crash and a seat cushion which showed that an explosive device appeared to have been on board' I wish in accordance with Regulation 7(1)(b) of the Civil Aviation (Investigation of Accidents) Regulations, 1951, to take statements from those concerned. I should be glad, therefore, if you would let me know the names of the persons responsible for the tests conducted by BEA in respect of the sabotage aspect.

On 11th January, John Veal noted a conversation he had had, probably with Jim Templeton, from the Air Registration Board:

Throughout the investigation there has been close cooperation with the BEA Flight Safety Branch and they have been kept informed of the progress of the investigation and, in particular, of the work which has been done at the RARDE into the explosion aspect. To the best of my knowledge there is no truth in the statement by Sir Anthony Milward about tests which they have carried out into the explosion aspect nor, as far as I know, have BEA been in touch with Scotland Yard. The Special Branch and Box 500[46] have been kept informed by me of the possible sabotage aspects so that they might make their own inquiries and I understand that the latest interim report which I have provided is being considered by the Assistant Commissioner and that the Director of Public Prosecutions is being consulted whether any further action should be taken.

Veal, however, was in no rush to make public the full details of his investigations. Writing to Marking on 9th January, he opined:

'Any expression of belief (in the cause of the crash) of this sort, or consideration of the need for it is, of course, a matter for you, but I am concerned that it is proposed to associate it with a report which is based to a considerable extent on information which I have released to BEA in confidence. Inclusion in it of a reference to the 'still confidential nature of relevant evidence, which has not been released by the Chief Inspector of Accidents' serves merely to make my position in the matter even more difficult.

I was under the impression from what had been written in the Press following the last statement in the House, and from the cessation of requests for more information, that there was now a general acceptance that the Comet accident resulted from detonation of a high explosive device in the cabin. If you have evidence that there still is public concern about the safety of the aircraft which needs to be allayed perhaps you

---

[46] *Box 500 is the pseudonym by which MI5 has traditionally been known, the label originating from the Post Office box used as its address. MI5 (Military Intelligence, Section 5) is also known as the Security Service, its role being counter-intelligence and domestic security. MI5 comes under the Home Office. However, Veal and his team refer to staff at 'Defence Intelligence', which might actually have been the 'Defence Intelligence Staff', a branch of the Ministry of Defence, possibly working in conjunction with MI6, the Secret Intelligence Service, which comes under the Foreign Office. As the existence of MI6 was kept secret at that time, it is likely that access to its staff would have been via MI5.*

could let me know so that consideration can be given to some further official statement about the progress of my investigation.'

As soon as he received them, Marking wrote two letters replying to Veal, in which he expressed his regrets for embarrassment caused and staying that had not been the intention. Marking offered to speak to the Air Safety Committee and ensure that they withheld publication of their report until a more suitable time. The second later, sent to Veal the same day, pointed out that Marking could not comment on the remarks attributed to his chairman, so he had referred Veal's letter to him. Details of any subsequent discussion on the matter, with or without coffee, between Marking and Gordon-Burge are not held in the files. On 25th January, Milward, however, did write something of an apology to Veal, though he could not help adding, *'I think, however, that Mallalieu's latest statement in the House has made our point adequately because he does make it clear that there was conclusive evidence of an explosion in the cabin.'*

On 15th January, the Greek Civil Aviation Administrator, Brig. Gen. A. Skarmaliorakis, replied to Veal. His take on events, and the outcome he desired, were significantly different from those of BEA. The text of the letter as delivered to the AIB was:

I hereby wish to thank you so much for having kindly kept me as informed on the progress of the investigation carried out with respect to the accident of BEA's Comet G-ARCO.

Nevertheless, with a view to avoid eventual mistakes which might lead to undesirable misunderstandings between those concerned, I would like to note the following:

As you also believe the complete investigation of an accident like the one in question, in spite of the difficulties encountered, is considered by us of a primary importance for the influenced fields of the air navigation.

Such a necessity not being covered yet from the elements into our hands up to now, calls certainly for a reconsideration of the possibility to raise the wreck from the sea or at least to use a teleoptic or photographic machine which might prove adequate for the investigation of the bottom of the sea.

We are of the opinion that the lack of complete evidence for the rejection or adoption of certain indications of the causes of the accident does not constitute a certainty for formulating any views.

I should not fail to tell you dear Group Captain Veal that, apart from other points of your informative letters, on the accident in question, the following are considered by us as not proving yet convincing indications on the causes of the accident occurred.

The detonation of a high explosive device within the cabin of the aircraft at an altitude of 29000 ft.

The damages caused to the fuel drop tank of the a/c F.100 due only to the impact on the sea and the fact that the adaptation points thereof on the a/c do not present indications of a forced

detachment (this may be ascertained only by a trial dropping of the tank).

The impossibility of ascertaining the date of the history of the tank and from which a/c has been dropped.

We would greatly appreciate any action on your part tending to clarify the aforementioned and contributing to the effective investigation of the accident in question, which is of great concern to both of us, to you as competent of the investigation and to us for sentimental and more general reasons.

On the occasion I would like to inform you that, following your invitation, two representatives of our Administration will be made available and leave for London very soon in order to follow the investigation of the accident in question.

The Greek authorities had as much interest in the actual cause as BEA, but they wished for a significantly different cause to be identified. For the airline, a security incident, involving the detonation of a bomb on a perfectly-serviceable and properly-operated and maintained aircraft would exonerate them completely. It would also allow the benighted Comet to retain its regained reputation as a safe aircraft in which crews and passengers could be absolutely confident. But that cause, much as it got BEA off the hook, would implicate security procedures at Athens airport and the accountable authority would ultimately be Brigadier-General Skarmaliorakis' Civil Aviation Administration. He, therefore, would rather have been informed that the cause was a mid-air collision with a non-Greek aircraft in international airspace.

The two representatives introduced by Skarmaliorakis were Mr. G. Papadimitropolous and Mr. Hazardas. On 20th January, along with Mr. M. Carder of Olympic Airways, who might have been a translator, they met with Messrs. Clancey of RARDE, Forsyth of RAE and Norman Head of the AIB. Clancey produced the cushion and accompanying photographs and explained the details of the evidence. He also showed the visitors x-ray photos of the passenger, Mr. Afatitis, injured by the explosion.

In the course of what was described[47] as 'a considerable discussion', Clancey went into the rationale for the theory that the bomb had been placed on the left-hand side of the aircraft, between the seat and the side of the fuselage[48]. The Greeks were then shown the available wreckage of Charlie Oscar, as well as the F.100 drop tank. Following this, Forsyth explained the wreckage plot and the evidence suggesting the break-up at 15,000 feet. The Greeks were apparently satisfied that the drop-tank had been jettisoned on a different occasion when it was pointed out that there was no drain plug in the tank. After being presented with relevant documentation, the Greek visitors expressed the opinion that they agreed with the findings, though they said they expected some difficulty in persuading some of the people in Athens that the cause had, in fact, been a bomb. They were offered the opportunity of further discussions with their own explosive experts should they so wish.

The picture of exactly how Charlie Oscar and her passengers came to grief was now as clear as it was ever likely to be. But an explanation of how and an explosive device came to be on the aircraft, who put it there and why, were questions beyond the scope of both Mason and Veal's expert teams.

---

[47] *Unattributed 'Note for the Record' – Meeting with representatives of the Greek Aviation Administration at RAE on 20.1.68, The National Archives, Avia101/218.*

[48] *Various descriptions of the locus place the bomb either underneath, just behind or at the side of the seat in question. However, the most compelling description is 11½ inches below and 4½ inches behind the back of the cushion. This is supported by sketches contained in the National Archives files.*

The Final Report is Produced

On 12th July 1968, John Veal was at last in a position to present his final report into the Charlie Oscar disaster. By way of introduction, he attached a comprehensive covering letter, which reiterated the basic facts of the crash and the thorough investigation. After highlighting the excellent work of those involved, including RARDE and the RAF Institute of Pathology and Tropical Medicine, Veal went further into the police investigation:

The Greek authorities, because of initial content, particularly in British newspapers, that the occurrence was an attempt on the life of General Grivas and because of the apparently adverse reflection on security at Athens, advanced the view that loss of the aircraft had resulted from a collision, probably with a Turkish fighter. When an F.100 drop tank was recovered from the sea three weeks later they pressed this view with renewed vigour, but investigation showed that the tank had been dropped from a U.S. fighter probably about three months before the Comet accident. The Greek authorities have been kept informed of the progress of the investigation and their representatives were shown the explosion evidence during a visit to London. I understand from our own police that security arrangements at Athens are now very strict and that access of unauthorised persons to the aircraft and apron is now effectively prevented.

Inquiries were initiated through the appropriate channels immediately after the accident against the possibility that there had been sabotage of the aircraft for political reasons, but with negative result. Immediately evidence was forthcoming that an explosive device had in fact been detonated on board, information was passed to the Special Branch. Subsequently arrangements were made through the. Home Office for the criminal aspects to be investigated by Scotland Yard; this was undertaken by Detective Superintendent Browne a copy of whose report is in the envelope at Doc. 2. There is circumstantial evidence which points to the possible involvement of one particular passenger whose body was not among those recovered. A copy of the police report has been sent to the Director of Public Prosecutions by the Commissioner of Police.

Veal finished off by spelling out the need to make it more difficult for bombs to be smuggled onto aircraft in the first place.

The feasibility of developing means of detecting the presence of explosive devices should be further studied with a view to assisting airlines and aerodrome authorities in their security measures. These recommendations are being followed up by the Director of Flight Safety. Developments currently taking place should lead to the achievement of the objective of (a), but it is necessary first to achieve adequate safeguards against inadvertent ejection.

The possibility of detecting explosive devices is already receiving a great deal of attention particularly in the military field in respect of mines, but civil aircraft freight and passengers introduce their own special problems. Although I have no great expectation that there will be any immediate break-through in this field, the feasibility study recommended would at least provide concrete evidence of effort if, unfortunately, we were faced with another event like the Comet; and it has to be remembered that there have been seven known cases of sabotage of civil aircraft by explosive during the last six years, while three of these occurred in 1967. At best, through the co-ordination of scientific effort and by application of advanced technology some advance might be made.

In this connection it is interesting to note that the final conclusion of a paper on accidents due to sabotage which is being prepared by the United States National Transportation Safety Board is, "Since the inflight bomb explosion problem is worldwide in nature, it is suggested that consideration be given to pooling international technical resources to achieve a successful solution to the bomb detection problem." The feasibility study recommended, which will be pursued with the appropriate Research Establishment through our scientific adviser, would make a practical contribution towards this objective.

At the Board of Trade, the new Minister of State, Bill Rodgers, commented: "An impressive, fascinating and convincing report. I support the recommendations." The President of the Board of Trade, Anthony Crosland, was equally complimentary:

"The thoroughness of this report reflects exceptional credit on Group Captain Veal and his staff. The recommendations are wholly acceptable. I imagine our thanks have been conveyed to RARDE and other outside bodies who co-operated so helpfully in the Inquiry."

Crosland suggested, as an afterthought, that if no 'thank you' letters had yet been sent, he would be quite prepared to write them himself.

The press, meanwhile, had lost none of its enthusiasm for generating dramatic headlines, no matter how carefully phrased any press releases or similar comments might be. On 21st November 1968, for example, the

Birmingham Post excitedly revealed, 'Comet death crash – it was a bomb meant for Grivas':

The British European Airways Comet 4b which crashed into the Mediterranean last October was destroyed by an explosion in the tourist class accommodation, states the report of the Board of Trade Accident Investigation Branch, published today.

And Scotland Yard investigations reveal that it was planted in a plot to kill former EOKA chief, Gen. Grivas, leader of the Cypriot armed forces...

After Board of Trade crash investigators had found the first signs that the aircraft had been damaged by an explosion at the end of January, detectives from Scotland Yard carried out a thorough investigation into the possibility of sabotage.

Superintendent Percy Browne and Det. Sgt. Peter Hill flew to Greece and Cyprus and spent most of February and March on the investigation. They interviewed relatives of passengers and looked into allegations that the explosive device was meant for Gen. Grivas, who was returning to Cyprus from Greece that day. He actually returned on a later flight.

A Scotland Yard spokesman said last night that Supt. Browne's report on the criminal aspects of the crash had been submitted to the Director of Public Prosecutions.

"It had been decided, that on the evidence available, no action should be taken," he said.

The crash investigators base their report that the Comet was destroyed by an explosion of a military-type explosive in a mild steel container on the evidence contained in a foam rubber seat cushion...the Board of Trade report blandly states that "the aircraft broke up in the air following the detonation of a high explosive device within the cabin."

But the report cannot completely answer the vital question – was the explosion accidental or was the aircraft sabotaged?

But at a press conference in London, Mr. V.J. Clancey, the explosives expert (from RARDE) who investigated the evidence, was in little doubt about how the blast was caused. He explained that his laboratory tests into the type of explosive used had proved beyond doubt that it had been a military-type explosive like TNT or RDX which had wrecked the Comet.

High-velocity explosive would not explode without a detonator or a timing device, he said. It was almost unknown for a detonator to go off by accident.

Home-made timing devices were another thing altogether, he said. The could go off at almost any time. But timing devices were not put on board an airliner with powerful high explosives without a purpose. The experts also ruled out the possibility of an accidental explosion of something like an aerosol hairspray in a passenger's handbag...

The Board of Trade investigators recommended in the report that flight recorders should be developed to detach themselves from an aircraft when it submerges after a crash at sea. The box could then float to the surface, and if fitted with a radio location device, recovery would be made far easier.

They also recommended that the Board of Trade should start studies into developing an effective device which would detect explosive devices in an aircraft or in passengers' luggage.

Scotland Yard Investigates...

The conclusion by RARDE, accepted by Veal, that the cause of the disaster was a bomb was not exactly a bolt from the blue. From the first day, there had been widespread speculation, in the press and elsewhere, that this was no accident, but a deliberate act of malice. Indeed, it was speculated, as stated above, that it was an assassination attempt on the life of General Georgios Grivas. As a potential offence of mass murder, therefore, the matter was of significant interest to the authorities, including the security services.

Two members of the Defence Intelligence section of the security services, identified as Suckling and Arnott, approached John Veal's team the day after the crash, asking for a list of passengers who joined at Athens, a booking list and also for a check to be made to see if Grivas had been booked as a passenger to Cyprus over the following week.

On 20th October, whilst the security services were doubtless digging around in the shadows, Michael Lester, the Company Secretary of BEA, wrote to Jan Riddoch, with details of a former BEA employee who had left the airline in acrimonious circumstances:

'Mr. Georgiou was employed as a loader and the corps of loaders does, of course, include some of the rougher elements of the community. I gather he was not popular and some of the loaders had sons in Cyprus and at least one of them had been killed. I think this gave rise to a certain amount of acrimony against Georgiou and the upshot of it was that he resigned from BEA. The (attached) file deals with Georgiou's subsequent complaint that he was improperly dismissed.

Georgiou made a number of verbal threats to blow up various bits of BEA property, including an aeroplane and in about the middle of April last year he went so far as to write to me threatening to blow up one of the aeroplanes. He was investigated by the police at the time and appears to have undertaken to behave himself.

One of the passengers on the Comet was a Mr. S. Georgiou[49] who is down on the passenger list as being an American citizen though I do not know what evidence there is to substantiate this as his body was not recovered. Mr. S. Georgiou was traveling on a 21-day excursion to Nicosia. He flew from New York to London on the 9th October on BA506 arriving on the morning of the 10th. He had a 24 hour stop-over in London

---

[49] *Sotiris Georgiou was in seat 4A. As stated, his body was never recovered.*

and left on BE284 for Athens and Nicosia on the 11th October. When he left London, he had 4 kilos of excess baggage and we are pursuing enquiries with BOAC to see whether he brought any excess baggage in with him from New York[50].

This passenger was checked in for the Athens / Nicosia flight but as his body was not recovered we do not know for certain that he actually boarded the aircraft and I understand there is some question of the aircraft having left Athens one passenger short – although this is not confirmed[51].

A handwritten 'PS' confirms, *'BOAC say he had <u>no</u> excess baggage New York – London.'*

Veal replied formally to the security services a fortnight later, on 26th October, enclosing a copy of the passenger list and a statement from Mr. Mastin. He added:

'It is understood that General Grivas travelled to Cyprus on the service which also departed from Athens later on 12th October.

Since Mr. Tench spoke to you, Mr. Lester, the Secretary of BEA has brought to our attention threats made by a Mr. George Georgiou, a Cypriot who is a former BEA employee…It seems somewhat unlikely that Mr. George Georgiou could be the same person as Mr. S. Georgiou who was stated as having US nationality. However, I should be glad if you would consider whether any follow-up can be made in respect of this particular threat '

Ronnie Martin, the BEA Manager in Beirut, also felt it would be useful to pass on an account from an unnamed friend of his, who had apparently been booked on Charlie Oscar but, due to a last-minute cancellation had been able to secure a seat on the Olympic Airways flight later on 12th October:

'When he got to the airport there was somewhat more commotion than usual, but eventually cleared the usual airport controls and went into the departure lounge. His flight was delayed and on enquiring into the reason was casually brushed off. Eventually a further delay was announced, and, on this occasion, he gathered that a VIP party was travelling. The further

---

[50] As Mr. Georgiou was travelling to visit family in Cyprus, he bought additional items whilst in London, thereby avoiding excess baggage charges from New York. Information to the author 2018.

[51] Nor does it appear to be mentioned elsewhere.

delay was bought about by Olympics (sic) bringing another aircraft out of the hangars and loading it with baggage etc. which had already been loaded on the aircraft which was supposed to have operated the service.

My informant was travelling economy and on boarding the aircraft found the 1st Class compartment closed. Whispers had it that General Grivas was aboard and that he should have been on the BEA Comet which left Athens early on the same morning. Even at that time none of the passengers seemed to be aware of the BEA disaster because on flying over the scene of the accident the Olympic stewardess was heard whispering to someone that that was the approx. point where the BEA Comet had crashed. This was heard by a few passengers and she was questioned – and informed them that an accident had occurred earlier that morning.

PS I understand that Grivas and his party disembarked off the Olympic service at Nicosia.

As with other correspondence, Veal passed this to a Mr. Sidwell, of DI6[52], a branch of the security services, commenting:

'...I think the delay referred to in the letter was occasioned by Olympic Airways changing the aircraft as a precaution in the knowledge that an accident had occurred.'

On 9th November Veal and Head discussed with Sidwell the relevant developments in the investigation, in relation to the sabotage aspects. Sidwell explained that the passenger lists were being followed up through Athens and Nicosia, but so far these had been negative. Sidwell assured the investigators that those concerned were aware of the urgency of the matter. It had, though, been established that George Georgiou was still living in London, so had not been on the aircraft.

Sidwell accepted the possibility that the damage to the cushion might have been caused by high explosive and pointed out that there were a very great number of 'experts' in Cyprus who would be capable of handling such a device. He did, however, find it difficult to believe that anyone would use the small amount of explosive suggested by the RARDE experiments. Sidwell thought it was a reasonable explanation that, in fact, it had been a bigger device and there had been incomplete combustion; in that case the peppering found on the body of Mr. Afatitis, since it showed evidence of high temperature, could have been incompletely burnt particles of explosive.

---

[52] *Possibly a branch of the Defence Intelligence Service, part of the Ministry of Defence.*

Sidwell was informed of the possible need for the AIB to put out a press release about the explosion. He did not think that it would prejudice the enquiries being carried out by DI6; in some respects, it might possibly help them.

The same day, Veal and Newton discussed the finding of RARDE with Chief Inspector Bryan, of Scotland Yard's Special Branch. They again mentioned the proposed press release and, after consulting his Commander, Bryan confirmed the police would have no objection, having regard to the elapsed time since the crash and what the two policemen considered to be the 'improbability of any successful criminal proceedings'.

On 17th November, Veal received a letter from one Frank Ellson-Jones, purportedly Technical Adviser to de Havilland, the original manufacturer of the Comet, speculating on the possible mechanism by which a bomb might have been triggered. It appears, on the face of it, entirely plausible and has, in fact been suggested to the author by other credible sources[53].

'When aircraft are operating through such a politically dangerous area the thought that hostile elements will be prepared to sacrifice the aircraft and its entire complement in an attempt on the life of one person cannot be excluded...the question of remotely detonating a bomb at the point on the route where the wreckage would fall into deep water arose...I realised that this would be a relatively easy mater since the construction of a battery-powered transistorised receiver is both simple and cheap. Such a receiver would make an excellent trigger because, if it were crystal controlled to the Nicosia FIR frequency (126.3 MHz), the first signal it would receive on the Athens-Nicosia leg would be at 30 deg E which is the changeover point between the FIRs and, by coincidence, is also in the area of the deepest water under airway RED 19.

The receiver specification would be very simple because there is always plenty of VHF signal around inside an aircraft cabin or baggage hold when the onboard transmitter is operated.'

Veal wrote again to Mr. Suckling at MI5 on 17th November. His letter covered both the threat from Middle Eastern terrorist groups and the thoughts of Mr. Ellson-Jones

I enclose a copy of a letter which I have received from our Civil Air Attaché in the Middle East which appears to refer to the Palestine

---

[53] *These include colleagues of the author with relevant experience in such matters, as well as Louis Loizou, who had military experience with the Cypriot defence forces.*

Liberation Army. I think you already know from Mr. Sidwell that one of the tourist seat cabin seat cushions has been found to have sustained damage consistent with that which would have been caused by an explosive device within the cabin at floor level. An interesting possibility of how such an explosive device might be remotely detonated is suggested in a letter from Mr. Ellson-Jones, a copy of which I also attach.

On 20th December, Veal had sent a copy of his interim report to Chief Inspector Bryan. In addition to the explanation given to other recipients reiterating the most likely cause as being a bomb explosion, Veal added in this letter:

You asked whether it would be possible to provide some interim report against which you could consider whether any police action could or should be taken in the matter and the purpose of this letter is provide this to you.

Shortly after the accident we got in touch with Mr. Suckling of Box 500 and asked him to look into the possible sabotage question. This of course was before we had any evidence whatsoever about the occurrence of an explosion. I have had no final report from him but when I previously enquired, I was told that nothing had come to light in Athens or Nicosia.

Chief Inspector Bryan spoke to Veal on the telephone on 4th January to acknowledge receipt of the interim report. He told Veal that preliminary consideration had been given to the matter but there was some doubt whether there was any police action that could be taken and sought Veal's views.

Veal replied that he had brought the matter to the attention of Scotland Yard because he felt that he had a responsibility to do so; however, it was not for him to decide what action the police should take. If they felt that nothing could be done, Veal thought that he would have to accept that decision, though he would like to have something in writing should that be the case, as he would need to refer to it when submitting his final report.

Chief Inspector Bryan was subsequently told that the Attorney General was taking an interest in the investigation and had asked for and been given a copy of the interim report. The Attorney General had also been advised that the matter had been referred to the Special Branch.

On 30th January, there having been a discussion involving Whittick, Veal and Riddoch, the latter wrote back setting out the reasons why there should be police inquiries. The Home Office man had raised the question of cost, as the Metropolitan Police was funded equally by the Treasury and the ratepayers of London.

Riddoch explained that the purpose of an accident investigation is to establish the cause, this having been done, adding that the AIB considered it important from the safety point of view to ascertain the means by which the explosive device was placed on board, so that precautions could be taken to prevent a recurrence. He pointed out that it was not known whether the bomb was put on board in Athens or the UK, but there was no doubt that the act was deliberate. Nor was it known whether the purpose was political or to obtain an insurance pay out. Riddoch stressed:

Whatever doubts you may have about the responsibility of the Metropolitan Police for investigating crimes on board British aircraft, I hope that there is no doubt whether such a serious crime as the Comet accident, involving the death of 66 people on a British aircraft (many of them British subjects) should be investigated.

You suggested a meeting to clarify the general responsibilities of the Police in investigating crimes on board aircraft. We would be grateful if you would arrange such a meeting. I confess I am in a state of confusion about the jurisdiction and responsibilities of the various authorities.'

On 31st January, Detective Superintendent Percy Browne, of Scotland Yard, telephoned Veal to say he had now taken over the investigation of the Comet accident.

The meeting suggested by Whittick took place in his office on 5th February. There were representatives from the Home Office, Riddoch and colleagues from the Board of Trade, Mr. John Macrae of the Foreign Office along with Mr. K. Parker and Assistant Commissioner P.E. Brodie of the Metropolitan Police.

The group agreed that if the Board of Trade so requested the Commissioner of the Metropolitan Police, that force would investigate the murder of the passengers (and, one assumes, the crew). The Board of Trade would pay for the investigation, subject to Treasury approval, and the Foreign Office would inform the Greek Government of the proposed investigation. Finally, they noted that the Director of Public Prosecutions had already agreed to bear the costs of any prosecution.

Veal, along with Head and Newton, met with Detective Superintendent Browne and Detective Sergeant Lee[54] on 12th February. They agreed to provide Scotland Yard with information on the passengers, including a passenger list and list of those missing. Also, they would forward correspondence with the American Life Insurance Company concerning

---

[54] *The name of the Detective Sergeant accompanying Detective Superintendent Browne is given variously as DS Peter Hill or DS Lee.*

one of the passengers, Mr. Michael Thomaides[55]. Reports from RARDE and Institute of Pathology would also be sent on. Browne wrote to his (unnamed) Chief Superintendent on 14th February, outlining his travel plans. He and DS Hill would:

'...travel by air to Athens on Wednesday 21st February 1968, arriving at approximately 3.30pm, GMT. On our arrival I will inform the British Embassy of our address in Athens.

It is not possible to say what line the enquiry will take or how we will be received by the Greek authorities. If, however, any difficulties arise an official of the British Embassy will be consulted.

I ask that this report be forwarded in triplicate to the Under Secretary of State, Home Office, with a request that a copy be forwarded to Mr. Macrae, Central Department, Foreign Office, for his information.'

It is interesting to note that the involvement of Det. Supt. Percy Browne in the investigation was not exactly a closely-guarded secret. The *Cyprus Mail* had already announced on February 10th:

'A top London murder detective has been named to head a probe (into the Comet crash) ...Scotland Yard police headquarters said Detective Superintendent Percy Browne will inquire into the cause of the cabin explosion...Supt. Browne, who normally investigates murders and other major crime, will start his inquiry soon, and will probably go to Greece and Cyprus.'

Browne and his bag-carrier, as such junior officers accompanying senior detectives were known, travelled to Athens as planned on 21st February. However, it appears that their arrival in the Greek capital came as something of a surprise to the staff of the British Embassy there. Macrae, having been contacted by his colleagues overseas, had telephoned Brodie's office to pass on the chagrin of the diplomatic service over what was seen as a somewhat unwelcome surprise. Brodie immediately sought to smooth the ruffled feathers, writing to Macrae:

'I am extremely sorry that you have not been made aware of the fact that Detective Superintendent Browne and his colleague had left this country.

---

[55] *Mr. Thomaides was well-insured because of the value of his business. There was never any suggestion that he was involved in anything improper and he did not feature further in the investigation.*

Several days ago, when I became aware that the enquiry had reached the stage when Browne was almost ready to go abroad, I was informed that he had been personally to the Foreign Office and had made all the necessary arrangements. Furthermore, a report left here at the end of last week to the Home Office giving full details of what was proposed. An additional copy of this report was made available to the Home Office who were requested to send it on to you. It appears that the individual in the Home Office who should have dealt with this matter was unavoidably not available for a day or two early this week and nobody else had taken any action on the report.

I write this letter not with the intention of trying to shift blame but merely to let you see that this appears to be one of those cases where "the best laid plans of mice and men..." I am only sorry that you appear to have been left in the dark. I can assure you that this was not intentional, and I do hope that you will accept my sincere regret.[56]

On 23rd February, Macrae wrote to Tom Bridges, concerning the unannounced arrival of Browne and Hill in Athens:

As I told you on the telephone...I am very sorry that two members of the Metropolitan Police should have arrived in Athens before we could warn you of their coming and explain some of the background. This is the story.

Macrae explained that Charlie Oscar had been lost following the detonation of the bomb, and that the AIB investigation was to establish the cause, not attribute blame. Further investigation into the cause was better carried out by the Metropolitan Police, he went on, as the police would not be constrained by the limitations of the Board of Trade's remit. Macrae then filled Bridges in with the agreement that the Board of Trade would formally request the Metropolitan Police to make enquiries into the events leading up to the explosion, and therefore to the deaths of the 66 people on board and would pay for the investigation. He added:

'We for our part agreed to alert you and ask you to take such action with the Greek authorities as deemed necessary and appropriate.

---

[56] *The Foreign Office seems to have been exceptionally annoyed, no matter how courteously their message to Brodie might appear. Similarly, his reply, couched in niceties, was little short of a grovelling apology, suggesting that the sudden appearance of the two policemen in Athens had given rise to a wave of severe anxiety in the British Embassy. It appeared that the Foreign Office had concerns about what Browne might uncover.*

We expected next to get a letter from the Police setting out the line of their investigation and their proposed plan of action. Instead of which I learnt from you that the two police officers had already arrived in Athens. **This is the more regrettable in that it seems quite possible that potentially tricky political questions could arise during the course of the investigation. For example, supposing the police should discover that the explosion was caused by a Greek (or for that matter a Turkish Cypriot) who was hoping to liquidate General Grivas**[57] **(something that has of course been canvassed in the Press).** *For this reason, it seems right that the police should keep in close touch with the Embassy about how their investigation is going, even if they make such day to day arrangements as are necessary with their Greek opposite numbers through their own channels. In view of the mix-up which has just happened, I am making sure that clear instructions in this sense are sent to Detective Superintendent Browne.*

As to the question of informing the Greek government about the investigation, I think this is entirely a matter for your discretion. As I mentioned on the telephone, it occurred to me that the action you were required to take (by the Foreign Office) provide a suitable starting point, but much would depend on how those instructions were carried out.

...I am sending a copy of this letter to Tony Tyler in the Commonwealth Office and to Timothy Daunt in Nicosia, as I believe it is possible that the police will wish to visit Cyprus in the course of their investigations. In that case the Commonwealth Office may well wish to inform the Cyprus government about the police investigation and, if you can find out about their plans to visit Cyprus, it would obviously be helpful for Tyler and Daunt to know about (the) plans.

Mr. SS Bampton, of Home Office department F2, wrote on 26th February to PE Brodie, Assistant Commissioner Crime at the Metropolitan Police:

'The Foreign Office are most anxious that your police officers should keep in close touch with the Embassy on this investigation, even if they

---

[57] *The Foreign Office was clearly concerned about this line of enquiry. As stated, it had indeed been touted in the press right from the day of the crash, so this might be a matter of the FO wishing to avoid any potentially embarrassing lines of enquiry. However, as it is so specific, is it possible that the FO had been privy to intelligence suggesting that this was, indeed, the root cause, which they needed to keep undercover? Such intelligence might, for example, have been from an SIS (MI6) source or even that the plot involved such a source who needed protection. Note: many EOKA fighters had given information to the security services during the Cyprus Emergency.*

make such day to day arrangements as are necessary with their Greek opposite numbers through their own channels, **as it is possible that potentially tricky political questions could arise during the course of the investigation.** *I imagine you will already have given instructions to this effect, but I have assured the Foreign Office that I would pass on this instruction to you immediately.'*

Brodie then took prompt action to ensure the sentiments of the Foreign Office were passed on to Browne. On 27th February, he sent a carefully-worded missive to the detective, being couched in such a way that it would not because embarrassment should it have inadvertently been viewed by unauthorised eyes, however that might have occurred:

'Bampton from the Home Office has been in to see me today and he tells me that someone from the Embassy in Athens has been in touch with Macrae in the Foreign Office here about your presence in Athens.

It appears that the Embassy staff in Athens are slightly apprehensive about any possible political repercussions should your enquiry develop in a certain direction. For instance, if you should find evidence to suggest that the explosion in the Comet was arranged in order to do harm to someone in politics in Cyprus or Greece then a very delicate situation would arise.

I think I need say no more than to ask you to keep very closely in touch with the Embassy staff and if anything, that savours of politics should arise, I know you would discuss the matter with them and would be most careful not to embarrass the Foreign Office.

Of necessity, this letter has to be in rather vague terms, but I am sure that you will take the point.

I wish you luck in your enquiry and I shall look forward to hearing all about it when you return to this country.'

The Assistant Commissioner forwarded the letter to Macrae, with a covering note stating:

'I enclose a secret and highly-confidential letter to Detective Superintendent Browne who is investigating the BEA Comet aircraft crash. I should be extremely grateful if you could arrange for this letter to be sent out to him in Athens through the Diplomatic Bag. We understand he is staying at the Hotel Stanley, 1 rue Odysseus, Place Kaiskis, Athens.

Macrae forwarded the letter to the Hon. Tom Bridges, with an additional level of cover:

In my recent undated letter to you I said that the police would be sending instructions to (Browne) to keep in touch with the Embassy in case of political developments arising during the course of his investigations.

I enclose, under Flying Seal[58], a letter from (Brodie) to Browne, which I should be grateful if you would pass on. I think the letter should serve its purpose from our point of view. Although the contents of the letter are not particularly startling you should know that **Brodie was most apprehensive that the letter should pass through unauthorised hands.** *He had hoped that it could be sent through the bag already sealed and when I explained that our rules did not permit this I had to assure him that you personally as the addressee of this letter would seal it and see that it was delivered by safe hand to Browne before he would entrust me with the letter!*

Bridges replied on 6th March, updating Macrae and giving him a bit of reassurance:

'We were a bit surprised when (Browne) arrived out of the blue but had been expecting a visit before very long as a result of what we had seen in the press and it did not matter much. With the help of the Foreign Ministry I arranged for Browne to meet the Greek Interpol Bureau. This meant a slight delay, but he has since told us that his enquiry has been making good progress and that the Greek authorities are being very helpful. I do not of course know the details, but I gather that the particular line of enquiry he is following does not involve politics.

On 19th April, RG Smith of CA4(1) of the Board of Trade sent a minute to a Captain Hunt in Veal's department. This noted that the Metropolitan Police would investigate the events leading up to the crash with the Board of Trade meeting the costs in certain circumstances. Smith wanted to know if the police had, as previously agreed, submitted any progress reports, adding wryly, *'Have you reached any conclusion so far as to whether there is sufficient progress to justify the public expenditure involved?'*

Veal responded four days later:

---

[58] *Under Flying Seal denotes a letter with a seal attached, but not closed, so that it may be read by the person entrusted with forwarding it to the addressee.*

...Superintendent Browne telephoned me about 15 days ago to tell me the current position regarding his enquiries and to ask about further reports by the RARDE.

Superintendent Browne and Sergeant Lee spent some five weeks in Cyprus and Greece pursuing their enquiries and their investigations included approaches to the close relatives[59] of all those killed in the accident.

Superintendent Browne told me that there were four main lines of investigation and that one of them appeared to be promising. He thought at the time that it would take them some four or five weeks to complete what he had to do and to make his report. On this basis we should expect to hear something within the next fortnight but if we do not I will get in touch with Superintendent Browne again. One item which is likely to hold up this final report is the availability of the RARDE report because this contains much important expert evidence.

Tom Bridges contacted John Macrae on 25th June in connection with the continuing Greek interest in criminal proceedings:

It was reported in the Athens press that further investigation of this subject was being undertaken by the Public Prosecutor in Athens. I am not sure exactly what the significance of this is, but I presume that some of the results of Detective Superintendent Browne's investigations have been made available to the Greek authorities by Scotland Yard and that the former wished to investigate the possibility of a prosecution[60] in the Greek courts. No doubt Scotland Yard know more about this.

I have now received a letter from the investigating authorities in the Athens Magistrates' Courts asking us to supply the Prosecutor of the Court of Misdemeanours here with a copy of the findings of the British authorities about the accident. I have replied to this letter by saying that, to the best of my knowledge, our own enquiries have not yet been

---

[59] *In the course of research for this book, the author has spoken to a number of close relatives of the victims, none of whom, when asked, remembered being 'approached' by the British detectives.*

[60] *Why the Greeks would consider a prosecution when Scotland Yard said there was no evidence is not made clear. It suggests that either Scotland Yard had inferred that there was, in fact, someone worth prosecuting or that the Greek authorities were using this as a 'legal' means of finding out what Scotland Yard knew.*

completed, but that I have forwarded their request to the appropriate authorities in London.

Bampton wrote to Veal on 16th July, concerning a request from the Greek authorities for a copy of the findings. It appeared that there was some slight confusion as to whether the findings referred to the Accident Report or the police investigation:

I have discussed this with the Assistant Commissioner of the Metropolitan Police and as you will appreciate from the nature of their report, it will be out of the question to send a copy of it to the Greek authorities, and it would be extremely difficult to prepare an edited edition.

One way of dealing with this, subject to your agreement, would be to let the Greek authorities have a copy of your report on the cause of the crash. At the same time, a covering note could be sent to our Ambassador explaining that if he were pressed for a copy of the police report he should tell them that the enquiry has now been completed, but it was inconclusive and there was insufficient evidence to indicate who might have been responsible. This approach would meet with the agreement of the Metropolitan Police and the Foreign Office and I should welcome your views on it.

Brodie acknowledged the letter to Veal, a copy of which Bampton had thoughtfully sent the Assistant Commissioner, adding:

'You will no doubt remember that when I spoke to you on the telephone I mentioned that Detective Superintendent Browne was still with the Director of Public Prosecutions. Perhaps, therefore, the proposed covering note to our Ambassador saying, "that the Police enquiry was inconclusive and there was insufficient evidence to indicate who might have been responsible" should be delayed until the Director of Public Prosecutions has given his decision.' Bampton acknowledged, *'I take the point that we should say nothing to pre-judge the decision of the Director of Public Prosecutions.'*

On 29th July, Brodie wrote to Bampton, confirming:

'A reply has now been received from the Director of Public Prosecutions to the effect that "no action can be taken on the present evidence". In the

absence of any further evidence, I do not think that the Director will take any action in the future[61].

Bampton sent a letter to Brodie on 1st August, in connection with the request from the Greek authorities for a copy of the 'findings'. There was still concern over the existence of the police investigations, and Bampton expanded on the earlier advice:

'The best way of dealing with this request would seem to be to give the Greek authorities a copy of the report prepared by the Chief Inspector of Accidents at the Board of Trade and omit all reference to the police investigation. The Board of Trade have no objection to this procedure, and I enclose a pre-print of their report. This will not be published until September, but the Board of Trade would not object if it were passed to the Greek authorities before this on the understanding that it is to be treated as confidential until the report is actually published. I have removed from the report the brief letter of submission to the President of the Board of Trade, as this does refer in passing to the investigation by the Metropolitan Police. Although this letter will be published in the report, it seems unnecessary to draw the attention of the Greek authorities to the police investigation[62] *and it would not be obvious that such a letter would be included in a pre-print copy.*

If our Ambassador in Athens is questioned about the police investigation, I suggest that he might say that the police inquiry was inconclusive and that there was insufficient evidence to indicate who might have been responsible.'

Macrae wrote to Bridges on 6th August, replying to his letter of 25th June:

Your enquiry has in fact placed us in a bit of difficulty since, unlike the report prepared by the Chief Inspector of Accidents, the contents of the report by the Metropolitan Police Officers are such that it would not do to supply it to the Greek authorities. Much of it is political dealing with the

---

[61] *A firm decision to finalise the matter suggested that the suspect was believed (Nicos Papapetrou) or known (Avraam Solomou) to be dead, and that any accomplices were unlikely to be brought to justice, either because of a lack of evidence or else because the chances of bringing them to trial in the UK were minimal or non-existent, e.g. in the case of Yiorkadjis.*

[62] *This contradicts the earlier correspondence, from the time of D/Supt. Browne's visit to Athens, that the Greek authorities were already aware of the police investigation, and that the Foreign Office had facilitated the detective's visit to the Greek Interpol Bureau.*

personal histories and allegiances of individuals concerned and the information could well be used (or misused) by the Greek authorities for their own purposes. In any case it is not normal practice for copies of police reports to be made available outside of the Home Office, even to other Government Departments. For your own information the report has been sent to the Director of Public Prosecutions who has confirmed the police's own view that there is insufficient evidence for further proceedings.

Macrae went on to suggest, as had Bampton to Brodie, that the Greek Prosecutor of the Court of Misdemeanours be given a copy of the Accident Report rather than that prepared by the police, along with the by-now standard line that, '*...the (police) enquiry was inconclusive...*'

By return, Bridges reassured Macrae that the Accident Report was probably what the Prosecutor actually wanted, as no mention of the police report had been made. He added that, should the Greek authorities wanted supplementary information, i.e. relating to the police investigation, there was no reason why they should not apply for it through Interpol. Bridges then proposed an alternative course of action:

The Director of Civil Aviation, Major-General A. Skarmaliorakis, RHAF (retired) has followed this matter with close interest and clearly resented the publication of the press reports last November indicating that the accident had been caused by an explosion on board the aircraft. He seemed to think that this implied some criticism of the Greek security arrangements at Athens airport, and issued a statement to the press implying that premature publication of these findings before the issue of the final report was irregular and unsatisfactory...Skarmaliorakis is a man of some political importance here, having been close to the leaders of the military coup last April, from the beginning. For these various reasons I would prefer him to obtain a copy of the report personally from the Air Attaché, rather than learn about its existence from his staff who are collaborating with the Public Prosecutor in investigating this accident.

Confirmation of the personal delivery to Skarmaliorakis of the report came in a telex on 28th August from Sir M. Stewart of the Athens Embassy, to the Foreign Office, stating that the Director of Civil Aviation, '*... made no comment of substance but was obviously pleased by the letter and glad to have copies before publication.*'

Details of the police investigation itself are still, at the time of writing, not available to the public. It is known that Browne and Hill spent around five weeks in Greece and Athens, but the witnesses they spoke to and material evidence they collected are still officially secret.

In April 1968 a 14-year-old schoolboy called Roy Tuthill was found murdered in the grounds of Lord Beaverbrook's estate in Givens Grove, Leatherhead, starting one of the Surrey Constabulary's longest police enquiries. Detective Constable Dave O'Connell was seconded to the murder squad assembled at Leatherhead. In an online post many years afterwards, he recalled,

> "Scotland Yard were asked to assist. In those days if a county force called in the Metropolitan Police within twenty-four hours of the murder being discovered the Home Office bore the cost of the enquiry. This was a great incentive for the counties to call in the Metropolitan Police. The Met maintained a murder squad consisting of five Chief Superintendents who rotated as the requests for assistance came in. They were assisted by a Detective Sergeant who became known as the "bag carrier".
>
> The officer appointed to lead this enquiry was Chief Superintendent Percy Brown[63] (sic). The enquiry in my opinion was doomed from the start and ranks as the worst led enquiry I have had any connection with.
>
> To start with detectives from all over the county were told to be at Leatherhead Police Station for briefing at a certain time. The senior officers arrived some two and a half hours later after clearly having enjoyed the benefits of a good lunch[64]. The first words dispensed by Chief Superintendent Brown were, "You will be lucky to detect this one." This was said from behind a cloud of smoke emitting from a huge cigar.
>
> Eventually the enquiry wound down with no detection and very little progress."

---

[63] Despite the omission of the 'e' from Brown, it is almost certain that the Percy Brown referred to here is the same Percy Browne. A search for other police officers named Percy Brown in the Met murder investigation departments at the time proved negative.

[64] It is inferred by this that the senior officers had consumed considerable alcohol in the course of their lunch.

Lines of Enquiry

In the *Evening News*, a London paper on February 17th 1968, a headline announced a *'Dragnet for Comet Killers – Disaster plotted in London'*, telling its readers,

'A police comb-out of 'Little Cyprus', the Greek Cypriot area of Camden Town, was going on today in a search for the men who plotted the Comet air disaster.

Fresh information has reached Scotland Yard about the Comet…police believe the object of the plan was to assassinate former EOKA leader General Grivas, who was wrongly thought to have been on board.

Det. Supt, Percy Browne, who has been transferred to Scotland Yard from his post at Paddington CID, has discovered that the plot was hatched in a Paddington gaming club.

A number of known Greek extremists are being sought by police.

Inquiries are being intensified in the Camden Town and Paddington areas and several clubs and cafes are being visited.

Three days later, the news was spiced up a bit by the *Daily Sketch*, which revealed,

'Murder squad detectives investigating the sabotage of the BEA Comet last October will fly to Athens tomorrow.

There, Detective Superintendent Percy Browne and a sergeant will interview a number of men in the presence of Greek police…Scotland Yard men have been told that a time bomb was put on the plane in a bid by political extremists to assassinate Colonel (sic) Georgios Grivas.

If that information is correct, the Greek Government could face insurance claims for millions of pounds.

Before Det. Supt. Browne leaves London, he will interview a Greek who fled to Britain as a political refugee after a split with Colonel Grivas.

Other Greeks also living in London have already been interviewed. An important statement has been taken from a Greek in a London jail.'

The *Daily Sketch* of 26th February was somewhat more detailed, and asserted that the perpetrator had died, stating,

'A man passenger among the 66 who died...had personal insurance for the flight worth many hundreds of thousands of pounds.

This development was revealed while Scotland Yard murder squad detectives are in Athens following leads to establish why the plane was sabotaged.

Greeks in London have claimed to police that the aircraft was blown up to assassinate the former EOKA leader, General Grivas.

Now the huge insurance cover has come to light, Det. Supt. Percy Browne, who leads the investigation has been briefed to establish whether there is any link between the insurance and the explosion...No insurance pay-out is likely until the Yard's investigation has ended.

Apart from personal insurance policies held by individual passengers, BEA stands to pay out more than £1 million in compensation for the loss of lives.

A newspaper report appeared in the Cyprus Mail of 5th September under the by-line of Anthony Chivers asked, *'Did saboteur die in Comet crash?'* It went on:

Scotland Yard know the name of the man who they believe was behind the bomb plot which resulted in the Comet crash off Cyprus last October.

He is alleged to be either a Greek or Greek Cypriot businessman. It is believed that his wife is living in London. But the one question which the Police cannot answer is this: Is the man behind the plot alive or dead?

For the bodies of eleven people were never recovered...and until they are all recovered – which is likely to be never – Scotland Yard would not be able to disentangle the final puzzle of this whole mystery.

Not until then would they be able to establish whether the man whose name they have was actually killed in the crash. Or whether someone else was using his name.

(The mystery) began a few weeks after the crash when Det. Supt. Percy Browne, accompanied by a detective sergeant, went to Greece and Cyprus.

He discovered that one of the passengers whose name was on the passenger list had taken out a large life insurance.

Then, Police believe, he somehow tricked another man into flying in his place, using his passport, his ticket and his seat.

After the plane had taken off, the organiser of the plot would disappear, leaving the people he had named as beneficiaries to claim full settlement.

In an official statement about the case, Scotland Yard said: "A Police investigation into the Comet disaster was carried out and a report was subsequently submitted to the Director of Public Prosecutions. It was decided on the evidence available that no action could be taken.

I learn it is extremely unlikely that the insurance policy in respect of the person known to the police will be paid out.

A spokesman for the Association of Insurance Companies said: "In such a case we should certainly refuse payment. It would have to be proved to our satisfaction that death was accidental and not due to some criminal act.

"It is a cardinal rule of law that no person should benefit from a criminal act and that would certainly apply to any beneficiary who was a party to that act, or who was party to any conspiracy."

Following the publication of the final AIB report, John Edmonds at the British Embassy in Ankara, contacted JMO Snodgrass at the FO's Central Department, advising him that,

'The Turkish press reported the Board of Trade's findings, but not in sensational terms. All newspapers said the bomb was placed in the aircraft to kill General Grivas, but they avoided speculation as to who was responsible.

For what it is worth, the local AP[65] correspondent, who is also the Times stringer, (said) that it had been "well established" that one of the passengers insured himself for £200,000 and then committed 'suicide'; but newspapers had been asked not to publish this because stories of this kind are even worse for airline business than assassination theories.

As this case could still have some political significance here, we should be grateful for any comments you may have, together with a copy of the official accident report.'

Edmonds received his reply from Macrae, who commented,

'...we do know – as the Press was told- that (the police) found insufficient evidence for further proceedings. Of the papers here, only The

---

[65] *Associated Press news agency.*

Sun carried headlines to the effect that the crash was caused by a bomb meant for Grivas, but the evidence does not really substantiate the story. We are therefore unable to comment authoritatively on the question of who was responsible for the accident. On the whole, the insurance theory seems the most likely, although we cannot corroborate the details (in your letter).'

The perpetrators of the atrocity would have needed access to a certain level of specialist knowledge to construct an explosive device sufficient to bring down an aircraft. In particular, the bomb maker would have needed access to the military-grade plastic explosive established by RARDE as the material used. In addition, there would need to be a means of detonation, in the case of Charlie Oscar this being a timer or a radio frequency (RF) detonator. Alternatively, for a suicide bomber, there would need to be a means of setting off the explosive device on demand.

EOKA had used bombs during its struggle against the British forces, so it is reasonable to assume that there were still people with the requisite skills on the island seven years after independence. The organisation had also been willing to use violence against women and children in pursuit of its aims, and indeed to destroy aircraft with civilians on board. On 3rd March 1956, a Handley Page Hermes, G-ALDW, of the charter airline Skyways was due to take 68 members of the British armed forces and their families from Nicosia back to the UK. A bomb, placed in a hat rack, exploded, destroying the aircraft though fortunately without casualties. The occupants were saved because the departure had been delayed by two and a half hours. Just over six weeks later, on 27th April, a bomb destroyed a Cyprus Airways Dakota on the ground, also without casualties.

International terrorism was still in its infancy, especially with aircraft and the travelling public as targets. Suicide bombings, as a political weapon, were also rare at that time in Europe. However, there were emerging threats, especially in the Middle East and, to a lesser extent in Northern Ireland, though the situation in the latter was to escalate dramatically in the following very few years. There had been one potential line of enquiry in this regard, however.

Just before the start of the 'Six Days War' in June 1967 between Israel and its Arab neighbours, there was a threat from Middle Eastern groups to target airlines which flew to Israel. This would have included both BEA and Cyprus Airways. On 15th June 1967, Colin Mastin of SA (I) 3, had written to Captain Woolfe, Chief Pilot of Cyprus Airways, asking, *'...Recent events in your part of the world have obviously affected Cyprus Airways operations; has this caused any problems that we should know about?*

Captain Woolfe then travelled to England with copies of the letter sent to Cyprus Airways and all airline operators operating into Israel. The letters in English and Arabic demanded that all airlines declare in the world press before mid-June that they would cease trading with Israel, and actually do so before mid-July, otherwise action would be taken against those airlines that continued their operations.

All operators involved, and the Lebanese government, took the letters seriously and various security actions were taken in Beirut. Captain Woolfe took matters further and imposed security at all stations that the Cyprus Airways Viscounts operated to. While the aircraft was on the ground at an outstation a steward remained at the cabin door and monitored persons coming on board the aircraft. One of the pilots kept watch under the aircraft and monitored the baggage. Normally the aircraft was not fuelled, catered or cleaned. Mr PCM Shillitoe and Captain AS Johnson of BEA knew about the threat as they subsequently went to Beirut to decide about BEA aircraft night-stopping once more.

Despite the existence of the 'Falcon Forces' letter, there has never been any suggestion that Charlie Oscar was brought down for terrorist purposes. Had it been, there would certainly have been claims from the group responsible, and others wishing to further their cause by suggesting they had the capability to destroy an airliner in flight. There were no such claims made.

Persons of Interest

It will be recalled that in early April, Detective Superintendent Browne told Veal that there were *'four main lines of enquiry, one of which was promising.'* It is likely, from the information contained in the National Archives files, that at the time these were:
1. Sotiris Georgiou, who was sitting in seat 4A on the London to Athens sector.
2. Andreas Antoniades and his associates, as named by Peter Georgeides.
3. Avraam Solomou, whose behaviour at Ellinikon Airport gave cause for concern, and who was named later as the carrier of the device.
4. Nicos Papapetrou who also had a number of insurance policies, these all being taken out shortly before his trip and covered him for one flight only.

Sotiris Georgiou

The threats to the airline made by former BEA employee George Georgiou raised an immediate suspicion that they were the same person. Sotiris Georgiou had also acquired an additional four kilogrammes of luggage during his day's stopover in London. The fact that he was sitting in one of the two seats considered most likely to have been where the device exploded would have been an immediate reason for suspicion.

The suspicions about Sotiris actually being George Georgiou were allayed when it was established that the latter was still alive and well in London after the crash. The excess baggage accumulated by Sotiris Georgiou was gifts and items purchased for family members that were not readily available in Cyprus. The luggage would have been carried in the hold so would not have included the bomb. There is no indication in the files of a specific motive for Sotiris Georgiou to blow up the aircraft. His body was amongst the missing, which means that he was quite possibly still in the same seat when the bomb exploded. If he was not responsible for the bomb, it would not, therefore, have been under seat 5A, the one in front of Georgiou. The bomb would have been brought on board by the person in seat 3A, immediately behind him, and who has not been identified.

Andreas Antoniades

There was, languishing in Brixton Prison, London, a man who believed he held to key to the mystery. Prisoner no. 41320 Peter Panayiotes Georgeides, originally from Cyprus, had been convicted of armed robbery and was imprisoned for a few years. Perhaps in an effort to gain some points for good behaviour, he wrote to the Chairman of BEA on 9th January 1968:

> *Sabotage is certainly the cause of the BEA Comet which crashed in flames off the coast of Cyprus.*
>
> *The man responsible (one of them) is Andreas Antoniades an ex-EOKA terrorist and expert in the "explosives squad" of General Georgios Grivas, head of the then EOKA and later supremo of the Cyprus National Guard. If you'd care to send someone to come and see me from your office, I will give them further details on the matter.*
>
> *Antoniades, or "Keravnos" as he is called, fell out with Grivas and was "sentenced" to death by the General, so Keravnos defected over to the British side SIB and gave away the organisation's secrets, and as a result many EOKA lieutenants got executed or imprisoned.*
>
> *Antoniades later came to this country so that he could escape the General's own "exterminating-traitor-squad".*
>
> *Early last year he, Keravnos, had ambitions to assassinate the Archbishop Makarios and Grivas and take over Cyprus.*
>
> *Before the trouble with the Turks started, the first step was to liquidate Grivas who was in control of the armed forces.*
>
> *Makarios would follow etc.*
>
> *I will not continue any further sir, but if you want to clear this dreadful matter, then you only have to come or send someone to see me.*
>
> *PS. I was present at a meeting (prior to the Comet explosion) when a top-ranking army person came to this country to discuss plans for a take-over.*

The letter to Milward was copied by someone in the Home Office, all prisoners' mail being subject to scrutiny. The copy was forwarded to the office of Anthony Crosland from where it made its way via Jan Riddoch to Veal. The covering letter stated that Milward had not been informed that the letter was also being sent to Crosland. A handwritten addendum stated, *'Action already taken in connection with BEA copy'*. The Chief Inspector of Accidents, on 23rd January, forwarded it to Chief Inspector Bryan at Scotland Yard.

In 2007, the BBC news website broke a story that some of Britain's leading heroin smuggling suspects were protected from police investigations because they were working as informers for HM Revenue & Customs and its predecessor units[66]. In one case in 2001, Foreign Office diplomats moved to secure the release of Antoniades, who was described in the article as 'an informer held in Germany on a warrant from the Greek authorities'. The allegations suggested a special form of protection was being given to several people suspected by police of being leading importers of heroin. A former officer of the National Crime Intelligence Service (NCIS) told the BBC:

> *"Customs told me he had been an informant and that he had been the best informant Customs ever had and what he had given the UK far exceeded the damage he had done, which was absolute rubbish."*

Antoniades, who was 75 at the time of the article, was by then believed to be living in Dubai, and had never been convicted of any drugs offence. A number of people, some from the Turkish and Greek communities, subsequently launched appeals against drug trafficking convictions based on his information. Antoniades, a Greek Cypriot, came to the UK in the late 1950s after working as an agent for British intelligence, according to the BBC, and was once jailed for four years after a shooting incident in west London. He went on to work as an informer until the 1990s when reports emerged he was involved in drug trafficking. The reason for protecting Antoniades from prosecution was that "...a public trial in Greece would reveal Mr Antoniades' long career as an informant for Customs and Excise and put his life at risk from criminal elements". Antoniades found himself charged with attempted murder and a letter[67] was sent by Antoniades' mother to the Under-Secretary of State at the Foreign Office on 30th July 1959, in which she states,

> *'My son worked for the Special Branch here in Cyprus during the recent emergency and his life was in constant danger throughout that period and in fact he was shot at many times and was seriously wounded by terrorists and for these reasons the British Government took him under their protection and flew him to England. I therefore feel that your Government is responsible for him and he would not be in this trouble if he had been properly cared for.*

---

[66] *Informer role protected drugs traffickers. www.news.bbc.co.uk, Sunday 4th March 2007*

[67] *FO 371/144714 Protection for former member of Special Branch of Cyprus, Code RGC file 1642, via Fanoulla Argyrou.*

> *In London my son is still in great danger from members of the Cypriot community who would be only too glad to get rid of him and would go to any extreme to do so and I am sure that my son has been framed in some way due to his work against the terrorists in Cyprus.'*

It is possible, of course, that Antoniades was, as alleged by Georgeides, involved in a plot to kill Grivas. There is no evidence to substantiate this, just as the suggestion that Antoniades was an informant, as opposed to being part of the Special Branch, is hearsay, although the institutionally circumspect BBC was confident in stating this on its website. There is nothing else about Antoniades himself in the CY284 files, and it would be necessary to establish whether he had any association with Avraam Solomou or Nicos Papapetrou in order to make a clearer link to the destruction of Charlie Oscar.

Given that both Antoniades and Georgeides moved to the UK some time before the Charlie Oscar incident, it is quite possible that their paths might have crossed. Both men were jailed in Britain for similar periods of time following convictions for violent crimes. The information that Antoniades arrived in the UK shortly before power in Cyprus passed to the former EOKA leaders, having been connected to the British authorities, suggests strongly that he would not have been a friend of Grivas, who was ruthless in his treatment of those he considered to be traitors. By the same token, it is equally unlikely that Antoniades would have found many allies elsewhere in the higher echelons of the new Cyprus government. From what little is known of Antoniades, he does not appear likely to have been well enough connected to 'take power in Cyprus.'

It might be the case that Georgeides had fallen out with Antoniades and his letter from prison was simply an opportunity at get at, or get rid of, Antoniades. If so, the ruse presumably failed as there is nothing available to show that Antoniades was ever arrested in connect with the loss of CY284.

Avraam Solomou

Avraam Solomou was first named as a suspect in an Evening Standard newspaper article by John Miller, published on 21st November 1967. The piece, titled *'Comet Bomb: Special Branch Step In'*, states:

> *The bomb was probably the size of a pencil and hidden in a brief case.*
>
> *But its base, a military type of explosive, was so powerful that it virtually ripped the airliner apart.*
>
> *The theory is that it was put in its briefcase under an innocent passenger's seat.*

> *The link seems to have been Cypriot chauffeur Mr. A. Solomou, one of the 66 people who died.*
>
> *He has been described variously as a henchman of General Grivas, commander of the Cyprus armed forces, or a bodyguard of Mr. Spyros Kyprianou, the Cyprus Foreign Minister.*
>
> *His presence could have misled saboteurs into thinking General Grivas was to have been aboard.*

The Sunday Telegraph article of 26th November also mentioned Solomou, suggesting that he was a body guard of General Grivas. Solomou drew attention to himself at Athens, prior to boarding the flight, due to a ticketing discrepancy which resulted in him forcefully demanding to be allowed onto the flight. Three days before the Sunday Telegraph article appeared, a Miss Roberts from MI5 had phoned Veal's office, having chased up their representative in Cyprus about Solomou:

> *Mr. Solomou, who is No. 55 on the list (of recovered victims) was chauffeur to the Foreign Minister, Mr. Kyprianou, and a former EOKA fighter during the Cyprus emergency of 1955-59. The Director of the Cyprus Special Branch completely discounts the possibility that this was an attempt against Grivas because he never travels at that time of day. They have no record of any of the Cypriot passengers in their index.*

There are two points of significance in this very concise reply to Veal's query concerning Solomou. Firstly, the Cyprus Special Branch came under the Cypriot Interior Ministry. The Interior Minister, Polycarpos Yiorkadjis, is of interest because of what some in Cyprus believed to be his involvement in the Charlie Oscar affair (see chapter 'Dark Deeds and Political Rivalry'). Secondly, the phrase '...*no record of any of the Cypriot passengers in their index*' infers that no Cypriot on the flight was known to them at all. This latter assertion is surprising in the context of their information that Solomou had been an EOKA fighter. It is highly unlikely that they would not keep a file on him as a former fighter and someone with direct access to a Government minister such as Kyprianou. It is, of course, entirely possible, that they actually meant 'no person other than Solomou'.

Leonidas Leonidou commented on the loss of Charlie Oscar in a biography of General Grivas. He wrote[68]:

---

[68] *Leonidou's original source is "Operation Kofinou" by Spyros Papageorgiou, page 43. Papageorgiou himself was considered to be a supporter of General Grivas and wrote a number of biographies about him.*

The scientific investigation carried out by British specialists took a number of months and showed that the crash was caused by the detonation on board of a bomb. It is considered most likely that the intention was to kill General Grivas, who is said to have cancelled his seat on this flight at the last minute.

Six years later, a close associate gave to Dhigenis, as Grivas was also known, information that he had subsequently received:

"I can tell you that I have authoritative information that the crash of the Cyprus Airways Comet, on the 12th October 1967, was aimed at you. It was known that you were to travel on that flight from Athens to Nicosia. You were saved because, at the last minute, you postponed the trip. They had placed a time bomb, which had been made by people trusted by the Cyprus Home Office. The postponement of your journey, which they did not expect, and the failure to reset the bomb, caused the aircraft to crash due to the explosion and for the person entrusted with placing the bomb to die, as he was supposed to cancel his departure from Athens if you did not board the aircraft. Are you aware of all this? Why did our newspapers not write about it?"

And the writer adds:

"These shocking details again involve the Minister for the Home Office, Polycarpos Yiorkadjis, because the explosion took place under the seat of Avraam Solomou, the then driver of the Foreign Minister of Cyprus, Spyros Kyprianou, and who was acting under orders from Yiorkadjis. If indeed General Grivas was the target of the attempt, then the timing of this action rather supports the view that this murderous attempt against Dhigenis is part of a wider, complex and sinister plan…"

Eleftherios Papadopoulos, also established this from other sources. Mr. Papadopoulos was imprisoned for his involvement in the coup against Makarios on 15 July 1974. In one of his books covering his testimonies to the Committee of the House of Representatives he wrote that, after he came out of prison, he was informed by two friends that a former official of the Cyprus Government wanted to have a meeting with him. Papadopoulos wrote:

When I was released from prison in 1984, my associate Andreas Paraskevas and late Pantelis Katelaris (doctor), told me of the wish of a former high-ranking government official, who knew a lot about a lot of people, to meet with me. Although I did not see what of common interest we had to discuss, I accepted.

He told me: "I am one step from my grave. I have cancer. I am fighting it, but I know I will not be the winner. I called you to tell you some secrets, which I do not want to take with me (to the grave). Come back tomorrow and bring with your paper and a tape recorder. I will name some people and events. I want you to promise me that you will not publicise all that I will tell you before 2016."

Indeed, he named some people and events. A lot I already knew from other sources. Nevertheless, all important. Many shocking. He also referred to the crash of the "Comet" near Kastellorizo. He told me:

"The explosives were sent by Polycarpos Yiorkadjis in a box with timing devices". Recipient was an employee of the Cyprus Embassy in Athens, who manufactured the bomb.

It was handed over to A. Solomou, driver of the Minister for Foreign Affairs Sp. Kyprianou, as a package for his Minister. Both of them knew nothing. The bomb was timed following a telephone call from Cyprus. Its target was Dhigenis".

When I told him that all these were extremely serious, however many were not proven, he showed me some pages from his diary. I begged him to allow me to go through its pages. He adamantly refused.

"No" he told me. "I myself have sins. Unfortunately, I also sinned in some instances with these thugs".

In the pages he showed me there were names, events, dates, times, dialogues and extracts from official documents. Unfortunately, 11 days later he died. His daughter, whom I begged to allow me to read through her father's diary, she told me that she was ordered to burn it together with four suitcases full of documents. I can only imagine what a rich archive had been lost"[69].

On 12th January, JE Papalexopoulos, a check-in clerk at Ellinikon Airport, probably employed by Olympic Airways had submitted a short report on Avraam Solomou's problem with his ticket when he presented himself for check-in on 12th October:

The late Mr. Solomou presented himself at the check-in counter on 12 Oct 1967 and asked to be processed for flight CY284 of that date. When asked for his ticket, Mr. Solomou stated due to a mix-up at Nicosia airport he was no longer in possession of his return ticket to Nicosia.

As Mr. Solomou did not have his ticket cover, nor did he know the number of his ticket, I explained to him that under the circumstances I could not possibly accept him for this flight. As an alternative I offered to signal Nicosia and ask for details of his ticket and also authority to issue

---

[69] 'My evidence to the Ad Hoc Committee of the House of Parliament of Cyprus for the "Cyprus File', Volume A' pages 534 to 536, published Nicosia 2010, Eleftherios Papadopoulos.

a new ticket against an indemnity form. I also informed the passenger that this, of course, would take some time and therefore he should consider as impossible to fly to Nicosia on that specific flight, i.e. CY284/1210.

Mr. Solomou, nevertheless, was quite determined to fly as he had planned and asked to speak to higher authority. Consequently, I had to turn him over to the duty officer, Mr. Coliandris, who listened to Mr. Solomou very carefully and then repeated to the passenger what I had already told him, i.e. that we could not possibly accept him on CY284/1210.

Being occupied with the closing of the service, I could not follow the rest of their conversation, but after a while Mr. Coliandris asked me to issue a new ticket against indemnity form and then send a signal to Nicosia for the relevant details and authority.

An indemnity form was prepared and duly signed by Mr. Solomou and a new ticket ATH/NIC was issued by me as per the D/O's instructions. As soon as the a/c departed I sent a signal to NICOSIA in accordance with the above.

To the best of my knowledge this signal remains unanswered.

The report was forwarded by PD Antram, BEA's Manager, Greece, to the airline's Air Safety Branch, on 15th January with a covering note outlining his own concerns:

In view of the suggestion that the cause of the accident to Comet GARCO was an explosion of a device carried on board, I believe the following information which has just come to light may be of some significance.

It appears that Mr. Solomou presented himself for carriage without any ticket and was quite adamant that he had to go on this flight.

I have called for statements from the staff who handled this passenger and attach them for your consideration.

You may consider Mr. Solomou's insistence on travelling as suspect. Perhaps he was carrying explosives which he wished to deliver as soon as possible.

Finally, although almost every other passenger on the police list of passengers has their personal address noted, Solomou's is given only as 'c/o the Embassy of the Republic of Cyprus in Athens'.

The account in the book '*Operation Kofinou*' by Spyros Papageorgiou, appears to be that the person entrusted with planting the bomb on the aircraft was to cancel his flight if Grivas did not board. This suggests that the actual plan, if Grivas had flown as anticipated, was for the person to board the aircraft as a passenger, conceal the bomb and then fabricate an excuse to leave the flight before it departed. How this would be achieved without rousing suspicion, and indeed without anyone noticing that the bomb had been placed surreptitiously and that the passenger and left without it, is not made clear. Sources have suggested to the author that the bomb planter did not manage to leave the flight and tried unsuccessfully to defuse the bomb. Again, this would not have gone unnoticed by the other passengers and the crew. Finally, if Solomou had intended all along to fly on CY284, he would certainly have ensured that his ticket was in order before turning up at the check-in desk. It is possible that the account has suffered somewhat in the retelling and translation.

In Solomou's defence, it is unlikely that he would have deliberately carried out the bombing as a suicidal venture. He was, by now, a family man with a job working for one of the most powerful men in Cyprus. The account given by George Papadopoulos, given to him by his contact who was in hopeless expectation of death, is similar in many respects to that of Papageorgiou, as related by Leonidou. The difference in detail is simply that, in the latter case, Solomou had no idea that he was carrying the device.

Solomou is described variously as chauffeur or personal assistant of the Foreign Minister of Spyros Kyprianou, this being an established fact, but also as a bodyguard or henchman of Grivas, which is not believed to have been the case. Sources have told the author that it is quite likely that Solomou was a *de facto* bodyguard of Kyprianou and might well have been a plain clothes police officer. Whether or not he would have been a member of the Cyprus Special Branch is impossible to say but, seven years after independence, it is feasible. That would explain why the Cyprus Special Branch did not mention Solomou as being on its records when contacting Veal. Certainly, Solomou had been a fighter with EOKA during the independence struggle so was no stranger to the use of force. However, that in itself certainly does not suggest he would have been prepared to destroy an airliner in more peaceful times, especially one carrying Cypriot cabin staff and passengers.

According to the few notes in the files, Solomou had been in Athens for a holiday. However, when he tried to check in at Ellinikon Airport in the early hours of 12th October, he was clearly determined to get on the flight. If, as asserted by the various sources above, he had been instructed to carry an urgent package for Spyros Kyprianou, and to get it to the Foreign Minister that very morning, it would explain why he was so hell-bent on being allowed to fly. Due to his role, it is certain that he would not have questioned the instruction to carry the package, or what it contained.

According to the files, however, there are two striking reasons why the carrier might not have been Solomou at all.

The seating plan for the ATH-NIC sector has Solomou sitting in seat 16C. However, it is noted that this is speculative, and no basis for the assumed seat allocation is given. The analysis by Fred Jones gives a clear rationale for the device detonating behind seats 4A or 5A, and this is borne out by the prevalence of extreme injuries and missing passengers from this part of the aircraft.

In addition, Solomou's body was in the 'slight injury' category. His injuries were described in the pathology report. These were facial injuries, lacerations on his right side, multiple rib fractures including a fractured sternum, dislocated pelvis and left knee. Internally, he had suffered a severe haemothorax and ruptured heart (the primary cause of death) and diaphragm. He also suffered from severe abdominal injuries. His injuries appeared consistent with a sudden and very violent, deceleration whilst strapped into his seat and possibly hitting his head on the seat in front of him. They were markedly different from those expected had he fallen from height into the sea or been caught in the blast of an exploding bomb.

If Solomou had indeed taken the device on board, deliberately or unwittingly, he had certainly not been sitting next to it when it exploded. His body was recovered amongst the 'Turkish group', which strongly suggested that Solomou had been in the forward part of the cabin when the fuselage broke at the wing spar. This would have been the case, had he been sitting in row 16, as indicated on the seating plan. It is, of course, entirely possible that Solomou was not sitting in row 16 but further back, in seat 3A or 4A. The only plausible hypothesis that would accord with the facts is if Solomou had left his bag in the footwell of his seat and had made his way forward for an unknown reason. He would certainly not have returned to his seat after the explosion and in all likelihood would have strapped himself into an empty seat some distance away from the damage.

Nicos Papapetrou

BEA's Insurance Manager, a Mr. Springbett, had been making enquiries into the insurance cover held by the victims of the crash. In late January, he contacted Veal to pass on information that passenger Nico Papapetrou had taken out three significant policies, shortly before travelling, these being two sums of £10,000 each with The Sun Alliance Group and The General Insurance Company of Cyprus, along with a policy for £5,000 with the Eagle Star company. Veal forwarded this information to Chief Inspector Bryan, adding:

It is understood that these insurances were taken out on 1st October in Cyprus. His body was not recovered.

It is understood that Mr. Papapetrou was a shoe salesman earning £80 a month but it is also apparently known that he was a professional gambler. In the twelve months prior to the accident he had made five visits by air from Cyprus to Greece but is believed never to have taken out any insurance except on this last occasion. In the winding up of his affairs after his presumed death in the accident his estate was sworn at less than £2,000. In view of the occurrence in North America of aircraft accidents in which insurance has been found to be an underlying factor it is felt that this aspect should be further investigated.

On 1st September 1968, an article in the *Sunday Times* pointed the finger of suspicion firmly in the direction of Papapetrou. Under the headline, *'Missing link in the Comet crash'* and the by-line of 'John Shirley in Cyprus and John Ball in London', it told its readers:

'It is better for me to die. My whole life has been a disaster.'

These are the words of a small-time Greek-Cypriot smuggler working as the manager of a shoe shop in the small town of Larnaca, Cyprus. He is almost certainly the missing link in the mystery explosion that sent a BEA Comet 4B crashing into the Mediterranean off Rhodes last October.

Nicos Papaetrou (sic), faced with gambling debts, two girlfriends in Athens and expensive fees to pay for his daughter's dental course in the Greek capital, was talking to a friend just 48 hours before a 16-ounce bomb – of military origin – blew a hole in the Comet's fuselage.

Papaetrou and 65 others were on the plane. They all died. In the fortnight before the crash, Papaetrou had taken out three insurance covers totalling £23,000. There may be a fourth.

Following in the tracks of a Scotland Yard team, headed by Detective Superintendent Percy Browne, who flew to Rhodes to examine the scant wreckage, we found this new witness whose memory of a conversation points directly to Papaetrou as the cause of the crash.

All documents concerning the flight were collected by the Yard and one by one the victims were crossed off his list. Then Supt. Browne came to 44-year-old Papaetrou and discovered the insurance covers.

It was Papaetrou's fifth journey between the island and the Greek capital that year; he had told his wife, Nina, at their blue-pained, double-

fronted rambling bungalow in 28th October Street, Larnaca, that they were business trips. But they were not for the Nicosia shoe firm of Galides Ltd., for whom he managed the local shop.

As he counted his meagre commission – he earned between £50 and £60 a month – he talked of breaking into the leather industry and manufacturing leather handbags. The journeys to Athens were to look for materials.

The detectives discovered Papaetrou had for years kept only one personal accident policy worth £2,000 with General Insurance Ltd. of Cyprus, which did not cover him for aviation risk.

But on September 30 last year he walked into the Larnaca branch office of the company and took out a personal accident cover for £8,000 – valid only for the month of October and covering a single journey abroad to Greece and England.

Within a few days he took out another policy, this time with the Cyprus branch of Eagle Star for £5,000. Then there was a third policy which he drew up with Sun Assurance Ltd. for £10,000.

A fortnight later the Comet exploded. Already it is understood Eagle Star have paid out to Papaetrou's widow. But the Sun company have been waiting for the official verdict on the crash before making final settlement. And General Insurance are contesting their obligation to pay on what their Nicosia manager termed "certain discrepancies in the claim".

Apparently, the dead man did not notify General Insurance of the two other policies he had taken out. The manager explained, "It is a technical matter. It is nothing to do with the cause of the accident."

But as the Yard probe went deeper, they discovered that Papaetrou, father of two daughters, had connections with a smuggling syndicate. In Athens he had two girlfriends called Helen and Titica. He gambled at casinos in Athens and on Corfu.

He spent most of the money he made through smuggling on the two girlfriends or in the casinos. But as his luck began to sour gambling debts built up and creditors demanded their money back.

Then he was thought to have been unable to pay for the goods he obtained for smuggling to Greece. A few days before his last trip he pleaded with an old friend, a retired shipping agent, who had travelled with him on some early trips, for a £1,000 loan. He only got £500.

But not only was his luck running out on the gambling tables, his marriage was beginning to crumble. However, he was still having to pay for his younger daughter, Christala, aged 19, who was undergoing expensive tuition at an Athens school of dentistry. Finally, he was almost caught red-handed with a consignment of watches worth £940 at Athens airport. Papaetrou's contact man, believed to be a customs official, failed to show up, and a brown leather suitcase stowed in the aircraft was opened. He denied it was part of his luggage and managed to hoodwink the customs investigators. But not only had he lost the consignment but also the smuggling link had been broken and he faced yet another debt.

In the introduction to his book *The Occult*[70], Colin Wilson wrote:

I open a weekend colour supplement and read that for a week before the explosion that destroyed a BEA Comet aircraft on October 12, 1967, Nicos Papapetrou was haunted by premonitions, and dreams of death and mourning, so that an hour before take-off, he tried to book on another flight. That is not past history, but then, Papapetrou was carrying the bomb that accidentally exploded. He was an explosives smuggler and had made six similar trips earlier that year; why did he get premonitions on this one?

The passage about Papapetrou is included by Wilson to support his contention that premonitions are still experienced in the present time, as well as historically. The colour supplement article appears to have been published in the Sunday magazine attached to *The Observer* newspaper. It contains a large amount of detail which bears the hallmarks of having been passed to the newspaper by the police or Foreign Office. It states with conviction that Papapetrou was smuggling explosives in his briefcase and, somehow, they had inadvertently detonated in the course of the flight. This appears to be speculative, however, as it is highly unlikely that a hitherto-successful smuggler of explosives would have transported the materials complete with a detonator attached. It is also at odds with the parallel speculation, by police and Foreign Office sources, that Papapetrou was intent on suicide for insurance purposes.

Elina Papapetrou, Nicos' daughter, confirmed that she was living in Athens at the time of the disaster. Nicos stayed with her whilst he was in Athens on business, as was perfectly usual. She recalls that he was his normal relaxed self, and that there was nothing to suggest that he was planning harm to himself or others. Elina saw Nicos off to the airport for his flight, and all was fine.

---

[70] *The Occult, by Colin Wilson (Hodder & Stoughton, 1971).*

The family was unaware of any military expertise he might have acquired that would enable him to construct an explosive device. Whilst he played cards, that was in any case a popular pastime and the family refutes any suggestion that Nicos was in significant debt or that he would be driven to such desperate measures as was mentioned in the British press.

Until the publication in 2018 of the first edition of *Bealine Charlie Oscar*, the Papapetrou family had not even been aware that Nicos was considered to be a suspect. The family rejects all the allegations made against Nicos Papapetrou[71].

On 11th September 1968, Jan Riddoch at the Foreign Office sought legal advice from the Board of Trade's solicitor on whether portions of the police report dealing with Papapetrou could be released to the Sun Alliance and London Insurance Group. He presumed that the insurance company would help to support or negate their assertion that (i) the death of Papapetrou had not been proved beyond doubt; (ii) that if he had died, then his death was due to suicide and (iii) that he had failed to disclose the existence of other insurance policies. The insurers had a significant interest in that they stood to pay out £10,000 unless they could show grounds why the policy was invalid. In the event, the police refused to make the report available, a situation that remains the same over fifty years later.

---

[71] *Elina Rossidou, daughter of Nicos Papapetrou, in conversation with the author, 2020.*

Watching the Detectives

The two Metropolitan Police officers sent to Athens and Cyprus were to investigate one of the biggest mass murders in modern British history. In later years, terrorist atrocities would become far more frequent but at the time, the Charlie Oscar incident was unprecedented for the British authorities.

The bombing of Pan Am flight 103 on 21st December 1988, resulting in the deaths of 270 people, was on a different scale to CY284, but the two crimes were similar in their nature. The police investigation into the Lockerbie atrocity had many times the limited resources given to Browne and Hill, involving the resources of the FBI as well as Dumfries and Galloway Constabulary. 15,000 witness statements were taken. The investigation into the downing of Charlie Oscar had been a much lower key affair.

The police report itself is still withheld from the public, but a cover note in the Metropolitan Police files, which contain fourteen pages of documents, notes that 266 other pages of documents have been removed, under Exemptions[72] S (2) 31, S (2) 38 and S (2) 40. Similarly, in the Home Office file (HO 287/2146), three sections are removed, totalling 255 pages. One of these is identifiable as the Pathology Report which was publicly available in full as AVIA101/255. A second section comprises 183 pages, removed under Exemptions 31 and 40. This was probably the compilation of witness statements. The third section, under the same Exemptions, comprises 29 pages and is annotated 'Report'.

The Schedule to Statements Relating to Deceased Passengers, contained in HO 287/2146 albeit redacted to remove the addresses of the passengers, shows that statement numbers 57 to 138 refer to the victims. It would be usual practice for there to be one statement from the next of kin confirming the planned journey and giving relevant background detail such as the purpose for traveling. In some cases, a married couple, such as the Griffiths, or a family group such as the Taskers, is covered by a single statement. Other individuals are covered by more than one statement. All told, this accounts for 82 statements covering the 59 passengers. There

---

[72] *Exemption 31 covers information relating to law enforcement, 38 to Health and Safety and 41 to 'information provided in confidence'. Exemptions 31 and 41 allow witness statements and the substantive police reports into the incident to be withheld. In this case, from correspondence challenging the withholding of these documents, it is known that Exemption 38 is used to withhold the Pathology Report as it contains images and information deemed to be too disturbing to view. As noted, the full report is available separately.*

would also have been statements for each of the crew, adding a further seven to the total. This would leave at least 49 statements from additional witnesses. However, a total of 183 pages for 138 statements is a paltry number considering the lines of enquiry that the two officers might reasonably have been expected to have recognised. There is the possibility of course that the documentation contains only a selection of the more substantial statements.

The additional 49 witness statements should have included the four BEA cabin staff on the London – Athens sector, the six passengers who disembarked, the airport staff at Athens and London Heathrow, the three flight deck crew of Mike Foxtrot, the air traffic controllers at Athens and Nicosia, the investigation teams at RARDE, the AIB and the Royal Aircraft Establishment. These would all be required to validate the documentary, aural and eye-witness evidence of all aspects of Charlie Oscar's last journey.

The 'passengers of interest' would have generated additional statements. **Avraam Solomou**'s behaviour had attracted attention at the airport which was witnessed by both JE Papalexopoulos, the check-in clerk, and Mr. C. Coliandris, the BEA Duty Manager, who authorised Solomou to travel at very short notice.

Even though the information quoted in the books by Leonidas Leonidou and Eleftherios Papadopoulos did not come to light until much later, Solomou was first named in the Evening Standard article on 21st November 1967 as the person carrying the bomb on board. The information is quite specific and although the article was played down, it would be a strange thing for someone to have dreamt up. Also, one identifying feature on Solomou's body noted by the pathologists was the presence of scars from bullet wounds from his time with EOKA. These should have been recorded as of possible significance.

The police team might have reasonably been expected to consider the following enquiries into Solomou's presence on the flight.

- Next-of-kin statement confirming that Solomou was planning to be on the flight, or at least to try to travel from Athens to Nicosia.
- Why was Solomou so determined to get onto the flight?
- If he had been told to be back in Nicosia the following morning, who had passed on that message and from whom had it originated?
- What was he carrying in the way of cabin baggage?
- Was he searched?
- What was his demeanour immediately prior to boarding, once his ticket had been sorted out?
- Where and when had he bought his original ticket?

- Was he travelling for personal purposes or for his work for Spiros Kyprianou.
- If travelling for work, had he visited the Cypriot Embassy in Athens, or had they had any contact with him?
- What were the exact purposes of his trip to Athens?
- Where had he stayed before checking in for CY284?
- Who had he visited?
- Had he been formally allocated seat 16C?
- If not, who provided the information that he was sitting there, and on what basis?
- What was known about his involvement in EOKA, and what specialist weapons-handling expertise did he have?
- What were his past and present relationships, if any, with Yiorkadjis and Grivas?

At the very least, statements should have been taken from Mr. Papalexopoulos, Mr. Coliandris, Mrs. Solomou, any other airline or airport staff who had direct contact with him, and finally an appropriate person in Mr. Kyprianou's office. If further details had emerged, it would be reasonable to obtain statements to substantiate or disprove the inference that Solomou's suspicious behaviour was in fact of significant concern. It would have been as important to eliminate Solomou as a suspect as to have shown there were grounds to dig even deeper. However, Avraam Solomou accounts for only two statements in the police file.

Sotiris Georgiou would have been more challenging as he originated in the USA. However, even in 1968 it would not have been beyond the realms of practicality for the FBI to assist with a next-of-kin statement. The lines of enquiry for Mr. Georgiou would have included:

- Purpose of his visit to Cyprus.
- Details of any military service, explosives expertise, or lack thereof.
- Links or otherwise, to George Georgiou, the disgruntled former BEA employee.
- Evidence of his seat allocation in 4A.
- Details of his cabin baggage.
- Evidence of any adverse behavioural indicators: was he unusually nervous, for a passenger?

The minimum requirement for statements for Sotiris Georgiou would have included his next-of-kin, check-in staff at London, cabin staff on the London – Athens sector and, if possible, George Georgiou. Only statement number 83 refers to Georgiou.

Had the investigation team made contact with the Georgiou family, they would ascertain the answers to the points above. The purpose of his trip to

Cyprus was simply to visit his parents, his brother Nick and family, as well as to explore the idea of finding a Cypriot future bride. Although, he had been in the US for less than four years, he was home sick and wanted to go back for a three-week visit. He had never served in the military and was never trained in the use of arms or explosives.

There was no link between Sotiris and George Georgiou, the disgruntled former employee of BEA. He did, coincidentally, have a brother named George who at the time of the disaster, was living a few thousand miles west of London, in Clairton Pennsylvania, where he managed a dry-cleaning business. During his stopover in London between his BOAC and BEA flights, Sotiris spent the time with his English in-laws and also shopping.

It is, of course, entirely possible that Sotiris may have changed seats while en route to Athens, or when reboarding Charlie Oscar after the stopover there. The BEA cabin staff make no mention of such a change, however.

Sotiris had two suitcases and a smaller carry-on bag. He was taking gifts to his family in Cyprus. The acquisition of further gifts in London accounts for the four kilos of excess baggage he was noted as checking in at London.

According to Sotiris' brother Polyvios[73], the people who knew him throughout his all-too-short life characterized Sotiris as a level-headed, handsome, even-tempered; socially involved, generous young man, who went to evening classes to improve his English. According to his two German employers he was well-disciplined and a hard worker that had dreams about opening his own car repair shop in New York. He was a trained car mechanic and at the time of his death was employed by Great Neck Imports, a firm specializing in Mercedes car models. He had acquired US citizenship in Wilmington, Delaware in 1965, fourteen months after arriving in the US. This rather quick naturalisation was the result of his father regaining his own US citizenship after a ruling by that country's Supreme Court.

Polyvios' mother-in-law and brothers-in-law were the last members of his extended family to see Sotiris alive as he boarded BE284 at Heathrow.

According to the *Sunday Telegraph* team, **Nicos Papapetrou** came to light when it transpired that he had taken out separate insurance policies with four different companies. In addition to the next-of-kin statement, it would also have been important to establish:

- Where and when did he buy the insurance policies?

---

[73] *Polyvios Georgiou in correspondence with the author, 2018.*

- Who had interacted with him in selling the insurance? Was it definitely Papapetrou who had bought the policies?
- Had he expressed suicidal thoughts at any time previously?
- What was he carrying in the way of cabin baggage?
- Was he searched?
- What was his demeanour immediately prior to boarding?
- Where and when had he bought his ticket?
- Was he travelling for personal purposes or for his work for Galides, his employer?
- What were the exact purposes of his trip to Athens?
- Where had he stayed before checking in for CY284?
- Who had he visited?
- Had he been formally allocated seat a seat?
- Was he associating with the group of Jehovah's Witnesses before boarding?
- What military or specialist weapons-handling expertise did he have?

This would entail the usual statements from his wife and check-in staff, along with the ticket seller, any surviving witnesses from the Athens departure lounge, his daughter in Athens and the four insurance agents. This would add up to at least seven statements; whilst Papapetrou was the subject of four statements, 135 to 138, it would have been reasonable to expect significantly more.

By way of comparison, a number of other passengers are the subject of several statements. Of note are the McComb family (six statements) and Mrs. Liassides (four). None of these victims rated any kind of a mention in terms of arousing suspicion, which under their apparent circumstances is entirely understandable. Yet they merited more statements than the named suspects.

On the face of it, to carry out a thorough investigation would require a much larger team of police officers than Detective Superintendent Browne and Detective Sergeant Hill. Nowadays, for a mass murder enquiry, the team would have reported to an Assistant Chief Constable in a county force or perhaps a Deputy Assistant Commissioner in the Metropolitan Police.

The cost of the investigation, which so exercised the minds of various parties, would mostly have comprised the time of the two officers, their travel, hotel and subsistence. The wages, in 2018 prices, of the two officers[74] for a two-month period would have amounted to around £20,000. Flights, depending on the number taken, would probably have added

---

[74] *Superintendent £85,000 p.a., Sergeant £40,000*

£10,000 for a number of round trips. Hotel accommodation would add perhaps £200 per night, and subsistence around £100 per day for the two officers. Taxi fares would probably amount to another £500 per week, if a lot of travelling was entailed. All told, the order of magnitude of the taxpayers' burden would have been £50,000 and £60,000. The cost of the Lockerbie investigation itself is not known, but the trial alone cost $60 million. When three Islamist terrorists plotted to blow up transatlantic airliners in August 2006, the investigation and trial were estimated to total £100 million. The investigation into Charlie Oscar would have been an absolute bargain, had the suspect been identified.

If the investigation was carried out today, Browne, or his equivalent, would manage a large team carrying out enquiries throughout Britain, Greece and Cyprus, digging into the backgrounds of each passenger, sifting through all available documentation, tracking down anybody who had any involvement at all with BE/CY284. Crucially, there would be intensive work going on behind the scenes exploring the potential political scenarios. The immediate assumption that the bomb was intended for General Grivas must have had some foundation for being so strongly held. If there was, indeed, some foundation for the belief, then it would have been in the interests of the Cypriot Government to determine what that was; at the very least, the reader might consider that Grivas himself would be keen to know.

The Metropolitan Police had not seemed particularly eager to take on the investigation in the first place. There was then considerable reticence to involve the Greek authorities, or even let them know that the investigation was going on. No mention at all is made of involving the Cypriot government or its agencies. The Foreign Office sent a clear message to Assistant Commissioner Brodie to tell Browne to raise any political angle to them before proceeding further. The importance of this message was clearly understood by Brodie, who sent a very secretive letter to Browne through the Diplomatic Bag system. If the instruction had been routine, and a matter of not treading on toes, it could have been handled by telephone, or perhaps by a member of the staff at the Athens Embassy having a quiet word with Browne and Hill about diplomatic niceties and protocols.

It seems that the Foreign Office had very great concerns about something being spoiled if Browne was not given the hard word. To this day, 'national security' remains one of the reasons given by the National Archives for not releasing some of the information in the files. Such measures, although likely to attract media criticism, are easier to understand if they are necessary to protect a highly-placed intelligence source, perhaps in a government position. During the Cyprus Emergency, EOKA was riddled with informants, leading to the extreme measures by Grivas, perhaps including what Georgeides had succinctly termed the General's *'exterminating-traitor-squad'*. It is unlikely that Grivas had succeeded in tracking them all down.

Analysis

No one will ever know what happened on board Charlie Oscar during her final few minutes of flight, and it is likely that the motive and the actual perpetrator will always be the subject of controversy. It is possible, though, to reconstruct the likely course of events after SFO Thomas started his greeting to Nicosia.

At that point, the bomb exploded in the passenger cabin. Sited in the passenger footwell of seat 3A or 4A, and partially under the seat in front of it, the device fragmented, forcing microscopic fragments of shrapnel in all directions, and at unimaginably high speeds. The occupant of the seat in whose footwell the bomb had been located, would have been very seriously wounded but, mercifully, would have known little about it. The over-pressure, of the order of several hundred pounds per square inch immediately next to the device, undoubtedly tore a significant hole in the fuselage, forcing the metal skin outward into the airstream. A smaller hole was left in the cabin floor. Initially measuring some thirty inches square, the breach in the pressure cabins wall immediately allowed all the air in the fuselage to escape. The sequence of events in explosive decompressions is well known. In a split second, the cabin temperature and pressure plummeted, causing a dense fog to form, compounded by dust and debris, though these were almost immediately displaced as the air forced its way out of the fuselage. The intense, though short-lived, rush may well have carried with it the shattered body of the occupant of the seat, never to be recovered. It is possible that this was Sotiris Georgiou, known to have been sitting in 4A on the London to Athens sector, strongly indicating that the bomb had been brought on to the aircraft by the person now sitting in 3A on the Athens to Nicosia flight. Whichever passenger was sitting in the seat below which the explosion occurred probably sustained serious lacerations to their back and legs and may also have been sucked out of the cabin breach as that happened.

The force of the blast diminished greatly with every foot from the centre of the explosion, especially as the aircraft seats provided a barrier to the wave of pressure.

Achillea Afatitis, one of the group of Jehovah's Witnesses, and who was probably standing in the aisle, four or five feet away, was peppered with shrapnel, but avoided being sucked out of the aircraft, probably because he was blocked by the row of seats between him and the hole in the cabin wall.

As the pressure within the cabin equalised with that outside, the mist cleared, and the temperature dropped. The emergency oxygen masks dropped and those who were still conscious and capable of doing so, donned them. The others remained mercifully oblivious to the traumatic situation developing around them.

The pilots would have put on their oxygen masks and run through the procedures for sudden loss of pressure. This involved a controlled descent to a lower altitude, flying at around 330 knots, with the airbrakes deployed and the throttles closed. In the case of explosive decompression, the Operations Manual advised *'...the stresses in the airframe should be kept at a minimum by holding the air speed within reasonable bounds by avoiding all unnecessary and violent manoeuvres.'*

The next stage in the procedure would come when they had descended to below 13,500 feet, which would be in four to five minutes. From their cruising height of 29,000 feet, this length of time would not present an overwhelming problem for the passengers, as they had access to the drop-down oxygen masks in the cabin. The role of the cabin staff would have been to instruct the passengers to remain in their seats with their seatbelts fastened, whilst they awaited the intentions of the captain. It is unlikely that Captain Blackwood anticipated ditching at that time, otherwise the passengers would have been instructed to put their lifejackets on.

The closest airport was now Rhodes, some 120 miles back along their track and 60 miles closer than Nicosia. Assuming the airport was open at that time of morning, it would probably have been the obvious choice of diversion airfield and was some 25 minutes flying time away.

Assessing the situation at first hand would have been the task of SFO Palmer. It would have been a scene of devastation, but it is fair to assume that he was trained to cope calmly with what he found. The noise of the engines and the slipstream, no longer mitigated by the cabin wall's soundproofing, would have been pronounced.

The cabin staff, by now doing their best to keep the passengers as calm as was possible in the circumstances, would try to move those nearest to the damage to empty seats away from the hole in the fuselage. There was a need to maintain the overall balance of the aircraft. It would not have been feasible to move all the passengers forward as that would have made the aircraft nose-heavy beyond its design limits, but it is quite likely that those passengers sitting on the left-hand side of the cabin, and behind the site of the explosion, would have been moved away first.

The situation would have merited a 'Mayday' call, but it is possible that the patchy radio coverage, which had necessitated Charlie Oscar's earlier transmission being relayed by Captain Emmerson in Mike Foxtrot, now let them down completely. No distress call was ever received.

Underneath the cabin floor, it is possible that one or more of the hydraulic pipes had been severed or critical components of the system disabled by the blast. In theory, the Comet's triplicated hydraulic system should have been able to cope with just such an emergency. Equally, it is possible that damage to the aileron servos, which were almost directly underneath seat row 5, affected the ability of the pilots to control the angle of roll of the aircraft. The five minutes or so indicated on the watches allowed Charlie Oscar time to descend to about 15,000 feet.

For whatever reason, the g-forces on the aircraft, resulting from the out-of-control situation it was now in, eventually became too much and Charlie Oscar broke in two, around the forward wing spar. The shock to the airframe caused the fire extinguishers to activate, and one broke free to be found amongst the floating debris. The front portion of the fuselage, from row 11 forward, devoid of wings, descended vertically at high speed whilst the rear part, from row 10 back, retained some slight forward motion, taking it some 2,000 feet to the south.

As stated at the start of this chapter, there is no direct evidence of the above account, but it is based on the emergency procedures outlined in the BEA Comet 4B Flight Manual. An uncontrolled, steepening turn would account for the distance of 25 to 30 nautical miles travelled in the five minutes between the explosion and disintegration, being so much greater than the straight-line distance of 10 nautical miles between the estimated location of the aircraft when the last call was made, and the place at which the wreckage was estimated to have fallen into the sea. It might also explain why the heading of Charlie Oscar when she disintegrated was believed to be south or south-east, rather than the west-north-west that would have taken her to Rhodes.

The account by Nikos Misomikes confirming that he saw no bodies wearing lifejackets, supports the notion that the disaster was not immediately considered catastrophic, and Captain Blackwood did not consider that it would be necessary to ditch the aircraft. Ditching far out at sea, with sporadic radio contact, in the dark, would in any case be a measure to be used only in extreme circumstances. It is therefore possible that the pilots were attempting to bring Charlie Oscar back under control, up until the point where the fuselage broke apart.

The movement of passengers to seats away from the hole in the fuselage might also account for five of the passengers originally seated in the rear of the aircraft being recovered in the northern wreckage field, which is where the front section of Charlie Oscar's fuselage came down. The ferrying of bodies recovered by the Kastellorizo sailors to the *Navarinon* would also possibly explain why six victims believed to have been travelling in the front section of Charlie Oscar were stated to have been amongst those found amongst the wreckage of the rear part of the aircraft.

The Metropolitan Police Investigation

The investigation into the criminal aspects of the incident was limited in its scope, resourcing and, apparently, in its enthusiasm, and has remained shrouded in secrecy. It is now more than half a century since Charlie Oscar was blown from the sky. After the initial flurry of activity around the recovery operation, analysis of the sparse wreckage and the pitiful remains of the victims and the prompt and effective accident investigation which showed conclusively that the cause was a bomb, there have been over fifty years of silence. Twenty-three files in the National Archives, comprising some 2,500 pages, provide a comprehensive record of the correspondence relating to almost every aspect of the work carried out by Ken Mason, John Veal, Eric Newton, Fred Jones and their teams.

Three files, relating to the police investigation, remain mostly unavailable to the public, and these have been a source of much speculation. These files remain wholly under lock and key with a further-delayed release date of 1st January 2067. In 2018 the National Archives secured permission from the Metropolitan Police and the Home Office to disclose part of their contents to the author.

It has long been assumed, by those having an interest in solving the mystery of flight CY284, that the Metropolitan Police files have the potential to reveal further details about the incident. The few newly-released documents in the closed files hold no 'smoking gun'; in fact, they reveal very little that was not already known. Unfortunately, the final 29-page police report, along with the 138 or so witness statements, are amongst the retained information in the files. The justification for continuing to retain these documents is three-fold. First, the Metropolitan Police recognises that the incident was a crime of mass murder, and they might reopen the case 'if new evidence comes to light'. Second, it comprises information given in confidence to the investigating officers and this might disclose the political sympathies fifty years ago of the witnesses, many of whom are most likely deceased now. Finally, some of the information might compromise national security as it might reveal the identity of intelligence sources, if any. After an appeal, the Met eventually decided that it could change its stance, that it would neither confirm nor deny that it held other information on Charlie Oscar, to a confirmation that in fact, it does not. All the remaining information gathered and retained by the Met sits in those three files in the National Archives. The National Archives Freedom of Information team explained to the author why they would not release further documents from the police files[75]

'Some of the information you have requested is being withheld under section 23 (1) and 24 (1) in the alternative. Section 23 (1), exempts information held by a public authority from disclosure if it was provided

---

[75] *The files are MEPO 2/11089, MEPO 2/11090 and HO 287/2146.*

to that public authority by the bodies dealing with security matters, or if that information relates to those bodies, and section 24 (1) exempts information from disclosure if its exemption is required for the purpose of safeguarding national security.

Sections 23 (1) and 24 (1) are being cited in the alternative as it is not appropriate, in the circumstances of the case, to say which of the two exemptions is actually engaged so as not to undermine national security or reveal the extent of any involvement, or not, of the bodies dealing with security matters.

Section 31(1) of the FOI Act exempts information if its disclosure would, or would be likely to, prejudice –

a) the prevention or detection of crime

b) the apprehension or prosecution of offenders

c) the administration of justice.

...Section 31(1)(a-c) is engaged for some of the information in MEPO 2/11089 & MEPO 2/11090 because it relates to evidence – in the form of investigation reports and related witness statements – about a crime that remains unsolved. The information is directly relevant to the investigation into the crash of BEA Comet G-Argo (sic) over the Mediterranean Sea that resulted in the death of all passengers and crew, as such the Metropolitan Police Service would desire that the details of the investigation remain confidential for the lifetime of any hypothetical suspect.

In relation to these specific files, it is not possible to identify particular information from investigation reports and witness statement that could be released into the public domain without the risk of compromising any future police actions. Information that appears innocuous may have significance to an experienced investigator that is not immediately obvious to the lay reader; or may assume a new significance in the light of newly discovered evidence or developments in forensic or investigative techniques.

The Metropolitan Police have confirmed that it is extremely difficult when considering any unsolved case as to the 'significant likelihood of future investigation' as it cannot be predicted what information or evidence may come to light in the future that would generate a renewed investigation. Increasingly police services throughout the country are setting up 'cold case' teams to review their case files on unsolved murders. As recently as last year, The National Archives provided case papers to police services in order to assist with enquiries into an unsolved murder from the late 1940s. In considering this exemption we therefore have to acknowledge that there does remain a possibility, however remote, that this case could be investigated at some point in the future and that the information contained in these records could be significant to it.

As a result section 31(1)(a-c) has been applied to all information created by the investigating authorities in these records, as we are unable to identify (and therefore redact) particular information that might be released into the public domain without the risk of compromising any future police actions.

The purpose of this exemption in this instance is to protect details that could be used in a future investigation should a suspect be identified, charged and brought to trial. The closure period is based on an assumption that the suspect(s) would have been at least 16 years old at the material time.

The premature release of this information into the public domain may be detrimental to any future investigation and subsequent prosecution. To release significant information which could potentially jeopardise a future prosecution for murder would not be in the public interest. Therefore it has been determined that the risk of prejudice outweighs the reasoning for disclosure in this specific case and the exemption at section 31(1)(a-c) of the Freedom of Information Act applies to the information...

...Section 38(1)(b) is engaged for a limited amount of information in these records because it contains the identities of police informants. While there is an important public interest in the transparency of police investigations and their investigative methods, in this case, this must be balanced against the risk of placing in the public domain, information that could put at risk the safety of an individual. It has been determined that release of the identities of these individuals would be likely to endanger these individuals and to prejudice their physical safety by exposing them to the risk of physical harm from reprisal attacks, thus section 38(1)(b) is engaged...

...It remains the expert opinion of the Metropolitan Police Service and therefore of TNA that, despite the passage of time, there continues to exist a real possibility of endangerment for these individuals, who could be at risk from retaliation or reprisal action if their names were to be released into the public domain. The public need the reassurance of knowing that FOI access rights are not going to be allowed to be exercised to their detriment. To release information which would be likely to expose

individuals to the risk of physical harm or pose a danger to their safety would not be in the public interest. Therefore, it has been determined that the risk of endangering the physical safety of the individuals identified in these records significantly outweighs any reasons for disclosure and the exemption at section 38(1)(b) of the FOI Act applies to this information...

...In your internal review request you mentioned that there are a number of open records related to this case and highlighted a lack of consistency between open and closed information.

I can confirm that I consulted a number of AVIA files in relation to your internal review request and can confirm that they do not contain the same information or investigation reports held within MEPO 2/11089 and MEPO 2/11090. This is because Metropolitan Police records (MEPO records) typically contain papers and reports directly relating to a criminal investigation including witness statements, information relating to possible suspects, forensic evidence and possible lines of enquiry.

The FOI Centre have referred three records, AVIA 101/225, AVIA 101/218 and AVIA 101/220[76] to be reviewed under our Reclosure policy.'

The Cypriot authorities have told sources that they hold no information whatsoever about the incident, this seemingly including the six copies of the AIB report they were sent in 1968. In 2014, the Cyprus Police reviewed the case, pursuant to a Presidential decree, but this apparently revealed no new information.

It is inconceivable in the current age that the criminal investigation into the loss of Charlie Oscar would have been so light-touch. Investigations into similar events, such as Lockerbie in the UK and the two separate losses of Malaysia Airlines Boeing 777s in 2014, were multinational affairs in which the cost, quite rightly, was not a deciding factor. With two officers dedicated to investigating CY284, the investigation plan should have been overwhelming; in fact, it appears to have taken Detective Superintendent Browne some six weeks to conduct an investigation spanning three countries, before concluding to the evident satisfaction the civil servants that there was no evidence upon which to proceed.

The very fact that the Metropolitan Police continues to retain the written evidence, in case new evidence comes to light half a century later, begs the

---

[76] *AVIA101/218 – Demarcation of Investigation; AVIA101/220 – Diaries and Documentation; AVIA101/225 – Pathology Reports. These files were publicly available at the time of writing, and their information is used throughout this book, under Open Licence V2.0.*

question of why their enquiries were wound down after such a short time. This is inconsistent with contemporaneous investigations into the murder of single individuals, let alone 66 people. Times have indeed changed.

It is clear from the correspondence available that the British Foreign Office was most concerned that no embarrassment be caused to its interests by the police investigation. John Macrae of the FO, in his letter of 13th February 1968 to his colleague John Edmonds in Ankara, felt that the most likely explanation was that the motive was an insurance scam. Whether that can be construed as an innocent comment on the various theories, or an indication of the way they had hoped the investigation would proceed, is open to conjecture. The Foreign Office and, at their behest, Assistant Commissioner Brodie went to considerable lengths get a 'secret' letter to Athens to instruct Browne not to dig too deeply into political lines of enquiry without consulting the FO first. This tends to suggest that there were some serious concerns on the part of the FO about where the investigation might well lead. There is no way of knowing what other documentation might have been excluded from the files, and it is not at all likely that any incriminating material would have been kept on file. However, the continued retention of material on the grounds of national security indicates that there is still sensitivity around certain information or its source.

During the 'Cyprus Emergency' or 'liberation struggle', depending on the viewpoint of the reader, it was, as stated earlier, known that the British Security Services, particularly the Secret Service, MI6, could rely on a flow of information from within EOKA. After the cessation of hostilities, there is rarely an amnesty for informants who have supplied sensitive intelligence to the enemy's security apparatus. If any such sources were inadvertently identified, for example in a criminal investigation, their lives would still be endangered; the seven years since Cypriot independence was unlikely to have led to a 'forgive and forget' attitude on the part of the more ruthless elements.

It has been suggested to the author that Polycarpos Yiorkadjis had been an informant for the British; perhaps his various escapes from British custody during the struggle had been more than simply fortuitous but had provided a cover for a covert debriefing by his handlers. If, indeed, this is the case, such a source, relying on continuing discretion by a foreign power, in the top level of government, would have been an asset worth preserving. The attitude of those tasked with handling him might have been outright repugnance at his involvement in mass murder, tempered by the reality that bringing him to justice would not help those lost.

The Metropolitan Police asserts to this day that it might reopen the criminal investigation if there is new evidence. The hearsay evidence, that Yiorkadjis had orchestrated the plot using Solomou as the carrier, appears to have come to light some time after Detective Superintendent Browne and Detective Sergeant Hill had returned to England, and moved on to their next cases. Whilst hearsay evidence itself is not generally admissible, it would be a good starting point to re-examine that area of the work of Browne and Hill. Nowadays, such a low-key nature of the original enquiries, along with implied direction by the Foreign Office and the paucity of the resources made available, would raise significant questions over the effectiveness of that investigation. The Sixties were an earlier era when power and influence were concentrated within the Establishment. Bodies such as Government departments and police forces were not expected to be transparent and accountable to the extent they are today. It is, surely, far from impossible that a senior police officer would have taken heed of some clear guidance from the Foreign Office to focus on certain areas and not be too concerned about others.

The police and Home Office in Britain have been willing to re-open cold cases and there would be merit in a thorough review of the original case, to identify missed opportunities and examine new leads. The mass murder of 66 people surely makes this worthwhile, notwithstanding the passage of half a century since the crime itself. The Metropolitan Police Service in the 21st century is far removed from the organisation it was in the Sixties, and it is to be hoped that they might be willing to take on this task, should a case be made to them.

Who Bombed Charlie Oscar?

The accident investigation proved beyond any doubt that a bomb brought down Charlie Oscar. Not only was there positive evidence of this, but every other plausible cause was considered and ruled out.

Terrorism is defined by NATO[77] as 'the unlawful use or threatened use of force or violence against individuals or property in an attempt to coerce or intimidate governments or societies to achieve political, religious or ideological objectives.' Although there had been a warning letter from the 'Falcon Forces' in June 1967, warning airlines flying to Israel to stop doing so, no group claimed responsibility for the destruction of Charlie Oscar, and nothing in the National Archives files so far released suggests that terrorism was progressed as a motive.

The attempted assassination of General Grivas has proved extremely resilient as a presumed motive for the bombing of Charlie Oscar. Grivas actually did travel from Athens to Nicosia later the same day as the crash of Charlie Oscar. The first-hand account by Louis Loizou and the information quoted by Leonidas Leonidou separately verify that Grivas originally planned to travel on CY284 and only the Cyprus Special Branch, under the auspices of Polycarpos Yiorkadjis, specifically says otherwise. The idea that Grivas was the intended target never truly went away, and indeed was resurrected in a headline in the *Birmingham Post* on 30th August 1968, under the headline, *'Comet death crash – it was a bomb meant for Grivas.'* However, this was countered the following day by an article in *The Sunday Times*, telling its readers, under the headline, *'Missing link in Comet crash'*, that Papapetrou has committed the atrocity for the insurance pay out. One of these must have been 'fake news' in today's parlance. It might be considered that the second article, rich in detail of the troubles of Nicos Papapetrou, had been fed to the paper's journalists by sources with a vested interest in ensuring that history recorded this version of the truth.

It appears that no one has suggested publicly that there was a Turkish dimension to the destruction of CY284 and nowhere in the National Archive's accessible files does that possibility arise. Yet the Turks, more than anyone other than a deadly political rival, might have had a clear interest in the removal from the stage of General Grivas. It is, perhaps, significant that the downing of Charlie Oscar preceded rather than followed an escalation of violence, for which Grivas was held responsible by many people.

---

[77] *NATO Glossary of Terms and Definitions, 2014.*

Whilst researching this book, it was suggested to the author that the British Secret Service, or the CIA, might have been behind the plot. However, it is not clear what they would have had to gain directly from the death of Grivas, especially considering the extreme measure the destruction of an airliner would represent. With Grivas no longer hiding furtively in the back streets of Limassol or Nicosia, those organisations would surely have been able to take him out, had they so wanted, without murdering 66 innocent people. There would have been hell to pay had the British Secret Service destroyed a British airliner carrying British passengers and crew. Equally, the Americans would have been unlikely to destroy a civilian aircraft belonging to one of their major allies, deliberately at least, and especially when their stock on the world stage was getting lower due to Vietnam. It is, however, interesting to note that a novel, *Cat's Paw*[78], is based on exactly the premise discounted here, the bomb being placed by a CIA agent working in collaboration with the British. The book was, according to its author, simply a work of fiction inspired by the intrigue surrounding the loss of Charlie Oscar.

Surrounding the established facts of the destruction of CY284 are other elements that certainly do not diminish the aura of subterfuge. The depth of the Mediterranean varies but is greatest in the vicinity of the Ionian Sea; Charlie Oscar fell in the vicinity of the Strabo Trench. It might have been coincidence but equally could have been by design. If the bomb had been triggered by the initial radio call as Charlie Oscar was about to enter the Nicosia Flight Information Region, its maker would have been reasonably certain that the aircraft would come down in an inaccessible part of the sea. The technology to construct such devices was certainly available at that time. Whilst a timing device could have caused the detonation at the same spot, it would be less precise and subject to the possibility of a delayed departure, as had happened to Hermes G-ALDW in 1956.

Speculation about the motive for the destruction of CY284 centred from the outset on an assassination attempt against General Georgios Grivas. This was reportedly confirmed by MI6 according to *The Sunday Telegraph* on 26th November 1967 (see p. 132), though the author remembers the theory being mentioned on the BBC News shortly after the crash. Later on 12th October, the reader will recall that Olympic Airways changed the aircraft assigned to their Athens – Nicosia flight. Whilst Veal considered that this might be a precaution, it suggests immediate concern on the part of Olympic Airways that their aircraft, now due to convey the General, might also have been targeted.

---

[78] *Cat's Paw by Christopher Malinger (Malinger Publishing, 2017).*

Half a century later, many Greek Cypriots remain convinced of this motive. The Cypriot authorities, however, have never accepted the theory. The alternative hypothesis, as noted and examined above, was that Nicos Papapetrou had destroyed the aircraft, with a bomb carried either by himself or by an unwitting stooge. This possible cause gained strength through the police investigation and was clearly more politically palatable to the British Foreign Office than the loss of the aircraft and occupants as collateral damage in an assassination attempt.

In order to identify the person most likely to have brought the bomb on board, it is necessary to specify exactly where the bomb was located, and who was sitting with it. The wording used when describing the location of the device is important. There are several versions of the precise position and a composite estimate, based on the damage to the seat cushion, was that it was between eleven and twelve inches below the rear of the seat cushion, up to four inches behind the rear edge and three inches to the side of the cushion. Therefore, when Jones et al describe the bomb as being under one of the numbered seats, this does not mean it was fully underneath. Rather, it was more or less directly under the back of that seat, slightly off centre and on the floor. This would be where a passenger would place a bag, under the back of the seat ahead of them, but where it would be readily accessible. For example, if the bomb was described in the files as 'under seat 4A', this means that it was probably in the footwell of seat 3A.

Jones based his assumption that the device was under the back of seats 4A or 5A on the basis that the bomb carrier was most probably amongst the missing passengers, and that the passenger with the shrapnel wounds, Achillea Afatitis, was sitting in the seat row behind the explosion, to account for the pattern of his injuries. Furthermore, he assumed that the passengers who had travelled from London and who were continuing to Nicosia from Athens did not change seats, and that the group of Jehovahs' Witnesses all sat in the block of seats in the rear cabin, primarily rows 4 to 7 inclusive. Reasonable though those assumptions might be, they are assumptions, nonetheless. The seating plan in Fred Jones' RAE report shows that Mr. and Mrs. Thiakou, both members of the Jehovah's Witnesses group, were sitting in seats 16D and 16E, across the gangway from Avraam Solomou. This shows that, in fact, at least some of the group were quite happy to find empty seats in other parts of the aircraft.

If Nicos Papapetrou had been carrying the device, he would, by Jones' reckoning, have been sitting in one of the seats that Jones then went on to assume would have been occupied by a Jehovah's Witness, whereas Papapetrou was not a member of that group.

There is very strong circumstantial evidence that Jones was close to the mark in his assessment of where the bomb went off, as there is a concentration of missing passengers along the port side of the cabin, and passengers with extreme injuries towards the rear.

Jones was the only person who assessed where the device was when it detonated, and he was a man with a solid reputation for deriving the causes of aircraft losses using impeccable logic. Therefore, the best guess remains that the device did indeed explode somewhere towards the rear of the cabin. This would also account for a loss of control of the aircraft resulting from damage to the hydraulic system and other controls directly underneath the seats indicated by Jones.

The possibility of an unidentified person at either Heathrow or Ellinikon airport smuggling the bomb on board was considered during the investigation, but the bomb was not positioned such that it would have been well-hidden. From the presumed position, the device would have been clearly visible to the passenger sitting in the seat adjacent to it. If someone had the opportunity to place it, the device might have been better concealed in the life-jacket housing or on the hat rack.

By far the most likely person to have brought the bomb on board was either Nicos Papapetrou or Avraam Solomou, resulting in two possible motives for the destruction of Charlie Oscar. Leonidas Leonidou and Eleftherios Papadopoulos, stated that Avraam Solomou carried the bomb onto the aircraft, albeit without knowing. Solomou was named in connection with the bombing at an early stage, when the investigation was still being carried out. As the journalist did not reveal his source it is impossible to know where this information came from, but it is quite explicit. Whilst the newspaper articles in November 1967 do not allege Solomou carried the bomb on board himself, they emphasise that his presence might have caused the plotters to identify CY284 as the flight on which Grivas was travelling. This should have been of immediate interest to the police investigation, but in fact resulted in only two statements being taken

However, as has been outlined above, the information in the pathologists' report shows that Solomou was not next to the bomb when it exploded, as his injuries showed no sign of blast damage. Also, his body was recovered in the northern debris field, indicating that he had been in the forward section of the aircraft when the fuselage broke apart. A plausible explanation is that Solomou was sitting in the rear of the tourist cabin, along with most of the passengers starting their journey at Athens. Half an hour before landing it is not unreasonable for a passenger to have left his seat to use the aircraft toilet compartment to freshen up, and therefore Solomou could easily have been away from the bomb when it exploded. Along with other passengers in the vicinity of the damage, he would then have had to move further forward as his seat would no longer exist. This would account for his injuries and the fact that he was found with passengers from the front of the aircraft when it hit the sea.

The absence of Nicos Papapetrou's body means that his proximity to the bomb cannot be proved or disproved. Other passengers were also missing from other parts of the cabin and so his disappearance in itself proves nothing. The accounts of his involvement in smuggling, his comments about it being better if he died, and his parlous financial situation are uncorroborated, and their provenance is uncertain; there is only one newspaper article to give any substance to these notions. The Papapetrou family consider the Sunday Times article to be lies. Of course, the fact that Papapetrou took out four insurance policies would arouse suspicion and, assuming it is true, would be a very clear indication that something was not right. But to prove Papapetrou's responsibility beyond reasonable doubt, or even on the balance of probabilities, requires more information about the man and all the circumstances surrounding his final, well-insured, journey.

There were possible precedents for the plots attributed to Papapetrou. On 16th November 1959, a National Airlines Douglas DC-7B airliner carrying 42 passengers and crew disappeared whilst flying over the Gulf of Mexico between Miami and New Orleans. In a case with similarities to Charlie Oscar, scattered debris and ten bodies were recovered. One theory advanced was that the perpetrator tricked another man to travel in his place; there was a bomb in his luggage and the plan was hatched so that the perpetrator's wife could collect on his life insurance. The passenger concerned, William Taylor, had boarded the flight using a ticket issued to a Robert Spears, a convicted criminal. It was believed that the two men had become friends whilst in prison. Despite using Spears' ticket, Taylor had purchased life insurance of his own at Miami airport before departure. His ex-wife applied to collect the insurance after the crash, and the substitution came to light. Spears disappeared after the crash but was arrested in Phoenix, Arizona, in 1969 in Taylor's car. He was never charged in connection with the loss of the aircraft, and there was no evidence ever produced connecting Spears directly with the disaster.

Less than two months later, on 6th January 1960, another National Airlines aircraft was lost, along with the lives of the 34 passengers and crew. Flight 2511, from New York to Miami, was a Douglas DC6, which was a substitute for the Boeing 707 originally scheduled to operate, but which was unserviceable. The aircraft crashed near the town of Bolivia, North Carolina. One part of the aircraft skin was found some 25 miles from the rest of the wreckage. As with CY284, pathological examination indicated that the body of one passenger, Julian Frank, had substantial evidence of the explosion of a dynamite bomb. Frank was under investigation of misappropriating up to one million dollars in charity scams. He had insurance policies totalling $900,000, including insurance cover bought on the day of the flight. The Civil Aeronautics Board (CAB), which carried out the investigation, concluded that the aircraft was brought down by a dynamite explosion in the passenger cabin, beneath the right-hand seat in row 7. This was close to Frank's seat, but as with the AIB report into Charlie Oscar, the CAB did not attribute blame to any named person. The case was referred to the FBI but was never concluded. It remains open to this day.

On May 22nd 1962, a Boeing 707 was operating Continental Airlines flight 11 from Chicago to Kansas City. 42 minutes into the flight, the aircraft disappeared from the ATC radar. An explosion had occurred in the right rear lavatory, leading to the separation of the rearmost 38 feet of the fuselage. The 707 crashed in a field near Unionville, Missouri, with the loss of the 45 souls on board. Thomas Doty, a passenger on the flight, had boarded at the very last minute and had, like Frank, bought additional insurance just before departure. He was covered to the extent of $300,000 and was being investigated on suspicion of armed robbery.

Doty had also bought six sticks of dynamite shortly before the flight. The FBI concluded that Doty had blown himself up in the rear lavatory, having carried the dynamite in his briefcase and then placed it in the used hand towel bin. His widow was refused the insurance pay-out.

The three cases cited were all domestic flights in the United States and the attacks were carried out before airport security was particularly intense. The latter two involved devices consisting of dynamite (the first case had no actual evidence of an explosion as the aircraft, like Charlie Oscar, crashed into the sea and little wreckage was recovered).

The supposed plot by Papapetrou was complex. The newspaper article *Did saboteur die in Comet crash?* which appeared in the *Cyprus Mail* on 5th September 1968 stated that *'...the Police believe he somehow tricked another man into flying in his place, using his ticket, and his seat.'* It would have been quite difficult to carry out this ruse on an international flight but not impossible. Papapetrou would have had to lend the unwitting victim his passport, in which case the man would have to bear a passable resemblance to him. Quite how Papapetrou might have persuaded the other man to undertake the task is not explained, though it is feasible that Papapetrou promised the man a significant amount of money. It is also plausible that the other man was a fellow smuggler, who thought the package in his bag was contraband, and that impersonating another smuggler was part of a cunning plan to fool the authorities. If the man with Papapetrou's documents was an impostor, then there would most likely have been a person similar to Papapetrou reported missing shortly after the crash.

Naturally any plot, whether suicide or murder, would not have succeeded without Papapetrou being able to acquire explosives and build a bomb, or perhaps by such a device from a bomb-maker. Either of these would require very specialised knowledge and suggest he had an even murkier past than that of a smuggler. Had Papapetrou, as suggested in the article cited by Colin Wilson, previously smuggled explosives, he would most likely have known that the only remotely safe way to do so would be to ensure that they did not have a detonator with them. The fact that the explosion occurred means that the device was indeed viable and therefore was inherently unsafe.

To assess whether Papapetrou had the capability to acquire or build a viable explosive device comprising military-grade plastic explosive, more information is needed about his background. If he was carrying the device, and had built it himself, he would necessarily have learned how to do so, either through military training or else with EOKA. The statement by the Cyprus Special Branch that they had no passenger names on file as being of interest makes the latter seem unlikely. Had they considered Papapetrou to be the culprit, and he was not involved in a political plot, they would have had good reason to suspect him, and to say so. It is quite unlikely that a skilled bomb maker would have avoided coming to their attention, especially as the number of EOKA activists with the required expertise would have been relatively small. Little information is available about Nicos Papapetrou, other than that already considered. It would certainly be a more compelling case if he was known to have been an EOKA fighter; his age would have made that possible. He might, equally, have served in the armed forces and still had contacts to help him in his task.

A further question is why Papapetrou would have blown himself up on his return journey, if it was a suicide. If he had made or acquired the device in Cyprus, as would probably have been more likely, it would have been expected that he would have carried out the deed on a flight from Cyprus. Otherwise he would have had to take the bomb on the outbound flight and then carry it around in Athens before activating it on the way home. That lacks credibility, meaning that he would have had to acquire the device, or its constituent parts, in Greece.

The *Sunday Times* article states that one insurance company had paid out on Papapetrou's policy, though the others had been awaiting the conclusion of the police investigation. No official statement was made that the investigation had been finalised, and that insurance fraud was believed to be the motive. The police line was that there was insufficient evidence to proceed against any person. This is, perhaps, understandable as Papapetrou's body was never recovered, so it was not possible to establish whether he had, in fact, travelled on the flight, losing his life in the process. If he had persuaded someone else to take his place, and the insurance policies were eventually honoured, the only way he could have benefited himself would be if his wife had colluded with him. It would have been a selfless, though perverse, act for Papapetrou to disappear leaving his wife, in total innocence, with all the money and it is not clear how he would have built a new life for himself with no apparent means of support. It might, however, have looked extremely suspicious if Mrs. Papapetrou had received the money and promptly left town.

If Papapetrou had detonated the bomb himself, it is highly unlikely that it would be on the cabin floor, partially under the seat, at the time. Therefore, he would need to have set it to explode, then sat and waited for the end to come. If he had given the bomb to an unwitting stooge, the question arises of who that might that have been. It would be useful to establish if an associate, similar enough to withstand the scrutiny of a passport check, had been reported missing in Greece or Cyprus at the time. If the plot had been, as postulated, to allow his family to collect the insurance and for him to meet up with them, this would have meant the entire family leaving Cyprus shortly after the event and starting their new life somewhere else, assuming the policies were eventually paid out.

The Papapetrou family, as stated earlier and confirmed in conference with the author, maintain that the theory that he was responsible is wholly untrue. He spent his time in Athens before the flight staying with his daughter, who clearly recalls that there was nothing unusual about his behaviour, Furthermore, until contacted by the author in the context of this book, the family had never even realised that Nicos Papapetrou was a suspect.

It is possible that the theory that Papapetrou was responsible was promulgated by the British authorities to selected journalists in order to put the whole incident to rest. If he was totally innocent, the damage done to his reputation, and that of his family, would have been immense but the dead cannot, under British law, be libelled. If, however, the bomb had in fact been detonated by Papapetrou, or by his unwitting stooge, the story would have ended there.

Suicide-by-bomb was the explanation preferred by the Foreign Office, especially as it would have avoided the diplomatic sensitivities around any remotely political motive for the attack. The *Sunday Times* journalists were apparently very thorough and capable, and put together a plausible explanation of why Papapetrou might have wanted to end his own life in such a way. They appear to have exceptionally well-informed and it is unfortunate that their account cannot be compared with the police report. They appear so well-informed that the reader might speculate on whether they were given information by, or on behalf of, the investigating officers. The reason for doing so might have been to ensure that the insurance scam story was accepted as the truth, and thereby finally lay to rest the Grivas theory.

It would have been a bizarre coincidence and a savage irony if General Grivas, whose life was considered to be potentially at risk from a political rival, had lost his life because he just happened to be travelling on an aircraft destroyed in a bomb attack carried out by another passenger for insurance fraud.

The documents relating to the police investigation, and to the involvement of the British Home Office and Foreign Office in the aftermath of the disaster, contain no information supporting the contention that Grivas was planning to fly on CY284. The only significant reference is the message to John Veal from MI5, relaying the assertion by the Cyprus Special Branch that Grivas never travelled at that time of day. In 2018, the author travelled to Cyprus to launch the first edition of *Bealine Charlie Oscar*. A public meeting and press conference were organised in Limassol by Cypriot journalist and broadcaster Christos Iacovou. This was attended by some seventy journalists, relatives of the victims and other interested parties, including a former member of EOKA who had sheltered Grivas during the conflict. At the end of the conference, the son of Avraam Solomou, who had been eight days old when his father was killed, told the meeting that his father had indeed attended the Cypriot Embassy in Athens shortly before boarding the flight. His family had been told that two envelopes were given to Solomou, addressed to Polycarpos Yiorkadjis and President Makarios. The envelopes had apparently been too small to contain a bomb. Mr. Solomou added, poignantly, that all his life he had borne the burden of being accused of being the son of a mass murderer.

Writer and journalist Nicos Papanastassiou has made separate enquiries at various times and provided further details of what then transpired.

An explosive device, in a 'safe' condition, was transported by courier to the Cypriot Embassy in Athens. It is believed that the courier was Avraam Solomou, who knew nothing about its contents. Solomou was travelling with a colleague, Miss Iacovidou. Solomou was called back to the Embassy on the evening of 11th October and told to take a package under diplomatic cover to Yiorkadjis. Such activities were a routine part of Solomou's duties. The package was to be carried in a cabin bag. The family of Avraam Solomou was told that the cabin bag containing the bomb was given to Solomou at the Cypriot Embassy[79].' The bomb was a wholly viable improvised explosive device with a timer, which was set shortly before it was packaged up and handed to Solomou. The device was timed to explode over the deepest part of the Mediterranean on the route from

---

[79] *Solomou family to Fanoulla Argyrou at open meeting in Limassol, October 2018.*

Athens to Nicosia. It was expected that there would be no trace of the flight, so no plot could subsequently be proved.

The person alleged to have handed the bag to Solomou was named to the author as Dinos Michaelides, who is known to be have been stationed at the Cypriot Embassy in Athens at the time of the bombing. It was not stated whether or not Michaelides was aware of its contents. He later rose to high office, serving as Interior Minister under Presidents Kyprianou and Clerides. However, in 1999, Michaelides resigned after allegations of corruption. In 2015, Michaelides and his son were convicted by a court in Athens of facilitating payments to former Greek defence minister Akis Tsohatzopoulos as kickbacks from a deal to supply Greece with Russian-made anti-aircraft missiles. Michaelides and his son were sentenced to fifteen years imprisonment, but Dinos Michaelides was allowed to remain under house arrest until his death in April 2020[80]. Despite attempts on behalf of the author to contact Michaelides, these were unsuccessful and Michaelides appears to have taken the secret of his true involvement, or innocence, to his grave. This information was passed on to the appropriate authorities but at the time of writing it is not known what, if any, action was taken.

Solomou travelled to Athens Airport in a Cypriot Embassy vehicle and, at the airport, he found that he had inadvertently brought Miss Iacovidou's flight ticket, rather than his own. This resulted in the somewhat heated discussion reported by the check-in staff at Athens airport.

Grivas, meanwhile, had prepared to travel to Athens airport and was in his car awaiting his driver. He was called back to take a telephone call. Neophytos Sofocleous, his staff officer, had become aware of what is described as 'suspicious activity by Yiorkadjis' men'. Grivas was told that he was required to attend an urgent meeting with Greek military personnel and that he would have to take the Olympic Airways flight later on 12th October. According to Grivas' biographer Leonidas Leonidou, it was some considerable time before Grivas became aware that he had been booked on to CY284.

Grivas was born in 1897 in Cyprus, attending school at the Pancyprian Gymnasium. In 1916, he left Cyprus, moving to Greece. Taking citizenship of the latter country, he enrolled at the Athens Military Academy. After completing his military studies, including time at the École Militaire in Paris, Grivas joined the Greek Army as a sub-Lieutenant. The Greco-Turkish War was in progress and he was duly posted to the 10th Division of the Greek Army, fighting in what is now Turkey. He participated in the Battle of Sakarya, in 1921. Grivas was decorated for his bravery in the

---

[80] *Cyprus Mail, April 7th 2020, Former interior minister Dinos Michaelides dies at 83.*

conflict and promoted to Lieutenant. Further promotions followed and, by 1935, Grivas was a Major.

Following the outbreak of the Second World War, Grivas was posted to the Albanian Front, serving as Chief of Staff of the 2nd Division. When Greece was occupied by the Axis powers, he set up and led a small guerrilla organisation, initially called Grivas Military Organisation and later known as Operation X, which comprised officers of the Greek Army. The group, which as well as fighting the occupiers was anti-communist, focussed its operations in parts of the Athens suburbs and expanded to between two and three thousand members.

By 1946 Grivas retired from the Greek Army in the rank of Colonel. In Athens he got acquainted with Archbishop Makarios III who eventually asked him to join forces and prepare for an armed struggle in Cyprus. Following some secret visits to the island in 1954 and clandestine arms shipments, the EOKA uprising began on 1st April 1955 for Enosis of Cyprus with Greece. With Makarios accepting Independence, Grivas left the island in 1959.

In the view of many Cypriots, the prime suspect for such an attempt on the life of Grivas is Polycarpos Yiorkadjis, the Interior Minister in the Makarios government. In this role, many considered that Yiorkadjis set up a vast information network and became notorious for using the police as his 'personal army'.

Yiorkadjis was born in 1932. During the 'Cyprus Emergency' he was an active member of EOKA, assuming the nom de guerre '*Laertes*'. He would rise to become the commander of EOKA operations in Nicosia. Captured by the British on a number of occasions, Yiorkadjis managed to escape on a number of occasions, earning himself the nickname '*Houdini*'. This apparent ability to escape from custody whenever he was captured might easily have given rise to the suspicion that Yiorkadjis was an informant for the British forces. As in any conflict, information and intelligence were passed from either side to the other by sympathisers or paid agents. This applied to the Cyprus Emergency; indeed, Peter Georgeides had referred in his letter from prison to the Chairman of BEA on 9th January 1968, that Grivas himself ran an 'exterminating-traitor-squad' (see p.179).

The inference of the Foreign Office input to Detective Superintendent Browne was that they had concerns about what might be revealed if the detective started making in-depth enquiries in the political arena.

According to some sources, Grivas was not the only prominent figure originally booked on CY284 on 12th October 1967. The Cypriot newspaper *Filelefteros* published an article on 1st October 2006, stating that Michalakis Triantafyllides, at that time Attorney General and head of the Supreme Court of Cyprus was to travel on the aircraft from Athens but changed his mind and returned to the island by ship. Glafkos Clerides, then

President of the House of Representatives and later to become President of the Republic of Cyprus, was also due to fly on CY284 from London but changed his mind because of some further business in England[81].

A Cypriot source, who wishes to remain anonymous, told the author in 2018:

"Yiorkadjis did have many reasons to want to get rid of Grivas, as Grivas was often opposing this man's attempt to control the armed forces of Cyprus. The fact that the two other government officials, Triantafyllides and Clerides, booked seats on this flight but cancelled their trips at the very last moment suggests that they knew about the bomb, and they had only booked on the flight to ensure that Grivas would not suspect anything. Also, the bomb was carried as a package by a person cooperating with the Ministry of Foreign Affairs. He was supposed to go to his assigned seat, leave his bag, and then find an excuse to deplane. Some sources state that, once onboard and realising that Grivas was not onboard, he decided to travel in order not to arouse

suspicion and cancel the timer of the explosive device, but he failed, killing himself and the others.

Other writers have suggested that the Greek junta was behind it, but at the time they did not have any real motives to do so, as Grivas at the time was not against them, and he was considered by the Greeks more useful for them as a 'tool'. The crazy thing is that while if you read most sources (albeit in Greek) the story is evident, but no-one has actually put it down as a complete plot. The complex relationships between President Makarios, General Grivas, the Greek junta, and Polycarpos Yiorkadjis, remain a sensitive issue among Cypriots to this day. Yiorkadjis did not like the independence that Grivas wanted for the military forces and he probably feared his popularity."

Neophytos Sofocleous, director of Grivas' office, was a close associate and confidante of the general. Mr. Sofocleous told the author, through Christos Iacovou, that he had personally made a booking for General Grivas to travel on flight CY284 from Athens to Nicosia on Thursday 12th October 1967. He rang Cyprus Airways to cancel the booking and

---

[81] *Polyvios and Renos Georgiou, brothers of passenger Sotiris Georgiou, knew Clerides well and met him many times in the years after the crash. Clerides knew that Sotiris had been killed and discussed the disaster on a number of occasions. At no time does Polyvios recall Clerides saying that he had been booked on the flight. (Polyvios Georgiou in conversation with the author, 2018).*

contacted General Grivas to tell him of the change of plan. Mr. Sofocleous said that he was not aware of a direct threat to CY284, thinking that an attack on Grivas would have been carried out on or shortly after his arrival in Cyprus. For that reason, he did not alert the airline to the possibility of an attack.

'Yiorkadjis asked me to disclose Grivas' movements before the attack on the aircraft, but I refused, as I knew why Yiorkadjis would ask for this. The attack (against Grivas) could not take place in Cyprus. I spoke to Grivas' brother-in-law and advised him not to board the aircraft, as I knew the Press would be aware that Grivas was travelling to Cyprus, so Yiorkadjis would also know. Avraam Solomou (the courier) was just sent by Yiorkadjis as a lamb to the slaughter, as were the other 65 people on the flight. Yiorkadjis and Makarios had no regrets at all over the attack, they didn't bat an eyelid. They even went to the funerals of some of the victims, such as Dr. Ioannides.

Yiorkadjis was acting on the orders of Makarios, as he did most of the time. He had also carried out various other acts for Makarios but the problem is there is no concrete evidence. Yiorkadjis had some incriminating recordings of Makarios, as I suspect other agencies had. That is why the (Met Police) files are sealed until 2040. Numerous politicians, some at a very high level, and various other people know all about this, but there is no concrete evidence until the files are opened. No one now wants to stir up the past; the Cypriot government is worried about compensation and the British government is worried about political reasons.'

The suggestion that President Makarios knew of, or even instigated, the bombing of CY284 raises very serious political considerations. It would be bad enough for a serving government minister to organise the destruction of a civilian airliner carrying, amongst others, nationals of his own country. For the Head of State of that country to condone or, worse, direct, such an act exacerbates it further. To deliberately destroy an airliner belonging to the flag carrier of another country, carrying nationals of three other nations, would today be considered tantamount to an act of war. The aftermath of Lockerbie, which saw Libya branded a pariah state, bears testimony to incidents of such gravity. One could understand why the British Foreign Office would see the emergence of evidence of 'a political dimension' to be fraught with danger.

The question of why Grivas' supposed political associates might want to kill him requires a detailed explanation. Grivas, who still ultimately controlled the Cyprus Defence Military High Command, was at odds with the Cypriot president, Archbishop Makarios III. Makarios, meanwhile, was supported by Polycarpos Yiorkadjis, who already controlled the police and Cyprus Special Branch. Certain actions against the Turkish Cypriot population had been directed by Makarios which Grivas was reluctant to support. Having had consultations in Athens with the Greek Defence Minister and army chiefs, Grivas therefore intended to return to Cyprus and take such a stance conflicting with the interests of Yiorkadjis and Makarios.

In the context of the complex relationships between Makarios, Yiorkadjis and Grivas, it becomes quite credible that they might turn on each other. Researcher and author[82] Leonidas Leonidou offered the following rationale to the author in 2021:

- After the London and Zurich Agreements in February 1959, Cyprus became independent, and Makarios was subsequently elected President. With time he became comfortable with Cyprus' independence and in his role as President. He no longer actively sought union with Greece. Grivas, who remained an enthusiastic advocate of Enosis, had returned to Greece, where he was promoted to General.
- In 1964, growing strife between the Greek and Turkish Cypriot communities, and Turkey's threats of military invasion, Grivas returned to Cyprus and organised the Greek Cypriot armed forces, becoming their Supreme Commander. Over and above the 900-strong army division specified by the London and Zurich agreements, the Greek government provided a further 10,000 troops to assist in protecting the Greek Cypriot community. Makarios, meanwhile, had appointed Yiorkadjis to the post of Minister of the Interior, which included control of the police. Yiorkadjis, according to commentators, also sought control of the armed forces in order to give him a complete grip on power, in support of Makarios.
- By 1967, Makarios' grip on the reins of power was complete and it was considered that nothing happened in the island's political life without his say-so. His relationship with Greece, however, had deteriorated and Georgios Papandreou, whose political career culminated in three periods as Prime Minister of Greece, lastly in 1964/5, wanted Makarios deposed. Although Grivas' standing in Greece was weakened following the military coup in April 1967 (Grivas was opposed to the Colonels who had seized power), Makarios still saw Grivas as a threat. Grivas, however, with the

---

[82] *Leonidas Leonidou, Georgios Grivas Digenis – Biography, Vol. III, p. 349-419 (2008). N.B. this book is in Greek.*

National Guard and Greek Division behind him, was in a strong position.
- Makarios wanted to take firm action in Cyprus to avoid the creation of further Turkish Cypriot cantons (zones under Turkish control.) Grivas insisted on the use of the police for that task and was opposed to the use of the military forces under his command, as he believed they should be used to counter external threats only. This made Yiorkadjis even more determined to take over the National Guard.
- Makarios decided that the time was right to remove Grivas from the scene. With the troops of the National Guard, and the Greek Division still under Grivas' command, it is likely that he considered it would be best if Grivas simply disappeared, as opposed to being seen to be assassinated, as that would have made Makarios a villain. Grivas' travel plans therefore gave rise to an opportunity for him to be involved in a mysterious accident.
- Neither Makarios nor Yiorkadjis would have had any qualms about killing innocent people in order to achieve their ends.
- It is therefore entirely credible that Makarios would have sanctioned or condoned an attack on a civilian airliner believed to be carrying Grivas. Yiorkadjis would have carried out Makarios' instructions without second thought.

The credibility of Yiorkadjis as the organiser of the plot is enhanced by his alleged involvement in other assassination attempts against key political figures. In 1968 he was linked to failed assassinations of Greek PM in that he assisted Alekos Panagoulis, a Greek political opponent of the junta, in his attempt to assassinate its leader, Georgios Papadopoulos. Following the attempt, the Greek regime forced Makarios to ask for Yiorkadjis' resignation. Following his effective removal from his post, Yiorkadjis became one of the President's principal political rivals.

On March 8th 1970 President Makarios intended to attend the annual memorial service for an EOKA fighter, Grigoris Afxentiou, which was to take place in the mountains of Marcheras. The president travelled by helicopter and, as he took off from the Archbishopric in Nicosia, shots were fired, damaging the helicopter and wounding the pilot. Despite this, the pilot carried out a successful forced landing. Makarios, helped by passers-by, managed to escape, taking the pilot to Nicosia General Hospital. The assassination attempt had failed. The same source who gave the author the account of Yiorkadjis' tracking of Grivas also said that he had attempted to warn Makarios not to travel to Afxentiou's memorial service but was ignored.

The President certainly believed that Yiorkadjis had played a part in this assassination bid. As he emerged from the wrecked helicopter, Makarios told onlookers, 'Yiorkadjis did this.'[83] Yiorkadjis, according to some sources, attempted to leave Cyprus and boarded a flight to Beirut. However, his attempted departure was discovered, and he was ordered off the aircraft. There are conflicting and uncorroborated accounts of the machinations that ensued, but it did not end well for Yiorkadjis. One week after the attempt on Makarios' life, Yiorkadjis was shot dead in a remote location near the village of Mia Milia, outside Nicosia.

Makarios was interviewed in a German newspaper, which was published on 16th April 1970. The article was cited by Greek writers[84] in 2014 and 2016. It was the first time, apparently, that Makarios spoke about the attempt on his life. The interviewer asked Makarios about a group of 'terrorists', known to Makarios and the government. There was no assurance that they were being kept under observation by the police. The journalist wanted to know if the six suspects, arrested after the attempt on Makarios' life, and Yiorkadjis himself, were part of that group.

Makarios replied:

"Whilst the police investigations are continuing, I do not think I am in a position to reply to your question in detail. I confine only in saying, that there is evidence implicating certain persons in relation to the attempt against my life and that the ex-Minister Yiorkadjis was associated with these persons and that he was implicated in the organisation of the attempt."

Polycarpos Yiorkadjis, the article noted, had proclaimed his innocence in the short time between the attack on Makarios and his own death. He had stated in the Athens newspaper 'BHMA' (VIMA) that Makarios' advisers were simply engaged in throwing mud at him and that he was, by then, sure that some people wanted to get him out of the way for their own interests.

---

[83] *"Under the Threat of Guns". Time Magazine. 30 March 1970.*
[84] *Greek academic (Larissa) Avgoustinos Avgousti quoted an account by authors P. Papademetri and A. Neophytou in a book 'Polycarpos Yiorkadjis, His Last Moments' (2014) Andreas Polycarpou posted the same information an article online, titled 'The historical timeline of Polycarpos Yiorkadjis murder':* https://www.offsite.com.cy/articles/kyria-themata/topika/83215-poioi-ithela-ton-polykarpo-giorkatzi-nekro-ti-gnorize-kai-poioi *(2016).*

The article was published the same day six persons were accused of making the attempt on Makarios' life. Among the charges was that the six of them, between 1st September 1969 and 8th March 1970, conspired in Nicosia together with the deceased P. Yiorkadjis and with other known persons to the prosecuting authority to bring about a change in government with the use of force or to show use of force and that they conspired together with the deceased P. Yiorkadjis and other persons to murder President Makarios.

More recent is a quote[85] from an article by University Historian Dr. Petros Papapolyviou:

> "...the court case was heard between September and November 1970. The would-be-killers belong to two totally different groups against Archbishop Makarios: A "historical compromise" brought together for the attempt devoted friends of Polycarpos Yiorkadjis, who felt pushed aside after his resignation, and men of the hardcore anti-Makarios opposition, who were of the opinion that the president of Cyprus had abandoned his policy in favour of enosis with Greece. For the attempt four persons were found guilty by the Nicosia Assize Court. The Court accepted that "it appears at first sight Polycarpos Yiorkadjis took part in the conspiracy".
>
> Another of the accused, Costas Ioannides... was found innocent due to not enough evidence that would have provided prima facie a case against him..."

The key individuals were men of their time. Grivas was a career soldier, even if his greatest impact had been as an insurgent or freedom fighter, depending on one's point of view. He was not the first such figure to have fought a war of liberation and achieved that aim only to then fall out over the new direction of his country with his fellow politicians. If, as implied, he was involved in the assassination attempts against Makarios and Papadopoulos, Yiorkadjis showed that he was a man capable of extreme violence for political ends. If he saw Grivas as an obstacle to be overcome, killing him would simply have been a tactical option. If he was acting on the orders of Makarios, he would have had little compunction in carrying out his orders.

It is a matter of supreme irony that, having allegedly been involved in the aforementioned two plots, and being implicated, according to the information provided to the author, in the attempt against Grivas, the only

---

[85] 'The attempted murder of Makarios' by Dr. Petros Papapolyviou, published 4th June 2018.

person amongst these prominent figures to meet a violent end was Yiorkadjis himself.

The final enigma in the whole sorry saga of the destruction of Charlie Oscar concerns the possibility of a cover up by the British Foreign Office, as evidenced by the documents and supporting information in the National Archives.

The correspondence between the British Foreign Office and Scotland Yard strongly suggests that Browne and Hill were not intended to find evidence that Grivas was the target, or that Makarios or Yiorkadjis were the perpetrators. In part, the deteriorating political situation would have been made significantly worse if Makarios was removed, rather than influenced.

Cyprus was of immense strategic value in the Cold War, due to its position in the Eastern Mediterranean. Makarios was, at the time, showing signs of becoming closer to the Soviet Union, and even to question whether he was involved could have made that situation worse.

There is circumstantial evidence to suggest that Yiorkadjis was, at the very least, fortunate in his earlier encounters with the British security forces. If he had been an informer in the Cyprus Emergency, he would not have been let off the hook afterwards, especially when he gained high political office.

It is possible that the destruction of Charlie Oscar and the deaths of 66 innocent people was viewed as wholly regrettable but risking national security by losing influence in Cyprus would bring no one back. In the Sixties, a nod and a wink from the Foreign Office to a senior police officer would have been good enough to ensure that no evidence was brought to light. It was not in the national interest to do so.

Conclusion

It is unlikely that there will ever be conclusive evidence of the identity of the perpetrators and the motive for the destruction of Charlie Oscar and her passengers and crew. Having said that, I believe that the true course of events is most likely to be as set out in the previous chapter. The population of Cyprus is small, in comparison with many other countries, and close-knit within its communities. Many people in Cyprus have, for the past half century, spoken amongst themselves about what happened on the evening of Wednesday 11th October 1967 and in the early hours of Thursday 12th October.

Of the various British and Cypriot authorities, the few who emerge from the incident and its aftermath with credit were those involved in the search and recovery operation, and in the subsequent accident investigation. In particular, the Hastings crews found the wreckage very quickly, enabling the recovery of the bodies of most of the victims, along with the seat covers with their vital evidence. The AIB team of John Veal and Eric Newton oversaw an investigation this is, to this day, considered exemplary. It was extraordinarily intricate and left no stone unturned. The work of the pathologists, Ken Mason and Stan Tarlton, is also considered to have been masterful, particularly under the most horrendous of circumstances.

It appears more unlikely that Nicos Papapetrou blew up himself, or a stooge, for insurance purposes, than it was that a courier such as Avraam Solomou unwittingly carried the bomb on board. The bomb appeared to the investigators to be a relatively sophisticated device, comprising military-grade plastic explosive with a detonator of unknown origin. The fact that it exploded at floor level, partially under a seat, would have made it more difficult for Papapetrou to detonate manually, and it was less likely that he would have relied on a timer. In October 2018, the Solomou family confirmed that they had been told Avraam Solomou had indeed called at the Cypriot Embassy the night before the flight and given packages to take to Nicosia on CY284. A number of separate sources stated that he was given the bomb there, without his knowledge. Avraam Solomou was no murderer, he was as much a victim as everyone else on the aircraft.

Much emphasis was placed throughout the investigation that there was no evidence that General Grivas was due to travel on CY284. For the first time, there is direct evidence that, in fact, Grivas was originally booked on the flight. Indeed, the crew had been told the day before the flight to expect him on board. The ultimate proof is that Neophytos Sofocleous, director of Grivas' office and a trusted confidante of the General, stated for this book that he had personally booked Grivas on to CY284 for 12th October 1967, and that he had cancelled the booking immediately before the flight, when he became aware of the intense interest of Yiorkadjis in Grivas' travel plans. The credibility of Mr. Sofocleous is beyond doubt; as a 20-year-old EOKA activist in 1956, he was involved in a plot to blow up the residence of the Governor of Cyprus, Field Marshal Sir John Harding.

The involvement of Yiorkadjis in the attempt to kill Grivas has been alleged previously, and that is now corroborated by Neophytos Sofocleous. Yiorkadjis proved himself capable of such a grotesquely violent act against a perceived rival, ultimately in his involvement in the assassination attempt against Makarios three years later. Shortly before his own death in a lonely spot outside Nicosia, Yiorkadjis said *"Anything can happen now. To Makarios, people are like lemons: when they are squeezed dry, he throws them away."* Perhaps, to Makarios in late 1967, Grivas had appeared equally dispensable.

It is unlikely that we will ever know the real reason why the British Foreign Office was so keen for the investigation to avoid concluding that there was a political motive. Cyprus was strategically important in what was the height of the Cold War and Makarios was believed, at the time, to have been getting uncomfortably friendly with the Soviet Union. Implicating the Interior Minister of a sovereign state would have caused a diplomatic furore; if it had transpired that the President himself had been involved there would have been hell to pay. The inference from the documents does point to interference by the British establishment in the police investigation. There was a very clear steer, from the Foreign Office via Assistant Commissioner Brodie to the two detectives to avoid making too much of any links to a political motive. It is, therefore, not surprising that John Macrae of the Foreign Office, wrote to a colleague that '*On the whole, the insurance theory seems the most likely...*' Whether this was wishful thinking, rather than Macrae trying to lay a trail away from anything remotely political, will never be known, but it appears indicative of what the Foreign Office hoped would be the conclusion of the police investigation.

If Yiorkadjis had been an informant for the British security services during the Cyprus Emergency a decade earlier, it is most unlikely that he would subsequently have been discarded as a source. As a high-ranking politician, he would have been valuable indeed. The security services would also have had a strong hold over him; he would not have wanted his previous role to become common knowledge to any political rival, especially if one really did have an 'Exterminating-Traitor-Squad', as suggested by Peter Georgeides. Under the British Freedom of Information Act there is an absolute exemption on releasing details of such informants, to protect their families and associates even after their own death. It also, of course, protects the reputation of the state.

The Metropolitan Police investigation, by today's standards, was woefully under-resourced and appears, at best, to have been superficial. The apparent allocation of only two detectives to the case suggests that the force saw the investigation as a potential waste of time and money; the comments of the former DC Dave O'Connell observed Detective Chief Superintendent Browne's apparently laid-back attitude in the Roy Tuthill murder investigation immediately after Browne's return from the Charlie Oscar case. A significant team of officers appears to have been involved for the murder of a single child; there were three children, two of them British, aboard Charlie Oscar along with everybody else.

In the absence of the full crime files it is not possible to assess how much effort Browne and his colleague put into their investigation. The author has asked all the families in Cyprus he spoke to in connection with this book if they knew of any contact from the detectives; none knew of any such enquiries.

The investigation into the Charlie Oscar atrocity was closed when Assistant Commissioner Brodie told Mr. Bampton of the Home Office: *'A reply has now been received from the Director of Public Prosecutions to the effect that "no action can be taken on the present evidence". In the absence of any further evidence, I do not think that the Director will take any action in the future.'* It is, as discussed earlier, unlikely that the closed files contain any such evidence, though we will need to wait to find out until January 1st 2067. However, there is evidence provided by witnesses, published for the first time in this book, that:

(i) General Grivas was booked to fly on CY284 in the early hours of 12th October 1967.

(ii) His political rival, Polycarpos Yiorkadjis, was actively monitoring Grivas' movements, which included contacting Grivas' office shortly before the flight.

(iii) Yiorkadjis and Makarios are heavily implicated in the destruction of Charlie Oscar, with the intention of killing Grivas.

(iv) Yiorkadjis had the propensity to become involved in complex attempts to kill his rivals. He was later implicated in two other assassination attempts, most strongly against Makarios three years later. The reality of such internecine violence was demonstrated when Yiorkadjis himself was shot dead shortly after the attempt against Makarios.

(v) A viable Improvised Explosive Device (IED) was packaged in a cabin bag and given by a man said to be Dinos Michaelides to Avraam Solomou at the Cypriot Embassy in Athens. Solomou was tasked with taking the bag to Nicosia and told he must fly on CY284. He knew nothing of the package's nature.

(vi) The Papapetrou family account for the movements of Nicos Papapetrou in the days before he flew on CY284, and refute the allegations leaked to the press in 1968.

There are still surviving witnesses who could, if asked, provide very useful and credible evidence to a new police investigation. Only this would truly bring closure to what is a devastating incident which is still felt deeply by the relatives and friends of the 66 victims.

This book has been publicly available since 2018, the British security services have been passed all relevant information, and there has been media coverage of the information that has come to light. The author has contacted the Yiorkadjis family to offer them the chance to reply, refute the information or set the record straight about the activities of Polycarpos Yiorkadjis. They have courteously replied, saying that they are unable to provide any information.

No one has yet challenged the conclusions set out in this book.

The destruction of Flight CY284 is yet another tragedy in the tormented history of Cyprus. It seems most likely that it was carried out by the Interior Minister Polycarpos Yiorkadjis at the direction of the president, Archbishop Makarios, in order to assassinate the head of the National Guard, General Grivas. That it appears to have been swept under the carpet by the British Foreign Office, whether to keep Makarios out of the Soviet sphere of influence, or to protect a highly placed intelligence source in Yiorkadjis, or perhaps both, is unforgiveable. Even half a century after this vile deed, the bombing of flight CY284 is still Britain's biggest officially undetected mass murder.

Acknowledgements

The research required for any book dealing with a complex subject is inevitably a daunting task. *Bealine Charlie Oscar* covers some areas in which I have some working knowledge; my working life has been in commercial aviation, policing and, latterly, in police aviation. However, I knew little about the intricacies of air crash investigation, much less about armaments research, and virtually nothing about the political intrigues of Greece and Cyprus in the Fifties and Sixties. Most significantly, I had almost no information about the people at the heart of this book, the passengers and crew who lost their lives in Charlie Oscar. The only exceptions were two of the pilots, Captain Gordon Blackwood and Senior First Officer Dennis Palmer.

As my research extended into Cyprus, both before and after publication of the first edition of this book, two things became clear. Firstly, the bombing of CY284 is remembered in that country to a far greater extent than in the UK and, secondly, it is still capable of attracting controversy and intense emotions. It has never been my intention to stir up old memories needlessly, but I have heard many views expressed that reinforce the sensitivity surrounding the incident. I would like to acknowledge the great courage shown by the people who believe that the truth must be told, and that my book will help them achieve that.

I have had a lifelong interest in the tragedy as Gordon was a neighbour, a close friend of my parents and a colleague of my father. I also remember Dennis Palmer, whom my parents knew as Tony, visiting our home. I had always assumed that the incident was closed and forgotten by everyone except those with distant memories of long-lost friends and relatives. Captain James Booth, a pilot friend and colleague of my own, suggested I post on the *Pprune* forum which immediately produced a response. The site connected me with Michael Thomaides, whose father was on flight CY284, and Fanoulla Argyrou, a London-based Greek Cypriot journalist. Together they have spent many years trying to make progress in establishing who was responsible for the disaster, and it has been a pleasure to join forces with them. Fanoulla's knowledge of where to find the relevant information, and Michael's many contacts in Cyprus, have really made the book possible. Rolandos Constantinides was also helpful in getting me started along the road to unravelling what had happened to CY284.

Much of that information is retained in the National Archives in London, and I am indebted to Fanoulla for her time and patience in helping me access it, and indeed for her return visits to gather small amounts of additional information on my behalf. I am obliged, but nonetheless pleased, to acknowledge access to the 2,500 or so pages of documents, that are available for reading, copying and reproducing in this book under the UK Government's Open Licence V2.0.

Contact with Michael and his family reassured me that I was not re-opening old wounds by publishing this book. On the contrary Michael, and every other family member I have spoken to, still feels the pain of their loss, exacerbated by the absence of closure and the apparent lack of official interest in determining once and for all why, and by whom, their loved ones were killed. I would also like to extend my gratitude to Michael for offering his facilities in support of my visit to Cyprus to promote this book and meet those of the families who were able to join us.

I am grateful to Jill Harper and Elizabeth Carey-Hughes, Gordon's daughters, for sharing information about their father's early life and for trusting me with scarce photographs of Gordon and Joyce. I hope that he, too would have approved of the book. Despite his best efforts, my father could not persuade Gordon to leave the Comet 4B fleet and join him on the Trident aircraft. As Gordon told his family, he would have flown the Comet without pay if BEA had wanted, such was the enjoyment he derived from flying the aircraft. Similarly, Mike Thomas' wife Sally and daughter Alison Whelan kindly supplied information and photos.

Louis Loizou, whose brother, John, was Senior Steward on the flight, provided a wealth of detail about Cyprus Airways' Comet operations, and the story of John and his girlfriend Josephine Coldicott. His recollection of the night of $11^{th} - 12^{th}$ October 1967 is understandably clear, and I thank him sincerely for being willing to share it in poignant detail. The story of John and Josephine's ill-fated romance is a tragedy in itself.

Many people have assisted me in gathering the information for what has become quite a complex writing project. Individual photographs are attributed to the person supplying them. In particular, I would like to thank the *Cyprus Mail* staff for supplying archive photographs of their newspaper coverage and Crysanthos Crysanthou, journalist of the *Filelefteros* newspaper, for the same facility. Simon Growcott made a special effort for me, gaining access to the freight hold of one of the very few intact Comet 4 aircraft still around, in order to obtain detailed photographs of the controls under the passenger cabin floor, in the vicinity of the device in Charlie Oscar. A picture paints a thousand words, especially when technical matters are concerned.

Roger Aves kindly carried out some research for me on the island of Kastellorizo. That put me in contact with Pantazis Houlis and Nikos Misomikes, who were able to shed some more light on the recovery operation.

The photographs come from many sources and are mostly from the time of the incident. Many were digital images created from old originals or have been scanned from copies of copies. As a result, there are some photographs which lack the quality associated with modern images. However, in most cases their relevance to the book and the scarcity of alternatives outweighs the low resolution of the picture. It is, as so often, a question for the author of 'Is this relatively low-quality image better than nothing at all?' I am very grateful for every one of them. Where possible they are attributed to the source who granted me permission to use them. A number, particularly relating to more generic and contextual material, are unattributed and come from multiple sources on the internet. I invite the original owners to contact me via the publisher.

Technical experts on an historic aircraft like the Comet 4B are hard to find, but I was very fortunate to find three men who could give me advice, guidance and pass a critical eye over many of the relevant details, putting me back on track when my lack of detailed knowledge was in danger of drawing me off-track. They are Graham M. Simons, author of *Comet! The World's First Jet Airliner*, Captain Simon Searle, formerly of Dan Air, who flew the last commercial flight by the type, and Captain Bill Innes, a BEA Comet 4B co-pilot at the time of the loss of Charlie Oscar. Bill, in particular, shed significant light on the culture in BEA, and especially on the Comet fleet, when some of those aspects had been misinterpreted by other sources. David Nicholas, who was on duty in the BEA Operations Control Centre at Heathrow on the night of the disaster, has provided a comprehensive overview of how the airline's operations were overseen.

Martin Painter's definitive work, *The DH.106 Comet – An Illustrated History*, published by Air Britain in 2002, provided invaluable details on the history of the Comet. I am grateful to Martin and his publisher, Air Britain ,for allowing me to collate the information on hull losses which I hope will help to dispel the enduring myth that the Comet was a death trap. It most certainly was not.

The labyrinthine world of 1960s Cypriot politics has been explained to me by Fanoulla Argyrou, and I am also grateful to journalists Christos Iacovou and Nicos Papanastassiou for the help they were able to provide. An excellent source of background information on the 'Cyprus Emergency' was the book of the same name, written by military historian Nik Van Der Bijl. I am grateful to Nik for his time during a lengthy phone call discussing the capabilities of EOKA in destroying aircraft, and for permission to use information from his book.

Author and researcher Leonidas Leonidou, who wrote a very comprehensive biography of Georgios Grivas amongst other works, played an invaluable part in explaining the complex relationships between Grivas, Makarios and Yiorkadjis. The information he provided is compelling in explaining why these leaders of a sovereign state thought nothing of destroying an airliner and killing 66 innocent people.

I contacted the family of Polycarpos Yiorkadjis, through his son Constantinos Yiorkadjis, the current Mayor of Nicosia, to offer them the opportunity to comment on the allegations in this book. Mr. Yiorkadjis courteously replied that he is unable to shed any light on his father's alleged involvement.

My son, William Hepworth, spent hours photographing documents for me and generally acting as my PA. As always, his enthusiasm and support have been outstanding, as has been the patience of my wife, Mandy, whose threshold of boredom is regularly breached once I start talking about matters such as this, but who supports me without wavering.

Above all, I could not, and would not, have accomplished the task of producing this book without the support of the family members of other victims of flight CY284. I particularly thank Helen Kyriakos (Rodosthenis Christou and Niki Rodosthenou), Ioannis Ioanniades (Dr. George Ioanniades), George Dimetriou and Andria Soteriou (Katerina Liassides), the Papapetrou family, and Macha Miller and family (the McComb family) and Louise Fawcett, family member of Jan and Guy Tasker. Makis Efraim, brother in law of stewardess Thelma Efremi, joined our number and hosted a visit to his splendid fish tavern, To Latsi, in Nicosia. The family of Avraam Solomou has provided useful information, including information that they were given by Cypriot authorities in the aftermath of the incident. Polyvios Georgiou was also very helpful in providing details of his brother, Sotiris. A special thank you to Christine and Bob Marlborough, who have been so very helpful and who persuaded British Airways to commemorate the victims.

It is important to stress that I have considered all the information passed to me or unearthed by the research I carried out along with others. Much of it is conflicting and I have used my best endeavours to sort the wheat from the chaff. However, even after half a century the Charlie Oscar incident, which is also referred to in Greece and Cyprus as the Kastellorizo Disaster, is very controversial. My conclusions are not accepted by everyone, but I have made them in good faith and on the basis of interpreting the evidence as objectively as possible.

I hope that, by presenting the evidence in a proportionate and considered way, I can help to bring closure to the families and friends of the victims. I have been thanked for my efforts by those with whom I have been in contact; that makes it all worthwhile. If the information as to the motive and the perpetrators is correct, and I do believe my sources to be credible, I can understand why there has been silence for half a century from the British and Cypriot establishments. It would not surprise me if that silence continues. This is no way excuses the apparent demonisation of Nicos Papapetrou, who appears to have been deliberately made a scapegoat to divert attention from the sinister political machinations that resulted in the downing of CY284. The families have always deserved better.

In June 2021, British Airways commissioned and paid for a permanent memorial to the victims of flight CY284, in the Memorial Garden in St. George's Chapel, Heathrow Airport. We are very grateful to BA's CEO, Sean Doyle, Head of Global PR Victoria Madden and her team.

The search, which spans four nations, goes on for others who lost a friend or relative on that dreadful night half a century ago. I would welcome contact with them, not least to tell them that their loved ones are not forgotten. I can be contacted via my publisher's e-mail address, mtwpublications@gmail.com

Simon Hepworth, July 2022.

Above: The commemorative plaque at the Chapel of St. George memorial garden, Heathrow Airport, kindly donated and organised by British Airways in 2021 (British Airways). Below: The wording on the plaque (author.) Επάνω: Η αναμνηστική πλακέτα στον κήπο του Παρεκκλησίου του Αγίου Γεωργίου, στο αεροδρόμιο Heathrow, ευγενική δωρεά και οργάνωση από την British Airways το 2021 (British Airways). Παρακάτω: Η διατύπωση στην πλακέτα (συγγραφέας)

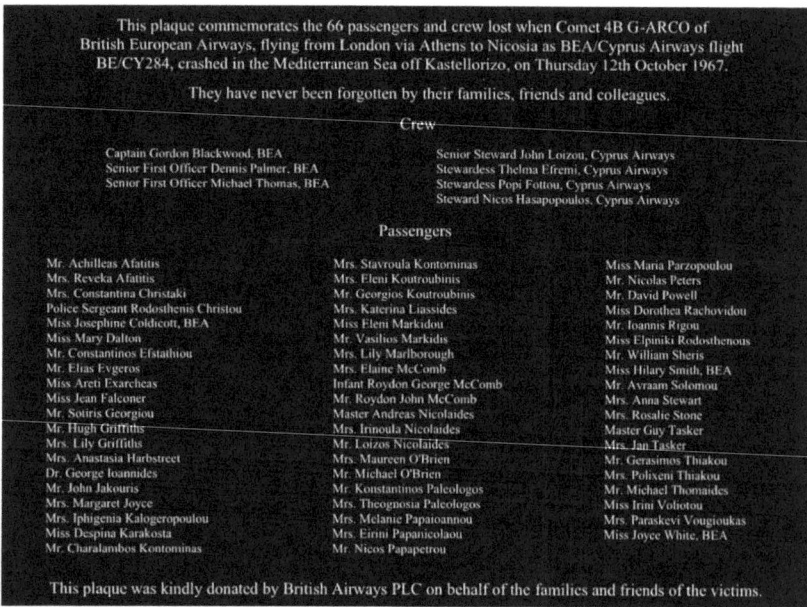

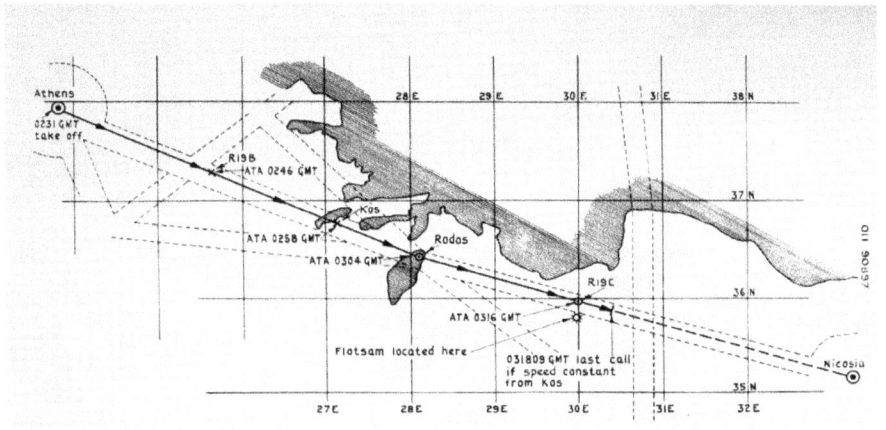

Times and locations of CY284 on 12th October 1967 (RAE Report).

Σχεδιάγραμμα της πτήσης (ώρες και τοποθεσίες) της πτήσης CY 284 (Αναφορά RAE).

The image and caption sent to the world's media on 12th October (AP.)

Αυτή η εικόνα στάλθηκαν στα διεθνή μέσα ενημέρωσης στις 12 Οκτωβρίου (AP.)

BEA Comet 4B G-ARCO, christened 'RMA John Hind', photographed at London Heathrow airport in 1962 (John Hamlin)

Ο Κομήτης της BEA 4B G-ARCO, που βαφτίστηκε «RMA John Hind», φωτογραφήθηκε στο αεροδρόμιο Heathrow του Λονδίνου το 1962 (John Hamlin)

Journey's End. Flight CY284 was supposed to terminate on the apron at Nicosia but it was not to be. This photograph, taken around the time of the disaster, shows, from left to right, a Cyprus Airways Vickers Viscount, and two Comet 4Bs, of Olympic Airways and BEA respectively (www.militaryhistories.com).

Τέλος ταξιδιού. Η πτήση CY284 έπρεπε να τερματίσει στη Λευκωσία, αλλά δεν έμελλε να γίνει. Αυτή η φωτογραφία, που τραβήχτηκε περίπου την ώρα καταστροφής, δείχνει, από αριστερά προς τα δεξιά, έναν Vickers Viscount της Cyprus Airways και δύο Comet 4B, της Olympic Airways και της BEA αντίστοιχα (www.militaryhistories.com).

Comet 4B G-ARCO as she appeared in the world's press after her loss (TNA).

Ο Κομήτης 4B G-ARCO όπως εμφανίστηκε στον παγκόσμιο τύπο μετά την απώλειά του (TNA)

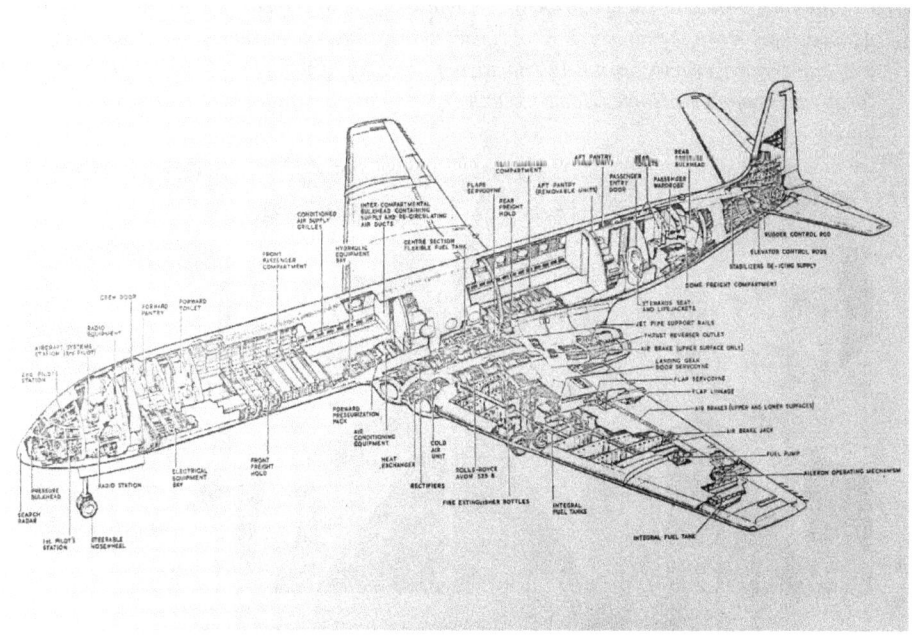

Comet 4B layout (Comet 4B Technical Manual, BEA October 1967)

Διάταξη Comet 4B (Τεχνικό Εγχειρίδιο Comet 4B, BEA Οκτώβριος 1967)

The flight deck crew of Charlie Oscar. Left to right: Captain Gordon Blackwood, Senior First Officer Mike Thomas and Senior First Officer Dennis Palmer. All three men were married, with children, had previously served in the RAF and lived in the Home Counties near their base at Heathrow.

Το πλήρωμα του θαλάμου πτήσης του Charlie Oscar. Από αριστερά προς τα δεξιά: Καπετάνιος Gordon Blackwood, , Ανώτερος Πρώτος Αξιωματικός Mike Thomas και Ανώτερος Πρώτος Αξιωματικός Dennis Palmer. Και οι τρεις άντρες ήταν παντρεμένοι, με παιδιά, είχαν υπηρετήσει προηγουμένως στη RAF (Βρετανική Βασιλική Αεροπορία – Royal Air Force) και ζούσαν στις κομητείες Home (Home Counties) κοντά στη βάση τους στο Heathrow.

Formal portrait photographs of the cabin staff were provided to the media by Cyprus Airways. From left to right: Popi Fottou, Thelma Efremi, Nicos Hasapopolous, John Loizou.

Επίσημες φωτογραφίες πορτρέτου του προσωπικού της καμπίνας δόθηκαν στα μέσα ενημέρωσης από τις Κυπριακές Αερογραμμές. Από αριστερά προς τα δεξιά: Πόπη Φώτου, Θέλμα Εφρέμη, Νίκος Χασαπόπουλου, Τζον Λοΐζου.

Above: Captain Gordon Blackwood (third from left) with the crew of a BEA Comet 4B, after the aircraft's inaugural service to Malta (Captain Maurice Hepworth). Below left: Gordon and Joyce Blackwood on their wedding day on October 14th 1944 at St. Peter's Church, Harold Wood, Essex. Right: Gordon, a very keen sailor, at the helm of a sailing boat. (both photos: Jill Harper)

Επάνω: Ο Καπετάνιος Gordon Blackwood (τρίτος από αριστερά) με το πλήρωμα ενός BEA Comet 4B, μετά την εναρκτήρια υπηρεσία του αεροσκάφους στη Μάλτα (ο καπετάνιος Maurice Hepworth). Κάτω αριστερά: Ο Gordon και η Joyce Blackwood την ημέρα του γάμου τους στις 14 Οκτωβρίου 1944 στην Εκκλησία του Αγίου Πέτρου, Harold Wood, Essex. Δεξιά: Ο Gordon ενθουσιώδης ναύτης, στο τιμόνι ενός ιστιοφόρου. (και οι δύο φωτογραφίες: Jill Harper)

Above: Senior First Officer Mike Thomas with (left) his bride Sally on their wedding day and (right) relaxing on his day off (Alison Whelan)

Επάνω: Ο Ανώτερος Πρώτος Αξιωματικός Mike Thomas (αριστερά) με τη σύζυγό του Sally την ημέρα του γάμου τους και (δεξιά) χαλαρώνουν την ημέρα του ρεπό του (Alison Whelan)

Hilary Smith (left) and Joyce White (right), who were good friends and colleagues at BEA's West London Air Terminal (BEA). They regularly travelled abroad together, as on this occasion (Hilary Smith's photo – Katie Kester. Joyce White's photo -Barry White.)

Η Hilary Smith (αριστερά) και η Joyce White (δεξιά), οι οποίες ήσαν καλές φίλες και συναδέλφισες στο Air Terminal της ΒΕΑ στο Ανατολικό Λονδίνο. Ταξίδευαν τακτικά μαζί στο εξωτερικό, όπως και σε αυτήν την περίπτωση (φωτογραφία της Hilary Smith – Katie Kester. φωτογραφία της Joyce White -Barry White.)

Above: The Loizou brothers with colleagues and friends at the Vasilis Tsitsanis nightclub in Athens. The photo was taken at 0220hrs on 12th October 1967, shortly before John left for work (there is no suggestion he had anything other than soft drinks before flying). From left: Louis Loizou, Adrin Cherchian, two unidentified friends, John Loizou, Nicos Hasapopolous, Vera Sophocleous. Adrin, Vera and Louis were operating CY264, scheduled to fly from Athens to Cyprus some twelve hours afterwards. Nicos was on CY284 with John (Louis Loizou).

Πάνω: Οι αδερφοί Λοΐζου με συναδέλφους και φίλους στο νυχτερινό μαγαζί Βασίλη Τσιτσάνη στην Αθήνα. Η φωτογραφία τραβήχτηκε στις 02:20 στις 12 Οκτωβρίου 1967, λίγο πριν φύγει ο John για δουλειά (δεν υπάρχει καμία ένδειξη ότι είχε κάτι άλλο εκτός από αναψυκτικά πριν πετάξει). Από αριστερά: Λούης Λοΐζου, Αντρίν Τσερτσιάν, δύο άγνωστοι φίλοι, Τζον Λοΐζου, Νίκος Χασαποπούλου, Βέρα Σοφοκλέους. Οι Adrin, Vera και Louis εκτελούσαν το CY264, το οποίο είχε προγραμματιστεί να πετάξει από την Αθήνα στην Κύπρο περίπου δώδεκα ώρες αργότερα. Ο Νίκος ήταν στο CY284 με τον Γιάννη (Λούης Λοΐζου).

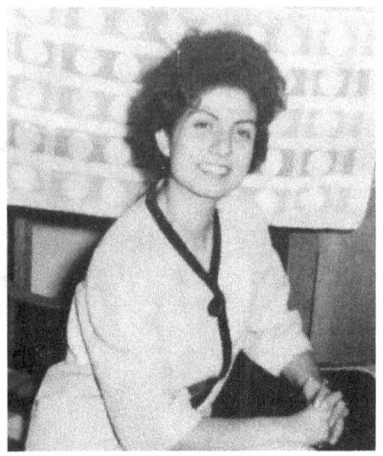

Above left: Stewardess Popi Fottou (Sandy Kontaktsi). Above right: Jan Tasker and her son Guy, who was three years old, seen in Mablethorpe in 1967. Jan's husband was at their home in Cyprus when CY284 was lost (Louise Fawcett).

Επάνω αριστερά: η αεροσυνοδός Πόπη Φώτου (Sandy Kontaktsi). Επάνω δεξιά: Η Jan Tasker και ο γιος της Guy, ο οποίος ήταν τριών ετών, στο Mablethorpe το 1967. Ο σύζυγος της Jan ήταν στο σπίτι τους στην Κύπρο όταν χάθηκε το CY284 (Louise Fawcett).

Above left: Michael Thomaides disembarking from a BEA Comet 4B on a previous flight to Nicosia. The 35-year-old businessman was a frequent traveller (Michael Thomaides). Right: Sotiris Georgiou, 23, was returning to visit his family and hoped to find a bride. The photograph, signed by Sotiris, is from his US citizenship certificate (Georgiou family).

Επάνω αριστερά: Ο Μιχαήλ Θωμαΐδης καθώς αποβιβάζεται από ένα BEA Comet 4B σε προηγούμενη πτήση για Λευκωσία. Ο 35χρονος επιχειρηματίας ήταν συχνός ταξιδιώτης (Μιχαήλ Θωμαΐδης). Δεξιά: Ο Σωτήρης Γεωργίου, 23 ετών, επέστρεφε για να επισκεφτεί την οικογένειά του και ήλπιζε να βρει νύφη. Η φωτογραφία, με την υπογραφή του Σωτήρη, είναι από το πιστοποιητικό αμερικανικής υπηκοότητας (οικογένεια Γεωργίου).

Police Sergeant Rodosthenis Christou, left, early in his career with Cyprus Police and right, with Eleni, the wife he met when she was nursing him in hospital (Helen Kyriakou).

Ο Αστυνομικός Λοχίας Ροδοσθένης Χρήστου, αριστερά, στην αρχή της καριέρας του στην Αστυνομία Κύπρου και δεξιά, με την Ελένη, τη σύζυγο που γνώρισε όταν νοσηλευόταν στο νοσοκομείο (Ελένη Κυριακού).

Left: 48-year-old Doctor George Ioannides (Ioannides family). Right: Costas Efstathiou, a hairdresser from Middleton, Manchester.

Αριστερά: Ο 48χρονος Ιατρός Γεώργιος Ιωαννίδης (οικογένεια Ιωαννίδη). Δεξιά: Κώστας Ευσταθίου, κομμωτής από το Middleton του Manchester.

Above: Roy and Elaine McComb at their wedding in 1965. Roy was serving with the RAF in Cyprus in 1967; he and Elaine were returning form a five-week holiday in England with their son, eighteen-month-old Roydon George (below left). Roydon and his father now lie together in Dekelia, Cyprus (below, right). Elaine was never found (McComb family).

Πάνω: Ο Roy και η Elaine McComb στο γάμο τους το 1965. Ο Roy υπηρετούσε στη RAF στην Κύπρο το 1967. Αυτός και η Elaine επέστρεφαν από διακοπές πέντε εβδομάδων στην Αγγλία με τον γιο τους, τον δεκαοκτώ μηνών Roydon George (κάτω αριστερά). Ο Roydon και ο πατέρας του βρίσκονται τώρα μαζί στη Δεκέλεια της Κύπρου (κάτω, δεξιά). Η Elaine δεν βρέθηκε ποτέ (οικογένεια McComb).

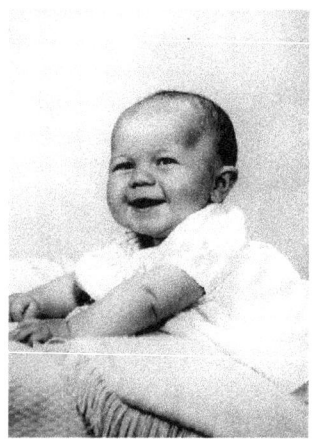

Top: Loizos and Irinoula Nicolaides and their son, Andreas (right). Above left: Mary Dalton (courtesy of Sheila Bond.). Right: Retired forestry worker Ioannis Tsiakouris.

Επάνω: Λοΐζος και Ειρηνούλα Νικολαΐδη και ο γιος τους, Ανδρέας (δεξιά). Επάνω αριστερά: Mary Dalton (ευγενική προσφορά της Sheila Bond.). Δεξιά: Συνταξιούχος δασολόγος Ιωάννης Τσιακούρης.

Above left: Lily Marlborough was on her way to visit her daughter Christine's family in Cyprus (Christine Marlborough). Above right: Michael and Maureen O'Brien had only been married thirteen days when they made the fateful decision to change their flight to avoid an overnight stay in London.

Επάνω αριστερά: Η Lily Marlborough ήταν καθ' οδόν για να επισκεφτεί την οικογένεια της κόρης της Christine στην Κύπρο (Christine Marlborough). Πάνω δεξιά: Ο Michael και η Maureen O'Brien είχαν παντρευτεί μόλις δεκατρείς μέρες όταν πήραν τη μοιραία απόφαση να αλλάξουν πτήση για να αποφύγουν μια διανυκτέρευση στο Λονδίνο.

Nicos Papapetrou, pictured sitting at the Parthenon, Athens. He had spent a few days in Athens, staying with his daughter who was a student there (Eleni Papapetrou).

Ο Νίκος Παπαπέτρου, φωτογραφία καθήμενος στον Παρθενώνα στην Αθήνα. Είχε περάσει λίγες μέρες στην Αθήνα, μένοντας με την κόρη του που ήταν φοιτήτρια εκεί (Ελένη Παπαπέτρου).

Avraam Solomou, left, had a particularly pressing reason to be on board CY284. Right: Avraam Solomou with his two children and those of his boss, Foreign Minister Spyros Kyprianou.

Ο Αβραάμ Σολωμού, αριστερά, είχε έναν ιδιαίτερα πιεστικό λόγο να βρίσκεται στο CY284. Δεξιά: Ο Αβραάμ Σολωμού με τα δύο του παιδιά και του προϊσταμένου του υπουργού Εξωτερικών Σπύρου Κυπριανού.

Four of the passengers who joined the flight at Athens. Above from left: Irini Papanicolaou, Ioannis Rigos, Rebecca and Achillea Afatitis. All four were part of the group travelling to an international convention of Jehovah's Witnesses in Cyprus.

Τέσσερις από τους επιβάτες που προστέθηκαν στην πτήση από Αθήνα. Πάνω από αριστερά: Ειρήνη Παπανικολάου, Ιωάννης Ρήγος, Ρεβέκκα και Αχιλλέα Αφατίτη. Και οι τέσσερις ήταν μέλη της ομάδας που ταξίδευε για μια διεθνή συνέλευση των Μαρτύρων του Ιεχωβά στην Κύπρο.

Press photos summing up the human emotions involved in the tragedy. Above left: Anguish on the face of Avraam Solomou's brother, having just identified the victim at Rhodes Hospital. Above right: Two colleagues of Steward Nicos Hasapopoulos, whose body was never recovered.

Φωτογραφίες του Τύπου που συνοψίζουν τα ανθρώπινα συναισθήματα που ενέχονται στην τραγωδία. Επάνω αριστερά: Αγωνία στο πρόσωπο του αδερφού του Αβραάμ Σολωμού, έχοντας μόλις αναγνωρίσει το θύμα στο Νοσοκομείο Ρόδου. Πάνω δεξιά: Δύο συνάδελφοι του αεροσυνοδού Νίκου Χασαπόπουλου, η σορός του οποίου δεν ανασύρθηκε ποτέ.

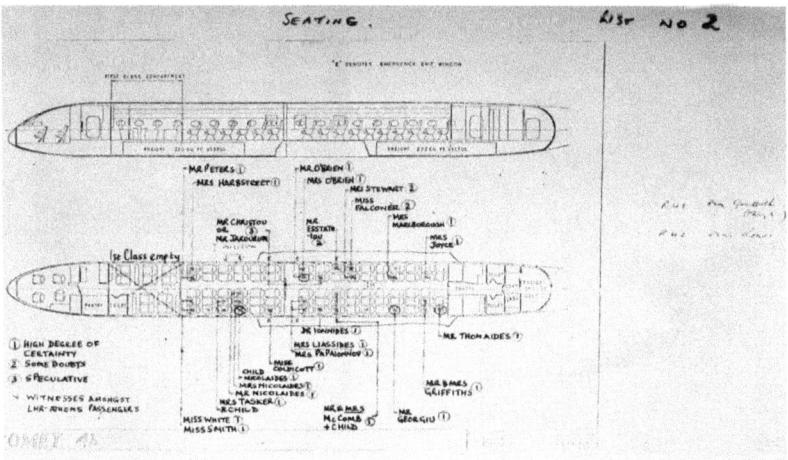

Seating of passengers travelling from London to Nicosia, based on recollections of BEA staff, crew and passengers disembarked at Athens.

Κάθισμα επιβατών που ταξίδευαν από το Λονδίνο στη Λευκωσία, με βάση τις αναμνήσεις του προσωπικού της ΒΕΑ, του πληρώματος και των επιβατών που αποβιβάστηκαν στην Αθήνα.

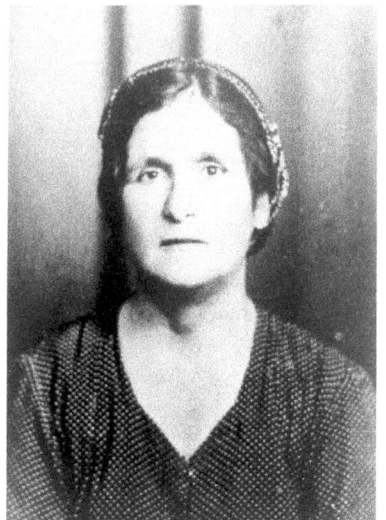 

Left: Katerina Liassides was returning to Cyprus in response to a family emergency. She just managed to secure a ticket on the afternoon of the flight (Andria Soteriou / George Demetriou.) Right: Melanie Papaioannou decided to surprise her family by returning home without telling them she was on the flight (Melanie Doritou.)

Αριστερά: Η Κατερίνα Λιασίδη επέστρεφε στην Κύπρο για οικογενειακή επείγουσα υπόθεση. Μόλις κατάφερε να εξασφαλίσει ένα εισιτήριο το απόγευμα της πτήσης (Άντρια Σωτηρίου / Γιώργος Δημητρίου.) Δεξιά: Η Μέλανι Παπαϊωάννου αποφάσισε να κάνει έκπληξη στην οικογένειά της επιστρέφοντας σπίτι χωρίς να τους πει ότι ήταν στην πτήση (Μελάνια Ντορίτου.)

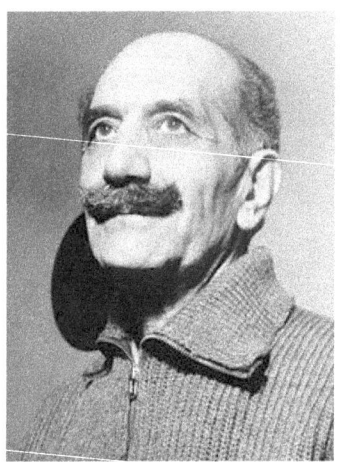 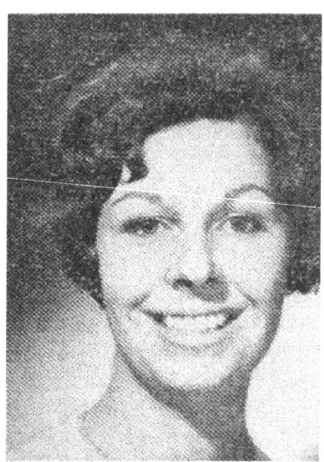

Left: General Georgios Grivas was expected by the cabin crew to be a passenger on the flight but travelled from Athens to Nicosia the following day. Right: Josephine Coldicott, who was travelling to spend a holiday with her boyfriend, Senior Steward John Loizou (BEA).

Αριστερά: Ο Στρατηγός Γεώργιος Γρίβας αναμενόταν από το πλήρωμα θαλάμου επιβατών να είναι επιβάτης στην πτήση, αλλά ταξίδεψε από την Αθήνα στη Λευκωσία αργότερα την ίδια μέρα. Δεξιά: Josephine Coldicott, η οποία ταξίδευε για να περάσει διακοπές με τον φίλο της, Senior Steward John Λοίζου (BEA).

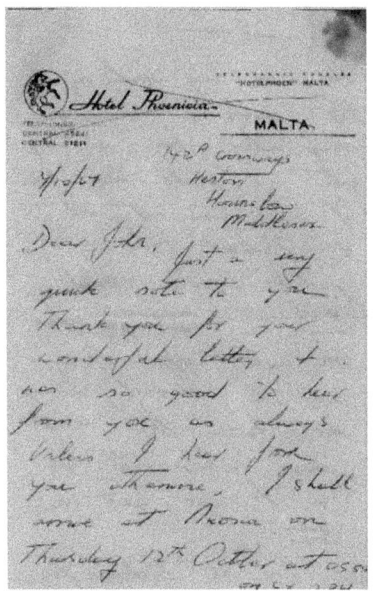
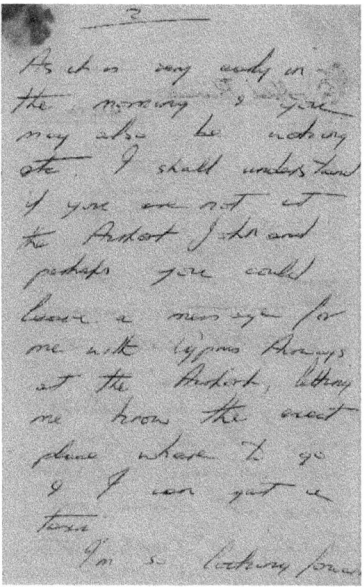
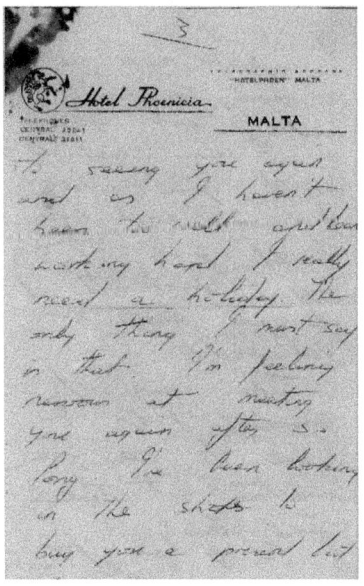
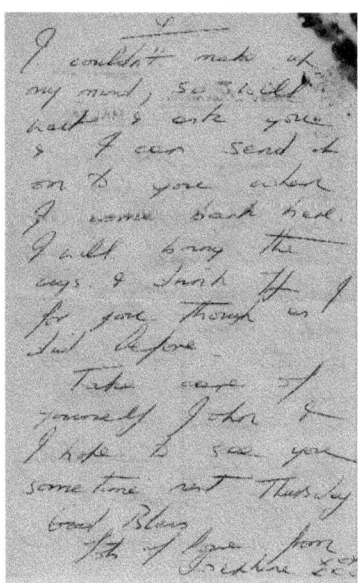

The letter from Josephine Coldicott to her boyfriend, John Loizou. The letter sealed the fate of both of them as John turned down an request from another steward to swap flights with him. (Louis Loizou).

Το γράμμα της Josephine Coldicott στον φίλο της, John Λοΐζου. Το γράμμα σφράγισε τη μοίρα και των δύο καθώς ο John απέρριψε αίτημα ενός άλλου αεροσυνοδού να ανταλλάξουν πτήσεις μαζί του. (Λούης Λοΐζου).

Mr. V.J. Clancey of RARDE, Fort Halstead, shows the blast-damaged seat cushion at a press conference. His work proved conclusively that the damage was caused by a device consisting of military-grade plastic explosive (TNA).

Ο κ. V.J. Ο Clancey του RARDE, στο Fort Halstead, δείχνει το μαξιλάρι του καθίσματος που έχει υποστεί ζημιά από την έκρηξη σε συνέντευξη Τύπου. Η εργασία του απέδειξε ότι η ζημιά προκλήθηκε από μια συσκευή αποτελούμενη από πλαστικό εκρηκτικό στρατιωτικής ποιότητας (TNA).

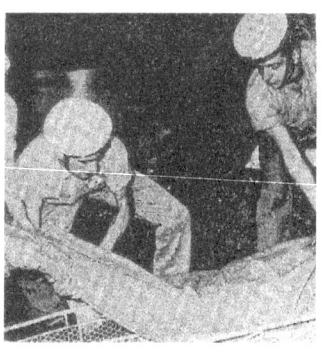 

Left: Sailors on the Navarinon carefully move a victim's body (all Chrystanthos Chrystanthou). Right: The stress and torment of dealing with the loss of one of his aircraft with all on board is evident on the face of BEA's General Manager, Captain William Baillie (TNA).

Αριστερά: Οι ναυτικοί στο Ναυαρίνο μετακινούν προσεκτικά το σώμα ενός θύματος (όλες του Χρύσανθου Χρυσάνθου). Δεξιά: Το άγχος και το μαρτύριο της αντιμετώπισης της απώλειας ενός από τα αεροσκάφη του είναι εμφανή στο πρόσωπο του Γενικού Διευθυντή της ΒΕΑ, Καπετάνιου William Baillie (TNA).

A press photo of Charlie Oscar landing at the end of an earlier flight. The date, location and original source were not stated. (TNA).

Μια φωτογραφία του Charlie Oscar κατά την προσγείωσή του στο τέλος μιας προηγούμενης πτήσης. Η ημερομηνία, η τοποθεσία και η αρχική πηγή δεν αναφέρθηκαν. (TNA).

Above: The cabin crew from BE284 on their arrival at Heathrow the day after the crash. The policy of changing from BEA to Cyprus Airways cabin staff saved their lives (TNA).

Πάνω: Το πλήρωμα καμπίνας από το ΒΕ284 κατά την άφιξή τους στο Heathrow την επόμενη μέρα της συντριβής. Η πολιτική αλλαγής από BEA σε προσωπικό καμπίνας της Cyprus Airways έσωσε τις ζωές τους (TNA).

The cockpit of the Comet 4B. The instruments and controls are a world away from today's electronic equipment but were very advanced at the time. To the right is the flight engineer (P3) station; the captain (P1) and co-pilot (P2) stations are shown very clearly in this photograph (HSA).

Το πιλοτήριο του Comet 4B. Τα όργανα και τα χειριστήρια απέχουν πολύ από τον σημερινό ηλεκτρονικό εξοπλισμό, αλλά ήταν πολύ προηγμένα εκείνη την εποχή. Στα δεξιά είναι ο σταθμός του μηχανικού πτήσης (P3). οι σταθμοί κυβερνήτη (P1) και συγκυβερνήτη(P2) φαίνονται πολύ καθαρά σε αυτή τη φωτογραφία (HSA).

Above: Handley Page Hastings TG524 of 70 Squadron, RAF, despatched to search the area underneath R19C. The wreckage of Charlie Oscar was located by her crew.

Επάνω: Handley Page Hastings TG524 of 70 Squadron, RAF, απεστάλη για να ερευνήσει την περιοχή κάτω από το R19C. Τα συντρίμμια του Charlie Oscar εντοπίστηκαν από το πλήρωμά του

Above left: This photograph of an RAF search and rescue crew based at RAF Akrotiri appeared in the Cypriot newspaper Filelefteros. It is thought it shows the crew of Flight Lieutenant Dennis King (Chrystanthos Chrystanthou). Above right: Turkish Navy patrol vessel P127 Bozcaada pictured in her wartime years when she was a Bangor-class minesweeper, HMCS Swift Current. (Mark Nelson, www.ReadyayeReady.com)

Επάνω αριστερά: Αυτή η φωτογραφία ενός συνεργείου έρευνας και διάσωσης της RAF που εδρεύει στη RAF Ακρωτήρι εμφανίστηκε στην κυπριακή εφημερίδα Φιλελεύθερος. Πιστεύεται ότι δείχνει το πλήρωμα του Flight Lieutenant Dennis King (Χρύσανθος Χρυσάνθου). Επάνω δεξιά: περιπολικό σκάφος P127 Bozcaada του Τουρκικού Πολεμικού Ναυτικού που απεικονίζεται στα χρόνια του πολέμου όταν ήταν ναρκαλιευτικό κλάσης Bangor, HMCS Swift Current. (Mark Nelson, www.ReadyayeReady.com)

MV Astrid, a German freighter, was diverted to the scene and assisted in recovering bodies and wreckage (Micke Asklander).

Το MV Astrid, ένα γερμανικό φορτηγό πλοίο, το οποίο άλλαξε πορεία προς το σημείο των ευρυμάτων και βοήθησε στην ανάκτηση πτωμάτων και συντριμμιών (Micke Asklander).

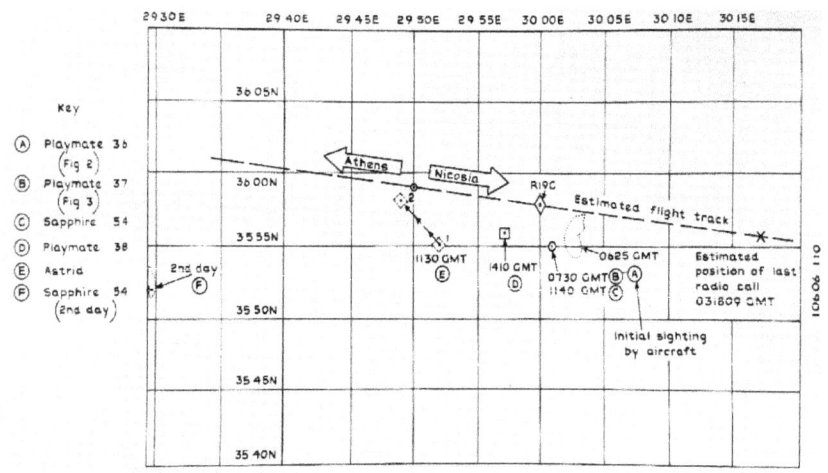

The location of the wreckage, as plotted by recovery crews.

Η θέση των συντριμμιών, όπως σχεδιάστηκε από τα συνεργεία ανάκτησης.

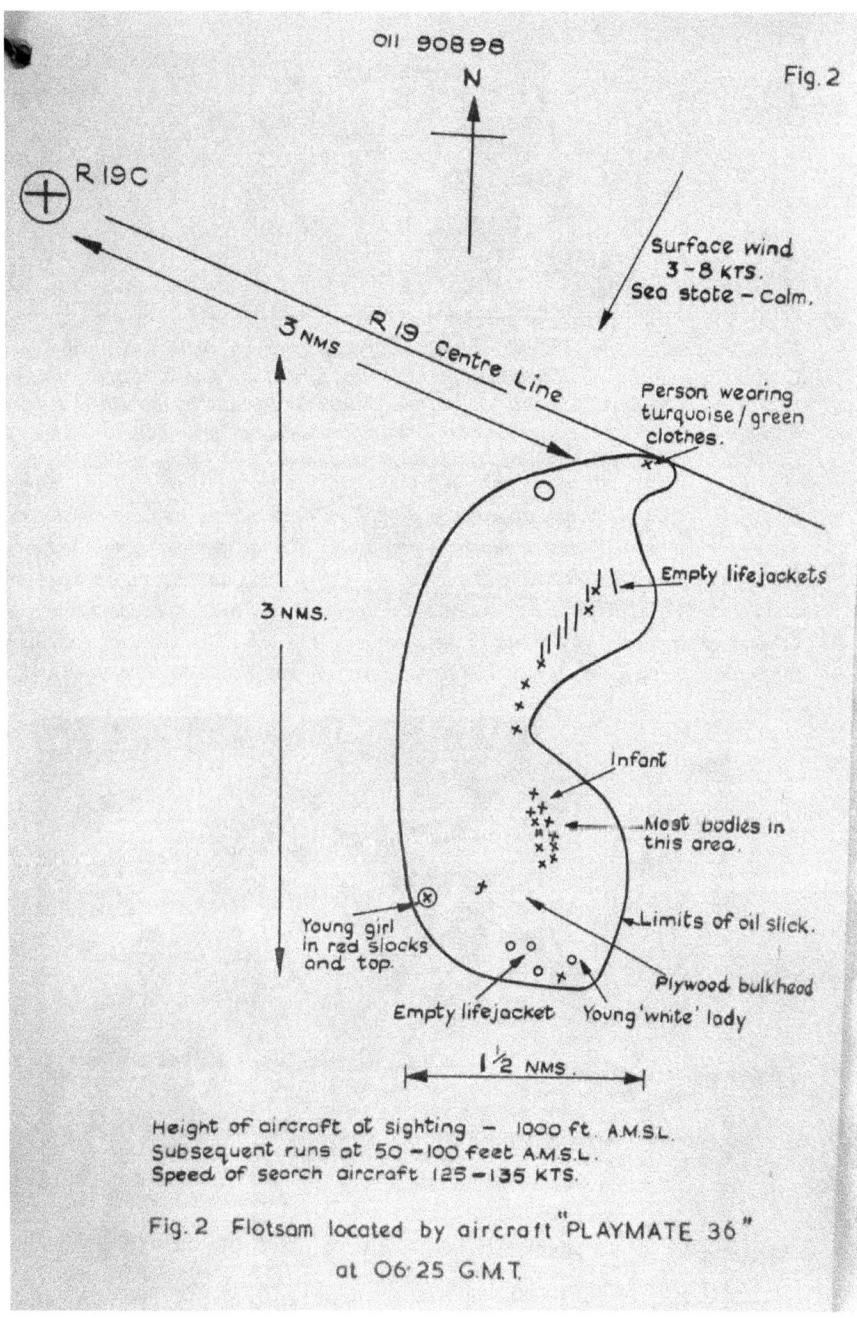

Flotsam located by aircraft 'Playmate 36' at 06.25 GMT (RAE Report)..

Συντρίμμια που εντόπισε το αεροπλάνο 'Playmate 36' στις 0625hrs GMT (RAE Report).

Filelefteros newspaper published a montage of photographs from the funerals in Cyprus. Cyprus Airways staff bearing the coffins of Thelma Efremi and John Loizou (second from left). Avraam Solomou's funeral at Tymbou (right) was attended by the wife of his boss, Foreign Minister Spyros Kyprianou (Chrystanthos Chrystanthou). Below: Crew of the Greek destroyer Navarino unload the body of a victim at Rhodes (Cyprus Mail).

Η εφημερίδα Φιλελεύθερος δημοσίευσε μοντάζ με φωτογραφίες από τις κηδείες στην Κύπρο. Το προσωπικό των Κυπριακών Αερογραμμών φέρει τα φέρετρα της Θέλμα Εφρέμη και του Γιάννη Λοΐζου (δεύτερος από αριστερά). Στην κηδεία του Αβραάμ Σολωμού στην Τύμπου (δεξιά) παρευρέθηκε η σύζυγος του προϊσταμένου του, Υπουργού Εξωτερικών Σπύρου Κυπριανού (Χρύσανθος Χρυσάνθου). Κάτω: Πλήρωμα του ελληνικού αντιτορπιλικού Navarino ξεφορτώνει τη σορό ενός θύματος στη Ρόδο (Cyprus Mail).

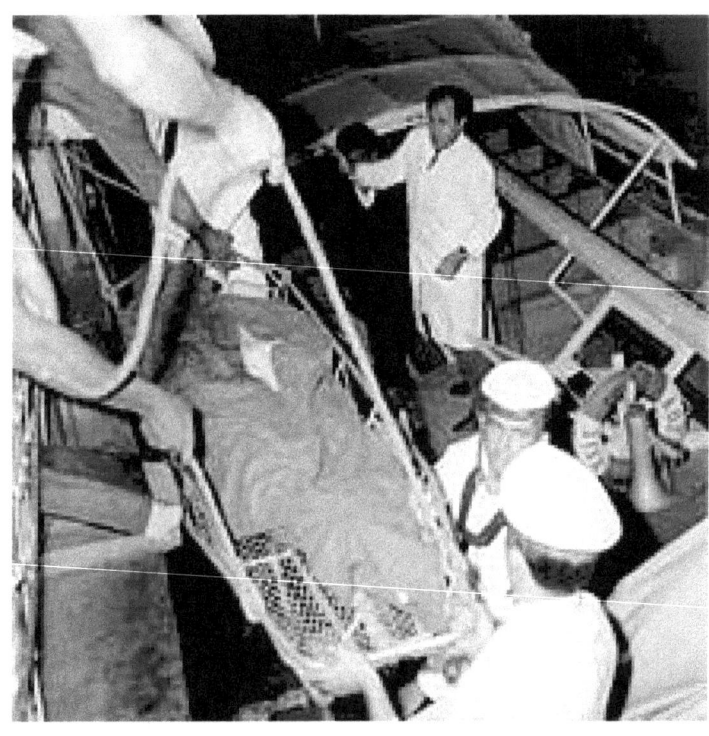

Nicosia Air Traffic Control Centre around the time of the crash. The controllers were responsible for aircraft movements in the Nicosia Flight Information Region and received the last call from Charlie Oscar. By the time they replied, it was too late to stop the chain of events unfolding (www.militaryhistories.co.uk). Below: Amongst the few pieces of wreckage recovered were seat cushions and covers. This cover, in a red fabric, was almost new at the time of the incident (Michael Thomaides).

Το Κέντρο Ελέγχου Εναέριας Κυκλοφορίας Λευκωσίας περίπου την ώρα της συντριβής. Οι ελεγκτές ήταν υπεύθυνοι για τις κινήσεις των αεροσκαφών στην Περιοχή Πληροφοριών Πτήσεων Λευκωσίας και έλαβαν την τελευταία κλήση από το Charlie Oscar. Όταν απάντησαν, ήταν πολύ αργά για να σταματήσει η αλυσίδα των γεγονότων που εκτυλίσσονταν (www.militaryhistories.co.uk). Κάτω: Ανάμεσα στα λίγα συντρίμμια που ανασύρθηκαν ήταν μαξιλάρια καθισμάτων και καλύμματα. Αυτό το εξώφυλλο, σε κόκκινο ύφασμα, ήταν σχεδόν καινούργιο την ώρα του συμβάντος (Μιχαήλ Θωμαΐδης).

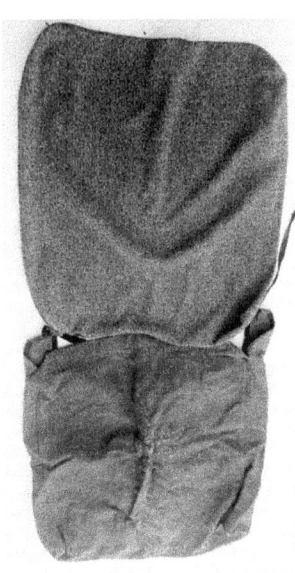

Chief Investigator Eric Newton (left) with colleague J. Letts, at the scene of the Stockport air disaster on 4th June 1967. Newton was a highly respected investigator and authority on air disasters (Manchester Evening News).

Ο επικεφαλής ερευνητής Eric Newton (αριστερά) με τον συνάδελφο του J. Letts, στη σκηνή της αεροπορικής καταστροφής στο Stockport στις 4 Ιουνίου 1967. Ο Newton ήταν ένας πολύ σεβαστός ερευνητής και ειδικός για αεροπορικές καταστροφές (Manchester Evening News).

The Aluminaut was a deep-sea salvage vessel and considered by many to be essential in determining the cause of Charlie Oscar's loss. Sadly, the operation was determined to be too impracticable to make the significant cost worthwhile (TNA).

Τυ Aluminaut ήταν ένα σκάφος διάσωσης βαθέων υδάτων και θεωρείτο από πολλούς απαραίτητο για τον προσδιορισμό της αιτίας της απώλειας του Charlie Oscar. Δυστυχώς, η επέμβαση κρίθηκε πολύ ανέφικτη για να δικαιολογηθεί το σημαντικό κόστος (TNA).

Above left: Photographed after conducting forensic examinations of victims of the Stockport air crash in April 1967, Group Captain Ken Mason (left) and Squadron Leader Stan Tarlton (right) were considered the foremost aviation pathologists of their time. Their expertise was to prove invaluable to the investigation. (Stephen Morrin). Above right: The limited facilities at the hospital on Rhodes are clear in this photograph from the Illustrated London News. The result was that the post-mortem examinations were not as thorough as the pathologists would have liked (ILN).

Επάνω αριστερά: η φωτογραφία πάρθηκε μετά από ιατροδικαστικές εξετάσεις των θυμάτων του αεροπορικού δυστυχήματος του Stockport τον Απρίλιο του 1967, ο Captain της ομάδας Ken Mason (αριστερά) και ο Squadron Leader Stan Tarlton (δεξιά) θεωρήθηκαν οι κορυφαίοι παθολόγοι της αεροπορίας της εποχής τους. Η τεχνογνωσία τους αποδείχθηκε ανεκτίμητη για την έρευνα. (Stephen Morrin). Επάνω δεξιά: Οι περιορισμένες διευκολύνσεις στο νοσοκομείο της Ρόδου είναι ξεκάθαρες σε αυτή τη φωτογραφία από το Illustrated London News. Το αποτέλεσμα ήταν ότι οι μεταθανάτιες εξετάσεις δεν ήταν τόσο ενδελεχείς όσο θα ήθελαν οι παθολόγοι (ILN).

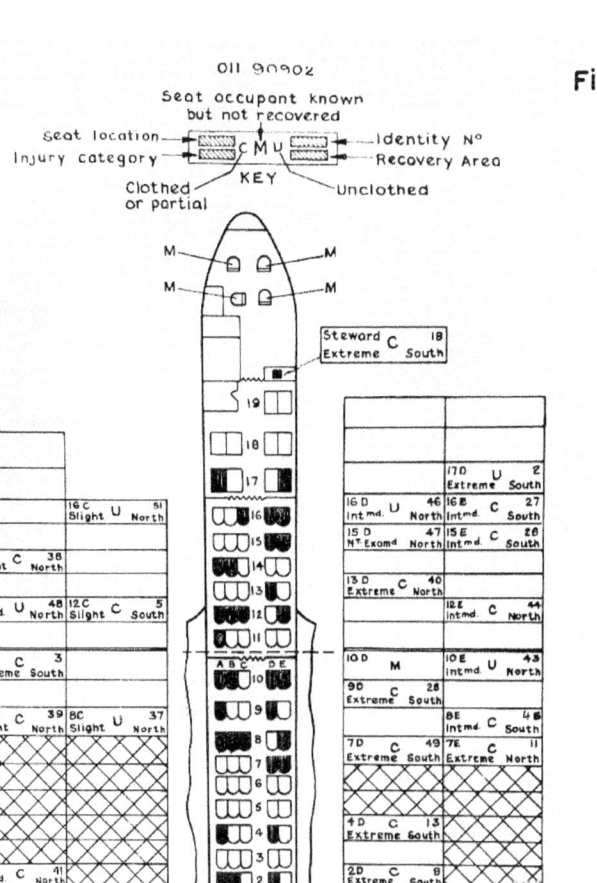

The seating plan of Charlie Oscar with relevant details considered by Mason and Tarlton in their pathology report (RAE Report via TNA)

Το σχέδιο θέσεων του Charlie Oscar με σχετικές λεπτομέρειες που εξέτασαν οι Mason και Tarlton στην παθολογική τους έκθεση (Αναφορά RAE μέσω TNA)

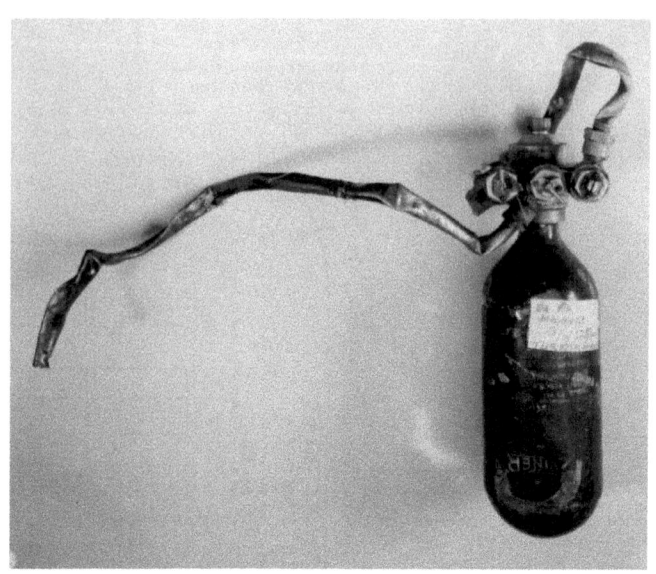

Above: The damaged Graviner fire extinguisher from Charlie Oscar which provided evidence that the aircraft had broken up in mid-air (TNA). Below: The layout of fixed fire extinguishers in the centre section of the Comet 4B and 4C. The bottle recovered from Charlie Oscar was that fitted next to No. 3 engine zone at position 6. (Comet 4B Technical Manual, BEA October 1967).)

Επάνω: Ο κατεστραμμένος πυροσβεστήρας Graviner από τον Charlie Oscar, ο οποίος παρείχε στοιχεία ότι το αεροσκάφος είχε κοπεί στον αέρα (TNA). Παρακάτω: Η διάταξη των σταθερών πυροσβεστήρων στο κεντρικό τμήμα των Comet 4B και 4C. Το μπουκάλι που ανακτήθηκε από το Charlie Oscar τοποθετήθηκε δίπλα στη ζώνη κινητήρα Νο. 3 στη θέση 6. (Τεχνικό Εγχειρίδιο Comet 4B, BEA Οκτωβρίου)

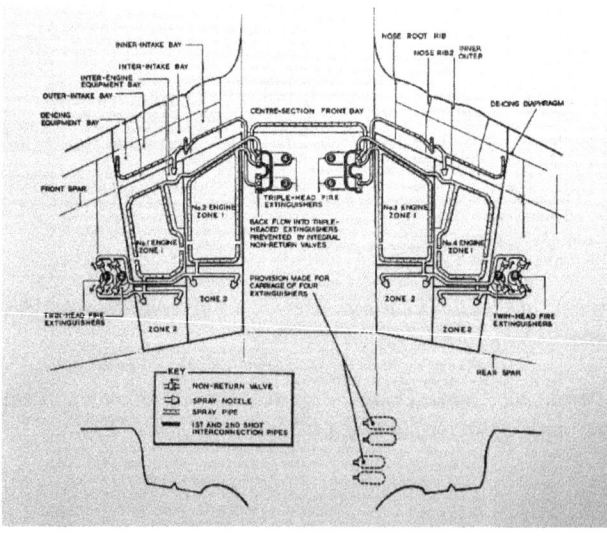

Above: A USAF North American F100 Super Sabre, carrying drop tanks, similar to that found in the vicinity of the crash site (US Air Force). Below: Diagram showing details of the fuel drop-tank (TNA).

Επάνω: Ένα USAF F100 Super Sabre της Βόρειας Αμερικής, που μεταφέρει drop tanks, παρόμοια με αυτά που βρέθηκαν κοντά στο σημείο της συντριβής (Αεροπορία των ΗΠΑ). Παρακάτω: Διάγραμμα που δείχνει λεπτομέρειες της δεξαμενής πτώσης καυσίμου (TNA).

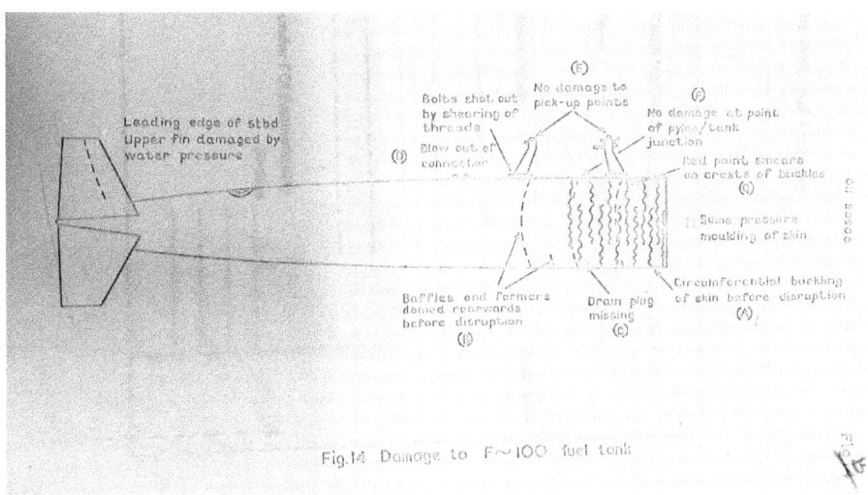

8"
4 1/4"
11 1/2"
FLOOR

1' 6½"
FOAM RUBBER CUSHION.
(TOURIST).
TOP
BOTTOM.
x Ray reveals numerous pieces of minute metal debris embedded in foam
Focal point (explain) checked by rod + angle.
4" behind + 12" below rear of cushion
Blackened area of damage.
Characteristic blast damage from below + slight behind.
slash rent marks made by high velocity particles of metal.
1' 3½"

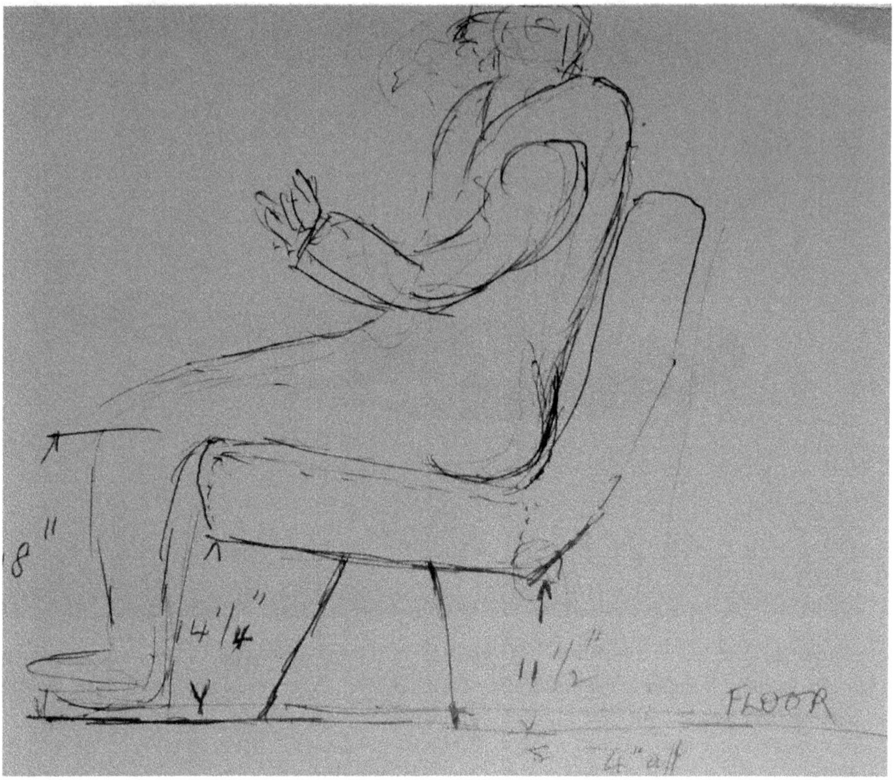

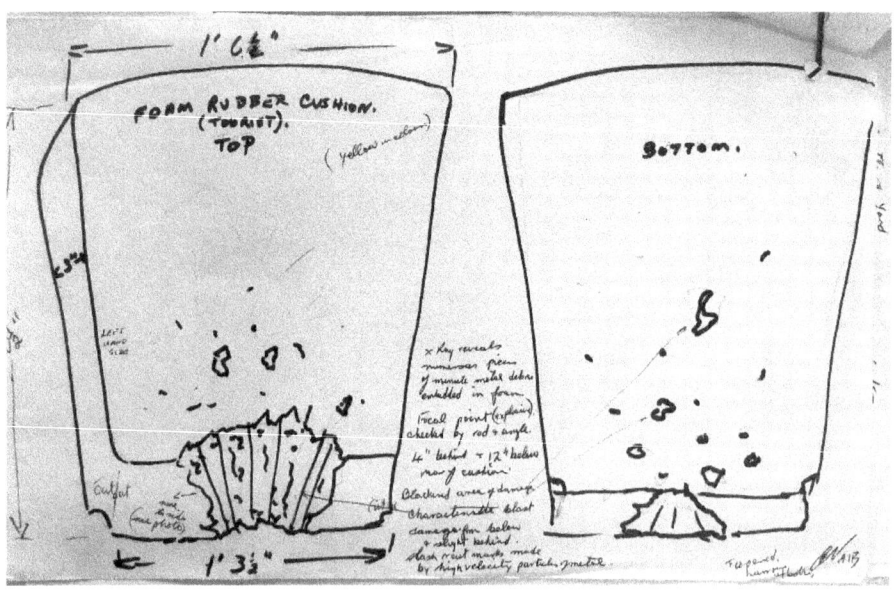

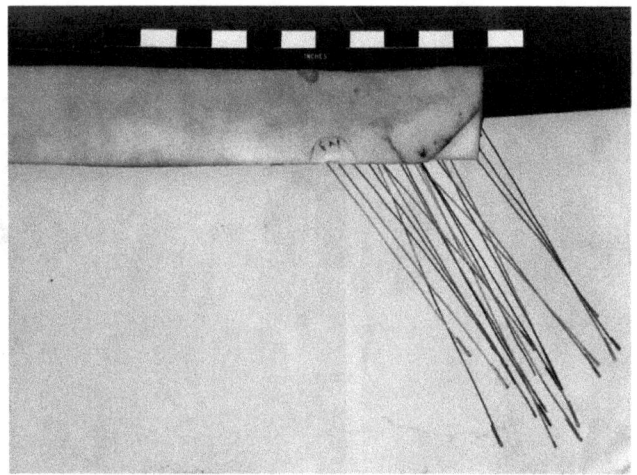

Left side (above) and rear (below) of the cushion from seat 4A or 5A. The wires extend back from the tracks made by very small fragments from the explosive device. They show that the device was on the floor of the cabin, next to the fuselage wall. Opposite page: annotated sketches showing the location of the device in relation to the seat cushion (TNA).

Αριστερή πλευρά (πάνω) και πίσω (κάτω) του μαξιλαριού από το κάθισμα 4Α ή 5Α. Τα καλώδια εκτείνονται πίσω από τις ράγες που δημιουργούνται από πολύ μικρά θραύσματα από τον εκρηκτικό μηχανισμό. Δείχνουν ότι η συσκευή βρισκόταν στο πάτωμα της καμπίνας, δίπλα στον τοίχο της ατράκτου. Απέναντι σελίδα: σχολιασμένα σκίτσα που δείχνουν τη θέση της συσκευής σε σχέση με το μαξιλάρι του καθίσματος (TNA).

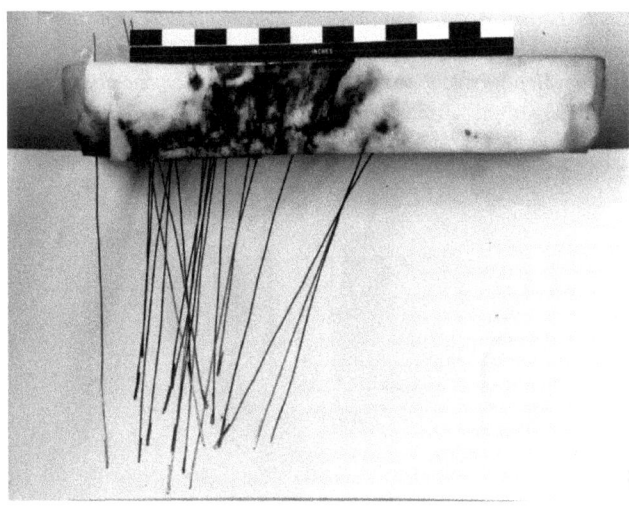

Above left: Fred Jones, OBE, C.Eng., AFRAeS, who examined the wreckage of G-ARCO at the Royal Aircraft Establishment. It was at least his fourth Comet examination (Lucas Black). Above right: A contemporary publicity photo of passengers enjoying their flight in a BEA Comet 4B (Captain Maurice Hepworth). Below: Compartments of the Comet 4B fuselage. Note position of the aileron servo unit bay, underneath row 5 seats (Comet 4B Technical Manual, BEA October 1967).

Επάνω αριστερά: Fred Jones, OBE, C.Eng., AFRAeS, ο οποίος εξέτασε τα συντρίμμια του G-ARCO στο Royal Aircraft Establishment. Ήταν τουλάχιστον η τέταρτη εξέταση του Κομήτη (Lucas Black). Επάνω δεξιά: Μια σύγχρονη διαφημιστική φωτογραφία επιβατών που απολαμβάνουν την πτήση τους σε ένα Κομήτη 4Β της ΒΕΑ (Captain Maurice Hepworth). Παρακάτω: Διαμερίσματα της ατράκτου του Κομήτη 4Β. Σημειώστε τη θέση aileron servo unit bay κάτω από τη σειρά θέσεων 5 (Τεχνικό Εγχειρίδιο Comet 4B, BEA Οκτώβριος 1967).

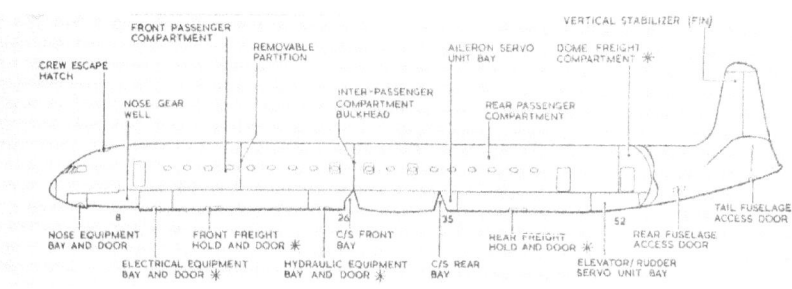

Above: The Tourist Class cabin of a Comet 4B. The bomb was believed to have been located in the footwell of the third or fourth row of seats from the back, against the left-hand cabin wall (Malcolm Hill). Below: G-ARCO on the apron at Heathrow, c. 1962. (JH). In both photographs the arrow indicates the place Fred Jones believed to be the likely site of the explosion.

Επάνω: Η καμπίνα τουριστικής κλάσης ενός Κομήτη 4B. Η βόμβα πιστεύεται ότι τοποθετήθηκε στο πόδι της τρίτης ή τέταρτης σειράς καθισμάτων από πίσω, στον αριστερό τοίχο της καμπίνας (Malcolm Hill). Παρακάτω: G-ARCO σταθμευμένο στο Heathrow, c. 1962. (JH). Και στις δύο φωτογραφίες το βέλος δείχνει το μέρος που ο Fred Jones πίστευε ότι ήταν η πιθανή τοποθεσία της έκρηξης.

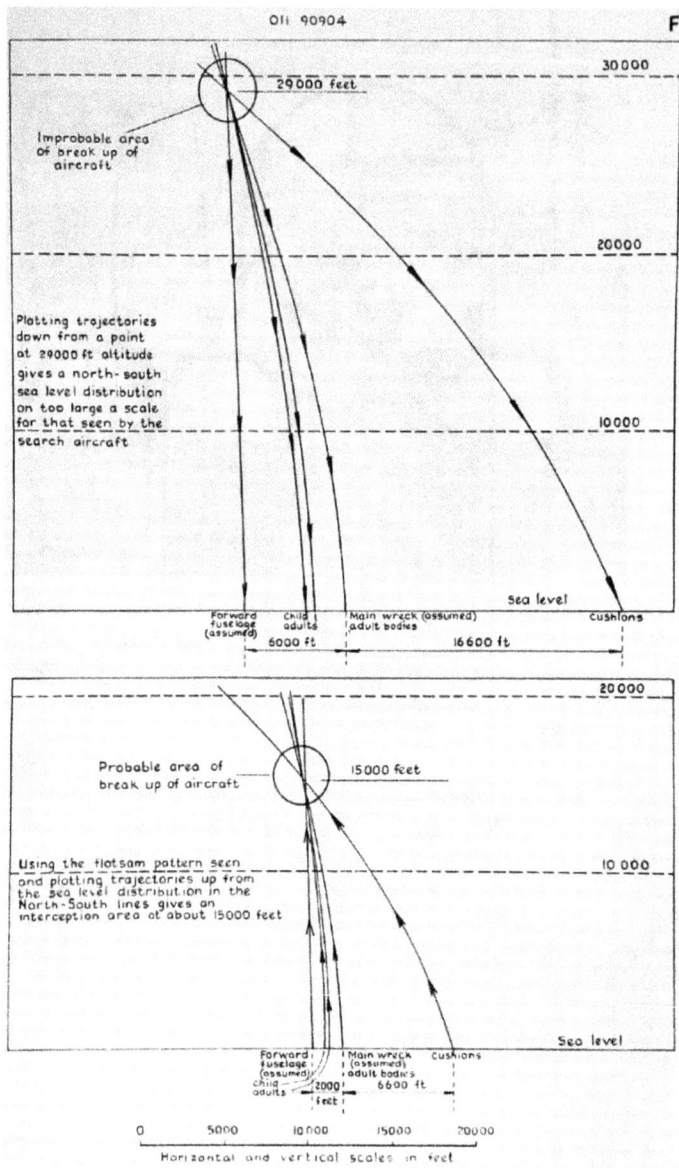

Fred Jones calculated the wreckage pattern that would have resulted from the airframe disintegrating at a number of different altitudes. The spread from the cruising altitude of 29,000 feet would have been much greater than the actual pattern. The best fit was from a disintegration at 15,000 feet (RAE Report).

O Fred Jones υπολόγισε το σχέδιο συντριμμιών που θα προέκυπτε από την αποσύνθεση του πλαισίου του αεροσκάφους σε πολλά διαφορετικά υψόμετρα.. Η εξάπλωση από το υψόμετρο πλεύσης των 29.000 ποδιών θα ήταν πολύ μεγαλύτερη από το πραγματικό μοτίβο. Η καλύτερη εφαρμογή ήταν από μια αποσύνθεση στα 15.000 πόδια (Αναφορά ΡΑΕ).

Reference: EW/A/0102

LOOSE MINUTE

IDENTIFICATION OF CUSHION

In order to establish as close as possible the identity of the cushion which reveals evidence consistent with explosive damage a sample of the material from it was sent to the material manufacturers i.e. Dunlops Ltd. They have replied that this is a piece of P.J. Super Gold material as supplied to Progress Mercantile Co. Ltd., 246, Brixton Hill, who make up the cushions for B.E.A. (see attached).

Progress Mercantile Co. Ltd., have examined the damaged cushion and another undamaged one salvaged from the Mediterranean at the same time. They identify the cushion as made from P.J. Super Gold material, and made up by them to a specific pattern for B.E.A. Comet 4B tourist seat (see attached).

Both B.E.A. & Hawker Siddeley Aviation, who have also seen the damaged cushion, identify it as a B.E.A. Comet 4B tourist seat. I have also satisfied myself that from size, shape and pattern that it conforms to a B.E.A. Comet 4B tourist seat.

The cushions salvaged from the sea following the crash of B.E.A. Comet G-ARCO were packed in a box under Mr. Head's (A.I.B.) supervision in Greece. The box was flown to the U.K. by B.E.A. and was opened by A.I.B. personnel at the R.A.E., and the cushions laid out in the hangar. From there they were taken to R.A.E. & D.E, Woolwich by myself. From all the evidence there appears to be no doubt that the cushion damaged by explosive was indeed from the B.E.A. Comet 4B G-ARCO which crashed in the Mediterranean on 12th October, 1967.

(E. NEWTON)
Chief Investigating Officer.

A.I.B.,
Room 427,
Shell Mex House.
Extn. 107.
1.12.1967.

Minute sheet confirming the provenance of the seat cushion with damage caused by blast from an explosive device. This audit trail links the seat cushion to the Comet 4B (TNA).

Σελίδα πρακτικών που επιβεβαιώνει την προέλευση του μαξιλαριού του καθίσματος με ζημιά που προκλήθηκε από έκρηξη εκρηκτικού μηχανισμού. Αυτή η διαδρομή έρευνας συνδέει το μαξιλάρι του καθίσματος με τον Κομήτη 4B (TNA).

SUNDAY TELEGRAPH 26 NOVEMBER 1967

M.I.6 in Comet Crash Inquiry

SUNDAY TELEGRAPH REPORTER

MR. WILSON is taking a personal interest in an investigation by British intelligence into the destruction by a plastic bomb of the B.E.A. Comet between Athens and Cyprus last month.

Following reports from M.I.6, it is almost certain that 66 people lost their lives because of an attempt to assassinate Gen. Grivas, commander of the Cyprus armed forces. Mr. Wilson is forced to play this down because of the Cyprus crisis.

Despite reports to the contrary, the whole investigation has been kept out of the hands of the British police. Normally Scotland Yard would be called in to discover who planted the bomb, and where.

This is invariably the case when a British plane and a Commonwealth country are involved.

BODYGUARD ON BOARD

Instead, the criminal aspect of the inquiry has been handled entirely by Government intelligence acting in conjunction with the Foreign Office and the Board of Trade.

Gen. Grivas flew from Athens to Cyprus in another Comet on the day of the crash. His bodyguard, Mr. A. Solemou, was on board the lost aircraft, and it is almost certain that those who planted the bomb thought the General was on the same plane.

There is little doubt that the bomb was planted at Athens airport. Political extremists owing allegiance outside Greece may well have been responsible.

COMPENSATION DELAY

If the assassination attempt had succeeded it would have touched off the crisis between Greece and Turkey a month ago.

Questions of international compensation are involved, but the Government is unwilling to aggravate the tense situation by pressing the matter immediately.

A B.E.A. spokesman said the airline had the relatives' interests very much in mind, but the investigation had been taken completely out of their hands by the Board of Trade.

The Sunday Telegraph article that caused ructions in Greece, and which was played down by Veal (TNA).

Το δημοσίευμα της Sunday Telegraph που προκάλεσε ανατροπές στην Ελλάδα και το οποίο υποβαθμίστηκε από τον Veal (TNA).

BRITISH EUROPEAN AIRWAYS

From the Chairman
Sir Anthony Milward, C.B.E.
Bealine House, Ruislip, Middlesex.

Telephone VIKing 1234 Telegrams BEALINE LONDON

CH/251

25th. January, 1968.

Group Captain J.B. Veal, C.B.E., A.F.C.,
Civil Aviation Department,
Board of Trade,
Shell Mex House,
Strand,
London, W.C.2.

Dear Group Captain Veal,

Thank you for your letter of the 22nd. January.

May I say at once that I do appreciate the necessity of you working in well with the scientists at RARDE and the other people who help you over these accidents, and we would certainly not want to do anything to upset this side of your work.

I am always told how very happy is the relationship between BEA and your Department and my remarks at Cardiff were not intended to spoil them in the least.

I think, however, that Mallalieu's latest statement in the House has made our point adequately because he does make it clear that there was conclusive evidence of an explosion in the cabin.

Yours sincerely,

Anthony Milward

Sir Anthony Milward's technical and somewhat-qualified letter of apology following his comments on the investigation made to a business audience in Cardiff (TNA).

Η τεχνική και κατά κάποιον τρόπο επιστολή συγγνώμης του Sir Anthony Milward μετά τα σχόλιά του σχετικά με την έρευνα που έγιναν σε επιχειρηματικό κοινό στο Κάρντιφ (TNA).

Two aircraft were destroyed by bombs at Nicosia airport in 1956. (Left) The departure of Handley Page Hermes G-ALDW of Skyways, on a charter flight carrying families of service personnel was delayed by two and a half hours. A bomb exploded whilst the aircraft was still on the ground. If the flight had left Nicosia on time, all on board would certainly have lost their lives. (Right) A Cyprus Airways Dakota was also destroyed by a bomb, six weeks after the Hermes. It is believed that EOKA was responsible for both attacks (www.militaryhistories.com) Below: C4 plastic explosive Its malleable nature means that it can be concealed in innocuous-looking items. Estimates of the amount used in the device on Charlie Oscar varied between four and sixteen ounces .

Δύο αεροσκάφη καταστράφηκαν από βόμβες στο αεροδρόμιο Λευκωσίας το 1956. (Αριστερά) Η αναχώρηση του Handley Page Hermes G-ALDW της Skyways, σε ναυλωμένη πτήση μεταφέροντας οικογένειες υπηρετικού προσωπικού καθυστέρησε δυόμιση ώρες. Μια βόμβα εξερράγη ενώ το αεροσκάφος ήταν ακόμα στο έδαφος. Αν η πτήση είχε φύγει έγκαιρα από τη Λευκωσία, όλοι οι επιβαίνοντες σίγουρα θα είχαν χάσει τη ζωή τους. (Δεξιά) Μια Dakota της Cyprus Airways (Κυπριακές Αερογραμμές) καταστράφηκε επίσης από βόμβα, έξι εβδομάδες μετά τον Hermes. Πιστεύεται ότι η ΕΟΚΑ ήταν υπεύθυνη και για τις δύο επιθέσεις (www.militaryhistories.com) Παρακάτω: C4 πλαστικό εκρηκτικό. Η εύπλαστη φύση του σημαίνει ότι μπορεί να κρυφτεί σε αβλαβή αντικείμενα. Οι εκτιμήσεις για την ποσότητα που χρησιμοποιήθηκε στη συσκευή στο Charlie Oscar κυμαίνονταν μεταξύ τεσσάρων και δεκαέξι ουγγιών.

Reference............... 30/1

C.I.A.

Miss Roberts telephoned from Box 500. She sent a telegram to their representative yesterday asking for a reply to her letter, and received a telegram back.

Mr. Solomou, who is No. 55 on the list, was chauffeur to the Foreign Minister, Mr. Kiprianou, and a former EOKA fighter during the Cyprus emergency of 1955-59. The Director of the Cyprus Special Branch completely discounts the possibility that this was an attempt against Grivas because he never travels at that time of the day. They have no record of any of the Cypriot passengers in their index.

23/11/67   A.I.

CODE 18-76

A minute in Veal's files notes information passed via the security services that Grivas '...never travelled at that time of day.' (TNA).

Ένα πρακτικό στα αρχεία του Veal σημειώνει την πληροφορία που πέρασε από τις υπηρεσίες ασφαλείας, ότι «ο Γρίβας ...δεν ταξίδευε ποτέ εκείνη την ώρα της ημέρας.» *(TNA).*

A2/17.   49A

In replying to this letter, please write on the envelope:—
Number 41320   Name GEORGEIDES. P.

H. M. PRISON,
JEBB AVENUE,
BRIXTON,
LONDON, S.W.2.

Dear sir,   9.1.68.

Sabotage is certainly the cause of the BEA comet which crashed in flames off the coast of Cyprus.

The man responsible, (one of them) is Andreas Antoniades an ex E.OKA terrorist and expert in the "explosives squad" of General George Grivas, head of the then EOKA and later supremo of the CYPRUS National guard.

If you'd care to send someone to come and see me from your office I will give them further details on the matter.

Antoniades or "Keravnos" as he is called fell out with Grivas and was "sentenced" to death by the General, so Keravnos →

P.T.P.

defected over to the british
side S.I.B. and gave away
organisations secrets, and
as a result many EOKA leaders
ants got executed or imprisoned

Antoniades, later came to this
Country so that he could
escape the Generals own
"exterminating-traitor-squad".

Early last year he, Keravnos,
had ambitions to assasinate
the Archibishop Makarios and
Grivas and take-over Cyprus.

Before the trouble with the
Turks started the first step
was to liquidate Grivas who
was in controll of the armed
forces
Makarios would follow etc.

I will not continue any further
sir, but if you want to clear
this dreadful matter, then you
have only to come, or send
someone to see me.

Yours very sincerely

I was present at a
meeting (prior to the
Comet explosion) when a
top ranking army person
came to this country
to discuss plans for a
take-over.

A copy of the letter sent to the Metropolitan Police by Peter Georgeides, a prisoner at HMP Brixton claiming to have inside knowledge of the plot to destroy Charlie Oscar (TNA).

Αντίγραφο της επιστολής που έστειλε στη Μητροπολιτική Αστυνομία ο Πέτρος Γεωργιάδης, κρατούμενος στο HMP Brixton, ο οποίος ισχυριζόταν ότι είχε εκ των έσω γνώση της συνωμοσίας για την καταστροφή του Charlie Oscar (TNA).

FROM   J E PAPALEXOPOULOS   Hellinikon A/P 12.1.68.
       Check-in-clerk

MR SOLOMOU ATH/NIC/6 CY284/12.10.67 G-ARCO

In accordance with your instructions to submit a short report as far as
the above mentioned passenger was concerned, I have to report the
following :-

1. The late Mr Solomou presented himself at the check-in counter
   on 12 Oct 1967 and asked to be processed for flight CY284 of
   that date. When asked for his ticket, Mr Solomou stated that
   due to a mix-up at NICOSIA A/P he was no longer in possession
   of his return ticket to NICOSIA.

2. As Mr Solomou did not have his ticket cover nor did he know
   the number of his ticket, I explained to him that under the
   circumstances I could not possibly accept him for this flight.
   As alternative I offered to signal NICOSIA and ask for details
   of his ticket and also authority to issue a new ticket against
   an indemnity form. I also informed the passenger that this, of
   course, would take some time and therefore he should consider
   as impossible to fly to NICOSIA on that specific flight, i.e.
   CY 284/1210

3. Mr Solomou, nevertheless, was quite determined to fly as he
   had planned and asked to speak to higher authority. Consequently
   I had to turn him over to the D/O, Mr Coliandris, who listened
   to Mr Solomou very carefully and then repeated to the passenger
   what I had already told him, i.e. that we could not possibly
   accept him on CY 284/1210.

4. Being occupied with the closing of the service, I could not
   follow the rest of their conversation, but after a while
   Mr Coliandris asked me to issue a new ticket against indemnity
   form and then send a signal to NICOSIA for the relevant details
   and authority.

5. An indemnity form was prepared and duly signed by Mr Solomou
   and a new ticket ATH/NIC/ was issued by me as per the D/O's
   instructions. As soon as the a/c departed I sent a signal to
   NICOSIA in accordance with the above.

6. To the best of my knowledge this signal remains unanswered.

The report from check-in clerk J E Papalexopolou concerning Solomou's behaviour at ATH when denied a seat on CY284 (TNA).

Η αναφορά του υπαλλήλου ελέγχου εισιτηρίων J. Ε. Παπαλεξοπούλου σχετικά με τη συμπεριφορά του Σολωμού στο ATH όταν του αρνήθηκαν μια θέση στο CY284 (TNA).

FROM: D/O Ch. Colliandris   13.1.68

Mr SOLOMOU ATHENS/NICOSIA CY284/1210 G-ARCO

The above named passenger reported at the Airport Check-In desk to
travel to Nicosia on the above flight.
He was in ~~possession of a carton ticket N° 0482/229985 in favour of~~
Miss Iacovidou Nicosia/Athens only and stated that when he checked in
at Nicosia airport the above wrong ticket was given to him by CAL
Official instead of his own which was a return one Nicosia/Athens/Nicosia
issued by CAL Town Office Nicosia on the 29th or 30th September, prior
to his departure.

He also stated that he was the personal driver of Cyprus Foreign Minister
Mr Kyprianou and he had to be back to Nicosia for duty on that day.
After a long discussion on the incident I realised that the liability
on the loss of the ticket was C.A.L's and gave instructions to our
Check-In staff to issue a ticket against indemnity form forwarding
immediately the attached signal to C A L Nicosia :

"NICAPCY NICTOCY
O/B CY284 MR SOLOMOU TRAVELLING ATH/NIC TKT N° 0602/8798588 ISSUED
AGAINST INDEMNITY FORM AS PAP STATED LOST ORIGINAL TKT NIC/ATH/NIC
ISSUED CAL T/O NIC 29 OR 30 SEP STOP PAP ALSO STATES HIS TKT MIXED DURING
CHECK-IN WORKS AND GIVEN COVER OF TICKET 0482/229985 FAVOUR MISS IACOVIDOU
NIC/ATH STOP ATTN NIC TO CY PSE ADV NUMBER OF ORIGINAL TICKET TO SUPPORT
FORM OF INDEMNITY. "

The report from Mr. Coliandris, Duty Officer at Athens for Olympic Airways, evidencing the conversation he had with Avraam Solomou, resulting in the latter being allowed to travel on CY284 (TNA).

Η αναφορά του κ. Κολιανδρή, Αξιωματικού Εφημερίας Αθηνών για την Ολυμπιακή Αεροπορία, μαρτυρία της συνομιλίας που είχε με τον Αβραάμ Σολωμού, με αποτέλεσμα να επιτραπεί στον τελευταίο να ταξιδέψει στο CY284 (TNA).

Telephone message from Mr. Springbett, Insurance Manager of BEA

Mr. Springbett was recently in Nicosia and Athens dealing with the claims from G-ARCO.

It has come to light that a Mr. Papapetrou insured himself for the following sums before the fatal flight -

£10,000 with The Sun
£10,000 with The General Insurance Co. of Cyprus
£5,000 with the Eagle Star.

He was a shoe salesman earning £80 a month. In the twelve months prior to the accident he made five visits by air to Greece at a cost of £35 each time but never took out any insurance except on this last occasion. He is also known to be a professional gambler.

BEA's solicitor in Cyprus is looking into this in the meantime.

Note to John Veal giving details of the suspicious insurance dealings by Nicos Papapetrou before his flight on CY284 (TNA)

Σημείωμα στον John Veal που δίνει λεπτομέρειες για τις ύποπτες ασφαλιστικές συναλλαγές του Νίκου Παπαπέτρου πριν από την πτήση του στο CY284 (TNA)

The Birmingham Post

66 died in plot to kill Cyprus army leader

Comet death crash —it was a bomb meant for Grivas

As Humphrey wins, the battle of Chicago rages

Dubcek dilemma as he faces take-over threat

Two boys hitch-hiked into an invasion

Tracker dogs find 'camp' site near murder scene

Union rule forces MP to withdraw

Operation on boy in farm outhouse

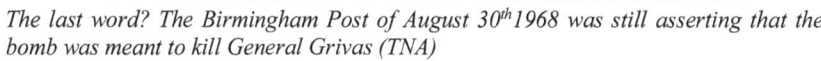

The last word? The Birmingham Post of August 30th 1968 was still asserting that the bomb was meant to kill General Grivas (TNA)

Η τελευταία λέξη; Η Birmingham Post της 30ης Αυγούστου 1968 ακόμη ισχυριζόταν ότι η βόμβα είχε σκοπό να σκοτώσει τον Στρατηγό Γρίβα (TNA)

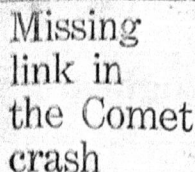

As if in response to the newspaper report saying Grivas was the target, two days later, on 1st September 1968, this article was published in The Sunday Times. Rich in detail, the article dismissed all notions of a political plot and supported the view of the Foreign Office that an insurance motive was more likely. The Papapetrou family does not accept the contents of the article. (TNA).

Λες και να απαντούσε στο δημοσίευμα της εφημερίδας που έλεγε ότι ο Γρίβας ήταν ο στόχος, δύο μέρες αργότερα, την 1η Σεπτεμβρίου 1968, αυτό το άρθρο δημοσιεύτηκε στους The Sunday Times. Πλούσιο σε λεπτομέρειες, το άρθρο απέρριψε όλες τις έννοιες περί πολιτικής πλοκής και υποστήριξε την άποψη του Φόρεϊν Όφις ότι ένα ασφαλιστικό κίνητρο ήταν πιο πιθανό. Η οικογένεια Παπαπέτρου δεν αποδέχεται το περιεχόμενο του άρθρου. (TNA).

Above: Grivas and some of his EOKA fighters in the Troodos Mountains during the campaign for Cypriot self-determination. The photo was on film stock subsequently seized by British troops (Nik van der Bijl).

Πάνω: Ο Γρίβας και κάποιοι από τους αγωνιστές του στην ΕΟΚΑ στα βουνά του Τροόδους κατά την εκστρατεία για την κυπριακή αυτοδιάθεση. Η φωτογραφία ήταν σε απόθεμα φιλμ που στη συνέχεια κατασχέθηκε από τα βρετανικά στρατεύματα (Nik van der Bijl).

Above: Whilst of poor quality, this is a rare photo of Archbishop Makarios visiting the scene of his attempted assassination. The pilot of the helicopter was seriously injured but survived. Below: The body of Polycarpos Yiorkadjis is carried away after he was murdered at Mia Milia (photo attribution sought).

Πάνω: Αν και κακής ποιότητας, αυτή είναι μια σπάνια φωτογραφία του Αρχιεπισκόπου Μακαρίου να επισκέπτεται τον τόπο της απόπειρας δολοφονίας του. Ο πιλότος του ελικοπτέρου τραυματίστηκε σοβαρά αλλά επέζησε. Παρακάτω: Το σώμα του Πολύκαρπου Γιωρκάτζη μεταφέρεται μετά τη δολοφονία του στη Μια Μηλιά (ζητείται η πηγή της φωτογραφίας).

Above: Friends and enemies... from left, General Grivas, Archbishop Makarios and Polycarpos Yiorkadjis share a platform (PIK). Below left: The studious appearance of Polycarpos Yiorkadjis belied his alleged involvement in attempts to assassinate the leaders of both Greece and Cyprus. He was to meet a violent end himself.

Πάνω: Φίλοι και εχθροί... από αριστερά, ο Στρατηγός Γρίβας, ο Αρχιεπίσκοπος Μακάριος και ο Πολύκαρπος Γιωρκάτζης μοιράζονται εξέδρα (ΡΙΚ). Κάτω αριστερά: Η φιλομαθής εμφάνιση του Πολύκαρπου Γιωρκάτζη διέψευσε την υποτιθέμενη συμμετοχή του σε απόπειρες δολοφονίας των ηγετών τόσο της Ελλάδας όσο και της Κύπρου. Ο ίδιος επρόκειτο να συναντήσει βίαιο τέλος

SPECIAL NOTICE
WANTED

WANTED in connection with the bomb incident at Government House, on 21st March, 1956:—

NEOPHYTOS SOPHOCLEOUS.

Born (Peyia, Paphos District) 1936, height 5' 6", black hair, brown eyes, slim build. Front teeth protrude slightly.

SPECIAL enquiries and observation must be maintained to effect arrest.

When arrested DO NOT INTERROGATE, but inform Police Headquarters (Criminal Investigation Department).

G. H. ROBINS,
Commissioner of Police.

Neophytos Sofocleous was an active member of EOKA who was wanted by the British authorities for attempting to bomb the residence of the Governor. He was trusted by Grivas, becoming director of the General's office. He told the author that he had booked Grivas onto CY284 but then cancelled the reservation at the last minute, warning Grivas not to board the flight (Crown Copyright).

Ο Νεόφυτος Σοφοκλέους ήταν ενεργό μέλος της ΕΟΚΑ που καταζητούνταν από τις βρετανικές αρχές για απόπειρα βομβιστικής επίθεσης στην κατοικία του Κυβερνήτη. Τον εμπιστεύτηκε ο Γρίβας και έγινε υπεύθυνος του γραφείου του Στρατηγού. Είπε στον συγγραφέα ότι είχε κάνει κράτηση για τον Γρίβα στο CY284, αλλά στη συνέχεια ακύρωσε την κράτηση την τελευταία στιγμή, προειδοποιώντας τον Γρίβα να μην επιβιβαστεί στην πτήση (Crown Copyright).

CY284 Passengers and Crew List - Κατάλογος πληρώματος και επιβατών CY284

Title	First name	Surname	Age	Nation	Boarded	Recovery Group	Seat No.
Mr	Achillea	Afatitis	28	Greek	Athens	Southern	JW
Mrs	Reveka	Afatitis	20	Greek	Athens	Southern	JW
Captain	Gordon	Blackwood	45	British	LHR	Missing	Pilot
Mrs	Constantina	Christaki		Greek	Athens	Southern	JW
Mr	Rodosthenis	Christou	40	Cypriot	LHR	Southern	9D
Miss	Josephine Yvonne	Coldicott	24	British	LHR	Northern	11A
Miss	Mary Elizabeth	Dalton	22	British	LHR	Missing	
Stewardess	Thelma	Efremi	c.20	Cypriot	Athens	Southern	
Mr	Costantinos	Efstathiou	34	Cypriot	LHR	Northern	08E
Mr	Elias	Evgeros	28	Greek	Athens	Northern	JW
Miss	Areti	Exarcheas	21	Greek	Athens	Northern	JW
Miss	Jean	Falconer	80	British	LHR	Southern	07E
Mr	Sotiris	Georgiou	23	US	LHR	Missing	04A
Mr	Hugh	Griffiths	65	British	LHR	Southern	02A/B
Mrs	Lily	Griffiths	63	British	LHR	Northern	02A/B
Mrs	Anastasia	Harbstreet	25	US	LHR	Northern	15B
Steward	Nicos	Hasapopoulos		Cypriot	Athens	Missing	Galley
Dr	George	Ioannides	48	Cypriot	LHR	Southern	09A
Mr	John	Jakouris		Cypriot	LHR	Southern	8E
Mrs	Margaret Mary	Joyce	56	British	LHR	Southern	02D
Mrs	Iphigenia	Kalogeropoulou		Greek	Athens	Southern	JW
Miss	Despina	Karakosta	60	Greek	Athens	Southern	JW
Mr	Charalambos	Kontominas		Greek	Athens	Southern	JW
Mrs	Stavroula	Kontominas		Greek	Athens	Southern	JW
Mrs	Eleni	Koutroubinis	54	Greek	Athens	Southern	JW
Mr	Georgios	Koutroubinis		Greek	Athens	Southern	JW
Mrs	Katarina Eleni	Liassides	51	Cypriot	LHR	Missing	10B
Sen. Steward	Yanakis	Loizou	27	Cypriot	Athens	Southern	
Miss	Eleni	Markidou	22	Greek	Athens	Southern	JW
Mr	Vasilios	Markidis		Greek	Athens	Missing	JW
Mrs	Lily	Marlborough	54	British	LHR	Greek	04D
Mrs	Elaine	McComb	23	British	LHR	Missing	08ABC
Master	Roydon George	McComb	18 mths	British	LHR	Northern	08ABC
Mr	Roydon John	McComb	24	British	LHR	Northern	08ABC
Master	Andreas	Nicolaides	4	Cypriot	LHR	Missing	13B
Mrs	Irinoula	Nicolaides	23	Cypriot	LHR	Northern	12A/B
Mr	Loizos	Nicolaides	30	Cypriot	LHR	Southern	12A/B
Mrs	Maureen	O'Brien	22	British	LHR	Northern	10E
Mr	Michael	O'Brien		US	LHR	Missing	10D
Mr	Konstantinos	Paleologos		Greek	Athens	Missing	11E
Mrs	Theognosia	Paleologos		Greek	Athens	Missing	11D
F/O	Dennis	Palmer	35	British	LHR	Missing	Pilot
Mrs	Melanie	Papaioannou	74	Cypriot	LHR	Southern	10A

Mrs	Eirini	Papanicolaou	61	Greek	Athens	Southern	JW
Mr	Nicos	Papapetrou		Cypriot	Athens	Missing	
Miss	Maria	Parzopoulou	60+	Greek	Athens	Southern	JW
Mr	Nicolas	Peters		US	LHR	Southern	15A
Stewardess	Poppy	Photiou	c.20	Cypriot	Athens	Southern	
Mr	David	Powell	27	British	LHR	Southern	1E
Mrs	Dorothea	Rachovidou	64	Cypriot	Athens	Southern	
Mr	Ioannis	Rigou	60	Greek	Athens	Northern	JW
Miss	Elpiniki	Rodosthenous	24	Cypriot	Athens	Northern	9E
Mr	William Theodore	Sheris		US	Athens	Missing	11A
Miss	Hilary C	Smith	32	British	LHR	Northern	17A
Mr	Avraam	Solomou		Cypriot	Athens	Northern	16C
Mrs	Anna	Stewart	68	British	LHR	Northern	07D
Mrs	Rosalie	Stone	72	British	LHR	Northern	13D
Master	Guy	Tasker	8	British	LHR	Northern	14A/B
Mrs	Jan	Tasker	30	British	LHR	Southern	14A/B
Mr	Gerasimos	Thiakou	48	Greek	Athens	Northern	16D/E
Mrs	Polixeni	Thiakou	22	Greek	Athens	Southern	16D/E
Mr	Michael	Thomaides	35	Cypriot	LHR	Northern	01A
SFO	Michael	Thomas	33	British	LHR	Missing	Pilot
Miss	Irini	Voliotou	25	Greek	Athens	Southern	JW
Mrs	Paraskevi	Vougioukas	31	Greek	Athens	Southern	JW
Miss	Joyce Pamela	White	29	British	LHR	Southern	17B

Correspondence between Police and Foreign Office – Αλληλογραφία μεταξύ Αστυνομίας και Υπουργείου Εξωτερικών

C-1/7

METROPOLITAN POLICE

Central Officer's Special Report

CRIMINAL INVESTIGATION DEPARTMENT,

New Scotland Yard,

14th day of February, 1968.

SUBJECT
COMET AIR CRASH
12.10.67

1.

Reference to Papers
225/67/28333

To Chief Superintendent

With reference to the meeting held at Home Office on the 5th February, 1968, between representatives of various Government departments respecting the Comet aircraft disaster on the 12th October, 1967, between Athens and Nicosia.

Arrangements have been made for myself (Detective Superintendent Browne) and Detective Sergeant Hill to travel by air to Athens on Wednesday, 21st February, 1968, arriving at approximately 3.30 p.m. (G.M.T). On our arrival I will inform the British Embassy of our address in Athens.

It is not possible at this stage to say what line the enquiry will take or how we will be received by the Greek authorities. If, however, any difficulties arise an official of the British Embassy will be consulted.

I ask that this report be forwarded in triplicate to the Under Secretary of State, Home Office, with a request that a copy be forwarded to Mr. Macrae, Central Department, Foreign Office, for his information.

[signature]
Detective Superintendent
Percy Browne

[signature]
Chief Superintendent C.O.C.1.

(CB 21/11)

CONFIDENTIAL

FOREIGN OFFICE,

LONDON, S.W.1.

CE 21/11

1. As I told you on the telephone when we spoke yesterday, I am very sorry that two members of the Metropolitan police should have arrived in Athens before we could warn you of their coming and explain some of the background. This is the story.

2. The Board of Trade's investigation following the loss of a B.E.A. Comet while on a flight between Athens and Nicosia led to the conclusion that the disappearance of the Comet was caused by an explosion on board the aircraft. The Board of Trade's responsibility is to find out the cause of an aircraft accident and not to impute blame. In the present case they felt the need for further investigation into how the crash occurred. They considered that such a further investigation could appropriately be carried out by the Metropolitan police. At the same time they recognised that the interests of the police, if they undertook the investigation, would not be limited by the Board of Trade's responsibility as discussed above.

3. Unfortunately there is no simple or general mechanism for invoking a police investigation into accidents of this type. Difficult questions over the responsibility of the police, payment for the investigation, and jurisdiction arise. But at an interdepartmental meeting on 5 February, it was agreed that the Board of Trade would formally request the Metropolitan police "to make enquiries into the events leading up to the explosion which resulted in the loss of the B.E.A. Comet in international waters in the Eastern Mediterranean on 12 October, 1967, and to the death of 66 people (some of them British)" and would pay for the investigation. We for our part agreed to alert you and ask you to take such action with the Greek authorities as seemed necessary and appropriate.

4. We expected next to get a letter from the Police setting out the lines of their investigation and their proposed plan of action. Instead of which I learnt from you that two police officers had already arrived in Athens. This is the more regrettable in that it seems quite possible that potentially trickly political questions could arise during the course of the investigation. For example, supposing the police should discover that the explosion was caused by a Greek (or for that matter a Turkish Cypriot) who was hoping to liquidate General Grivas (something that has of course been canvassed in the Press). For this reason it seems right that the police should keep in close touch with the Embassy about how their investigation is going, even if they make such day to day arrangements as are necessary with their Greek opposite numbers through their own channels. In view of the mix-up which has just happened, I am making sure that clear instructions in this sense are sent to Detective Superintendent Brown.

5. As to the question of informing the Greek Government about the investigation, I think this is entirely a matter for your discretion. As I mentioned on the telephone, it occurred to me that the action you were required to take in para. 1 of Foreign Office telegram No. 1414 of 8 November might provide a suitable starting point, but much would obviously depend on how those instructions were carried out.

The Hon. T. E. Bridges,
ATHENS.

CONFIDENTIAL

CONFIDENTIAL

6. I understand that the police will be asking you for help with interpreting facilities. I am sure this does not mean that they want to press into service your own already hard-pressed staff, but rather wish for assistance in finding a reliable and trustworthy Greek/English speaker (I do not see that payment will be a problem), but I expect that Detective Superintendent Brown will already have explained this to you.

7. I am sending a copy of this letter to Tony Tyler in the Commonwealth Office and to Timothy Daunt in Nicosia, as I believe it is possible that the police will wish to visit Cyprus during the course of their investigations. In that case the Commonwealth Office may well wish to inform the Cyprus Government about the police investigation and, if you can find out about their plans to visit Cyprus, it would obviously be helpful for Tyler and Daunt to know about any plans the police may have for visiting Cyprus.

(J. M. C. Macrae)
Central Department

CONFIDENTIAL

NEW SCOTLAND YARD,
BROADWAY, LONDON, S.W.1

P. E. Brodie, O.B.E.   27th February, 1968

Dear Macrae,

    I enclose a secret and highly-confidential letter to Detective Superintendent Browne who is investigating the B.E.A. Comet aircraft crash.

    I should be extremely grateful if you could arrange for this letter to be sent out to him in Athens through the Diplomatic Bag. We understand that he is staying at the Hotel Stanley, 1 rue Odysseus, Place Kaiskis, Athens.

                  Yours sincerely,

                  Assistant Commissioner Crime

J. E. C. Macrae, Esq.,
Foreign Office,
Whitehall,
S.W.1.

CRIMINAL INVESTIGATION DEPARTMENT
NEW SCOTLAND YARD
LONDON S.W.1

27th February, 1968

...die, O.B.E.

Dear Browne,

    Bampton from the Home Office has been to see me today and he tells me that someone from the Embassy in Athens has been in touch with Macrae in the Foreign Office here about your presence in Athens.

    It appears that the Embassy staff in Athens are slightly apprehensive about any possible political repercussions should your enquiry develop in a certain direction. For instance, if you find evidence to suggest that the explosion in the Comet was arranged in order to do harm to someone in politics in Cyprus or Greece then a very delicate situation would arise.

    I think I need say no more than to ask you to keep very closely in touch with the Embassy staff and if anything that savours of politics should arise, I know you would discuss the matter with them and would be most careful not to embarrass the Foreign Office.

    Of necessity, this letter has to be in rather vague terms but I am sure that you will take the point.

    I wish you luck in your enquiry and I shall look forward to hearing all about it when you return to this country.

                              Yours sincerely,

                              Assistant Commissioner Crime

Det. Supt. P. Browne,
Hotel Stanley,
1 rue Odysseus,
Place Kaiskis,
Athens.

Greek Translation of

The Destruction of Flight CY284

Η Καταστροφή της Πτήσης CY284

Αυτό το βιβλίο είναι αφιερωμένο στους 66 επιβάτες και το πλήρωμα της πτήσης των Κυπριακών Αερογραμμών CY284, που χάθηκαν όταν το αεροπλάνο Comet 4B G-ARCO συνετρίβη στη Μεσόγειο περίπου στις 03:25 GMT στις 12 Οκτωβρίου 1967, και στις οικογένειες και τους φίλους τους, που δεν τους ξέχασαν ποτέ.

Πρόλογοι

Με μεγάλη χαρά γνώρισα τον Simon Hepworth και τον γιο του William στο Εθνικό Αρχείο του Ηνωμένου Βασιλείου στο Kew Gardens στο Surrey. Ήταν επίσης προνόμιο να ενώσω τις δυνάμεις μου με τον Simon με σκοπό να εμβαθύνουμε περισσότερο στο θέμα επιδιώκοντας ένα «τρομακτικό έργο»: προσπαθώντας να βρούμε κάποιες δίκαιες απαντήσεις στα αναπάντητα ερωτήματα που, για περισσότερα από 50 χρόνια, βασανίζουν τους συγγενείς των θυμάτων της βομβιστικής επίθεσης που είχε ως αποτέλεσμα τη συντριβή του Bealine Charlie Oscar, αλλιώς γνωστής ως πτήσης CY 284 των Κυπριακών Αερογραμμών, στις 12 Οκτωβρίου 1967.

Τι ακριβώς συνέβη με την πτήση CY284 στις 12 Οκτωβρίου 1967; Γιατί βομβαρδίστηκε; Και ποιος ήταν υπεύθυνος;

Η έρευνά μου για αυτήν την τεράστια τραγωδία είχε αρχικά υποκινηθεί από τον Μιχαήλ Θωμαΐδη, του οποίου ο πατέρας ήταν ένα από τα 66 άτομα που σκοτώθηκαν με την βομβιστική εκείνη ανατίναξη. Ως αποτέλεσμα, και έχοντας μελετήσει όλα τα αρχεία που ήταν διαθέσιμα εκείνη την εποχή στο Εθνικό Αρχείο του Ηνωμένου Βασιλείου στο Kew Gardens στο Surrey, δημοσιεύσαμε τα ευρήματά μας σε ένα άρθρο μας το 2011 στην εβδομαδιαία εφημερίδα *Ελευθερία*, που εκδίδεται στο Λονδίνο, στο www.eleftheria.co.uk .

Στην εξέλιξη των γεγονότων, ο Simon ενίσχυσε τις προσπάθειές μας. Το έκανε εντελώς τυχαία αφού επικοινώνησε με τον Μιχαήλ Θωμαΐδη, μετά από μια ανάρτηση στο φόρουμ Pprune (The Professional Pilots Rumor Network). Ο Μιχαήλ έφερε τον Simon σε επαφή μαζί μου και έτσι, η συνεργασία μας για αυτό το θέμα ξεκίνησε στα Αναγνωστήρια του Εθνικού Αρχείου στο Kew. Σε αυτό το μοναδικό «κατάστημα γνώσης και επίσημης τεκμηρίωσης», όπως αποκαλώ αυτό το υπέροχο ίδρυμα, που επισκέφτηκα για πρώτη φορά στα μέσα της δεκαετίας του 1980 και έκτοτε δεν σταμάτησαν ποτέ να το επισκέπτονται για τις έρευνές μου.

Δράττομαι αυτής της ευκαιρίας να ευχαριστήσω το προσωπικό του Εθνικού Αρχείου για το ρόλο τους στη διευκόλυνση της έρευνας πίσω από αυτό το βιβλίο.

Η εμπειρία του Simon Hepworth στην υπηρεσία της Αστυνομικής έρευνας και την Αεροπορία υπήρξε για μένα τεράστια βοήθεια, καθώς και για τον Μιχαήλ και για τους άλλους συγγενείς των θυμάτων αυτής της τραγωδίας. Η συμμετοχή του Simon ενίσχυσε την αναζήτηση για την αλήθεια πίσω από τον βομβαρδισμό του Bealine Charline Oscar, ποιος ήταν υπεύθυνος και γιατί. Ο Simon γνώριζε πολύ περισσότερα από εμένα για τέτοιου είδους έρευνες. Ειδικά για αεροπορικά δυστυχήματα, τη μεθοδολογία και τις διαδικασίες αεροπορικών ατυχημάτων. Έχει επίσης δεσμούς με την αστυνομία και εμπειρία από αστυνομικές έρευνες και πληροφορίες για εγκλήματα. (Police investigations and criminal intelligence). Το ιστορικό του Simon όχι μόνο αποδείχθηκε σημαντικό εργαλείο για εμάς. Έγινε επίσης το κλειδί για την εξήγηση περίπλοκων μεθόδων με τις οποίες ο Μιχαήλ και εγώ δεν γνωρίζαμε.

Ζωντανή απόδειξη της εμπειρίας και της γνώσης του Simon βρίσκεται στη ετοιμασία –σε σχετικά σύντομο χρονικό διάστημα– αυτού του αξιοσημείωτου βιβλίου. Βασίζεται σε όλα σχεδόν τα επίσημα έγγραφα στα αρχεία που κυκλοφόρησαν στο Kew και πολλά άλλα από άλλες πηγές.

Με ευαίσθητο και σοβαρό τρόπο, το βιβλίο αντιμετωπίζει τα ερωτήματα που προσδιορίστηκαν παραπάνω. Πλησιάζει στο να δώσει σωστές απαντήσεις και, με αυτόν τον τρόπο, απεικονίζει με τρόπους που ζωντανεύουν την ταραχώδη περίοδο της ιστορίας όταν έλαβε χώρα ο βομβαρδισμός. Το βιβλίο τελειώνει με ένα δίκαιο σύνολο συμπερασμάτων που βασίζονται στις πληροφορίες που ήταν διαθέσιμες στο δημόσιο τομέα τη στιγμή της συγγραφής.

Εύχομαι το βιβλίο να παρακινήσει οποιονδήποτε «γνωρίζει», να μιλήσει και να καλύψει τα κενά που απομένουν. Ελπίζω επίσης το βιβλίο να παροτρύνει όσους βρίσκονται στην εξουσία να αποκαλύψουν και να αποδεσμεύσουν την επίσημη τεκμηρίωση που παραμένει απόρρητη. Με τέτοια μέσα μπορεί να αποδοθεί δικαιοσύνη, έστω και καθυστερημένα.

Το βιβλίο είναι ταπεινά αφιερωμένο στους 66 επιβάτες και το πλήρωμα που χάθηκαν στην πτήση CY284 των Κυπριακών Αερογραμμών και στις οικογένειες και τους φίλους τους που δεν τους ξέχασαν ποτέ. Το βιβλίο είναι επίσης αφιερωμένο στην Cyprus Airways, (Κυπριακές Αερογραμμές) την πολυαγαπημένη αεροπορική εταιρεία της πατρίδας μου, την οποία είχα την τιμή και τη χαρά να υπηρετήσω για σχεδόν έξι χρόνια από το 1965 έως το 1971, χρονιά κατά την οποία εγκαταστάθηκα μόνιμα στο Λονδίνο.

Simon Hepworth, ευχαριστώ.

Φανούλλα Αργυρού
Ερευνητής/δημοσιογράφος/συγγραφέας, Λονδίνο, 22 Σεπτεμβρίου 2018

***

Σε ηλικία 36 ετών ο πατέρας μου, Μιχαλάκης Θωμαΐδης, ήταν ένας επιτυχημένος επιχειρηματίας στην Κύπρο όταν τόσο άδικα έχασε τη ζωή του μαζί με άλλους 65 επιβάτες και πλήρωμα στην πτήση CY 284 της Cyprus Airways στις 12 Οκτωβρίου 1967 στο Καστελλόριζο, Ελλάδα.

Να αναπαύονται πάντα εν ειρήνη!

Εμείς, οι σύζυγοι, τα παιδιά και τα εγγόνια, θα τους θυμόμαστε με αγάπη και δεν θα σταματήσουμε ποτέ να αγωνιζόμαστε για δικαιοσύνη για τη δολοφονία 66 αθώων ανθρώπων από κάποιον που πιστεύουμε ότι πρέπει να ήταν δειλός φανατικός.

Ευχαριστώ τον Simon Hepworth και τη Φανούλλα Αργυρού για την όλη έρευνα που έκαναν μέσω των Βρετανικών Εθνικών Αρχείων και για την έκδοση αυτού του βιβλίου!

Μαρία-Νίκη Μ Θωμαΐδη
Κόρη του αποθανόντος επιβάτη Μιχαλάκη Θωμαΐδη

Σε Προσωπικό Σημείωμα

Θυμάμαι πολύ καθαρά την ημέρα της συντριβής. Οκτώ χρονών εκείνη την εποχή, ήμουν στο σχολείο όπου ο δάσκαλος είχε επικεντρωθεί σε αυτό που μας είπαν ότι ήταν η ανακάλυψη της Αμερικής από τον Χριστόφορο Κολόμβο εκείνη την ημέρα, το 1492. Όταν οι αδερφές μου και εγώ φτάσαμε σπίτι, το αυτοκίνητο του Gordon Blackwood ένα blue Singer saloon, ήταν σταθμευμένο στη λωρίδα στο τέλος της αυλής μας.

Η μητέρα μου καθόταν δίπλα στο παράθυρο της κουζίνας και μας περίμενε. Μπαίνοντας στο σπίτι, τη ρώτησα τι συνέβη και μας είπε ότι ο Gordon είχε σκοτωθεί. Ήταν στενός φίλος και κοντινός γείτονας της οικογένειάς μας, καθώς και συνάδελφος του πατέρα μου, εκείνη την εποχή Πρώτος Αξιωματικός (First Officer) με την ΒΕΑ στον στόλο των αεροπλάνων Trident.

Η μητέρα μου, στην ερώτησή μας για το τι είχε συμβεί, μας είπε απλώς ότι το αεροσκάφος του είχε συντριβεί και θα ήταν στις ειδήσεις της τηλεόρασης. Όλα έμοιαζαν τόσο άδικα, όπως και στους πολλούς άλλους ανθρώπους που επλήγησαν από την τραγωδία.

Τους επόμενους λίγους μήνες, η καταστροφή αναφέρθηκε σποραδικά, στη συνέχεια σπάνια, και τελικά εξαφανίστηκε από τις ειδήσεις και, από την ευαισθητοποίηση του κοινού. Οι γονείς μου μιλούσαν ζεστά για τον Gordon για την υπόλοιπη ζωή τους και κράτησαν επαφή με την Joyce Blackwood για το υπόλοιπο της ζωής της.

Το 1981, όταν εργαζόμουν τότε για τη British Aerospace, βρήκα ένα αντίγραφο της έκθεσης του Κλάδου Διερεύνησης Ατυχημάτων στην τεχνική βιβλιοθήκη. Τουλάχιστον μου είπε τι είχε συμβεί, αλλά όχι γιατί.

Η έλευση του Διαδικτύου και το αυξανόμενο ενδιαφέρον μου για τη συγγραφή βιβλίων για την αεροπορία, με οδήγησαν να αρχίσω να εξετάζω το περιστατικό του *Τσάρλι Όσκαρ (Charlie Oscar)* σε μεγαλύτερο βάθος. Είχα χρησιμοποιήσει τους πόρους του Εθνικού Αρχείου στο Λονδίνο όταν ερευνούσα την εξαφάνιση του μεγάλου θείου μου και του πληρώματος του στο Lancaster τους το 1944. Στο διάστημα που μεσολάβησε μισό αιώνα, η πρόσβαση σε έγγραφα και άλλες πληροφορίες κατέστησε δυνατή την άρση του *πέπλου* του απορρήτου που φαινόταν, κατά τη γνώμη μου, να είχε κατασταλάξει σε όλη την υπόθεση.

Επομένως, παραδέχομαι ένα εντελώς προσωπικό κίνητρο συγγραφής αυτού του βιβλίου. Δεν υπήρξε ποτέ κανένα πραγματικό κλείσιμο για την οικογένεια και τους φίλους των 66 ανθρώπων που έχασαν τη ζωή τους στη Μεσόγειο λίγο πριν τα ξημερώματα της 12ης Οκτωβρίου 1967. Ως παιδί, η απώλεια κάποιου κοντά στον οικογενειακό μας κύκλο είχε πολύ σημαντικό αντίκτυπο. Η αίσθηση της απώλειας μου, όμως, δεν συγκρίνεται με αυτή των συζύγων, των παιδιών και των αδερφών των θυμάτων. Ο μισός αιώνας σιωπής το έκανε όλο και πιο δύσκολο να το αντέξουμε. Αφιερώνω αυτό το βιβλίο στους 66 και τις οικογένειές τους.

Simon Hepworth

«Μια πτήση χωρίς προβλήματα»

"Καλημέρα Nicky, Bealine Golf Alpha Romeo Charlie Osc… [86]"

Ο Ανώτερος Πρώτος Αξιωματικός Mike Thomas, ο συγκυβερνήτης ενός αεροσκάφους Comet 4B της British European Airways, (Βρετανικές Ευρωπαϊκές Αερογραμμές) δεν είχε την ευκαιρία να ολοκληρώσει το εναρκτήριο μήνυμά του προς τον Έλεγχο Εναέριας Κυκλοφορίας Λευκωσίας. Το γιατί ακριβώς κόπηκε στη μέση της πρότασης δεν θα γίνει ποτέ γνωστό, αλλά μεταξύ δύο και επτά λεπτών αργότερα η ζωή του έληξε τραγικά.

Ο καιρός ήταν το συνηθισμένο φθινοπωρινό χαμηλό σύννεφο, καθώς ο Καπετάνιος Blackwood και το πλήρωμα του θαλάμου πτήσης, μαζί με τους 38 επιβάτες τους, συν μια γάτα που ξεκουραζόταν σε υπέροχη μοναξιά στο κλουβί της στο πίσω μέρος, είχαν ξεκινήσει το ταξίδι τους από το αεροδρόμιο Heathrow του Λονδίνου στις 22:45 ώρα Ηνωμένου Βασιλείου το προηγούμενο βράδυ. Το πρώτο σκέλος της πτήσης, ήταν ως πτήση BE284 της British European Airways, προς το αεροδρόμιο του Ελληνικού, στην Αθήνα. Στη συνέχεια, το αεροσκάφος θα πετούσε στη Λευκωσία, στην Κύπρο, για λογαριασμό της Cyprus Airways (Κυπριακές Αερογραμμές) που θα λειτουργούσε ως CY284[87]. Το BE/CY284 ήταν ένα

---

[86] Το «Bealine» ήταν το διακριτικό της αεροπορικής εταιρείας που χρησιμοποιούσε η British European Airways. Το «Golf Alpha Rome Charlie Oscar» ήταν η φωνητική μορφή των επιστολών εγγραφής του αεροσκάφους, G-ARCO. Αυτή η εγγραφή ήταν διαδοχικά στο Βρετανικό Μητρώο Πολιτικών Αεροσκαφών και όχι με κάποια ιδιαίτερη σημασία. Το πλήρωμα παρουσίασε τον εαυτό του σε κάθε υπηρεσία Ελέγχου Εναέριας Κυκλοφορίας καθ' οδόν με το πλήρες διακριτικό κλήσης και βεβαιώνοντας ότι δεν υπήρχε άλλο αεροσκάφος με παρόμοιο διακριτικό που θα μπορούσε να προκαλέσει σύγχυση, οι επόμενες μεταδόσεις συντομεύθηκαν σε «Golf Charlie Oscar», «Bealine Charlie Oscar» ή απλά «Charlie Oscar».)

[87] Η Cyprus Airways, ο κυπριακός αερομεταφορέας, ήταν μια νέα αεροπορική εταιρεία καθώς πράγματι η Κύπρος ήταν ένα πρόσφατα ανεξάρτητο κράτος. Ως κληρονομιά της μακροχρόνιας σχέσης της Βρετανίας με το νησί της Μεσογείου, η BEA κατείχε το 22,7% των μετοχών της Cyprus Airways και την υποστήριζε με τζετ σε μια σειρά από μεγάλα δρομολόγια για λογαριασμό της, συμπεριλαμβανομένου αυτού μεταξύ Λευκωσίας και Αθήνας. Αυτή η διαδρομή ήταν πολιτικά η πιο σημαντική για την πλειοψηφία των Κυπρίων, που ήταν ελληνικής καταγωγής. Η Ένωση, με την ελληνική πατρίδα, ήταν ακόμα ο απώτερος στόχος πολλών Κυπρίων πολιτικών, αν και υπήρχαν άλλοι στο νησί, ειδικά μεταξύ της δεύτερης μεγαλύτερης εθνικής ομάδας, τουρκικής καταγωγής, που σίγουρα δεν συμμερίζονταν αυτό το όνειρο.

προγραμματισμένο δρομολόγιο ρουτίνας, το οποίο εκτελούσε το δρομολόγιο τέσσερις φορές την εβδομάδα. Εκτός από τους επιβάτες, τις αποσκευές τους και τη γάτα, μεταφέρθηκαν στο αμπάρι μικροαντικείμενα φορτίου υψηλής αξίας. Σε αυτή την πτήση, ως εθνικός αερομεταφορέας η ΒΕΑ μετέφερνε επίσης το ταχυδρομείο του Royal Mail.

Καθώς ο Κομήτης ανέβαινε μέσα από το σύννεφο για καθαρότερο αέρα, οι επιβάτες χαλάρωναν κατά τη διάρκεια της πτήσης για Αθήνα, ενώ το προσωπικό της καμπίνας ετοιμαζόταν να προσφέρει καφέ, τσάι και αναψυκτικά. Η πτήση ήταν προγραμματισμένη να διαρκέσει λιγότερο από τρεισήμισι ώρες. Η ΒΕΑ εκτελούσε το δρομολόγιο ως πτήση Night Tourist, ενώ η καμπίνα πρώτης θέσης παρέμενε κενή. Η υπηρεσία απευθυνόταν σε άτομα για τα οποία η ταλαιπωρία της πτήσης στη μέση της νύχτας αντισταθμιζόταν από μειωμένα ναύλα[88].

Το Charlie Oscar ολοκλήρωσε το πρώτο σκέλος του ταξιδιού και προσγειώθηκε στην Αθήνα στις 01:11, GMT, 03:11 τοπική ώρα και τέσσερα λεπτά νωρίτερα από το χρονοδιάγραμμα. Ενώ το Charlie Oscar ετοιμαζόταν για την πτήση του προς τη Λευκωσία, άλλοι 31 επιβάτες προστέθηκαν στην πτήση από Αθήνα.

Σε αυτόν τον δεύτερο σκέλος της πτήσης, ο SFO (Senior First Officer – Ανώτερος Πρώτος Αξιωματικός) Thomas θα ενεργούσε ως συγκυβερνήτης, χειριζόμενος τις ραδιοεπικοινωνίες και την πλοήγηση ενώ ο Καπετάνιος Blackwood πετούσε το αεροσκάφος. Ο SFO Palmer κάθισε πίσω από τους δύο άλλους πιλότους, ο ρόλος του σε αυτή την πτήση ήταν να διαχειρίζεται τα πολύπλοκα συστήματα του αεροσκάφους και να παρακολουθεί τους δύο πιλότους που πετούσαν το αεροσκάφος.

Η παραμονή 75 λεπτών στην Αθήνα έδωσε στους επιβάτες και το πλήρωμα την ευκαιρία να τεντώσουν τα πόδια τους στο αεροδρόμιο. Με εξαίρεση τρεις επιβάτες και τον Καπετάνιο, όλοι όσοι ταξίδευαν προς τη Λευκωσία εκμεταλλεύτηκαν την ευκαιρία. Για λόγους ασφαλείας, οι επιβάτες δεν μπορούσαν να μείνουν μόνοι στο αεροσκάφος. Για να μπορεί να παρακολουθεί τη δραστηριότητα των καθαριστριών και των τροφοδοτών, καθώς και να ασχολείται με τη γραφειοκρατία για τον επόμενο τομέα, ο Καπετάνιος Blackwood κάθισε στην καμπίνα πρώτης τάξεως κατά τη διάρκεια της παραμονής.

---

[88] *Το ναύλο της τουριστικής θέσης μετ' επιστροφής στην πτήση 284 ήταν £76 8s για Αθήνα και £85 για Λευκωσία. Για μία διαδρομή μόνο τα ναύλα ήταν £56.4 και £65 αντίστοιχα, επομένως για τους επιβάτες που σκόπευαν να ταξιδέψουν μετ' επιστροφής, η νυχτερινή πτήση αντιπροσώπευε κάτι σαν ευκαιρία. Η τιμή των £85 το 1967 ισοδυναμούσε εντυπωσιακά με £1.500 το 2018. Ο μέσος μισθός στο Ηνωμένο Βασίλειο εκείνη την εποχή ήταν £891 ετησίως. ή £74. 5 (£74,25) το μήνα, επομένως η πτήση δεν ήταν ακόμη ένα προσιτό μέσο ταξιδιού για τους περισσότερους ανθρώπους. Πηγή: ΒΕΑ.*

Κατά τη διάρκεια του πρώτου τομέα, που αργότερα επρόκειτο να περιγραφεί στον Τύπο απλώς ως «μια πτήση χωρίς προβλήματα», το μόνο τεχνικό ζήτημα που ενοχλούσε τον Καπετάνιο Blackwood ήταν ένα λάθος με μία από τις πυξίδες του αεροσκάφους. Αυτή ήταν μέρος του συστήματος προσγείωσης του Comet, αλλά ήταν διπλή, επομένως δεν παρουσίαζε σοβαρά προβλήματα. Την είχε σημειώσει στο τεχνικό ημερολόγιο του αεροσκάφους και την ανέφερε στον εφημερεύοντα μηχανικό κ. Ν. Καραΐνδρο στην Αθήνα. Με τη σειρά του, ο κ. Καραΐνδρος, ο οποίος εργαζόταν στην Ολυμπιακή Αεροπορία και ήταν υπεύθυνος του πληρώματος εξυπηρέτησης, έδωσε εντολή στον κ. Α. Καλεσίδη, ειδικό των μηχανημάτων, να αναλάβει το θέμα.

Ο κ. Καλεσίδης έκανε έλεγχο και με μια μικρή ρύθμιση το μηχάνημα φάνηκε πλέον να λειτουργεί. Έκανε μια κατάλληλη καταχώριση στο ημερολόγιο τεχνολογίας και εξήγησε στον Καπετάνιο Blackwood ότι το μηχάνημα φαινόταν τώρα να είναι διορθωμένο.

Εν τω μεταξύ, το υπόλοιπο προσωπικό εδάφους συνέχισε με τις συνήθεις εργασίες που περιλάμβαναν την προετοιμασία του Charlie Oscar για την μετέπειτα πτήση προς τη Λευκωσία. Ο κ. Δ. Αργυρού επέβλεψε τους ελέγχους πριν από την αναχώρηση, συμπεριλαμβανομένου του ανεφοδιασμού. Βοηθήθηκε στους ελέγχους από τον κ. Α. Αναγκούστο, μηχανικό αεροσκαφών. Και οι δύο άνδρες ήταν ικανοποιημένοι ότι δεν υπήρχαν εκκρεμή προβλήματα.

Ο κ. Γεώργιος Διαμαντάρας, Traffic and Administration officer της BEA, ήταν υπεύθυνος για τη φροντίδα των επιβατών.

Αρκετά άλλα μέλη του προσωπικού της BEA συμμετείχαν στην εξυπηρέτηση του Charlie Oscar στο έδαφος στην Αθήνα. Ο κ. Σαμπελάριος ήταν υπεύθυνος για τον καθαρισμό στις τουαλέτες και φόρτωσε βαλίτσες στο υπ' αριθ. 2 hold. Ο Traffic Clerk κ. Παγώνης, φρόντισε για τη σωστή φόρτωση του φορτίου, με εφημερίδες, αλληλογραφία και μια παρτίδα παπουτσιών, με βάρος 328 κιλά. Το φορτίο περιελάμβανε επίσης τέσσερα κιβώτια με τσάντες, εμπορεύματα που πιστεύεται ότι ανήκαν στον ανώτερο αεροσυνοδό της Cyprus Airways, Φρίξο Μιχαήλ. Στο Hold 2 υπήρχαν 24 αποσκευές και είκοσι σακούλες αλληλογραφίας. Η αλληλογραφία που φορτώθηκε στην Αθήνα προερχόταν από διάφορα μέρη σε όλη την Ευρώπη, καθώς και τη Νέα Υόρκη. Μέρος της αλληλογραφίας ήταν για την αποστολή των Ηνωμένων Εθνών στην Κύπρο. Το Hold 3 περιείχε οκτώ αποσκευές, που φορτώθηκαν στο Heathrow και ανήκαν σε επιβάτες της τελευταίας στιγμής, συμπεριλαμβανομένων τριών υπαλλήλων της BEA που ταξίδευαν εκτός υπηρεσίας. Άλλες δεκαοκτώ ή δεκαεννέα τσάντες, που ανήκαν σε επιβάτες από το Λονδίνο, βρίσκονταν στο Hold 4. Τέλος, στο Hold 5, βρίσκονταν οι υπόλοιπες αποσκευές του Λονδίνου, συνολικά δεκαέξι ή δεκαεπτά, μαζί με περίπου 500 κιλά φορτίου. Δεν υπήρχε τίποτα το αξιοσημείωτο ή το ύποπτο σε οποιοδήποτε από τα φορτία, που τώρα ενώθηκαν με τη γάτα στο ταξίδι της.

Ο κ. Μορσετάκης, Traffic Officer, ετοίμασε τα χαρτιά του αεροπλάνου, τα οποία παρέδωσε στον Καπετάνιο Blackwood και έφυγε από το αεροσκάφος αφού υπογράφτηκε το έγγραφο φόρτωσης. Ο Μιχαήλ Ζωγράφος, Operations Officer, πήρε το φάκελο καιρού και έβαλε μέσα ένα σχέδιο πτήσης, το οποίο είχε ετοιμάσει η Ολυμπιακή Αεροπορία. Είχε μια συνομιλία με τον Καπετάνιο Blackwood, ο οποίος καθόταν κοντά στην είσοδο της καμπίνας. Ο Καπετάνιος υπέγραψε το σχέδιο πτήσης και το φορτίο καυσίμων.

Ο Καπετάνιος Blackwood έλεγξε τις λεπτομέρειες του καιρού κατά τη διαδρομή, οι οποίες έδειχναν καλές και καθαρές συνθήκες, με κάποια διάσπαρτα σύννεφα πολύ κάτω από το προγραμματισμένο υψόμετρο πτήσης 29.000 ποδιών, με μικρή πιθανότητα νεφών συσσωρευμένων από 3.000 έως 30.000 πόδια. Δεν υπήρχε καμία προσδοκία πάγου ή αναταράξεων. Στη Λευκωσία, θα υπήρχε διάσπαρτη νέφωση στα περίπου 5.000 πόδια με ορατότητα έως και 40 χιλιόμετρα. Συνολικά, ο καιρός δεν φαινόταν ότι θα δημιουργούσε κανένα πρόβλημα.

Ο κ. Τελεβάντος ήταν ο φορτωτής και οδηγός τρακτέρ. Από το Τελωνείο, μετέφερε στο αεροσκάφος τις τσάντες των επιβατών Αθηνών-Λευκωσίας, χωρίς όμως να πραγματοποιήσει ο ίδιος καμία φόρτωση.

Ο κ. Καλαϊτζής, φορτωτής Catering, έφερε δίσκους από το Τμήμα Catering και μάζεψε από το εστιατόριο του αεροδρομίου τα πρωινά που θα σερβίρονταν κατά την πτήση προς τη Λευκωσία. Με τη βοήθεια του κ. Χηλαδάκη, τα φόρτωσε στο Charlie Oscar .Ο καθαρισμός της καμπίνας του αεροσκάφους έγινε από τον κ. Λεμνέων, ο οποίος σημείωσε ότι κάποιοι επιβάτες παρέμειναν στο αεροσκάφος, σχεδόν σίγουρα οι τρεις που αναφέρονται από το υπόλοιπο προσωπικό.

Ο έλεγχος του προσωπικού της καμπίνας και η φόρτωση των επιβατών ήταν ευθύνη του κ. Καρνεμίδα, Tarmac Controller. Γνώριζε ότι οι τρεις επιβάτες και ο Καπετάνιος Blackwood βρίσκονταν ακόμη στο αεροσκάφος, επομένως ένας φρουρός έμεινε στο αεροσκάφος κατά τη διάρκεια του ανεφοδιασμού σε καύσιμα σε περίπτωση περιστατικού ασφαλείας που θα απαιτούσε την εκκένωση τους.

Ο αξιωματικός υπηρεσίας της ΒΕΑ, κ. Χ. Κολιανδρής, δεν συνάντησε τον Καπετάνιο Blackwood. Στην έκθεσή του σημείωσε ότι είχε κρυφακούσει τον κ. Καραϊνδρο, τον μηχανικό της Ολυμπιακής Αεροπορίας, να σχολιάζει κάτι που λέει ότι «... κάποιες σελίδες έλειπαν από το Τεχνικό Μητρώο». Το είχε συζητήσει με τον κ. Καραϊνδρο, ο οποίος διευκρίνισε το θέμα, εξηγώντας ότι είχε γίνει ένα μικρό λάθος στις ώρες πτήσης στα χαρτιά, το οποίο διόρθωσε.

Ο κ. Κολιανδρής συνέχισε και σημείωσε ότι το Charlie Oscar αναχώρησε για τη Λευκωσία στις 04:25 τοπική ώρα, πέντε λεπτά νωρίτερα από τη προγραμματισμένη ώρα.

66 Ψυχές στο Αεροπλάνο

Ο Καπετάνιος Gordon Blackwood 45 ετών, από το Bracknell, Berkshire, ήταν επικεφαλής του αεροσκάφους, με συγκυβερνήτη τον SFO Mike Thomas, από το Farnborough, Hampshire. Επίσης στο θάλαμο πτήσης ήταν ένας τρίτος πλήρως καταρτισμένος πιλότος, ο SFO Dennis Palmer.
Και οι τρεις άνδρες ήταν πολύ έμπειροι και όλοι είχαν υπηρετήσει στη Βασιλική Πολεμική Αεροπορία πριν ενταχθούν στη ΒΕΑ. Ο Καπετάνιος Blackwood είχε ενταχθεί στη RAF το 1942, σε ηλικία είκοσι ετών. Στάλθηκε στον Καναδά για να εκπαιδευτεί ως πιλότος, οι βαθμοί του ήταν αρκετά υψηλοί που τον κράτησαν ως εκπαιδευτή, αντί να τον αποσπάσουν κατευθείαν στη Βρετανία. Αυτό σχεδόν σίγουρα θα του έσωζε τη ζωή. Εκείνη την εποχή οι περισσότεροι νέοι πιλότοι της RAF μεταφέρθηκαν κατευθείαν στη Διοίκηση Βομβαρδιστικών, όπου το επίπεδο των θανάτων ήταν πολύ υψηλό. Όταν τελικά άφησε τον εκπαιδευτικό του ρόλο, μεταφέρθηκε στο Μεσογειακό Θέατρο Επιχειρήσεων. Ο 33χρονος Mike Thomas, ο οποίος είχε ενταχθεί στη ΒΕΑ δέκα χρόνια νωρίτερα, ήταν παντρεμένος με έναν γιο και μια κόρη. Ο Dennis Palmer, 35 ετών, ήταν μέλος της Βασιλικής Βοηθητικής Αεροπορίας πριν ενταχθεί στην ΒΕΑ το 1957 και ήταν βιομηχανικός χημικός σε μια εταιρεία κατασκευής χαρτιού στο Aberdeen. Τώρα ζούσε με τη σύζυγο του, τον γιο και την κόρη τους, στο Goring-on-Thames, κοντά στο Reading.
Τα τρία μέρη του πληρώματος γνώρισαν ο ένας τον άλλον καλά, ο στόλος της ΒΕΑ με Comet 4Β αριθμούσε τότε δεκατρία αεροσκάφη. Τις προηγούμενες επτά ημέρες, ο Dennis Palmer και ο Mike Thomas είχαν πετάξει μαζί δύο φορές. Ο Mike Thomas δεν είχε αρχικά συμπεριληφθεί στον κατάλογο για το BE/CY284. Ένας συνάδελφος, ο John Weldon, μόλις είχε ανακαλύψει ότι η σύζυγός του είχε διαγνωστεί με καρκίνο, οπότε ο Mike προσφέρθηκε να ανταλλάξει καθήκοντα μαζί του.
Το προσωπικό καμπίνας για το πρώτο μέρος του ταξιδιού, ο ανώτερος αεροσυνοδός Tony Talaska, οι αεροσυνοδοί Clive Hummerstone και Alan Heard και η αεροσυνοδός Wendy Gibbs, ήταν επίσης Βρετανοί. Θα άφηναν την πτήση στην Αθήνα και θα πραγματοποιούσαν μια πτήση επιστροφής για Λονδίνο με άλλη υπηρεσία ΒΕΑ Comet, φτάνοντας πίσω στο Heathrow την επόμενη μέρα. Αφού έφτανε στη Λευκωσία, ο Charile Oscar θα περνούσε λίγο περισσότερες από τέσσερις ώρες εκεί πριν ξεκινήσει το ταξίδι της επιστροφής στην Αθήνα και το Λονδίνο Heathrow ως CY/BE265. Οι τρεις πιλότοι θα χειρίζονταν το CY/BE265 την επόμενη μέρα.
Η διάταξη του de Havilland DH106 Comet 4B ήταν ελαφρώς διαφορετική από τα περισσότερα αεροσκάφη, τότε και σήμερα. Η

μπροστινή είσοδος και έξοδος ήταν στη δεξιά πλευρά του αεροσκάφους[89]. Ωστόσο, καθώς οι σύγχρονες αερογέφυρες δεν ήταν καθόλου συνηθισμένες, οι περισσότεροι άνθρωποι έπρεπε να επιβιβασθούν και να αποβιβασθούν με μεταφερόμενες σκάλες με τροχούς μέχρι την πόρτα του αεροσκάφους, επομένως αυτό δεν ήταν εμπόδιο στη διαδικασία επιβίβασης και αποβίβασης. Εξίσου άγνωστη θα ήταν η αρίθμηση των θέσεων στον κομήτη. Η σειρά 1, που είναι συνήθως η πρώτη σειρά καθισμάτων επιβατών, ήταν στο πίσω μέρος, με τις επόμενες σειρές καθισμάτων να αριθμούνται μπροστά. Στη διαμόρφωση της ΒΕΑ, η καμπίνα Tourist (Economy) Class περιείχε 79 θέσεις, σε δεκαπέντε σειρές των πέντε και μία από τέσσερις. Τρία καθίσματα, με τα γράμματα Α, Β και C, βρίσκονταν σε μια ενιαία μονάδα στην αριστερή πλευρά της καμπίνας, με μια μονάδα δύο θέσεων, D και Ε, στη δεξιά πλευρά.

Στη θέση 1Α, ο επιχειρηματίας Μιχαήλ (Michael) Κώστα Θωμαΐδης ήταν τακτικός ταξιδιώτης στο δρομολόγιο Λονδίνο προς Λευκωσία. Γιος ιδιοκτήτη πορτοκαλεώνα, στα τέλη της δεκαετίας του 1950 είχε ξεκινήσει ως αντιπρόσωπος προμήθειας πωλήσεων, μελετώντας τα βράδια για να πάρει το δίπλωμά του από το κολέγιο Pitman. Στη συνέχεια ίδρυσε μια επιχείρηση συσκευασίας φρούτων και λαχανικών, με εξειδίκευση στις πατάτες, τα καρότα, τα σταφύλια και τα εσπεριδοειδή. Το εγχείρημα σύντομα αποδείχθηκε επιτυχημένο, και εξελίχθηκε σε έναν από τους μεγαλύτερους εμπόρους γεωργικών προϊόντων στην Κύπρο. Μέχρι το 1967 η εταιρεία έκανε εξαγωγές στο Ηνωμένο Βασίλειο, με γραφεία στη Long Acre Street, στο Covent Garden στο Λονδίνο, καθώς και στο Rotterdam. Μεταξύ των πελατών της, η εταιρεία του Μιχαήλ εξήγαγε πατάτες στην οικογένεια Smith, που φημίζεται για τη σειρά σνακ "Smith's Crisps", με την οποία έγινε στενός φίλος.

Λόγω του όγκου της εργασίας, που επεκτάθηκε στην Αίγυπτο, την Ελλάδα, ακόμη και την Τουρκία, πριν από τα προβλήματα του 1963, ο Μιχαήλ αποφάσισε να ασχοληθεί με τη ναυτιλία αντί να ναυλώνει πλοία. Μέχρι το 1965, μαζί με τον αδερφό του και τους Βρετανούς εταίρους του, Anthony και Robert Beeson, ήταν ένας από τους πρώτους Κύπριους πλοιοκτήτες, με ένα πλοίο-ψυγείο, το *Cyprian Trader* και ένα πλοίο μεταφοράς το *Cyprian Producer*. Βρήκε ότι έπρεπε να ναυλώσει ακόμα ένα, επιπλέον χωρητικότητας για να αντεπεξέλθει στον όγκο της εργασίας.

---

[89] *Ο συγγραφέας έχει χρησιμοποιήσει τη συμβατική ορολογία της αεροπορίας σε όλο αυτό το βιβλίο, για να είναι συνεπής με τη γλώσσα που χρησιμοποιείται στις εκθέσεις έρευνας. Ως θύρα (port) αναφέρεται στην αριστερή πλευρά του αεροσκάφους που κοιτάζει προς τα εμπρός, δεξιά προς τα δεξιά. Οι όροι «εμπρός» και «πίσω» αναφέρονται στο μπροστινό και πίσω μέρος του αεροσκάφους αντίστοιχα.*

Ο Μιχαήλ είχε υπογράψει συμφωνία πώλησης με την Smith's Potato Crisps, η οποία κάλυπτε 25 χώρες στη Μέση Ανατολή και την Ανατολική Μεσόγειο. Αυτό περιελάμβανε την εταιρεία του Μιχαήλ που κατασκεύασε το πιο προηγμένο εργοστάσιο σνακ στην Ευρώπη. Αγόρασε τη γη, κοντά στην Αμμόχωστο στην Κύπρο, το καλοκαίρι του 1967[90]. Ο Μιχαήλ είχε καλό λόγο να ανυπομονεί να επιστρέψει στην πατρίδα του μετά από λίγες εβδομάδες μακριά σε ένα επιτυχημένο επαγγελματικό ταξίδι. Η σύζυγος του περίμενε το τρίτο τους παιδί μέσα στον επόμενο μήνα.

Αμέσως μπροστά στον Μιχαήλ Θωμαΐδη στις θέσεις 2Α και Β, καθόταν ένα ζευγάρι Ουαλών, ο Hugh Seymour Griffiths και η σύζυγός του, Lily, που κατάγονταν από το χωριό Cosheston, μερικά μίλια από το Pembroke Dock. Ο Hugh ήταν φαρμακοποιός, και λειτουργούσε ένα τοπικό φαρμακείο. Έπαιρναν την πρώτη τους πτήση για την Κύπρο, όπου θα επισκέπτονταν τον αδερφό του Hugh, δημόσιο υπάλληλο, ο οποίος επρόκειτο να φύγει από το νησί. Αυτή θα ήταν η μοναδική τους ευκαιρία να πραγματοποιήσουν την επίσκεψη, έτσι η Lily ήταν έτοιμη να ξεπεράσει την απροθυμία της να πετάξει για να μπορέσουν να απολαύσουν τις διακοπές.

Η κυρία Margaret Joyce κάθισε στον διάδρομο απέναντι από τους Griffiths, στο κάθισμα 2D. Παρά το γεγονός ότι ήταν περίπου δέκα χρόνια νεότερη από το ζευγάρι απέναντι, θα τους είχε βρει συντροφιά στο ταξίδι. Η σύζυγος του αιδεσιμότατου Henry Joyce, εφημέριου του Hathersage στο Derbyshire, η Margaret καταγόταν από πολύ πιο βόρεια, έχοντας γεννηθεί στο Cumberland. Ήταν καθ' οδόν για να επισκεφτεί την κόρη της που εκείνη την ώρα νοσηλευόταν σε νοσοκομείο της Κύπρου.

Ο 23χρονος Αμερικανός επιβάτης κυπριακής καταγωγής, Σωτήρης Γεωργίου, είχε το κάθισμα στο πλαϊνό παράθυρο, 4Α. Είχε φτάσει στο Λονδίνο από τη Νέα Υόρκη, όπου δύο αυτοκίνητα φίλων και συγγενών τον είχαν συνοδεύσει στο αεροδρόμιο Kennedy για να τον αποχαιρετήσουν. Διανυχτέρευσε στο Λονδίνο σε συγγενικά του πρόσωπα πριν μεταφερθεί στο ΒΕ284 για το επόμενο ταξίδι του στην Κύπρο. Επέστρεφε στο Νέο Χωρίο Κυθρέας, μια πόλη βορειοανατολικά της Λευκωσίας, για να επισκεφτεί την οικογένεια που είχε αφήσει τέσσερα

---

[90] *Η σύζυγος και ο αδερφός του Μιχαήλ συνέχισαν το έργο μετά τον θάνατό του, ολοκληρώνοντας το εργοστάσιο το 1969. Αργότερα, φοιτητές από το Πανεπιστήμιο του Reading θα επισκέπτονταν για εκπαιδευτικούς σκοπούς. Έχασαν το εργοστάσιο το 1974 από τις τουρκικές δυνάμεις εισβολής αλλά συνέχισε να χρησιμοποιείται υπό την κατοχική δύναμη. Ο Όμιλος Θωμαΐδη συνεχίζει να ευδοκιμεί στην Κύπρο, υπό την ηγεσία του πρώτου γιου του Μιχαήλ, τον Αρτέμη, της κόρης του Μαρίας και του Μιχαήλ, που γεννήθηκε τον Νοέμβριο του 1967, ο οποίος φέρει το όνομα του πατέρα του που δεν είχε ποτέ την ευκαιρία να γνωρίσει.*

χρόνια νωρίτερα όταν μετακόμισε στις ΗΠΑ. Ο Σωτήρης εργαζόταν ως μηχανικός αυτοκινήτων, με ειδίκευση στα οχήματα Mercedes. Επίσης στη σειρά 4, κατά μήκος του διαδρόμου σε 4D, ήταν η 54χρονη χήρα, η κυρία Lily Marlborough, από το Stockton-on-Tees. Η μικρόσωμη κυρία, μόλις 5 πόδια 1 ίντσα σε ύψος, με καστανόξανθα και γκρίζα μαλλιά, πήγαινε να επισκεφτεί την 20χρονη κόρη της, Christine, η οποία είχε μετακομίσει στην Κύπρο με τον 18 μηνών γιο της, Graham και τον σύζυγό της ,Bob, ο οποίος υπηρετούσε με τους Royal Signals σε τριετή απόσπαση. Στις 11 Οκτωβρίου, η Christine με έκπληξη και χαρά έλαβε γράμμα από την μητέρα της Lily, που έλεγε ότι θα έφτανε στις 6 το πρωί της επόμενης ημέρας. Η Lily ήταν ακόμα ένα άτομο που πετούσε για πρώτη φορά, σύμφωνα με τον γιο της στα δημοσιεύματα του Τύπου, είχε τρομερό φόβο να πετάξει, τον οποίο ξεπέρασε για να επισκεφτεί την κόρη της. Η σύζυγος και το παιδί του γιου της είχαν προγραμματίσει να συνοδεύσουν τη Lily αλλά ακύρωσαν τα σχέδιά τους λόγω της αδιαθεσίας του τετράχρονου γιου τους.

Η 68χρονη Anna Stewart συνόδευε την επί χρόνια φίλη της, δεσποινίς Jean Falconer, η οποία ήταν συνταξιούχος δασκάλα. Οι δύο κυρίες, που κάθονταν στις θέσεις 7D και E, ήταν από το Edinburgh, όπου ο σύζυγος της Άννας ασκούσε το επάγγελμα του δικηγόρου. Η Jean είχε μετακομίσει στο Balloch, στο Inverness-shire, αλλά παρέμεινε σε επαφή με τη φίλη της. Ήταν καθ' οδόν για διακοπές στην Κύπρο.

Η οικογένεια McComb, που κατείχε τις θέσεις 8A, B και Γ, επέστρεφε στην Κύπρο μετά από παρατεταμένες διακοπές πέντε εβδομάδων. Ο 24χρονος Roy υπηρετούσε στη RAF στην Κύπρο και πετούσε μαζί με τη σύζυγό του Elaine και τον δεκαοκτώ μηνών γιο τους, Roydon George. . Έμειναν με την οικογένεια της Elaine στο Mexborough, κοντά στο Doncaster. Η οικογένεια του Roy καταγόταν από το Osmotherly του North Yorkshire, όπου ζούσαν στο The Lady Chapel. Ο Roy πήγε σχολείο στο Northallerton και, σε ηλικία 16 ετών, εντάχθηκε στη RAF ως Aircraft Apprentice.

Το 1965 παντρεύτηκε την Elaine και τον επόμενο χρόνο γεννήθηκε ο γιος τους, Roydon George.

Απέναντι από τους McCombs στο διάδρομο, στη θέση 8E, βρισκόταν ο Κώστας Ευσταθίου, που περιγράφεται ως ένας σωματώδης άνδρας, ύψους 5 πόδια 7 ίντσες. Σε ηλικία 34 ετών, ήταν κομμωτής που ζούσε στο Alkrington, Middleton, στο βόρειο άκρο του σημερινού οικισμού του Manchester, και είχε ζήσει στην Αγγλία για πολλά χρόνια.

Ο γιατρός Γεώργιος Ιωαννίδης, 48 ετών, στη θέση 9A, ήταν γιος του Διευθυντή του φημισμένου Παγκυπρίου Γυμνασίου στη Λευκωσία (Κύπρο) και της Αθηνάς Ιωαννίδου, μιας πολύ γνωστής και σεβαστής γυναίκας στην Κύπρο, η οποία διηύθυνε την Παγκύπρια Ακαδημία Κοριτσιών Λευκωσίας. Ο Γιώργος παρακολούθησε το δημοτικό σχολείο τη δεκαετία του 1920 στη Γερμανία, όπου ο πατέρας του σπούδαζε στο Πανεπιστήμιο της Λειψίας για το διδακτορικό του. Ο μικρότερος αδερφός του Γιώργου Χρήστος έγινε δικηγόρος και αργότερα δικαστής στην Κύπρο, ενώ ο Γιώργος απέκτησε το πτυχίο ιατρικής από το Πανεπιστήμιο Αθηνών και, τη δεκαετία του 1950, άσκησε το επάγγελμά του στο Νοσοκομείο Victoria, στο Accrington, στο Lancashire. Συνεχίζοντας την ιατρική για αρκετά χρόνια στο Λονδίνο, διορίστηκε ως σύμβουλος υπεύθυνος για τα νοσοκομεία της περιοχής North Paddington. Ήταν επίσης υπεύθυνος του Παθολογικού Τμήματος στο National Temperance Hospital του Λονδίνου. Όταν επέστρεψε μόνιμα στην Κύπρο, παντρεύτηκε την Ιωάννα Καλλιμάχου. Ο γιατρός Ιωαννίδης ήταν λοιπόν εξοικειωμένος με το ιατρικό σύστημα στο Λονδίνο, έχοντας πολλές επαφές. Σε αυτό το ταξίδι είχε συνοδεύσει στο Λονδίνο ένα σοβαρά τραυματισμένο παιδί στενού φίλου του που είχε τροχαίο ατύχημα στη Λευκωσία. Επέστρεφε εγκαίρως για το ετήσιο μνημόσυνο του πατέρα του, ο οποίος είχε πεθάνει στις 13 Οκτωβρίου, και για τα δεύτερα γενέθλια της κόρης του στις 14 Οκτωβρίου.

Στο κάθισμα 9D καθόταν ο Αστυνομικός Λοχίας Ροδοσθένης Χρήστου, ο οποίος είχε γεννηθεί στο χωριό Αρμίνου Πάφου, στη Κύπρο στις 17 Σεπτεμβρίου 1927, γιος της Αθηνάς Σαλούμη και του Χρήστου Μεσαρίτη. Μετά τη γέννησή του, οι γονείς του μετακόμισαν σε ένα άλλο χωριό, τα Μαντριά Λεμεσού, όπου φοίτησε στη Σχολή Μιτσή Λεμίθου. Ήταν ένα από τέσσερα παιδιά.

Τελειώνοντας το σχολείο ο Ροδοσθένης πήγε στην Αστυνομική Ακαδημία, όπου αποφοίτησε και αργότερα χαρακτηρίστηκε ως πρότυπο αστυνομικού. Μερικά χρόνια αργότερα μετατέθηκε στην αστυνομική δύναμη Αμμοχώστου. Σε μια περίπτωση, λόγω ασθένειας, εισήχθη στο νοσοκομείο Αμμοχώστου όπου γνωρίστηκε με μια από τις νοσοκόμες που τον φρόντιζαν, την Ελένη Κακούρη Πέτρου. Της ζήτησε ραντεβού, ερωτεύτηκαν και παντρεύτηκαν. Απέκτησαν τέσσερα παιδιά, τον Σώτο, την Αθηνά, τον Πέτρο και τη Βάσω. Ως εισαγγελέας της αστυνομίας, ήθελε να συνεχίσει τις σπουδές του και να γίνει δικηγόρος. Ήταν καλά μορφωμένος και μιλούσε τέσσερις γλώσσες. Με αυτή την πρόθεση κατά νου, αποφάσισε να ταξιδέψει στην Αγγλία για να βρει τρόπους να συνεχίσει την εκπαίδευσή του μέσω της εκπαίδευσης εξ αποστάσεως.

Ο Ροδοσθένης έκλεισε απευθείας πτήση για Λονδίνο όπου τον υποδέχτηκε η οικογενειά του και έμεινε για ένα μήνα. Για την επιστροφή του ήθελε επίσης να κλείσει απευθείας πτήση αλλά έπρεπε να συμβιβαστεί με το BE/CY284 το οποίο, παρά τη στάση στην Αθήνα όπου επιβιβάστηκαν επιπλέον επιβάτες, ήταν μια ενδιάμεση πτήση, με την οποία τουλάχιστον θα ολοκλήρωνε το ταξίδι με το ίδιο αεροσκάφος. Από την Αθήνα μαζί με τον Ροδοσθένη θα ταξίδευε και η βαφτιστήρα του, η 24χρονη Νίκη Ροδοσθένους, αισθητικός. Πίσω στο σπίτι στην Κύπρο, η οικογένειά του τον περίμενε με ανυπομονησία και είχε προγραμματίσει μια οικογενειακή συγκέντρωση για να γιορτάσει την επιστροφή του.

Στις θέσεις 10Α και Β κάθονταν η κυρία Κατερίνα Λιασίδη, 52 ετών, που ζούσε στο Muswell Hill του Λονδίνου, και η 74χρονη κυρία Μέλανι Παπαϊωάννου, ο γιος της οποίας ζούσε στο Kingston Hill του Surrey. Η 53χρονη κυρία Λιασίδη είχε λάβει τηλεγράφημα νωρίτερα εκείνη την ημέρα που την καλούσε να ταξιδέψει στην Κύπρο το συντομότερο δυνατό, καθώς ο αδερφός της ήταν βαριά άρρωστος[91]. Παρά τη συμβουλή της οικογένειάς της να περιμένει το Σαββατοκύριακο, επέμεινε να κλείσει το εισιτήριό της για την επόμενη διαθέσιμη πτήση.

Ο Αμερικανός λοχίας πεζοναυτών Michael O'Brien, ταξίδευε με την 22χρονη Βρετανίδα σύζυγό του, Maureen. Το ζευγάρι υπηρετούσε στην Κύπρο, με τις αντίστοιχες μονάδες υπηρεσίας, η Maureen ήταν μέλος του Γυναικείου Βασιλικού Σώματος Στρατού. Ο Michael ήταν από το New Jersey ενώ η Maureen από το Warrington. Αν και αρχικά επρόκειτο να ταξιδέψουν την επόμενη μέρα, άλλαξαν για την προηγούμενη πτήση για να αποφύγουν διανυκτέρευση στο Λονδίνο. Το ζευγάρι, που καθόταν στις θέσεις 10D και Ε, είχε παντρευτεί μόλις πριν δεκατρείς ημέρες.

Στις θέσεις 12Α και Β κάθονταν ο κ. Λοΐζος Νικολαΐδης, 30 ετών, και η 23χρονη σύζυγός του Ειρηνούλα, από το χωριό Πέρα Πεδί. Στη σειρά μπροστά τους βρισκόταν ο γιος τους Ανδρέας, του οποίου η ηλικία δεν καταγράφηκε, αλλά μια φωτογραφία του Τύπου δείχνει ότι ήταν περίπου τεσσάρων ετών. Ο κ. Νικολαΐδης εργάστηκε στην Εταιρεία Γενικών Ασφαλίσεων Κύπρου, μέρος της Τράπεζας Κύπρου. Η οικογένεια επέστρεφε από το Λονδίνο, όπου είχε πάρει τον Ανδρέα για ιατρικές εξετάσεις.

Μια άλλη οικογένεια με στρατιωτικές διασυνδέσεις ήταν οι Taskers, στις θέσεις 14Α και Β. Η κυρία Jan Tasker επέστρεφε στη Κύπρο με τον 3χρονο γιο της Guy, όπου ο σύζυγός της ήταν Υπαξιωματικός στις βρετανικές ένοπλες υπηρεσίες.

Στις θέσεις 15Α και Β, η 25χρονη Anne Harbstreet και ο πατέρας της Nicolas Peters, ταξίδευαν μαζί από την Elizabeth του New Jersey των ΗΠΑ. Ο σύζυγος της Άννας είχε αποσπαστεί πρόσφατα στο Βιετνάμ, όπου μαινόταν ο πόλεμος, και ο Nicolas σκέφτηκε ότι θα βοηθούσε την κόρη του να αντεπεξέλθει αν πήγαιναν να επισκεφτούν συγγενείς στην Κύπρο.

Στην κυρία Λιασίδη αρχικά είπαν ότι η πτήση ήταν γεμάτη, οπότε αναγκάστηκε να φύγει από τον ταξιδιωτικό πράκτορα. Ωστόσο, την κάλεσαν πίσω στο γραφείο και της είπαν ότι υπήρχε, στην πραγματικότητα, μια εφεδρική θέση στην πτήση. Η Μέλανι Παπαϊωάννου

---

[91] Κατά ειρωνικό τρόπο, ο αδερφός της έζησε για άλλους έξι μήνες.

ζούσε στο χωριό Παρεκκλησιά, δεκατρία μίλια ανατολικά της Λεμεσού, όπου ο σύζυγός της ήταν ιερέας. Το ζευγάρι είχε έξι γιους και μια κόρη. Η Μέλανι Παπαϊωάννου χαρακτηρίστηκε στον συγγραφέα ως ένα πολύ δυναμικό άτομο με έντονη προσωπικότητα. Μία ή δύο φορές το χρόνο, ταξίδευε στο Λονδίνο για να επισκεφτεί τους δύο γιους της, που ασχολούνταν με εστιατόρια. Ήταν άνετη στο να ταξιδεύει μόνη της, μια φορά επισκέφτηκε τη Νέα Υόρκη για να δει τον μεγαλύτερο γιο της. Σε αυτή τη περίπτωση, η Μέλανι βρισκόταν στο Surrey για ένα μήνα και αποφάσισε να επιστρέψει στο σπίτι χωρίς να ειδοποιήσει την οικογένειά της εκεί, προκειμένου να τους κάνει έκπληξη. Η κόρη και η οικογένεια της Μέλανι έλαβαν τα νέα λίγες μέρες αργότερα, χωρίς να συνειδητοποιήσουν ότι η Μέλανι ήταν στην πτήση.

Η 22χρονη Mary Dalton ταξίδευε για να επισκεφτεί τον πατέρα της, που υπηρετούσε με τους Royal Signals στο νησί. Δεν τον είχε δει για περισσότερο από ένα χρόνο, έτσι ήταν κατανοητός ο ενθουσιασμένος για την συνάντησή τους. Σκόπευε να μείνει στην Κύπρο για έξι εβδομάδες.

Η Hilary Smith, 32, και η Joyce White, 29, ήταν συνάδελφοι και πολύ καλές φίλες που συναναστρέφονταν συχνά μαζί και αξιοποιούσαν στο έπακρο τις ταξιδιωτικές παραχωρήσεις του προσωπικού της ΒΕΑ για να ταξιδέψουν στο εξωτερικό. Συχνά σχεδίαζαν μαζί διακοπές και αυτή ήταν η τρίτη φορά που το δίδυμο επισκεπτόταν την Κύπρο. Και οι δύο γυναίκες εργάζονταν για την ΒΕΑ ως ταμίες στο West London Air Terminal. Ο πατέρας της Hilary ήταν Βαπτιστής ιερέας σε εκκλησία στο Richmond, Surrey. Η Joyce ζούσε στο Twickenham, όχι πολύ μακριά από τη φίλη της και σε εξίσου βολική απόσταση για τον κοινό χώρο εργασίας τους. Είχαν ολοκληρώσει τις βάρδιες τους εκείνη την ημέρα πριν κατευθυνθύν στο αεροδρόμιο του Heathrow για να προλάβουν την πτήση τους. Σύμφωνα με το πρόγραμμα ταξιδιών προσωπικού, μπορούσαν να πετάξουν με έκπτωση 90% μόνο εάν υπήρχαν κενές θέσεις στην πτήση. Είχαν θεωρήσει τους εαυτούς των τυχερές που το αεροπλάνο δεν ήταν γεμάτο έτσι και οι δύο έγιναν δεκτές για την πτήση. Η καλή τους τύχη αυξήθηκε ακόμη περισσότερο όταν τους πρόσφεραν θέσεις στο κατά τα άλλα άδειο διαμέρισμα πρώτης θέσης από τους συναδέλφους τους στο προσωπικό καμπίνας.

Από το Λονδίνο ταξίδευε επίσης ένας συνταξιούχος δασολόγος από το Στρόβολο (ή Στροβίλια; δεν ξεκαθαρίζει στο κατάλογο ονομάτων). Ο κ. Ιωάννης Τσιακούρης, είχε πάρει τον γιο του στο σχολείο στο Λονδίνο. Ο κ. David Powell, 27 ετών, που ζούσε στο Eltham Park Gardens, στο νοτιοανατολικό Λονδίνο, και η κυρία Rosalie Stone, 72 ετών, που είχε κλείσει την πτήση της στο Λονδίνο επισκεπτόταν τον γιο της που ζούσε στη Λευκωσία.

Εκτός από το πλήρωμα καμπίνας της ΒΕΑ, έξι επιβάτες από το Λονδίνο αποβιβάστηκαν στην Αθήνα. Η δεσποινίς P. Downie, η οποία ζούσε στο

Battersea, ήταν άλλη μια επιβάτης του προσωπικού της ΒΕΑ, που εργαζόταν στο τμήμα Ground Communication στον σταθμό Ανατολικού Λονδίνου. Ο κ. P.C. Βουλγαρίδης, ο οποίος εργαζόταν για την Greek Line, ταξίδευε από την Αθήνα στη Ρώμη και τη Γένοβα πριν επιστρέψει στο Λονδίνο . Ο Έλληνας ναυτικός, κ. Τσολακάκης, έχοντας αγοράσει το εισιτήριό του στο Londonderry της Βόρειας Ιρλανδίας, τελείωνε το ταξίδι του στην Αθήνα. Η δεσποινίς Πετροπούλου, που εργαζόταν στο ξενοδοχείο Pembridge Gardens στο West End, είχε αγοράσει νωρίτερα εκείνη την ημέρα ένα εισιτήριο μετ' επιστροφής από το Λονδίνο στην Αθήνα. Δύο εισιτήρια είχαν εκδώσει η Ολυμπιακή Αεροπορία, ο εθνικός αερομεταφορέας της Ελλάδας. Ο κ. Παπαδόπουλος είχε ξεκινήσει το ταξίδι του στην Αθήνα, πετώντας για Ζυρίχη, Γενεύη, Παρίσι και Λονδίνο. Αυτό ήταν το τελευταίο σκέλος του ταξιδιού του. Ο κ. Τσοπουρίδης, από τη Θεσσαλονίκη της Ελλάδας, είχε πετάξει στην Αθήνα και από εκεί στη Φρανκφούρτη, το Ντίσελντορφ και το Λονδίνο. Από την Αθήνα θα έπαιρνε άλλη πτήση για το σπίτι του στη Θεσσαλονίκη. Και οι έξι μάζεψαν τα πράγματά τους όταν ο Charlie Oscar προσγειώθηκε στο αεροδρόμιο του Ελληνικού και ακολούθησαν χωριστούς δρόμους για να συνεχίσουν την υπόλοιπη ζωή τους.

Είκοσι από τους 31 επιβάτες που επιβιβάστηκαν στην Αθήνα αποτελούνταν από μια ομάδα Μαρτύρων του Ιεχωβά, οι οποίοι ταξίδευαν για μια διεθνή συνέλευση στην Κύπρο με μέλη της πίστης τους. Είχαν κάνει μαζική κράτηση, τα ονόματα όσων ταξίδευαν είχαν τροποποιηθεί, αλλά ο συνολικός αριθμός στην ομάδα παρέμεινε αμετάβλητος. Τα τελικά μέλη της ομάδας στην πτήση ήταν: ο κ. Αχιλλέας Αφατίτης, 28 ετών, εργολάβος ζωγραφικής από το Νέο Ηράκλειο και η νέα σύζυγός του, Ρεβέκα, 20 ετών, η οποία είχε αρχικά κάνει κράτηση με το πατρικό της όνομα, Σιφναίου. Είχαν αποφασίσει να συνδυάσουν το μήνα του μέλιτος με ένα ταξίδι στη συνέλευση των Μαρτύρων του Ιεχωβά. Την ομάδα αποτελούσε επίσης η κυρία Αρετή Εξαρχέα, 21 ετών από το Αιγάλεο . Η κα Κωνσταντίνα Χριστάκη από την Πολιτεία. Η κα Ιφιγένεια Καλογεροπούλου από το Παλαιό Ψυχικό. Δέσποινα Καρακώστα, 60 από την Ιωνία. Ο κ. Χαράλαμπος Κοντομηνάς και η σύζυγός του Σταβούλα από τον Πειραιά. Ο κ. Γεώργιος Κουτρουμπίνης και η 54 ετών σύζυγός του, Ελένη. Ο κ. Γεράσιμος Διάκου, 48 ετών και η σύζυγός του Πολυξένη, 22 ετών, από την Αθήνα, ο κ. Βασίλειος Μαρκίδης και η 22χρονη κόρη του Ελένη, επίσης από την Αθήνα. Η κ. Ειρήνη Παπανικολάου, 61 ετών, και ο κ. Ιωάννης Ρήγου, 60 ετών, ήταν και οι δύο από το Ηράκλειο. Η δεσποινίς Μαρία Παρζοπούλου, επίσης εξήντα ετών καταγόταν από την Αγία Παρασκευή. Η κυρία Ειρήνη Βολιώτου, 25 ετών, ήταν από την Αθήνα. Η 31χρονη κυρία Παρασκευή Βουγιούκα ήταν επίσης από την Ιωνία. Το τελευταίο μέλος της ομάδας πιστεύεται ότι ήταν ο κ. Ηλίας Ευγέρος, 28 ετών, από την Πέτρα.

Οι άλλοι επιβάτες της Αθήνας ήταν ένα μείγμα ατόμων και ζευγαριών. Όπως ήταν αναμενόμενο, η Νίκη Ροδοσθένους ήταν μαζί με τον Ροδοσθένη Χρήστου. Ο William Sheris, Αμερικανός, ταξίδευε από το Fairfax της Virginia. Η 64χρονη κυρία Δωροθέα Ραχωβίδου επέστρεφε στη Λεμεσό από επίσκεψη στην κόρη της, η οποία έμενε στην ελληνική πρωτεύουσα. Ο κ. Νίκος Παπαπέτρου ήταν πωλητής υποδημάτων από τη Λάρνακα. Επέστρεφε από το πέμπτο ταξίδι του στην Ελλάδα τους τελευταίους δώδεκα μήνες. Συμπλήρωνε το εισόδημά του των 80 λιρών το μήνα με τα χρήματα που κέρδιζε ως επαγγελματίας τζογαδόρος, ενώ ανέπτυξε μια παράπλευρη επιχείρηση εισαγωγής δερμάτινων ειδών και ρολογιών. Ο κ. Κωνσταντίνος Παλαιολόγου και η σύζυγός του Θεογνωσία, από τον Πειραιά, επισκέπτονταν την κόρη τους στην Κύπρο.

Ένας επιβάτης που ήθελε να συμμετάσχει στην πτήση την τελευταία στιγμή διαπίστωσε ότι έπρεπε να εργαστεί πολύ σκληρά για να το πραγματοποιήσει. Ο Αβραάμ Σολωμού εργαζόταν απευθείας για τον τότε Κύπριο υπουργό Εξωτερικών Σπύρο Κυπριανού. Τα επίσημα καθήκοντά του ήταν αυτά του οδηγού και του προσωπικού βοηθού. Ωστόσο, ο κ. Σολωμού υπήρξε ενεργό μέλος της οργάνωσης της ΕΟΚΑ[92], η οποία είχε αναλάβει παραστρατιωτική δραστηριότητα τη δεκαετία του 1950 κατά τη διάρκεια του κυπριακού αγώνα (για Ένωση της Κύπρου με την Ελλάδα) αλλά επιτεύχθηκε αντί αυτού ανεξαρτησία από το Ηνωμένο Βασίλειο. Είχε μόνιμες ουλές από τραύματα από σφαίρες για να επαληθεύσει τα διαπιστευτήριά του ως μαχητής της ελευθερίας[93].

Ο κ. Σολωμού χρειαζόταν να επιστρέψει στη Λευκωσία για ένα σημαντικό ραντεβού την επόμενη μέρα, αλλά του είχε εκδοθεί λάθος εισιτήριο και δεν μπορούσε να μπει στην πτήση. Είχε γίνει αρκετά κατηγορηματικός, σύμφωνα με το προσωπικό του check-in, επιμένοντας ότι ήταν απαραίτητο να ήταν στο CY284 και αρνούμενος να περιμένει την πτήση αργότερα εκείνο το πρωί. Τελικά, το θέμα λύθηκε και ο κ. Σολωμού αφέθηκε να πάρει μια από τις κενές θέσεις, που πιστεύεται ότι ήταν η 16 C.

Ο ανώτερος αεροσυνοδός Ιωάννης Λοΐζου ήταν υπεύθυνος του πληρώματος καμπίνας και την εν πτήσει εξυπηρέτηση από την γαλέρα εμπρός με βοηθό την αεροσυνοδό Καλλιόπη Φώτου. Ο Ιωάννης ήταν γνωστός με την αγγλική εκδοχή του ονόματός του, John, ενώ η Καλλιόπη ήταν γνωστή στους φίλους και τους συναδέλφους της ως Πόπη. Από την

---

[92] *ΕΟΚΑ [Εθνική Οργάνωση ΚυπρίωνΑγωνιστών]*

[93] *Ο Σπύρος Κυπριανού ήταν εξέχων Κύπριος πολιτικός και αργότερα διετέλεσε Πρόεδρος της Κύπρου από το 1977 έως το 1988.*

πίσω γαλέρα εργάζονταν ο αεροσυνοδός Νίκος Χασαπόπουλος και η αεροσυνοδός Θέλμα Εφρέμη.

Οι Κυπριακές Αερογραμμές ήταν μια ακόμη πιο δεμένη κοινότητα από την ΒΕΑ. Ο Ιωάννης Λοΐζου και ο Νίκος Χασαπόπουλος ήταν στο ίδιο σχολείο για δώδεκα χρόνια πριν ενταχθούν στην αεροπορική εταιρεία. Ο αδερφός του John (Ιωάννη), Λούης, επίσης αεροσυνοδός στην Cyprus Airways, ήταν συμμαθητής του αδελφού του Νίκου. Ο Λούης εργαζόταν συχνά στις πτήσεις Comet και επρόκειτο να πραγματοποιήσει την πτήση Αθήνα προς Λευκωσία, CY264, αργότερα εκείνη την ημέρα. Καθώς οι αδερφοί Λοΐζου έμεναν και οι δύο στην Αθήνα πριν από τις πτήσεις τους, είχαν μοιραστεί ένα γεύμα με συναδέλφους και φίλους το βράδυ πριν εμφανιστεί ο John για υπηρεσία στο αεροδρόμιο της Αθήνας. Αυτό περιελάμβανε τον Νίκο Χασαπόπουλο καθώς και δύο αεροσυνοδούς από την πτήση του Λούη. Καθώς απολάμβαναν τη βραδινή τους έξοδο, ο John είπε στον Λούη ότι περίμενε έναν VIP επιβάτη, τον Στρατηγό Γεώργιο Γρίβα, να ταξιδέψει στην πτήση. Τα αδέρφια το συζήτησαν εκτενώς, καθώς είχαν προηγουμένως συναντήσεις που ο Λούης, αργότερα περιέγραψε ως θυελλώδεις συναντήσεις με μέλη της ακολουθίας του Στρατηγού. Ο Γρίβας είχε ηγηθεί της οργάνωσης της ΕΟΚΑ κατά τη διάρκεια του αγώνα της χώρας για ανεξαρτησία από τη Βρετανία και τώρα ήταν αρχηγός της Κυπριακής Εθνικής Φρουράς. Η Κύπρος περνούσε ακόμη μια περίοδο αναταραχής, στην οποία ο Γρίβας ήταν εξέχουσα προσωπικότητα.

Ο ανώτερος αεροσυνοδός Φρίξος Μιχαήλ είχε προσφερθεί να ανταλλάξει πτήσεις με τον John Λοΐζου, καθώς έστελνε μια ακριβή αποστολή με τσάντες στη Λευκωσία. Ενώ συνήθως θα το έκανε, σε αυτήν την περίπτωση ο John αρνήθηκε, για έναν πολύ ιδιαίτερο λόγο. Είχε σχέση εξ αποστάσεως με μία αεροσυνοδό της ΒΕΑ που ζούσε στο Λονδίνο.

Σύμφωνα με τον Λούη, ο αδερφός του ήταν πολύ ερωτευμένος με τη Josephine Coldicott, η οποία είχε την έδρα της στο Λονδίνο. Ο John και η Josephine είχαν περιορισμένες ευκαιρίες να περάσουν χρόνο μαζί και όταν εκείνη έγραψε ότι είχε δέκα μέρες άδεια για να περάσει μαζί του στην Κύπρο, δεν θα μπορούσε να είναι πιο ευχαριστημένος. Ο Λούης θυμάται τον αδερφό του να του εκμυστηρεύεται ότι ήθελε να κάνει πρόταση γάμου στη Josephine γιατί ήταν, για εκείνον, «η μία». Η Josephine, η οποία δικαιούταν να χρησιμοποιήσει το πρόγραμμα ευνοϊκών ταξιδιών της ΒΕΑ, είχε γράψει στον John λίγες μέρες νωρίτερα, για να του πει ότι σχεδίαζε να είναι στην πτήση Λονδίνου προς Λευκωσία το βράδυ της 11ης Οκτωβρίου, στην πτήση που θα αναχωρούσε από την Αθήνα ως CY284 :

7/10/67
Αγαπητέ John.

Απλά μια πολύ γρήγορη σημείωση για να πω ευχαριστώ για την υπέροχη επιστολή σου. Ήταν τόσο καλό που άκουσα από σένα όπως πάντα. Εκτός και αν ακούσω από σένα διαφορετικά, θα φτάσω στη Λευκωσία στις 0550 με το CY284. Καθώς είναι πολύ νωρίς το πρωί, μπορεί επίσης να εργάζεσαι κ.λπ. Θα καταλάβω αν δεν είσαι στο αεροδρόμιο John και ίσως θα μπορούσες να μου αφήσεις ένα μήνυμα με τη Cyprus Airways στο αεροδρόμιο, να με ενημερώσεις για το ακριβές μέρος όπου να πάω και να πάρω ταξί.

Ανυπομονώ να σε ξαναδώ και καθώς δεν ήμουν πολύ καλά και δούλευα σκληρά, χρειάζομαι πραγματικά διακοπές. Το μόνο πράγμα που πρέπει να πω είναι ότι νιώθω άγχος που θα σε ξανασυναντήσω μετά από τόσο καιρό. Έψαχνα στα καταστήματα να σου αγοράσω ένα δώρο, αλλά δεν μπορούσα να αποφασίσω, οπότε θα περιμένω και θα σε ρωτήσω και μπορώ να σου το στείλω όταν επιστρέψω εδώ.

Θα σου φέρω τα τσιγάρα και θα πιω στην υγειά σου όπως έκανα πριν.

Φρόντισε τον εαυτό σου John και ελπίζω να σε δω κάποια στιγμή την επόμενη Πέμπτη.

Ο Θεός να ευλογεί.

Πολλή αγάπη από
Josephine xxxxx

Ο John είχε κάθε πρόθεση να είναι σε εκείνη την πτήση, αν και δεν της είχε αναφέρει το γεγονός, και ήταν αποφασισμένος να εκπλήξει τη Josephine όταν ανέλαβε στην Αθήνα ως ανώτερος αεροσυνοδός για την πτήση προς Λευκωσία.

Όλοι οι επιβάτες επιβιβάστηκαν στο αεροσκάφος. Η Josephine Coldicott ήταν πολύ χαρούμενη που την υποδέχτηκε ο John Λοΐζου τόσο νωρίτερα από όσο περίμενε. Δεν υπήρχε κανένα σημάδι του Στρατηγού Γρίβα, έτσι οι επιβάτες του προσωπικού BEA, μεταξύ των οποίων τώρα και η Josephine, οδηγήθηκαν στην κατά τα άλλα αχρησιμοποίητη καμπίνα πρώτης θέσης, ένα κανονικό προνόμιο για όσους πετούσαν μεταξύ φίλων. Ο John και η Josephine, ειδικά, ήθελαν αυτό να είναι ένα αξέχαστο ταξίδι.

Μέσα στην νύχτα

Οι πόρτες έκλεισαν και το αεροσκάφος ασφαλίστηκε από το προσωπικό της καμπίνας, οι τρεις πιλότοι πέρασαν μεθοδικά τις διαδικασίες που έφεραν ξανά στη ζωή το Charlie Oscar. Η ισχύς εδάφους χρησιμοποιήθηκε για την τροφοδοσία των ηλεκτρικών συστημάτων, μέχρι να λειτουργήσουν τα τέσσερα turbo jet της Rolls-Royce Avon. Η επίγεια μονάδα ισχύος, μια τεράστια ρυμουλκούμενη γεννήτρια, απομακρύνθηκε από το δρόμο, δεν χρειαζόταν πλέον. Οι λίστες ελέγχου επιβεβαίωσαν ότι όλα ήταν εντάξει και το Charlie Oscar ήταν έτοιμο να αναχωρήσει για τη Λευκωσία. Μόλις ο Καπετάνιος Blackwood έμεινε ικανοποιημένος, ο SFO Thomas ζήτησε από τον Ελεγκτή Εναέριας Κυκλοφορίας (ATC) την άδεια να ξεκινήσει τις μηχανές του. Και οι τέσσερις κινητήρες Avon λειτουργούσαν ομαλά, το πλήρωμα ολοκλήρωσε τους ελέγχους και στη συνέχεια ζήτησε άδεια να κινηθεί προς τον αεροδιάδρομο.

Ο SFO Thomas ξεκίνησε ελιγμούς με τον Charlie Oscar προσεκτικά προς τον αεροδιάδρομο. Μακριά από τις φωταγωγημένες κερκίδες, οι πιλότοι καθοδηγήθηκαν από τα φώτα εκατέρωθεν του μονοπατιού της ασφάλτου που οδηγούσε στον διάδρομο 33. Στη συνέχεια, ο SFO Thomas επικοινώνησε με τον πύργο ελέγχου λαμβάνοντας άδεια για τη διέλευση των αεραγωγών που θα ήταν η διαδρομή τους προς τη Λευκωσία.

Απογειώνοντας το αεροσκάφος προς τα βόρεια βορειοδυτικά, λόγω του βόρειου ανέμου που φυσούσε με δέκα κόμβους, αυτό σκαρφάλωνε ευθεία ενώ οι τροχοί αποσύρθηκαν, οι ρυθμίσεις του πτερυγίου προσαρμόστηκαν και η ταχύτητα αέρα αυξήθηκε στο σημείο όπου μπορούσε να ξεκινήσει μια σταθερή ανάβαση. Μόλις μπορούσε να το κάνει με ασφάλεια, και συνήθως πριν φτάσει τα 500 πόδια, ο Καπετάνιος Blackwood άρχιζε μια στροφή προς τα αριστερά. Αυτό θα απομακρύνει το αεροσκάφος από τις κατοικημένες περιοχές στην Αθήνα και το λιμάνι του Πειραιά, προκειμένου να μειωθεί η ενόχληση στον τοπικό πληθυσμό που δημιουργείται από έναν Κομήτη σε αναρρίχηση. Καθώς το Charlie Oscar αντέστρεφε την πορεία του, θα κατευθυνόταν προς τα νότια του αεροδρομίου μέχρι να φτάσει τα τέσσερεις χιλιάδες πόδια, όταν θα κατευθυνόταν κατευθείαν για έναν άλλο φάρο αεροναυτιλίας, στο Ακρωτήριο Σούνιο.

Ο τροχιόδρομος, εκείνη την εποχή, δεν εκτεινόταν στο νότιο άκρο του αερο-διαδρόμου 33, οπότε ο Κομήτης έπρεπε να χρησιμοποιήσει τον ίδιο τον διάδρομο για να φτάσει στην περιοχή στροφής στο άκρο του. Παρά το μέγιστο βάρος απογείωσης, η κοινή λογική και οι βέλτιστες πρακτικές σήμαιναν να ξεκινούσε την απογείωση με όσο το δυνατόν μεγαλύτερο μέρος του διαδρόμου μπροστά από το αεροσκάφος.

Το Charlie Oscar είχε φτάσει στο τέλος του διαδρόμου 33 και είχε γυρίσει να ευθυγραμμιστεί με την κεντρική γραμμή του διαδρόμου. Το πλήρωμα καμπίνας είχε πραγματοποιήσει τους ελέγχους ασφαλείας και είχε πάρει τις θέσεις του. Οι τελικοί έλεγχοι πριν από την απογείωση ήταν σωστοί. Κατόπιν αιτήματος του Mike Thomas, το Athens ATC του έδωσε το πράσινο φως για να πάρει μπροστά με την απογείωση, να αφήσει τα φρένα και να επιταχύνει μέχρι να σηκωθούν από το έδαφος. Τονίστηκε για άλλη μια φορά η οδηγία για στροφή προς τα αριστερά. Κάπου μεταξύ τριάντα πέντε και σαράντα δευτερόλεπτα αργότερα, το Charlie Oscar βρισκόταν στο αέρα.

Η ATC επιβεβαίωσε την ώρα αναχώρησης στις 02:31. Με ασφάλεια στην ανάβαση, ο Mike Thomas συντόνισε ξανά το VHF του αεροσκάφους στα 119.1 MHz, τη συχνότητα για την προσέγγιση Athens Approach, υπεύθυνη για το συντονισμό των κινήσεων των αεροσκαφών κοντά στο αεροδρόμιο της Αθήνας.

Ο Κομήτης ανέβηκε γρήγορα. Δεν υπήρχε πλήρες φορτίο, είτε επιβατών είτε καυσίμων, οπότε υπήρχε άφθονη ισχύς. Το Charlie Oscar είχε φτάσει τα 4.000 πόδια όπως είχε προηγουμένως καθοριστεί.

Τρία λεπτά αργότερα, ο Mike Thomas έδωσε μια περαιτέρω ενημέρωση στο Athens Approach, με το Charlie Oscar να έχει φτάσει στον φάρο του Σουνίου σε υψόμετρο 10.500 ποδιών. Όπως είχε προηγουμένως καθοριστεί ο Καπετάνιος Blackwood συνέχιζε την ανάβασή του στο καθορισμένο ύψος διαδρομής των 29.000 ποδιών. Περίμενε να ενταχθεί στον αεραγωγό μεγάλου υψομέτρου, R19, και να περάσει το επόμενο σημείο αναφοράς, R19B, στις 0246. Καθώς τώρα έφευγαν από την περιοχή του αεροδρομίου της Αθήνας, μεταφέρθηκαν στο Κέντρο Ελέγχου Αθηνών (ACC), το οποίο συντόνιζε πτήσεις μεγάλου ύψους στην περιοχή. Ο SFO Thomas άλλαξε τη συχνότητα για άλλη μια φορά, στα 124.4 MHz.

Ο SFO Thomas επιβεβαίωσε ότι είχαν περάσει τον φάρο του Σουνίου στις 02:36 και περνούσαν πάνω από την Ιουλίδα, περίπου δέκα μίλια νοτιοανατολικά του Ακρωτηρίου Σουνίου. Το πλήρωμα επιβεβαίωσε ότι περίμενε να φτάσει στο R19B στις 02:46.

Στην καμπίνα, ο John Λοΐζου και η ομάδα καμπίνας ζέσταιναν τα κουτιά γευμάτων που περιείχαν τα ζεστά πρωινά για τους επιβάτες. Σε μια τόσο σύντομη πτήση, η προετοιμασία και το σερβίρισμα των γευμάτων έπρεπε να ολοκληρωθεί χωρίς καθυστέρηση. Θα προσφερόταν επίσης τσάι και καφές, μαζί με πωλήσεις ποτών. Με τις πινακίδες της ζώνης ασφαλείας κλειστές και το αεροσκάφος να σκαρφαλώνει σε ήρεμο αέρα, οι επιβάτες ήταν πλέον ελεύθεροι να σηκωθούν και να μετακινηθούν στην καμπίνα, κάτι που δυσκόλεψε την υπηρεσία γευμάτων, αλλά το πλήρωμα τα κατάφερε θαυμάσια.

Στη συνέχεια, το Charlie Oscar έλαβε μήνυμα από τον Κομήτη BEA[94] που εκτελούσε το αντίστοιχο δρομολόγιο από τη Λευκωσία στην Αθήνα. Ωστόσο, σε αυτό το σημείο, είναι προφανές ότι δεν μπόρεσαν να ακούσουν το μήνυμα και το έθεσαν υπόψη του Κέντρου Ελέγχου Αθηνών. Ο Charlie Oscar βρισκόταν τώρα στα 21.500 πόδια και εξακολουθούσε να σκαρφαλώνει. Έχοντας επίγνωση της προσέγγισης του Bealine Mike Foxtrot, η Αθήνα έδωσε εντολή στο Charlie Oscar να σκαρφαλώσει όσο το δυνατόν γρηγορότερα, για να ανέβει πάνω από το άλλο αεροσκάφος πριν διασταυρωθούν οι δρόμοι τους.

Είχαν περάσει λιγότερο από δεκαπέντε λεπτά από τότε που είχαν απογειωθεί από την Αθήνα. Είχαν ανέβει στα 28.000 πόδια όσο το δυνατόν γρηγορότερα, κάτι που αναγνώρισε ο ελεγκτής. Ένα λεπτό αργότερα, το Charlie Oscar πέρασε το σημείο αναφοράς στο Red 19B και ενημέρωσε την Αθήνα για αυτό, όπως χρειαζόταν. Ο Thomas πρόσθεσε ότι βρίσκονταν στο υψόμετρο πλεύσης των 29.000 ποδιών και αναμένεται να περάσουν τη Ρόδο στις 03:03. Η ATC Αθηνών αναγνώρισε το μήνυμα, δίνοντας εντολή στο πλήρωμα να διατηρήσει αυτό το υψόμετρο και να κάνει αναφορά πάνω από τη Ρόδο.

Εκτός από τα αστέρια, λίγα λεπτά με απόλυτο σκοτάδι έμειναν, πριν αρχίσει να φωτίζει ο ανατολικός ουρανός[95]. Ο Captain Emmerson, στο Bealine Mike Foxtrot, είδε τα φώτα προσγείωσης του Charlie Oscar να πλησιάζουν από τα δυτικά, χίλια πόδια πάνω από αυτόν, που ήταν ο ελάχιστος νόμιμος διαχωρισμός ανά ύψος. Ο χαιρετισμός, «Καλημέρα», ήρθε μέσω του ασυρμάτου VHF, στον οποίο απάντησε με τον ίδιο τρόπο, αναβοσβήνοντας τα φώτα προσγείωσης του δικού του αεροσκάφους. Την ανταλλαγή εντόπισε το Κέντρο Ελέγχου Αθηνών. Τέτοιες ευγένειες δεν ήταν ασυνήθιστες τις μικρές ώρες σε μια κατά τα άλλα έρημη τοποθεσία.

Ο SFO Thomas ενημέρωσε την Αθήνα ότι το Charlie Oscar περνούσε τη Ρόδο στις 03:04 ώρες, ακόμα στα 29.000 πόδια, και ότι υπολόγισαν το σημείο αναφοράς στους R19 C στις 03:16. Δεν έγινε καμία αναφορά για κάτι κακό στο αεροσκάφος. Στην καμπίνα, ο John Λοΐζου και η ομάδα του είχαν καθαρίσει τα απομεινάρια από τα ζεστά πρωινά των επιβατών και

---

[94] *Το δρομολόγιο της επιστροφής, που λειτουργούσε ως CY285 προς Αθήνα, μετά BE285 και μετά στο Heathrow του Λονδίνου, εκτελούνταν εκείνο τη νύχτα από τον Captain L. Emmerson, στον Comet 4B G-APMF, φωνητικά Golf Alpha Papa Mike Foxtrot. Η πτήση είχε καθυστερήσει στη Λευκωσία λόγω τεχνικών προβλημάτων.*

[95] *Η ανατολή του ηλίου στην Αττάλεια στις 12 Οκτωβρίου είναι 0705LT / 0505Z. Ο Ήλιος ανατέλλει έξι λεπτά νωρίτερα στα 29.000 πόδια. επομένως η ανατολή του ηλίου θα ήταν 0659LT/0459Z. Το Twilight (αστρονομικό) ήταν 0635LT στο έδαφος και 0529LT/0229Z στα 29.000 πόδια.*

βρίσκονταν στο πίσω μέρος, ετοιμάζοντας να μετρήσουν και να σφραγίσουν. Ο Λούης Λοΐζου θυμάται ότι, σε αυτό το σημείο της σχετικά σύντομης πτήσης, ο διάδρομος θα καταλαμβανόταν από πολλούς επιβάτες όρθιους για να τεντώσουν τα πόδια τους για λίγα λεπτά πριν το αεροσκάφος ξεκινήσει την κάθοδό του στη Λευκωσία.

Στις 03:16, δώδεκα λεπτά μετά την τελευταία του κλήση στην Αθήνα, ο SFO Thomas είχε προσπαθήσει να επικοινωνήσει με τον ελεγκτή για να επιβεβαιώσει ότι το Charlie Oscar περνούσε το δεύτερο σημείο αναφοράς, το R19C. Ήταν πλέον εκτός εμβέλειας του ασυρμάτου, οπότε ο Καπετάνιος Emmerson στο Mike Foxtrot, ακούγοντας το μήνυμα, το μετέδωσε στην Αθήνα. Για άλλη μια φορά, αυτή ήταν μια πρακτική ρουτίνας εκείνη την εποχή.

Δύο λεπτά αργότερα, στις 03:18, ο SFO Mike Thomas πληκτρολόγησε το μικρόφωνό του και ξεκίνησε την αρχική του κλήση επικοινωνίας στο ATC της Λευκωσίας, «Καλημέρα, Nicky, Bealine Golf Alpha Romeo Charlie Osc...»

Καθώς μιλούσε, στην καμπίνα των επιβατών, ξέσπασε όλη η κόλαση...

Στα Βαθιά Νερά

Από την αρχή, αναγνωρίστηκε ότι η έλλειψη συντριμμιών, ιδίως τμημάτων του πλαισίου του αεροσκάφους και των κινητήρων, και η απουσία του καταγραφέα δεδομένων πτήσης, ήταν πιθανό να παρεμποδίσουν ή να αποτρέψουν την έρευνα για τον προσδιορισμό της αιτίας της συντριβής. Ωστόσο, το Charlie Oscar, είχε πέσει στη Μεσόγειο σε ένα μέρος όπου το βάθος του ήταν μεταξύ εννέα και δεκαπέντε χιλιάδες πόδια. Αυτό ήταν πιθανό να είναι ένα τεράστιο πρόβλημα, αν όχι ανυπέρβλητο. Ο ανώμαλος βυθός της θάλασσας κατέστησε πολύ δύσκολο να εκτιμηθεί ακριβώς πόσο βαθιά μπορεί να βρίσκονται τα συντρίμμια του Charlie Oscar. Στις 16 Οκτωβρίου, ο κ. Riddoch και ο Eric Newton, μαζί με τον John Veal, είχαν συνάντηση με τον κ. Peter Flett, Αξιωματικό Ναυτικής Διάσωσης στο Υπουργείο Άμυνας. Παρευρέθηκε επίσης ο διοικητής Sims-Ross, του Πολεμικού Ναυτικού των Ηνωμένων Πολιτειών. Ο κ. Flett εξήγησε ότι ο εξοπλισμός του Βασιλικού Ναυτικού ήταν ανεπαρκής για το έργο, ειδικά λαμβάνοντας υπόψη το βάθος του νερού στο οποίο βρισκόταν πλέον το Charlie Oscar. Το Υπουργείο Εξωτερικών θεώρησε ότι το Πολεμικό Ναυτικό των ΗΠΑ ήταν πολύ καλύτερα εξοπλισμένο, και πράγματι το τελευταίο είχε χρήσιμη εμπειρία στη διάσωση σε πολύ βαθιά νερά[96]. Ο διοικητής Sims-Ross είπε στη συνάντηση, μετά από επικοινωνία που είχε με την Ουάσιγκτον το Σαββατοκύριακο, ότι δύο πλοία, το *Aluminaut* και το *Alvin*, θα μπορούσαν χρησιμοποιηθούν εάν αποφάσιζαν τον εντοπισμό και την ανάκτηση των συντριμμιών.

Το *Aluminaut*, ένα υποβρύχιο από αλουμίνιο, είχε χρησιμοποιηθεί για την αναζήτηση μιας χαμένης αμερικανικής βόμβας υδρογόνου στα ανοιχτά του Palomares το 1966. Η Reynolds Aluminium Company, η οποία είχε κατασκευάσει και χειριστεί την *Aluminaut*, ήθελε να εμπλακεί. Είχε δοθεί μια εκτίμηση κόστους, το μηνιαίο ποσό των $200.000 ανά μήνα συμπεριλαμβανομένου του πληρώματος. Ωστόσο, αποκαλύφθηκε ότι το *Aluminaut* ήταν σκάφος έρευνας και όχι ανάκτησης και δεν θα μπορούσε να διασώσει συντρίμμια από το Charlie Oscar.

---

[96] *Τον Ιανουάριο του 1966, ένα βομβαρδιστικό Β-52, που μετέφερε τρεις βόμβες υδρογόνου, συγκρούστηκε με ένα εναέριο δεξαμενόπλοιο KC-135 κατά τη διάρκεια μιας επιχείρησης ανεφοδιασμού στον αέρα πάνω από το Palomares της Ισπανίας. Δύο από τις βόμβες έπεσαν στη στεριά, αλλά η τρίτη έπεσε στη Μεσόγειο Θάλασσα. Το Πολεμικό Ναυτικό των ΗΠΑ είχε καταφέρει να εντοπίσει τις δύο τοποθεσίες και να ανακτήσει την εξαφανισμένη βόμβα Η, προς ανακούφιση τουλάχιστον του τοπικού πληθυσμού.*

Το *Alvin*, αντίθετα, ήταν εξοπλισμένο για επιχειρήσεις διάσωσης και μπορούσε επίσης να λειτουργήσει μέχρι τα 6.000 πόδια νερού. Ουσιαστικά, τα δύο σκάφη θα μπορούσαν να λειτουργούν παράλληλα, το *Aluminaut* να ψάχνει και το *Alvin* να ανασύρει όσα συντρίμμια μπορούσε να φτάσει. Υπήρχε πρόβλημα όμως όσον αφορά το σχεδιασμό και το βαθμό ακρίβειας που απαιτείται.

Η μεταφορά των δύο σκαφών από και προς τις Ηνωμένες Πολιτείες θα χρειαζόταν περίπου ένα μήνα προς κάθε κατεύθυνση και ο χρόνος στον σταθμό για την έρευνα εκτιμήθηκε ότι ήταν ένας ακόμη μήνας, ανεβάζοντας το εκτιμώμενο κόστος, αν όλα πήγαιναν καλά, σε περίπου $2.000.000. Αυτό θα κάλυπτε μια περιοχή αναζήτησης περίπου 15 τετραγωνικών μιλίων, υποθέτοντας ότι οι επιχειρήσεις θα συνεχίζονταν κάθε μέρα. Σημειώθηκε ότι η θέση της σύγκρουσης, εκείνη τη στιγμή, δεν ήταν πιο ακριβής από συν ή πλην πέντε μίλια, πράγμα που σημαίνει ότι η πιθανή περιοχή αναζήτησης θα ήταν επομένως της τάξης των εκατό τετραγωνικών μιλίων. Δεδομένης της εποχής του χρόνου, καθώς και του χρόνου για να φτάσει ο εξοπλισμός στη σκηνή, η Ανατολική Μεσόγειος θα βιώσει σχεδόν σίγουρα περιόδους κακοκαιρίας, αυξάνοντας ακόμη περισσότερο το συνολικό κόστος, αλλά και πάλι θεωρήθηκε ότι δεν θα είχαν περισσότερο από 10% πιθανότητα επιτυχίας.

Στη συνάντηση εξετάστηκε επίσης η δυνατότητα χρήσης τηλεοπτικών καμερών για την εξερεύνηση του βυθού. Ο κατάλληλος εξοπλισμός στις ΗΠΑ μπορούσε να λειτουργεί σε βάθη έως και 4.700 πόδια, αν και θα μπορούσε να επεκταθεί στα 6.000 με πρόσθετο καλώδιο. Αυτός ο εξοπλισμός προσφέρθηκε χωρίς κόστος εκτός από τα πραγματοποιηθέντα έξοδα.

Στις 9 Νοεμβρίου, ο John Veal συναντήθηκε με τον Bill Mallalieu, τον Υπουργό Εμπορίου στο Λονδίνο. Μαζί τους συμμετείχαν ο κ. Riddoch, ο κ. Flett, ο Διοικητής Sims-Ross και ο Captain Searle, Επόπτης της Διάσωσης Αμερικανικού Ναυτικού. Ο κ. Mallalieu εξήγησε στους Αμερικανούς ότι ήταν ευγνώμων για τη συνεργασία τους τις τελευταίες εβδομάδες και ότι ήθελε πολύ να βρεθούν τα συντρίμμια του G-ARCO προκειμένου να ανακαλυφθεί η αιτία της τραγωδίας. Ωστόσο, επεσήμανε, η κυβέρνηση χρειαζόταν κάποια ένδειξη για τις πιθανότητες επιτυχίας εάν αποφάσιζε να ακολουθήσει τον πολύ δαπανηρό δρόμο της πρόσληψης του *Aluminaut*.

Ο Captain Searle εξήγησε ότι το *Aluminaut* μπορούσε να λειτουργήσει για αρκετά μεγάλες περιόδους σε σημαντικά βάθη. Ωστόσο, δεν ήταν ασφαλισμένο να εργάζεται σε βάθη περισσότερα από 8.000 πόδια και μεγαλύτερα βάθη θα ήταν ακόμη πιο επικίνδυνο.

Στο τέλος, ο Malllalieu αποφάσισε ότι ήταν καιρός να τραβήξει μια γραμμή. Λαμβάνοντας υπόψη τις συμβουλές από διάφορες πλευρές, εμφανίστηκε ενώπιον της Βουλής των Κοινοτήτων στις 22 Νοεμβρίου για να πει:

«Η πιθανότητα διάσωσης έχει εξεταστεί προσεκτικά με εμπειρογνώμονες του Υπουργείου Άμυνας και του Ναυτικού των Ηνωμένων Πολιτειών και έχω συζητήσει προσωπικά το θέμα με τον Επόπτη του Ναυτικού των Ηνωμένων Πολιτειών. Είναι σαφές ότι η διάσωση των συντριμμιών θα ήταν ανέφικτη και ότι μια προσπάθεια ανάκτησης μόνο του καταγραφέα πτήσης θα ήταν μια εξαιρετικά δύσκολη, χρονοβόρα και ίσως επικίνδυνη επιχείρηση με ελάχιστες προοπτικές επιτυχίας. Λαμβάνοντας υπόψη αυτό, καθώς και στοιχεία που υποδεικνύουν την έκρηξη ισχυρής εκρηκτικής ύλης στην καμπίνα του αεροσκάφους, (έχει αποφασιστεί) ότι το ζήτημα της διάσωσης δεν πρέπει να επιδιωχθεί.»

Πτώματα Αποδείξεων

Το έργο της διενέργειας νεκροψίας για τα θύματα που ανασύρθηκαν έπεσε στον Captain Ken Mason, της ομάδας του Τμήματος Αεροπορίας και Ιατροδικαστικής Παθολογίας της RAF. Γεννημένος το 1920, ο Mason επρόκειτο να περάσει τριάντα χρόνια δουλεύοντας ως παθολόγος της RAF, έχοντας χαρακτηριστεί από τους συναδέλφους του στην μετέπειτα καριέρα του στο Πανεπιστήμιο του Εδιμβούργου[97] ως «...πρωτοπόρος της παθολογίας της αεροπορίας».

Η δουλειά του Mason και του συναδέλφου του, του Squadron Leader Stan Tarlton, ήταν εξαιρετικά επίπονη. Έχοντας ενημερωθεί για τη συντριβή το πρωί της 12ης Οκτωβρίου, το δίδυμο ταξίδεψε στην Ελλάδα, φεύγοντας από το Heathrow στις 2245 το ίδιο βράδυ και φτάνοντας στην Αθήνα στις 02:15 της 13ης Οκτωβρίου, ακριβώς 24 ώρες αφότου το Charlie Oscar είχε κάνει το ίδιο ταξίδι. Όταν έφτασαν στην Αθήνα, ενημερώθηκαν ότι η πλειονότητα των σορών μεταφέρονταν στη Ρόδο, όπου αναμένονταν νωρίς το ίδιο πρωί. Ταξίδεψαν λοιπόν στη Ρόδο, φτάνοντας στις 09:30.

Ο Mason και ο Tarlton είχαν συνάντηση στις 11:30 με τον Captain Baillie και τον Dr. Preston, Chief Medical Officer της ΒΕΑ, μαζί με δύο Έλληνες εκπροσώπους, τον κ. Π. Αποστολίδη του Υπουργείου Εξωτερικών και τον Κ. Χριστόπουλο, Συμβούλιο Υγείας Πολιτικής Αεροπορίας. Παρόντες ήταν επίσης ανώνυμοι εκπρόσωποι των Κυπριακών Αερογραμμών και ο κ. Canyon, από τη Βρετανική Ένωση Βαλσαμοποιών. Ο κ. Χριστόπουλος περιέγραψε την επίσημη θέση σχετικά με τις υγειονομικές πτυχές της ταυτοποίησης, της ταρίχευσης και της ταφής των σορών. Ο Mason και ο Tarlton ήταν αντίθετοι με την ιδέα να προσκαλούνταν συγγενείς των θυμάτων για να αναγνωρίσουν τα πτώματα, καθώς κάτι τέτοιο, κατά την άποψή τους, θα παρενοχλούσε τη δουλειά τους. Ο κ. Χριστόπουλος απέρριψε τις διαμαρτυρίες τους,

---

[97] Ο John Kenyon («Ken») French Mason CBE υπηρέτησε για τρεις δεκαετίες ως ιατροδικαστής στη Βασιλική Πολεμική Αεροπορία. Εστιάζοντας στην αεροπορική ιατρική, ανέβηκε στις τάξεις για να γίνει Captain της ομάδας και διευθυντής του Τμήματος Αεροπορίας και Ιατροδικαστικής Παθολογίας της RAF και καλούνταν τακτικά για να ερευνήσει αεροπορικά ατυχήματα. Ως αναγνώριση της συμβολής του στην ιατροδικαστική παθολογία των αεροπορικών ατυχημάτων, το 1973 του απονεμήθηκε ο Τίτλος του Διοικητή του Τάγματος της Βρετανικής Αυτοκρατορίας (Στρατιωτική Μεραρχία). Στη συνέχεια κατείχε τη θέση του Καθηγητή Ιατροδικαστικής στο Πανεπιστήμιο του Εδιμβούργου. Στη συνέχεια ανέπτυξε μια τρίτη καριέρα στο ιατρικό δίκαιο. Η καριέρα του διήρκεσε τελικά 74 χρόνια. Πέθανε στις 26 Ιανουαρίου 2017 σε ηλικία 97 ετών. Ο Stan Tarlton πέθανε το 2014.

εξηγώντας ότι η παρουσία συγγενών ήταν απαραίτητη για τη διαδικασία ταυτοποίησης.

Στη συνέχεια, ο Mason και ο Tarlton πήγαν στο Νοσοκομείο της Ρόδου για να οργανώσουν τις μεταθανάτιες εξετάσεις. Ενώ προσπαθούσαν να το κάνουν, διακόπτονταν συνεχώς από υποτιθέμενα επείγοντα τηλεφωνήματα, τα περισσότερα από τα οποία αποδείχτηκε ότι ήταν από τον Τύπο. Ως αποτέλεσμα, δεν κατάφεραν να ξεκινήσουν τις νεκροψίες μέχρι τις 15:00, οπότε μέχρι τότε είχαν μείνει τριάντα ώρες χωρίς ύπνο. Ο Mason θεώρησε ότι οι συνθήκες δεν ήταν ιδανικές. Το νεκροτομείο στην πραγματικότητα αποτελείτο από ένα τραπέζι χωρίς αποχέτευση. Υπήρχε ένας νιπτήρας που γρήγορα βουλώθηκε. Η τοποθεσία του νεκροτομείου σήμαινε επίσης ότι ήταν αδύνατο να εργαστεί κανείς δίχως παιδιά και ενήλικες να κοιτάζουν από το παράθυρο. Μέχρι τώρα, φυσικά, ο Mason και ο Tarlton ήταν εξαιρετικά κουρασμένοι και κατάφεραν να ολοκληρώσουν έξι εξετάσεις πριν χρειαστεί να σταματήσουν στις 19:00 για να παρευρεθούν σε διάσκεψη με τον Captain Baillie.

Οι ελληνικές αρχές ήταν δυσαρεστημένες, σύμφωνα με τον Mason στην μεταγενέστερη έκθεσή του[98] και η ομάδα ένιωσε ότι δεχόταν μεγάλη πίεση που επηρέασε το έργο της. Την επόμενη μέρα η πίεση αυξήθηκε περισσότερο όταν ο τοπικός Λειτουργός Υγείας εξέφρασε τις ανησυχίες του σχετικά με τον γενικό κίνδυνο για την υγεία που ενέχει η έρευνα. Ο Mason αισθάνθηκε ένα βαθμό συμπάθειας με αυτή την άποψη. Δεν υπήρχε δυνατότητα ψύξης των σορών που βρίσκονταν στη θάλασσα και στη συνέχεια σε διαμετακόμιση για περίπου 24 ώρες πριν καν φτάσουν στη Ρόδο. Ωστόσο, ο Υπεύθυνος Υγείας κατάλαβε την κατάσταση των παθολόγων και συμφώνησε να τους αφήσει να συνεχίσουν.

Ωστόσο, η άφιξη των δεκαεννέα σορών από την Τουρκία, που παραδόθηκαν στο νεκροτομείο το απόγευμα της 13ης Οκτωβρίου, είχε ως αποτέλεσμα ο Εισαγγελέας να διατάξει όλα τα πτώματα να σφραγιστούν σε φέρετρα μέχρι το τέλος της επόμενης ημέρας, Σάββατο 14 Οκτωβρίου. Κατά τη διάρκεια της 13[ης] ο Mason και ο Tarlton δούλεψαν ηρωικά και ολοκλήρωσαν συνολικά 21 περαιτέρω αυτοψίες. Το έργο τους διεκόπη περαιτέρω από την επίσκεψη ενός αεροπλάνου γεμάτο συγγενείς που είχαν νόμιμο δικαίωμα να επιθεωρήσουν κάθε πτώμα. Ο Χριστόπουλος ανέφερε αργότερα ότι «*η αναγνώριση των σορών έγινε ευκολότερη από τα αξιόπιστα στοιχεία και τις δηλώσεις των συγγενών που είχαν φτάσει και σε μια δύσκολη περίπτωση από άλλα στοιχεία της ιατρικής νομολογίας (ουλές*

---

[98] *Έκθεση Παθολογίας Αεροπορίας No. 15 1967, Ινστιτούτο Παθολογίας και Τροπικής Ιατρικής RAF. AVIA101/225 The National Archives, Λονδίνο.*

εγχειρήσεις, προσωπικά αντικείμενα κ.λπ.)[99] Προς μεγάλη απογοήτευση του Mason, οι επισκέπτες περιλάμβαναν επίσης, μετά από επιμονή του Δημόσιου Κατήγορου, και αρκετούς Ιταλούς φωτογράφους του Τύπου[100]. Για να προστεθεί στα προβλήματα της ομάδας, το μόνο ψυγείο κατάψυξης που ήταν διαθέσιμο για τη διατήρηση δειγμάτων αίματος και παρόμοιων δειγμάτων ήταν σε ένα ξενοδοχείο και ο Mason θεώρησε ότι ήταν παράλογο να πιέσει τη διοίκηση για περισσότερες από μία ημέρα.

Ο Mason και ο Tarlton ολοκλήρωσαν τις υπόλοιπες αυτοψίες, εκτός από τέσσερεις, σε συνθήκες που θεωρούσαν ότι ήταν κάπως μη ικανοποιητικές. Τα άλλα τέσσερα πτώματα, τα πήραν οι οικογένειές των πριν γίνουν οι νεκροψίες.

Ο Δημόσιος Κατήγορος συνέχιζε την πίεση για ταχεία ολοκλήρωση των νεκροψιών πριν από το σούρουπο, με τα εναπομείναντα άγνωστα πτώματα να σφραγίζονται σε φέρετρα και να θάβονται τοπικά. Ωστόσο, ακολούθησε μια λογική προσέγγιση όταν έγινε φανερό την καθορισμένη ώρα ότι μόνο έξι πτώματα δεν είχαν ακόμη κατονομαστεί.

Υπήρχε περισσότερη δουλειά για το ζευγάρι την επόμενη μέρα, 15 Οκτωβρίου, καθώς συναντήθηκαν με τον Norman Head of AIB για να εξετάσουν τα σωσίβια και τη μικρή ποσότητα συντριμμιών που είχαν ανακτηθεί. Μετά από αυτό, ο Mason και ο Tarlton ολοκλήρωσαν τη διαδικασία αναγνώρισης των υπόλοιπων έξι σορών[101], πριν δώσουν συνέντευξη Τύπου με τον Norman Head εκείνο το βράδυ.

Στην έκθεσή του, ο Mason αναγνώρισε τη βοήθεια που τους δόθηκε από την BEA, τις Κυπριακές Αερογραμμές και τις τοπικές αρχές. Ιδιαίτερα ευγνώμονες για την παρουσία φωτογράφου και διερμηνέα.

Εν τω μεταξύ, ελλείψει πειστικής αιτίας για την απώλεια του αεροσκάφους, η πιθανότητα μιας βόμβας δεν μπορούσε ακόμα να αποκλειστεί οριστικά. Στις 13 Οκτωβρίου ο Norman Head είχε ζητήσει από τον Ken Mason να επιστραφούν στο AIB (Accident Investigation

---

[99] *Έκθεση Χριστόπουλου (όπως μεταφράστηκε), AVIA101/210 Chief Investigating Officer's Report – TNA.*

[100] *Φωτογραφίες από έναν αριθμό νεκρών, ανάμεσά τους και ένα μικρό παιδί, εμφανίστηκαν στον διεθνή Τύπο. Ο βρετανικός Τύπος ήταν, και παραμένει, συγκρατημένος ως προς αυτό. Αυτές οι φωτογραφίες, αν και τέθηκαν στη διάθεση του συγγραφέα, δεν εμφανίζονται σε αυτό το βιβλίο.*

[101] *Ο Χριστόπουλος σημείωσε, «Από τα 51 πτώματα που υποβλήθηκαν σε νεκροψία σε δύο από αυτά δεν διαπιστώθηκε πλήρης ταυτοποίηση, εκτός από την εθνικότητα. Αυτά μεταφέρθηκαν στο Λονδίνο για περαιτέρω συλλογή στοιχείων ιατροδικαστικής αναγνώρισης.»*

Board) επειγόντως όλα τα κομμάτια μετάλλου που ανακτήθηκαν από πτώματα με το ταχύτερο μέσο και επίσης πρότεινε όλοι οι σοροί να υποβληθούν σε ακτινογραφία. Υπήρξαν προηγούμενες περιπτώσεις, κυρίως στη Βόρεια και Νότια Αμερική, κατά τις οποίες αεροσκάφη είχαν καταρριφθεί από έκρηξη εκρηκτικών στην καμπίνα επιβατών ή στο αμπάρι. Η έρευνα στα συντρίμμια είχε αποκαλύψει αξιοσημείωτα θραύσματα μετάλλου. Στην περίπτωση της αυτοκτονίας, το κυρίαρχο χαρακτηριστικό ήταν η χρήση χειροβομβίδων, οι οποίες διασκόρπισαν μεγάλα κομμάτια μετάλλου, και θεωρήθηκε πολύ πιθανό ότι ένα παρόμοιο περιστατικό στο Charlie Oscar θα είχε αφήσει τέτοια στοιχεία στα λείψανα των θυμάτων.

Ο Mason και ο Tarlton αφού ολοκλήρωσαν όσο καλύτερα μπορούσαν το ασυνήθιστα δύσκολο έργο τους το Σαββατοκύριακο, πήγαν σπίτι τους για να ετοιμάσουν την ενδιάμεση έκθεσή τους[102]. Υπήρχαν αρχικά δηλώσεις, από το πλήρωμα της RAF και άλλους, ότι ορισμένα από τα πτώματα φορούσαν σωσίβια. Μόνο μετά τις νεκροτομές η ομάδα μπόρεσε να ξεκαθαρίσει ότι κανείς δεν είχε σωσίβιο. Ο Mason και ο Tarlton σημείωσαν ότι, μέχρι την ενδιάμεση έκθεση, οι θέσεις των 28 επιβατών που επιβιβάστηκαν στο Λονδίνο ήταν γνωστές, οι πληροφορίες αυτές προέρχονταν από το πλήρωμα καμπίνας Λονδίνου - Αθήνας. Αναγνώρισαν επίσης μια πιθανή σημασία στην κατανομή των σορών, όσον αφορά την ανάκτησή τους είτε στην «ελληνική» (νότια) ή στην «τουρκική» (βόρεια) ομάδα.

Ο Mason και ο Tarlton σχολίασαν τις διαφορές στην αναλογία των ακραίων προς τους ελαφρούς εξωτερικούς τραυματισμούς μεταξύ των βόρειων και νότιων ομάδων. Η νότια ομάδα είχε σημαντικό αριθμό περιπτώσεων «ακραίου τραυματισμού» και λιγότερες με ελαφρά ορατά τραύματα. Αν και δεν ήταν από μόνη της οριστική, η διαφορά ήταν σημαντική.

Η ομοιομορφία του τραυματισμού μεταξύ εκείνων που παρουσίαζαν ακραίο τραυματισμό ήταν εντυπωσιακή. Βασικά, η εικόνα ήταν μια μαζική κρανιοεγκεφαλική κάκωση σε συνδυασμό με σοβαρό τραυματισμό στη θωρακική μοίρα της σπονδυλικής στήλης (συνήθως κάτι σαν τομή) και πλήρες κάταγμα του στέρνου. Η κολποκοιλιακή ρήξη ήταν συχνή και η κοιλιακή ρήξη αμετάβλητη. Αυτό μπορεί να είναι αποτέλεσμα βίαιου πετάγματος γύρω από την καμπίνα καθώς ο Κομήτης κατέβαινε.

---

[102] *AVIA13 1383 Διερεύνηση Ατυχήματος – Εθνικά Αρχεία.*

Οι περισσότεροι από την ομάδα των «ελαφρώς τραυματισμένων»[103] είχαν πεθάνει από μεμονωμένα τραύματα στο καρδιαγγειακό σύστημα, αλλά η συχνότητα των κοιλιακών τραυμάτων ακόμη και σε αυτήν την ομάδα ήταν αξιοσημείωτη.

Η ενδιάμεση έκθεση εξέτασε ομοιότητες μεταξύ των θυμάτων που ανακτήθηκαν από το Charlie Oscar και εκείνων από τις συντριβές του Κομήτη της Έλβα και της Νάπολης δεκατρία χρόνια νωρίτερα. Ενώ δεν υπήρξε καμία ένδειξη ότι οι διάφοροι τραυματισμοί και η διατήρηση ή η απώλεια ρούχων αφορούσαν συγκεκριμένα ατυχήματα που αφορούσαν τον συγκεκριμένο τύπο αεροσκάφους, όλα είχαν συμβεί στη Μεσόγειο και αφορούσαν βρετανικά αεροσκάφη. Τα αποτελέσματα των προηγούμενων ερευνών ήταν, επομένως, άμεσα διαθέσιμα για σύγκριση. Ο Mason και ο Tarlton σημείωσαν την κοινή υψηλή συχνότητα τραυματισμών στο κεφάλι, σοβαρών τραυματισμών του θώρακα και εσωτερικού τραυματισμού με απουσία σοβαρής εξωτερικής βλάβης σε πολλά από τα σώματα. Αυτό υποδηλώνει ότι υπήρχε ένας βαθμός ομοιότητας στη διαδικασία καθόδου μετά από μια καταστροφική αποτυχία και την καταστροφή των διαφόρων αεροσκαφών κατά επαφή/σύγκρουση με τη θάλασσα.

Σύμφωνα με το στοιχειώδες σχέδιο καθισμάτων[104] που ανακατασκευάστηκε με τη βοήθεια του πληρώματος καμπίνας Λονδίνου-Αθηνών και των επιβατών, όλοι οι «ελαφρά τραυματισμένοι» επιβάτες, των οποίων οι θέσεις μπορούσαν να αναγνωριστούν, βρίσκονταν μεταξύ των σειρών 6 και 12, στην αριστερή (port) πλευρά του αεροσκάφους. Η έκθεση θεώρησε ότι η εικοσαμελής ομάδα των Μαρτύρων του Ιεχωβά, κυρίως ηλικιωμένων, πιθανότατα θα καθόντουσαν μαζί στο πίσω μέρος της καμπίνας.

Οι Mason και Tarlton τόνισαν ότι οποιαδήποτε εξήγηση του μηχανισμού με τον οποίο υπέστησαν τα τραύματα πρέπει ταυτόχρονα να εξηγεί την παρουσία της ομάδας των «ελαφρώς τραυματισμένων». Θεώρησαν ότι ήταν αναπόφευκτο ότι τα ευρήματα θα μπορούσαν να ικανοποιηθούν μόνο με βάση το γεγονός ότι η ομάδα «ελαφρά τραυματισμένη» πετάχτηκε μακριά από το αεροσκάφος είτε πριν είτε την ίδια στιγμή που τα άλλα

---

[103] Αν και μπορεί να φαίνεται ανώμαλο να αναφέρονται τα θύματα που είχαν υποστεί θανατηφόρα τραύματα ως «ελαφρώς τραυματισμένα», αυτή ήταν η διατύπωση που υιοθέτησαν οι Mason και Tarlton και έτσι χρησιμοποιείται σε αυτό το πλαίσιο.

[104] Οι σκέψεις που έγιναν για το τελικό μοτίβο θέσεων βασίζονται στο ότι κανείς δεν έχει αλλάξει θέση μετά τον ενδιάμεσο σταθμό στην Αθήνα. Με τις καμπίνες Tourist Class να είναι άδειες κατά το ένα τρίτο, δεν υπάρχει καμία εγγύηση ότι αυτό ίσχυε στην πραγματικότητα. Ωστόσο, είναι απίθανο ένας σημαντικός αριθμός επιβατών να άλλαζε θέσεις εκτός αν υπήρχε κάποιος λόγος να το κάνει.

θύματα είχαν πεταχτεί μέσα στην άτρακτο. Στη συνέχεια εξέτασαν μια σειρά από πιθανά σενάρια με βάση την προϋπόθεση ότι όλοι οι επιβάτες κάθονταν σύμφωνα με το σχέδιο θέσεων που τους δόθηκε στις συνεντεύξεις των επιβατών και του πληρώματος που αποβιβάστηκαν στην Αθήνα.

Μετά τις προηγούμενες τραγωδίες του Comet Mk1, η πρώτη αιτία απώλειας που εξέτασαν οι Mason και Tarlton ήταν αστοχία στη πίεση στην καμπίνα. Ήταν επίσης προφανές σε αυτούς ότι τα τραύματα στο κεφάλι στα προηγούμενα ατυχήματα ήταν παρόμοια με αυτά που βρέθηκαν στο Charlie Oscar. Ωστόσο, σημείωσαν ότι καμία παρόμοια σειρά ατυχημάτων δεν είχε συμβεί σε κανένα άλλο σημαντικό τύπο αεροσκάφους, γι' αυτό προειδοποίησαν για μη βιαστικά συμπεράσματα. Τόνισαν επίσης ότι ο Κομήτης 4Β ήταν πολύ διαφορετικός από το προηγούμενο μοντέλο και ότι πιθανώς είχε δοκιμαστεί πιο διεξοδικά από οποιοδήποτε άλλο αεροσκάφος σε υπηρεσία. Αν είχε συμβεί μια αστοχία καμπίνας παρόμοιας κλίμακας με τους προηγούμενους Κομήτες, ήταν φαινομενικά αδύνατο να εξηγηθεί γιατί πολλοί επιβάτες στο κέντρο της καμπίνας είχαν γλιτώσει από τις επιπτώσεις των αναταράξεων. Εάν ήταν σε σημαντικά μικρότερη κλίμακα, θα μπορούσε να ήταν ακόμα αρκετό για να καταστρέψει την πλευρά του αεροσκάφους, επιτρέποντας την εκτίναξη της ομάδας των «ελαφρώς τραυματισμένων». Η δεύτερη πιθανότητα, ωστόσο, υπονοούσε ότι οι επιβαίνοντες μπορεί να είχαν πέσει από διαφορετικά ύψη, με την ομάδα των «ελαφρώς τραυματισμένων» να είχε πέσει από μεγαλύτερη απόσταση[105]. Τα στοιχεία από την ανάκτηση των σορών, με δύο ξεχωριστές ομάδες σε απόσταση περίπου μισού μιλίου, υποδηλώνουν ότι οποιαδήποτε εκτίναξη των θυμάτων είχε συμβεί σε ύψος σημαντικά χαμηλότερο από το υψόμετρο πλεύσης των 29.000 ποδιών του Charlie Oscar. Συγκεκριμένα, μια σειρά από την ομάδα των «ελαφρώς τραυματισμένων» διατήρησαν μερικά από τα ρούχα τους, τα οποία ήταν σε αντίθεση με τα πειράματα που διεξήχθησαν μετά τις καταστροφές του Κομήτη Mk 1.

Η δεύτερη πιθανότητα ήταν η απώλεια του ελέγχου του αεροσκάφους, η οποία μπορεί να προκλήθηκε από έναν ή περισσότερους διάφορους

---

[105] *Προηγούμενες εργασίες είχαν καταλήξει στο συμπέρασμα ότι επιβάτες που έπεσαν από ύψος γλίτωσαν από το φαινόμενο του «μίκτη τσιμέντου» που πέταξε γύρω από την καμπίνα και ότι η πρόσκρουση με τη θάλασσα θα είχε προκαλέσει θανατηφόρους εσωτερικούς τραυματισμούς, αλλά χωρίς το εξωτερικό τραύμα όσων βρίσκονταν μέσα στην άτρακτο. Παρομοίως, πειράματα μετά τη συντριβή του Κομήτη Mk 1 έδειξαν ότι μια πτώση στη θάλασσα από ύψος μεγαλύτερο από μερικές εκατοντάδες πόδια θα είχε τόσο σκίσει τα ρούχα που θα απομακρυνόταν είτε σε επαφή με τη θάλασσα είτε από τη δράση των κυμάτων προτού το σώμα ανασυρθεί.*

παράγοντες. Αυτά θα μπορούσαν να περιλαμβάνουν, πρότειναν οι παθολόγοι, αδυναμία χειριστή, αποσύνθεση του κινητήρα, δολιοφθορά, σύγκρουση ή κεραυνό. Καθώς και οι τρεις πιλότοι ήταν μεταξύ των αγνοουμένων, δεν υπήρχαν στοιχεία που να δείχνουν ή να διαψεύδουν την ανικανότητα. Μια σύγκρουση στην περιοχή της καμπίνας επιβατών θα είχε δημιουργήσει ένα λιγότερο ομοιόμορφο μοτίβο τραυματισμών, αν και δέχτηκαν ότι το σημείο σύγκρουσης μπορεί να βρισκόταν κοντά στο θάλαμο πτήσης ή έξω από την ίδια την καμπίνα πίεσης. Το χτύπημα κεραυνού δεν μπορούσε να αποκλειστεί εντελώς, αλλά οι παθολόγοι παρατήρησαν ότι δεν βρέθηκαν αντικείμενα από χάλυβα στην κατοχή των επιβατών, όπως αυτά που είχαν ανασυρθεί. Το ενδεχόμενο διάσπασης του κινητήρα ή δολιοφθοράς, δήλωσαν, θα πρέπει να συζητηθεί σε σχέση με την Υπόθεση Νο. 6, του 28χρονου κ. Αχιλλέας Αφατίτη, ο οποίος ταξίδευε με τη νέα του σύζυγο ως μέλος της ομάδας των είκοσι, ως επί τω πλείστον μεγαλύτερης ηλικίας, Μαρτύρων του Ιεχωβά.

Το σώμα του κ. Αφατίτη ήταν ξεχωριστό για πολλούς λόγους:

Α. Είχε τραύματα στο χέρι, τα οποία υπέστη πριν πεθάνει, που υποδηλώνουν κάποια αδυναμία στην υγεία.

Β. Το πάνω μέρος του σώματός του ήταν γεμάτο από μικρές μαύρες κηλίδες.

Γ. Η τραχεία του φάνηκε να επηρεάζεται έντονα από τη ζέστη.

Δ. Το πουκάμισό του είχε επίσης μικρές τρύπες παρόμοιες με αυτές στο στήθος του.

Οι βλάβες στο δέρμα του φάνηκαν να είναι πολύ επιφανειακά τραύματα που έδειξαν έντονη θερμική πήξη. Οι μικρές βλάβες, μαζί με την πήξη της θερμότητας στο λαιμό, έδειξαν αγγειακή αντίδραση, φλεγμονή που προκλήθηκε από μικρά αιμοφόρα αγγεία, υποδηλώνοντας ότι ο κ. Αφατίτης ήταν ακόμη ζωντανός τη στιγμή που προκλήθηκε η βλάβη. Αυτό έμελλε να αποδείξει μια πολύ σημαντική εξέλιξη. Ενώ δεν βρέθηκε τίποτα στο δέρμα που εξετάστηκε , οι Mason και Tarlton παρατήρησαν ότι οποιοδήποτε τέτοιο ξένο σώμα θα είχε εξαφανιστεί αν ήταν υγρό και θα είχε χαθεί κατά τη διαδικασία ανάκτησης και εξέτασης, εάν ήταν μεταλλικό αντικείμενο.

Μελετώντας το σαμποτάζ ως την αιτία της καταστροφής, ο Mason και ο Tarlton αναφέρθηκαν σε αμερικανική εμπειρία ότι θα υπήρχαν μεγάλα μεταλλικά θραύσματα, και κανένα από αυτά δεν βρέθηκε, είτε πάνω στο σώμα του κ. Αφανιτη, είτε στις ακτινογραφίες ή σε οποιοδήποτε άλλο θύμα.

Αν η αιτία ήταν μια βόμβα ή παρόμοιο συμβάν, ανέφεραν οι παθολόγοι, τα ιατρικά στοιχεία πρότειναν τρεις επόμενες αλληλουχίες στην καταστροφή του Charlie Oscar :

1. Ότι δημιουργήθηκε ένα τεράστιο ελάττωμα στο αεροσκάφος στα 29.000 πόδια.
2. Ότι το αεροσκάφος τέθηκε εκτός ελέγχου και διαλύθηκε υπό αυξανόμενη πίεση σε πολύ χαμηλότερο ύψος.
3. Ότι, όντας εκτός ελέγχου, το αεροσκάφος χτύπησε το νερό, πιθανώς πρώτα την αριστερή πτέρυγα (port wing), και διαλύθηκε καθώς περνούσε με ταχύτητα πάνω από το νερό, εκτοξεύοντας τα θύματα καθώς προχωρούσε.

Θεώρησαν ότι ήταν πιθανό τα μηχανικά στοιχεία θα υποστήριζαν σθεναρά ότι ένα τεράστιο ελάττωμα εμφανίστηκε σε υψόμετρο και ότι η διαθέσιμη ιατρική διαφορά θα βοηθούσε ελάχιστα στη διάκριση μεταξύ των πιθανοτήτων 2 και 3. Ενώ οι εμφανίσεις των πνευμόνων στην ομάδα «ελαφρώς τραυματισμένων» ήταν συγκρίσιμες με εκείνες που αποδίδονται σε πρόσκρουση νερού ελεύθερης πτώσης στις προηγούμενες συντριβές του Κομήτη, δεν υπήρχε λόγος να μην μπορούσαν και τα θύματα του Charlie Oscar να υποστούν το ίδιο όταν πετάχτηκαν και το αεροπλάνο χτύπησε την επιφάνεια της θάλασσας. Ομοίως, οι πιο σοβαροί εξωτερικοί τραυματισμοί που υπέστησαν άλλα θύματα ήταν αρκετά ομοιόμορφοι ώστε να είχαν προκληθεί με θανατηφόρο πέταγμα, με όλες τις προθέσεις και σκοπούς, μιας σύγκρουσης στη θάλασσα και όχι μια ελεγχόμενη προσγείωση στο νερό. Όμως, μια προσχεδιασμένη προσγείωση στο νερό, όσο ανεπιτυχής κι αν ήταν, θα ήταν αναμενόμενο ότι οι επιβάτες θα φορούσαν σωσίβια. Ο Mason ο Tarlton μπόρεσαν να εξετάσουν μερικά σωσίβια, αλλά δεν βρήκαν κανένα στοιχείο ότι κάποιο είχε στερεωθεί σε επιβάτη, επιβεβαιώνοντας την παρατήρηση του Νίκου Μισομίκη. Εξέφρασαν όντως κάποια έκπληξη που τόσα πολλά σωσίβια φαινόταν να είχαν βγει από τη θέση τους κάτω από τα καθίσματα χωρίς κάποια προσπάθεια από τους επιβάτες, αλλά οι ερευνητές της AIB τους έπεισαν ότι δεν έπρεπε να εξαχθούν ιδιαίτερα συμπεράσματα από αυτό.

Μεταξύ των συγγενών στη Ρόδο ήταν και ο Πολύβιος Γεωργίου, ο οποίος αντιμετώπισε τώρα την περαιτέρω αγωνία να μάθει ότι ο αδελφός του Σωτήρης ήταν μεταξύ των έντεκα επιβατών και τεσσάρων του πληρώματος των οποίων οι σοροί δεν είχαν ανασυρθεί. Ανάμεσα στα πιο παράξενα περιστατικά σε μια αδιάκοπα φρικτή εμπειρία ήταν αυτό που ο Πολύβιος αργότερα περιέγραψε στον συγγραφέα ως «...*μια αδυσώπητη προσπάθεια από ορισμένους Μάρτυρες του Ιεχωβά να προσηλυτίσουν τον αδελφό μου και εμένα από Έλληνες Ορθόδοξους σε Μάρτυρες του Ιεχωβά».*

«Η απάντηση βρίσκεται κάπου ανάμεσα σε αυτήν τη λίστα»

Στην αρχή της έρευνας, ο προσδιορισμός της αιτίας πέρα από κάθε εύλογη αμφιβολία φαινόταν να ήταν πολύ δύσκολος. Σχεδόν κανένα ουσιαστικό συντρίμμι δεν είχε ανακτηθεί και δεν υπήρχε κανένα σημάδι του καταγραφέα δεδομένων πτήσης του «μαύρου κουτιού». Το Charlie Oscar είχε πέσει στη Μεσόγειο ακριβώς στο σημείο όπου υπήρχε μια άβυσσος, με το νερό να έχει βάθος περίπου 9.000 πόδια.

Οι εικασίες σχετικά με την αιτία της απώλειας του Charlie Oscar ήταν έντονες από την αρχή. Με τα πρότυπα της εποχής, σε μια εποχή πριν από τα social media και την άμεση επικοινωνία, η επιχείρηση συλλογής ειδήσεων ήταν εκπληκτικά αποτελεσματική. Ο Τύπος δεν έχασε χρόνο να συμπληρώσει τα λιγοστά στοιχεία της συντριβής και τα ονόματα των θυμάτων, με προσωπικά στοιχεία, ερμηνείες και εικασίες. Οι βρετανικές εφημερίδες κάλυψαν την ιστορία από τις 13 Οκτωβρίου, αρχικές αναφορές όπως αυτή της Daily Telegraph έδωσαν τον τόνο. Ενημέρωσαν τους αναγνώστες των πως «*Η αιτία της συντριβής παραμένει ένα πλήρες μυστήριο*», παρόλο που μόλις 24 ώρες είχαν περάσει από τότε που χάθηκε το Charlie Oscar .Παρά την απουσία μέχρι στιγμής οποιωνδήποτε αποδεικτικών στοιχείων, επικαλούνταν μια σειρά από αίτια.

Οι ερευνητές είχαν πολύ λίγα μπροστά τους στην αρχή. Εκτός από τα 51 πτώματα που βρέθηκαν, τα στοιχεία αποτελούνταν από συντρίμμια, τα οποία σχεδόν όλα αναγνωρίστηκαν ως θραύσματα των εξαρτημάτων της καμπίνας. Υπήρχαν, φυσικά, τα δεδομένα που συγκεντρώθηκαν από την αρχή. Οι καταγραφές ATC και τα αρχεία καιρού κατασχέθηκαν σωστά και έγκαιρα για λεπτομερή έλεγχο.

Σύμφωνα με τα λόγια του Sherlock Holmes, «Όταν έχεις εξαλείψει το αδύνατο, ό,τι απομένει, όσο απίθανο κι αν είναι, πρέπει να είναι η αλήθεια»[106].

Ξεκίνησαν τώρα μια σειρά από συγκεκριμένες γραμμές έρευνας, οι οποίες λειτουργούσαν παράλληλα, προκειμένου να επιβεβαιωθούν ή να εξαλειφθούν διάφορες πιθανές αιτίες της καταστροφής.

Μεταξύ των συντριμμιών που ανασύρθηκαν από το σημείο της συντριβής ήταν ένας τρικέφαλος αυτόματος πυροσβεστήρας Graviner τύπου 71Α, μέρος του εγκατεστημένου εξοπλισμού του αεροσκάφους. Διαπιστώθηκε ότι προερχόταν από τη δεξιά (starboard side) πλευρά του κεντρικού τμήματος του Charlie Oscar. Μετά την επιστροφή στην Αγγλία, το μπουκάλι στάλθηκε στην κατασκευάστρια εταιρεία για εξέταση.

---

[106] *The Sign of the Four*, του Sir Arthur Conan Doyle.

Εξήχθη το συμπέρασμα ότι ο πυροσβεστήρας είχε πυροδοτηθεί ηλεκτρικά από διακόπτη αδράνειας (σύγκρουσης) και ότι όλα τα μέρη του μηχανισμού λειτουργίας φαινόταν να λειτούργησαν σωστά.

Ο διακόπτης αδράνειας ήταν τοποθετημένος στη μύτη του αεροσκάφους με το μπουκάλι που ανακτήθηκε να βρίσκεται, όπως αναφέρθηκε, στο κεντρικό τμήμα. Η ηλεκτρική καλωδίωση περνά από τη μύτη κατά μήκος του κάτω μέρους της μπροστινής ατράκτου στο κεντρικό τμήμα του αεροσκάφους. Η εκκένωση της φιάλης μπορεί να ενεργοποιηθεί μόνο με θετική ηλεκτρική ενεργοποίηση, καθώς δεν επαρκεί ένα βραχυκύκλωμα. Αυτό οδήγησε στο συμπέρασμα ότι το ηλεκτρικό κύκλωμα ήταν πλήρες τη στιγμή της εκφόρτωσης.

Είναι σημαντικό ότι το μπουκάλι είχε ανακτηθεί από τη βόρεια περιοχή, μακριά από άλλα συντρίμμια και τα πτώματα που σχετίζονται με το κεντρικό τμήμα του Charlie Oscar. Θεωρήθηκε πολύ απίθανο να είχε διαχωριστεί κατά την πρόσκρουση με τη θάλασσα και οι εξεταστές κατέληξαν στο συμπέρασμα ότι πιθανότατα αποκολλήθηκε λόγω της διάσπασης του αεροσκάφους στον αέρα. Η HSA (Hawker Siddeley Aviation) υπολόγισε ότι, εάν η μπροστινή άτρακτος αποκολληθεί ξαφνικά, για παράδειγμα λόγω αδρανειακής φόρτισης προς τα κάτω, το φορτίο θα ήταν αρκετό για να ενεργοποιήσει τον διακόπτη σύγκρουσης, προκαλώντας την εκφόρτωση της φιάλης. Μια προς τα κάτω περιστροφή της ατράκτου προς τα εμπρός, προκαλώντας ουσιαστικά την «απόσπαση» της, θα διατηρούσε την ηλεκτρική καλωδίωση για αρκετό καιρό ώστε η φιάλη να αποφορτιστεί πλήρως. Ο μόνος πυροσβεστήρας που ανακτήθηκε είχε ως εκ τούτου πολύ ισχυρές αποδείξεις ότι το Charlie Oscar είχε κοπεί στον αέρα.

Συνολικά ανασύρθηκαν δέκα ρολόγια χειρός από τα πτώματα των θυμάτων κατά τη διάρκεια των νεκροτομών. Ένας εξέχων ωρολογοποιός που εξέτασε όλα τα ρολόγια διαπίστωσε ότι τα περισσότερα είχαν σταματήσει ξαφνικά, αν και τρία είχαν, σταματήσει παρά το καταστροφικό κτύπημα μόνο όταν έληξε το κούρδισμα τους. Σημειώθηκε με ενδιαφέρον ότι αυτά έτειναν να είναι τα φθηνότερα ρολόγια. Επτά από τα ρολόγια είχαν σταματήσει μεταξύ είκοσι και είκοσι πέντε περασμένης της ώρας είτε στις τέσσερεις ή πέντε ακριβώς[107].

Συνολικά, η ισορροπία των αποδεικτικών στοιχείων ήταν ότι τα ρολόγια είχαν σταματήσει περίπου στις 03:25 GMT. Οκτώ ρολόγια μολύνθηκαν από κηροζίνη. Αν αυτό μπορούσε να συνδεθεί με μεμονωμένους επιβάτες, σημειώθηκε ότι προέρχονταν από τη νότια ομάδα πτωμάτων. Οι ερευνητές μπόρεσαν να καταλήξουν στο συμπέρασμα ότι ο πρώτος χρόνος

---

[107] *Η διαφορά της ώρας θα μπορούσε να εξηγηθεί από τη διαφορά στην τοπική ώρα μεταξύ Λονδίνου και Αθήνας και Λευκωσίας.*

πρόσκρουσης που υποδεικνύεται από τα ρολόγια ήταν, επομένως, το πολύ δύο λεπτά μετά την τελευταία επικοινωνία ασυρμάτου, με την πλειοψηφία να υποδηλώνει ότι η πρόσκρουση σημειώθηκε περίπου επτά λεπτά μετά τα τελευταία λόγια του SFO Thomas.

Εν τω μεταξύ, η κατεύθυνση της έρευνας πήρε μια ξαφνική στροφή στις 5 Νοεμβρίου, όταν η ομάδα έρευνας αντιλήφθηκε ότι ένα μεταλλικό αντικείμενο, προφανώς από αεροσκάφος, ανασύρθηκε από τη θάλασσα κοντά στο νησί της Σύμης, δέκα με δεκαπέντε μίλια δυτικά της Ρόδου, λίγες μέρες πριν. Αναγνωρίστηκε ως δεξαμενή πτώσης καυσίμου, που προοριζόταν για χρήση σε ένα βορειοαμερικανικό μαχητικό βομβαρδιστικό F100D/F Super Sabre, ένα αεροσκάφος που χρησιμοποιείται από την USAF και τις αεροπορικές δυνάμεις πολλών άλλων εθνών. Ένα ρεπορτάζ της 2ας Νοεμβρίου στην ελληνική εφημερίδα Έθνος, συνέδεε το εύρημα με το Charlie Oscar, παρά τη διόλου ευκαταφρόνητη απόσταση από το σημείο του δυστυχήματος, επισημαίνοντας ότι σε παραλία στη Ρόδο είχε βρεθεί και μια αστυνομική ταυτότητα που ανήκε σε κάποια «Μις Exeshea»[108], έχοντας παρασυρθεί περίπου 100 μίλια από το σημείο της συντριβής.

Είναι χαρακτηριστικό ότι η δεξαμενή πτώσης έφερε ένα μικρό ίχνος κόκκινης μπογιάς. Το αντικείμενο είχε διαβιβαστεί στις ελληνικές αρχές όπου εξετάστηκε από την Ελληνική Υπηρεσία Πολιτικής Αεροπορίας, τη Βασιλική Αεροπορία και την Ολυμπιακή Αεροπορία. Παρόλο που γρήγορα αναγνωρίστηκε ως στρατιωτικής προέλευσης και όχι ως μέρος του Charlie Oscar το ίχνος του κόκκινου υποδήλωνε ότι μπορούσε να είχε συγκρουστεί με αεροσκάφος που έφερε βαφή αυτού του χρώματος. Το αεροσκάφος της ΒΕΑ είχε κόκκινα φτερά και το λογότυπο της αεροπορικής εταιρείας ήταν, στην πραγματικότητα, ένα κόκκινο τετράγωνο. Προέκυψε η ενδιαφέρουσα πιθανότητα: είχε το Charlie Oscar συγκρουστεί με άλλο αεροσκάφος;

Μια σύγκρουση στον αέρα θα μπορούσε σίγουρα να εξηγήσει την ξαφνική διακοπή του τελευταίου μηνύματος (ασυρμάτου) του SFO Thomas. Ήταν επίσης μια λύση που θα είχε αφαιρέσει κάθε υποψία ότι υπήρχαν ελαττώματα ασφαλείας στο αεροδρόμιο του Ελληνικού. Για το λόγο αυτό, οι ελληνικές αρχές επιθυμούσαν πολύ να διερευνηθεί η πιθανότητα σύγκρουσης στο μέγιστο δυνατό βαθμό.

Η ομάδα έρευνας, όπως είναι λογικό, είχε ζητήσει να μεταφερθεί το αντικείμενο στην Αγγλία για εξέταση. Η δεξαμενή πτώσης έφτασε κανονικά στις 20 Νοεμβρίου. Το επίχρισμα της κόκκινης μπογιάς

---

[108] Πιθανώς η 21χρονη δεσποινίς Αρετή Εξαρχέα που ήταν μέλος της ομάδας των Μαρτύρων του Ιεχωβά στο Charlie Oscar

θεωρήθηκε ότι ήταν η πιο πιθανή ένδειξη για να αποδείξει ή να αναιρέσει τη άμεση επαφή με τον Charlie Oscar, έτσι ανατέθηκε στη Κυβερνητική Χημική Αρχή, στο Royal Arsenal, στο Woolwich, να πραγματοποιήσει μια λεπτομερή εξέταση. Στις 29 Νοεμβρίου, τα πολύ-αναμενόμενα αποτελέσματα της εξέτασης της βαφής στάλθηκαν στον Eric Newton, σε μια έκθεση του κ. Η Wells. Για άλλη μια φορά, οι λεπτομέρειες που δόθηκαν δείχνουν τον εξαιρετικά εμπεριστατωμένο και μεθοδικό τρόπο με τον οποίο πραγματοποιήθηκε η εξέταση. Ο κ. Wells σημείωσε ότι η βαφή στο αντικείμενο εξετάστηκε και συγκρίθηκε με κόκκινη βαφή που είχαν ορισμένοι Κομήτες της ΒΕΑ.

Ο κ. Wells ήταν αρκετά σαφής στο συμπέρασμά του:

«Οι παραπάνω παρατηρήσεις, οι μετρήσεις των φυσικών χαρακτηριστικών και η χημική ανάλυση δείχνουν ξεκάθαρα ότι η κηλίδα της κόκκινης βαφής στο κομμάτι της δεξαμενής πτώσης διαφέρει σημαντικά στη σύνθεση από τη βαφή Κομήτη της ΒΕΑ και ότι η κηλίδα δεν είναι αποτέλεσμα βίαιης πρόσκρουσης με κόκκινο βαμμένο αντικείμενο».

Δύο μέρες μετά την αναφορά του κ. Wells, λήφθηκε μήνυμα από τον κ. van Cott της Πρεσβείας των ΗΠΑ. Είχε ενημερωθεί ότι το drop tank (το εν λόγω αντικείμενο) ήταν ένα από ένα ζευγάρι τέτοιων που έπεσε από ένα USAF F100, με αριθμό ουράς 50-3970, στις 14 Ιουλίου 1967 κάτω από καθαρές συνθήκες σε θέση 15 μίλια νότια της αεροπορικής βάσης Ιντσιρλίκ, στην Τουρκία, από όπου είχαν φτάσει τα εν λόγω drop tanks. Το αεροσκάφος ρυμουλκούσε ένα target drogue sleeve και τα drop tanks είχαν εκτοξευθεί για να κάνουν σίγουρο ότι όταν απελευθερωθεί το drogue, το καλώδιο δεν θα επηρεάζε τα tanks. . Ο πιλότος παρακολούθησε τα tanks μέχρι να χτυπήσουν στο νερό. Η απόρριψη είχε γίνει σύμφωνα με τη διεθνή διαδικασία.

Το Charlie Oscar σίγουρα δεν είχε συγκρουστεί στον αέρα με το αεροσκάφος που μετέφερε το tanks, και κανένα αεροσκάφος δεν έλειπε ή δεν είχε ζημιά που να υποδηλώνει επαφή με τον Κομήτη.

Η θεωρία της βόμβας

Περίπου 27 μαξιλάρια καθισμάτων, που ανασύρθηκαν από τη θάλασσα δόθηκαν στο RARDE από τον Eric Newton, όπου η έρευνα διεξήχθη από τον κ. V.J. Clancey, τον Επικεφαλής Επιστημονικό Υπεύθυνο, με τη βοήθεια άλλων ειδικών[109]. Χρησιμοποίησαν εξελιγμένες τεχνικές, για εκείνη την εποχή, όπως στερεοσκοπικό μικροσκόπιο σάρωσης, ακτίνες Χ, ανάλυση μικρο-ανιχνευτών ηλεκτρονίων και μικροχημική ανάλυση.

Η RARDE είχε κληθεί να συμμετάσχει λόγω των εγκαταστάσεων και της εμπειρίας της στην τεχνολογία εκρηκτικών. Είχε επίσης εξειδικευμένη εμπειρία σε εγκληματολογικές εργασίες σε σχέση με εκρηκτικά, καθώς και στη διερεύνηση τυχαίων εκρήξεων καθώς και βομβών.

Οι αποδείξεις έκρηξης ενός ισχυρού εκρηκτικού υλικού, που προσδιορίστηκε ως στρατιωτικού ή παρόμοιου τύπου, αντί της συνηθισμένης ζελατοδυναμίτιδας (gelignite) προήλθαν κυρίως από τη λεπτομερή εξέταση ενός συγκεκριμένου μαξιλαριού, που προσδιορίστηκε ότι προερχόταν από την τουριστική καμπίνα του Charlie Oscar. Αυτό υποστηρίχθηκε από ελαφρά ζημιά σε άλλο μαξιλάρι, μέρος ενός σκισμένου πουκάμισου και επίσης παθολογική εξέταση ορισμένων πτωμάτων, ένα εκ των οποίων είχε τραύματα που πιστεύεται ότι προήλθαν από έκρηξη.

Οι λεπτομέρειες των αποδεικτικών στοιχείων[110] ήταν, πρώτον, η επιφανειακή ζημιά στο μαξιλάρι, η οποία αποτελούταν από ένα κομμάτι σε σχήμα βεντάλιας κομμένο από το μαξιλάρι και μαύρισμα της επιφάνειας, ενός τυπικού είδους έκρηξης. Οι ευθείες τομές ακτινοβολούνταν από μια κοινή προέλευση και πρέπει να είχαν παραχθεί από έναν αριθμό μεμονωμένων αντικειμένων που κινούνταν με πολύ μεγάλη ταχύτητα, όπως με τον τρόπο θραυσμάτων υλικού από μια έκρηξη. Στο μαξιλάρι υπήρχαν διατρήσεις, μέσα από τις οποίες σπρώχνονταν σύρματα. Αυτά καθόρισαν τις τροχιές των θραυσμάτων που προκάλεσαν τις διατρήσεις ως προερχόμενες από την ίδια προέλευση με

---

[109] Αυτοί ονομάζονται στην παραπάνω έκθεση RARDE ως: κ. *Alfred Nichol-Smith, Chief Experimental Officer (in charge of metallurgical studies) Dr. George Todd, Principal Scientific Officer (analytical studies)*, κ. *R.L. Durant, Principal Scientific Officer (X-ray)*, κ. *J. Markham, Experimental Officer ((Stero-scan electron microscope)*, κ. *D.F.T Winter* και κ. *K.J. Jarvis (fragment velocity measurements)* και κ. *H.J. Yallop* και κ. *D.P. Lidstone (explosive trials.)* Όλοι είναι άξιοι αναφοράς για το έργο τους.

[110] Ατύχημα στον Κομήτη 4Β, G-ARCO – Ενδιάμεση έκθεση για την εξέταση ενός μαξιλαριού καθίσματος. D.F. Runnicles, Principal Superintendent, Explosives Division, RARDE, 1η Ιανουαρίου 1968, μέσω The National Archives (Εθνικού Αρχείου).

τα κοψίματα. Οι ακτίνες Χ έδειξαν την παρουσία στο μαξιλάρι μεγάλου αριθμού μικροσκοπικών σωματιδίων μετάλλου. Το πολύ μικρό τους μέγεθος, από 10 χιλιοστόγραμμα βάρους έως μικροσκοπικό, συμφωνούσε ότι ήταν αποτέλεσμα έκρηξης. Η παρουσία και η διανομή τέτοιων μικροσκοπικών σωματιδίων μετάλλου απεδείχθη επίσης σε εργαστηριακές δοκιμές με ένα εκρηκτικό σε μια ελαφριά μεταλλική θήκη.

Οι εξεταστές στη συνέχεια πραγματοποίησαν δοκιμές πυροδοτώντας μικρά σωματίδια σε ένα παρόμοιο μαξιλάρι, καθώς μετρούσαν τις ταχύτητες. Η διείσδυση στο ύποπτο μαξιλάρι προκλήθηκε από σωματίδια που ταξίδευαν με ταχύτητα μεταξύ 5.000 και 10.000 πόδια ανά δευτερόλεπτο (3.000 έως 6.000 μίλια την ώρα). Τέτοιες ταχύτητες μπορούσαν να παραχθούν μόνο με έκρηξη. Όταν η ομάδα εξέτασε τα σωματίδια που ανακτήθηκαν από το μαξιλάρι από το Charlie Oscar κάτω από ηλεκτρονικό μικροσκόπιο, ανακάλυψε πολλά επιφανειακά χαρακτηριστικά των εκρηκτικών φαινομένων[111]. Στη συνέχεια έκαναν σύγκριση των σωματιδίων που παρήχθησαν στη δοκιμαστική τους έκρηξη και βρήκαν σημάδια τόσο παρόμοια που αυτό θεωρήθηκε πειστικό στοιχείο. Περαιτέρω επιβεβαίωση προέκυψε από τη μεταλλογραφική εξέταση των ανακτημένων θραυσμάτων, η οποία έδειξε χαρακτηριστικά κρυσταλλικής δομής εκρηκτικών φαινομένων. Τέλος, εργαστηριακές δοκιμές έδειξαν ότι παρόμοια μεταλλικά θραύσματα μπορούσαν να παραχθούν μόνο με χρήση στρατιωτικού ή παρόμοιου ισχυρού εκρηκτικού. Σημειωτέον, δεν θα μπορούσαν να παραχθούν (λ.χ.) από το σκάσιμο ενός δοχείου αεροζόλ ή άλλης «αθώας» πηγής.

Έχοντας διαπιστώσει πέραν πάσης αμφιβολίας ότι η ζημιά στο μαξιλάρι είχε προκληθεί από έναν ισχυρό εκρηκτικό μηχανισμό, που μερικές φορές αναφέρεται ως «μηχανή της κολάσεως», οι εξεταστές ξεκίνησαν στη συνέχεια να προσδιορίσουν την ακριβή θέση της συσκευής όταν εξερράγη. Βοηθήθηκαν από το σχήμα των μαξιλαριών για καθεμία από τις πέντε θέσεις στην τουριστική καμπίνα του Κομήτη.

Η γεωμετρία της ζημιάς στο μαξιλάρι, η θέση των θραυσμάτων και οι τροχιές έδειχναν μια θέση όπου ορισμένα μέρη του μαξιλαριού καλύπτονταν από τη δομή του καθίσματος. Επειδή οι δύο πλευρές του καθίσματος ήταν διαφορετικές, η μία συνόρευε με το καμπύλο τοίχωμα της ατράκτου και η άλλη από το διάδρομο, και οι δύο πλευρές της

---

[111]. «*Τα σωματίδια έχουν παραχθεί κυρίως με ξεφλούδισμα και έχουν κυρίως σχήμα κυπέλου με τυλιγμένες άκρες. Στις επιφάνειές τους παρουσιάζουν διαγνωστικά χαρακτηριστικά, όπως το ράγισμα, τα αποτελέσματα της πλύσης με ζεστό αέριο και ο βομβαρδισμός από μικροσωματίδια υψηλής ταχύτητας. Σε ορισμένες περιπτώσεις, έχουν προκαλέσει το υλικό του μαξιλαριού να λιώσει και να προσκολληθεί στις επιφάνειές τους.*» -

καμπίνας απαιτούσαν τα σχέδια να αντικατοπτρίζονται, η μόνη δυνατή θέση για το συγκεκριμένο μαξιλάρι ήταν στην αριστερή πλευρά του αεροσκάφους, δηλαδή κάτω από ένα κάθισμα με αριθμό «Α», με τη συσκευή να βρίσκεται μεταξύ του στηρίγματος του καθίσματος και του τοίχου της καμπίνας. Η ακριβής τοποθεσία ήταν «...*μια προέλευση σε περιορισμένο μέγεθος περίπου 12 ίντσες κάτω από το κάθισμα, περίπου στο κατακόρυφο επίπεδο της πίσω άκρης του μαξιλαριού και περίπου 3 ίντσες από την αριστερή άκρης του μαξιλαριού*». Αυτό υποδηλώνει ότι η θέση θα ήταν επομένως συνεπής με τη συσκευή να βρίσκεται στο χώρο των ποδιών του επιβάτη του καθίσματος ακριβώς πίσω από αυτό από το οποίο προήλθε το μαξιλάρι και όπου θα ήταν καθαρά ορατό σε όλους τους επιβάτες σε παρακείμενα καθίσματα. Ο ανιχνευτής ηλεκτρονίων και η ανάλυση ακτίνων Χ των μεταλλικών θραυσμάτων έδειξαν ότι μερικά ήταν από χάλυβα και μερικά κράμα αλουμινίου. Αποδείχθηκε, με μία εξαίρεση, ότι διαφέρουν αρκετά από τα λίγα μικρά εξαρτήματα από χάλυβα και τα πιο διαδεδομένα κράματα που χρησιμοποιούνται στη δομή και τα καθίσματα αεροσκάφους. Ήταν επίσης διαφορετικά από τα μέταλλα που χρησιμοποιούνται στους βρετανικούς πυροκροτητές και η ομάδα ήθελε να συνεχίσει την εξέταση που θα περιλάμβανε σύγκριση με πυροκροτητές ξένης προέλευσης. Η μόνη εξαίρεση ήταν ένα κομμάτι μετάλλου με μια κηλίδα χρώματος καφέ. Αυτό ταίριασε με ένα που χρησιμοποιήθηκε σε κάθισμα επιβάτη του Κομήτη. Είναι σημαντικό ότι δεν βρέθηκαν στο δάπεδο θραύσματα κράματος (fragments of alloy). Αυτό απέδειξε ότι η συσκευή δεν τοποθετήθηκε κάτω από το πάτωμα της καμπίνας, όπως στο χώρο αποσκευών. Αυτό επιβεβαιώθηκε από την απουσία ινών στο χαλί. Πολλές ίνες ανακτήθηκαν από το κατεστραμμένο μαξιλάρι του καθίσματος, που εισχώρησαν σ'αυτό από τη δύναμη της έκρηξης. Αυτά υποβλήθηκαν σε χημική, μικροσκοπική και ακτινογραφική εξέταση η οποία έδειξε ότι η προέλευσή τους ήταν το ύφασμα που κάλυπτε τα καθίσματα.

Υπήρξε επίσης ζημιά, μαύρισμα και σκισίματα στην κάτω επιφάνεια του μαξιλαριού, γεγονός που έδειξε ότι η έκρηξη έγινε ενώ το μαξιλάρι βρισκόταν στην κανονική του θέση στο πλαίσιο του καθίσματος και ότι βαρούσε κάτω χαρακτηριστικό όταν υπάρχει επιβάτης. καθισμένος πάνω του εκείνη την ώρα.

Ένα δεύτερο μαξιλάρι καθίσματος είχε μικρές ζημιές που φαινόταν σύμφωνο με το πρώτο. Οι διατρήσεις στο δεύτερο μαξιλάρι υποδήλωναν, αν και όχι οριστικά, ότι το κάθισμα βρισκόταν λίγο πίσω στη δεξιά πλευρά της έκρηξης. Για άλλη μια φορά, υπήρχε μαύρισμα στην κάτω επιφάνεια, εκτός από εκεί που είχε καλυφθεί από το πλέγμα του καθίσματος.

Τα πρακτικά του Veal σημειώνουν ότι είχε μια συνάντηση στις 13 Νοεμβρίου, όπου παρευρέθησαν μαζί του οι Harper, Gordon-Burge, Head και Newton.. Η ομάδα συζήτησε τη θέση σχετικά με την εξέταση του μαξιλαριού του καθίσματος, με τον Harper είχε αναλάβει το ρόλο να καθορίσει μια σίγουρη αναγνώριση του μαξιλαριού. Αυτό ακολουθήθηκε στη συνέχεια μέσω των κατασκευαστών του αεροσκάφους, μέσω των εταιρειών της αλυσίδας εφοδιασμού, στο Dunlopillo στο Aberdare της Νότιας Ουαλίας, που είχε κατασκευάσει το υλικό /γέμιση (foam material) για το κατεστραμμένο αντικείμενο (μαξιλάρι). Ως αποδεικτική αλυσίδα ήταν υποδειγματική. Σημείωσε ο Veal:

«... Εξετάστηκε η πιθανή επίδραση στη δομή μιας έκρηξης του υποτιθέμενου μεγέθους. Θεωρήθηκε ότι ως εναλλακτική λύση για την πρόκληση βλάβης στην καμπίνα, θα μπορούσε να προκληθεί ζημιά που θα προκαλούσε τοπική κατάρρευση του δαπέδου με επακόλουθη ζημιά στα χειριστήρια του αεροσκάφους που θα μπορούσε να δημιουργήσει μια καταστροφική κατάσταση. Στον κ. Harper δόθηκαν τα χαρακτηριστικά της εκρηκτικής πίεσης και συμφώνησε να εξετάσει τις επιπτώσεις στη δομή της καμπίνας και του δαπέδου.»

Μέρος ενός λευκού νάιλον πουκάμισου είχε μερικές μικρές διατρήσεις στην περιοχή του δεξιού μπροστινού μέρους που θα μπορούσαν, σκέφτηκαν οι ερευνητές, να είχαν παραχθεί από σωματίδια υψηλής ταχύτητας. Ωστόσο, δεν μπορούσαν να είναι σίγουροι για αυτό.

Οι ερευνητές εξέτασαν την ποσότητα της εκρηκτικής ύλης που απαιτείται για να προκληθεί η ακριβής ζημιά που καταγράφηκε. Από προηγούμενες εμπειρίες και εργαστηριακές δοκιμές, υπολόγισαν ότι η ζημιά θα μπορούσε να είχε προκληθεί από «περίπου ένα κιλό ισχυρής εκρηκτικής ύλης» που πιθανόν να βρισκόταν μέσα σε σωλήνα από μαλακό χάλυβα ή παρόμοιο δοχείο.

Με βάση τα στοιχεία που προέρχονται από τα μαξιλάρια των καθισμάτων ο Ken Mason κλήθηκε να επαναξιολογήσει το εύρημα από την υπόθεση Νο. 6, κ. Αφατίτη. Οι ακτινογραφίες που λήφθηκαν κατά τη μεταθανάτια εξέταση εξετάστηκαν ξανά και παρατηρήθηκαν αδιαφανή σωματίδια, τα οποία ήταν πολύ παρόμοια με αυτά που βρέθηκαν στα μαξιλάρια. Περαιτέρω αποδεικτικά στοιχεία, που δεν είναι από μόνα τους οριστικά αλλά θεωρούνται πιθανό να συμβούν σε περιπτώσεις έκρηξης, βρέθηκαν σε μεμονωμένες περιπτώσεις ακρωτηριασμού των ποδιών τριών επιβατών, σε ένα αριθμό εκρήξεων στην κοιλιά, στη βλάβη πνεύμονος επιβάτη που αρχικά θεωρήθηκε πως είχε πνιγεί, και τραυματισμό στους γλουτούς μιας ηλικιωμένης επιβάτιδας, της δίδας Παρζοπούλου[112].

Ο Mason σημείωσε, ωστόσο, ότι ήταν αδύνατο να πει κανείς ότι αυτοί οι τραυματισμοί δεν ήταν συμβατοί με εκείνους που θα αναμένονταν σε ένα σοβαρό αεροπορικό ατύχημα λόγω άλλης αιτίας εκτός από την έκρηξη. Ειδικότερα, προέτρεψε να είναι προσεκτικοί όσον αφορά τον χαρακτηρισμό της δολιοφθοράς ως βέβαιης αιτίας, λαμβάνοντας υπόψη:

1. Ο κ. Αφατίτης ήταν η μόνη περίπτωση που παρουσίασε τέτοιους τραυματισμούς. Το σώμα της συζύγου του δεν παρείχε τέτοια στοιχεία, αν και ήταν ένα από τα τελευταία θύματα που εξετάστηκαν και η χρήση του πατρικού της ονόματος σήμαινε ότι η σχέση δεν ήταν γνωστή *(εννοείται στους εξεταστές)* παρά μόνο εβδομάδες αργότερα.
2. Οι βλάβες στο δέρμα, ήταν πολύ επιφανειακές. Ωστόσο, οι εμπειρογνώμονες των εκρηκτικών θεώρησαν ότι αυτό δεν ήταν ασυμβίβαστο με τη θεωρία της έκρηξης.

Ο Mason και ο Tarlton δεν μπορούσαν να δηλώσουν ότι τα τραύματα που υπέστη ο κ. Αφατίτης παρείχαν εκ πρώτης όψεως στοιχεία για έναν εκρηκτικό μηχανισμό που να είχε προκαλέσει την καταστροφή. Ωστόσο, πίστευαν ότι τέτοια ιατρικά στοιχεία θα μπορούσαν να επιβεβαιώσουν οποιοδήποτε τέτοιο συμπέρασμα βασισμένο σε στοιχεία μηχανολογικής μαρτυρίας. Επιπλέον, πίστευαν ότι πρόκειται για μια συσκευή που περιείχε πλαστικό εκρηκτικό αντί για χειροβομβίδα, και ότι αυτό είχε κάνει τη διαφορά στην ικανότητά τους να θεωρούν τους τραυματισμούς στα σώματα ως εκ πρώτης όψεως αποδεικτικά στοιχεία. Κατά την απώλεια του Charlie Oscar, είχαν πραγματοποιηθεί προηγούμενες βομβιστικές επιθέσεις σε αεροσκάφη που θεωρήθηκαν τότε ως να έγιναν με συμβατικά εκρηκτικά, συμπεριλαμβανομένης της σκόπιμης ανατίναξης χειροβομβίδων ή συσκευασιών δυναμίτη ή gelignite από επιβάτες αυτοκτονίας, και η χρήση «πλαστικής βόμβας» ήταν μοναδική[113].

---

[112] *Οι επιβάτες που περιγράφονται έτσι ήταν όλοι μεταξύ της ομάδας των Μαρτύρων του Ιεχωβά που επιβιβάστηκαν στην Αθήνα και πιστεύεται ότι κάθονταν μαζί στην πίσω καμπίνα της Τουριστικής Κατηγορίας.*

[113] *Είχε επίσης δοθεί προσοχή σε μια περιβόητη δολοφονία του 1943 στο Rayleigh του Essex, κατά την οποία ένας άνδρας σε μια καρέκλα μπάνιου είχε σκοτωθεί από μια συσκευή που ήταν τοποθετημένη κάτω από αυτό. Σε εκείνη την περίπτωση, το εκρηκτικό ήταν μια αντιαρματική νάρκη.*

Λαμβάνοντας υπόψη τη ζημιά στα μαξιλάρια των καθισμάτων, όμως, εκείνο που είδαν στα πτώματα και μπορούσε να θεωρηθεί ως περιστασιακό στοιχείο, ήταν πλέον επαρκή για να επιβεβαιώσουν αυτό που πίστευαν τώρα συλλογικά οι ειδικοί: ένας εκρηκτικός μηχανισμός ήταν η βασική αιτία της καταστροφής.

Η AIB συνεργάστηκε τώρα με το Τμήμα Δομών (Structures Deparment) του Royal Aircraft Establishment (RAE) στο Farnborough, με την ελπίδα (να μάθουν) αν θα μπορούσαν να βάλουν τον εκρηκτικό μηχανισμό μεσα στην άτρακτο ενός Κομήτη 4Β εν πτήση στα 29.000 πόδια. Την επίβλεψη του έργου είχε ο Fred Jones ένας 47χρονος δομικός εμπειρογνώμονας, ο οποίος είχε αποκτήσει φήμη ως εμπειρογνώμονα εναέριας ασφάλειας, λόγω της συμμετοχής του στην εξέταση των συντριμμιών από τις προηγούμενες συντριβές του Κομήτη της BOAC. Ο Fred Jones έλαβε τελικά ένα OBE[114].

Ο Jones ήταν ένας σχολαστικός άνθρωπος, με εξαιρετικό ιστορικό να συνάγει την αιτία των απωλειών αεροσκαφών από τα ελάχιστα διαθέσιμα στοιχεία. Στην περίπτωση του Charlie Oscar , ωστόσο, έπρεπε να καλύψει τα κενά λόγω της απουσίας σημαντικών συντριμμιών αεροσκάφους και να εργαστεί με τις θύμισες του προσωπικού εδάφους και των αποβιβαζόμενων επιβατών (εννοείται στην Αθήνα) και του πληρώματος ως προς το ποιος πιθανότατα καθόταν πού. Δεν τον βοήθησε το γεγονός ότι αγνοούνταν δεκαπέντε επιβάτες και τέσσερις δεν είχαν υποβληθεί σε νεκροψία. Ο Jones είχε σίγουρα πρόβλημα με τον Charlie Oscar .

Η αναφορά του Jones[115] ξεκίνησε με μια επισκόπηση της πτήσης, το υλικό που ανακτήθηκε από τη σκηνή της συντριβής και όσα ήταν γνωστά για τους επιβάτες. Σημείωσε:

«Τα επιφανειακά σκάφη, που ασχολούνταν με την ανάκτηση, αναπτύχθηκαν στις δύο περιοχές «Βόρεια» και «Νότια», και όλα τα σώματα και συντρίμμια ταυτοποιήθηκαν σε πρώτη φάση, από αυτές τις περιοχές. Έγινε φανερό στους παθολόγους που εξέταζαν τα πτώματα, ότι αυτά μπορούσαν να χωριστούν σε δύο γενικές ομάδες – εξαιρετικά τραυματίες και άλλες. Επιπλέον, με ελάχιστες εξαιρέσεις, εκείνοι στην ομάδα ακραίων τραυματισμών είχαν μολυνθεί με κηροζίνη, ενώ εκείνοι

---

[114] https://moretimespace.wordpress.com/2009/02/21/fred-jones-obe-mraes-ceng. Ο Fred Jones ήταν ο συγγραφέας του «Air Crash: The Clues in the Wreckage». Έφυγε από τη ζωή το 2003 σε ηλικία 82 ετών.

[115] Σημείωση Ατυχήματος Αρ. Structures 337: Σημείωμα για την απώλεια του Κομήτη BEA G-ARCO πάνω από τη Μεσόγειο Θάλασσα στις 12 Οκτωβρίου 1967 από τον F.H. Jones C.Eng., AFRAeS., Royal Aircraft Establishment, Μάρτιος 1968.

που τραυματίστηκαν ελαφρά ήταν «καθαροί». Οι ερευνητές παρατήρησαν επίσης ότι κάποια flotsam (συντρίμμια) ήταν πολύ μολυσμένα με κηροζίνη. Τα μολυσμένα πτώματα και τα flotsam ανασύρθηκαν όλα από τη νότια περιοχή. (η έμφαση του Jones).»

Ο Jones συνέχισε να εξετάζει όσα ήταν γνωστά για τους επιβάτες και το πλήρωμα καμπίνας, όπως συζητήθηκε στο Κεφάλαιο 2. Ο Jones θεώρησε ότι ήταν απίθανο οι επιβάτες αρχικά από το Λονδίνο να είχαν μετακινηθεί των θέσεών τους σε σημαντικό βαθμό κατά την επιστροφή τους στο αεροπλάνο στην Αθήνα μετά την ενδιάμεση στάση. Σχολίασε ότι μια ομάδα επιβατών, που τώρα προσδιορίζεται ως το κόμμα των Μαρτύρων του Ιεχωβά που εντάχθηκαν στην πτήση στην Αθήνα, είχαν κλείσει ομαδικά θέσεις στην πίσω τουριστική καμπίνα. Ωστόσο, αν και είχε εξακριβωθεί το τμήμα της καμπίνας που κατέλαβαν μέλη της ομάδας, ήταν αδύνατο να προσδιοριστεί ποια άτομα κάθονταν σε συγκεκριμένες θέσεις. Το σώμα ενός μέλους της ομάδας, σχολίασε, δεν είχε ανακτηθεί.

Ο Jones σημείωσε κατά προσέγγιση τα μετεωρολογικά δεδομένα την στιγμή του ατυχήματος, προσθέτοντας ότι η ισχύς και οι κατευθύνσεις του ανέμου σε διάφορα ύψη σχετίζονταν ειδικά με τους υπολογισμούς του για τις τροχιές των αντικειμένων που πέφτουν.

Η RARDE είχε δώσει στον Jones ορισμένες πληροφορίες που προέκυψαν από την εξέταση των μαξιλαριών, παθολογικά στοιχεία και τα πειράματά τους να αναπαράγουν την έκρηξη στην καμπίνα. Τον συμβούλεψαν:

α) Η έκρηξη είχε σημειωθεί ακριβώς πάνω από το δάπεδο του αεροσκάφους.

β) Η έκρηξη είχε συμβεί κάτω από το πίσω μέρος καθίσματος τουριστικού τύπου.

γ) Το κάθισμα αυτό ήταν κατειλημμένο την ώρα της έκρηξης.

δ) Αυτό το κάθισμα βρισκόταν στην ακραία αριστερή πλευρά του αεροσκάφους.

ε) Ένα πτώμα, αυτό του κ. Αφατίτη, τραυματίστηκε με τρόπο που υποδηλώνει ότι βρισκόταν σε κάθισμα μια σειρά πίσω και ένα κάθισμα δεξιά, από αυτό κάτω από το οποίο έγινε η έκρηξη.

ζ) Κανένα άλλο πτώμα που ανακτήθηκε δεν περιείχε στοιχεία παρόμοιας φύσης που να υποδηλώνουν ότι η έκρηξη ήταν πολύ κοντά[116]

---

[116] *Αυτά τα σημεία συνοψίζονται στην έκθεση του Jones. Είναι κάπως πιο συνοπτικοί από τους πιο προσεκτικούς Mason και Tarlton, οι οποίοι σημείωσαν κάποιους άλλους τραυματισμούς που θα μπορούσαν να προκλήθηκαν από τη βόμβα και επίσης δήλωσαν ότι υπήρχαν πολλά σώματα που μπορεί να είχαν θραύσματα, τα οποία δεν αναγνωρίστηκαν με τις βεβιασμένες μεταθανάτιες εξετάσεις τους.*

Όπως ήταν η πρακτική του, όποτε ήταν δυνατόν, όταν διεξήγαγε εξετάσεις συντριμμιών, ο Jones κανόνισε να τοποθετηθούν τα αντικείμενα σε μια διάταξη όπως ακριβώς στον Κομήτη, στο πάτωμα του εργαστηρίου στο Farmborough. Ο Jones βρήκε ότι όλα τα flotsam (συντρίμμια) προέρχονταν από την άτρακτο του Κομήτη και σημείωσε ότι όλα από το μπροστινό πτερύγιο ήταν μολυσμένα από κηροζίνη και όλα τα επόμενα δεν ήταν. Τα ρούχα που σχετίζονται με μεμονωμένους επιβάτες, των οποίων η θέση ήταν γνωστή, θα μπορούσαν επίσης να ταξινομηθούν με αυτόν τον τρόπο. Ο Jones κατέληξε επίσης στο συμπέρασμα, από την εξέταση των δέκα ρολογιών χειρός, ότι το Charlie Oscar είχε χτυπήσει τη θάλασσα περίπου στις 03:25 GMT, 0525 τοπική ώρα, περίπου επτά λεπτά μετά την τελευταία κλήση του SFO Thomas. Η έκθεσή του συνόψιζε την ανάλυση και τα συμπεράσματά του, τα οποία στη συνέχεια αντιπροσώπευσαν ένα σημαντικό συμπέρασμα για την τελική Έκθεση Ατυχήματος.

Οι έρευνες από την AIB καθόρισαν το χρόνο και τις θέσεις του αεροσκάφους κατά τη διάρκεια της πτήσης του... τα συντρίμμια (flotsam) και τα πτώματα βρέθηκαν σχεδόν είκοσι μίλια πίσω κατά μήκος της διαδρομής από την εκτιμώμενη θέση του τελευταίου μηνύματος.

Παρόλο που δεν ανακτήθηκαν από την θάλασσα συντρίμμια του σκελετού του αεροσκάφους, βρέθηκε αρκετό υλικό με τη μορφή χαλιών, επίπλων, μαξιλαριών καθισμάτων, επιβατών κ.λπ., ώστε να καθοδηγήσουν ως προς τις πιθανές θέσεις των κύριων τμημάτων της ατράκτου στη θάλασσα. Η φυσική διαίρεση όλου αυτού του υλικού, περιοχή ανάκτησης και ταυτότητα, σε δύο ομάδες έδειξε έντονα ότι η μπροστινή άτρακτος είχε προσγειωθεί στη θάλασσα στη βόρεια περιοχή και η πίσω άτρακτος, και τα συναφή φτερά που περιείχαν δεξαμενές καυσίμου, στη νότια περιοχή. Ορισμένα μαξιλάρια καθισμάτων βρέθηκαν στα νότια μεταξύ 1 έως 1 ½ μίλια από τη νότια περιοχή. Θεωρείται ότι ο διαχωρισμός της ατράκτου σε τουλάχιστον δύο μεγάλα τμήματα πρέπει να είχε συμβεί πριν το αεροσκάφος χτυπήσει στη θάλασσα, για να εξηγηθεί η κατανομή και η κατάσταση των συντριμμιών και των αμαξωμάτων.

Η εξέταση των flotsam (συντριμμιών) έδειξε ότι η διαίρεση της ατράκτου, με την μπροστινή και την πισινή έννοια, θα μπορούσε να έχει συμβεί περίπου στην εγκάρσια θέση αναφοράς (transverse datum position). Η εξέταση του γενικού προτύπου τραυματισμού επιβατών υποστήριξε αυτό το εύρημα. Γενικά, οι επιβάτες που βρίσκονταν μπροστά στην εγκάρσια θέση αναφοράς είχαν υποστεί σχετικά ελαφρούς ή ενδιάμεσους τραυματισμούς, ενώ εκείνοι που βρίσκονταν πίσω είχαν υποστεί ενδιάμεσους ή ακραίους τραυματισμούς. Είναι προφανές ότι μια τέτοια διαίρεση θα μπορούσε να προκύψει μόνο από τους επιβάτες που αντιμετώπισαν πολύ διαφορετικές συνθήκες, όπως στην περίπτωση θραύσης μιας ατράκτου στον αέρα.

Ως εκ τούτου, οι υπολογισμοί της τροχιάς έγιναν με την προϋπόθεση ότι ο διαχωρισμός της ατράκτου συνέβη στον αέρα στην μπροστινή θέση (front spar position). Η εταιρεία σχεδιασμού ανέφερε ότι αυτό θα ήταν ένα πιθανό σημείο διαχωρισμού σε περίπτωση φόρτωσης.

Πειράματα καταρχήν έγιναν με συγκεκριμένο ύψους 29.000 ποδιών και σημειώθηκε η προκύπτουσα διασπορά συντριμμιών και πτωμάτων στο επίπεδο της θάλασσας. Αυτή η κατανομή ήταν πολύ μεγάλη για να συμβιβαστεί με αυτή που είδε το αεροσκάφος έρευνας. Στη συνέχεια σχεδιάστηκαν τροχιές από το επίπεδο της θάλασσας προς τα πάνω, από τις γενικές θέσεις των αντικειμένων, σύμφωνα με σχέδια και χάρτες από το αεροσκάφος αναζήτησης. Μια πολύ κοντινή περιοχή αναχαίτισης βρέθηκε σε περίπου 15.000 πόδια υψόμετρο. Έφθασαν στο συμπέρασμα ότι το αεροσκάφος δεν είχε διαλυθεί στο ύψος της πτήσης του, αλλά σε χαμηλότερο υψόμετρο, για να δημιουργήσει το γενικό μοτίβο στη θάλασσα με τα flotsam και πτώματα, και το μοτίβο ζημιών και τραυματισμών στα πτώματα. Αυτό το συμπέρασμα υποστηρίχθηκε από την αναφορά των παθολόγων ότι δεν υπήρχαν ενδείξεις εκρηκτικής αποσυμπίεσης σε κανένα από τα πτώματα, αν και αυτό θα ήταν αναμενόμενο εάν είχε συμβεί μεγάλη διακοπή του αεροσκάφους σε μεγαλύτερο ύψος.

Μια περαιτέρω ένδειξη ότι διαχωρισμός της ατράκτου πιθανό να συνέβη στον αέρα δόθηκε από τα στοιχεία της άδειας φιάλης. Από το σημείο ανάκτησης της φιάλης βγήκε το συμπέρασμα ότι αυτή είχε αδειάσει στον αέρα λόγω της λειτουργίας του διακόπτη σύγκρουσης αδράνειας, που βρίσκεται στην υποδοχή, στη μύτη της ατράκτου, και ότι αυτή η λειτουργία θα μπορούσε να συσχετιστεί με φορτία αδράνειας. περίπου κατά τη διάρκεια θραύσης της ατράκτου στην μπροστινή θέση (spar).

Εάν το αεροσκάφος είχε διαλυθεί στα περίπου 15.000 πόδια, τότε τα πιο βαρετά συντρίμμια, που περιείχαν επιβάτες, ή τα πτώματα των επιβατών που έπεφταν, θα χρειάζονταν περίπου δύο λεπτά για να πέσουν στη θάλασσα. Εάν, επομένως, ο χρόνος της τελικής πρόσκρουσης που προκύπτει από τα ρολόγια (δηλαδή 0325 GMT) είναι σωστός, τότε η διάσπαση του αεροσκάφους θα είχε συμβεί περίπου στις 0323 GMT. Αυτό είναι πέντε λεπτά μετά το τελευταίο ηχογραφημένο μήνυμα από το αεροσκάφος και θα επέτρεπε αρκετό χρόνο στο αεροσκάφος να περάσει την τελευταία εκτιμώμενη θέση του στην τροχιά στα 29.000 πόδια και να επιστρέψει στη θέση διάσπασης στα 15.000 πόδια. Δεν βρέθηκαν στοιχεία από τη ΡΑΕ που να παρέχουν οποιαδήποτε ένδειξη της διαδρομής πτήσης του αεροσκάφους κατά την κάθοδο από τα 29.000 πόδια στα 15.000 πόδια, ή να εξηγούν την τελική διάσπαση.

Έγινε προσπάθεια εντοπισμού του πιθανού σημείου έκρηξης, που άλλες έρευνες έδειξαν ότι συνέβη πριν το αεροσκάφος χτυπήσει στη θάλασσα. Ανακεφαλαιώνοντας, φαίνεται ότι η έκρηξη σημειώθηκε κάτω από ένα τουριστικό κάθισμα στα αριστερά με μια σειρά από τρία (καθίσματα), ότι το κάθισμα ήταν κατειλημμένο, ότι το σώμα του επιβάτη δεν ανασύρθηκε και ότι το μόνο πτώμα που ανασύρθηκε με τραύματα του αναμενόμενου τύπου από έκρηξη, (δηλαδή αρ.6), ήταν αυτό του επιβάτη του μεσαίου καθίσματος στη σειρά πίσω. Δυστυχώς, ο επιβάτης αρ. 6 ήταν ένας από μια ομάδα με «καθίσματα σε μπλοκ», έτσι ώστε η ακριβής θέση του στην καμπίνα δεν ήταν γνωστή, αν και θα ήταν στη γραμμή Β σε μία από τις σειρές 3,4,5,6,7. Οι θέσεις στην αριστερή πλευρά σε αυτήν την περιοχή θα είχαν επίσης καταληφθεί από μέλη της ομάδας, αλλά καμία από αυτές δεν είχε τραυματιστεί με τρόπο που να υποδηλώνει ότι ήταν κοντά σε έκρηξη. Ωστόσο, ένας από την ομάδα δεν ανακτήθηκε.

Η φύση της ζημιάς στο κάθισμα, από την έκρηξη, και στο πτώμα αρ. 6 στη γραμμή Β, υποδηλώνει ότι το αποτέλεσμα της έκρηξης δεν ήταν μονοκατευθυντικό. Είναι πιθανό τότε ένα άτομο που καθόταν αμέσως στο πίσω μέρος της έκρηξης επίσης να τραυματιστεί από αυτήν. Δεδομένου ότι κανένα τέτοιο άτομο δεν έχει ανασυρθεί, είναι πιθανό ότι αυτό ήταν το άτομο που καθόταν στη θέση 4Α (γνωστό αλλά δεν βρέθηκε) ή ήταν το μέλος της ομάδας που έλειπε, το οποίο μπορεί να καθόταν στις θέσεις 3Α ή 7Α, δηλαδή πίσω από ένα από από τους δύο γνωστούς αλλά όχι ανακτημένους επιβάτες. Φαίνεται τότε ότι η έκρηξη θα μπορούσε να είχε συμβεί κάτω από τη θέση 4Α, 5Α ή 8Α και ότι ο επιβάτης αρ. 6 βρισκόταν στη θέση 3Β, 4Β ή 7Β.

Το ίδιο το αεροσκάφος δεν έφταιγε. Τα αποτελέσματα των βοηθητικών γραμμών έρευνας υποστήριξαν την άποψη ότι η αιτία ήταν η έκρηξη βόμβας και όχι οτιδήποτε άλλο. Είχαν περάσει μόλις έξι εβδομάδες από τότε που χάθηκε το Charlie Oscar, αλλά οι ερευνητές είχαν αξιοποιήσει στο έπακρο τα λίγα που είχαν στην διάθεσή τους να δουλέψουν. Διαπιστώθηκε τώρα ότι δεν είχε χαθεί σε σύγκρουση στον αέρα με άλλο αεροσκάφος, δεν είχε καταρριφθεί λόγω αποσύνθεσης κινητήρα ή βλάβης του πλαισίου του αεροσκάφους. Στις 20 Νοεμβρίου, με σχετικά μικρές φανφάρες, ο στόλος του Κομήτη αποδεσμεύθηκε για άλλη μια φορά να πετάξει σε κανονικά υψόμετρα. Το μόνο που έμενε ήταν να μάθουμε ποιος είχε τοποθετήσει τη βόμβα και γιατί.

Διαπιστώθηκε η πιθανή αιτία

Μετά την εργασία που έκανε η ομάδα στο RARDE και την διερευνητική δραστηριότητα που την συνόδεψε ο Veal πίστευε τώρα ότι είχε βρει την πιθανή αιτία του θανάτου του Charlie Oscar . Οι δηλώσεις του περιορίζονταν σε γεγονότα και περιείχαν επιφυλάξεις που επέτρεπαν τη δυνατότητα περαιτέρω εξελίξεων. Την Παρασκευή 10 Νοεμβρίου 1967, δόθηκε τηλεφωνικώς στον Τύπο το ακόλουθο δελτίο τύπου:

«Ο κλάδος διερεύνησης ατυχημάτων του Board of Trade (Τμήμα Εμπορίου) ακολουθεί μια σειρά από έρευνες, με βάση τα συντρίμμια του Κομήτη που ανακτήθηκαν από τη Μεσόγειο και άλλα στοιχεία.

Ένα από τα μαξιλάρια καθίσματος, το οποίο πιστεύεται ότι προέρχεται από την τουριστική καμπίνα, βρέθηκε να έχει υποστεί ζημιά, σύμφωνη με αυτή που θα προκαλείτο από εκρηκτικό μηχανισμό μέσα στο δάπεδο της καμπίνας. Υπάρχουν άλλα στοιχεία, τα οποία συνάδουν ότι αυτό συνέβη, αλλά θα ήταν πρόωρο να πούμε ότι επιβεβαιώνουν ένα τέτοιο ενδεχόμενο. Θα απαιτηθούν περαιτέρω πειραματικές εργασίες και άλλες έρευνες προτού καταλήξουμε σε κάποιο συγκεκριμένο συμπέρασμα σχετικά με τη σχέση αυτών των στοιχείων με την αιτία του ατυχήματος του Κομήτη και προτού γίνει οποιαδήποτε περαιτέρω δήλωση.»

Το σκεπτικό του Veal ήταν πιθανώς ότι ήταν απίθανο να αποδειχτεί κάποια άλλη, πιο πιθανή, αιτία, και επομένως ήταν προς το δημόσιο συμφέρον να γίνει γνωστό ότι η καταστροφή του αεροσκάφους ήταν σκόπιμη και όχι λόγω εγγενούς σφάλματος του Κομήτη.

Τα μέσα ενημέρωσης δεν είναι γνωστά να αργούν να κάνουν εικασίες για δραστηριότητες παρασκηνίων, και στις 26 Νοεμβρίου η *The Sunday Telegraph* δημοσίευσε ένα σύντομο και μη αποδιδόμενο άρθρο, με τον τίτλο *Η ΜΙ6 στην έρευνα για το ατύχημα του Κομήτη* στο οποίο συνέδεσε τον τότε πρωθυπουργό, Harold Wilson με το θέμα:

« Ο κ. Wilson ενδιαφέρεται προσωπικά για μια έρευνα της βρετανικής υπηρεσίας πληροφοριών σχετικά με την καταστροφή από πλαστική βόμβα του Κομήτη BEA μεταξύ Αθήνας και Κύπρου τον περασμένο μήνα.

Σύμφωνα με πληροφορίες από την ΜΙ6 είναι σχεδόν βέβαιο ότι 66 άνθρωποι έχασαν τη ζωή τους εξαιτίας απόπειρας δολοφονίας του Στρατηγού Γρίβα, διοικητή των ενόπλων δυνάμεων της Κύπρου. Ο κ. Wilson αναγκάζεται να το υποβαθμίσει λόγω της Κυπριακής κρίσης.

Παρά τις πληροφορίες περί του αντιθέτου, η όλη έρευνα έχει κρατηθεί μακριά από τα χέρια της βρετανικής αστυνομίας. Υπό κανονικές συνθήκες η Scotland Yard έπρεπε να καλεστεί να ανακαλύψει ποιος τοποθέτησε τη βόμβα και πού.

Αυτό συμβαίνει πάντα όταν εμπλέκονται ένα βρετανικό αεροπλάνο και μια χώρα της Κοινοπολιτείας.

Αντίθετα, την εγκληματική πτυχή της έρευνας χειρίζεται εξ ολοκλήρου η κυβερνητική υπηρεσία πληροφοριών σε συνεργασία με το Υπουργείο Εξωτερικών και το Συμβούλιο (Τμήμα) Εμπορίου.

Ο Στρατηγός Γρίβας πέταξε από την Αθήνα στην Κύπρο με άλλο Κομήτη την ημέρα της συντριβής. Ο σωματοφύλακάς του κ. Α Σολωμού[117] επέβαινε στο χαμένο αεροσκάφος και είναι σχεδόν βέβαιο ότι όσοι τοποθέτησαν τη βόμβα νόμιζαν ότι ο Στρατηγός ήταν στο ίδιο αεροπλάνο.

Ελάχιστες αμφιβολίες υπάρχουν ότι η βόμβα τοποθετήθηκε στο αεροδρόμιο της Αθήνας. Πολιτικοί εξτρεμιστές εκτός Ελλάδας μπορεί κάλλιστα να ήταν υπεύθυνοι.

Εάν η απόπειρα δολοφονίας είχε πετύχει, θα είχε αγγίξει την κρίση μεταξύ Ελλάδας και Τουρκίας πριν από ένα μήνα.»

Το άρθρο της *Sunday Telegraph*, μαζί με το συνοπτικό δελτίο τύπου του Veal που προσδιορίζει μια βόμβα ως την πιο πιθανή αιτία, προκάλεσαν αναταραχές στην Ελλάδα. Την ίδια μέρα, η Διοίκηση Πολιτικής Αεροπορίας στην Αθήνα έβγαλε τη δική της ανακοίνωση[118] 44 διαψεύδοντας :

« Μετά από εκπομπή του BBC και σχόλια στον εγχώριο και ξένο τύπο... δηλώνουμε και πάλι ότι σύμφωνα με λεπτομερείς αποδείξεις που λάβαμε μέχρι τις 20 Νοεμβρίου τα παραπάνω σχόλια από τον Τύπο και το BBC δεν έχουν καμία σχέση με τα αληθινά αίτια του ατυχήματος. Συμβουλεύουμε όσους βιάζονται να βγάλουν ανεύθυνα συμπεράσματα να περιμένουν έως ότου η αρμόδια νόμιμη αρχή υποβάλει την επίσημη έκθεσή της. Αυτή η νομική αρχή... είναι το Board of Trade, Μεγάλης Βρετανίας. Θα πρέπει επίσης να περιμένουν τη σύμφωνη γνώμη των αρμόδιων ελληνικών αρχών.»

Το δελτίο τύπου των Ελλήνων προκάλεσε κάποια αναστάτωση στη Βρετανική Πρεσβεία, η οποία έστειλε τηλε-μήνυμα την επομένη στον Veal :

---

[117] *Δεν υπάρχουν στοιχεία ότι ο Αβραάμ Σολωμού ενεργούσε ως σωματοφύλακας του Στρατηγού Γρίβα.*

[118] *Η πηγή είναι ένα τέλεξ από τη Βρετανική Πρεσβεία στην Αθήνα, το κείμενο είναι μετάφραση της Πρεσβείας από τα ελληνικά.*

«Αναμφίβολα θα έχετε δει τη στήλη στη χθεσινή Sunday Telegraph... Κατά τη γνώμη μας, τέτοιες εικασίες δεν μπορούν παρά να εκνευρίσουν την Ελληνική Υπηρεσία Πολιτικής Αεροπορίας υπονοώντας κριτική για τις ρυθμίσεις ασφαλείας στο αεροδρόμιο του Ελληνικού. Ως εκ τούτου, θα πρέπει να είμαστε ευγνώμονες εάν μπορούσατε να μας αφήσετε το σχόλιό σας για τη στήλη της ST και τυχόν περαιτέρω στοιχεία σχετικά με τον «εκρηκτικό μηχανισμό» που αναφέρεται στις δικές σας δηλώσεις.»

Ο Veal απάντησε αμέσως, σε μια προσπάθεια να δώσει διαβεβαίωση:

«Εάν το άρθρο της Sunday Telegraph δεν είναι πλήρης εικασία ή πέταγμα χαρταετού, δεν γνωρίζουμε πηγές πληροφοριών. Οι μόνες πληροφορίες που δίνονται από εμάς σχετικά με την έκρηξη είναι το δελτίο τύπου που ήδη έχετε και η απάντηση σε ερώτηση στη Βουλή των Κοινοτήτων στις 22 Νοεμβρίου σχετικά με τη διάσωση του Κομήτη που λέγει ότι «Λόγω αυτού (ανέφικτο της γενικής διάσωσης και δυσκολίες και απιθανότητα επιτυχούς διάσωσης του καταγραφέα πτήσης) και στοιχεία που υποδηλώνουν έκρηξη ισχυρής εκρηκτικής ύλης στη καμπίνα του αεροσκάφους, ο Εντιμότατος φίλος[119] αποφάσισε ότι το ζήτημα της διάσωσης δεν πρέπει να επιδιωχθεί». Επιστολή για την παρούσα θέση σε σχέση με την έρευνα είναι καθ' οδόν. Αναμένετε η διερεύνηση της εκρηκτικής πτυχής να ολοκληρωθεί σύντομα επιβεβαιώνοντας ότι συνέβη η έκρηξη.»

Ο Veal έγραψε στον JWG James, Διευθυντή Επιχειρήσεων της ΒΕΑ, στις 12 Δεκεμβρίου, δηλώνοντας:

«Βρίσκομαι σε αλληλογραφία με τον Στρατηγό Σκαρμαλιωράκη, τον Διευθυντή Πολιτικής Αεροπορίας στην Αθήνα, και με το Forbes-Johnson για στοιχεία που βρέθηκαν κατά την έρευνα. Καταρχήν έγραψα για πρώτη φορά στον Διαχειριστή στις 15 Νοεμβρίου λέγοντάς του, μεταξύ άλλων, για το μαξιλάρι που βρέθηκε με τα συντρίμμια της καμπίνας, το οποίο έδειξε ζημιά που συνάδει με αυτό που θα μπορούσε να προκληθεί από εκρηκτικό μηχανισμό στο δάπεδο της καμπίνας. Ακολούθησα με περαιτέρω επιστολή στις 28 Νοεμβρίου στην οποία έλεγα ότι η περαιτέρω έρευνα του μαξιλαριού, της ζημιάς σε αυτό και των σωματιδίων που περιείχε, έδειχναν την έκρηξη ενός ισχυρού εκρηκτικού μηχανισμού μέσα

---

[119] *Κοινοβουλευτικός όρος που χρησιμοποιείται όταν αναφέρεται σε ανώτερο στέλεχος του ίδιου πολιτικού κόμματος με τον ομιλητή.*

στην καμπίνα στο επίπεδο του δαπέδου. Του είπα επίσης ότι τα ιατρικά στοιχεία επιβεβαίωσαν την πυροδότηση εκρηκτικού μηχανισμού.

Φυσικά δεν έχουμε στοιχεία ότι η υπεύθυνη δαιμόνια μηχανή (infernal machine)[120] εισήχθη στο αεροσκάφος στην Αθήνα. Αν και κάποιοι θα μπορούσαν να το θεωρήσουν αυτό ως μια λογική υπόθεση, υποθέτω ότι οι Έλληνες μπορούν να ισχυριστούν ότι κάποιος έβαλε τον μηχανισμό αυτό στο Λονδίνο κατά την επιβίβασή του και τον άφησε εκεί όταν αποβιβάστηκε στην Αθήνα. Προσωπικά, δεν βλέπω ότι είναι πιθανό να λάβουμε ποτέ αποδεικτικά στοιχεία για την επίλυση αυτής της πτυχής. Αυτό μπορεί να υποδηλώνει ότι οι άνθρωποί σας θα πρέπει να είναι πολύ προσεκτικοί πώς χειρίζονται το θέμα με τις Ελληνικές αρχές, αλλά με βάση αυτό πιστεύω ότι έχω ήδη πει στον Στρατηγό Σκαρμαλιωράκη αρκετά ώστε να λάβετε κάποια μέτρα σχετικά με προληπτικά μέτρα.»

Το έργο των επιθεωρητών του ατυχήματος συνεχίστηκε και στις 12 Δεκεμβρίου, ο Veal συγκάλεσε συνάντηση για να συγκεντρώσει τα διάφορα σκέλη της έρευνας, με τους συνήθεις εκπροσώπους από το RARDE, RAE, Hawker Siddeley και την AIB. Ο κ. Clancey της RARDE έδωσε μια σύνοψη της δουλειάς των συναδέλφων του, δείχνοντας φωτογραφίες των θραυσμάτων μετάλλου που ανασύρθηκαν από το μαξιλάρι.

Η πολύ υψηλή ταχύτητα των διαφόρων σωματιδίων που ανιχνεύθηκαν, μεταξύ 2.000 και 5.000 ποδιών ανά δευτερόλεπτο για τα μεγαλύτερα θραύσματα και ίσως έως 15.000 πόδια ανά δευτερόλεπτο για τα μικρότερα, βοήθησε τον κ. Clancey να σχηματίσει την άποψη ότι υπήρχε «μια πλήρη βεβαιότητα για την έκρηξη ισχυρής εκρηκτικής ύλης».

Ο κ. Clancey συνέχισε, εξηγώντας ότι, αν και αρχικά θεώρησαν ότι τα στοιχεία υποδήλωναν ότι είχε πυροδοτηθεί μια ουγγιά εκρηκτικής ύλης, τώρα φαινόταν πιθανό ότι η συσκευή περιείχε τουλάχιστον τέσσερις ουγγιές. Όπως αναφέρθηκε προηγουμένως, πιστεύεται ότι ο τόπος ήταν στο αριστερό άκρο μιας αριστερής σειράς καθισμάτων.

Ο συνάδελφος του κ. Clancey στο RARDE, ο κ. Jarvis, πρόσθεσε ότι οι πιέσεις που σχετίζονται με μια ουγγιά εκρηκτικής ύλης θα ήταν 200 psi σε απόσταση ενός ποδιού από το σημείο της έκρηξης, μειώνοντας στα 30 psi στα δύο πόδια και στα 13 psi στα 3 πόδια. Ωστόσο, αυτές οι πιέσεις θα τετραπλασιάζονταν εάν η συσκευή περιείχε τέσσερις ουγγιές εκρηκτικής ύλης. Ήταν σαφές ότι η έκρηξη ενός εκρηκτικού μηχανισμού θα μπορούσε να προκαλέσει δυνητικά καταστροφικές ζημιές και σχεδόν άμεση διάσπαση της δομής της ατράκτου.

---

[120] Το «Infernal Machine» είναι ένας αρχαϊκός όρος για έναν εκρηκτικό μηχανισμό.

Στις 18 Δεκεμβρίου, ο Veal ήταν τελικά έτοιμος να καταθέσει την επίσημη ενδιάμεση έκθεσή του:

«Λόγω της μη διαθεσιμότητας των κύριων συντριμμιών του αεροσκάφους, η διερεύνηση του ατυχήματος επικεντρώθηκε στην εξέταση των συντριμμιών της καμπίνας που ανασύρθηκαν από τη Μεσόγειο, στα αποτελέσματα της παθολογικής εξέτασης των πτωμάτων των θυμάτων, στις γενικές συνθήκες της πτήσης και μια δεξαμενή πτώσης F.100 που ανασύρθηκε στη συνέχεια κοντά στη Ρόδο. Παράλληλα με αυτό έχουν μελετηθεί το ιστορικό ελαττωμάτων και τα δεδομένα του προηγούμενου καταγραφέα πτήσης της G-ARCO και έχει γίνει λεπτομερής μηχανική έρευνα άλλων αεροσκαφών Comet. Τα σημερινά συμπεράσματα επί του θέματος είναι ότι: -

(i) Κανένα από τα θύματα του ατυχήματος φορούσε σωσίβιο και δεν φάνηκαν συντρίμμια, εκτός από συντρίμμια καμπίνας και ένα μπουκάλι πυροσβεστήρα, στην περιοχή της σύγκρουσης, με πιθανή εξαίρεση ένα κυκλικό αντικείμενο που μπορεί να ήταν θόλος πίεσης καμπίνας (cabin pressure dome).

(ii) Η εξέταση μιας φιάλης πυροσβεστήρα, η οποία ήταν τοποθετημένη στη δεξιά πτέρυγα του αεροσκάφους, δείχνει ότι έχει αποφορτιστεί ως αποτέλεσμα της δράσης των διακοπτών αδράνειας και ότι υπέστη ζημιά από πρόσκρουση κατά τη διαδικασία εκφόρτωσης. Από τη διερεύνηση της πιθανής ακολουθίας διάσπασης φαίνεται ότι η εκκένωση της φιάλης και η ζημιά από την πρόσκρουση που υπέστη σχετίζονται με τη διάσπαση του αεροσκάφους σε ύψος. Υπάρχει σαφής διαχωρισμός μεταξύ μολυσμένης κηροζίνης και μη μολυσμένα συντρίμμια καμπίνας και πτώματα θυμάτων, γεγονός που υποδηλώνει τουλάχιστον μερική διάσπαση της καμπίνας σε διόλου ευκαταφρόνητο ύψος. Λόγω των ανακριβή πληροφοριών σχετικά με τα σημεία στα οποία ανακτήθηκαν τα διάφορα κομμάτια των συντριμμιών καμπίνας δεν είναι δυνατό να κατασκευαστεί ένα ακριβές σχέδιο τροχιάς από το οποίο θα μπορούσε να προσδιοριστεί το πιθανό ύψος της διάσπασης. Ωστόσο, η εργασία που έγινε σε αυτή τη σύνδεση και η ποσότητα της διασποράς υποδηλώνουν ότι η διάσπαση ήταν πολύ κάτω από το αρχικό υψόμετρο πλεύσης και μπορεί να ήταν μεταξύ 10.000 και 20.000 ποδιών.

(iii) Το μοτίβο τραυματισμού των θυμάτων, το 80% των οποίων υπέστη κακώσεις στο κεφάλι και σε άλλη μέρη του σώματος και το 20% μικρό εξωτερικό τραυματισμό, έχει διερευνηθεί με βάση τις περιορισμένες διαθέσιμες πληροφορίες για τις θέσεις των καθισμάτων και λαμβάνοντας υπόψη τους τραυματισμούς που υπέστησαν τα θύματα άλλων ατυχημάτων στα οποία έχει συμβεί δομική διάσπαση σε υψόμετρο. Ο παθολόγος, εξετάζοντας εάν θα μπορούσε να είχε συμβεί δολιοφθορά, είχε υπόψη ότι αυτό θα απαιτούσε την παρουσία μεγάλων μεταλλικών θραυσμάτων στα πτώματα. Δεν βρέθηκαν τέτοια θραύσματα στις ακτίνες X, αν και βρέθηκαν τρία κομμάτια υλικού αεροσκάφους ως αποτέλεσμα οπτικής εξέτασης. Ως αποτέλεσμα των στοιχείων που ελήφθησαν από ένα μαξιλάρι καθίσματος πραγματοποιήθηκε περαιτέρω διερεύνηση των φωτογραφιών με ακτίνες X και αυτό εξετάζεται παρακάτω μαζί με τις επιπτώσεις των παθολογικών ευρημάτων.

(iv) Ένα μαξιλάρι που βρέθηκε με τα συντρίμμια της καμπίνας, το οποίο αναγνωρίστηκε θετικά ως μαξιλάρι τουριστικής καμπίνας Κομήτη, έδειξε ζημιά η οποία, ως αποτέλεσμα εξαντλητικής έρευνας και πειραματικών εργασιών στο Royal Armament Research and Development Establishment είχε προκληθεί από έκρηξη ενός ισχυρού εκρηκτικού μηχανισμού. Η κύρια απόδειξη για αυτό είναι η μεγάλη ζημιά στο πίσω μέρος του μαξιλαριού, οι οπές διείσδυσης μέσα από το μαξιλάρι και η συμπερίληψη στο μαξιλάρι ενός αριθμού σιδηρούχων υλικών και σωματιδίων κράματος αλουμινίου. Η εξέταση των σωματιδίων πραγματοποιήθηκε με τη χρήση ηλεκτρονικής μικροσκοπίας και άλλων μεθόδων που δείχνουν ότι τα τεμάχια σιδήρου και κράματος αλουμινίου που ανακτήθηκαν έχουν τα χαρακτηριστικά ζημιάς λόγω υψηλής εκρηκτικής έκρηξης και επέτρεψαν να εξακριβωθεί η προέλευση των σωματιδίων. Η διερεύνηση των αυλακώσεων διείσδυσης δείχνει ότι η προέλευση της έκρηξης ήταν περίπου στο επίπεδο του δαπέδου της καμπίνας και μεταξύ δύο σειρών θέσεων. Υπάρχουν ενδείξεις ότι το μαξιλάρι βρισκόταν στο αριστερό κάθισμα μιας αριστερής σειράς, δηλαδή δίπλα της ατράκτου. Ένα άλλο από τα μαξιλάρια που ανακτήθηκαν βρέθηκε επίσης να έχει υποστεί μια σειρά από διεισδύσεις που δείχνουν ότι αυτό το μαξιλάρι βρισκόταν στη σειρά πίσω από αυτό στην οποία βρισκόταν το άλλο μαξιλάρι. Η ζημιά των μαξιλαριών λόγω έκρηξης και εναποθέσεων άνθρακα εντός των αυλακώσεων διείσδυσης και των δύο μαξιλαριών παρέχει αποδεικτικά στοιχεία για την εκδήλωση έκρηξης. Έχει υπολογιστεί ότι η ταχύτητα των μεγαλύτερων σωματιδίων που βρέθηκαν ήταν μεταξύ 2.000 και 5.000 πόδια ανά δευτερόλεπτο και έως 15.000 πόδια ανά δευτερόλεπτο σε σχέση με τα πραγματικά μικρά.

(v) Αρχικά προτάθηκε ότι μια δεξαμενή πτώσης καυσίμου F.100 που ανακτήθηκε από τη θάλασσα, η οποία είχε υποστεί σοβαρή ζημιά από πρόσκρουση και έφερε ίχνη κόκκινου χρώματος, μπορεί να σχετιζόταν με τις συνθήκες του ατυχήματος του Κομήτη. Κατά την οπτική εξέταση (όμως) το κόκκινο χρώμα φάνηκε να έχει ουσιαστικά διαφορετικό χρώμα από το χρώμα στους Κομήτες της ΒΕΑ και η χημική ανάλυση έδειξε ότι είναι ουσιαστικά διαφορετικό. Κατά την εξέταση η βαφή φάνηκε ότι ήταν σε υγρή κατάσταση όταν ήρθε σε επαφή με τη δεξαμενή καυσίμου και φαίνεται ότι η προέλευσή της ήταν κάτι πάνω στο οποίο ακουμπούσε η δεξαμενή ή που είχε τριβεί η δεξαμενή. Η ζημιά στη δεξαμενή συνάδει με τη ζημιά από πρόσκρουση νερού και ερευνώντας μέσω αμερικανικών πηγών, μάθαμε ότι ήταν ένα από δύο τέτοιες δεξαμενές (tanks) που έπεσαν από αεροσκάφος των Ηνωμένων Πολιτειών τον Ιούλιο.

(vi) ΟΙ μετεωρολογικές εξετάσεις έδειξαν ότι δεν υπήρχε λόγος να θεωρηθεί ότι ο καιρός ήταν παράγοντας στην αιτία του ατυχήματος.

...Όταν από τα συντρίμμια της καμπίνας βρέθηκαν στοιχεία έκρηξης στο αεροσκάφος, τα στοιχεία που ήταν διαθέσιμα από τις παθολογικές εξετάσεις των σορών ερευνήθηκαν εκ νέου σε μια προσπάθεια να διαπιστωθεί εάν αυτό έδειχνε ζημιά που να συνάδει με έκρηξη. Αυτό ήταν περίπλοκο από το γεγονός ότι ανασύρθηκαν μόνο 51 πτώματα, αν και 66 άτομα σκοτώθηκαν στο ατύχημα και ήταν αδύνατο να πραγματοποιηθεί πλήρης παθολογική εξέταση όλων των διαθέσιμων σορών. Επιπλέον, η έκταση της παθολογικής εξέτασης περιορίστηκε από τις διαθέσιμες εγκαταστάσεις. Αυτή η εκ νέου έρευνα έδειξε σε σχέση με ένα από τα πτώματα επαρκή ιατρικά στοιχεία για να επιβεβαιωθεί το συμβάν εκρηκτικού μηχανισμού. Επιπλέον αυτή η ιατρική επιβεβαίωση είναι ότι ο μηχανισμός ήταν πλαστικού εκρηκτικού τύπου και όχι τύπου χειροβομβίδας.

Αυτό το σημείωμα αποτελεί ουσιαστικά μια ενδιάμεση περιγραφή της παρούσας θέσης της έρευνας, αλλά έχει σκοπό να καταστήσει σαφές ότι η έκρηξη ενός ισχυρού εκρηκτικού μηχανισμού σχετίζεται με την απώλεια του αεροσκάφους.»

Ως συμπληρωματικό, ένα σημείωμα από τον Veal προς τον Riddoch στις 21 Δεκεμβρίου προσθέτει:

«Η RARDE... έχει φτάσει τώρα σε θέση βεβαιότητας ότι υπήρξε έκρηξη ενός ισχυρού εκρηκτικού μηχανισμού και ότι ήταν μεγαλύτερος από ό,τι είχε αρχικά υπολογιστεί, πιθανόν της τάξης των 4 ουγγιών[121].»

Μια χειρόγραφη προσθήκη στο αντίγραφο αυτού του σημειώματος του Veal αναφέρει: «Ευχαριστώ. Ο Πρόεδρος σχολίασε: «Πρώτης τάξεως και λεπτομερής ενδιάμεση έκθεση».

Ο Veal βρήκε επίσης την ευκαιρία να ενημερώσει τον Riddoch ότι η τελική του έκθεση εξαρτιόταν από την ολοκλήρωση των επικουρικών ερευνών και ότι ήταν απίθανο να ήταν διαθέσιμη μέχρι τα τέλη Μαρτίου.
Ο Veal είχε σημειώσει, σε ένα μήνυμα προς τον Ken Mason, επίσης στις 21 Δεκεμβρίου, ότι είχε ετοιμάσει την έκθεση ως μια περίληψη της έρευνας. Περίμενε ακόμη την τελική έκθεση της RARDE, η οποία υπολόγιζε θα ακολουθούσε μέχρι τα τέλη Ιανουαρίου. Σημείωσε επίσης:

---

[121] 4 ουγγιές είναι περίπου 113 γραμμάρια.

«Με πιέζουν να υποβάλω την επίσημη έκθεσή μου το συντομότερο δυνατό, και έχω δηλώσει ότι ελπίζω να το κάνω αυτό εντός δύο ή τριών μηνών. Αυτό εξαρτάται, φυσικά, από το ότι θα λάβω την τελική σας αναφορά και αυτή της RARDE μέχρι τα τέλη Ιανουαρίου».

Ο Mason απάντησε στις 5 Ιανουαρίου:
«Ευχαριστώ πολύ για την (έκθεσή σας) της 19ης Δεκεμβρίου 1967 και το αντίγραφο της έκθεση του κ. Χριστόπουλου. Όπως σας είπα στο τηλέφωνο, με ανησυχεί λίγο για το τι θα γίνει με αυτήν την έκθεση. Για το συμφέρον της διεθνούς συνεργασίας, δεν θέλω να διαφωνήσω μαζί της δημόσια και ελπίζω ότι θα μπορέσετε απλώς να την αγνοήσετε.»

Είναι προφανές από αυτό ότι ο Veal γνώριζε τις πιέσεις από διάφορες πλευρές, ιδίως και από τη ΒΕΑ και τον Τύπο, να δηλώσει κατηγορηματικά ποια θεωρούσε ότι ήταν η αιτία. Υπήρχαν επίσης ερωτήματα από τις ελληνικές και τις κυπριακές αρχές που ήταν εξίσου πρόθυμες να δουν το θέμα να ξεκαθαρίζει. Για το σκοπό αυτό, ο Veal έστειλε αντίγραφο της ενδιάμεσης έκθεσής του στον Στρατηγό Σκαρμαλιωράκη της Ελληνικής Διοίκησης Πολιτικής Αεροπορίας και περίμενε την απάντησή του.

Ο John Veal είχε συμπεριλάβει και τον Γενικό Εισαγγελέα στον κατάλογο περιορισμένης κυκλοφορίας της ενδιάμεσης έκθεσης. Ο Γενικός Εισαγγελέας, αφού την διάβασε, θεώρησε ξεκάθαρα ότι το θέμα ήταν σημαντικό καθώς, στις 3 Ιανουαρίου, στάλθηκε ένα μήνυμα στον Veal που του ζητούσε να έχει πρόσβαση και σε περαιτέρω εκθέσεις , συμπεριλαμβανομένης της τελικής έκθεσης, όταν θα ήταν διαθέσιμη.

Εν τω μεταξύ, πίσω στις 19 Δεκεμβρίου, ο Hugh Gordon-Burge είχε εκδώσει μια προκαταρκτική έκθεση του Τμήματος Αεροπορικής Ασφάλειας της ΒΕΑ (ASB). Αναπόφευκτα η έκθεση της ASB αντικατόπτριζε εκείνη του Veal, αν και πρόσθεσε τα ακόλουθα προκαταρκτικά συμπεράσματα:

1. Τα χαρτιά του αεροσκάφους ήταν εντάξει.

2. Οι πιλότοι είχαν την κατάλληλη άδεια.

3. Ενώ το αεροσκάφος πετούσε μεταξύ Ρόδου και Κύπρου, ένας εκρηκτικός μηχανισμός πυροδοτήθηκε στο επίπεδο του δαπέδου σε κάποιο σημείο της τουριστικής καμπίνας.

4. Η έκρηξη εντός της καμπίνας πιθανότατα προκάλεσε ζημιές στο αεροσκάφος ώστε να το καταστήσει ουσιαστικά ανεξέλεγκτο. Στη συνέχεια, και στην επακόλουθη αναγκαστική κάθοδο, το αεροσκάφος κόπηκε.

Η αρχική προκαταρτική έκθεση περιελάμβανε επίσης μια γραμμή που δήλωνε την πρώτη πιθανή αιτία: *«Το ατύχημα πιθανόν να προήλθε από την έκρηξη εκρηκτικού μηχανισμού μέσα στην καμπίνα».*

Δεν υπάρχει αμφιβολία ότι η ΒΕΑ ανέπνευσε έναν εταιρικό αναστεναγμό ανακούφισης όταν φάνηκε πολύ πιθανό ότι ούτε ο Κομήτης ως αεροσκάφος ούτε η ίδια η εταιρεία ως χειριστής του αεροσκάφους, θα θεωρούνταν υπεύθυνοι για την τραγωδία. Ήταν ξεκάθαρο προς όφελος της αεροπορικής εταιρείας ότι η αιτία, μια κακόβουλη πράξη μαζικής δολοφονίας, μπορούσε να συμβεί σε οποιοδήποτε αεροσκάφος και σε οποιανδήποτε εταιρεία. Το ταξιδιωτικό κοινό δεν θα είχε κανέναν ιδιαίτερο λόγο να αποφύγει την ΒΕΑ ή να αποφύγει την κράτηση πτήσης σε Κομήτη. Βασισμένη όπως ήταν στα έσοδα από τους επιβάτες, η ΒΕΑ έπρεπε να διασφαλίσει ότι αυτές οι πληροφορίες κοινοποιούνταν το συντομότερο δυνατό.

Ο Sir Anthony Milward, Πρόεδρος της ΒΕΑ, φάνηκε οπωσδήποτε να αισθάνεται την ανάγκη να καθησυχάσει το κοινό όταν μίλησε σε έναν ανταποκριτή της εφημερίδας The Times κατά τη διάρκεια μιας επίσκεψης στο Cardiff Business Club στις 8 Ιανουαρίου. Ο ανώνυμος ρεπόρτερ ίσως να νόμισε ότι βρήκε λαυράκι όταν η εφημερίδα τους αποκάλυψε την επόμενη μέρα, με τον τίτλο «*Η ΒΕΑ λέγει ο Κομήτης έπαθε σαμποτάζ*». Αποδίδοντας τις πληροφορίες στον Sir Anthony, το άρθρο συνέχισε:

«Οι ντετέκτιβ της Scotland Yard κλήθηκαν από την αεροπορική εταιρεία να ερευνήσουν . Ξεχωριστή έρευνα από τον επιθεωρητή του Συμβουλίου Εμπορικών Ατυχημάτων (Board of Trade) συνεχίζεται. Απόψε ένας αξιωματούχος είπε ότι δεν μπορούσε να γίνει κανένα σχόλιο.

(Ο Sir Anthony) μου είπε: «Οι δοκιμές μας απέδειξαν ότι ήταν δολιοφθορά. Κάναμε και δική μας έρευνα για την καταστροφή και ένα μαξιλάρι καθίσματος έδειξε ότι φαινόταν να υπήρξε εκρηκτικός μηχανισμός στο σκάφος».

Δεν είχε σίγουρη θεωρία γιατί το αεροσκάφους ... υπέστη σαμποτάζ. «Φαίνεται ότι κάποιος πίστευε ότι ο πρώην αρχηγός της ΕΟΚΑ Στρατηγός Γρίβας ή κάποιος από τους ανθρώπους του μπορεί να ήταν στο αεροσκάφος, αν και δεν έχω στοιχεία ότι ήταν έτσι», είπε.

«Οι δικές μας έρευνες έχουν πλέον τελειώσει και έχουμε παραδώσει τα πάντα στη Scotland Yard . Η επίσημη έρευνα του υπουργείου βρίσκεται ακόμη σε εξέλιξη. Δεν ξέρω αν αυτό θα συμφωνήσει με τα ευρήματά μας».

Εν τω μεταξύ, η σελίδα Londoners Diary της εφημερίδας *Evening Standard* επανέλαβε ορισμένους από τους ισχυρισμούς του Sir Anthony την επόμενη μέρα σε ένα σύντομο κομμάτι με τίτλο «*Comet Delay*» («Καθυστέρηση στον Κομήτη») :

«Η χθεσινή δήλωση του προέδρου της ΒΕΑ Sir Anthony Milward ότι η συντριβή του Κομήτη στα ανοιχτά της Τουρκίας τον περασμένο Οκτώβριο προκλήθηκε σίγουρα από δολιοφθορά δεν υποδηλώνει ότι το

Συμβούλιο Εμπορίου (Board of Trade) είναι έτοιμο να κάνει οποιαδήποτε ανακοίνωση σχετικά με το αποτέλεσμα των ερευνών του.

Τον Νοέμβριο έκαναν μια προσεκτική δήλωση ότι «ένα από τα μαξιλάρια καθισμάτων που πιστεύεται ότι προέρχεται από την τουριστική καμπίνα πιστεύεται ότι έχει υποστεί ζημιά αντίστοιχη με αυτή που θα προκαλούνταν από εκρηκτικό μηχανισμό», αλλά το αντιστάθμισαν με παρατηρήσεις όπως: «Περαιτέρω πειραματική εργασία και έρευνες θα χρειαστούν πριν καταλήξουν σε οριστικά συμπεράσματα».

Και πρέπει να περάσουν ακόμη πολλοί μήνες μέχρι να δημοσιοποιηθεί η τελική έκθεση.»

Στη συνέχεια, η εφημερίδα έστριψε το μαχαίρι περαιτέρω αναφέροντας ότι ο Captain William Baillie είχε εκφράσει:

«...κάποια δυσαρέσκεια σήμερα με την καθυστέρηση για μια έκθεση σαν αυτή. Είπε: «Ο John Veal μου είπε πριν από περίπου δύο μήνες ότι υπήρχαν σαφείς αποδείξεις ότι είχε εκραγεί μια βόμβα κάτω από το κάθισμα – (υπήρχαν) βαλλιστικά και χημικά στοιχεία.

« Κατά πόσο τοποθετήθηκε εκεί με αποκλειστικό σκοπό να ανατινάξουν το αεροσκάφος ή όχι, δεν το γνωρίζουμε. Η ΒΕΑ πρέπει να μετέφερε πολλούς επιβάτες στη Λευκωσία με πολεμικές συσκευές στις αποσκευές τους». Ο Captain Baillie τείνει να πιστεύει ότι η βόμβα δεν είχε στόχο τον στρατηγό Γρίβα.»

Είναι δίκαιο να πούμε ότι ο John Veal δεν ήταν ιδιαίτερα ευχαριστημένος με τα σχόλια των ανδρών της ΒΕΑ στον Τύπο. Στις 10 Ιανουαρίου, έστειλε μια κάπως ενοχλημένη επιστολή στον Henry Marking, τον Διευθύνοντα Σύμβουλο της αεροπορικής εταιρείας.

«Οι The Times της 9ης Ιανουαρίου περιείχαν μια αναφορά μιας συνέντευξης με τον Sir Anthony Milward, στην οποία μίλησε για δοκιμές που διεξήγαγε η ΒΕΑ κατά τη διερεύνηση του ατυχήματος του Κομήτη.

Καθώς η ΒΕΑ δεν μου παρείχε στοιχεία σχετικά με τις «δοκιμές σας που απέδειξαν ότι ήταν δολιοφθορά» ή «την έρευνά σας για τη καταστροφή και ένα μαξιλάρι καθίσματος που έδειξε ότι υπήρχε εκρηκτικός μηχανισμός στο αεροσκάφος», θα ήθελα σύμφωνα με τον Κανονισμό 7(1)(β) των Κανονισμών Πολιτικής Αεροπορίας (Διερεύνηση Ατυχημάτων) 1951, για μιλήσω και να πάρω δηλώσεις από όλους (όσους εμπλέκονταν στις έρευνες της εταιρείας). Επομένως θα χαρώ, αν με ενημερώσατε για τα ονόματα των υπεύθυνων για τις δοκιμές που διεξήγαγε η ΒΕΑ όσον αφορά την πτυχή της δολιοφθοράς.»

Στις 11 Ιανουαρίου, ο John Veal σημείωσε μια συνομιλία που είχε, πιθανότατα με τον Jim Templeton, από το Air Registration Board:

«Καθ' όλη τη διάρκεια της έρευνας υπήρξε στενή συνεργασία με το Τμήμα Ασφάλειας Πτήσεων της BEA και ενημερώθηκαν για την πρόοδο της έρευνας και, ειδικότερα, για το έργο που έχει γίνει στο RARDE σχετικά με την πτυχή της έκρηξης. Από όσο γνωρίζω, δεν υπάρχει καμία αλήθεια στη δήλωση του Sir Anthony Milward σχετικά με τις δοκιμές που έχουν πραγματοποιήσει στην πτυχή της έκρηξης ούτε, από όσο γνωρίζω, η BEA ήταν σε επαφή με τη Scotland Yard. Το Special Branch και το Box 500[122] ενημερώθηκαν από εμένα για τις πιθανές πτυχές της δολιοφθοράς, ώστε να μπορούν να κάνουν τις δικές τους έρευνες και καταλαβαίνω ότι η τελευταία ενδιάμεση έκθεση που έχω υποβάλει εξετάζεται από τον Βοηθό Επιθεωρητή και ότι συμβουλεύονται τον Δημόσιο Κατήγορο εάν πρέπει να ληφθούν περαιτέρω μέτρα.»

Ο Veal, ωστόσο, δεν βιάστηκε να δημοσιοποιήσει όλες τις λεπτομέρειες των ερευνών του. Γράφοντας στο Marking στις 9 Ιανουαρίου, είπε:

«Οποιαδήποτε έκφραση πεποίθησης (για την αιτία της συντριβής) αυτού του είδους ή σκέψη για ανάγκη τέτοιας, φυσικά, είναι θέμα για εσάς, αλλά με ανησυχεί ότι προτείνεται να συσχετιστεί με μια έκθεση που είναι βασισμένη σε σημαντικό βαθμό σε πληροφορίες που έχω κοινοποιήσει στη BEA εμπιστευτικά. Η συμπερίληψη σε αυτό αναφοράς ότι «ακόμη είναι εμπιστευτικού χαρακτήρα σχετικά αποδεικτικά στοιχεία, τα οποία δεν έχουν δημοσιοποιηθεί από τον Αρχι-επιθεωρητή Ατυχημάτων» χρησιμεύει απλώς στο να κάνει ακόμη πιο δύσκολη τη θέση μου στο θέμα. Μου έκανε εντύπωση από όσα γράφτηκαν στον Τύπο μετά την τελευταία δήλωση στη Βουλή, και την απόφαση να μην απαντώνται

---

[122] Το Box 500 είναι το ψευδώνυμο με το οποίο ήταν παραδοσιακά γνωστή η MI5, η ετικέτα προέρχεται από το κουτί Post Office (ταχυδρομείου) που χρησιμοποιείται ως διεύθυνσή του. Η MI5 (Στρατιωτική Υπηρεσία πληροφοριών Τμήμα 5) είναι επίσης γνωστή ως Υπηρεσία Ασφαλείας, με ρόλο την αντικατασκοπεία και την εσωτερική ασφάλεια. Η MI5 υπάγεται στο Υπουργείο Εσωτερικών. Ωστόσο, ο Veal και η ομάδα του αναφέρονται στο προσωπικό της «Defence Intelligence», το οποίο θα μπορούσε στην πραγματικότητα να ήταν το «Defence Intelligence Staff», ένα τμήμα του Υπουργείου Άμυνας, που πιθανώς συνεργάζεται με την MI6, τη Secret Intelligence Service, η οποία υπάγεται το Υπουργείο Εξωτερικών. Καθώς η ύπαρξη της MI6 κρατήθηκε μυστική εκείνη την εποχή, είναι πιθανό ότι η πρόσβαση στο προσωπικό της να γινόταν μέσω της MI5.

ερωτήσεις για περισσότερες πληροφορίες, ότι υπήρχε πλέον η γενική αποδοχή ότι το ατύχημα του Κομήτη προήλθε από έκρηξη ισχυρού εκρηκτικού μηχανισμού στην καμπίνα. Εάν έχετε αποδείξεις ότι εξακολουθεί να υπάρχει δημόσια ανησυχία για την ασφάλεια του αεροσκάφους που πρέπει να αμβλυνθεί ίσως θα μπορούσατε να με ενημερώσετε ώστε να μπορεί να ληφθεί υπόψη κάποια περαιτέρω επίσημη δήλωση σχετικά με την πρόοδο της έρευνάς μου.»

Μόλις τα έλαβε, ο Marking έγραψε δύο επιστολές απαντώντας στον Veal, στις οποίες εξέφραζε τη λύπη του για την αμηχανία που προκάλεσε και αυτό δεν ήταν πρόθεσή του. Ο Marking προσφέρθηκε να μιλήσει στην Επιτροπή Ασφάλειας Αεροπορίας και να κάνει σίγουρο ότι δεν δημοσίευαν έκθεσής τους μέχρι κάποια πιο κατάλληλη στιγμή. Η Επιτροπή ενημέρωσε τον Veal την ίδια μέρα, ότι ο Marking δεν μπορούσε να σχολιάσει τις παρατηρήσεις που αποδίδονταν στον πρόεδρό της, επομένως τον είχε παραπέμψει στην επιστολή του Veal. Λεπτομέρειες οποιασδήποτε μεταγενέστερης συζήτησης για το θέμα, μεταξύ Marking και Gordon-Burge δεν υπάρχουν στους φακέλους των Αρχείων. Στις 25 Ιανουαρίου, ο Milward ωστόσο, έγραψε κάτι σαν συγγνώμη στον Veal, αν και δεν μπόρεσε να μην προσθέσει: «*Πιστεύω, ωστόσο, ότι η τελευταία δήλωση του Mallalieu στη Βουλή κατέστησε επαρκώς την άποψή μας, διότι όντως διευκρινίζει ότι υπάρχουν πειστικές αποδείξεις έκρηξης στην καμπίνα*».

Στις 15 Ιανουαρίου, ο Έλληνας Διευθυντής Πολιτικής Αεροπορίας, Ταξίαρχος Α. Σκαρμαλιωράκης, απάντησε στο Veal. Η αντίληψή του για τα γεγονότα, και το αποτέλεσμα που επιθυμούσε, ήταν σημαντικά διαφορετικά από αυτά της BEA. Το κείμενο της επιστολής όπως παραδόθηκε στην AIB ήταν:

«Με το παρόν θα ήθελα να σας ευχαριστήσω πολύ που με κρατήσατε ευγενικά ενήμερο για την πρόοδο της έρευνας που διενεργήθηκε σχετικά με το ατύχημα του Κομήτη G-ARCO της BEA.

Ωστόσο, για να αποφευχθούν τυχόν λάθη που θα μπορούσαν να οδηγήσουν σε ανεπιθύμητες παρεξηγήσεις μεταξύ των ενδιαφερομένων, θα ήθελα να σημειώσω τα εξής:

Όπως επίσης και εσείς πιστεύετε, η πλήρης διερεύνηση ενός ατυχήματος όπως το εν λόγω, παρά τις δυσκολίες που αντιμετωπίζουμε, θεωρείται από εμάς πρωταρχικής σημασίας για τα επηρεαζόμενα πεδία της αεροναυτιλίας.

Μια τέτοια αναγκαιότητα που δεν καλύπτεται ακόμη από τα στοιχεία στα χέρια μας μέχρι τώρα, απαιτεί ασφαλώς επανεξέταση της δυνατότητας ανάκτησης του ναυαγίου από τη θάλασσα ή τουλάχιστον χρήσης μιας τηλεοπτικής ή φωτογραφικής μηχανής που θα μπορούσε να αποδειχθεί επαρκής για τη διερεύνηση του βυθού της θάλασσας.

Πιστεύουμε ότι η έλλειψη πλήρους αποδείξεων για την απόρριψη ή την υιοθέτηση ορισμένων ενδείξεων για τα αίτια του ατυχήματος δεν αποτελεί βεβαιότητα για τη διατύπωση οποιωνδήποτε απόψεων.

Δεν θα παραλείψω να σας πω αγαπητέ Group Captain Veal ότι, εκτός από άλλα σημεία των ενημερωτικών επιστολών σας, για το εν λόγω ατύχημα, τα ακόλουθα δεν θεωρούνται ακόμα από εμάς ως πειστικές ενδείξεις για τα αίτια του ατυχήματος.

Α) Η έκρηξη ενός ισχυρού εκρηκτικού μηχανισμού εντός της καμπίνας του αεροσκάφους σε υψόμετρο 29000 ποδιών.

Β) Οι ζημιές που προκλήθηκαν στη δεξαμενή πτώσης καυσίμου του κλιματιστικού F.100 οφείλονται μόνο στην πρόσκρουση στη θάλασσα και στο γεγονός ότι τα σημεία προσαρμογής του στο κλιματιστικό δεν παρουσιάζουν ενδείξεις αναγκαστικής αποκόλλησης (αυτό μπορεί να διαπιστωθεί μόνο με δοκιμαστική ρίψη της δεξαμενής).

Γ) Η αδυναμία εξακρίβωσης της ημερομηνίας του ιστορικού της δεξαμενής και από ποίο αεροπλάνο έχει πέσει.

Θα εκτιμούσαμε ιδιαίτερα κάθε ενέργεια εκ μέρους σας που τείνει να διευκρινίσει τα προαναφερθέντα και συμβάλλει στην αποτελεσματική διερεύνηση του εν λόγω ατυχήματος, που μας απασχολεί πολύ και τους δύο, εσάς ως αρμόδιους της έρευνας και εμάς για συναισθηματικούς και άλλους γενικούς λόγους.

Με την ευκαιρία θα ήθελα να σας ενημερώσω ότι, μετά από πρόσκλησή σας, δύο εκπρόσωποι της Διοίκησης μας θα αναχωρήσουν για το Λονδίνο πολύ σύντομα προκειμένου να παρακολουθήσουν τη διερεύνηση του εν λόγω ατυχήματος.»

Οι ελληνικές αρχές είχαν τόσο ενδιαφέρον για την πραγματική αιτία όσο και η ΒΕΑ, αλλά επιθυμούσαν να εντοπιστεί μια πολύ διαφορετική αιτία. Για την αεροπορική εταιρεία, ένα περιστατικό ασφαλείας, που συνεπάγεται την έκρηξη βόμβας σε ένα αεροσκάφος που κατά τα άλλα λειτουργεί και συντηρείται σε άριστη κατάσταση, θα τους απαλλάσσει εντελώς από κάθε ευθύνη. Θα επέτρεπε επίσης στον Κομήτη να διατηρήσει την ανακτημένη φήμη του ως ασφαλούς αεροσκάφους στο οποίο τα πληρώματα και οι επιβάτες θα μπορούσαν να έχουν απόλυτη εμπιστοσύνη. Αλλά αυτό, όσο και αν βοηθούσε την ΒΕΑ, θα εμπλέκει τις διαδικασίες ασφαλείας στο αεροδρόμιο της Αθήνας και η υπόλογη αρχή θα ήταν τελικά η Διοίκηση Πολιτικής Αεροπορίας του Ταξίαρχου Σκαρμαλιωράκη. Θα προτιμούσε, λοιπόν, να είχαν (οι Ελληνικές αρχές) ενημερωθεί ότι η αιτία ήταν μια σύγκρουση στον αέρα με μη ελληνικό αεροσκάφος στον διεθνή εναέριο χώρο.

Οι δύο εκπρόσωποι που εισηγήθηκε ο Σκαρμαλιωράκης ήταν ο κ. Γ. Παπαδημητροπούλου και ο κ. Χαζάρδας. Στις 20 Ιανουαρίου, μαζί με τον κ. Μ. Carder της Ολυμπιακής Αεροπορίας, ο οποίος θα μπορούσε να ήταν μεταφραστής, συναντήθηκαν με τους κκ. Clancey του RARDE, Forsyth της RAE και Norman Head της AIB. Ο Clancey τους έδειξε το μαξιλάρι και τις συνοδευτικές φωτογραφίες και εξήγησε τις λεπτομέρειες των αποδεικτικών στοιχείων. Επίσης, έδειξε στους επισκέπτες φωτογραφίες με ακτίνες Χ του τραυματισμένου από την έκρηξη επιβάτη κ. Αφατίτη.

Κατά τη διάρκεια αυτού που περιγράφηκε ως «μια σημαντική συζήτηση»[123], ο Clancey μπήκε στο σκεπτικό της θεωρίας ότι η βόμβα είχε τοποθετηθεί στην αριστερή πλευρά του αεροσκάφους, μεταξύ του καθίσματος και της πλευράς της ατράκτου[124].

Στη συνέχεια παρουσιάστηκαν στους Έλληνες τα διαθέσιμα συντρίμμια του Charlie Oscar , καθώς και το drop tank (δεξαμενή πτώσης) F.100. Μετά από αυτό, ο Forsyth εξήγησε τα συντρίμμια και τα στοιχεία που υποδηλώνουν το μοίρασμα του αεροσκάφους στα 15.000 πόδια. Οι Έλληνες ήταν προφανώς ικανοποιημένοι που η δεξαμενή πτώσης είχε εκτοξευθεί σε διαφορετική περίπτωση όταν επισημάνθηκε ότι δεν υπήρχε βύσμα αποστράγγισης στη δεξαμενή. Μετά την παρουσίαση σχετικής τεκμηρίωσης, οι Έλληνες επισκέπτες εξέφρασαν την άποψη ότι συμφωνούν με τα ευρήματα, αν και δήλωσαν ότι ανέμεναν κάποια δυσκολία να πείσουν κάποιους από τους ανθρώπους στην Αθήνα ότι η αιτία ήταν στην πραγματικότητα μια βόμβα. Τους προσφέρθηκε η ευκαιρία περαιτέρω συζητήσεων με τους δικούς τους εκρηκτικούς εμπειρογνώμονες εάν το επιθυμούσαν.

Η εικόνα του πώς ακριβώς ο Charlie Oscar και οι επιβάτες έπαθαν το κακό ήταν τώρα τόσο ξεκάθαρη όσο ήταν πιθανό να είναι ποτέ. Αλλά εξήγηση για το πώς ένας εκρηκτικός μηχανισμός βρέθηκε στο αεροσκάφος, ποιος τον έβαλε εκεί και γιατί, ήταν ερωτήματα που ξεπερνούσαν το πεδίο των ομάδων ειδικών τόσο του Mason όσο και του Veal.

---

[123] *Unattributed 'Note for the Record'* – *Συνάντηση με εκπροσώπους της Ελληνικής Διοίκησης Αεροπορίας στη PAE στις 20.1.68, The National Archives (Εθνικό Αρχείο) Avia101/218.*

[124] *Διάφορες περιγραφές του τόπου τοποθετούν τη βόμβα είτε από κάτω, ακριβώς πίσω ή στο πλάι του εν λόγω καθίσματος. Ωστόσο, η πιο συναρπαστική περιγραφή είναι 11½ ίντσες κάτω και 4½ ίντσες πίσω από το πίσω μέρος του μαξιλαριού. Αυτό υποστηρίζεται από σκίτσα που περιέχονται στους φακέλους των Εθνικών Αρχείων.*

Εκδόθηκε η Τελική Έκθεση

Στις 12 Ιουλίου 1968, ο John Veal ήταν επιτέλους σε θέση να παρουσιάσει την τελική του έκθεση για την καταστροφή του Charlie Oscar . Ως εισαγωγή, επισύναψε μια περιεκτική συνοδευτική επιστολή, η οποία επαναλάμβανε τα βασικά στοιχεία της συντριβής και την ενδελεχή έρευνα. Αφού τόνισε την εξαιρετική δουλειά των εμπλεκομένων, συμπεριλαμβανομένου του RARDE και του Ινστιτούτου Παθολογίας και Τροπικής Ιατρικής της RAF, ο Veal προχώρησε περαιτέρω στην αστυνομική έρευνα:

«Οι Ελληνικές αρχές, λόγω του αρχικού περιεχομένου, ιδίως σε βρετανικές εφημερίδες, ότι το περιστατικό ήταν απόπειρα κατά της ζωής του Στρατηγού Γρίβα και λόγω του προφανώς δυσμενούς προβληματισμού για την ασφάλεια στην Αθήνα, εξέφρασαν την άποψη ότι η απώλεια του αεροσκάφους προήλθε από σύγκρουση, πιθανότατα με τουρκικό μαχητικό. Όταν τρεις εβδομάδες αργότερα ένα F.100 ανασύρθηκε από τη θάλασσα, πίεσαν αυτήν την άποψη με ανανεωμένη δύναμη, αλλά η έρευνα έδειξε ότι το tank είχε πέσει από ένα αμερικανικό μαχητικό πιθανώς περίπου τρεις μήνες πριν από το ατύχημα του Κομήτη . Οι Ελληνικές αρχές κρατήθηκαν ενήμερες για την πρόοδο της έρευνας και στους εκπροσώπους τους που ήλθαν στο Λονδίνο επιδείχθηκαν τα στοιχεία της έκρηξης. Καταλαβαίνω από τη δική μας αστυνομία ότι οι ρυθμίσεις ασφαλείας στην Αθήνα είναι πλέον πολύ αυστηρές και ότι η πρόσβαση μη εξουσιοδοτημένων ατόμων στο αεροσκάφος και στην περιοχή στάθμευσης αεροπλάνων αποτρέπεται πλέον αποτελεσματικά.

Αμέσως μετά το ατύχημα ξεκίνησαν έρευνες από τα αρμόδια διάφορα τμήματα για την πιθανότητα δολιοφθοράς στο αεροσκάφος για πολιτικούς λόγους, αλλά με αρνητικό αποτέλεσμα. Αμέσως προέκυψαν στοιχεία ότι όντως είχε πυροδοτηθεί εκρηκτικός μηχανισμός στο αεροσκάφος και οι πληροφορίες διαβιβάστηκαν στο Special Branch. Στη συνέχεια έγιναν διευθετήσεις μέσω του Υπουργείου Εσωτερικών για τις ποινικές πτυχές που έπρεπε να ερευνηθούν από τη Scotland Yard. Αυτό το ανέλαβε ο Αστυνομικός Επιθεωρητής (Ντετέκτιβ) Browne , αντίγραφο της έκθεσής του βρίσκεται στον φάκελο στο Έγγρ. 2. Υπάρχει έμμεση απόδειξη που υποδεικνύει την πιθανή εμπλοκή ενός συγκεκριμένου επιβάτη του οποίου η σορός δεν ήταν μεταξύ αυτών που ανασύρθηκαν. Αντίγραφο της αστυνομικής έκθεσης εστάλη από τον Επιθεωρητή Αστυνομίας στον Δημόσιο Κατήγορο (Γενική Εισαγγελία).»

Ο Veal ολοκλήρωσε τονίζοντας την ανάγκη να γίνει πιο δύσκολη η λαθραία μεταφορά βομβών σε αεροσκάφη.

«Η ανάγκη ανάπτυξης μέσων ανίχνευσης της παρουσίας εκρηκτικών μηχανισμών θα πρέπει να μελετηθεί περαιτέρω με σκοπό να βοηθηθούν οι αεροπορικές εταιρείες και οι αρχές των αεροδρομίων στα μέτρα ασφαλείας τους. Αυτές οι συστάσεις ακολουθούνται από τον Διευθυντή Ασφάλειας Πτήσεων. Οι τρέχουσες εξελίξεις θα πρέπει να οδηγήσουν στην επίτευξη του στόχου (α), αλλά είναι απαραίτητο πρώτα να επιτευχθούν οι κατάλληλες διασφαλίσεις κατά ακούσιας εκτίναξης.

Η δυνατότητα ανίχνευσης εκρηκτικών μηχανισμών ήδη τυγχάνει μεγάλης προσοχής ιδιαίτερα στον στρατιωτικό τομέα όσον αφορά τις νάρκες, αλλά η μεταφορά εμπορευμάτων και επιβατών με πολιτικά αεροσκάφη παρουσιάζουν τα δικά τους ειδικά προβλήματα. Αν και δεν έχω μεγάλες προσδοκίες ότι θα υπάρξει κάποια άμεση πρόοδος σε αυτόν τον τομέα, η προτεινόμενη μελέτη σκοπιμότητας θα παρείχε τουλάχιστον συγκεκριμένες αποδείξεις προσπάθειας εάν, δυστυχώς, βρισκόμασταν αντιμέτωποι με ένα άλλο γεγονός όπως αυτό του Κομήτη. Και πρέπει να θυμόμαστε ότι υπήρξαν επτά γνωστές περιπτώσεις δολιοφθοράς πολιτικών αεροσκαφών με εκρηκτικά τα τελευταία έξι χρόνια, ενώ τρεις από αυτές συνέβησαν το 1967. Στην καλύτερη περίπτωση, μέσω του συντονισμού της επιστημονικής προσπάθειας και με την εφαρμογή προηγμένης τεχνολογίας, μπορεί να γίνει κάποια πρόοδος.

Σε αυτό το πλαίσιο, είναι ενδιαφέρον να σημειωθεί ότι το τελικό συμπέρασμα ενός εγγράφου για τα ατυχήματα λόγω δολιοφθοράς, το οποίο προετοιμάζεται από το Εθνικό Συμβούλιο Ασφάλειας Μεταφορών των Ηνωμένων Πολιτειών είναι, «Δεδομένου ότι το πρόβλημα της έκρηξης βόμβας εν πτήσει είναι παγκόσμιο, προτείνεται ότι πρέπει να εξεταστεί η συγκέντρωση διεθνών τεχνικών πόρων για την επίτευξη επιτυχούς λύσης στο πρόβλημα ανίχνευσης βομβών». Η προτεινόμενη μελέτη σκοπιμότητας, η οποία θα διεξαχθεί από το κατάλληλο Ερευνητικό Ίδρυμα μέσω του επιστημονικού μας συμβούλου, θα συμβάλει έμπρακτα σε αυτόν τον στόχο.»

Στο Συμβούλιο Εμπορίου, ο νέος υπουργός Επικρατείας, Bill Rodgers, , σχολίασε: *«Μια εντυπωσιακή, συναρπαστική και πειστική έκθεση. Υποστηρίζω τις συστάσεις».* Ο Πρόεδρος του Board of Trade, Anthony Crosland, ήταν εξίσου υποστηρικτικός :

«Η σωστή επιμέλεια αυτής της έκθεσης κατοπτρίζει εξαιρετικά εύσημα στον Group Captain Veal και στο προσωπικό του. Οι συστάσεις είναι απολύτως αποδεκτές. Φαντάζομαι ότι οι ευχαριστίες μας έχουν μεταφερθεί στο RARDE και σε άλλους εξωτερικούς φορείς που συνεργάστηκαν τόσο βοηθητικά στην έρευνα.»

Ως δεύτερη σκέψη, ο Crosland πρότεινε, ότι αν δεν είχαν σταλεί ακόμη «ευχαριστήριες» επιστολές ήταν έτοιμος να τις γράψει ο ίδιος.

Ο Τύπος, εν τω μεταξύ, δεν είχε χάσει καθόλου τον ενθουσιασμό του για τη δημιουργία δραματικών πρωτοσέλιδων, ανεξάρτητα από το πόσο προσεκτικά διατυπώνονταν τυχόν δελτία τύπου ή παρόμοια σχόλια. Στις 21 Νοεμβρίου 1968, για παράδειγμα, η *Birmingham Post* αποκάλυψε με ενθουσιασμό με τίτλο : «*Η συντριβή του θανάτου του Κομήτη – ήταν μια βόμβα που προοριζόταν για τον Γρίβα*»:

«Ο Κομήτης 4Β της British European Airways που συνετρίβη στη Μεσόγειο τον περασμένο Οκτώβριο καταστράφηκε από έκρηξη στη τουριστική θέση (του αεροπλάνου), αναφέρει η έκθεση του Τμήματος Διερεύνησης Εμπορικών Ατυχημάτων που δημοσιεύτηκε σήμερα.

Και οι έρευνες της Scotland Yard αποκαλύπτουν ότι είχε τοποθετηθεί στο πλαίσιο σχεδίου δολοφονίας του πρώην αρχηγού της ΕΟΚΑ, Στρατηγού Γρίβα, αρχηγού των κυπριακών ενόπλων δυνάμεων...

Αφού οι ερευνητές του Board of Trade βρήκαν τα πρώτα σημάδια ότι το αεροσκάφος είχε υποστεί ζημιά από έκρηξη περί τα τέλη Ιανουαρίου, ντετέκτιβς από τη Scotland Yard διεξήγαγαν ενδελεχή έρευνα για την πιθανότητα δολιοφθοράς.

Ο Αστυνομικός Επιθεωρητής Percy Browne και ο Ντετέκτιβ Peter Hill πέταξαν στην Ελλάδα και την Κύπρο και πέρασαν το μεγαλύτερο μέρος του Φεβρουαρίου και του Μαρτίου ερευνόντας. Πήραν συνεντεύξεις από συγγενείς επιβατών και εξέτασαν καταγγελίες ότι ο εκρηκτικός μηχανισμός προοριζόταν για τον Στρατηγό Γρίβα, ο οποίος επέστρεφε από την Ελλάδα στην Κύπρο εκείνη την ημέρα. Στην πραγματικότητα επέστρεψε με την επόμενη πτήση.

Εκπρόσωπος της Scotland Yard χθες βράδυ είπε ότι η έκθεση του Επιθεωρητή Browne σχετικά με τις ποινικές πτυχές της συντριβής είχε κατατεθεί στην Εισαγγελία (Γραφείο Δημόσιου Κατήγορου).

«Είχε αποφασιστεί, με βάση τα διαθέσιμα στοιχεία, να μην ληφθούν μέτρα», είπε.

Οι ερευνητές βασίζουν την έκθεσή τους στο ότι ο Κομήτης καταστράφηκε από έκρηξη εκρηκτικού στρατιωτικού τύπου σε δοχείο από μαλακό χάλυβα από στοιχεία που περιέχονται σε ένα μαξιλάρι καθίσματος ... η έκθεση του Board of Trade αναφέρει ξεκάθαρα ότι «το αεροσκάφος κόπηκε στον αέρα μετά από έκρηξη ενός ισχυρού εκρηκτικού μηχανισμού μέσα στην καμπίνα».

Αλλά η έκθεση δεν μπορεί να απαντήσει πλήρως το ζωτικής σημασίας ερώτημα - ήταν η έκρηξη τυχαία ή το αεροσκάφος υπέστη σαμποτάζ ;

Όμως σε συνέντευξη Τύπου στο Λονδίνο, ο κ. V.J. Ο Clancey, ο ειδικός στα εκρηκτικά (από το RARDE) που ερεύνησε τα στοιχεία, δεν είχε καμία αμφιβολία για το πώς προκλήθηκε η έκρηξη. Εξήγησε ότι οι εργαστηριακές δοκιμές του για τον τύπο του εκρηκτικού που χρησιμοποιήθηκε απέδειξαν χωρίς αμφιβολία ότι ήταν μια στρατιωτικού τύπου εκρηκτική ύλη όπως το TNT ή το RDX που κατέστρεψε τον Κομήτη.

Εκρηκτικό υψηλής ταχύτητας δεν μπορεί να εκραγεί χωρίς πυροκροτητή ή συσκευή χρονισμού, είπε. Ήταν σχεδόν άγνωστο να εκραγεί ένας πυροκροτητής κατά λάθος.

Οι οικιακές συσκευές χρονισμού ήταν εντελώς άλλο πράγμα, είπε. Μπορούσαν να σβήσουν σχεδόν οποιαδήποτε στιγμή. Αλλά συσκευές χρονισμού δεν τοποθετούνται σε ένα αεροπλάνο με ισχυρά εκρηκτικά χωρίς σκοπό. Οι ειδικοί απέκλεισαν επίσης την πιθανότητα τυχαίας έκρηξης π.χ. κάτι σαν αεροζόλ σπρέι μαλλιών στην τσάντα κάποιου επιβάτη ...

Οι ερευνητές του Board of Trade συνέστησαν στην έκθεση ότι θα πρέπει να αναπτυχθούν συσκευές καταγραφής πτήσης για να αποσπώνται από ένα αεροσκάφος όταν αυτό βυθίζεται στη θάλασσα μετά από συντριβή. Στη συνέχεια, το κουτί θα μπορούσε να επιπλεύσει στην επιφάνεια και, εάν εξοπλισμένο με συσκευή εντοπισμού ασυρμάτου, η ανάκτηση θα είναι πολύ πιο εύκολη.

Συνέστησαν επίσης στο Συμβούλιο Εμπορίου να ξεκινήσει μελέτες για την ανάπτυξη μιας αποτελεσματικής συσκευής που θα ανιχνεύει εκρηκτικούς μηχανισμούς σε ένα αεροσκάφος ή στις αποσκευές των επιβατών.»

Η Scotland Yard ερευνά...

Το συμπέρασμα του RARDE, το οποίο αποδέχτηκε ο Veal, ότι η αιτία της καταστροφής ήταν μια βόμβα δεν ήταν ακριβώς έκπληξη. Από την πρώτη μέρα, υπήρξαν ευρέως διαδεδομένες εικασίες, στον Τύπο και αλλού, ότι αυτό δεν ήταν τυχαίο, αλλά μια σκόπιμη πράξη κακίας. Πράγματι, εικάστηκε, όπως προαναφέρθηκε, ότι επρόκειτο για απόπειρα δολοφονίας κατά της ζωής του Στρατηγού Γεωργίου Γρίβα. Ως δυνητικό αδίκημα μαζικής δολοφονίας, επομένως, το θέμα ήταν μεγάλου ενδιαφέροντος για τις αρχές, συμπεριλαμβανομένων των υπηρεσιών ασφαλείας.

Δύο μέλη του τμήματος Αμυντικών Πληροφοριών των υπηρεσιών ασφαλείας, που αναγνωρίζονται ως Suckling και Arnott, πλησίασαν την ομάδα του John Veal την επόμενη μέρα της συντριβής, ζητώντας μια λίστα με τους επιβάτες που επιβιβάστηκαν στην Αθήνα, μια λίστα κρατήσεων και επίσης να γινόταν έλεγχος για να φανεί αν ο Γρίβας είχε κλείσει ως επιβάτης για την Κύπρο την επόμενη εβδομάδα.

Στις 20 Οκτωβρίου, ενώ οι υπηρεσίες ασφαλείας έσκαβαν αναμφίβολα στα θολά, ο Michael Lester, ο γραμματέας της εταιρείας ΒΕΑ, έγραψε στον Jan Riddoch, με στοιχεία ενός πρώην υπαλλήλου της ΒΕΑ που είχε εγκαταλείψει την αεροπορική εταιρεία σε δύσκολες συνθήκες:

«Ο κ. Γεωργίου εργαζόταν ως φορτωτής και το σώμα των φορτωτών περιλαμβάνει φυσικά μερικά από τα πιο τραχιά στοιχεία της κοινότητας. Φαντάζομαι ότι δεν ήταν δημοφιλής και κάποιοι από τους φορτωτές είχαν γιους στην Κύπρο και τουλάχιστον ένας από αυτούς είχε σκοτωθεί. Νομίζω ότι αυτό οδήγησε σε μια ορισμένη σκληρότητα εναντίον του Γεωργίου και το αποτέλεσμα ήταν ότι παραιτήθηκε από τη ΒΕΑ. Ο (επισυναπτόμενος) φάκελος ασχολείται με την επακόλουθη καταγγελία του Γεωργίου ότι απολύθηκε αδικαιολόγητα.

Ο Γεωργίου έκανε πολλές φραστικές απειλές για να ανατινάξει διάφορα κομμάτια ιδιοκτησίας της ΒΕΑ, συμπεριλαμβανομένου ενός αεροπλάνου και περίπου στα μέσα Απριλίου του περασμένου έτους έφτασε στο σημείο να μου γράψει απειλώντας ότι θα ανατινάξει ένα από τα αεροπλάνα. Είχε ερευνηθεί από την αστυνομία τότε και φαίνεται ότι είχε υποσχεθεί να διορθώσει τη συμπεριφορά του.

Ένας από τους επιβάτες του Κομήτη ήταν ο κ. Σ. Γεωργίου[125], ο οποίος βρίσκεται στη λίστα επιβατών ως Αμερικανός πολίτης, αν και δεν ξέρω τι στοιχεία υπάρχουν για να το τεκμηριώσουν αυτό, καθώς το σώμα του δεν

---

[125] *Στη θέση 4Α ήταν ο Σωτήρης Γεωργίου. Όπως αναφέρθηκε, η σορός του δεν βρέθηκε ποτέ.*

βρέθηκε. Ο κ. Σ. Γεωργίου ταξίδευε για εκδρομή για 21 ημέρες στη Λευκωσία. Πέταξε από τη Νέα Υόρκη στο Λονδίνο στις 9 Οκτωβρίου με ΒΑ506 και έφτασε το πρωί της 10ης Οκτωβρίου. Είχε μια 24ωρη στάση στο Λονδίνο και έφυγε με τη πτήση ΒΕ284 για Αθήνα και Λευκωσία στις 11 Οκτωβρίου. Όταν έφυγε από το Λονδίνο, είχε 4 κιλά περίσσευμα στις αποσκευές του και συνεχίζουμε τις έρευνες με την ΒΟΑC για να δούμε αν έφερε επιπλέον αποσκευές μαζί του από τη Νέα Υόρκη.[126]

Αυτός ο επιβάτης έγινε check-in για την πτήση Αθήνα / Λευκωσία, αλλά καθώς το σώμα του δεν ανασύρθηκε, δεν γνωρίζουμε με βεβαιότητα αν όντως επιβιβάστηκε στο αεροσκάφος και καταλαβαίνω ότι υπάρχει κάποιο ερώτημα αν το αεροσκάφος έφυγε από την Αθήνα με έναν επιβάτη μείων- αν και αυτό δεν έχει επιβεβαιωθεί[127].»

Μία χειρόγραφη σημείωση «PS» επιβεβαιώνει, «Η ΒΟΑC λέει ότι δεν είχε επιπλέον αποσκευές Νέα Υόρκη – Λονδίνο»
Ο Veal απάντησε επίσημα στις υπηρεσίες ασφαλείας ένα δεκαπενθήμερο αργότερα, στις 26 Οκτωβρίου, επισυνάπτοντας αντίγραφο της λίστας επιβατών και μια δήλωση του κ. Mastin. Αυτός πρόσθεσε:

«Αντιλαμβανόμαστε ότι ο Στρατηγός Γρίβας ταξίδεψε στην Κύπρο με το δρομολόγιο που αναχώρησε επίσης από την Αθήνα αργότερα στις 12 Οκτωβρίου.» Και πρόσθεσε:

«Από τη στιγμή που σας μίλησε ο κ. Tench, κύριε Lester, ο Γραμματέας της ΒΕΑ έφερε στην αντίληψή μας τις απειλές του κ. Γιώργου Γεωργίου, Κύπριου πρώην υπαλλήλου της ΒΕΑ... Φαίνεται κάπως απίθανο ο κ. Γιώργος Γεωργίου να είναι το ίδιο πρόσωπο με τον κ. Σ. Γεωργίου που δηλώθηκε ότι έχει αμερικανική υπηκοότητα. Ωστόσο, θα ήθελα να ακούσω εάν τυχόν μπορεί να δοθεί συνέχεια σε σχέση με αυτήν τη συγκεκριμένη απειλή.»

Ο Ronnie Martin, ο Διευθυντής της ΒΕΑ στη Βηρυτό, επίσης θεώρησε ότι θα ήταν χρήσιμο να αναφέρει μια περίπτωση από έναν ανώνυμο φίλο του, ο οποίος προφανώς είχε κρατήσει θέση για το Charlie Oscar αλλά, λόγω ακύρωσης της τελευταίας στιγμής, κατάφερε να εξασφαλίσει θέση στην πτήση της Ολυμπιακής Αεροπορίας αργότερα στις 12 Οκτωβρίου:

---

[126] *Καθώς ο κ. Γεωργίου ταξίδευε για να επισκεφθεί την οικογένειά του στην Κύπρο, αγόρασε επιπλέον αντικείμενα ενώ βρισκόταν στο Λονδίνο, αποφεύγοντας έτσι τις επιπλέον χρεώσεις αποσκευών από τη Νέα Υόρκη. Πληροφορίες στον συγγραφέα το 2018.*

[127] *Ούτε φαίνεται να αναφέρεται αλλού.*

«Όταν έφτασε στο αεροδρόμιο επικράτησε κάπως περισσότερη ταραχή από τη συνηθισμένη, αλλά τελικά πέρασε από τους ελέγχους του αεροδρομίου και πήγε στο σαλόνι αναχωρήσεων. Η πτήση του καθυστέρησε και ερωτώντας για την καθυστέρηση τον αγνόησαν. Τελικά ανακοινώθηκε μια περαιτέρω καθυστέρηση και, και στην περίπτωση αυτή κατάλαβε ότι ταξίδευε μια ομάδα VIP. Η περαιτέρω καθυστέρηση είχε ως αποτέλεσμα να αλλάξει αεροπλάνο η Ολυμπιακή στο οποίο φορτώθηκαν οι αποσκευές κτλ από το αεροπλάνο στο οποίο είχαν φορτωθεί και που υποτίθεται θα εκτελούσε την πτήση.
Ο πληροφοριοδότης μου ταξιδεύει στην οικονομική θέση και επιβιβαζόμενος στο αεροσκάφος βρήκε το διαμέρισμα της 1ης θέσης κλειστό. Οι ψίθυροι έλεγαν ότι ο Στρατηγός Γρίβας επέβαινε του ιδίου αεροπλάνου και ότι αυτός θα έφευγε με τον Κομήτη της ΒΕΑ που έφυγε από την Αθήνα νωρίς το ίδιο πρωί. Ακόμα και εκείνη την ώρα κανένας από τους επιβάτες φαινόταν να γνώριζε για την καταστροφή του αεροπλάνου της ΒΕΑ. Μόνο πετώντας πάνω από τη σκηνή του ατυχήματος ακούστηκε η αεροσυνοδός του Ολυμπιακής να ψιθυρίζει σε κάποιον ότι αυτό ήταν περίπου το σημείο συντριβής του Κομήτη της ΒΕΑ. Αυτό ακούστηκε από μερικούς επιβάτες και ρωτήθηκε η αεροσυνοδός – και τους ενημέρωσε ότι νωρίτερα το πρωί είχε συμβεί ατύχημα.
Υ.Γ. Αντιλαμβάνομαι ότι ο Γρίβας και η παρέα του αποβιβάστηκαν από το αεροπλάνο της Ολυμπιακής Αεροπορίας στη Λευκωσία.»

Όπως και με άλλη αλληλογραφία, ο Veal ενημέρωσε σχετικά των Sidwell , του DI6[128], ενός κλάδου των υπηρεσιών ασφαλείας, σχολιάζοντας:
«...Πιστεύω ότι η καθυστέρηση που αναφέρεται στην επιστολή προκλήθηκε από την αλλαγή του αεροσκάφους από την Ολυμπιακή Αεροπορία ως προληπτικό μέτρο, εν όψει του ατυχήματος.»

Στις 9 Νοεμβρίου ο Veal και ο Head συζήτησαν με τον Sidwell τις σχετικές εξελίξεις στην έρευνα, σε σχέση με τις πτυχές της δολιοφθοράς. Ο Sidwell εξήγησε ότι οι λίστες επιβατών μελετούνταν μέσω Αθήνας και Λευκωσίας, αλλά μέχρι στιγμής ήταν αρνητικές. Ο Sidwell διαβεβαίωσε τους ερευνητές ότι οι ενδιαφερόμενοι γνώριζαν τον επείγοντα χαρακτήρα του θέματος. Είχε, ωστόσο, διαπιστωθεί ότι ο Γιώργος Γεωργίου ζούσε ακόμα στο Λονδίνο, επομένως δεν ήταν στο αεροσκάφος.

---

[128] Ενδεχομένως παράρτημα της Υπηρεσίας Πληροφοριών Άμυνας, τμήμα του Υπουργείου Άμυνας.

Ο Sidwell αποδέχτηκε την πιθανότητα ότι η ζημιά στο μαξιλάρι μπορεί να προκλήθηκε από ισχυρή εκρηκτική ύλη και επεσήμανε ότι υπήρχε πολύ μεγάλος αριθμός «ειδικών» στην Κύπρο που θα μπορούσαν να χειριστούν μια τέτοια συσκευή. Ωστόσο, δυσκολευόταν να πιστέψει ότι κάποιος θα χρησιμοποιούσε τη μικρή ποσότητα εκρηκτικής ύλης που πρότειναν τα πειράματα RARDE. Ο Sidwell θεώρησε ότι μια λογική εξήγηση ήταν ότι, στην πραγματικότητα, ήταν μια μεγαλύτερη συσκευή και ότι υπήρχε ατελής καύση. Σε εκείνη την περίπτωση, εκείνα που βρέθηκαν στο σώμα του κ. Αφατίτη, καθώς έδειχναν υψηλή θερμοκρασία, θα μπορούσε να ήταν ημιτελώς καμένα σωματίδια εκρηκτικής ύλης.

Ο Sidwell ενημερώθηκε για την πιθανή ανάγκη της AIB να εκδώσει ένα δελτίο τύπου σχετικά με την έκρηξη. Δεν πίστευε ότι θα έθιγε τις έρευνες που διενεργούνταν από την DI6. Εν μέρει, μπορούσε να τους βοηθήσει.

Την ίδια μέρα, ο Veal και ο Newton συζήτησαν τα ευρύματα του RARDE με τον Αρχι-επιθεωρητή Bryan, από το Special Branch της Scotland Yard. Ανέφεραν ξανά το προτεινόμενο δελτίο τύπου και, μετά από διαβούλευση με τον Διοικητή του, ο Bryan επιβεβαίωσε ότι η αστυνομία δεν θα είχε αντίρρηση, λαμβάνοντας υπόψη τον χρόνο που πέρασε από τη συντριβή και αυτό που οι δύο αστυνομικοί θεώρησαν ως «απίθανη επιτυχία για ποινική διαδικασία».

Στις 17 Νοεμβρίου, ο Veal έλαβε μια επιστολή από έναν Frank Ellson-Jones, υποτιθέμενο Τεχνικό Σύμβουλο της εταιρείας de Havilland, αρχικού κατασκευαστή του Κομήτη, με εικασίες για τον πιθανό μηχανισμό με τον οποίο θα μπορούσε να είχε πυροδοτηθεί μια βόμβα. Φαίνεται, εκ πρώτης όψεως, απολύτως εύλογο και έχει μάλιστα, προταθεί στον συγγραφέα από άλλες αξιόπιστες πηγές[129].

«Όταν αεροσκάφη πετούν μέσα από μια τόσο πολιτικά επικίνδυνη περιοχή, δεν μπορεί να αποκλειστεί η σκέψη ότι εχθρικά στοιχεία θα είναι έτοιμα να θυσιάσουν το αεροσκάφος και ολόκληρο το συμπλήρωμά του σε μια απόπειρα για τη ζωή ενός ατόμου... προέκυψε το ζήτημα της εξ αποστάσεως πυροδότησης μιας βόμβας στο σημείο που στη διαδρομή τα συντρίμμια θα έπεφταν σε βαθιά νερά ... Συνειδητοποίησα ότι αυτό θα ήταν σχετικά εύκολο, καθώς η κατασκευή ενός τρανζίστορ δέκτη που λειτουργεί με μπαταρία είναι απλή και φθηνή. Ένας τέτοιος δέκτης θα έκανε μια πολύ καλή ενεργοποίηση γιατί, αν ήταν κρυσταλλικά ελεγχόμενος στη συχνότητα FIR Λευκωσίας (126,3 MHz), το πρώτο σήμα που θα λάμβανε ο έλεγχος Αθήνας-Λευκωσίας θα ήταν στις 30 μοίρες

---

[129] Σε αυτούς περιλαμβάνονται συνάδελφοι του συγγραφέα με σχετική εμπειρία σε τέτοια θέματα, καθώς και ο Λούης Λοΐζου, ο οποίος είχε στρατιωτική εμπειρία με τις κυπριακές αμυντικές δυνάμεις.

που είναι το σημείο εναλλαγής μεταξύ των FIRs και, κατά σύμπτωση, βρίσκεται επίσης στην περιοχή του βαθύτερου νερού κάτω από τον αεραγωγό (airway) RED 19.

Η προδιαγραφή του δέκτη θα ήταν πολύ απλή, επειδή υπάρχει πάντα άφθονο σήμα VHF μέσα στην καμπίνα του αεροσκάφους ή στο χώρο αποσκευών όταν λειτουργεί ο επί αεροσκάφου πομπός.»

Ο Veal έγραψε ξανά στον κ. Suckling στην ΜΙ5 στις 17 Νοεμβρίου. Η επιστολή του κάλυπτε τόσο την απειλή από τρομοκρατικές ομάδες της Μέσης Ανατολής όσο και τις σκέψεις του κ. Ellson-Jones.

«Επισυνάπτω αντίγραφο επιστολής που έλαβα από τον Ακόλουθό μας, της Πολιτικής Αεροπορίας στη Μέση Ανατολή, η οποία φαίνεται να αναφέρεται στον Απελευθερωτικό Στρατό της Παλαιστίνης. Νομίζω ότι γνωρίζετε ήδη από τον κ. Sidwell ότι ένα από τα μαξιλάρια του καθίσματος της καμπίνας τουριστικών καθισμάτων βρέθηκε να έχει υποστεί ζημιά που συνάδει με αυτή που θα προκαλείτο από έναν εκρηκτικό μηχανισμό μέσα στην καμπίνα στο επίπεδο του δαπέδου. Μια ενδιαφέρουσα πιθανότητα για το πώς θα μπορούσε να πυροδοτηθεί εξ αποστάσεως ένας τέτοιος εκρηκτικός μηχανισμός προτείνεται σε μια επιστολή του κ. Ellson-Jones, αντίγραφο της οποίας επισυνάπτω επίσης.»

Στις 20 Δεκεμβρίου, ο Veal είχε στείλει ένα αντίγραφο της ενδιάμεσης έκθεσής του στον Αρχι-επιθεωρητή Browne. Εκτός από την εξήγηση που δόθηκε σε άλλους παραλήπτες που επαναλάμβαναν την πιο πιθανή αιτία ως έκρηξη βόμβας, ο Veal πρόσθεσε σε αυτή την επιστολή:

«Ρωτήσατε εάν θα ήταν δυνατό να παρασχεθεί κάποια ενδιάμεση έκθεση κατά της οποίας θα μπορούσατε να εξετάσετε εάν θα υπάρξει κάποια ενέργεια της αστυνομίας ή που πρέπει να ληφθεί και ο σκοπός αυτής της επιστολής είναι να σας το παράσχει.

Λίγο μετά το ατύχημα ήρθαμε σε επαφή με τον κ. Suckling του Box 500 και του ζητήσαμε να εξετάσει την πιθανή περίπτωση δολιοφθοράς. Αυτό φυσικά έγινε πριν έχουμε οποιαδήποτε απόδειξη για την εκδήλωση έκρηξης. Δεν είχα καμία τελική αναφορά από αυτόν, αλλά όταν ρώτησα προηγουμένως, μου λέχθηκε ότι τίποτα δεν είχε βγει στο φως στην Αθήνα ή στη Λευκωσία.»

Ο επικεφαλής επιθεωρητής Bryan μίλησε στον Veal στο τηλέφωνο στις 4 Ιανουαρίου για να επιβεβαιώσει τη λήψη της ενδιάμεσης έκθεσης. Είπε στον Veal ότι είχε δοθεί προκαταρκτική εξέταση για το θέμα, αλλά υπήρχε κάποια αμφιβολία εάν υπήρχε κάποια αστυνομική ενέργεια που θα μπορούσε να γίνει και ζήτησε τις απόψεις του Veal.

Ο Veal απάντησε ότι είχε γνωστοποιήσει το θέμα στη Scotland Yard επειδή ένιωθε ότι είχε ευθύνη να το πράξει. Ωστόσο, δεν εναπόκειτο σε αυτόν να αποφασίσει ποια μέτρα έπρεπε να λάβει η αστυνομία. Αν ένιωθαν ότι δεν μπορούσε να γίνει τίποτα, ο Veal σκέφτηκε ότι θα έπρεπε να αποδεχτεί την απόφαση, αν και θα ήθελε να έχει κάτι γραπτώς σε περίπτωση που συνέβαινε αυτό, καθώς θα έπρεπε να αναφερθεί στο θέμα κατά την υποβολή της τελικής του έκθεσης.

Ο επικεφαλής επιθεωρητής Bryan ενημερώθηκε στη συνέχεια ότι ο Γενικός Εισαγγελέας ενδιαφερόταν για την έρευνα και ζήτησε και του δόθηκε ένα αντίγραφο της ενδιάμεσης έκθεσης. Ο Γενικός Εισαγγελέας είχε επίσης ενημερωθεί ότι το θέμα είχε παραπεμφθεί στο Special Branch.

Στις 30 Ιανουαρίου, αφού υπήρξε μια συζήτηση με τους Whittick, Veal και Riddoch, ο τελευταίος απάντησε γραπτώς αναφέροντας τους λόγους για τους οποίους θα έπρεπε να γίνει αστυνομική έρευνα. Ο άνθρωπος του Υπουργείου Εσωτερικών έθεσε το ζήτημα του κόστους, καθώς η Μητροπολιτική Αστυνομία χρηματοδοτούνταν εξίσου από το Υπουργείο Οικονομικών και τους φορολογούμενους του Λονδίνου.

Ο Riddoch εξήγησε ότι σκοπός μιας έρευνας ατυχήματος είναι να εξακριβωθεί η αιτία, αυτό έγινε, προσθέτοντας ότι η ΑΙΒ θεώρησε σημαντικό από την άποψη της ασφάλειας να εξακριβώσει τον τρόπο με τον οποίο τοποθετήθηκε ο εκρηκτικός μηχανισμός στο αεροσκάφος, ώστε να λαμβάνονται προφυλάξεις για να μην ξανασυμβεί κάτι τέτοιο. Επεσήμανε ότι δεν ήταν γνωστό εάν η βόμβα τοποθετήθηκε στο αεροπλάνο στην Αθήνα ή στο Ηνωμένο Βασίλειο, αλλά δεν υπήρχε αμφιβολία ότι η πράξη ήταν εσκεμμένη. Ούτε έγινε γνωστό αν ο σκοπός ήταν πολιτικός ή για εξασφάλιση ασφαλιστικής πληρωμής. Ο Riddoch τόνισε:

«Όποιες και αν είναι οι αμφιβολίες σας σχετικά με την ευθύνη της Μητροπολιτικής Αστυνομίας για τη διερεύνηση εγκλημάτων σε βρετανικά αεροσκάφη, ελπίζω ότι δεν υπάρχει καμία αμφιβολία κατά πόσο ένα τόσο σοβαρό έγκλημα όπως το ατύχημα του Κομήτη , με το θάνατο 66 ατόμων σε ένα βρετανικό αεροσκάφος (πολλοί ήσαν οι βρετανοί υπήκοοι) θα πρέπει να ερευνηθεί.

Εισηγηθήκατε συνάντηση για να διευκρινιστούν οι γενικές αρμοδιότητες της Αστυνομίας για τη διερεύνηση εγκλημάτων στα αεροσκάφη. Θα είμαστε ευγνώμων αν κανονίσετε μια τέτοια συνάντηση. Ομολογώ ότι βρίσκομαι σε κατάσταση σύγχυσης σχετικά με τη δικαιοδοσία και τις ευθύνες των διαφόρων αρχών».

Στις 31 Ιανουαρίου, ο ντετέκτιβ Επιθεωρητής Percy Brown, από τη Scotland Yard , τηλεφώνησε στον Veal για να πει ότι είχε τώρα αναλάβει την έρευνα για το ατύχημα του Κομήτη.

Η συνάντηση που πρότεινε ο Whittick πραγματοποιήθηκε στο γραφείο του στις 5 Φεβρουαρίου. Υπήρχαν εκπρόσωποι από το Υπουργείο Εσωτερικών, ο Riddoch και συνάδελφοι από το Board of Trade, ο κ. John Macrae του Foreign Office μαζί με τον κ. Κ. Parker και τον βοηθό Αστυνόμο P.E Brodie της Μτροπολιτικής Αστυνομίας.

Η ομάδα συμφώνησε ότι εάν το Συμβούλιο Εμπορίου το ζητούσε από τον Αστυνόμο της Μητροπολιτικής Αστυνομίας, η δύναμη θα ερευνούσε τη δολοφονία των επιβατών (και, μάλλον και του πληρώματος). Το Συμβούλιο Εμπορίου (Board of Trade) θα πλήρωνε για την έρευνα, εννοείται αφού την ενέκρινε το Υπουργείο Οικονομικών, και το Υπουργείο Εξωτερικών (Foreign Office) θα ενημέρωνε την Ελληνική κυβέρνηση για την προτεινόμενη έρευνα. Τέλος, σημείωσαν ότι ο Δημόσιος Κατήγορος είχε ήδη συμφωνήσει να αναλάβει τα έξοδα οποιασδήποτε δίωξης.

Ο Veal μαζί με τον Head και τον Newton, συναντήθηκαν με τον ντετέκτιβ Επιθεωρητή Browne και τον ντετέκτιβ Λοχία Lee[130] στις 12 Φεβρουαρίου. Συμφώνησαν να παράσχουν στη Scotland Yard πληροφορίες για τους επιβάτες, συμπεριλαμβανομένης της λίστας επιβατών και του καταλόγου των αγνοουμένων. Επίσης, θα έστελναν αλληλογραφία με την American Life Insurance Company που αφορούσε έναν από τους επιβάτες, τον κ. Μιχάλη Θωμαΐδη[131]. Θα έστελλαν επίσης αναφορές από το RARDE και το Ινστιτούτο Παθολογίας. Ο Browne έγραψε στον (άγνωστο) Διευθυντή του στις 14 Φεβρουαρίου, περιγράφοντας τα ταξιδιωτικά του σχέδια. Μαζί με τον DS Hill:

«...ταξιδεύουμε αεροπορικώς στην Αθήνα την Τετάρτη 21 Φεβρουαρίου 1968, φτάνοντας περίπου στις 3.30 μ.μ., GMT. Κατά την άφιξή μας θα ενημερώσω τη Βρετανική Πρεσβεία για τη διεύθυνσή μας στην Αθήνα.
Δεν είναι δυνατόν να πούμε ποια γραμμή θα ακολουθήσει η έρευνα ή πώς θα μας υποδεχθούν οι ελληνικές αρχές. Εάν, ωστόσο, προκύψουν οποιεσδήποτε δυσκολίες θα ζητηθεί η γνώμη ενός αξιωματούχου της Βρετανικής Πρεσβείας.
Ζητώ να διαβιβαστεί αυτή η έκθεση εις τριπλούν στον Υφυπουργό Εσωτερικών, στο Υπουργείο Εσωτερικών, με αίτημα να διαβιβαστεί

---

[130] *Το όνομα του ντετέκτιβ λοχία που συνοδεύει τον ντετέκτιβ Επιθεωρητή Browne δίνεται ποικιλοτρόπως ως DS Peter Hill ή DS Lee.*

[131] *Ο κ. Θωμαΐδης ήταν καλά ασφαλισμένος λόγω της αξίας της επιχείρησής του. Δεν υπήρξε ποτέ καμία υπόνοια ότι εμπλέκεται σε κάτι ανάρμοστο και δεν εμφανίστηκε περαιτέρω στην έρευνα.*

αντίγραφο στον κ. Macrae, Central Department, Foreign Office, προς ενημέρωσή του».

Είναι ενδιαφέρον να σημειωθεί ότι η εμπλοκή του ντετ. Επιθεωρητή Percy Browne στην έρευνα δεν ήταν ένα καλά φυλαγμένο μυστικό. Η *Cyprus Mail* την είχε ήδη ανακοινώσει στις 10 Φεβρουαρίου:

«Ένας κορυφαίος ντετέκτιβ του Λονδίνου για δολοφονίες ορίστηκε επικεφαλής έρευνας (για τη συντριβή του Κομήτη)...Το αρχηγείο της αστυνομίας της Scotland Yard είπε ότι ο ντετέκτιβ Επιθεωρητής Percy Browne θα ερευνήσει την αιτία της έκρηξης στην καμπίνα... Ο Browne ο οποίος συνήθως ερευνά δολοφονίες και άλλα μεγάλα εγκλήματα, θα ξεκινήσει την έρευνά του σύντομα και πιθανότατα θα πάει στην Ελλάδα και την Κύπρο».

Ο Browne και ο συνάδελφός του, όπως ήταν γνωστό κατώτεροι αξιωματικοί συνόδευαν ανώτερους ντετέκτιβ, ταξίδεψαν στην Αθήνα όπως είχε προγραμματιστεί στις 21 Φεβρουαρίου. Ωστόσο, φαίνεται ότι η άφιξή τους στην ελληνική πρωτεύουσα προκάλεσε έκπληξη για το προσωπικό της βρετανικής πρεσβείας εκεί. Ο Macrae, επικοινώνησε με τους συναδέλφους του στο εξωτερικό, και τηλεφώνησε στο γραφείο του Brodie για να του μεταφέρει την δυσαρέσκεια της διπλωματικής υπηρεσίας για αυτό που θεωρήθηκε ως μια κάπως ανεπιθύμητη έκπληξη. Ο Brodie προσπάθησε αμέσως να τον καθησυχάσει γράφοντας στον Macrae:

«Λυπάμαι πολύ που δεν ενημερώθηκες για το γεγονός ότι ο ντετέκτιβ Επιθεωρητής Browne και ο συνάδελφός του είχαν φύγει από αυτή τη χώρα.

Πριν λίγες μέρες, όταν συνειδητοποίησα ότι η έρευνα είχε φτάσει στο στάδιο που ο Browne ήταν σχεδόν έτοιμος να πάει στο εξωτερικό, ενημερώθηκα ότι είχε πάει προσωπικά στο Υπουργείο Εξωτερικών και είχε κάνει όλες τις απαραίτητες ρυθμίσεις. Επιπλέον, μια έκθεση που άφησαν εδώ στα τέλη της περασμένης εβδομάδας για το Υπουργείο Εσωτερικών περιέχει πλήρεις λεπτομέρειες για το τι προτάθηκε. Ένα επιπλέον αντίγραφο αυτής της αναφοράς τέθηκε στη διάθεση του Υπουργείου Εσωτερικών, το οποίο κλήθηκε να σας το στείλει. Φαίνεται ότι το άτομο στο Υπουργείο Εσωτερικών που θα έπρεπε να είχε ασχοληθεί με αυτό το θέμα δεν ήταν διαθέσιμο για μια ή δύο μέρες στις αρχές αυτής της εβδομάδας και κανείς άλλος δεν είχε προβεί σε κάποια ενέργεια σχετικά με την έκθεση.

Γράφω την επιστολή αυτή όχι με σκοπό να προσπαθήσω να μετατοπίσω την ευθύνη, αλλά απλώς για να σας ενημερώσω ότι αυτή φαίνεται να είναι μια από εκείνες τις περιπτώσεις όπου «τα καλύτερα σχεδιασμένα σχέδια ποντικών και ανθρώπων...» Λυπάμαι μόνο που φαίνεστε να μείνατε στο σκοτάδι. Μπορώ να σας διαβεβαιώσω ότι αυτό δεν έγινε σκόπιμα, και ελπίζω ότι θα αποδεχτείτε την ειλικρινή μου λύπη»[132].

Στις 23 Φεβρουαρίου, ο Macrae έγραψε στον Tom Bridges, σχετικά με την απροειδοποίητη άφιξη των Browne and Hill στην Αθήνα:

«Όπως σας είπα στο τηλέφωνο... Λυπάμαι πολύ που δύο μέλη της Μητροπολιτικής Αστυνομίας έφθασαν στην Αθήνα προτού μπορέσουμε να σας προειδοποιήσουμε για τον ερχομό τους και να εξηγήσουμε λίγο το ιστορικό. Αυτή είναι η ιστορία.»

Ο Macrae εξήγησε ότι ο Charlie Oscar είχε χαθεί μετά την έκρηξη της βόμβας και ότι η έρευνα της AIB επρόκειτο να εξακριβώσει την αιτία και όχι να αποδώσει ευθύνες. Περαιτέρω έρευνα για την αιτία διεξήχθη καλύτερα από τη Μητροπολιτική Αστυνομία, συνέχισε, καθώς η αστυνομία δεν θα περιοριζόταν από τους περιορισμούς των αρμοδιοτήτων του Board of Trade. Στη συνέχεια, ο Macrae ενημέρωσε τον Bridges για την συμφωνία ότι το Board of Trade θα ζητούσε επίσημα από τη Μητροπολιτική Αστυνομία να διεξαγάγει έρευνες για τα γεγονότα που οδήγησαν στην έκρηξη και ως εκ τούτου στους θανάτους των 66 επιβαινόντων και θα πλήρωνε για την έρευνα. Αυτός πρόσθεσε:

«Εμείς από την πλευρά μας συμφωνήσαμε να σας ειδοποιήσουμε και να σας ζητήσουμε να προβείτε σε τέτοιες ενέργειες με τις ελληνικές αρχές όπως κρίνεται απαραίτητο και κατάλληλο.
Στη συνέχεια περιμέναμε να λάβουμε μια επιστολή από την Αστυνομία που θα καθόριζε τη γραμμή της έρευνάς της και το προτεινόμενο σχέδιο δράσης της. Αντί αυτού μάθαμε από εσάς ότι οι δύο αστυνομικοί είχαν ήδη φτάσει στην Αθήνα. **Αυτό είναι το πιο λυπηρό καθώς φαίνεται πολύ πιθανό να προκύψουν δυνητικά δύσκολα πολιτικά ερωτήματα κατά τη διάρκεια της έρευνας. Για παράδειγμα, ας υποθέσουμε ότι η αστυνομία ανακαλύπτει ότι η έκρηξη προκλήθηκε από έναν Έλληνα (ή από έναν Τουρκοκύπριο) που ήλπιζε να εκκαθαρίσει τον Στρατηγό Γρίβα**[133] (κάτι που φυσικά έχει δημοσιευτεί στον Τύπο). Για το λόγο

---

[132] *Το Φόρεϊν Όφις φαίνεται να έχει ενοχληθεί εξαιρετικά, ανεξάρτητα από το πόσο ευγενικό μπορεί να εμφανιστεί το μήνυμά τους στον Brodie Παρομοίως, η απάντησή του, καλυμμένη με κομψές αναφορές, ήταν πολύ κοντά σε μια συγγνώμη, υποδηλώνοντας ότι η ξαφνική εμφάνιση των δύο αστυνομικών στην Αθήνα είχε προκαλέσει κύμα έντονης ανησυχίας στη Βρετανική Πρεσβεία. Φάνηκε ότι το Υπουργείο Εξωτερικών είχε ανησυχίες για το τι θα μπορούσε να ανακαλύψει ο Browne.*

[133] *Το Φόρεϊν Όφις ανησυχούσε σαφώς για αυτή τη γραμμή έρευνας. Όπως αναφέρθηκε, είχε πράγματι διαφημιστεί στον Τύπο από την ημέρα της συντριβής, επομένως αυτό μπορεί να είναι θέμα του FO που επιθυμεί να αποφύγει τυχόν ενοχλητικές γραμμές έρευνας. Ωστόσο,*

αυτό, φαίνεται σωστό η αστυνομία να πρέπει να διατηρεί στενή επαφή με την Πρεσβεία για το πώς εξελίσσεται η έρευνά της, ακόμα κι αν κάνει τις καθημερινές διευθετήσεις που είναι απαραίτητες με τους Έλληνες συνάδελφούς της μέσω των δικών της καναλιών. Ενόψει της σύγχυσης που μόλις συνέβη, υπό αυτή τη έννοια, φροντίζω να αποστέλλονται σαφείς οδηγίες στον ντετέκτιβ Browne.

Όσον αφορά το ζήτημα της ενημέρωσης της Ελληνικής κυβέρνησης για την έρευνα, νομίζω ότι αυτό είναι αποκλειστικά θέμα δικής σας διακριτικότητας. Όπως ανέφερα στο τηλέφωνο, σκέφτηκα ότι εκείνο που εσείς θα κάνατε (ως Υπουργείο Εξωτερικών) αποτελεί το κατάλληλο σημείο εκκίνησης, αλλά πολλά θα εξαρτηθούν από τον τρόπο εκτέλεσης αυτών των οδηγιών.

…Στέλνω αντίγραφο αυτής της επιστολής στον Tony Tyler στο Γραφείο της Κοινοπολιτείας και στον Timothy Daunt στη Λευκωσία, καθώς πιστεύω ότι είναι πιθανό η αστυνομία να επιθυμεί να επισκεφθεί την Κύπρο κατά τη διάρκεια των ερευνών της. Σε αυτήν την περίπτωση, το Γραφείο της Κοινοπολιτείας μπορεί κάλλιστα να επιθυμεί να ενημερώσει την Κυπριακή Κυβέρνηση για την αστυνομική έρευνα και, εάν μπορείτε να μάθετε για τα σχέδιά τους να επισκεφθούν την Κύπρο, θα ήταν προφανώς χρήσιμο για τον Tyler και τον Daunt να ενημερωθούν γι'αυτά.»

Ο κ. SS Bampton, του τμήματος F2 του Υπουργείου Εσωτερικών, έγραψε στις 26 Φεβρουαρίου στον PE Brodie, Assistant Commissioner Crime στη Μητροπολιτική Αστυνομία:

«Το Φόρεϊν Όφις ανησυχεί πολύ όπως οι αστυνομικοί σας διατηρήσουν στενή επαφή με την Πρεσβεία για αυτήν την έρευνα, ακόμα κι αν κάνουν καθημερινές διευθετήσεις με τους Έλληνες συναδέλφους των μέσω των δικών τους καναλιών, καθώς είναι πιθανό δυνητικά δύσκολα πολιτικά ερωτήματα να προκύψουν κατά τη διάρκεια της έρευνας. Φαντάζομαι ότι θα έχετε ήδη δώσει οδηγίες για αυτό το σκοπό, αλλά έχω διαβεβαιώσει το Φόρεϊν Όφις ότι θα σας διαβιβάσω αμέσως αυτήν την οδηγία».

δεδομένου ότι είναι τόσο συγκεκριμένο, είναι δυνατόν στο FO να γνώριζαν πληροφορίες που υποδηλώνουν ότι αυτή ήταν, πράγματι, η βασική αιτία, την οποία έπρεπε να κρατήσουν κρυφά; Τέτοιες πληροφορίες μπορεί, για παράδειγμα, να προέρχονταν από πηγή SIS (MI6) ή ακόμα και ότι η πλοκή περιλάμβανε μια τέτοια πηγή που χρειαζόταν προστασία. Σημείωση: πολλοί μαχητές της ΕΟΚΑ είχαν δώσει πληροφορίες στις υπηρεσίες ασφαλείας κατά τη διάρκεια της Κυπριακής Έκτακτης Ανάγκης.

Ο Brodie ανέλαβε αμέσως να μεταβιβάσει τα συναισθήματα του Υπουργείου Εξωτερικών στον Browne. Στις 27 Φεβρουαρίου, έστειλε μια προσεκτικά διατυπωμένη επιστολή στον ντετέκτιβ, με τέτοιο τρόπο που δεν θα τους έβαζε σε δύσκολη θέση αν την έβλεπαν ακούσια μη εξουσιοδοτημένα μάτια, όμως ίσως να είχε συμβεί:

«Ο Bampton από το Υπουργείο Εσωτερικών ήρθε να με δει σήμερα και μου λέει ότι κάποιος από την Πρεσβεία στην Αθήνα είχε επαφή με τον Macrae στο Υπουργείο Εξωτερικών εδώ για την παρουσία σας στην Αθήνα.
Φαίνεται ότι το προσωπικό της Πρεσβείας στην Αθήνα είναι ελαφρώς ανήσυχο για τυχόν πιθανές πολιτικές επιπτώσεις σε περίπτωση που η έρευνά σας εξελιχθεί προς μια συγκεκριμένη κατεύθυνση. Για παράδειγμα, εάν βρείτε στοιχεία που να υποδεικνύουν ότι η έκρηξη στον Κομήτη κανονίστηκε για να κάνει κακό σε κάποιον στην πολιτική στην Κύπρο ή την Ελλάδα, τότε θα προέκυπτε μια πολύ λεπτή κατάσταση.
Νομίζω ότι δεν χρειάζεται να πω περισσότερα από το να σας ζητήσω να διατηρήσετε πολύ στενή επαφή με το προσωπικό της Πρεσβείας αν προκύψει οτιδήποτε με πολιτική ανάμιξη. Γνωρίζω ότι θα συζητούσατε το θέμα μαζί τους και θα προσέχετε πολύ να μην φέρετε σε δύσκολη θέση το Φόρεϊν Όφις.
Αναγκαστικά, αυτή η επιστολή πρέπει να είναι με μάλλον αόριστους όρους, αλλά είμαι σίγουρος θα καταλάβετε.
Σας εύχομαι καλή τύχη στην έρευνά σας και ανυπομονώ να ακούσω τα πάντα σχετικά με αυτή όταν επιστρέψετε σε αυτή τη χώρα.»

Ο Βοηθός Επιθεωρητής διαβίβασε την επιστολή στον Macrae, με συνοδευτικό σημείωμα που ανέφερε:

«Επισυνάπτω μια μυστική και άκρως εμπιστευτική επιστολή προς τον ντετέκτιβ Επιθεωρητή Browne , ο οποίος ερευνά τη συντριβή του Κομήτη της ΒΕΑ. Θα σας ήμουν εξαιρετικά ευγνώμων εάν μπορούσατε να κανονίσετε να του σταλεί αυτή η επιστολή στην Αθήνα μέσω του Διπλωματικού σάκου. Πιστεύουμε ότι διαμένει στο Hotel Stanley, 1 rue Odysseus 1, Place Kaiskis, Αθήνα.»

Ο Macrae διαβίβασε την επιστολή στον Tom Bridges, και με δική του συνοδευτική επιστολή :
«Στην πρόσφατη, χωρίς ημερομηνία επιστολή μου προς εσάς, είπα ότι η αστυνομία θα έστελνε οδηγίες (στο Browne) να διατηρεί επαφή με την Πρεσβεία σε περίπτωση που προκύψουν πολιτικές εξελίξεις κατά τη διάρκεια των ερευνών του.

Επισυνάπτω, κάτω από το Flying Seal[134], μια επιστολή από τον (Brodie) προς τον Browne, την οποία θα ήμουν ευγνώμων αν την διαβιβάζατε. Νομίζω ότι η επιστολή πρέπει να εξυπηρετήσει τον σκοπό της από τη δική μας σκοπιά. Αν και το περιεχόμενο της επιστολής δεν είναι ιδιαίτερα εντυπωσιακό, θα πρέπει να ξέρετε ότι ο **Brodie ήταν πολύ ανήσυχος η επιστολή να μην περάσει από μη εξουσιοδοτημένα χέρια**. Ήλπιζε ότι θα μπορούσε να σταλεί μέσω του σφραγισμένου σάκου και όταν του εξήγησα ότι οι κανόνες μας δεν το επέτρεπαν, έπρεπε να τον διαβεβαιώσω ότι εσείς προσωπικά ως αποδέκτης αυτής της επιστολής θα τη σφραγίζατε και θα κάνατε σίγουρο ότι παραδόθηκε με ασφαλές χέρι στον Browne πριν μου εμπιστευθεί την επιστολή!»

Ο Bridges απάντησε στις 6 Μαρτίου, ενημερώνοντας τον Macrae και δίνοντάς του λίγη διαβεβαίωση:

«Ήμασταν λίγο έκπληκτοι όταν (ο Browne) έφτασε αυθόρμητα, αλλά περιμέναμε μια επίσκεψη πριν από πολύ καιρό ως αποτέλεσμα αυτού που είχαμε δει στον Τύπο και δεν είχε μεγάλη σημασία. Με τη βοήθεια του Υπουργείου Εξωτερικών κανόνισα να συναντηθεί ο Browne με το Ελληνικό Γραφείο της Ιντερπόλ. Αυτό σήμαινε μια μικρή καθυστέρηση, αλλά από τότε μας είπε ότι η έρευνά του έχει σημειώσει καλή πρόοδο και ότι οι Ελληνικές αρχές βοηθούν πολύ.
Δεν γνωρίζω φυσικά τις λεπτομέρειες, αλλά καταλαβαίνω ότι η συγκεκριμένη γραμμή έρευνας που ακολουθεί δεν περιλαμβάνει πολιτικούς λόγους.»

Στις 19 Απριλίου, ο RG Smith του CA4(1) του Board of Trade έστειλε ένα σημείωμα σε κάποιο Captain Hunt στο τμήμα του Veal. Σημείωνε ότι η Μητροπολιτική Αστυνομία θα διερευνήσει τα γεγονότα που οδήγησαν στη συντριβή με το Συμβούλιο Εμπορίου να πληρώνει το κόστος σε ορισμένες περιπτώσεις. Ο Smith ήθελε να μάθει εάν η αστυνομία, όπως είχε συμφωνηθεί προηγουμένως, είχε υποβάλει εκθέσεις προόδου, προσθέτοντας ειρωνικά: *«Έχετε καταλήξει σε κάποιο συμπέρασμα μέχρι στιγμής για το εάν υπάρχει επαρκής πρόοδος που να δικαιολογεί τις σχετικές δημόσιες δαπάνες;»*

Ο Veal απάντησε τέσσερις μέρες αργότερα:

---

[134] *Η αναφορά σε Flying Seal υποδηλώνει επιστολή με επικολλημένη σφραγίδα, αλλά όχι κλειστή, ώστε να μπορεί να διαβαστεί από το άτομο στο οποίο έχει ανατεθεί η διαβίβασή του στον παραλήπτη.*

«...Ο Επιθεωρητής Browne μου τηλεφώνησε πριν από περίπου 15 ημέρες για να με ενημερώσει για την τρέχουσα κατάσταση σχετικά με τις έρευνές του και να ρωτήσει για περαιτέρω αναφορές από το RARDE. Ο Επιθεωρητής Browne και ο Λοχίας Lee πέρασαν περίπου πέντε εβδομάδες στην Κύπρο και την Ελλάδα συνεχίζοντας τις έρευνές τους και οι έρευνές τους περιλάμβαναν συναντήσεις με τους στενούς συγγενείς[135] όλων εκείνων που σκοτώθηκαν στο ατύχημα.
Ο Επιθεωρητής Browne μου είπε ότι υπήρχαν τέσσερις κύριες γραμμές έρευνας και ότι μία από αυτές φαινόταν να είχε προοπτικές. Πίστευε ότι θα τους έπαιρνε περίπου τέσσερις ή πέντε εβδομάδες για να ολοκληρώσουν αυτό που έπρεπε να κάνουν και να ετοιμάσουν την έκθεσή τους. Με αυτό το δεδομένο θα πρέπει να περιμένουμε να ακούσουμε κάτι μέσα στο επόμενο δεκαπενθήμερο, αλλά αν δεν το κάνουν, θα έρθω ξανά σε επαφή με τον Επιθεωρητή Browne. Ένα στοιχείο που είναι πιθανό να καθυστερήσει αυτήν την τελική έκθεση είναι η διαθεσιμότητα της έκθεσης RARDE επειδή περιέχει πολύ σημαντικά στοιχεία εμπειρογνωμόνων.»

Ο Tom Bridges επικοινώνησε με τον John Macrae στις 25 Ιουνίου σε σχέση με το συνεχιζόμενο ελληνικό ενδιαφέρον για ποινικές διαδικασίες:

«Αναφέρθηκε στον Τύπο της Αθήνας ότι περαιτέρω έρευνα για το θέμα αυτό αναλάμβανε ο Εισαγγελέας Πλημμελειοδικών Αθηνών. Δεν είμαι σίγουρος ποια ακριβώς είναι η σημασία αυτού, αλλά υποθέτω ότι ορισμένα από τα αποτελέσματα των ερευνών του ντετέκτιβ Επιθεωρητή Browne έχουν τεθεί στη διάθεση των Ελληνικών αρχών από τη Scotland Yard και ότι οι Ελληνικές αρχές ήθελαν να διερευνήσουν την δυνατότητα δίωξης[136] στα ελληνικά δικαστήρια. Αναμφίβολα η Scotland Yard γνωρίζει περισσότερα για αυτό.
Τώρα έλαβα μια επιστολή από τις ανακριτικές αρχές στο Ειρηνοδικείο Αθηνών που μας ζητούν να παράσχουμε στον Εισαγγελέα Πλημμελειοδικών εδώ αντίγραφο των πορισμάτων των βρετανικών αρχών για το ατύχημα. Απάντησα σε αυτήν την επιστολή λέγοντας ότι, εξ όσων

---

[135] *Κατά τη διάρκεια της έρευνας για αυτό το βιβλίο, ο συγγραφέας μίλησε με αρκετούς στενούς συγγενείς των θυμάτων, κανένας από τους οποίους, όταν ρωτήθηκε, δεν θυμήθηκε να τον «πλησίασαν» οι Βρετανοί ντετέκτιβ.*

[136] *Το γιατί οι Έλληνες θα εξετάσουν το ενδεχόμενο δίωξης όταν η Scotland Yard είπε ότι δεν υπάρχουν αποδείξεις δεν έχει διευκρινιστεί. Υποδηλώνει ότι είτε η Scotland Yard είχε συμπεράνει ότι υπήρχε, στην πραγματικότητα, κάποιος που αξίζει να διωχθεί, είτε, ότι οι Ελληνικές αρχές το χρησιμοποιούσαν ως «νομικό» μέσο για να μάθουν τι ήξερε η Scotland Yard.*

γνωρίζω, οι δικές μας έρευνες δεν έχουν ακόμη ολοκληρωθεί, αλλά έχω διαβιβάσει το αίτημά τους στις αρμόδιες αρχές στο Λονδίνο.»

Ο Bampton έγραψε στον Veal στις 16 Ιουλίου, σχετικά με ένα αίτημα από τις ελληνικές αρχές για αντίγραφο των ευρημάτων. Φάνηκε ότι υπήρχε κάποια μικρή σύγχυση ως προς το εάν τα ευρήματα αναφέρονται στην Έκθεση Ατυχήματος ή στην αστυνομική έρευνα:

«Το έχω συζητήσει με τον Βοηθό Επιθεωρητή της Μητροπολιτικής Αστυνομίας και, όπως θα καταλάβετε από τη φύση της έκθεσής τους, θα αποκλείεται να σταλεί αντίγραφό της στις Ελληνικές αρχές και θα ήταν εξαιρετικά δύσκολο να προετοιμαστεί μια επεξεργασμένη έκδοση.
Ένας τρόπος αντιμετώπισης αυτού, αν συμφωνείτε, θα ήταν να επιτρέψετε στις Ελληνικές αρχές να έχουν αντίγραφο της έκθεσής σας για την αιτία της συντριβής. Ταυτόχρονα, ένα συνοδευτικό σημείωμα θα μπορούσε να σταλεί στον Πρέσβη μας που να εξηγεί ότι, εάν πιεστεί για αντίγραφο της έκθεσης της αστυνομίας, θα πρέπει να τους πει ότι η έρευνα έχει πλέον ολοκληρωθεί, αλλά ήταν ασαφή και δεν υπήρχαν επαρκή στοιχεία που να υποδεικνύουν ποιος μπορεί να ήταν υπεύθυνος. Αυτή η προσέγγιση θα γίνει δεκτή από την Μητροπολιτική Αστυνομία και το Υπουργείο Εξωτερικών και θα ήθελα τις απόψεις σας επ' αυτού.»

Ο Brodie ενημέρωσε τον Veal για την παραλαβή της επιστολής, αντίγραφο της οποίας ο Bampton είχε στείλει στον Βοηθό Επιθεωρητή προσθέτοντας:

«Αναμφίβολα θα θυμάστε ότι όταν μίλησα μαζί σας στο τηλέφωνο ανέφερα ότι ο ντετέκτιβ Επιθεωρητής Browne ήταν ακόμα με τον Δημόσιο Κατήγορο στην Εισαγγελία. Ίσως, επομένως, το προτεινόμενο συνοδευτικό σημείωμα προς τον Πρέσβη μας που έλεγε, «ότι η έρευνα της αστυνομίας ήταν ασαφής και ότι υπήρχαν ανεπαρκή στοιχεία για να δείξει ποιος θα μπορούσε να ήταν υπεύθυνος» θα έπρεπε να καθυστερήσει έως ότου ο Δημόσιος Κατήγορος δώσει την απόφασή του.» Ο Bampton συμφώνησε «Θεωρώ ότι δεν πρέπει να πούμε τίποτα για να προδικάσουμε την απόφαση του Δημόσιου Κατήγορου».
Στις 29 Ιουλίου, ο Brodie έγραψε στον Bampton, επιβεβαιώνοντας:

«Έχει ληφθεί τώρα απάντηση από το γραφείου του Διευθυντή του Δημόσιου Κατήγορου ότι «δεν μπορεί να γίνει καμία ενέργεια επί των παρόντων αποδεικτικών στοιχείων». Ελλείψει περαιτέρω στοιχείων, δεν νομίζω ότι ο Διευθυντής θα προβεί σε οποιαδήποτε ενέργεια στο μέλλον[137].

Ο Bampton έστειλε επιστολή στον Brodie την 1η Αυγούστου, σε σχέση με το αίτημα των ελληνικών αρχών για αντίγραφο των «ευρημάτων». Υπήρχε ακόμη ανησυχία για την ύπαρξη των αστυνομικών ερευνών και ο Bampton επεκτάθηκε στις προηγούμενες συμβουλές:

«Ο καλύτερος τρόπος αντιμετώπισης αυτού του αιτήματος φαίνεται είναι να δοθεί στις ελληνικές αρχές ένα αντίγραφο της έκθεσης που συνέταξε ο επικεφαλής επιθεωρητής ατυχημάτων στο Συμβούλιο Εμπορίου και να παραλειφθεί κάθε αναφορά στην αστυνομική έρευνα. Το Board of Trade δεν έχει αντίρρηση για αυτή τη διαδικασία και επισυνάπτω μια προ-εκτύπωση της έκθεσής τους. Αυτό δεν θα δημοσιευθεί πριν από τον Σεπτέμβριο, αλλά το Συμβούλιο Εμπορίου δεν θα είχε αντίρρηση εάν διαβιβαζόταν στις Ελληνικές αρχές πριν από αυτό, με την προϋπόθεση ότι θα πρέπει να αντιμετωπίζεται ως εμπιστευτικό μέχρι να δημοσιευθεί η έκθεση. Έχω αφαιρέσει από την έκθεση τη σύντομη επιστολή υποβολής προς τον Πρόεδρο του Συμβουλίου Εμπορίου, καθώς αυτή παραπέμπει στην έρευνα της Μητροπολιτικής Αστυνομίας. Αν και αυτή η επιστολή θα δημοσιευθεί στην έκθεση, δεν είναι αναγκαίο να επιστήσουμε την προσοχή των Ελληνικών αρχών στην αστυνομική έρευνα[138] και δεν θα φαίνεται ότι μια τέτοια επιστολή θα έπρεπε να περιλαμβάνεται σε προ-εκτυπωμένο αντίγραφο.

Εάν ο Πρέσβης μας στην Αθήνα ανακριθεί σχετικά με την αστυνομική έρευνα, προτείνω να πει ότι η αστυνομική έρευνα ήταν ασαφής και ότι δεν υπήρχαν επαρκή στοιχεία για να δείξει ποιος μπορεί να ήταν υπεύθυνος».

Ο Macrae έγραψε στον Bridges στις 6 Αυγούστου, απαντώντας στην επιστολή του της 25ης Ιουνίου:

---

[137] *Μια σταθερή απόφαση να οριστικοποιηθεί το θέμα υποδηλώνει ότι ο ύποπτος (Νίκος Παπαπέτρου) ή γνωστός (Αβραάμ Σολωμού) ήταν νεκρός και ότι τυχόν συνεργοί ήταν απίθανο να οδηγηθούν στη δικαιοσύνη, είτε λόγω έλλειψης αποδεικτικών στοιχείων είτε επειδή οι πιθανότητες να οδηγηθούν σε δίκη στο Ηνωμένο Βασίλειο ήταν ελάχιστες ή ανύπαρκτες, π.χ. στην περίπτωση του Γιωρκάτζη.*

[138] *Αυτό έρχεται σε αντίθεση με την προηγούμενη αλληλογραφία, από την εποχή του D/Supt. Επίσκεψη του Browne στην Αθήνα, ότι οι ελληνικές αρχές γνωρίζαν ήδη την αστυνομική έρευνα και ότι το Φόρεϊν Όφις είχε διευκολύνει την επίσκεψη του ντετέκτιβ στο Ελληνικό Γραφείο της Ιντερπόλ.*

«Πράγματι, η έρευνά σας μας έφερε σε μια μικρή δυσκολία, καθώς, σε αντίθεση με την έκθεση που συνέταξε ο Αρχι-επιθεωρητής Ατυχημάτων, το περιεχόμενο της έκθεσης των Αξιωματικών της Μητροπολιτικής Αστυνομίας είναι τέτοιο που δεν θα έκανε να δοθεί στις Ελληνικές αρχές. Μεγάλο μέρος του είναι πολιτικό που ασχολείται με προσωπικά δεδομένα (ιστορικά) και τις συμμαχίες ενδιαφερομένων ατόμων και οι πληροφορίες θα μπορούσαν κάλλιστα να χρησιμοποιηθούν (ή να τύχουν κατάχρησης) από τις Ε λληνικές αρχές για δικούς τους σκοπούς. Σε κάθε περίπτωση, δεν είναι συνήθης πρακτική να διατίθενται αντίγραφα των αστυνομικών εκθέσεων εκτός του Υπουργείου Εσωτερικών, ακόμη και σε άλλα Κυβερνητικά Υπουργεία. Για δική σας ενημέρωση, η αναφορά έχει σταλεί στον Δημόσιο Κατήγορο (Εισαγγελία) ο οποίος επιβεβαίωσε την άποψη της ίδιας της αστυνομίας ότι δεν υπάρχουν επαρκή στοιχεία για περαιτέρω διαβήματα.»

Ο Macrae συνέχισε να προτείνει, όπως και ο Bampton στον Brodie, να δοθεί στον Έλληνα Εισαγγελέα Πλημμελειοδικών αντίγραφο της Έκθεσης Ατυχήματος και όχι αυτό που συνέταξε η αστυνομία, μαζί με την μέχρι τώρα τυπική γραμμή ότι, «...Η (αστυνομική) έρευνα ήταν ασαφής...»

Στη συνέχεια ο Bridges διαβεβαίωσε τον Macrae ότι η Έκθεση Ατυχήματος ήταν πιθανώς αυτό που ήθελε στην πραγματικότητα ο Κατήγορος, καθώς δεν είχε γίνει καμία αναφορά στην έκθεση της αστυνομίας. Πρόσθεσε ότι, εάν οι Ελληνικές αρχές ήθελαν συμπληρωματικές πληροφορίες, δηλαδή σχετικά με την αστυνομική έρευνα, δεν υπήρχε λόγος να μην υποβάλουν αίτηση για αυτές μέσω της Ιντερπόλ. Στη συνέχεια, ο Bridges πρότεινε μια εναλλακτική πορεία δράσης:

Ο Διευθυντής Πολιτικής Αεροπορίας, Υποστράτηγος Α. Σκαρμαλιωράκης, RHAF (συνταξιούχος) παρακολούθησε το θέμα με πολύ ενδιαφέρον και δυσανασχετούσε σαφώς με τα δημοσιεύματα τον περασμένο Νοέμβριο που έδειχναν ότι το ατύχημα προκλήθηκε από έκρηξη στο αεροσκάφος. Φαινόταν να σκέφτεται ότι αυτό υπονοούσε κάποια κριτική για τις ρυθμίσεις ασφαλείας της Ελλάδας στο αεροδρόμιο της Αθήνας και εξέδωσε μια δήλωση στον Τύπο υπονοώντας ότι η πρώρη δημοσίευση αυτών των ευρημάτων πριν από την έκδοση της τελικής έκθεσης ήταν παράτυπη και μη ικανοποιητική... Ο Σκαρμαλιωράκης είναι ένας άνθρωπος με κάποια πολιτική θέση εδώ, αφού από την αρχή ήταν κοντά στους ηγέτες του στρατιωτικού πραξικοπήματος τον περασμένο Απρίλιο. Για αυτούς τους διάφορους λόγους, θα προτιμούσα να λάβει ένα αντίγραφο της έκθεσης προσωπικά από τον Αεροπορικό Ακόλουθο (Air Attaché) αντί να μάθει για την ύπαρξή της από το προσωπικό του που συνεργάζεται με τον Εισαγγελέα στη διερεύνηση αυτού του ατυχήματος.»

Η επιβεβαίωση της προσωπικής παράδοσης στον Σκαρμαλιωράκη της αναφοράς ήρθε με τηλεμήνυμα στις 28 Αυγούστου από τον Sir M. Stewart της Πρεσβείας Αθηνών στο Υπουργείο Εξωτερικών, τονίζοντας ότι ο Διευθυντής Πολιτικής Αεροπορίας, «... *δεν έκανε κανένα σχόλιο επί της ουσίας, αλλά προφανώς χάρηκε για την επιστολή και τα αντίγραφα πριν από τη δημοσίευση»*.

Λεπτομέρειες της ίδιας της αστυνομικής έρευνας δεν είναι ακόμη διαθέσιμες στο κοινό, τη στιγμή που γράφονται αυτές οι γραμμές. Είναι γνωστό ότι ο Browne και ο Hill πέρασαν περίπου πέντε εβδομάδες στην Ελλάδα και την Αθήνα, αλλά οι μάρτυρες με τους οποίους μίλησαν και τα υλικά στοιχεία που συγκέντρωσαν εξακολουθούν να είναι επίσημα μυστικά.

Τον Απρίλιο του 1968, ένας 14χρονος μαθητής που ονομαζόταν Roy Tuthill βρέθηκε δολοφονημένος στο κτήμα του Λόρδου Beaverbrook, στο Givens Grove. στο Leatherhead, όταν ξεκίνησε μια από τις μεγαλύτερες αστυνομικές έρευνες του Αστυνομικού Σώματος στο Surrey . Ο ντετέκτιβ αστυφύλακας Dave O'Connell αποσπάστηκε στην ομάδα δολοφονιών που συγκεντρώθηκε στο Leatherhead. Σε μια διαδικτυακή ανάρτηση πολλά χρόνια αργότερα, θυμήθηκε:

«Ζητήθηκε από τη Scotland Yard να βοηθήσει. Εκείνες τις μέρες, αν μια δύναμη κομητείας καλούσε τη Μητροπολιτική Αστυνομία εντός είκοσι τεσσάρων ωρών από την ανακάλυψη της δολοφονίας, το Υπουργείο Εσωτερικών ανελάμβανε το κόστος της έρευνας. Αυτό ήταν ένα μεγάλο κίνητρο για τους νομούς να καλούν τη Μητροπολιτική Αστυνομία. Η Μητροπολιτική Αστυνομία διατηρούσε μια ομάδα από πέντε Επικεφαλής –Επιθεωρητές για δολοφονίες που εναλλάσσονταν καθώς έφταναν τα αιτήματα για βοήθεια. Τους βοηθούσε ένας ντετέκτιβ λοχίας ο οποίος ήταν γνωστός ως ο "κουβαλητής".

Ο αξιωματικός που διορίστηκε για να ηγείτο αυτής της έρευνας ήταν ο Επικεφαλής Επιθεωρητής Percy Brown[139] (sic). Η έρευνα κατά τη γνώμη μου ήταν καταδικασμένη από την αρχή και κατατάσσεται ως η χειρότερη καθοδηγούμενη έρευνα με την οποία είχα οποιαδήποτε σχέση.

Αρχικά, οι ντετέκτιβς από όλη την χώρα καλέστηκαν να βρίσκονται στον αστυνομικό τμήμα Leatherhead για ενημέρωση σε κάποια

---

[139] *Παρά την παράλειψη του «e» από τον Brown , είναι σχεδόν βέβαιο ότι ο Percy Brown που αναφέρεται εδώ είναι ο ίδιος Percy Browne. Η έρευνα για άλλους αστυνομικούς με το όνομα Percy Brown στα τμήματα έρευνας δολοφονίας της Μ.Α εκείνη την εποχή αποδείχθηκε αρνητική.*

συγκεκριμένη ώρα. Οι ανώτεροι αξιωματικοί έφτασαν περίπου δυόμισι ώρες αργότερα αφού προφανώς είχαν απολαύσει τα οφέλη ενός καλού γεύματος[140]. Οι πρώτες λέξεις που έδωσε ο Επικεφαλής Επιθεωρητής Browne ήταν: «Θα είστε τυχεροί να το διαλευκάνετε αυτό ». Αυτό ειπώθηκε πίσω από ένα σύννεφο καπνού που εξέπεμπε από ένα τεράστιο πούρο.

Τελικά η έρευνα ολοκληρώθηκε χωρίς ανίχνευση και πολύ μικρή πρόοδο».

---

[140] *Από αυτό συνάγεται ότι οι ανώτεροι αξιωματικοί είχαν καταναλώσει σημαντικό αλκοόλ κατά τη διάρκεια του μεσημεριανού τους γεύματος.*

Γραμμές έρευνας

Στην *Evening News*, μια εφημερίδα του Λονδίνου, στις 17 Φεβρουαρίου 1968, ένας τίτλος ανήγγειλε ένα «*Δίκτυ δολοφώνων του Κομήτη – Καταστροφή που σχεδιάστηκε στο Λονδίνο*», λέγοντας στους αναγνώστες του:

«Αστυνομική χτένα βρίσκεται σε εξέλιξη στην «Μικρή Κύπρο», την ελληνοκυπριακή περιοχή του Camden Town σε αναζήτηση των ανδρών που σχεδίασαν την αεροπορική καταστροφή του Κομήτη.

Νέες πληροφορίες έφτασαν στη Scotland Yard για τον Κομήτη... η αστυνομία πιστεύει ότι στόχος του σχεδίου ήταν η δολοφονία του πρώην αρχηγού της ΕΟΚΑ Στρατηγού Γρίβα, ο οποίος εσφαλμένα θεωρήθηκε ότι επέβαινε στο αεροσκάφος.

Ο ντετέκτιβ Επιθεωρητής Percy Browne, ο οποίος έχει μεταγραφεί στη Scotland Yard από τη θέση του στο Paddington CID, ανακάλυψε ότι η πλοκή σχεδιάστηκε σε ένα κλαμπ παιχνιδιών στο Paddington.

Ένας αριθμός Ελλήνων εξτρεμιστών αναζητούνται από την αστυνομία.

Οι έρευνες εντείνονται στη περιοχή του Camden Town και του Paddington και επισκέπτονται πολλά κλαμπ και καφέ.»

Τρεις μέρες αργότερα, η είδηση χρωματίστηκε κάπως από τη *Daily Sketch*, η οποία αποκάλυψε:

«Οι ντετέκτιβ της ομάδας δολοφονιών που ερευνούν τη δολιοφθορά του Κομήτη ΒΕΑ τον περασμένο Οκτώβριο θα πετάξουν αύριο στην Αθήνα.

Εκεί, ο ντετέκτιβ Επιθεωρητής Percy Browne και ένας λοχίας θα πάρουν συνεντεύξεις από αρκετούς άντρες παρουσία της ελληνικής αστυνομίας... Οι άνδρες της Scotland Yard έχουν ενημερωθεί ότι τοποθετήθηκε ωρολογιακή βόμβα στο αεροπλάνο σε μια προσπάθεια από πολιτικούς εξτρεμιστές να δολοφονήσουν τον συνταγματάρχη (sic) Γεώργιο Γρίβα.

Εάν αυτές οι πληροφορίες είναι σωστές, η Ελληνική κυβέρνηση μπορεί να αντιμετωπίσει ασφαλιστικές αποζημιώσεις εκατομμυρίων λιρών.

Προτού ο Επιθεωρητής Browne φύγει από το Λονδίνο, θα πάρει συνέντευξη από έναν Έλληνα που διέφυγε στη Βρετανία ως πολιτικός πρόσφυγας μετά από διαφωνία με τον Συνταγματάρχη Γρίβα.

Ήδη έχουν πάρει συνεντεύξεις και από άλλους Έλληνες που ζουν στο Λονδίνο. Μια σημαντική δήλωση έγινε από έναν Έλληνα σε μια φυλακή του Λονδίνου.»

Η *Daily Sketch* της 26ης Φεβρουαρίου ήταν κάπως πιο λεπτομερής και υποστήριξε ότι ο δράστης είχε πεθάνει, τονίζοντας:

«Ένας άνδρας επιβάτης μεταξύ των 66 που πέθανε... είχε προσωπική ασφάλεια για την πτήση αξίας πολλών εκατοντάδων χιλιάδων λιρών.

Αυτή η εξέλιξη αποκαλύφθηκε ενώ οι ντετέκτιβς της ομάδας δολοφονιών της Scotland Yard βρίσκονταν στην Αθήνα ερευνώντας τα αίτια της δολιοφθοράς του αεροπλάνου.

Έλληνες του Λονδίνου ισχυρίστηκαν στην αστυνομία ότι το αεροσκάφος ανατινάχθηκε για να δολοφονηθεί ο πρώην αρχηγός της ΕΟΚΑ, Στρατηγός Γρίβας.

Τώρα ήρθε στο φως η τεράστια ασφάλεια ζωής , και ο Επιθεωρητής Percy Browne που ηγείται της έρευνας, έχει ενημερωθεί για να διαπιστώσει εάν υπάρχει κάποια σχέση μεταξύ της ασφάλισης και της έκρηξης... Δεν είναι πιθανή η πληρωμή της ασφάλισης μέχρι να τελειώσει η έρευνα της Yard.

Εκτός από τα προσωπικά ασφαλιστήρια συμβόλαια που κατέχονται από μεμονωμένους επιβάτες, η ΒΕΑ πρόκειται να πληρώσει πάνω από £1 εκατομμύριο ως αποζημίωση για την απώλεια ζωών.»

Ένα ρεπορτάζ της εφημερίδας *Cyprus Mail* της 5ης Σεπτεμβρίου κάτω από τον υπότιτλο ο Anthony Chivers ρώτησε : *«Πέθανε ο σαμποτέρ στη συντριβή του Κομήτη ;»* και συνέχισε:

«Η Scotland Yard γνωρίζει το όνομα του ανθρώπου που πιστεύουν ότι βρισκόταν πίσω από το σχέδιο βόμβας που είχε ως αποτέλεσμα τη συντριβή του Κομήτη στα ανοιχτά της Κύπρου τον περασμένο Οκτώβριο.

Υποτίθεται ότι είναι είτε Έλληνας είτε Ελληνοκύπριος επιχειρηματίας. Πιστεύεται ότι η γυναίκα του ζει στο Λονδίνο. Αλλά το ένα ερώτημα στο οποίο η Αστυνομία δεν μπορεί να απαντήσει είναι το εξής: Είναι ο άνδρας πίσω από την πλοκή ζωντανός ή νεκρός;

Επειδή τα πτώματα έντεκα ανθρώπων δεν ανασύρθηκαν ποτέ... και μέχρι να ανακτηθούν όλοι –κάτι που είναι πιθανό να μην γίνει ποτέ– η Scotland Yard δεν θα μπορέσει να ξεκαθαρίσει και το τελευταίο κομμάτι του μυστηρίου αυτού.

Μόνο τότε θα είναι σε θέση να διαπιστώσουν εάν ο άνδρας του οποίου το όνομα έχουν, πράγματι σκοτώθηκε στη συντριβή. Ή αν κάποιος άλλος χρησιμοποιούσε το όνομά του.

(Το μυστήριο) ξεκίνησε λίγες εβδομάδες μετά τη συντριβή όταν ο ντετέκτιβ Percy Browne συνοδευόμενος από έναν λοχία ντετέκτιβ, πήγε στην Ελλάδα και την Κύπρο.

Ανακάλυψε ότι ένας από τους επιβάτες του οποίου το όνομα ήταν στη λίστα επιβατών είχε συνάψει μεγάλη ασφάλεια ζωής.

Στη συνέχεια, η αστυνομία πιστεύει ότι με κάποιο τρόπο ξεγέλασε έναν άλλο άνδρα να πετάξει στη θέση του, χρησιμοποιώντας το διαβατήριό του, το εισιτήριό του και τη θέση του.

Μετά την απογείωση του αεροπλάνου, ο διοργανωτής της δολιοφθοράς θα εξαφανιζόταν, αφήνοντας τα άτομα που είχε κατονομάσει ως δικαιούχους να διεκδικήσουν πλήρη διευθέτηση.

Σε επίσημη δήλωση σχετικά με την υπόθεση, η Scotland Yard είπε: «Έγινε έρευνα της αστυνομίας για την καταστροφή του Κομήτη και στη συνέχεια υποβλήθηκε έκθεση στον Δημόσιο Κατήγορο στην Εισαγελία . Αποφασίστηκε, βάσει των διαθέσιμων αποδεικτικών στοιχείων, ότι δεν μπορούσε να γίνει καμία ενέργεια.

Μαθαίνω ότι είναι εξαιρετικά απίθανο να πληρωθεί το ασφαλιστήριο συμβόλαιο για το πρόσωπο που είναι γνωστό στην αστυνομία.

Εκπρόσωπος του Συνδέσμου Ασφαλιστικών Εταιρειών είπε: «Σε μια τέτοια περίπτωση θα πρέπει οπωσδήποτε να αρνηθούμε την πληρωμή. Θα πρέπει να αποδειχθεί προς ικανοποίησή μας ότι ο θάνατος ήταν τυχαίος και όχι από κάποια εγκληματική ενέργεια.

«Είναι βασικός κανόνας δικαίου ότι κανένα άτομο δεν πρέπει να επωφελείται από μια εγκληματική πράξη και αυτό σίγουρα θα ισχύει για οποιονδήποτε δικαιούχο που συμμετείχε σε αυτήν την πράξη ή συμμετείχε σε οποιαδήποτε συνωμοσία».

Μετά τη δημοσίευση της τελικής έκθεσης της AIB, ο John Edmonds στη Βρετανική Πρεσβεία στην Άγκυρα, επικοινώνησε με τον JMO Snodgrass στο Κεντρικό Τμήμα του Φόρειν Όφις , συμβουλεύοντάς τον ότι:

«Ο τουρκικός Τύπος ανέφερε τα πορίσματα του Board of Trade, αλλά όχι με εντυπωσιακούς όρους. Όλες οι εφημερίδες ανέφεραν ότι η βόμβα τοποθετήθηκε στο αεροσκάφος για να σκοτώσει τον Στρατηγό Γρίβα, αλλά απέφυγαν τις εικασίες για το ποιος ήταν υπεύθυνος.
Ο τοπικός ανταποκριτής του AP (Associated Press)[141], ο οποίος είναι επίσης και των Times, (είπε) ότι ήταν «καλά αποδεδειγμένο» ότι ένας από τους επιβάτες ασφαλίστηκε για 200.000 λίρες και στη συνέχεια «αυτοκτόνησε». αλλά είχε ζητηθεί από τις εφημερίδες να μην το δημοσιεύσουν, επειδή οι ιστορίες αυτού του είδους είναι ακόμη χειρότερες για τις αεροπορικές εταιρείες από τις θεωρίες δολοφονίας.
Καθώς αυτή η υπόθεση θα μπορούσε να έχει ακόμη κάποια πολιτική σημασία εδώ, θα πρέπει να είμαστε ευγνώμονες για τυχόν σχόλια που

---

[141] Πρακτορείο ειδήσεων Associated Press.

μπορεί να έχετε, μαζί με ένα αντίγραφο της επίσημης έκθεσης του ατυχήματος.»

Ο Edmonds έλαβε την απάντησή του από τον Macrae, ο οποίος σχολίασε:

«...γνωρίζουμε –όπως ειπώθηκε στον Τύπο– ότι (η αστυνομία) βρήκε ανεπαρκή στοιχεία για περαιτέρω διαδικασίες. Από τις εφημερίδες εδώ, μόνο η *Sun* είχε τίτλους ότι η συντριβή προκλήθηκε από βόμβα που προοριζόταν για τον Γρίβα, αλλά τα στοιχεία δεν τεκμηριώνουν πραγματικά την ιστορία. Επομένως, δεν μπορούμε να σχολιάσουμε έγκυρα το ερώτημα ποιος ευθύνεται για το ατύχημα. Συνολικά, η ασφαλιστική θεωρία φαίνεται η πιο πιθανή, αν και δεν μπορούμε να επιβεβαιώσουμε τις λεπτομέρειες (στην επιστολή σας).»

Οι δράστες της θηριωδίας θα χρειάζονταν πρόσβαση σε ένα ορισμένο επίπεδο εξειδικευμένων γνώσεων για να κατασκευάσουν έναν εκρηκτικό μηχανισμό ικανό να καταρρίψει ένα αεροσκάφος. Ειδικά , ο κατασκευαστής της βόμβας θα χρειαζόταν πρόσβαση στο πλαστικό εκρηκτικό στρατιωτικής ποιότητας που καθιέρωσε η RARDE ως το χρησιμοποιούμενο υλικό. Επιπλέον, θα χρειαζόταν ένα μέσο πυροδότησης, στην περίπτωση του Charlie Oscar , όπως ένα χρονοδιακόπτη ή ένα πυροκροτητή ραδιοσυχνοτήτων (RF).

Εναλλακτικά, ένας βομβιστής αυτοκτονίας, θα πρέπει να χρειαζόταν ένα μέσο πυροδότησης του εκρηκτικού μηχανισμού κατά παραγγελία.

Η ΕΟΚΑ είχε χρησιμοποιήσει βόμβες κατά τη διάρκεια του αγώνα της εναντίον των βρετανικών δυνάμεων, επομένως είναι λογικό να υποθέσουμε ότι υπήρχαν ακόμη άνθρωποι με τις απαραίτητες ικανότητες στο νησί επτά χρόνια μετά την ανεξαρτησία. Η οργάνωση ήταν επίσης πρόθυμη να χρησιμοποιήσει βία κατά των γυναικών και των παιδιών για την επιδίωξη των στόχων της, και μάλιστα να καταστρέψει αεροσκάφη με πολίτες επί του σκάφους. Στις 3 Μαρτίου 1956, ένα Handley Page Hermes, G-ALDW, της αεροπορικής εταιρείας τσάρτερ Skyways επρόκειτο να πάρει 68 μέλη των βρετανικών ενόπλων δυνάμεων και τις οικογένειές τους από τη Λευκωσία πίσω στο Ηνωμένο Βασίλειο. Μια βόμβα, τοποθετημένη σε σχάρα καπέλων, εξερράγη, καταστρέφοντας το αεροσκάφος αν και ευτυχώς χωρίς θύματα. Οι επιβαίνοντες σώθηκαν γιατί η αναχώρηση είχε καθυστερήσει δύομιση ώρες. Λίγο περισσότερο από έξι εβδομάδες αργότερα, στις 27 Απριλίου, μια βόμβα κατέστρεψε μια Dakota των Κυπριακών Αερογραμμών στο έδαφος, επίσης χωρίς θύματα.

Η διεθνής τρομοκρατία βρισκόταν ακόμη στα σπάργανα, ειδικά με στόχο τα αεροσκάφη και το επιβατικό κοινό. Οι βομβιστικές επιθέσεις αυτοκτονίας, ως πολιτικό όπλο, ήταν επίσης σπάνιες εκείνη την εποχή στην Ευρώπη. Ωστόσο, υπήρξαν αναδυόμενες απειλές, ειδικά στη Μέση Ανατολή και, σε μικρότερο βαθμό στη Βόρεια Ιρλανδία, αν και η κατάσταση στην τελευταία επρόκειτο να κλιμακωθεί δραματικά τα επόμενα πολύ λίγα χρόνια. Ωστόσο, υπήρχε μια πιθανή γραμμή έρευνας σχετικά με αυτό.

Λίγο πριν από την έναρξη του «Πολέμου των Έξι Ημερών» τον Ιούνιο του 1967 μεταξύ του Ισραήλ και των Αράβων γειτόνων του, υπήρχε απειλή από ομάδες της Μέσης Ανατολής να στοχοποιήσουν αεροπορικές εταιρείες που πετούσαν στο Ισραήλ. Αυτό θα περιλάμβανε τόσο την ΒΕΑ όσο και την Cyprus Airways. Στις 15 Ιουνίου 1967, ο Colin Mastin της SA (I) 3, είχε γράψει στον Captain Woolfe, Chief Pilot (Αρχι-πιλότο) της Cyprus Airways, ρωτώντας:

«...Τα πρόσφατα γεγονότα στη περιοχή επηρέασαν προφανώς τις δραστηριότητες των Κυπριακών Αερογραμμών. Μήπως έχει προκαλέσει προβλήματα που πρέπει να γνωρίζουμε;»

Στη συνέχεια, ο Captain Woolfe ταξίδεψε στην Αγγλία με αντίγραφα της επιστολής που εστάλη στις Κυπριακές Αερογραμμές και σε όλους τους αερομεταφορείς που δραστηριοποιούνται στο Ισραήλ. Οι επιστολές στα αγγλικά και τα αραβικά απαιτούσαν από όλες τις αεροπορικές εταιρείες να δηλώσουν στον παγκόσμιο Τύπο πριν από τα μέσα Ιουνίου ότι θα σταματήσουν τις συναλλαγές τους με το Ισραήλ και στην πραγματικότητα θα το έκαναν πριν από τα μέσα Ιουλίου, διαφορετικά θα έπαιρναν μέτρα εναντίον εκείνων των αεροπορικών εταιρειών που συνέχιζαν τις δραστηριότητές τους.

Όλοι οι εμπλεκόμενοι φορείς, και η κυβέρνηση του Λιβάνου, έλαβαν σοβαρά υπόψη τις επιστολές και πάρθηκαν διάφορα μέτρα ασφαλείας στη Βηρυτό. Ο Captain Woolfe προχώρησε περαιτέρω και επέβαλε ασφάλεια σε όλους τους σταθμούς στους οποίους λειτουργούσαν τα Viscounts των Κυπριακών Αερογραμμών . Καθώς αεροσκάφος των ΚΑ βρισκόταν στο έδαφος σε έναν σταθμό (άλλης χώρας) ένας αεροσυνοδός παρέμενε στην πόρτα της καμπίνας και παρακολουθούσε τα άτομα που επέβαιναν στο αεροσκάφος. Ένας από τους πιλότους παρακολουθούσε τις αποσκευές. Κανονικά το αεροσκάφος δεν έπαιρνε καύσιμα, ούτε φαγητό ούτε καθαριζόταν. Ο κ. PCM Shillitoe και ο καπετάνιος AS Johnson της ΒΕΑ γνώριζαν για την απειλή καθώς στη συνέχεια πήγαν στη Βηρυτό για να αποφασίσουν για άλλη μια φορά για τις πτήσεις της ΒΕΑ που διανυχτέρευαν.

Παρά την ύπαρξη της επιστολής «Falcon Forces», δεν υπήρξε ποτέ καμία υπόνοια ότι το Charlie Oscar καταρρίφθηκε για τρομοκρατικούς σκοπούς. Αν ήταν, σίγουρα θα υπήρχαν αξιώσεις από την αρμόδια ομάδα, και άλλους που επιθυμούσαν να προωθήσουν τον σκοπό τους υποδηλώνοντας ότι είχαν την ικανότητα να καταστρέψουν ένα αεροσκάφος κατά την πτήση. Δεν υπήρξαν τέτοιοι ισχυρισμοί.

Πρόσωπα Ενδιαφέροντος

Υπενθυμίζεται ότι στις αρχές Απριλίου, ο ντετέκτιβ Επιθεωρητής Browne είπε στον Veal ότι υπήρχαν «τέσσερις κύριες γραμμές έρευνας,», η μία από τις οποίες ήταν πολύ υποσχόμενη.» Είναι πιθανό, από τις πληροφορίες που περιέχονται στα αρχεία του Εθνικού Αρχείου, ότι εκείνη τη στιγμή αυτές οι έρευνες ήταν:
1. Σωτήρης Γεωργίου, που καθόταν στη θέση 4Α στη πτήση Λονδίνο προς Αθήνα.
2. Ο Ανδρέας Αντωνιάδης και οι συνεργάτες του, όπως κατονομάζονται από τον Πέτρο Γεωργιάδη.
3. Αβραάμ Σολωμού, η συμπεριφορά του οποίου στο αεροδρόμιο του Ελληνικού προκάλεσε ανησυχία και ο οποίος αργότερα κατονομάστηκε ως φορέας της συσκευής.
4. Νίκος Παπαπέτρου ο οποίος είχε και μια σειρά από ασφάλειες ζωής, τις οποίες αγόρασε λίγο πριν το ταξίδι του και τον κάλυπταν για μία μόνο πτήση.

Σωτήρης Γεωργίου
Οι απειλές προς την αεροπορική εταιρεία που έκανε ο πρώην υπάλληλος της ΒΕΑ Γιώργος Γεωργίου δημιούργησαν άμεση υποψία ότι επρόκειτο για το ίδιο πρόσωπο. Ο Σωτήρης Γεωργίου είχε επίσης αποκτήσει επιπλέον τέσσερα κιλά αποσκευών κατά τη διάρκεια της ημερήσιας παραμονής του στο Λονδίνο. Το γεγονός ότι καθόταν σε ένα από τα δύο καθίσματα που θεωρούνται ως πιο πιθανό να ήταν εκεί που εξερράγη ο μηχανισμός θα αποτελούσε άμεσο λόγο υποψίας.
Οι υποψίες ότι ο Σωτήρης ήταν όντως ο Γιώργος Γεωργίου κάηκαν όταν διαπιστώθηκε ότι ο τελευταίος ήταν ακόμα ζωντανός και καλά στο Λονδίνο μετά τη συντριβή. Οι πλεονάζουσες αποσκευές που συγκέντρωσε ο Σωτήρης Γεωργίου ήταν δώρα και αντικείμενα που αγοράστηκαν για μέλη της οικογένειας που δεν ήταν άμεσα διαθέσιμα στην Κύπρο. Οι αποσκευές θα είχαν μεταφερθεί στο αμπάρι, επομένως δεν θα περιελάμβαναν τη βόμβα. Δεν υπάρχει καμία ένδειξη στα αρχεία για συγκεκριμένο κίνητρο του Σωτήρη Γεωργίου να ανατινάξει το αεροσκάφος. Το σώμα του ήταν μεταξύ των αγνοουμένων, πράγμα που σημαίνει ότι ήταν πολύ πιθανόν να καθόταν στο κάθισμα όταν εξερράγη η βόμβα. Αν δεν ήταν υπεύθυνος για τη βόμβα, δεν θα ήταν, λοιπόν, κάτω από το κάθισμα 5Α, αυτό μπροστά από τον Γεωργίου. Η βόμβα θα είχε μεταφερθεί από το άτομο στο κάθισμα 3Α, αμέσως πίσω του, και το οποίο δεν έχει αναγνωριστεί.

Ανδρέας Αντωνιάδης

Στη φυλακή Brixton, στο Λονδίνο, βρισκόταν ένας άντρας που πίστευε ότι κρατούσε το κλειδί του μυστηρίου. Κρατούμενος αρ. 41320 Πέτρος Παναγιώτης Γεωργιάδης, με καταγωγή από την Κύπρο, είχε καταδικαστεί για ένοπλη ληστεία και φυλακίστηκε για λίγα χρόνια. Ίσως σε μια προσπάθεια να κερδίσει κάποιους βαθμούς για καλή συμπεριφορά, έγραψε στον Πρόεδρο της ΒΕΑ στις 9 Ιανουαρίου 1968:

«Η δολιοφθορά είναι σίγουρα η αιτία του Κομήτη της ΒΕΑ που καταστράφηκε στα ανοικτά των ακτών της Κύπρου.

Ο υπεύθυνος (ένας από αυτούς) είναι ο Ανδρέας Αντωνιάδης, πρώην τρομοκράτης της ΕΟΚΑ και ειδικός στην «ομάδα εκρηκτικών» του Στρατηγού Γεωργίου Γρίβα, αρχηγού της τότε ΕΟΚΑ και μετέπειτα ανώτατου της Εθνικής Φρουράς Κύπρου. Εάν θέλετε να στείλετε κάποιον από τα γραφεία σας να έρθει να με δει, θα του δώσω περισσότερες λεπτομέρειες για το θέμα.

Ο Αντωνιάδης ή «Κεραυνός» όπως τον λένε, συγκρούστηκε με τον Γρίβα και «καταδικάστηκε» σε θάνατο από τον Στρατηγό, έτσι ο Κεραυνός αυτομόλησε στη βρετανική πλευρά SIB και έδωσε τα μυστικά της οργάνωσης, και ως αποτέλεσμα πολλοί ανθυπολοχαγοί της ΕΟΚΑ εκτελέστηκαν ή φυλακίστηκαν.

Αργότερα ο Αντωνιάδης ήρθε σε αυτή τη χώρα για να μπορέσει να ξεφύγει από την «ομάδα εξοντωτικών-προδοτών» του ίδιου του Στρατηγού.

Στις αρχές του περασμένου έτους αυτός, ο Κεραυνός, είχε φιλοδοξίες να δολοφονήσει τον Αρχιεπίσκοπο Μακάριο και Γρίβα και να καταλάβει την Κύπρο.

Πριν ξεκινήσουν τα προβλήματα με τους Τούρκους, το πρώτο βήμα ήταν η εκκαθάριση του Γρίβα που είχε τον έλεγχο των ενόπλων δυνάμεων.

θα ακολουθούσε ο Μακάριος κ.λπ.

Δεν θα συνεχίσω άλλο κύριε, αλλά αν θέλετε να ξεκαθαρίσετε αυτό το τρομερό θέμα, δεν έχετε παρά να έρθετε ή να στείλετε κάποιον να με δει.

ΥΣΤΕΡΟΓΡΑΦΟ. Ήμουν παρών σε μια συνάντηση (πριν από την έκρηξη του Κομήτη) όταν ένας υψηλόβαθμος στρατιώτης ήρθε σε αυτή τη χώρα για να συζητήσει τα σχέδια για κατάληψη.»

Αντίγραφο της επιστολής προς τον Milward (ΒΕΑ) στάλθηκε σε κάποιον στο Υπουργείο Εσωτερικών, καθώς όλη η αλληλογραφία των κρατουμένων υπόκειται σε έλεγχο. Το αντίγραφο προωθήθηκε στο γραφείο του Anthony Crosland από όπου μέσω του Jan Riddoch δόθηκε στον Veal. Η συνοδευτική επιστολή ανέφερε ότι ο Milward δεν είχε ενημερωθεί πως η επιστολή διοχετεύθηκε επίσης στο Crosland. Ένα χειρόγραφο σημείωμα ανέφερε, *«Έχει ήδη γίνει ενέργεια σε σχέση με το αντίγραφο της ΒΕΑ»*. Ο Επικεφαλής Επιθεωρητής Ατυχημάτων, στις 23

Ιανουαρίου, το διαβίβασε στον Αρχι-επιθεωρητή Bryan στη Scotland Yard

Το 2007, ο ειδησεογραφικός ιστότοπος του BBC δημοσίευσε μια είδηση ότι ορισμένοι από τους κορυφαίους υπόπτους για λαθρεμπόριο ηρωίνης της Βρετανίας προστατεύονταν από τις αστυνομικές έρευνες επειδή εργάζονταν ως πληροφοριοδότες για την HM Revenue & Customs (Βρετανικές Αρχές Φόρου Εισοδήματος και Τελωνείου) και τις προκατόχους μονάδες[142]. Σε μια περίπτωση το 2001, διπλωμάτες του Φόρεϊν Όφις ενέργησαν για να εξασφαλίσουν την απελευθέρωση του Αντωνιάδη, ο οποίος περιγράφεται στο άρθρο ως «πληροφοριοδότης που κρατείται στη Γερμανία μετά από ένταλμα των Ελληνικών αρχών». Οι ισχυρισμοί υποδηλώνουν ότι δόθηκε ειδική μορφή προστασίας σε πολλά άτομα που θεωρούνται ύποπτα από την αστυνομία ως κύριοι εισαγωγείς ηρωίνης. Ένας πρώην αξιωματικός της Εθνικής Υπηρεσίας Πληροφοριών του Εγκλήματος (NCIS) είπε στο BBC:

«Το τελωνείο μού είπε ότι ήταν πληροφοριοδότης και ότι ήταν ο καλύτερος πληροφοριοδότης που είχε ποτέ η Τελωνειακή υπηρεσία και αυτό που είχε δώσει στο Ηνωμένο Βασίλειο ξεπέρασε κατά πολύ τη ζημιά που είχε κάνει, η οποία δεν άξιζε τίποτα».

Ο Αντωνιάδης, ο οποίος ήταν 75 ετών την εποχή του άρθρου, πιστεύεται ότι ζούσε στο Ντουμπάι και δεν είχε καταδικαστεί ποτέ για παράβαση ναρκωτικών. Αρκετοί άνθρωποι, ορισμένοι από την τουρκική και την ελληνική κοινότητα, άσκησαν στη συνέχεια προσφυγές κατά των καταδικαστικών αποφάσεων για διακίνηση ναρκωτικών με βάση τις πληροφορίες του. Ο Αντωνιάδης, Ελληνοκύπριος, ήρθε στο Ηνωμένο Βασίλειο στα τέλη της δεκαετίας του 1950 αφού εργάστηκε ως πράκτορας των βρετανικών μυστικών υπηρεσιών, σύμφωνα με το BBC, και κάποτε φυλακίστηκε για τέσσερα χρόνια μετά από ένα περιστατικό με πυροβολισμούς στο δυτικό Λονδίνο. Συνέχισε να εργάζεται ως πληροφοριοδότης μέχρι τη δεκαετία του 1990, όταν εμφανίστηκαν αναφορές ότι εμπλεκόταν σε διακίνηση ναρκωτικών. Ο λόγος για την προστασία του Αντωνιάδη από τη δίωξη ήταν ότι «...μια δημόσια δίκη στην Ελλάδα θα αποκάλυπτε τη μακρά καριέρα του κ. Αντωνιάδη ως πληροφοριοδότη για τα Τελωνεία και θα έθετε σε κίνδυνο τη ζωή του από εγκληματικά στοιχεία». Ο Αντωνιάδης βρέθηκε κατηγορούμενος για

---

[142] *Ο ρόλος του πληροφοριοδότη προστάτευε τους εμπόρους ναρκωτικών*. www.news.bbc.co.uk, Κυριακή 4 Μαρτίου 2007 (*Ο τίτλος της είδησης στον ιστότοπο του BBC)*

απόπειρα ανθρωποκτονίας και μια επιστολή[143] εστάλη από τη μητέρα του Αντωνιάδη στον Υφυπουργό Εξωτερικών στο Υπουργείο Εξωτερικών στις 30 Ιουλίου 1959, στην οποία αναφέρει:

«Ο γιος μου εργάστηκε για το Ειδικό Τμήμα εδώ στην Κύπρο κατά τη διάρκεια της πρόσφατης έκτακτης ανάγκης και η ζωή του βρισκόταν σε διαρκή κίνδυνο όλη εκείνη την περίοδο και μάλιστα πυροβολήθηκε πολλές φορές και τραυματίστηκε σοβαρά από τρομοκράτες και για αυτούς τους λόγους η βρετανική κυβέρνηση τον προστάτευσε και τον πέταξε στην Αγγλία. Επομένως, πιστεύω ότι η κυβέρνησή σας είναι υπεύθυνη γι' αυτόν και δεν θα βρισκόταν σ΄αυτή τη θέση εάν του είχε παρασχεθεί ασφάλεια.

Στο Λονδίνο ο γιος μου εξακολουθεί να βρίσκεται σε μεγάλο κίνδυνο από μέλη της κυπριακής κοινότητας που θα ήταν πολύ χαρούμενοι να τον ξεφορτωθούν και θα έφταναν σε κάθε άκρο για να το κάνουν και είμαι σίγουρη ότι ο γιος μου έχει κατηγορηθεί άδικα με κάποιο τρόπο λόγω της δουλειάς του κατά των τρομοκρατών στην Κύπρο».

Πιθανόν βέβαια ο Αντωνιάδης να ενεπλάκη, όπως ισχυρίζεται ο Γεωργιάδης, σε σχέδιο δολοφονίας του Γρίβα. Δεν υπάρχουν στοιχεία που να το τεκμηριώνουν αυτό, όπως και η υπόδειξη ότι ο Αντωνιάδης ήταν πληροφοριοδότης, σε αντίθεση με το ότι ήταν μέλος του Special Branch, είναι φήμες, αν και το θεσμικά ενημερωμένο BBC ήταν σίγουρο για την αναφορά στην ιστοσελίδα του. Δεν υπάρχει τίποτα άλλο για τον ίδιο τον Αντωνιάδη στα αρχεία του CY284 και θα ήταν απαραίτητο να εξακριβωθεί εάν είχε κάποια σχέση με τον Αβραάμ Σολωμού ή τον Νίκο Παπαπέτρου για να γίνει σαφέστερη σύνδεση με την καταστροφή του Charlie Oscar.

Δεδομένου ότι τόσο ο Αντωνιάδης όσο και ο Γεωργιάδης μετακόμισαν στο Ηνωμένο Βασίλειο λίγο καιρό πριν από το περιστατικό με τον Charlie Oscar , είναι πολύ πιθανό οι δρόμοι τους να είχαν διασταυρωθεί. Και οι δύο άνδρες φυλακίστηκαν στη Βρετανία για παρόμοια χρονικά διαστήματα μετά από καταδίκες για βίαια εγκλήματα. Η πληροφορία ότι ο Αντωνιάδης έφτασε στο Ηνωμένο Βασίλειο λίγο πριν περάσει η εξουσία στην Κύπρο στους πρώην ηγέτες της ΕΟΚΑ, έχοντας συνδεθεί με τις βρετανικές αρχές, υποδηλώνει έντονα ότι δεν θα ήταν φίλος του Γρίβα, ο οποίος ήταν αδίστακτος στη αντιμετώπιση εκείνων που θεωρούσε προδότες. Με την ίδια λογική, είναι εξίσου απίθανο ο Αντωνιάδης να είχε βρει πολλούς συμμάχους αλλού στα ανώτερα κλιμάκια της νέας κυπριακής κυβέρνησης. Από όσα λίγα είναι γνωστά για τον Αντωνιάδη, δεν φαίνεται

---

[143] *FO 371/144714 Προστασία πρώην μέλους Ειδικού Κλάδου Κύπρου, Κωδικός RGC αρχείο 1642, μέσω Φανούλλας Αργυρού.*

να ήταν αρκετά καλά συνδεδεμένος για να «αναλάβει την εξουσία στην Κύπρο».

Ίσως ο Γεωργιάδης να είχε τσακωθεί με τον Αντωνιάδη και το γράμμα του από τη φυλακή ήταν απλώς μια ευκαιρία να του επιτεθεί ή να τον ξεφορτωθεί. Αν ναι, το τέχνασμα προφανώς απέτυχε καθώς δεν υπάρχει τίποτα διαθέσιμο που να αποδεικνύει ότι ο Αντωνιάδης συνελήφθη ποτέ σε σχέση με την απώλεια του CY284.

Αβραάμ Σολωμού

Ο Αβραάμ Σολωμού κατονομάστηκε για πρώτη φορά ως ύποπτος σε άρθρο της εφημερίδας *Evening Standard* από τον John Miller, που δημοσιεύτηκε στις 21 Νοεμβρίου 1967. Το άρθρο, με τίτλο «*Comet Bomb: Special Branch Step In»* («*Βόμβα Κομήτη: Αναλαμβάνει το Special Branch*») αναφέρει:

«Η βόμβα ήταν πιθανώς στο μέγεθος ενός μολυβιού και κρυμμένη σε μια θήκη.
Αλλά η βάση του, ένας στρατιωτικός μηχανισμός εκρηκτικής ύλης, ήταν τόσο ισχυρή που ουσιαστικά διέλυσε το αεροσκάφος.
Η θεωρία είναι ότι το έβαλαν στον χαρτοφύλακα ενός αθώου επιβάτη κάτω από το κάθισμά του.
Ο σύνδεσμος φαίνεται να ήταν ο Κύπριος σοφέρ κ. Α. Σολωμού, ένας από τους 66 νεκρούς.
Έχει χαρακτηριστεί ποικιλοτρόπως ως ένας πιστός του Στρατηγού Γρίβα, διοικητή των ενόπλων δυνάμεων της Κύπρου, ή σωματοφύλακας του κύπριου υπουργού Εξωτερικών κ. Σπύρου Κυπριανού.
Η παρουσία του θα μπορούσε να παραπλανήσει τους σαμποτέρ ώστε να πιστέψουν ότι ο Στρατηγός Γρίβας επρόκειτο να επέβαινε του αεροσκάφους.»

Το άρθρο της *Sunday Telegraph* της 26ης Νοεμβρίου επίσης ανέφερε τον Σολωμού, υπονοώντας ότι ήταν σωματοφύλακας του Στρατηγού Γρίβα. Ο Σολωμού προκάλεσε την προσοχή (των αρχών) στον εαυτό του στην Αθήνα, πριν επιβιβαστεί στην πτήση, λόγω της διαφωνίας με το εισιτήριο του που είχε ως αποτέλεσμα να απαιτήσει με βίαιο τρόπο να του επιτραπεί να επιβιβαστεί του αεροσκάφους. Τρεις μέρες πριν από την εμφάνιση του άρθρου της Sunday Telegraph, μια δίδα Roberts από την MI5 είχε τηλεφωνήσει στο γραφείο του Veal, έχοντας ζητήσει πληροφορίες από τον εκπρόσωπό τους στην Κύπρο για τον Σολωμού (και τους ενημέρωσε πως) :
«Ο κ. Σολωμού, ο οποίος βρίσκεται στην αρ. 55 της λίστας (των ανακτηθέντων θυμάτων) ήταν σοφέρ του υπουργού Εξωτερικών κ.

Κυπριανού και πρώην αγωνιστής της ΕΟΚΑ κατά τη διάρκεια της κυπριακής έκτακτης ανάγκης του 1955-59. Ο Διοικητής του Κυπριακού Special Branch απορρίπτει παντελώς το ενδεχόμενο να ήταν απόπειρα κατά του Γρίβα γιατί (ο Γρίβας) δεν ταξίδευε ποτέ εκείνη την ώρα της ημέρας. Δεν είχαν στοιχεία για κανέναν από τους Κύπριους επιβάτες στο αρχείο τους».

Υπάρχουν δύο σημεία σημασίας σε αυτή την πολύ συνοπτική απάντηση στο ερώτημα του Veal σχετικά με Σολωμού. Πρώτον, το Κυπριακό Special Branch υπαγόταν στο Υπουργείο Εσωτερικών. Ο υπουργός Εσωτερικών, Πολύκαρπος Γιωρκάτζης, παρουσιάζει ενδιαφέρον εξαιτίας λόγω του ότι κάποιοι στην Κύπρο πίστευαν ότι είχε εμπλοκή στην υπόθεση του Charlie Oscar (βλ. κεφάλαιο «**Ποιος βομβάρδισε το Charlie Oscar;**»). Δεύτερον, η φράση «...δεν υπάρχουν στοιχεία για κανένα από τους Κύπριους επιβάτες στο αρχείο τους» συνεπάγεται ότι κανένας Κύπριος στην πτήση δεν τους ήταν γνωστός. Ο τελευταίος αυτός ισχυρισμός προκαλεί έκπληξη, δηλαδή να μην γνώριζαν ότι ο Σολωμού ήταν αγωνιστής της ΕΟΚΑ. Είναι πολύ απίθανο να μην κρατούσαν φάκελο για αυτόν ως πρώην αγωνιστή και κάποιον με άμεση πρόσβαση σε υπουργό της κυβέρνησης όπως ο Κυπριανού. Είναι, βεβαίως, απολύτως πιθανό, να εννοούσαν στην πραγματικότητα «κανένα άτομο εκτός από τον Σολωμού».

Την απώλεια του Charlie Oscar σχολίασε ο Λεωνίδας Λεωνίδου σε μια βιογραφία του Στρατηγού Γρίβα.[144] Έγραψε :

«Η επιστημονική έρευνα που διεξήχθη από Βρετανούς ειδικούς διήρκεσε αρκετούς μήνες και έδειξε ότι η συντριβή προκλήθηκε από την έκρηξη βόμβας στο σκάφος. Θεωρείται πιθανότατα ότι η πρόθεση ήταν να σκοτωθεί ο Στρατηγός Γρίβας, ο οποίος φέρεται να ακύρωσε τη θέση του σε αυτή την πτήση την τελευταία στιγμή.

Έξι χρόνια αργότερα, ένας στενός συνεργάτης έδωσε στον Διγενή, όπως ήταν επίσης γνωστός ο Γρίβας, πληροφορίες που είχε εν τω μεταξύ λάβει:

«Μπορώ να σας πω ότι έχω έγκυρες πληροφορίες ότι η συντριβή του Κομήτη των Κυπριακών Αερογραμμών, στις 12 Οκτωβρίου 1967, είχε στόχο εσάς. Ήταν γνωστό ότι επρόκειτο να ταξιδέψετε με εκείνη την πτήση από την Αθήνα στη Λευκωσία. Σωθήκατε γιατί την τελευταία στιγμή αναβάλατε το ταξίδι. Είχαν τοποθετήσει μια ωρολογιακή βόμβα,

---

[144] . *Η αρχική πηγή του Λεωνίδου είναι η «Επιχείρηση Κοφίνου» του Σπύρου Παπαγεωργίου, σελ. 43. Ο ίδιος ο Παπαγεωργίου θεωρήθηκε υποστηρικτής του Στρατηγού Γρίβα και έγραψε μια σειρά βιογραφιών για αυτόν.*

την οποία είχαν φτιάξει άνθρωποι έμπιστοι του Υπουργείου Εσωτερικών της Κύπρου. Η αναβολή του ταξιδιού σας, που δεν περίμεναν, και η αποτυχία να απενεργοποιήσουν τη βόμβα, προκάλεσαν τη συντριβή του αεροσκάφους λόγω της έκρηξης και τον θάνατο του ατόμου στον οποίο είχε ανατεθεί η τοποθέτηση της βόμβας, καθώς αυτός υποτίθεται έπρεπε να ακύρωνε την αναχώρησή του αν εσείς δεν επιβιβαζόσασταν στο αεροσκάφος. Γνωρίζετε όλα αυτά; Γιατί οι εφημερίδες μας δεν έγραψαν γι' αυτό;».

Και ο συγγραφέας προσθέτει:
«Αυτές οι συγκλονιστικές λεπτομέρειες αφορούν και πάλι τον Υπουργό Εσωτερικών, Πολύκαρπο Γιωρκάτζη, γιατί η έκρηξη έγινε κάτω από το κάθισμα του Αβραάμ Σολωμού, του τότε οδηγού του υπουργού Εξωτερικών της Κύπρου Σπύρου Κυπριανού και ο οποίος ενεργούσε με εντολή Γιωρκάτζη (εννοείται ο Σολωμού). Αν πράγματι ο Στρατηγός Γρίβας ήταν ο στόχος της απόπειρας, τότε η χρονική στιγμή αυτής της ενέργειας μάλλον υποστηρίζει την άποψη ότι αυτή η δολοφονική απόπειρα κατά του Διγενή είναι μέρος ενός ευρύτερου, πολύπλοκου και απαίσιου σχεδίου...»

Ο Ελευθέριος Παπαδόπουλος το διαπίστωσε και από άλλες πηγές. Ο κ. Παπαδόπουλος φυλακίστηκε για τη συμμετοχή του στο πραξικόπημα κατά του Μακαρίου στις 15 Ιουλίου 1974. Σε ένα από τα βιβλία του στο οποίο κάλυψε τις καταθέσεις του στην Επιτροπή της Κυπριακής Βουλής των Αντιπροσώπων, έγραφε ότι μετά την έξοδό του από τη φυλακή ενημερώθηκε από δύο φίλους ότι πρώην στέλεχος της Κυπριακής Κυβέρνησης ήθελε να έχει συνάντηση μαζί του. Ο Παπαδόπουλος έγραψε:

«Όταν βγήκα από τη φυλακή το 1984, ο συνεργάτης μου Ανδρέας Παρασκευάς και ο αείμνηστος Παντελής Κατελάρης (γιατρός), μου ανέφεραν την επιθυμία ενός πρώην υψηλόβαθμου κυβερνητικού στελέχους, ο οποίος γνώριζε πολλά για πολλούς ανθρώπους για να με συναντήσει. Αν και δεν είδα τι κοινό ενδιαφέρον είχαμε να συζητήσουμε, δέχτηκα.

Μου είπε: «Είμαι ένα βήμα από τον τάφο. Έχω καρκίνο. Το παλεύω, αλλά ξέρω ότι δεν θα είμαι ο νικητής. Σε πήρα τηλέφωνο για να σου πω μερικά μυστικά, που δεν θέλω να τα πάρω μαζί μου (στον τάφο). Έλα πίσω αύριο και φέρε μαζί χαρτί και ένα μαγνητόφωνο. Θα αναφέρω μερικά πρόσωπα και γεγονότα. Θέλω να μου υποσχεθείς ότι δεν θα δημοσιοποιήσεις όλα αυτά που θα σου πω πριν από το 2016».

Πράγματι, κατονόμασε ορισμένα πρόσωπα και γεγονότα. Πολλά τα γνώριζα ήδη από άλλες πηγές. Ωστόσο, όλα σημαντικά. Πολλά συγκλονιστικά. Αναφέρθηκε και στη συντριβή του «Κομήτη» κοντά στο Καστελλόριζο. Μου είπε:

«Τα εκρηκτικά στάλθηκαν από τον Πολύκαρπο Γιωρκάτζη σε κουτί με ωρολογιακές συσκευές». Παραλήπτης ήταν υπάλληλος της Κυπριακής Πρεσβείας στην Αθήνα, ο οποίος κατασκεύασε τη βόμβα. Δόθηκε στον Α. Σολωμού, οδηγό του Υπουργού Εξωτερικών Σπ. Κυπριανού, ως πακέτο για τον Υπουργό του. Και οι δύο δεν ήξεραν τίποτα. Ρυθμίστηκε ο χρόνος έκρηξης της βόμβας μετά από τηλεφώνημα από την Κύπρο. Στόχος του ήταν ο Διγενής».

Όταν του είπα ότι όλα αυτά ήταν εξαιρετικά σοβαρά, ωστόσο πολλά δεν αποδείχθηκαν, μου έδειξε μερικές σελίδες από το ημερολόγιό του. Τον παρακάλεσα να μου επιτρέψει να διαβάσω από τις σελίδες του. Εκείνος αρνήθηκε κατηγορηματικά.

«Όχι» μου είπε. «Εγώ ο ίδιος έχω αμαρτίες. Δυστυχώς, αμάρτησα και εγώ σε ορισμένες περιπτώσεις με αυτούς τους κακοποιούς».

Στις σελίδες που μου έδειξε υπήρχαν ονόματα, γεγονότα, ημερομηνίες, ώρες, διάλογοι και αποσπάσματα από επίσημα έγγραφα. Δυστυχώς, 11 μέρες αργότερα πέθανε. Η κόρη του, την οποία παρακάλεσα να μου επιτρέψει να διαβάσω το ημερολόγιο του πατέρα της, μου είπε ότι διετάχθη να το κάψει μαζί με τέσσερις βαλίτσες γεμάτες έγγραφα. Μπορώ μόνο να φανταστώ τι πλούσιο αρχείο είχε χαθεί»[145]. Δυστυχώς, ο Ελευθέριος (Λευτέρης) Παπαδόπουλος απεβίωσε λίγο πριν εκδοθεί το τρίτο βιβλίο του συγγραφέα.

Στις 12 Ιανουαρίου, ο Ι.Ε. Παπαλεξόπουλος, υπάλληλος check-in στο αεροδρόμιο του Ελληνικού, ίσως υπάλληλος της Ολυμπιακής Αεροπορίας, είχε υποβάλει μια σύντομη αναφορά για το πρόβλημα του Αβραάμ Σολωμού με το εισιτήριό του όταν παρουσιάστηκε για check-in στις 12 Οκτωβρίου:

«Ο μ. κ. Σολωμού παρουσιάστηκε στο check-in στις 12 Οκτωβρίου 1967 και ζήτησε να πετάξει για την πτήση CY284 εκείνης της ημέρας. Όταν του ζητήθηκε το εισιτήριό του, ο κ. Σολωμού δήλωσε πως λόγω μπερδέματος στο αεροδρόμιο Λευκωσίας δεν είχε πλέον το εισιτήριο της επιστροφής για Λευκωσία.

Καθώς ο κ. Σολωμού δεν είχε το κάλυμμα του εισιτηρίου του, ούτε γνώριζε τον αριθμό του εισιτηρίου του, του εξήγησα ότι υπό τις συνθήκες δεν μπορούσα να τον δεχτώ για αυτή την πτήση. Εναλλακτικά, προσφέρθηκα να δώσω σήμα στη Λευκωσία και να ζητήσω λεπτομέρειες

---

[145] Τα στοιχεία μου στην Ad Hoc Επιτροπή της Βουλής της Βουλής της Κύπρου για τον «Φάκελο της Κύπρου», Τόμος Α' σελίδες 534 έως 536, έκδοση Λευκωσία 2010, Ελευθέριος Παπαδόπουλος.

για το εισιτήριό του και επίσης εξουσιοδότηση έκδοσης νέου εισιτηρίου έναντι εντύπου αποζημίωσης. Ενημέρωσα επίσης τον επιβάτη ότι αυτό, φυσικά, θα πάρει κάποιο χρόνο και ως εκ τούτου θα έπρεπε να θεωρήσει αδύνατον να πετάξει στη Λευκωσία με τη συγκεκριμένη πτήση, δηλαδή CY284/1210.

Ο κ. Σολωμού, ωστόσο, ήταν αρκετά αποφασισμένος να πετάξει όπως είχε σχεδιάσει και ζήτησε να μιλήσει με ανώτερες αρχές. Κατά συνέπεια, αναγκάστηκα να τον μεταφέρω στον αξιωματικό υπηρεσίας κ. Κολιανδρή, ο οποίος άκουσε τον κ. Σολωμού πολύ προσεκτικά και στη συνέχεια επανέλαβε στον επιβάτη αυτό που του είχα ήδη πει, δηλαδή ότι δεν μπορούσαμε να τον δεχθούμε στο CY284/1210..

Καθώς ήμουν απασχολημένος με το κλείσιμο της πτήσης, δεν μπόρεσα να παρακολουθήσω την υπόλοιπη συνομιλία τους, αλλά μετά από λίγο ο κ. Κολιανδρής μου ζήτησε να του εκδώσω νέο εισιτήριο στη βάση αποζημίωσης και μετά να στείλω σήμα στη Λευκωσία για τις σχετικές λεπτομέρειες και εξουσιοδότηση.

Συντάχθηκε έντυπο αποζημίωσης και υπογράφηκε δεόντως από τον κ. Σολωμού και εκδόθηκε νέο εισιτήριο Αθήνα/Λευκωσία από εμένα σύμφωνα με τις οδηγίες του κ. Κολιανδρή. Μόλις έφυγε το αεροπλάνο έστειλα σήμα στη ΛΕΥΚΩΣΙΑ σύμφωνα με τα παραπάνω.

Από όσο γνωρίζω αυτό το σήμα παραμένει αναπάντητο.»

Η αναφορά διαβιβάστηκε από τον PD Antram, Διευθυντή της ΒΕΑ στην Ελλάδα, στον κλάδο αεροπορικής ασφάλειας της αεροπορικής εταιρείας, στις 15 Ιανουαρίου με ένα συνοδευτικό σημείωμα που περιγράφει τις δικές του ανησυχίες:

«Λαμβάνοντας υπόψη την υπόνοια ότι η αιτία του ατυχήματος στον Κομήτη GARCO ήταν μια έκρηξη μιας συσκευής που μεταφέρθηκε στο αεροσκάφος, πιστεύω ότι οι ακόλουθες πληροφορίες που μόλις ήρθαν στο φως μπορεί να έχουν κάποια σημασία.

Φαίνεται ότι ο κ. Σολωμού παρουσιάστηκε για πτήση χωρίς εισιτήριο και ήταν αρκετά ανένδοτος ότι έπρεπε να πάει σε αυτή την πτήση.

Ζήτησα δηλώσεις από το προσωπικό που χειρίστηκε αυτόν τον επιβάτη και τις επισυνάψω για να τις λάβετε υπόψη σας.

Ίσως να θέλετε να λάβετε υπόψη την επιμονή του κ. Σολωμού να ταξιδέψει ως ύποπτη. Ίσως μετέφερε εκρηκτικά τα οποία ήθελε να παραδώσει το συντομότερο δυνατό.»

Τέλος, αν και σχεδόν όλοι οι υπόλοιποι επιβάτες στον κατάλογο της αστυνομίας, έχουν σημειωμένες τις προσωπικές των διευθύνσεις, αυτή του Σολωμού αναφέρεται μόνο ως «*πρεσβεία της Κυπριακής Δημοκρατίας στην Αθήνα*».

Ο αναφορά στο βιβλίο «Επιχείρηση Κοφίνου» του Σπύρου Παπαγεωργίου φαίνεται να είναι ότι το άτομο στο οποίο είχε ανατεθεί η τοποθέτηση της βόμβας στο αεροσκάφος επρόκειτο να ακυρώσει την πτήση του αν δεν επιβιβαζόταν ο Γρίβας. Αυτό υποδηλώνει ότι το πραγματικό σχέδιο, εάν ο Γρίβας είχε πετάξει όπως αναμενόταν, ήταν να επιβιβαστεί το άτομο στο αεροσκάφος ως επιβάτης, να κρύψει τη βόμβα και στη συνέχεια να κατασκευάσει μια δικαιολογία για να φύγει από την πτήση πριν αναχωρήσει. Το πώς θα γινόταν αυτό χωρίς να δημιουργηθούν υποψίες, και μάλιστα χωρίς να εντοπίσει κάποιος ότι η βόμβα είχε τοποθετηθεί κρυφά και ότι ο επιβάτης έφυγε χωρίς αυτήν, δεν διευκρινίζεται. Πηγές ανέφεραν στον συγγραφέα ότι εκείνος που τοποθέτησε την βόμβα δεν κατάφερε να φύγει από την πτήση και προσπάθησε ανεπιτυχώς να την εξουδετερώσει. Και πάλι, αυτό δεν θα περνούσε απαρατήρητο από τους άλλους επιβάτες και το πλήρωμα. Τέλος, αν ο Σολωμού είχε σκοπό να πετάξει με το CY284, σίγουρα θα είχε εξασφαλίσει ότι το εισιτήριό του ήταν εντάξει πριν εμφανιστεί στο check-in. Είναι πιθανό η εξιστόρηση να υποφέρει κάπως στην ανα-διήγηση και τη μετάφραση.

Προς υπεράσπιση του Σολωμού, είναι απίθανο να είχε πραγματοποιήσει σκόπιμα τη βομβιστική επίθεση ως αυτοκτονικό εγχείρημα. Ήταν, πλέον, οικογενειάρχης, δουλεύοντας για λογαριασμό ενός από τους πιο ισχυρούς άνδρες στην Κύπρο. Ο απολογισμός που έδωσε ο Ελευθέριος Παπαδόπουλος, που του έδωσε ο άνθρωπος που βρισκόταν σε απελπιστική κατάσταση θανάτου, μοιάζει από πολλές απόψεις με αυτή του Παπαγεωργίου, όπως αναφέρει ο Λεωνίδου. Η διαφορά στη λεπτομέρεια είναι απλώς ότι, στην τελευταία περίπτωση, ο Σολωμού δεν είχε ιδέα ότι κουβαλούσε τη συσκευή.

Ο Σολωμού χαρακτηρίζεται ποικιλοτρόπως ως σοφέρ ή προσωπικός βοηθός του υπουργού Εξωτερικών του Σπύρου Κυπριανού, γεγονός που είναι αλήθεια , αλλά και ως σωματοφύλακας ή έμπιστος του Γρίβα, κάτι που δεν πιστεύεται ότι ίσχυε. Πηγές είπαν στον συγγραφέα ότι είναι πολύ πιθανό ο Σολωμού να ήταν de facto σωματοφύλακας του Κυπριανού και να ήταν κάλλιστα αστυνομικός με πολιτικά ρούχα. Το αν θα ήταν ή όχι μέλος του Κυπριακού Special Branch είναι αδύνατο να διευκρινιστεί, αλλά, επτά χρόνια μετά την ανεξαρτησία, ήταν εφικτό. Αυτό θα εξηγούσε γιατί το Κυπριακό Special Branch δεν ανέφερε το Σολωμού ότι ήταν στα αρχεία του όταν επικοινώνησε μαζί του ο Veal. Ασφαλώς, ο Σολωμού ήταν μαχητής της ΕΟΚΑ κατά τη διάρκεια του αγώνα της ανεξαρτησίας, οπότε δεν ήταν άγνωστος στη χρήση βίας. Ωστόσο, αυτό από μόνο του σίγουρα δεν υποδηλώνει ότι θα ήταν έτοιμος να καταστρέψει ένα αεροσκάφος σε πιο ειρηνικές στιγμές, ειδικά ένα αεροσκάφος που μετέφερε Κύπριο προσωπικό καμπίνας και επιβάτες.

Σύμφωνα με τις ελάχιστες σημειώσεις στους φακέλους (του Εθνικού Αρχείου στο Λονδίνο), ο Σολωμού είχε βρεθεί στην Αθήνα για διακοπές. Ωστόσο, όταν προσπάθησε να κάνει check-in στο αεροδρόμιο του Ελληνικού τα ξημερώματα της 12ης Οκτωβρίου, ήταν ξεκάθαρα αποφασισμένος να ανέβει στην πτήση. Εάν, όπως υποστηρίζουν οι διάφορες παραπάνω πηγές, του είχε δοθεί εντολή να μεταφέρει ένα επείγον δέμα για τον Σπύρο Κυπριανού και να το πάει στον Υπουργό Εξωτερικών το ίδιο πρωί, θα εξηγούσε γιατί ήταν τόσο επίμονος να του επιτρέψουν να πετάξει. Λόγω του ρόλου του, είναι βέβαιο ότι δεν θα είχε αμφισβητήσει την οδηγία μεταφοράς του πακέτου, ή τι περιείχε.

Σύμφωνα με τα αρχεία, ωστόσο, υπάρχουν δύο εντυπωσιακοί λόγοι για τους οποίους ο αερομεταφορέας μπορεί να μην ήταν καθόλου ο Σολωμού.

Το σχέδιο θέσεων για τον τομέα ATH-NIC έχει τον Σολωμού να κάθεται στη θέση 16C. Ωστόσο, σημειώνεται ότι αυτό είναι κερδοσκοπικό και όχι βάση για την υποτιθέμενη κατανομή θέσεων. Η ανάλυση του Fred Jones δίνει ένα σαφές σκεπτικό για τη συσκευή που εκρήγνυται πίσω από τα καθίσματα 4Α ή 5Α, και αυτό επιβεβαιώνεται από τους ακραίους τραυματισμούς και αγνοουμένων επιβατών από αυτό το τμήμα του αεροσκάφους. Επιπλέον, το σώμα του Σολωμού ήταν στην κατηγορία «ελαφρώς τραυματισμένων». Τα τραύματά του περιγράφονται στην παθολογική έκθεση. Αυτά ήταν τραύματα στο πρόσωπο, ρήξεις στη δεξιά πλευρά, πολλαπλά κατάγματα πλευρών συμπεριλαμβανομένου ενός κατάγματος στέρνου, εξάρθρωση της λεκάνης και του αριστερού γονάτου. Εσωτερικά, είχε υποστεί σοβαρό αιμοθώρακα και ρήξη καρδιάς (η κύρια αιτία θανάτου) και το διάφραγμα. Υπέστη επίσης σοβαρά τραύματα στην κοιλιά. Τα τραύματά του φάνηκαν να συνάδουν με μια ξαφνική και πολύ βίαιη κίνηση ενώ ήταν δεμένος στο κάθισμά του και πιθανόν χτυπώντας το κεφάλι του στο κάθισμα μπροστά του. Ήταν αισθητά διαφορετικά από αυτά που αναμένονταν αν είχε πέσει από ύψος στη θάλασσα ή είχε άμεση επαφή με μια έκρηξη βόμβας. Αν ο Σολωμού είχε όντως πάρει τη συσκευή στο αεροσκάφος, ηθελημένα ή άθελά του, σίγουρα δεν είχε καθίσει δίπλα της όταν εξερράγη. Η σορός του ανασύρθηκε ανάμεσα στην «τουρκική ομάδα», η οποία υποδηλώνει έντονα ότι ο Σολωμού βρισκόταν στο μπροστινό μέρος της καμπίνας όταν έσπασε η άτρακτος στο φτερό. Αυτό θα συνέβαινε, αν καθόταν στη σειρά 16, όπως υποδεικνύεται στο σχέδιο θέσεων. Είναι, βέβαια, απολύτως πιθανό ο Σολωμού να μην καθόταν στη σειρά 16 αλλά πιο πίσω, στη θέση 3Α ή 4Α. Η μόνη εύλογη υπόθεση που θα συμφωνούσε με τα γεγονότα είναι αν ο Σολωμού είχε αφήσει την τσάντα του στο πόδι του καθίσματος του και είχε προχωρήσει για άγνωστο λόγο. Σίγουρα δεν θα είχε επιστρέψει στη θέση του μετά την έκρηξη και κατά πάσα πιθανότητα θα είχε δεθεί σε ένα άδειο κάθισμα σε κάποια απόσταση από τη ζημιά.

Νίκος Παπαπέτρου

Ο Διευθυντής Ασφαλίσεων της ΒΕΑ, ένας κ. Springbett, έκανε έρευνες για την ασφαλιστική κάλυψη που είχαν τα θύματα του δυστυχήματος. Στα τέλη Ιανουαρίου, επικοινώνησε με τον Veal για να διαβιβάσει την πληροφορία ότι ο επιβάτης Νίκο Παπαπέτρου είχε αγοράσει τρείς ασφάλειες ζωής λίγο πριν ταξιδέψει, δύο ποσά των £10.000 τη κάθε μία, μία με την εταιρεία Sun Alliance και μία με την Γενική Ασφαλιστική Εταιρεία Κύπρου, και $3^η$ ασφάλεια ζωής για £5.000 με την εταιρεία Eagle Star. Ο Veal διαβίβασε αυτές τις πληροφορίες στον Αρχι-επιθεωρητή Browne, προσθέτοντας:

«Εννοείται ότι αυτές οι ασφάλειες αγοράστηκαν την 1η Οκτωβρίου στην Κύπρο. Το σώμα του δεν ανασύρθηκε. Αντιλαμβανόμαστε ότι ο κ. Παπαπέτρου ήταν πωλητής παπουτσιών και κέρδιζε 80 λίρες το μήνα αλλά είναι επίσης γνωστό ότι ήταν επαγγελματίας τζογαδόρος. Τους δώδεκα μήνες πριν από το ατύχημα είχε κάνει πέντε αεροπορικές επισκέψεις από την Κύπρο στην Ελλάδα, αλλά πιστεύεται ότι δεν είχε προηγουμένως εκτός σε αυτή τη τελευταία περίπτωση αγοράσει ασφάλεια . Κατά το κλείσιμο των υποθέσεών του μετά τον υποτιθέμενο θάνατό του στο ατύχημα, η περιουσία του εκτιμήθηκε λιγότερο από £2.000. Λαμβάνοντας υπόψη ότι ατυχήματα αεροσκαφών στη Βόρεια Αμερική στα οποία η ασφάλεια διαπιστώθηκε ότι ήταν ένας βασικός παράγοντας, θεωρείται ότι αυτή η πτυχή θα πρέπει να διερευνηθεί περαιτέρω.»

Την 1η Σεπτεμβρίου 1968, ένα άρθρο των *Sunday Times* έριξε σθεναρά το δάκτυλο υποψίας προς την κατεύθυνση του Παπαπέτρου. Κάτω από τον τίτλο, «*Χαμένος κρίκος στη συντριβή του κομήτη*» γραμμένο από τους « John Shirley στην Κύπρο και John Ball στο Λονδίνο», είπε η εφημερίδα στους αναγνώστες της :

«Είναι καλύτερα για μένα να πεθάνω. Όλη μου η ζωή ήταν μια καταστροφή».
«Αυτά λέει ένας μικροκαμωμένος Ελληνοκύπριος λαθρέμπορος που εργαζόταν ως υπεύθυνος καταστήματος υποδημάτων στη μικρή πόλη της Λάρνακας της Κύπρου. Είναι σχεδόν σίγουρα ο χαμένος κρίκος στη μυστηριώδη έκρηξη που οδήγησε ένα Κομήτη της ΒΕΑ 4Β να συντριβεί στη Μεσόγειο στα ανοιχτά της Ρόδου τον περασμένο Οκτώβριο.
Ο Νίκος Παπαπέτρου (sic), αντιμέτωπος με χρέη από τζόγο, δύο φιλενάδες στην Αθήνα και ακριβά δίδακτρα για να πληρώσει για τα μαθήματα οδοντο-ιατρικής της κόρης του στην ελληνική πρωτεύουσα, μιλούσε με έναν φίλο του μόλις 48 ώρες προτού μια βόμβα 16 ουγγιών – στρατιωτικής προέλευσης ανατίναξε την άτρακτο του Κομήτη.

Στο αεροπλάνο επέβαιναν ο Παπαπέτρου και άλλοι 65. Όλοι πέθαναν. Το δεκαπενθήμερο πριν από τη συντριβή, ο Παπαπέτρου είχε συνάψει τρεις ασφάλειες ζωής συνολικού ύψους 23.000 λιρών. Μπορεί να υπάρχει και τέταρτη.

Ακολουθώντας τα ίχνη μιας ομάδας της Scotland Yard , με επικεφαλής τον ντετέκτιβ Επιθεωρητή Percy Browne, ο οποίος πέταξε στη Ρόδο για να εξετάσει τα λιγοστά συντρίμμια, βρήκαμε αυτόν τον νέο μάρτυρα του οποίου η θύμηση μιας συνομιλίας δείχνει απευθείας στον Παπαπέτρου ως την αιτία της συντριβής.

Όλα τα έγγραφα σχετικά με την πτήση συγκεντρώθηκαν από τη Scotland Yard και ένα προς ένα τα θύματα διαγράφηκαν από τη λίστα του. Στη συνέχεια, ο Μπράουν ήρθε στον 44χρονο Παπαπέτρου και ανακάλυψε τις ασφάλειες ζωής του.

Ήταν το πέμπτο ταξίδι του Παπαπέτρου μεταξύ του νησιού και της ελληνικής πρωτεύουσας εκείνη τη χρονιά. Είχε πει στη σύζυγό του, Νίνα, στο σπίτι τους στην οδό 28ης Οκτωβρίου, στη Λάρνακα, μπογιατισμένο μπλέ χρώμα, με διπλή πρόσοψη, ότι ήταν επαγγελματικά ταξίδια. Όμως, δεν ήταν για την εταιρεία υποδημάτων Galides Ltd. στη Λευκωσία, για την οποία διαχειριζόταν το τοπικό τους κατάστημα.

Καθώς μετρούσε την πενιχρή προμήθεια του – κέρδιζε μεταξύ £50 και £60 το μήνα – έλεγε ότι θα έμπαινε στη βιομηχανία δέρματος για την κατασκευή δερμάτινων τσαντών. Τα ταξίδια στην Αθήνα ήταν για αναζήτηση υλικών.

Οι ντετέκτιβς ανακάλυψαν ότι ο Παπαπέτρου είχε για χρόνια κρατήσει μόνο μία ασφάλεια για προσωπικό ατύχημα αξίας £2.000 στη General Insurance Ltd Κύπρου, το οποίο δεν τον κάλυπτε για αεροπορικούς κινδύνους.

Όμως, στις 30 Σεπτεμβρίου πέρυσι μπήκε στο υποκατάστημα της εταιρείας στη Λάρνακα και έβγαλε ασφάλεια προσωπικού ατυχήματος για £8.000 – με ισχύ μόνο για τον μήνα Οκτώβριο και καλύπτοντας ένα μόνο ταξίδι στο εξωτερικό στην Ελλάδα και την Αγγλία.»

Εντός ορισμένων ημερών αγόρασε ακόμα μια ασφάλεια, αυτή τη φορά από το παράρτημα Κύπρου της Eagle Star για £5,000. Μετά υπήρξε και τρίτη ασφάλεια που αγόρασε από την Sun Alliance Ltd για £10,000.

Δεκαπέντε μέρες αργότερα ανατινάχτηκε ο Κομήτης. Ήδη είναι γνωστό ότι η Eagle Star πλήρωσε τη χήρα του Παπαπέτρου. Όμως η εταιρεία Sun αναμένει την επίσημη απόφαση για το ατύχημα πριν ολοκληρώσει την διευθέτηση. Και η Γενική Ασφαλιστική αμφισβητούν την υποχρέωσή τους να πληρώσουν με το σκεπτικό του διευθυντή της στη Λευκωσία «υπάρχουν κάποιες εκκρεμότητες στο αίτημα».

Προφανώς, ο νεκρός άνδρας δεν είχε ενημερώσει τη Γενική Ασφαλιστική για τις άλλες δύο ασφάλειες που είχε κάνει. Ο διευθυντής εξήγησε, πως «Είναι τεχνικό θέμα. *Δεν έχει να κάνει με την αιτία του δυστυχήματος».*

Αλλά καθώς η έρευνα της Scotland Yard προχώρησε πιο βαθιά, ανακάλυψαν ότι ο Παπαπέτρου, πατέρας δύο κοριτσιών, είχε διασυνδέσεις με ένα συνδικάτο λαθρεμπόρων. Στην Αθήνα είχε δύο φιλενάδες ονόματι Ελένη και Τιτίκα. Έπαιζε στα καζίνο στην Αθήνα και στη Κέρκυρα.

Ξόδευε τα περισσότερα λεφτά που έπαιρνε από το λαθρεμπόριο στις δύο φιλενάδες του ή στα καζίνο. Αλλά η τύχη του άρχισε να στενεύει, τα χρέη του τζόγου μεγάλωναν και οι πιστωτές απαιτούσαν τα λεφτά τους πίσω.

Πιστεύεται τότε δεν ήταν εις θέση να πληρώσει για τα λαθραία που έπαιρνε στην Ελλάδα. Λίγες μέρες πριν το τελευταίο του ταξίδι παρακαλούσε ένα παλαιό του φίλο, συνταξιούχο ναυτιλιακό πράκτορα, ο οποίος είχε ταξιδέψει μαζί του σε κάποια από τα ταξίδια του, για £1,000 δάνειο. Πήρε μόνο £500.

Αλλά όχι μόνο η τύχη του τελείωσε στα τραπέζια του τζόγου, αλλά και ο γάμος του είχε αρχίσει να καταρρέει. Ωστόσο, εξακολουθούσε να πληρώνει για τη μικρότερη κόρη του, Χρυστάλλα, 19 ετών, η οποία σπούδαζε σε οδοντιατρική σχολή της Αθήνας με ακριβά δίδακτρα. Τελικά, λίγο έλειψε να συλληφθεί στο αεροδρόμιο της Αθήνας για μια βαλίτσα με ρολόγια αξίας 940 λιρών. Ο σύνδεσμος του Παπαπέτρου, που πιστεύεται ήταν τελωνειακός, δεν εμφανίστηκε και μια καφέ δερμάτινη βαλίτσα που ήταν στοιβαγμένη στο αεροσκάφος άνοιξε. Αρνήθηκε ότι ήταν μέρος των αποσκευών του και κατάφερε να ξεγελάσει τους τελωνειακούς ανακριτές. Αλλά όχι μόνο έχασε το εμπόρευμα, αλλά χάλασε και ο σύνδεσμος του λαθρεμπορίου και αντιμετώπισε ένα ακόμη χρέος.»

Στην εισαγωγή του βιβλίου του *The Occult* ο Colin Wilson[146] έγραψε:

«Ανοίγω ένα έγχρωμο ένθετο για το Σαββατοκύριακο και διαβάζω ότι για μια εβδομάδα πριν από την έκρηξη που κατέστρεψε ένα αεροσκάφος Κομήτη της ΒΕΑ στις 12 Οκτωβρίου 1967, ο Νίκος Παπαπέτρου στοιχειωνόταν από προαισθήσεις , και ονειρευόταν θάνατο και πένθος έτσι ώστε μια ώρα πριν την απογείωση, προσπάθησε να κάνει κράτηση για άλλη πτήση. Αυτό δεν είναι παρελθόν, αλλά τότε ο Παπαπέτρου κουβαλούσε τη βόμβα που εξερράγη κατά λάθος. Ήταν λαθρέμπορος εκρηκτικών και είχε κάνει έξι παρόμοια ταξίδια νωρίτερα το ίδιο έτος. γιατί είχε προαισθήσεις για αυτό;»

---

[146] *The Occult*, του *Colin Wilson (Hodder & Stoughton, 1971).*

Ο Wilson περιλαμβάνει το απόσπασμα για τον Παπαπέτρου για να υποστηρίξει τον ισχυρισμό του ότι τα προαισθήματα εξακολουθούν να βιώνονται στον παρόντα χρόνο, καθώς και ιστορικά. Το άρθρο στο έγχρωμο ένθετο φαίνεται να είχε δημοσιευθεί στο περιοδικό της Κυριακής που επισυνάπτεται στην εφημερίδα *The Observer*. Περιέχει μεγάλη ποσότητα λεπτομέρειας που φέρει τα χαρακτηριστικά ότι είχε διαβιβαστεί στην εφημερίδα από την αστυνομία ή το Υπουργείο Εξωτερικών. Ανέφερε (το δημοσίευμα) με πεποίθηση ότι ο Παπαπέτρου μετέφερε λαθραία εκρηκτικά στον χαρτοφύλακά του και, κατά κάποιο τρόπο, είχαν κατά λάθος πυροδοτηθεί κατά τη διάρκεια της πτήσης. Αυτό φαίνεται να είναι εικαστικό, καθώς είναι πολύ απίθανο ένας επιτυχημένος μέχρι τότε λαθρέμπορος εκρηκτικών να μετέφερε τα υλικά μαζί με έναν πυροκροτητή. Επίσης, έρχεται σε αντίθεση με την παράλληλη εικασία, από αστυνομικές πηγές και πηγές του Φόρεϊν Όφις, ότι ο Παπαπέτρου είχε πρόθεση να αυτοκτονήσει για ασφαλιστικούς λόγους.

Η Ελίνα Παπαπέτρου, η κόρη του Νίκου, επιβεβαίωσε ότι ζούσε στην Αθήνα την ώρα της καταστροφής. Ο Νίκος έμεινε μαζί της όσο ήταν στην Αθήνα για επαγγελματικούς λόγους, όπως ήταν απόλυτα συνηθισμένο. Θυμάται ότι ήταν ο κανονικός χαλαρός εαυτός του και ότι δεν υπήρχε τίποτα που να υποδηλώνει ότι σχεδίαζε κακό στον εαυτό του ή στους άλλους. Η Ελίνα οδήγησε τον Νίκο στο αεροδρόμιο για την πτήση του και όλα ήταν καλά.

Η οικογένεια δεν γνώριζε καμία στρατιωτική εμπειρία που θα μπορούσε να είχε αποκτήσει που θα του επέτρεπε να κατασκευάσει έναν εκρηκτικό μηχανισμό. Έπαιζε χαρτιά, αυτό ήταν ούτως ή άλλως ένα δημοφιλές χόμπι και η οικογένεια διαψεύδει κάθε αναφορά ότι ο Νίκος είχε σημαντικά χρέη ή ότι θα οδηγούνταν σε τέτοια μέτρα απελπισίας, όπως αναφέρθηκε στον βρετανικό Τύπο.

Μέχρι τη δημοσίευση το 2018 της πρώτης έκδοσης του *Bealine Charlie Oscar*, η οικογένεια Παπαπέτρου δεν γνώριζε καν ότι ο Νίκος θεωρούνταν ύποπτος. Η οικογένεια απορρίπτει όλες τις κατηγορίες σε βάρος του Νίκου Παπαπέτρου[147].

Στις 11 Σεπτεμβρίου 1968, ο Jan Riddoch στο Υπουργείο Εξωτερικών ζήτησε νομική συμβουλή από τον δικηγόρο του Board of Trade σχετικά με το εάν τμήματα της αστυνομικής αναφοράς που αφορούσαν τον Παπαπέτρου θα μπορούσαν να κοινοποιηθούν στη Sun Alliance και στην London Insurance Group. Υπέθεσε ότι η ασφαλιστική εταιρεία θα βοηθούσε να υποστηρίξει ή να αναιρέσει τον ισχυρισμό τους ότι (i) ο θάνατος του Παπαπέτρου δεν είχε αποδειχτεί πέραν αμφιβολίας (ii) ότι εάν

---

[147] Η Έλμα Ρωσίδου, κόρη του Νίκου Παπαπέτρου, σε συνομιλία με τον συγγραφέα, 2020.

είχε πεθάνει, τότε ο θάνατός του οφειλόταν σε αυτοκτονία και (iii) ότι δεν είχε αποκαλύψει την ύπαρξη άλλων ασφαλειών ζωής. Οι ασφαλιστές είχαν σημαντικό συμφέρον στο ότι επρόκειτο να πληρώσουν £ 10.000 εκτός αν μπορούσαν να αποδείξουν τους λόγους για τους οποίους το συμβόλαιο ήταν άκυρο. Στην περίπτωση αυτή, η αστυνομία αρνήθηκε να κάνει διαθέσιμη την αναφορά, μια κατάσταση που παραμένει ίδια πάνω από πενήντα χρόνια αργότερα.

Παρακολουθώντας τους Ντετέκτιβ

Οι δύο αξιωματικοί της Μητροπολιτικής Αστυνομίας που στάλθηκαν στην Αθήνα και την Κύπρο επρόκειτο να ερευνήσουν μια από τις μεγαλύτερες μαζικές δολοφονίες στη σύγχρονη βρετανική ιστορία. Τα επόμενα χρόνια, οι τρομοκρατικές θηριωδίες θα γίνονταν πολύ πιο συχνές, αλλά εκείνη την εποχή, το περιστατικό του Charlie Oscar ήταν πρωτοφανές για τις βρετανικές αρχές.

Ο βομβαρδισμός της πτήσης 103 της Pan Am στις 21 Δεκεμβρίου 1988, με αποτέλεσμα τον θάνατο 270 ατόμων, ήταν διαφορετικής κλίμακας από το CY284, αλλά τα δύο εγκλήματα ήταν παρόμοια στη φύση τους. Η αστυνομική έρευνα για την θηριωδία του Λόκερμπι (Lockerbie) (στη Σκωτία όπου έπεσε το αεροπλάνο) είχε πολλές φορές τους περιορισμένους πόρους που δόθηκαν στους Browne and Hill, που αφορούσαν τους πόρους του FBI καθώς και στις αστυνομικές δυνάμεις των Dumfries και Galloway Constabulary. Έγιναν 15.000 καταθέσεις μαρτύρων. Η έρευνα για την κατάρριψη του Charlie Oscar ήταν μια πολύ χαμηλότερης σημασίας υπόθεση.

Η ίδια η αναφορά της αστυνομίας εξακολουθεί να αποκρύπτεται από το κοινό, αλλά ένα συνοδευτικό έγγραφο στα αρχεία της Μητροπολιτικής Αστυνομίας, που περιέχει δεκατέσσερις σελίδες εγγράφων, σημειώνει ότι έχουν αφαιρεθεί άλλες 266 σελίδες εγγράφων, σύμφωνα με τις Εξαιρέσεις[148] S (2) 31, S (2) 38 και S (2) 40. Ομοίως, στο αρχείο του υπ. Εσωτερικών (HO 287/2146), αφαιρέθηκαν τρεις ενότητες, συνολικού αριθμού 255 σελίδων. Ένα από αυτά μπορεί να αναγνωριστεί ως η Αναφορά Παθολογίας, η οποία είναι δημόσια διαθέσιμη πλήρως ως AVIA101/255. Μια δεύτερη ενότητα περιλαμβάνει 183 σελίδες, αφαιρέθηκε και αυτή βάση της νομοθεσίας 31 και 40. Αυτή ήταν πιθανώς η συλλογή καταθέσεων μαρτύρων. Η τρίτη ενότητα, κάτω από τις ίδιες Εξαιρέσεις, περιλαμβάνει 29 σελίδες και αναφέρεται ως «Έκθεση».

---

[148] Η εξαίρεση 31 καλύπτει πληροφορίες που σχετίζονται με την επιβολή του νόμου, 38 για την Υγεία και την Ασφάλεια και 41 για τις «πληροφορίες που παρέχονται εμπιστευτικά». Οι εξαιρέσεις 31 και 41 επιτρέπουν την απόκρυψη των καταθέσεων μαρτύρων και των ουσιαστικών αστυνομικών εκθέσεων για το συμβάν. Σε αυτήν την περίπτωση, από αλληλογραφία που αμφισβητεί την απόκρυψη αυτών των εγγράφων, είναι γνωστό ότι η Εξαίρεση 38 χρησιμοποιείται για την απόκρυψη της Αναφοράς Παθολογίας καθώς περιέχει εικόνες και πληροφορίες που θεωρούνται πολύ ενοχλητικές για προβολή. Όπως σημειώθηκε, η πλήρης αναφορά είναι διαθέσιμη χωριστά.

Το Πρόγραμμα δηλώσεων σχετικά με τους νεκρούς επιβάτες, το οποίο περιέχεται στο HO 287/2146, αν και έχουν αφαιρεθεί οι διευθύνσεις των επιβατών, δείχνει ότι οι αριθμοί δηλώσεων 57 έως 138 αναφέρονται στα θύματα. Θα ήταν συνήθης πρακτική να υπάρχει μια δήλωση από τον πλησιέστερο συγγενή που να επιβεβαιώνει το προγραμματισμένο ταξίδι και να δίνει σχετικές λεπτομέρειες του ιστορικού, όπως ο σκοπός του ταξιδιού. Σε ορισμένες περιπτώσεις, ένα παντρεμένο ζευγάρι, όπως οι Griffiths, ή μια οικογενειακή ομάδα όπως οι Taskers, καλύπτεται από μια ενιαία δήλωση. Άλλα άτομα καλύπτονται με περισσότερο από μια δήλωση. Συνολικά 82 δηλώσεις καλύπτουν 59 επιβάτες. Θα έπρεπε επίσης να υπάρχουν δηλώσεις για το πλήρωμα, προσθέτοντας ακόμα επτά σε σύνολο. Θα έπρεπε να υπάρχουν τουλάχιστον και 49 επιπρόσθετες δηλώσεις από μάρτυρες. Όμως, 183 σελίδες για 138 δηλώσεις είναι ασήμαντος αριθμός έχοντας υπόψη τον τρόπο της έρευνας που αναμενόταν από τους δύο αξιωματούχους. Υπάρχει βέβαια η πιθανότητα ότι η συλλογή εγγράφων να αποτελεί μια επιλογή των σημαντικότερων δηλώσεων.

Οι επιπλέον 49 δηλώσεις μαρτύρων θα έπρεπε να περιλαμβάνουν εκείνες των τεσσάρων αεροσυνοδών της ΒΕΑ στη πτήση από Λονδίνο προς Αθήνα, των έξι επιβατών που αποβιβάστηκαν (στην Αθήνα), των υπαλλήλων στο αεροδρόμιο του Ελληνικού της Αθήνας και του Λονδίνου (Heathrow), των τριών του πληρώματος του Mike Foxtrot, τους ελεγκτές εναέριας κυκλοφορίας στην Αθήνα και τη Λευκωσία, της ομάδας έρευνας του RARDE, του AIB και του Royal Aircraft Establishment. Όλα αυτά θα απαιτούνταν για την επικύρωση των τεκμηρείων, ακουστικών και αυτοπτών μαρτύρων όλων των πτυχών του τελευταίου ταξιδιού του Charlie Oscar.

Οι «επιβάτες ενδιαφέροντος» θα είχαν δημιουργήσει πρόσθετες δηλώσεις. Η συμπεριφορά του **Αβραάμ Σολωμού** είχε τραβήξει την προσοχή στο αεροδρόμιο, την οποία παρακολούθησαν τόσο ο Τζ.Ε. Παπαλεξόπουλος, ο υπάλληλος ελέγχου εισιτηρίων, όσο και ο κ. Χ. Κολιανδρής, ο Διευθυντής Εφημεριών ΒΕΑ, ο οποίος εξουσιοδότησε το Σολωμού να ταξιδέψει σε πολύ σύντομο χρονικό διάστημα.

Παρόλο που οι πληροφορίες που αναφέρονται στα βιβλία του Λεωνίδα Λεωνίδου και του Ελευθέριου Παπαδόπουλου δεν ήρθαν στο φως παρά πολύ αργότερα, ο Σολωμού κατονομάστηκε για πρώτη φορά στο άρθρο της Evening Standard στις 21 Νοεμβρίου 1967 ως το άτομο που μετέφερε τη βόμβα στο αεροσκάφος. Οι πληροφορίες είναι αρκετά συγκεκριμένες και παρόλο που το άρθρο υποβαθμίστηκε, θα ήταν περίεργο να το είχε ονειρευτεί κάποιος. Επίσης, ένα αναγνωριστικό στοιχείο στο σώμα του Σολωμού που σημείωσαν οι παθολόγοι ήταν η παρουσία ουλών από τραύματα από σφαίρες από την εποχή του με την ΕΟΚΑ. Αυτά θα έπρεπε να είχαν καταγραφεί ως πιθανής σημασίας.

Εύλογα να αναμενόταν από την αστυνομική ομάδα, να εξετάσει τις ακόλουθες έρευνες σχετικά με την παρουσία του Σολωμού στην πτήση.
• Δήλωση συγγενών που επιβεβαίωνε ότι ο Σολωμού σχεδίαζε να είναι στην πτήση ή τουλάχιστον να προσπαθήσει να ταξιδέψει από την Αθήνα στη Λευκωσία.
• Γιατί ο Σολωμού ήταν τόσο αποφασισμένος να ανέβει στην πτήση;
• Εάν του είχαν πει να επιστρέψει στη Λευκωσία το επόμενο πρωί, ποιος του είχε περάσει αυτό το μήνυμα και από ποιον προήλθε;
• Τι κουβαλούσε στις χειραποσκευές του;
• Ερευνήθηκαν (οι χειραποσκευές του);
• Ποια ήταν η συμπεριφορά του αμέσως πριν την επιβίβαση, αφού είχε πλέον τακτοποιηθεί το εισιτήριό του;
• Πού και πότε είχε αγοράσει το αρχικό του εισιτήριο;
• Ταξίδευε για προσωπικούς λόγους ή για δουλειά για τον Σπύρο Κυπριανού;
• Αν ταξίδευε για δουλειά, είχε επισκεφθεί την Κυπριακή Πρεσβεία στην Αθήνα ή είχαν κάποια επαφή μαζί του;
• Ποιοι ήταν οι ακριβείς στόχοι του ταξιδιού του στην Αθήνα;
• Πού είχε μείνει πριν κάνει check-in για CY284;
• Ποιους είχε επισκεφτεί;
• Του είχε επισήμως κατανεμηθεί η θέση 16C;
• Εάν όχι, ποιος έδωσε τις πληροφορίες ότι καθόταν εκεί και σε ποια βάση;
• Τι ήταν γνωστό για την εμπλοκή του στην ΕΟΚΑ και ποία ειδικευμένη τεχνογνωσία είχε στον χειρισμό όπλων;
• Ποιες ήταν οι προηγούμενες και οι παρούσες σχέσεις του, αν υπάρχουν, με τον Γιωρκάτζη και τον Γρίβα;
Τουλάχιστον, θα έπρεπε να είχαν ληφθεί δηλώσεις από τον κ. Παπαλεξόπουλο, τον κ. Κολιανδρή, την κυρία Σολωμού, οποιονδήποτε άλλο στο προσωπικό αεροπορικής εταιρείας ή αεροδρομίου που είχε άμεση επαφή μαζί του και τέλος από κατάλληλο πρόσωπο στο γραφείο του κ. Κυπριανού. Εάν είχαν προκύψει περαιτέρω λεπτομέρειες, θα ήταν λογικό να είχαν ληφθεί δηλώσεις που να τεκμηριώνουν ή να διαψεύδουν το συμπέρασμα ότι η ύποπτη συμπεριφορά του Σολωμού ήταν στην πραγματικότητα σημαντική ανησυχία. Θα ήταν τόσο σημαντικό να αποκλειστεί ο Σολωμού ως ύποπτος όσο και να είχε αποδειχθεί ότι υπήρχαν λόγοι να ερευνούταν βαθύτερα. Ωστόσο, μόνο δύο καταθέσεις υπάρχουν για Αβραάμ Σολωμού στον αστυνομικό φάκελο.

Ο Σωτήρης Γεωργίου θα ήταν μεγαλύτερου ενδιαφέροντος καθώς κατάγεται από τις ΗΠΑ. Ωστόσο, ακόμη και το 1968 δεν θα ήταν δύσκολο για το FBI να βοηθήσει με μια δήλωση συγγενών. Οι γραμμές έρευνας για τον κ. Γεωργίου θα περιλάμβαναν:
• Σκοπός της επίσκεψής του στην Κύπρο.

• Στοιχεία στρατιωτικής θητείας, εμπειρογνωμοσύνης σε εκρηκτικά ή έλλειψής τους.
• Διασυνδέσεις ή αλλιώς, με τον Γιώργο Γεωργίου, τον δυσαρεστημένο πρώην υπάλληλο της ΒΕΑ.
• Αποδεικτικά της κατανομής της έδρας του στην θέση 4Α.
• Στοιχεία για τις χειραποσκευές του.
• Στοιχεία τυχόν δυσμενών δεικτών συμπεριφοράς: ήταν ασυνήθιστα νευρικός για επιβάτη;
Το ελάχιστο θα έπρεπε να υπήρχαν δηλώσεις από τους συγγενείς του Σωτήρη Γεωργίου το προσωπικό check-in στο Λονδίνο, το προσωπικό καμπίνας στη πτήση Λονδίνο – Αθήνα και, αν δυνατόν, δήλωση από τον ίδιο το Γιώργο Γεωργίου. Μόνο η δήλωση με αριθμό 83 αναφέρεται στον Γεωργίου.

Αν η ανακριτική ομάδα είχε έρθει σε επαφή με την οικογένεια Γεωργίου, θα εξασφάλιζε τις απαντήσεις στα παραπάνω σημεία. Σκοπός του ταξιδιού του στην Κύπρο ήταν απλώς να επισκεφτεί τους γονείς του, τον αδερφό του Νίκο και την οικογένειά του, καθώς και να βολιδοσκοπήσει αν μπορούσε να βρει μια Κύπρια μέλλουσα νύφη. Παρόλο που βρισκόταν στις ΗΠΑ για λιγότερο από τέσσερα χρόνια, νοσταλγούσε το σπίτι του στην Κύπρο και ήθελε να επιστρέψει για ένα ταξίδι τριών εβδομάδων. Δεν είχε υπηρετήσει ποτέ στον στρατό και ποτέ δεν είχε εκπαιδευτεί στη χρήση όπλων ή εκρηκτικών.

Δεν υπήρχε σχέση μεταξύ του Σωτήρη και του Γιώργου Γεωργίου, του δυσαρεστημένου πρώην υπαλλήλου του ΒΕΑ. Είχε, συμπτωματικά, έναν αδερφό ονόματι Γιώργο , ο οποίος τη στιγμή της καταστροφής ζούσε μερικές χιλιάδες μίλια δυτικά του Λονδίνου, στο Clairton Pennsylvania, όπου διαχειριζόταν μια επιχείρηση στεγνοκαθαριστηρίου. Κατά τη διάρκεια της ενδιάμεσης στάσης του στο Λονδίνο μεταξύ των πτήσεων BOAC και ΒΕΑ, ο Σωτήρης πέρασε το χρόνο με συγγενείς του. και για ψώνια.

Είναι, βεβαίως, απολύτως πιθανό ο Σωτήρης να άλλαξε θέση καθ' οδόν προς την Αθήνα ή κατά την επανεπιβίβαση του στο Charlie Oscar μετά τη στάση εκεί. Ωστόσο, το προσωπικό της καμπίνας της ΒΕΑ δεν κάνει καμία αναφορά σε μια τέτοια αλλαγή.

Ο Σωτήρης είχε δύο βαλίτσες και μια μικρότερη χειραποσκευή με δώρα για την οικογενειά του στην Κύπρο. Η αγορά περαιτέρω δώρων στο Λονδίνο αντιπροσωπεύει τα τέσσερα πλεονάζων κιλά που σημειώθηκε ότι είχε όταν έκανε check- in στο Λονδίνο.

Σύμφωνα με τον αδελφό του Σωτήρη, τον Πολύβιο[149], οι άνθρωποι που τον γνώριζαν σε όλη τη σύντομη ζωή του, χαρακτήριζαν τον Σωτήρη ως

---

[149] *Πολύβιος Γεωργίου σε αλληλογραφία με τον συγγραφέα, 2018.*

έναν ευθυγραμμισμένο, όμορφο, εύθυμο, κοινωνικό, γενναιόδωρο νεαρό, που πήγαινε σε βραδινά μαθήματα για να βελτιώσει τα αγγλικά του. Σύμφωνα με τους δύο Γερμανούς εργοδότες του, ήταν καλά πειθαρχημένος και εργατικός που ονειρευόταν να ανοίξει το δικό του συνεργείο αυτοκινήτων στη Νέα Υόρκη. Ήταν εκπαιδευμένος μηχανικός αυτοκινήτων και τη στιγμή του θανάτου του εργαζόταν στην Great Neck Imports, μια εταιρεία που ειδικεύεται στα αυτοκίνητα Mercedes

Είχε αποκτήσει την αμερικανική υπηκοότητα στο Wilmington του Delaware το 1965, δεκατέσσερις μήνες μετά την άφιξή του στις ΗΠΑ. Αυτή η μάλλον γρήγορη πολιτογράφηση ήταν αποτέλεσμα της ανάκτησης της αμερικανικής υπηκοότητας από τον πατέρα του μετά από απόφαση του Ανώτατου Δικαστηρίου των ΗΠΑ.

Η πεθερά και οι κουνιάδοι του Πολύβιου ήταν τα τελευταία μέλη της ευρύτερης οικογενειάς του που είδαν τον Σωτήρη ζωντανό καθώς επιβιβαζόταν στο ΒΕ284 στο Heathrow.

Σύμφωνα με την ομάδα της *Sunday Telegraph*, ο **Νίκος Παπαπέτρου** ήρθε στο φως όταν αποκαλύφθηκε ότι είχε συνάψει χωριστές ασφάλειες ζωής με τέσσερις διαφορετικές εταιρείες. Εκτός από τη δήλωση συγγενών, θα ήταν επίσης σημαντικό να καθοριστεί:
• Από πού και πότε αγόρασε τις ασφάλειες ζωής ;
• Ποιος είχε αλληλεπιδράσει μαζί του για την πώληση των ασφαλειών ;
Ήταν σίγουρα ο Παπαπέτρου που είχε αγοράσει τις ασφάλειες ;
• Είχε εκφράσει σκέψεις αυτοκτονίας οποιαδήποτε στιγμή στο παρελθόν;
• Τι κουβαλούσε στις χειραπυσκευές του;
• Έγινε έρευνα των χειραποσκευών του;
• Ποια ήταν η συμπεριφορά του αμέσως πριν την επιβίβαση;
• Πού και πότε είχε αγοράσει το εισιτήριό του;
• Ταξίδευε για προσωπικούς λόγους ή για τη δουλειά του για τον Γαλίδη, τον εργοδότη του;
• Ποιοι ήταν οι ακριβείς στόχοι του ταξιδιού του στην Αθήνα;
• Πού είχε μείνει πριν κάνει check -in για CY284;
• Ποιους είχε επισκεφτεί;
•Του είχε επισήμως παραχωρηθεί μια θέση;
• Σχετιζόταν με την ομάδα των Μαρτύρων του Ιεχωβά πριν από την επιβίβαση;
• Τι στρατιωτική ή εξειδικευμένη εμπειρία στο χειρισμό όπλων είχε;

Αυτό θα περιλάμβανε και τις συνήθεις δηλώσεις της συζύγου του και του προσωπικού του check-in, μαζί με τον πωλητή εισιτηρίων, τυχόν επιζώντες μάρτυρες από το σαλόνι αναχώρησης της Αθήνας, την κόρη του στην Αθήνα και τους τέσσερις ασφαλιστικούς πράκτορες. Αυτό θα πρόσθετε τουλάχιστον επτά δηλώσεις. Ενώ ο Παπαπέτρου αναφέρεται σε τέσσερεις δηλώσεις, 135 προς 138, θα ήταν λογικό να περιμένουμε πολύ περισσότερα.

Συγκριτικά, ορισμένοι άλλοι επιβάτες αποτελούν αντικείμενο πολλών δηλώσεων. Όπως η οικογένεια McComb (έξι δηλώσεις) και η κυρία Λιασίδη (τέσσερις). Κανένα από αυτά τα θύματα δεν είχε προκαλέσει υποψίες, κάτι που υπό τις προφανείς συνθήκες είναι απολύτως κατανοητό. Ωστόσο, είχαν περισσότερες δηλώσεις από τους κατονομαζόμενους ύποπτους.

Εκ πρώτης όψεως, για να διεξαχθεί μια ενδελεχής έρευνα θα χρειαζόταν μια πολύ μεγαλύτερη ομάδα αστυνομικών από τον ντετέκτιβ Επιθεωρητή Browne και τον ντετέκτιβ Λοχία Hill. Σήμερα, για μια έρευνα μαζικής δολοφονίας, η ομάδα θα έδινε αναφορά σε έναν Βοηθό Αρχηγό Αστυνομίας στη αστυνομική δύναμη της περιοχής, ή ίσως σε έναν Αναπληρωτή Βοηθό Επιθεωρητή στη Μητροπολιτική Αστυνομία.

Το κόστος της έρευνας, που συζητήθηκε από διάφορους, θα περιλάμβανε κυρίως τον χρόνο των δύο αξιωματικών, το ταξίδι, το ξενοδοχείο και τη διαμονή τους. Οι αμοιβές, σε τιμές 2018, των δύο αξιωματικών[150] για ένα δίμηνο θα ήταν περίπου £20.000 λίρες. Οι πτήσεις, ανάλογα με τον αριθμό που πραγματοποιούνταν, πιθανότατα θα πρόσθεταν £10.000 για μια σειρά από ταξίδια μετ' επιστροφής. Η διαμονή σε ξενοδοχείο θα πρόσθετε ίσως £200 ανά διανυκτέρευση και για διατροφή άλλες περίπου £ 100 την ημέρα για τους δύο αξιωματικούς. Τα μεταφορικά μέσα (ταξί) θα ανέρχονταν πιθανώς σε άλλες £500 λίρες την εβδομάδα, εάν συνεπάγονταν πολλά ταξίδια. Συνολικά, η επιβάρυνση του φορολογούμενου πολίτη θα ήταν £50.000 και £60.000. Το κόστος της ίδιας της έρευνας στο Λόκερμπι δεν είναι γνωστό, αλλά μόνο η δίκη κόστισε £60 εκατομμύρια δολάρια. Όταν τρεις ισλαμιστές τρομοκράτες σχεδίασαν να ανατινάξουν υπερατλαντικά αεροσκάφη τον Αύγουστο του 2006, η έρευνα και η δίκη υπολογίστηκαν συνολικά σε £100 εκατομμύρια. Η έρευνα για τον Charlie Oscar αν είχε εντοπιστεί ο ύποπτος, θα ήταν μια τιμή ευκαιρίας.

Εάν η έρευνα γινόταν σήμερα, ο Browne, ή όποιος την ανελάμβανε, θα διαχειριζόταν μια μεγάλη ομάδα που θα διενεργούσε έρευνες σε όλη τη Βρετανία, την Ελλάδα και την Κύπρο, σκάβοντας το ιστορικό κάθε επιβάτη, κοσκινίζοντας όλα τα διαθέσιμα έγγραφα, εντοπίζοντας οποιονδήποτε είχε οποιαδήποτε ανάμειξη με BE/CY284. Το κρίσιμο είναι ότι θα υπήρχε εντατική εργασία σε εξέλιξη στα παρασκήνια για τη διερεύνηση των πιθανών πολιτικών σεναρίων. Η άμεση υπόθεση ότι η βόμβα προοριζόταν για τον Στρατηγό Γρίβα πρέπει να είχε κάποια βάση

---

[150] *Επιθεωρητής £85.000 ετ., Λοχίας £40.000*

για να κρατηθεί τόσο ισχυρά. Εάν υπήρχε, πράγματι, κάποια βάση γι'αυτή , τότε θα ήταν προς το συμφέρον της κυπριακής κυβέρνησης να καθορίσει αυτή τι βάση. Τουλάχιστον, ο αναγνώστης θα μπορούσε να θεωρήσει ότι και ο ίδιος ο Γρίβας θα ήθελε να μάθει.

Η Μητροπολιτική Αστυνομία δεν φαινόταν εξαρχής ιδιαίτερα πρόθυμη να αναλάβει την έρευνα. Υπήρχε τότε μεγάλη επιφυλακτικότητα για εμπλοκή των Ελληνικών αρχών ή ακόμη και να γνωστοποιηθεί ότι η έρευνα συνεχιζόταν. Δεν γίνεται καμία απολύτως αναφορά για εμπλοκή της κυπριακής κυβέρνησης ή των φορέων της. Το Φόρεϊν Όφις έστειλε ένα σαφές μήνυμα στον Βοηθό Επίτροπο Brodie να πει στον Browne να θίξει οποιαδήποτε πολιτική ανάμιξη πρώτα σ'αυτούς (Φ.Οφις) πριν προχωρήσει περαιτέρω. Η σημασία αυτού του μηνύματος έγινε ξεκάθαρα κατανοητή από τον Brodie, ο οποίος έστειλε μια πολύ μυστική επιστολή στον Browne μέσω του διπλωματικού σάκου. Εάν η οδηγία ήταν ρουτίνα θα μπορούσε να είχε διεκπεραιωθεί τηλεφωνικά, ή ίσως από ένα μέλος του προσωπικού της Πρεσβείας της Αθήνας να είχε μια σιωπηρή κουβέντα με τους Browne και Hill για διπλωματικές ανταλλαγές και πρωτόκολλα.

Φαίνεται ότι το Φόρεϊν Όφις είχε πολύ μεγάλες ανησυχίες μήπως χαλάσει κάτι αν δεν δινόταν μια σκληρή εντολή στον Browne. Μέχρι σήμερα, η «εθνική ασφάλεια» παραμένει ένας από τους λόγους που χρησιμοποιούν τα Εθνικά Αρχεία για τη μη δημοσιοποίηση ορισμένων πληροφοριών των αρχείων. Τέτοια μέτρα, αν και είναι πιθανό να προσελκύσουν κριτική από τα μέσα ενημέρωσης, είναι ευκολότερα κατανοητά εάν είναι απαραίτητα για την προστασία μιας πηγής πληροφοριών με υψηλή θέση, ίσως σε κυβερνητική θέση. Κατά τη διάρκεια της Κυπριακής Έκτακτης Ανάγκης, η ΕΟΚΑ ήταν γεμάτη πληροφοριοδότες, που οδήγησαν στα ακραία μέτρα του Γρίβα, συμπεριλαμβανομένου ίσως αυτού που ο Γεωργιάδης είχε περιληπτικά αποκαλέσει «εξοντωτική-προδοτική ομάδα» του Στρατηγού. Είναι απίθανο ο Γρίβας να είχε καταφέρει να τους εντοπίσει όλους.

Αναλύσεις και Συμπεράσματα

Κανείς δεν θα μάθει ποτέ τι συνέβη στο Charlie Oscar κατά τη διάρκεια των τελευταίων λεπτών της πτήσης του και είναι πιθανό το κίνητρο και ο πραγματικός δράστης να αποτελούν πάντα αντικείμενο διαμάχης. Είναι δυνατό, ωστόσο, να ανασυνθέσουμε την πιθανή εξέλιξη των γεγονότων αφού ο SFO Thomas ξεκίνησε τον χαιρετισμό του στη Λευκωσία.

Σε εκείνο το σημείο, η βόμβα εξερράγη στην καμπίνα των επιβατών. Τοποθετημένη στο πέλμα των ποδιών του επιβάτη του καθίσματος 3Α ή 4Α, και εν μέρει κάτω από το κάθισμα μπροστά του, η συσκευή κατακερματίστηκε, αναγκάζοντας μικροσκοπικά θραύσματα να σκορπιστούν προς όλες τις κατευθύνσεις και σε αφάνταστα υψηλές ταχύτητες. Ο επιβάτης του καθίσματος στο πόδι του οποίου είχε εντοπιστεί η βόμβα, θα είχε τραυματιστεί πολύ σοβαρά, αλλά, ευτυχώς, θα ήξερε λίγα γι' αυτό. Η υπερ-πίεση, της τάξης των πολλών εκατοντάδων pounds (αγγλικός ζυγιστικός όρος – 2 ½ pounds ένα κιλό) ανά τετραγωνική ίντσα ακριβώς δίπλα στη συσκευή, αναμφίβολα άφησε μια σημαντική τρύπα στην άτρακτο, αναγκάζοντας το μεταλλικό δέρμα προς τα έξω στο αέρα. Μια μικρότερη τρύπα έμεινε στο πάτωμα της καμπίνας. Αρχικά μετρούσε περίπου τριάντα ίντσες σε τετράγωνο, το ρήγμα στον τοίχο της καμπίνας και η πίεση επέτρεψε αμέσως να διαφύγει όλος ο αέρας από την άτρακτο. Η αλληλουχία των γεγονότων στις εκρηκτικές αποσυμπιέσεις είναι γνωστή. Σε ένα κλάσμα του δευτερολέπτου, η θερμοκρασία και η πίεση της καμπίνας έπεσαν κατακόρυφα, προκαλώντας τη δημιουργία πυκνής ομίχλης, που επιδεινώθηκε από σκόνη και συντρίμμια, αν και αυτά μετατοπίστηκαν σχεδόν αμέσως καθώς ο αέρας έβγαινε από την άτρακτο.

Η έντονη, αν και βραχύβια, βιασύνη του αέρα κάλλιστα να παρέσυρε το θρυμματισμένο σώμα του επιβάτη του καθίσματος, για να μην ανακτηθεί ποτέ. Πιθανόν να επρόκειτο για τον Σωτήρη Γεωργίου, που είναι γνωστό ότι καθόταν στο 4Α στη πτήση Λονδίνο-Αθήνα, υποδεικνύοντας έντονα ότι η βόμβα είχε τοποθετηθεί στο αεροσκάφος από το άτομο που κάθεται τώρα στο 3Α της πτήσης Αθήνα-Λευκωσία. Όποιος επιβάτης καθόταν στο κάθισμα κάτω από το οποίο σημειώθηκε η έκρηξη πιθανότατα να προκάλεσε σοβαρές ρωγμές στην πλάτη και στα πόδια του και μπορεί επίσης να ρουφήχτηκε από το ρήγμα της καμπίνας καθώς συνέβη αυτό.

Η δύναμη της έκρηξης μειώθηκε κατά πολύ με κάθε πόδι (απόστασης) από το κέντρο της έκρηξης, ειδικά καθώς τα καθίσματα του αεροσκάφους ήσαν εμπόδιο στο κύμα πίεσης.

Ο Αχιλλέας Αφατίτης, ένας από την ομάδα των Μαρτύρων του Ιεχωβά, και που πιθανό να στεκόταν στο διάδρομο, τέσσερα ή πέντε πόδια μακριά, να γέμισε με αιχμηρά (shrapnel), αλλά απέφυγε να τον ρουφήξει ο αέρας, ίσως επειδή τον εμπόδισε η σειρά των καθισμάτων ανάμεσα σε αυτόν και την τρύπα στον τοίχο της καμπίνας.

Καθώς η πίεση εντός της καμπίνας εξισωνόταν με την εξωτερική, η ομίχλη καθαρίστηκε και η θερμοκρασία έπεσε. Οι μάσκες οξυγόνου έκτακτης ανάγκης έπεσαν και όσοι είχαν ακόμη τις αισθήσεις τους και μπορούσαν να το κάνουν, τις φόρεσαν. Οι άλλοι παρέμειναν στο έλεος της τραυματικής κατάστασης που εξελισσόταν γύρω τους.

Οι πιλότοι θα είχαν φορέσει τις μάσκες οξυγόνου τους και θα είχαν κάνει τις διαδικασίες για ξαφνική απώλεια πίεσης. Αυτό περιλάμβανε μια ελεγχόμενη κάθοδο σε χαμηλότερο υψόμετρο, πετώντας γύρω στους 330 κόμβους, με τα αερόφρενα ανοιχτά και βαλβίδες κλειστές. Στην περίπτωση της εκρηκτικής από-συμπίεσης, το Εγχειρίδιο Λειτουργίας συμβούλευε «...*οι πιέσεις στο αεροσκάφος θα πρέπει να διατηρούνται στο ελάχιστο διατηρώντας την ταχύτητα του αέρα εντός λογικών ορίων, αποφεύγοντας όλους τους περιττούς και βίαιους ελιγμούς»*.

Το επόμενο στάδιο της διαδικασίας θα ερχόταν όταν είχαν κατέβει κάτω από τα 13.500 πόδια, που θα ήταν σε τέσσερα έως πέντε λεπτά. Από το ύψος πλεύσης των 29.000 ποδιών, αυτό το χρονικό διάστημα δεν θα αποτελούσε υπερβολικό πρόβλημα για τους επιβάτες, καθώς θα είχαν πρόσβαση στις μάσκες οξυγόνου στην καμπίνα. Ο ρόλος του προσωπικού της καμπίνας θα ήταν να δώσει εντολή στους επιβάτες να παραμείνουν στις θέσεις τους με δεμένες τις ζώνες ασφαλείας, αναμένοντας τις προθέσεις του Καπετάνιου. Είναι απίθανο ο Καπετάνιος Blackwood να υπολόγιζε εγκατάλειψη εκείνη τη στιγμή, διαφορετικά οι επιβάτες θα είχαν λάβει οδηγίες να φορέσουν τα σωσίβια τους.

Το πλησιέστερο αεροδρόμιο τώρα ήταν η Ρόδος, περίπου 120 μίλια πίσω κατά μήκος της διαδρομής τους και 60 μίλια πιο κοντά στη Λευκωσία. Αν υποθέσουμε ότι το αεροδρόμιο ήταν ανοιχτό την πρωινή εκείνη ώρα , θα ήταν πιθανώς η προφανής επιλογή ως το αεροδρόμιο εκτροπής και θα ήταν περίπου 25 λεπτά πτήσης μακριά.

Η αξιολόγηση της κατάστασης από πρώτο χέρι θα ήταν καθήκον του SFO Palmer. Θα ήταν μια σκηνή καταστροφής, αλλά είναι δίκαιο να υποθέσουμε ότι είχε εκπαιδευτεί να αντιμετωπίζει ήρεμα την κατάσταση. Ο θόρυβος των κινητήρων και η ολίσθηση, που δεν μετριάζονταν πλέον από την ηχομόνωση του τοίχου της καμπίνας, θα ήταν έντονοι.

Το προσωπικό της καμπίνας, κάνοντας τώρα ότι μπορούσε για να κρατήσει τους επιβάτες όσο το δυνατόν πιο ήρεμους υπό τις περιστάσεις, θα προσπαθούσε να μετακινήσει όσους ήσαν πλησιέστερα της ζημιάς στο αεροσκάφος, σε άδεια καθίσματα μακριά από την τρύπα στην άτρακτο. Υπήρχε ανάγκη να διατηρηθεί η συνολική ισορροπία του αεροσκάφους. Δεν θα ήταν εφικτό να μετακινηθούν όλοι οι επιβάτες προς τα εμπρός, καθώς αυτό θα βάρυνε το αεροσκάφος πέρα από τα σχεδιαστικά του όρια, αλλά είναι πολύ πιθανό οι επιβάτες που κάθονται στην αριστερή πλευρά της καμπίνας και πίσω από την τοποθεσία της έκρηξης, να είχαν απομακρυνθεί πρώτοι.

Η κατάσταση θα άξιζε ένα κάλεσμα «Mayday», αλλά είναι πιθανό η αποσπασματική κάλυψη του ασυρμάτου, η οποία ανάγκασε τον Charlie Oscar να μεταδώσει το μήνυμα στον Καπετάνιο Emmerson στο Mike Foxtrot, τώρα να τους εγκατέλειψε εντελώς. Δεν ελήφθη ποτέ κλήση κινδύνου.

Κάτω από το δάπεδο της καμπίνας, είναι πιθανό ένας ή περισσότεροι από τους υδραυλικούς σωλήνες να είχαν κοπεί ή κρίσιμα εξαρτήματα του συστήματος να απενεργοποιήθηκαν από την έκρηξη. Θεωρητικά, το τριπλό υδραυλικό σύστημα του Κομήτη θα έπρεπε να ήταν σε θέση να αντιμετωπίσει ακριβώς μια τέτοια έκτακτη ανάγκη. Ομοίως, είναι πιθανό ότι η βλάβη στους σερβομηχανισμούς του αεροπλάνου, που βρίσκονταν σχεδόν ακριβώς κάτω από τη σειρά καθισμάτων 5, επηρέασε την ικανότητα των πιλότων να ελέγχουν τη γωνία κύλισης του αεροσκάφους. Τα πέντε περίπου λεπτά που υποδεικνύονταν στα ρολόγια επέτρεψαν στο Charlie Oscar να κατέβει περίπου στα 15.000 πόδια.

Για οποιονδήποτε λόγο, οι δυνάμεις g-forces στο αεροσκάφος, που προέκυψαν από την κατάσταση εκτός ελέγχου που βρισκόταν τώρα, τελικά έγιναν υπερβολικές και το Charlie Oscar κόπηκε στα δύο, γύρω από το προφυλακτήρα της μπροστινής πτέρυγας. Το χτύπημα στο πλαίσιο του αεροσκάφους προκάλεσε την ενεργοποίηση των πυροσβεστήρων και ένας απελευθερώθηκε και βρέθηκε ανάμεσα στα επιπλέοντα συντρίμμια. Το μπροστινό τμήμα της ατράκτου, από τη σειρά 11 προς τα εμπρός, χωρίς φτερά, κατέβηκε κατακόρυφα με μεγάλη ταχύτητα, ενώ το πίσω μέρος, από τη σειρά 10 πίσω, διατήρησε κάποια ελαφριά κίνηση προς τα εμπρός, οδηγώντας το περίπου 2.000 πόδια προς τα νότια.

Όπως αναφέρθηκε στην αρχή αυτού του κεφαλαίου, δεν υπάρχει άμεση απόδειξη των παραπάνω, αλλά βασίζονται στις διαδικασίες έκτακτης ανάγκης που περιγράφονται στο Εγχειρίδιο πτήσης ΒΕΑ Comet 4B. Μια ανεξέλεγκτη, απότομη στροφή θα αντιπροσώπευε την απόσταση 25 έως 30 ναυτικών μιλίων που διανύθηκαν στα πέντε λεπτά μεταξύ της έκρηξης και της αποσύνθεσης, όντας πολύ μεγαλύτερη από την ευθεία απόσταση των 10 ναυτικών μιλίων μεταξύ της εκτιμώμενης θέσης του αεροσκάφους όταν έγινε η τελευταία κλήση και το σημείο στο οποίο τα συντρίμμια εκτιμήθηκε ότι έπεσαν στη θάλασσα. Θα μπορούσε επίσης να εξηγήσει γιατί ο προσανατολισμός του Charlie Oscar όταν διαλύθηκε πιστεύεται ότι ήταν νότιος ή νοτιοανατολικός, παρά δυτικο-βορειοδυτικά που θα το πήγαινε στη Ρόδο.

Η αφήγηση του Νίκου Μισομίκη που επιβεβαιώνει ότι δεν είδε πτώματα να φορούν σωσίβια, υποστηρίζεται από την άποψη ότι η καταστροφή δεν θεωρήθηκε αμέσως καταστροφική και ο Καπετάνιος Blackwood δεν θεώρησε ότι θα ήταν απαραίτητο να εγκαταλείψει το αεροσκάφος. Το να εγκαταλειφθεί το αεροσκάφος στη θάλασσα, με σποραδική ραδιοεπικοινωνία, στο σκοτάδι, θα ήταν σε κάθε περίπτωση ένα μέτρο που θα έπρεπε να χρησιμοποιείται μόνο σε ακραίες περιστάσεις. Είναι λοιπόν πιθανό οι πιλότοι να προσπαθούσαν να επαναφέρουν το Charlie Oscar υπό έλεγχο, μέχρι το σημείο όπου η άτρακτος κόπηκε.

Στη μετακίνηση των επιβατών σε καθίσματα μακριά από την τρύπα στην άτρακτο μπορεί επίσης να οφείλεται το γεγονός ότι πέντε από τους επιβάτες που κάθονταν αρχικά στο πίσω μέρος του αεροσκάφους να ανασύρθηκαν στο βόρειο πεδίο συντριμμιών, όπου κατέβηκε το μπροστινό τμήμα της ατράκτου του Charlie Oscar . Η μεταφορά των σορών που ανασύρθηκαν από τους ναύτες του Καστελλόριζου στο *Ναυαρίνο* θα εξηγούσε επίσης γιατί έξι θύματα που πιστεύεται ότι ταξίδευαν στο μπροστινό τμήμα του Charlie Oscar φέρεται να ήταν μεταξύ αυτών που βρέθηκαν ανάμεσα στα συντρίμμια του πίσω μέρους του αεροσκάφους.

Έρευνα της Μητροπολιτικής Αστυνομίας

Η έρευνα για τις ποινικές πτυχές του περιστατικού ήταν περιορισμένη ως προς το εύρος, τους πόρους και, προφανώς, στον ενθουσιασμό της και παρέμεινε μυστική. Έχει περάσει περισσότερο από μισός αιώνας από τότε που το Charlie Oscar ανατινάχθηκε στον ουρανό. Μετά την αρχική αναταραχή της δραστηριότητας γύρω από την επιχείρηση ανέλκυσης, ανάλυση των αραιών συντριμμιών και των θλιβερών υπολειμμάτων των θυμάτων και η άμεση και αποτελεσματική έρευνα ατυχήματος που έδειξε οριστικά ότι η αιτία ήταν μια βόμβα, έχουν περάσει πάνω από πενήντα χρόνια σιωπής. Είκοσι τρεις φάκελοι στο Εθνικό Αρχείο , που περιλαμβάνουν περίπου 2.500 σελίδες, παρέχουν μια ολοκληρωμένη καταγραφή της αλληλογραφίας που σχετίζεται σχεδόν με κάθε πτυχή της δουλειάς που πραγματοποιήθηκε από τους Ken Mason, John Veal, Eric Newton, Fred Jones και τις ομάδες τους.

Τρεις φάκελοι, που σχετίζονται με την αστυνομική έρευνα, παραμένουν ως επί το πλείστον μη διαθέσιμοι στο κοινό, και αυτοί έχουν αποτελέσει πηγή πολλών εικασιών. Αυτά τα αρχεία παραμένουν πλήρως κλειδωμένα με μια περαιτέρω καθυστερημένη ημερομηνία κυκλοφορίας την 1η Ιανουαρίου 2067. Το 2018 τα Εθνικά Αρχεία εξασφάλισαν άδεια από τη Μητροπολιτική Αστυνομία και το Υπουργείο Εσωτερικών για να αποκαλύψουν μέρος του περιεχομένου τους στον συγγραφέα.

Από εκείνους που ενδιαφέρονται να λύσουν το μυστήριο της πτήσης CY284, εικάζεται εδώ και καιρό ότι τα αρχεία της Μητροπολιτικής Αστυνομίας έχουν τη δυνατότητα να αποκαλύψουν περισσότερες λεπτομέρειες για το περιστατικό. Τα λίγα έγγραφα που κυκλοφόρησαν πρόσφατα στα κλειστά αρχεία δεν περιέχουν «τίποτα το συγκεκριμένο». Στην πραγματικότητα, αποκαλύπτουν πολύ λίγα που δεν ήταν ήδη γνωστά.

Δυστυχώς, η τελική έκθεση της αστυνομίας 29 σελίδων, μαζί με τις 138 περίπου καταθέσεις μαρτύρων, συγκαταλέγονται στις πληροφορίες που διατηρούνται στους φακέλους. Η αιτιολόγηση για τη συνέχιση της διατήρησης αυτών των εγγράφων είναι τριπλή. Πρώτον, η Μητροπολιτική Αστυνομία αναγνωρίζει ότι το περιστατικό ήταν έγκλημα μαζικής δολοφονίας και μπορεί να ανοίξει ξανά την υπόθεση «αν έρθουν στο φως νέα στοιχεία». Δεύτερον, περιλαμβάνει πληροφορίες που δίνονται εμπιστευτικά στους ανακριτές και αυτό μπορεί να αποκαλύψει τις πολιτικές συμπάθειες πριν από πενήντα χρόνια των μαρτύρων, πολλοί από τους οποίους είναι πιθανότατα νεκροί τώρα. Τέλος, ορισμένες από τις πληροφορίες ενδέχεται να θέσουν σε κίνδυνο την εθνική ασφάλεια καθώς ενδέχεται να αποκαλύψουν την ταυτότητα των πηγών πληροφοριών, εάν υπάρχουν. Μετά από έφεση, η Μητροπολιτική Αστυνομία αποφάσισε τελικά ότι θα μπορούσε να αλλάξει τη στάση της , ότι δεν θα επιβεβαίωνε ούτε θα αρνούνταν ότι είχε άλλες πληροφορίες για το Charlie Oscar , σε επιβεβαίωση ότι στην πραγματικότητα δεν έχει . Όλες οι υπόλοιπες πληροφορίες που συγκεντρώθηκαν και διατηρήθηκαν από τη Μητροπολιτική Αστυνομία βρίσκονται σε αυτούς τους τρείς φακέλους στο Εθνικό Αρχείο . Η ομάδα υπεύθυνη για την Ελευθερία στην Πληροφόρηση (Freedom of Information) του Εθνικού Αρχείου εξήγησε στον συγγραφέα γιατί δεν θα δημοσιοποιήσει περαιτέρω έγγραφα από τους φακέλους της αστυνομίας[151].

«Ορισμένες από τις πληροφορίες που ζητήσατε αποκρύπτονται σύμφωνα με την ενότητα 23 (1) και 24 (1) εναλλακτικά. Το άρθρο 23 παράγραφος 1 εξαιρεί από τη δημοσιοποίηση πληροφορίες που κατέχει μια δημόσια αρχή εάν παρασχέθηκαν σε αυτήν τη δημόσια αρχή από φορείς που ασχολούνται με θέματα ασφαλείας ή εάν αυτές οι πληροφορίες σχετίζονται με αυτούς τους φορείς και το άρθρο 24 παράγραφος 1 εξαιρεί τις πληροφορίες από την αποκάλυψη εάν απαιτείται η εξαίρεση του για λόγους διασφάλισης της εθνικής ασφάλειας.
Τα τμήματα 23 (1) και 24 (1) αναφέρονται καθώς δεν είναι σκόπιμο, υπό τις περιστάσεις της υπόθεσης, να προσδιοριστεί ποιο από τις δύο εξαιρέσεις σχετίζεται ώστε να μην υπονομεύεται η εθνική ασφάλεια ή να αποκαλύπτεται η έκταση οποιασδήποτε εμπλοκής ή όχι των φορέων που ασχολούνται με θέματα ασφάλειας.
Το άρθρο 31 παράγραφος 1 του νόμου FOI (Freedom of Information) εξαιρεί πληροφορίες εάν η αποκάλυψή τους θα έθιγε ή θα ήταν πιθανό να βλάψει -

---

[151] Τα αρχεία είναι MEPO 2/11089, MEPO 2/11090 και HO 287/2146.

α) την πρόληψη ή τον εντοπισμό εγκληματικότητας
β) τη σύλληψη ή δίωξη παραβατών
γ) την απονομή της δικαιοσύνης.

...Η ενότητα 31(1)(α-γ) σχετίζεται σε ορισμένες από τις πληροφορίες στο ΜΕΡΟ 2/11089 & ΜΕΡΟ 2/11090, επειδή σχετίζεται με αποδεικτικά στοιχεία – με τη μορφή αναφορών έρευνας και σχετικές καταθέσεις μαρτύρων – σχετικά με ένα έγκλημα που παραμένει ανεξιχνίαστο. Οι πληροφορίες σχετίζονται άμεσα με την έρευνα για τη συντριβή του BEA Comet G-Argo (sic) πάνω από τη Μεσόγειο Θάλασσα που είχε ως αποτέλεσμα το θάνατο όλων των επιβατών και του πληρώματος, καθώς η Μητροπολιτική Αστυνομική Υπηρεσία θα ήθελε να παραμείνουν οι λεπτομέρειες της έρευνας εμπιστευτικές καθ'όλη τη διάρκεια ζωής οποιουδήποτε υποθετικού υπόπτου.

Σε σχέση με αυτούς τους συγκεκριμένους φακέλους, δεν είναι δυνατό να εντοπιστούν συγκεκριμένες πληροφορίες από αναφορές έρευνας και καταθέσεις μαρτύρων που θα μπορούσαν να δημοσιοποιηθούν χωρίς τον κίνδυνο να διακυβευθούν οι μελλοντικές αστυνομικές ενέργειες. Οι πληροφορίες που φαίνονται αβλαβείς μπορεί να έχουν σημασία για έναν έμπειρο ερευνητή αλλά δεν είναι άμεσα προφανείς στον απλό αναγνώστη, ή μπορούν να αποκτήσουν νέα σημασία υπό το πρίσμα των πρόσφατα ανακαλυφθέντων στοιχείων ή των εξελίξεων σε εγκληματολογικές ή ερευνητικές τεχνικές.

Η Μητροπολιτική Αστυνομία επιβεβαίωσε ότι είναι εξαιρετικά δύσκολο όταν εξετάζεται οποιαδήποτε ανεξιχνίαστη υπόθεση ως προς τη «σημαντική πιθανότητα μελλοντικής έρευνας», καθώς δεν μπορεί να προβλεφθεί ποιες πληροφορίες ή αποδεικτικά στοιχεία μπορεί να έρθουν στο φως στο μέλλον που θα οδηγήσουν σε ανανεωμένη έρευνα. Όλο και περισσότερες αστυνομικές υπηρεσίες σε όλη τη χώρα συγκροτούν ομάδες «ψυχρής υπόθεσης» για να εξετάσουν τους φακέλους υποθέσεών τους για ανεξιχνίαστες δολοφονίες. Μόλις πέρυσι, τα Εθνικά Αρχεία παρείχαν έγγραφα υποθέσεων στις αστυνομικές υπηρεσίες προκειμένου να βοηθήσουν στις έρευνες για μια ανεξιχνίαστη δολοφονία από τα τέλη της δεκαετίας του 1940. Ως εκ τούτου, εξετάζοντας αυτήν την εξαίρεση, πρέπει να αναγνωρίσουμε ότι εξακολουθεί να υπάρχει μια πιθανότητα, όσο απομακρυσμένη κι αν είναι, ότι η υπόθεση αυτή θα μπορούσε να διερευνηθεί κάποια στιγμή στο μέλλον και ότι οι πληροφορίες που περιέχονται σε αυτά τα αρχεία θα μπορούσαν να είναι σημαντικές για αυτήν.

Ως αποτέλεσμα, η ενότητα 31(1)(α-γ) έχει εφαρμοστεί σε όλες τις πληροφορίες που δημιουργούνται από τις ανακριτικές αρχές σε αυτά τα αρχεία, καθώς δεν είμαστε σε θέση να προσδιορίσουμε (και επομένως να διαγράψουμε) συγκεκριμένες πληροφορίες που ενδέχεται να διατεθούν στο δημόσιο τομέα χωρίς τον κίνδυνο να διακυβευτούν τυχόν μελλοντικές αστυνομικές ενέργειες.

Ο σκοπός αυτής της εξαίρεσης σε αυτήν την περίπτωση είναι η προστασία των λεπτομερειών που θα μπορούσαν να χρησιμοποιηθούν σε μια μελλοντική έρευνα σε περίπτωση που ένας ύποπτος εντοπιστεί, κατηγορηθεί και παραπεμφθεί σε δίκη. Η περίοδος κλεισίματος βασίζεται στην υπόθεση ότι ο ύποπτος ή οι ύποπτοι θα ήταν τουλάχιστον 16 ετών κατά τον κρίσιμο χρόνο.

Η πρόωρη δημοσιοποίηση αυτών των πληροφοριών μπορεί να είναι επιζήμια για οποιαδήποτε μελλοντική έρευνα και επακόλουθη δίωξη. Η δημοσιοποίηση σημαντικών πληροφοριών που θα μπορούσαν ενδεχομένως να θέσουν σε κίνδυνο μια μελλοντική δίωξη για φόνο δεν θα ήταν προς το δημόσιο συμφέρον. Ως εκ τούτου, έχει καθοριστεί ότι ο κίνδυνος προκατάληψης υπερτερεί του συλλογισμού για αποκάλυψη στη συγκεκριμένη περίπτωση και η εξαίρεση στο άρθρο 31 παράγραφος 1 στοιχείο α-γ) του νόμου περί ελευθερίας της πληροφόρησης ισχύει για τις πληροφορίες...

...Το τμήμα 38(1)(β) αφορά περιορισμένο αριθμό πληροφοριών σε αυτά τα αρχεία, επειδή περιέχει τις ταυτότητες των αστυνομικών πληροφοριοδοτών. Ενώ υπάρχει σημαντικό δημόσιο συμφέρον για τη διαφάνεια των αστυνομικών ερευνών και των μεθόδων διερεύνησής τους, στην περίπτωση αυτή, αυτό πρέπει να εξισορροπηθεί με τον κίνδυνο διάθεσης στο δημόσιο τομέα, πληροφοριών που θα μπορούσαν να θέσουν σε κίνδυνο την ασφάλεια ενός ατόμου. Έχει καθοριστεί ότι η απελευθέρωση της ταυτότητας αυτών των ατόμων θα μπορούσε να θέσει σε κίνδυνο αυτά τα άτομα και να θέσει σε κίνδυνο τη σωματική τους ασφάλεια εκθέτοντάς τους στον κίνδυνο σωματικής βλάβης από επιθέσεις αντιποίνων, επομένως εφαρμόζεται το άρθρο 38(1)(β)...

...Παραμένει η έμπειρη άποψη της Μητροπολιτικής Υπηρεσίας Αστυνομίας και κατά συνέπεια του TNA ότι, παρά την πάροδο του χρόνου, εξακολουθεί να υπάρχει πραγματική πιθανότητα κινδύνου για τα άτομα αυτά, τα οποία θα μπορούσαν να κινδυνεύσουν από αντίποινα ή αντίποινα εάν τα ονόματά τους κυκλοφορήσουν στο δημόσιο τομέα. Το κοινό χρειάζεται τη διαβεβαίωση να γνωρίζει ότι τα δικαιώματα πρόσβασης στο FOI δεν πρόκειται να επιτρέψουν οτιδήποτε εις βάρος του. Η δημοσιοποίηση πληροφοριών που ενδέχεται να εκθέσουν τα άτομα σε κίνδυνο σωματικής βλάβης ή να θέσουν σε κίνδυνο την ασφάλειά τους δεν θα ήταν προς το δημόσιο συμφέρον. Ως εκ τούτου, έχει καθοριστεί ότι ο κίνδυνος να τεθεί σε κίνδυνο η φυσική ασφάλεια των ατόμων που προσδιορίζονται σε αυτά τα αρχεία υπερτερεί σημαντικά των λόγων αποκάλυψης και η εξαίρεση στην ενότητα 38 παράγραφος 1 στοιχείο β) του νόμου FOI ισχύει για αυτές τις πληροφορίες...

...Στο αίτημά σας για εσωτερική επανεξέταση αναφέρατε ότι υπάρχουν ορισμένα ανοιχτά αρχεία που σχετίζονται με αυτήν την υπόθεση και επισημάνατε την έλλειψη συνοχής μεταξύ ανοικτών και κλειστών πληροφοριών.

Μπορώ να επιβεβαιώσω ότι συμβουλεύτηκα έναν αριθμό αρχείων AVIA σε σχέση με το αίτημα εσωτερικής επανεξέτασης και μπορώ να επιβεβαιώσω ότι δεν περιέχουν τις ίδιες πληροφορίες ή εκθέσεις έρευνας που περιλαμβάνονται στο ΜΕΡΟ 2/11089 και στο ΜΕΡΟ 2/11090. Αυτό συμβαίνει επειδή τα αρχεία της Μητροπολιτικής Αστυνομίας (αρχεία ΜΕΡΟ) συνήθως περιέχουν έγγραφα και αναφορές που σχετίζονται άμεσα με μια ποινική έρευνα, συμπεριλαμβανομένων καταθέσεων μαρτύρων, πληροφοριών σχετικά με πιθανούς υπόπτους, ιατροδικαστικά στοιχεία και πιθανές γραμμές έρευνας.

Το FOI Centre έχει παραπέμψει τρεις φακέλους, AVIA 101/225, AVIA 101/218 και AVIA 101/220[152] για έλεγχο στο πλαίσιο της Πολιτικής μας περί εκ νέου κλεισίματος.»

Οι κυπριακές αρχές ανέφεραν σε πηγές ότι δεν κατέχουν καμία πληροφορία για το περιστατικό, συμπεριλαμβανομένων των έξι αντιγράφων της έκθεσης της AIB που τους εστάλησαν το 1968. Το 2014, η Κυπριακή Αστυνομία εξέτασε την υπόθεση, σύμφωνα με προεδρικό διάταγμα, αλλά αυτό προφανώς δεν αποκάλυψε νέες πληροφορίες.

Είναι αδιανόητο στη σημερινή εποχή η ποινική έρευνα για την απώλεια του Charlie Oscar να ήταν τόσο ελαφριά. Οι έρευνες για παρόμοια γεγονότα, όπως το Lockerbie στο Ηνωμένο Βασίλειο και οι δύο ξεχωριστές απώλειες των Boeing 777 της Malaysia Airlines το 2014, ήταν πολυεθνικές υποθέσεις στις οποίες το κόστος, πολύ σωστά, δεν ήταν καθοριστικός παράγοντας. Με δύο αξιωματικούς αφοσιωμένους στη διερεύνηση του CY284, το σχέδιο έρευνας θα έπρεπε να ήταν συντριπτικό. Στην πραγματικότητα, φαίνεται ότι ο ντετέκτιβ Επιθεωρητής Browne χρειάστηκε (μόνο) περίπου έξι εβδομάδες για να διεξαγάγει μια έρευνα σε τρεις χώρες, προτού καταλήξει σε προφανή ικανοποίηση των δημοσίων υπαλλήλων ότι δεν υπήρχαν στοιχεία βάσει των οποίων να προχωρήσουν.

Το ίδιο το γεγονός ότι η Μητροπολιτική Αστυνομία συνεχίζει να διατηρεί τα γραπτά αποδεικτικά στοιχεία, σε περίπτωση που έρθουν στο φως νέα στοιχεία μισό αιώνα αργότερα, θέτει το ερώτημα γιατί οι έρευνές

---

[152] *AVIA101/218 – Οριοθέτηση της έρευνας. AVIA101/220 – Ημερολόγια και Τεκμηρίωση. AVIA101/225 – Αναφορές Παθολογίας. Αυτά τα αρχεία ήταν δημόσια διαθέσιμα τη στιγμή της σύνταξης και οι πληροφορίες τους χρησιμοποιούνται σε αυτό το βιβλίο, υπό την Open License V2.0.*

τους περατώθηκαν μετά από τόσο σύντομο χρονικό διάστημα. Αυτό δεν συνάδει με τις σύγχρονες έρευνες για τη δολοφονία μεμονωμένων ατόμων, πόσο μάλλον 66 ατόμων. Οι καιροί όντως έχουν αλλάξει.

Είναι σαφές από τη διαθέσιμη αλληλογραφία ότι το βρετανικό Υπουργείο Εξωτερικών ανησυχούσε περισσότερο να μην προκληθεί καμία αμηχανία στα συμφέροντά του από την αστυνομική έρευνα. Ο John Macrae του FO, στην επιστολή του της 13ης Φεβρουαρίου 1968 προς τον συνάδελφό του John Edmonds στην Άγκυρα, θεώρησε ότι η πιο πιθανή εξήγηση ήταν ότι το κίνητρο ήταν μια ασφαλιστική απάτη. Το αν αυτό μπορεί να ερμηνευθεί ως ένα αθώο σχόλιο για τις διάφορες θεωρίες ή ως ένδειξη του τρόπου με τον οποίο ήλπιζαν ότι θα προχωρήσει η έρευνα, είναι ανοιχτό σε εικασίες.

Το υπ. Εξωτερικών (Foreign Office) και, κατόπιν εντολής τους, ο Βοηθός Αστυνόμος Επιθεωρητής Brodie μπήκαν σε μεγάλο κόπο για να σταλεί μια «μυστική» επιστολή στην Αθήνα με εντολή στον Browne να μην εμβαθύνει σε πολιτικές γραμμές έρευνας χωρίς να συμβουλευτεί πρώτα το FO. Αυτό τείνει να υπονοεί ότι υπήρχαν ορισμένες σοβαρές ανησυχίες από την πλευρά του FO σχετικά με το πού θα μπορούσε να οδηγήσει η έρευνα. Δεν υπάρχει τρόπος να γνωρίζουμε ποια άλλη τεκμηρίωση θα μπορούσε να είχε αποκλειστεί από τα αρχεία, και δεν είναι καθόλου πιθανό ότι κάποιο ενοχοποιητικό υλικό θα είχε κρατηθεί στο αρχείο. Ωστόσο, η συνεχής διατήρηση υλικού για λόγους εθνικής ασφάλειας δείχνει ότι εξακολουθεί να υπάρχει ευαισθησία σχετικά με ορισμένες πληροφορίες ή την πηγή τους.

Κατά τη διάρκεια της «Κυπριακής Έκτακτης Ανάγκης» ή «απελευθερωτικού αγώνα», ανάλογα με την άποψη του αναγνώστη, ήταν γνωστό, όπως αναφέρθηκε προηγουμένως, ότι οι Βρετανικές Υπηρεσίες Ασφαλείας, ιδιαίτερα η Μυστική Υπηρεσία, ΜΙ6, μπορούσαν να βασιστούν σε μια ροή πληροφοριών από το εσωτερικό της ΕΟΚΑ. Μετά την παύση των εχθροπραξιών, σπάνια υπάρχει αμνηστία για πληροφοριοδότες που έχουν παράσχει ευαίσθητες πληροφορίες στον μηχανισμό ασφαλείας του εχθρού. Εάν οποιεσδήποτε τέτοιες πηγές ταυτοποιούνταν κατά λάθος, για παράδειγμα σε μια ποινική έρευνα, η ζωή τους θα εξακολουθούσε να τίθεται σε κίνδυνο. τα επτά χρόνια από την ανεξαρτησία της Κύπρου ήταν απίθανο να οδήγησαν σε μια στάση «συγχωρήστε και ξεχάστε» από την πλευρά των πιο αδίστακτων στοιχείων.

Έχει προταθεί στον συγγραφέα ότι ο Πολύκαρπος Γιωρκάτζης ήταν πληροφοριοδότης των Βρετανών. Ίσως οι διάφορες αποδράσεις του από τη βρετανική κράτηση κατά τη διάρκεια του αγώνα να ήταν κάτι παραπάνω από τυχαίες, αλλά να προκάλεσαν μια κρυφή ενημέρωση από τους χειριστές του. Εάν, πράγματι, συμβαίνει αυτό, μια τέτοια πηγή, που στηρίζεται στη συνεχιζόμενη διακριτικότητα μιας ξένης δύναμης, στο ανώτατο επίπεδο της κυβέρνησης, θα ήταν ένα αγαθό που αξίζει να διατηρηθεί. Η στάση όσων ήταν επιφορτισμένοι με τον χειρισμό του μπορεί να ήταν η απόλυτη απέχθεια για τη συμμετοχή του σε μαζικές δολοφονίες, μετριασμένη από την πραγματικότητα ότι η προσαγωγή του στη δικαιοσύνη δεν θα βοηθούσε τους χαμένους.

Η Μητροπολιτική Αστυνομία ισχυρίζεται μέχρι σήμερα ότι ενδέχεται να ξανανοίξει την ποινική έρευνα εάν υπάρχουν νέα στοιχεία. Οι φήμες, ότι ο Γιωρκάτζης είχε ενορχηστρώσει την πλοκή χρησιμοποιώντας τον Σολωμού ως φορέα, φαίνεται ότι ήρθαν στο φως λίγο καιρό αφότου ο ντετέκτιβ Έφορος Μπράουν και ο Ντετέκτιβ Σέρτζαντ Χιλ επέστρεψαν στην Αγγλία και προχώρησαν στις επόμενες υποθέσεις τους. Αν και τα στοιχεία από φήμες δεν είναι γενικά αποδεκτά, θα ήταν ένα καλό σημείο εκκίνησης να επανεξεταστεί αυτός ο τομέας του έργου των Browne and Hill. Σήμερα, ένας τόσο χαμηλών τόνων χαρακτήρας των αρχικών ερευνών, μαζί με τις υπονοούμενες οδηγίες του Υπουργείου Εξωτερικών και την έλλειψη των διαθέσιμων πόρων, θα εγείρουν σημαντικά ερωτήματα σχετικά με την αποτελεσματικότητα αυτής της έρευνας. Η δεκαετία του '60 ήταν μια παλαιότερη εποχή όπου η εξουσία και η επιρροή συγκεντρώνονταν στο κατεστημένο. Φορείς όπως τα κυβερνητικά τμήματα και οι αστυνομικές δυνάμεις δεν αναμενόταν να είναι διαφανείς και υπόλογοι στον βαθμό που είναι σήμερα. Είναι, σίγουρα, κάθε άλλο παρά αδύνατο ένας ανώτερος αξιωματικός της αστυνομίας να είχε λάβει υπόψη κάποιες σαφείς οδηγίες από το Υπουργείο Εξωτερικών για να επικεντρωθεί σε ορισμένους τομείς και να μην ανησυχεί πολύ για άλλους.

Η Μητροπολιτική Αστυνομία και το Υπουργείο Εσωτερικών στη Βρετανία ήταν πρόθυμες να ανοίξουν εκ νέου ψυχρές υποθέσεις και θα ήταν χρήσιμο να γίνει ενδελεχής επανεξέταση της αρχικής υπόθεσης, να εντοπιστούν χαμένες ευκαιρίες και να εξεταστούν νέα στοιχεία. Η μαζική δολοφονία 66 ανθρώπων σίγουρα αξίζει τον κόπο, παρά το πέρασμα μισού αιώνα από το ίδιο το έγκλημα. Η Μητροπολιτική Αστυνομική Υπηρεσία του 21ου αιώνα απέχει πολύ από την οργάνωση που ήταν τη δεκαετία του '60, και μπορούμε να ελπίζουμε ότι μπορεί να είναι διατεθειμένες να αναλάβουν αυτό το έργο, εάν τους τεθεί μια υπόθεση.

Ποιος βομβάρδισε το Charlie Oscar;

Η έρευνα του ατυχήματος απέδειξε πέραν πάσης αμφιβολίας ότι μια βόμβα κατέστρεψε το Charlie Oscar. Όχι μόνο υπήρχαν θετικά στοιχεία γι' αυτό, αλλά και κάθε άλλη εύλογη αιτία εξετάστηκε και αποκλείστηκε. Η τρομοκρατία ορίζεται από το NATO[153] ως «η παράνομη χρήση ή η απειλούμενη χρήση βίας ή βίας κατά ατόμων ή περιουσιακών στοιχείων σε μια προσπάθεια εξαναγκασμού ή εκφοβισμού κυβερνήσεων ή κοινωνιών να επιτύχουν πολιτικούς, θρησκευτικούς ή ιδεολογικούς στόχους.» Αν και υπήρχε μια προειδοποιητική επιστολή από το «Falcon Forces» τον Ιούνιο του 1967, προειδοποιώντας τις αεροπορικές εταιρείες που πετούν προς το Ισραήλ να σταματήσουν να το κάνουν, καμία ομάδα δεν ανέλαβε την ευθύνη για την καταστροφή του Charlie Oscar και τίποτα στα αρχεία των Εθνικών Αρχείων που έχουν δημοσιευτεί μέχρι στιγμής δεν υποδηλώνει ότι η τρομοκρατία τέθηκε ως κίνητρο.

Η απόπειρα δολοφονίας του Στρατηγού Γρίβα αποδείχθηκε εξαιρετικά ανθεκτική ως υποτιθέμενο κίνητρο για τη βομβιστική επίθεση στο Charlie Oscar. Ο Γρίβας στην πραγματικότητα ταξίδεψε από την Αθήνα στη Λευκωσία αργότερα την ίδια μέρα με τη συντριβή του Charlie Oscar. Η προσωπική αφήγηση του Λούη Λοΐζου και οι πληροφορίες που παραθέτει ο Λεωνίδας Λεωνίδου επιβεβαιώνουν χωριστά ότι ο Γρίβας σχεδίαζε αρχικά να ταξιδέψει με το CY284 και μόνο το Special Branch της Κύπρου, υπό την αιγίδα του Πολύκαρπου Γιωρκάτζη, λέει συγκεκριμένα διαφορετικά. Η ιδέα ότι ο Γρίβας ήταν ο επιδιωκόμενος στόχος δεν εξαφανίστηκε ποτέ, και πράγματι αναστήθηκε σε έναν τίτλο στο Birmingham Post στις 30 Αυγούστου 1968, υπό τον τίτλο, «*Ο θάνατος του Κομήτη– ήταν μια βόμβα που προοριζόταν για τον Γρίβα*». Που αντικρούστηκε την επόμενη μέρα με άρθρο των The Sunday Times, που έλεγε στους αναγνώστες του, με τίτλο «*Χαμένος κρίκος στη συντριβή του κομήτη*», ότι ο Παπαπέτρου διέπραξε τη θηριωδία για την πληρωμή των ασφαλειών ζωής του. Ένα από αυτά πρέπει να ήταν «ψευδείς ειδήσεις- fake news » στη σημερινή γλώσσα. Θα μπορούσε να θεωρηθεί ότι το δεύτερο άρθρο, πλούσιο σε λεπτομέρειες από τα δεινά του Νίκου Παπαπέτρου, είχε τροφοδοτηθεί στους δημοσιογράφους της εφημερίδας από πηγές με έννομο συμφέρον να διασφαλίσουν ότι η ιστορία θα καταγράψει αυτή την εκδοχή της αλήθειας.

Φαίνεται ότι κανείς δεν υπέδειξε δημόσια ότι υπήρχε τουρκική διάσταση στην καταστροφή του CY284 και πουθενά στα προσβάσιμα αρχεία του Εθνικού Αρχείου δεν προκύπτει αυτή η πιθανότητα. Ωστόσο, οι Τούρκοι,

---

[153] *Γλωσσάρι Όρων και Ορισμών NATO, 2014.*

περισσότερο από οποιονδήποτε άλλον εκτός από έναν θανάσιμο πολιτικό αντίπαλο, θα μπορούσαν να είχαν σαφές ενδιαφέρον για την απομάκρυνση από το βήμα του Στρατηγού Γρίβα. Είναι, ίσως, σημαντικό ότι η κατάρριψη του Charlie Oscar προηγήθηκε παρά ακολούθησε μια κλιμάκωση της βίας, για την οποία ο Γρίβας θεωρήθηκε υπεύθυνος από πολλούς.

Κατά την έρευνα αυτού του βιβλίου, προτάθηκε στον συγγραφέα ότι η βρετανική μυστική υπηρεσία ή η CIA μπορεί να ήταν πίσω από την πλοκή. Ωστόσο, δεν είναι ξεκάθαρο τι θα είχαν να κερδίσουν άμεσα από τον θάνατο του Γρίβα, ειδικά αν σκεφτεί κανείς το ακραίο μέτρο που θα είχε η καταστροφή ενός αεροσκάφους.

Με τον Γρίβα να μην κρύβεται πλέον κρυφά στους πίσω δρόμους της Λεμεσού ή της Λευκωσίας, αυτές οι οργανώσεις σίγουρα θα μπορούσαν να τον ξεκάνουν, αν το ήθελαν, χωρίς να δολοφονήσουν 66 αθώους ανθρώπους. Θα ήταν κόλαση αν η βρετανική μυστική υπηρεσία κατέστρεφε ένα βρετανικό αεροσκάφος που μετέφερε Βρετανούς επιβάτες και πλήρωμα. Ομοίως, οι Αμερικανοί θα ήταν απίθανο να καταστρέψουν ένα πολιτικό αεροσκάφος που ανήκε σε έναν από τους σημαντικότερους συμμάχους τους, σκόπιμα τουλάχιστον, και ειδικά όταν η αξιοπρέπειά τους στην παγκόσμια σκηνή μειώνονταν λόγω του Βιετνάμ. Είναι, ωστόσο, ενδιαφέρον να σημειωθεί ότι ένα μυθιστόρημα, το *Cat's Paw*[154], βασίζεται ακριβώς στην υπόθεση που απορρίπτεται εδώ, ότι η βόμβα τοποθετείται από έναν πράκτορα της CIA που εργάζεται σε συνεργασία με τους Βρετανούς. Το βιβλίο ήταν, σύμφωνα με τον συγγραφέα του, απλώς ένα έργο φαντασίας εμπνευσμένο από την ίντριγκα γύρω από την απώλεια του Charlie Oscar.

Γύρω από τα διαπιστωμένα γεγονότα της καταστροφής του CY284 υπάρχουν και άλλα στοιχεία που σίγουρα δεν μειώνουν την αύρα της υπονόμευσης. Το βάθος της Μεσογείου ποικίλει αλλά είναι μεγαλύτερο στην περιοχή του Ιονίου. Το Charlie Oscar έπεσε κοντά στην τάφρο του Στράβωνα (Strabo Trench) . Μπορεί να ήταν σύμπτωση, αλλά εξίσου θα μπορούσε να ήταν από σχέδιο. Εάν η βόμβα είχε ενεργοποιηθεί από την αρχική κλήση ασυρμάτου καθώς το Charlie Oscar επρόκειτο να εισέλθει στην Περιοχή Πληροφοριών Πτήσεων Λευκωσίας, ο κατασκευαστής της θα ήταν εύλογα σίγουρος ότι το αεροσκάφος θα έπεφτε σε δυσπρόσιτο μέρος της θάλασσας. Η τεχνολογία για την κατασκευή τέτοιων συσκευών ήταν σίγουρα διαθέσιμη εκείνη την εποχή. Ενώ μια συσκευή χρονισμού θα μπορούσε να προκαλέσει την έκρηξη στο ίδιο σημείο, θα ήταν λιγότερο

---

[154] *Cat's Paw* βιβλίο *(μυθοπλασία)* του *Christopher Malinger (Malinger Publishing, 2017).*

ακριβής και θα υπόκειται στην πιθανότητα καθυστερημένης αναχώρησης, όπως είχε συμβεί με τον Hermes G-ALDW το 1956.

Οι εικασίες για το κίνητρο της καταστροφής του CY284 επικεντρώθηκαν εξαρχής σε μια απόπειρα δολοφονίας κατά του Στρατηγού Γεώργιου Γρίβα. Αυτό φέρεται να επιβεβαιώθηκε από την ΜΙ6 σύμφωνα με την The Sunday Telegraph στις 26 Νοεμβρίου 1967 αν και ο συγγραφέας θυμάται ότι η θεωρία αναφέρθηκε στο BBC News λίγο μετά τη συντριβή. Αργότερα, στις 12 Οκτωβρίου, ο αναγνώστης θα θυμηθεί ότι η Ολυμπιακή Αεροπορία άλλαξε το αεροσκάφος που είχε καθοριστεί για την πτήση Αθήνα – Λευκωσία. Παρόλο που ο Veal θεώρησε ότι αυτό θα μπορούσε να ήταν προληπτικό μέτρο, υποδηλώνει άμεση ανησυχία εκ μέρους της Ολυμπιακής Αεροπορίας ότι τα αεροσκάφη της, τώρα που επρόκειτο να μεταφέρουν τον Στρατηγό, ενδέχεται να ήτν επίσης στόχος.

Μισό αιώνα αργότερα, πολλοί Ελληνοκύπριοι παραμένουν πεπεισμένοι για αυτό το κίνητρο. Οι κυπριακές αρχές, ωστόσο, δεν αποδέχθηκαν ποτέ τη θεωρία. Η εναλλακτική υπόθεση, όπως σημειώθηκε και εξετάστηκε παραπάνω, ήταν ότι ο Νίκος Παπαπέτρου είχε καταστρέψει το αεροσκάφος, με μια βόμβα που κουβάλησε είτε ο ίδιος είτε κάποιος άλλος εν αγνοία του. Αυτή η πιθανή αιτία ενισχύθηκε μέσω της αστυνομικής έρευνας και ήταν σαφώς πιο πολιτικά βολική για το Βρετανικό Υπουργείο Εξωτερικών παρά η απώλεια ενός αεροσκάφους και των επιβαινόντων ως παράπλευρη ζημιά από μια απόπειρα δολοφονίας.

Προκειμένου να εντοπιστεί το άτομο που είναι πιο πιθανό να έφερε τη βόμβα στο αεροσκάφος, είναι απαραίτητο να διευκρινιστεί πού ακριβώς βρισκόταν η βόμβα και ποιος καθόταν απάνω της. Το λεξιλόγιο που χρησιμοποιείται περιγράφοντας το σημείο της συσκευής είναι σημαντικό. Υπάρχουν πολλές εκδοχές για την ακριβή θέση και μια σύνθετη εκτίμηση, με βάση τη ζημιά στο μαξιλάρι του καθίσματος, ήταν πως αυτή ήταν μεταξύ έντεκα και δώδεκα ίντσες κάτω από το πίσω μέρος του μαξιλαριού του καθίσματος, μέχρι τέσσερις ίντσες πίσω από το πίσω άκρο και τρεις ίντσες στο πλάι του μαξιλαριού. Επομένως, όταν ο Jones και άλλοι περιγράφουν τη βόμβα ως κάτω από ένα από τα αριθμημένα καθίσματα, αυτό δεν σημαίνει ότι ήταν εντελώς από κάτω. Μάλλον, ήταν πάνω κάτω ακριβώς κάτω από την πίσω πλευρά αυτού του καθίσματος, ελαφρώς εκτός κέντρου και στο πάτωμα. Εκεί όπου ένας επιβάτης θα τοποθετούσε μια τσάντα, κάτω από το πίσω μέρος του καθίσματος μπροστά του, αλλά όπου θα ήταν εύκολα προσβάσιμη. Για παράδειγμα, εάν η βόμβα περιγραφόταν στα αρχεία ως «κάτω από το κάθισμα 4Α», αυτό σημαίνει ότι πιθανότατα βρισκόταν στο χώρο των ποδιών του καθίσματος 3Α.

Ο Jones στήριξε την υπόθεσή του ότι η συσκευή βρισκόταν κάτω από την πλάτη των καθισμάτων 4Α ή 5Α βάση του ότι ο φορέας της βόμβας ήταν κατά πάση πιθανότητα μεταξύ των αγνοουμένων επιβατών και ότι ο επιβάτης με τα θραύσματα, Αχιλλέα Αφατίτης, καθόταν στη σειρά καθισμάτων πίσω , για να εξηγηθεί και το μοτίβο των τραυματισμών του. Επιπλέον, υπέθεσε ότι οι επιβάτες που ταξίδεψαν από το Λονδίνο και συνέχιζαν για τη Λευκωσία από την Αθήνα δεν άλλαξαν θέσεις και ότι όλοι της ομάδας των Μαρτύρων του Ιεχωβά κάθονταν στο μπλοκ καθισμάτων στην πίσω καμπίνα, κυρίως στις σειρές 4 έως 7 περιλαμβανομένης. Όσο λογικές κι αν είναι αυτές οι υποθέσεις, είναι υποθέσεις, ωστόσο παραμένουν υποθέσεις. Το σχεδιάγραμμα θέσεων στην έκθεση RAE του Fred Jones δείχνει ότι ο κύριος και η κυρία Θιάκου, και οι δύο μέλη της ομάδας των Μαρτύρων του Ιεχωβά, κάθονταν στις θέσεις 16D και 16E, απέναντι από τον Αβραάμ Σολωμού. Αυτό δείχνει ότι, στην πραγματικότητα, τουλάχιστον κάποιοι από την ομάδα ήταν πολύ χαρούμενοι που βρήκαν κενές θέσεις σε άλλα μέρη του αεροσκάφους.

Αν κατά την εκτίμηση του Jones, ο Νίκος Παπαπέτρου κουβαλούσε τη συσκευή, θα καθόταν σε μια από τις θέσεις που ο Jones στη συνέχεια πίστευε ότι θα είχε καταληφθεί από Μάρτυρα του Ιεχωβά, ενώ ο Παπαπέτρου δεν ήταν μέλος αυτής της ομάδας.

Υπάρχουν πολύ ισχυρές έμμεσες αποδείξεις ότι ο Jones πλησίαζε πολύ στην εκτίμησή του για το πού εξερράγη η βόμβα, καθώς υπάρχει συγκέντρωση αγνοουμένων επιβατών κατά μήκος της αριστερής πλευράς της καμπίνας , και επιβατών με ακραία τραύματα προς τα πίσω.

Ο Jones ήταν το μόνο άτομο που εκτίμησε πού βρισκόταν η συσκευή όταν πυροδοτήθηκε και ήταν ένας άνθρωπος με ισχυρή φήμη ότι εξήγαγε τα αίτια των απωλειών αεροσκαφών χρησιμοποιώντας άψογη λογική. Επομένως, η καλύτερη εικασία παραμένει ότι η συσκευή όντως εξερράγη κάπου προς το πίσω μέρος της καμπίνας. Αυτό θα μπορούσε επίσης να οφείλεται σε απώλεια ελέγχου του αεροσκάφους ως αποτέλεσμα ζημιάς στο υδραυλικό σύστημα και άλλα χειριστήρια ακριβώς κάτω από τα καθίσματα που υποδεικνύονται από τον Jones.

Η πιθανότητα ενός αγνώστου προσώπου είτε στο αεροδρόμιο Heathrow είτε στο αεροδρόμιο του Ελληνικού να μεταφέρει λαθραία τη βόμβα στο αεροσκάφος, μελετήθηκε κατά την έρευνα αλλά η βόμβα δεν ήταν τοποθετημένη έτσι ώστε να ήταν καλά κρυμμένη. Από την υποτιθέμενη θέση, η συσκευή θα ήταν καθαρά ορατή στον επιβάτη που κάθεται στο κάθισμα δίπλα της. Αν κάποιος είχε την ευκαιρία να την τοποθετήσει, η συσκευή θα μπορούσε να ήταν καλύτερα κρυμμένη στο περίβλημα του σωσίβιου ή στη σχάρα καπέλων.

Τα πιο πιθανά άτομα να είχαν φέρει μέσα στο αεροπλάνο τη βόμβα ήταν είτε ο Νίκος Παπαπέτρου είτε ο Αβραάμ Σολωμού, με αποτέλεσμα δύο πιθανά κίνητρα για την καταστροφή του Charlie Oscar. Ο Λεωνίδας Λεωνίδου και ο Ελευθέριος Παπαδόπουλος δήλωσαν ότι ο Αβραάμ Σολωμού μετέφερε τη βόμβα στο αεροσκάφος, εν αγνοία του. Ο Σολωμού κατονομάστηκε σε σχέση με τη βομβιστική επίθεση σε πρώιμο στάδιο, όταν ακόμη διενεργούνταν η έρευνα. Καθώς ο δημοσιογράφος δεν αποκάλυψε την πηγή του, είναι αδύνατο να γνωρίζουμε από πού προερχόντουσαν εκείνες οι πληροφορίες, αλλά είναι αρκετά σαφές. Ενώ τα δημοσιεύματα των εφημερίδων τον Νοέμβριο του 1967 δεν ισχυρίζονται ότι ο Σολωμού μετέφερε τη βόμβα ο ίδιος στο αεροπλάνο, τονίζουν ότι η παρουσία του μπορεί να έκανε τους συνωμότες να αναγνωρίσουν το CY284 ως την πτήση με την οποία θα ταξίδευε ο Γρίβας. Αυτό θα έπρεπε να είχε άμεσο ενδιαφέρον για την αστυνομική έρευνα, αλλά στην πραγματικότητα είχε ως αποτέλεσμα να ληφθούν μόνο δύο καταθέσεις.

Ωστόσο, όπως προαναφέρθηκε, οι πληροφορίες στην έκθεση των παθολόγων δείχνουν ότι ο Σολωμού δεν ήταν δίπλα στη βόμβα όταν εξερράγη, καθώς τα τραύματά του δεν έδειχναν σημάδια τραυμάτων από την έκρηξη. Επίσης, το σώμα του ανασύρθηκε στο βόρειο πεδίο συντριμμιών, υποδεικνύοντας ότι βρισκόταν στο μπροστινό τμήμα του αεροσκάφους όταν έσπασε η άτρακτος. Μια εύλογη εξήγηση είναι ότι ο Σολωμού καθόταν στο πίσω μέρος της τουριστικής καμπίνας, μαζί με τους περισσότερους επιβάτες που ξεκινούσαν το ταξίδι τους στην Αθήνα. Μισή ώρα πριν από την προσγείωση δεν είναι παράλογο ένας επιβάτης να έχει εγκαταλείψει τη θέση του για να χρησιμοποιήσει την τουαλέτα του αεροσκάφους για να φρεσκαριστεί, και επομένως ο Σολωμού θα μπορούσε εύκολα να ήταν μακριά από τη βόμβα όταν εξερράγη. Μαζί με άλλους επιβάτες κοντά στη ζημιά, θα έπρεπε στη συνέχεια να προχωρήσει πιο μπροστά καθώς η θέση του δεν θα υπήρχε πλέον. Αυτό θα εξηγούσε τα τραύματά του και το γεγονός ότι βρέθηκε με επιβάτες από το μπροστινό μέρος του αεροσκάφους όταν χτύπησε στη θάλασσα.

Η απουσία της σορού του Νίκου Παπαπέτρου σημαίνει ότι η εγγύτητά του με τη βόμβα δεν μπορεί να αποδειχθεί ή να διαψευστεί. Άλλοι επιβάτες έλειπαν επίσης από άλλα σημεία της καμπίνας και έτσι η εξαφάνισή του από μόνη της δεν αποδεικνύει τίποτα. Οι αναφορές για τη συμμετοχή του στο λαθρεμπόριο, τα σχόλιά του σχετικά με το ότι θα ήταν καλύτερα αν πέθαινε και η άθλια οικονομική του κατάσταση δεν επιβεβαιώνονται και η προέλευσή τους είναι αβέβαιη. Υπάρχει μόνο ένα άρθρο εφημερίδας που δίνει ουσία σε αυτές τις έννοιες. Η οικογένεια Παπαπέτρου θεωρεί το άρθρο στους Sunday Times να είναι ψέμα. Φυσικά, το γεγονός ότι ο Παπαπέτρου συνήψε τέσσερεις ασφάλειες ζωής θα δημιουργούσε υποψίες και, αν υποτεθεί ότι ισχύει, θα αποτελούσε σαφέστατη ένδειξη ότι κάτι δεν πήγαινε καλά. Αλλά για να αποδειχθεί η ευθύνη του Παπαπέτρου πέρα από εύλογη αμφιβολία, ή ακόμα και στο ισοζύγιο πιθανοτήτων, απαιτούνται περισσότερες πληροφορίες για τον άνδρα και όλες τις συνθήκες γύρω από το τελικό, καλά ασφαλισμένο, ταξίδι του.

Υπήρχαν πιθανά προηγούμενα για τις συνωμοσίες που αποδίδονταν στον Παπαπέτρου. Στις 16 Νοεμβρίου 1959, ένα αεροσκάφος Douglas DC-7B της National Airlines που μετέφερε 42 επιβάτες και πλήρωμα εξαφανίστηκε ενώ πετούσε πάνω από τον Κόλπο του Μεξικού μεταξύ του Μαϊάμι και της Νέας Ορλεάνης. Σε μια υπόθεση με ομοιότητες με το Charlie Oscar, βρέθηκαν διάσπαρτα συντρίμμια και δέκα πτώματα. Μια θεωρία που προωθήθηκε ήταν ότι ο δράστης ξεγέλασε έναν άλλο άνδρα για να ταξιδέψει στη θέση του, υπήρχε μια βόμβα στις αποσκευές του και το σχέδιο ήταν η γυναίκα του δράστη να εισπράξει την ασφάλεια ζωής του. Ο εν λόγω επιβάτης, ο William Taylor, είχε επιβιβαστεί στην πτήση χρησιμοποιώντας ένα εισιτήριο σε κάποιο Robert Spears, έναν καταδικασθέντα εγκληματία. Πιστεύεται ότι οι δύο άνδρες είχαν γίνει φίλοι ενώ βρίσκονταν στη φυλακή. Πέρα από την χρήση του εισιτηρίου του Spears, ο Taylor είχε αγοράσει δική του ασφάλεια ζωής στο αεροδρόμιο του Μαϊάμι πριν από την αναχώρηση. Η πρώην σύζυγός του έκανε αίτηση να εισπράξει την ασφάλεια μετά το δυστύχημα και έτσι φανερώθηκε η αντικατάσταση του επιβάτη. Ο Spears εξαφανίστηκε μετά το δυστύχημα, αλλά συνελήφθη στο Φοίνιξ της Αριζόνα το 1969 στο αυτοκίνητο του Taylor. Ποτέ δεν κατηγορήθηκε σε σχέση με την απώλεια του αεροσκάφους και δεν υπήρχαν ποτέ στοιχεία που να συνδέουν τον Spears απευθείας με την καταστροφή.

Λιγότερο από δύο μήνες αργότερα, στις 6 Ιανουαρίου 1960, χάθηκε ένα άλλο αεροσκάφος της National Airlines, μαζί με τις ζωές των 34 επιβατών και του πληρώματος. Η πτήση 2511, από τη Νέα Υόρκη στο Μαϊάμι, έγινε με ένα Douglas DC6, το οποίο ήταν ένα υποκατάστατο του Boeing 707 που αρχικά είχε προγραμματιστεί να κάνει την πτήση αλλά το οποίο δεν ήταν σε κατάσταση λειτουργίας. Το αεροσκάφος συνετρίβη κοντά στην πόλη της Βολιβίας, στη Βόρεια Καρολίνα. Ένα μέρος του σκελετού του αεροσκάφους βρέθηκε περίπου 25 μίλια από τα υπόλοιπα συντρίμμια. Όπως και με το CY284, η παθολογική εξέταση έδειξε ότι το σώμα ενός επιβάτη, του Julian Frank, είχε ουσιαστικά στοιχεία από έκρηξη βόμβας δυναμίτη. Ο Frank βρισκόταν υπό έρευνα για υπεξαίρεση έως και ενός εκατομμυρίου δολαρίων σε φιλανθρωπικές απάτες. Είχε ασφάλειες ζωής συνολικού ύψους $900.000 συμπεριλαμβανομένης της ασφαλιστικής κάλυψης που αγόρασε την ημέρα της πτήσης. Το Συμβούλιο Πολιτικής Αεροναυτικής (CAB), το οποίο διεξήγαγε την έρευνα, κατέληξε στο συμπέρασμα ότι το αεροσκάφος καταρρίφθηκε από έκρηξη δυναμίτη στην καμπίνα επιβατών, κάτω από το δεξί κάθισμα στη σειρά 7. Αυτό ήταν κοντά στο κάθισμα του Frank, αλλά όπως και η έκθεση της AIB για το Charlie Oscar η CAB δεν απέδωσε ευθύνες σε κανένα επώνυμο πρόσωπο. Η υπόθεση παραπέμφθηκε στο FBI αλλά δεν ολοκληρώθηκε ποτέ. Παραμένει ανοιχτή μέχρι σήμερα.

Στις 22 Μαΐου 1962, ένα Boeing 707 εκτελούσε την πτήση 11 της Continental Airlines από το Σικάγο στο Κάνσας Σίτι. 42 λεπτά μετά την πτήση, το αεροσκάφος εξαφανίστηκε από το ραντάρ ATC. Μια έκρηξη σημειώθηκε στην πίσω δεξιά τουαλέτα, που οδήγησε στον διαχωρισμό 38 ποδιών της ατράκτου. Το 707 συνετρίβη σε χωράφι κοντά στο Unionville του Μιζούρι, με την απώλεια των 45 ψυχών που επέβαιναν σ΄αυτό. Ο Thomas Doty, ένας επιβάτης της πτήσης, είχε επιβιβαστεί την τελευταία στιγμή και, όπως ο Frank, είχε αγοράσει πρόσθετη ασφάλεια λίγο πριν από την αναχώρηση. Καλυπτόταν με το ποσό $300.000 δολαρίων και ερευνούνταν ως ύποπτος για ένοπλη ληστεία.

Ο Doty είχε αγοράσει επίσης έξι ξυλάκια δυναμίτη λίγο πριν την πτήση. Το FBI κατέληξε στο συμπέρασμα ότι ο Doty ανατινάχθηκε στην πίσω τουαλέτα, έχοντας κουβαλήσει τον δυναμίτη στον χαρτοφύλακά του και στη συνέχεια τον τοποθέτησε στον κάδο χρησιμοποιημένης πετσέτας. Η χήρα του δεν έλαβε την ασφαλιστική πληρωμή.

Οι τρεις περιπτώσεις που αναφέρθηκαν ήταν όλες εσωτερικές πτήσεις στις Ηνωμένες Πολιτείες και οι επιθέσεις πραγματοποιήθηκαν πριν παρθούν αυστηρά μέτρα ασφάλειας στα αεροδρόμια. Οι δύο τελευταίες αφορούσαν συσκευές που αποτελούνταν από δυναμίτη (η πρώτη περίπτωση δεν είχε πραγματικά στοιχεία έκρηξης καθώς το αεροσκάφος, όπως το Charlie Oscar, συνετρίβη στη θάλασσα και ανασύρθηκαν μικρά συντρίμμια).

Η υποτιθέμενη πλοκή του Παπαπέτρου ήταν πολύπλοκη. Το άρθρο της εφημερίδας *«Πέθανε ο σαμποτέρ σε συντριβή Κομήτη;»* το οποίο εμφανίστηκε στην *Cyprus Mail* στις 5 Σεπτεμβρίου 1968 ανέφερε ότι «...*η αστυνομία πιστεύει ότι με κάποιο τρόπο ξεγέλασε έναν άλλον άνδρα να πετάξει στη θέση του, χρησιμοποιώντας το εισιτήριό του και τη θέση του.*» Θα ήταν πολύ δύσκολο να πραγματοποιηθεί αυτό το τέχνασμα σε μια διεθνή πτήση αλλά όχι αδύνατη. Ο Παπαπέτρου θα έπρεπε να δανείσει στο ακούσιο θύμα το διαβατήριό του, οπότε ο άνδρας θα έπρεπε να έχει εύλογη ομοιότητα μαζί του. Το πώς θα μπορούσε ο Παπαπέτρου να πείσει τον άλλον να αναλάβει το έργο δεν εξηγείται, αν και είναι εφικτό ο Παπαπέτρου να είχε υποσχεθεί στον άνδρα ένα σημαντικό χρηματικό ποσό. Είναι επίσης εύλογο ότι ο άλλος άνδρας ήταν συνάδελφος λαθρέμπορος, ο οποίος νόμιζε ότι το δέμα στην τσάντα του ήταν λαθρεμπόριο και ότι η πλαστοπροσωπία ενός άλλου λαθρέμπορου ήταν μέρος ενός πονηρού σχεδίου για να ξεγελάσουν τις αρχές. Εάν ο άνδρας με τα έγγραφα του Παπαπέτρου ήταν απατεώνας, τότε πιθανότατα θα υπήρχε ένα άτομο παρόμοιο με τον Παπαπέτρου που δηλώθηκε αγνοούμενο λίγο μετά το δυστύχημα.

Φυσικά, οποιαδήποτε συνωμοσία, είτε αυτοκτονία είτε δολοφονία, δεν θα είχε πετύχει χωρίς ο Παπαπέτρου να μπορέσει να αποκτήσει εκρηκτικά και να κατασκευάσει μια βόμβα ή ίσως ένα τέτοιο μηχανισμό από έναν κατασκευαστή βομβών. Οποιοδήποτε από αυτά θα απαιτούσε πολύ εξειδικευμένες γνώσεις και υποδηλώνει ότι είχε ένα ακόμη πιο σκοτεινό παρελθόν από αυτό ενός λαθρέμπορου. Αν ο Παπαπέτρου, όπως προτείνεται στο άρθρο που επικαλείται ο Colin Wilson, είχε προηγουμένως διακινήσει εκρηκτικά, πιθανότατα θα ήξερε ότι ο μόνος ασφαλής τρόπος για να το κάνει θα ήταν να διασφαλίσει ότι δεν είχαν πυροκροτητή μαζί τους. Το γεγονός ότι σημειώθηκε η έκρηξη σημαίνει ότι η συσκευή ήταν πράγματι βιώσιμη και επομένως ήταν εγγενώς μη ασφαλής.

Για να εκτιμηθεί εάν ο Παπαπέτρου είχε τη δυνατότητα να αποκτήσει ή να κατασκευάσει βιώσιμο εκρηκτικό μηχανισμό που να περιλαμβάνει πλαστικό εκρηκτικό στρατιωτικής ποιότητας, χρειάζονται περισσότερες πληροφορίες για το ιστορικό του. Αν κουβαλούσε τη συσκευή και την είχε κατασκευάσει μόνος του, θα είχε αναγκαστικά μάθει πώς να το κάνει, είτε μέσω στρατιωτικής εκπαίδευσης ή αλλιώς με την ΕΟΚΑ. Η δήλωση του Special Branch της Κύπρου ότι δεν είχε ονόματα επιβατών στο αρχείο του που να ενδιαφέρουν καθιστά το τελευταίο να φαίνεται απίθανο. Αν θεωρούσαν ένοχο τον Παπαπέτρου, και δεν είχε εμπλακεί σε πολιτική πλοκή, θα είχαν βάσιμους λόγους να τον υποψιαστούν και να το πουν. Είναι πολύ απίθανο ένας έμπειρος κατασκευαστής βομβών να ξέφευγε της αντίληψή τους, ειδικά καθώς ο αριθμός των ακτιβιστών της ΕΟΚΑ με την απαιτούμενη τεχνογνωσία θα ήταν σχετικά μικρός. Ελάχιστες πληροφορίες είναι διαθέσιμες για τον Νίκο Παπαπέτρου, εκτός από αυτές που έχουν ήδη εξεταστεί. Θα ήταν σίγουρα πιο επιβλητική περίπτωση αν ήταν γνωστός αγωνιστής της ΕΟΚΑ. η ηλικία του θα το επιβεβαίωνε. Θα μπορούσε, εξίσου, να είχε υπηρετήσει στις ένοπλες δυνάμεις και να διατηρούσε ακόμα επαφές για να τον βοηθήσουν στο έργο του.

Ένα άλλο ερώτημα είναι γιατί ο Παπαπέτρου θα είχε ανατιναχθεί στο ταξίδι της επιστροφής, αν επρόκειτο για αυτοκτονία. Αν είχε κατασκευάσει ή αποκτήσει τη συσκευή στην Κύπρο, όπως θα ήταν πιο πιθανό, θα ήταν αναμενόμενο ότι θα είχε πραγματοποιήσει την πράξη σε πτήση από την Κύπρο. Διαφορετικά, θα έπρεπε να πάρει τη βόμβα στην πτήση της εξερχόμενης πτήσης και στη συνέχεια να τη μεταφέρει στην Αθήνα πριν την ενεργοποιήσει στο δρόμο για το σπίτι. Αυτό στερείται αξιοπιστίας, πράγμα που σημαίνει ότι θα έπρεπε να αποκτήσει τη συσκευή, ή τα συστατικά μέρη της, στην Ελλάδα.

Το άρθρο των *Sunday Times* αναφέρει ότι μια ασφαλιστική εταιρεία πλήρωσε για το συμβόλαιο του Παπαπέτρου, αν και οι υπόλοιπες περίμεναν την ολοκλήρωση της αστυνομικής έρευνας. Δεν έγινε επίσημη δήλωση ότι η έρευνα είχε οριστικοποιηθεί και ότι το κίνητρο πιστεύεται ότι ήταν η ασφαλιστική απάτη. Η γραμμή της αστυνομίας ήταν ότι δεν υπήρχαν επαρκή στοιχεία για να κινηθεί εναντίον οποιουδήποτε ατόμου. Αυτό είναι, ίσως, κατανοητό καθώς η σορός του Παπαπέτρου δεν ανασύρθηκε ποτέ, επομένως δεν κατέστη δυνατό να εξακριβωθεί εάν όντως είχε ταξιδέψει στην πτήση, χάνοντας τη ζωή του στη διαδικασία. Αν είχε πείσει κάποιον άλλον να πάρει τη θέση του και τα ασφαλιστήρια συμβόλαια τελικά τιμούνταν, ο μόνος τρόπος που θα μπορούσε να ωφεληθεί θα ήταν εάν η γυναίκα του είχε συνεννοηθεί μαζί του. Θα ήταν μια ανιδιοτελής, αν και διεστραμμένη, πράξη να εξαφανιστεί ο Παπαπέτρου αφήνοντας τη γυναίκα του, στην απόλυτη αθωότητα, με όλα τα χρήματα και δεν είναι ξεκάθαρο πώς θα είχε χτίσει μια νέα ζωή για τον εαυτό του χωρίς εμφανή μέσα υποστήριξης. Θα μπορούσε, ωστόσο, να φαινόταν εξαιρετικά ύποπτο εάν η κυρία Παπαπέτρου είχε λάβει τα χρήματα και έφευγε αμέσως από την πόλη.

Αν ο Παπαπέτρου είχε πυροδοτήσει τη βόμβα ο ίδιος, είναι πολύ απίθανο αυτή να βρισκόταν στο πάτωμα της καμπίνας, εν μέρει κάτω από το κάθισμα, εκείνη τη στιγμή. Ως εκ τούτου, θα έπρεπε να την είχε διευθετήσει να εκραγεί και μετά να κάτσει και να περιμένει να έρθει το τέλος. Αν είχε δώσει τη βόμβα σε ένα άβουλο κολλητό του (που τηρούσε εν πλήρη άγνοια) τίθεται το ερώτημα ποιος μπορεί να ήταν αυτός. Θα ήταν χρήσιμο να εξακριβωθεί εάν κάποιος συνεργάτης, αρκετά παρόμοιος ώστε να αντέξει τον έλεγχο ενός ελέγχου διαβατηρίου, είχε δηλωθεί αγνοούμενος στην Ελλάδα ή την Κύπρο εκείνη την εποχή. Εάν η πλοκή ήταν, όπως έχει ο ισχυρισμός, να επιτρέψει στην οικογένειά του να εισπράξει την ασφάλεια και να συναντηθεί μαζί τους, αυτό θα σήμαινε ότι ολόκληρη η οικογένεια θα έφευγε από την Κύπρο λίγο μετά το συμβάν και θα ξεκινούσε τη νέα της ζωή κάπου αλλού, υποθέτοντας ότι οι ασφάλειες ζωής θα είχαν πληρωθεί.

Η οικογένεια Παπαπέτρου, όπως αναφέρθηκε νωρίτερα και επιβεβαιώθηκε σε συνδιάσκεψη με τον συγγραφέα, υποστηρίζει ότι η θεωρία ότι ήταν υπεύθυνος είναι εντελώς αναληθής. Πέρασε το χρόνο του στην Αθήνα πριν από την πτήση μένοντας με την κόρη του, η οποία θυμάται ξεκάθαρα ότι δεν υπήρχε τίποτα ασυνήθιστο στη συμπεριφορά του. Επιπλέον, μέχρι να έρθει σε επαφή με τον συγγραφέα στο πλαίσιο αυτού του βιβλίου, η οικογένεια δεν είχε καν συνειδητοποιήσει ότι ο Νίκος Παπαπέτρου ήταν ένας ύποπτος.

Δεν αποκλείεται η θεωρία ότι ευθύνεται ο Παπαπέτρου να κυκλοφόρησε από τις βρετανικές αρχές σε επιλεγμένους δημοσιογράφους προκειμένου να κλείσει το όλο θέμα . Εάν ήταν τελείως αθώος, η ζημιά που προκλήθηκε στη φήμη του και στην φήμη της οικογένειάς του θα ήταν τεράστια, αλλά οι νεκροί δεν μπορούν, σύμφωνα με το βρετανικό δίκαιο, να κατηγορηθούν με λίβελλο. Αν, όμως, η βόμβα είχε όντως πυροδοτηθεί από τον Παπαπέτρου, ή από τον άβουλο κολλητό του, η ιστορία θα είχε τελειώσει εκεί.

Αυτοκτονία-βόμβα ήταν η εξήγηση που προτιμούσε το Φόρεϊν Όφις, ειδικά καθώς θα είχαν αποφευχθεί οι διπλωματικές ευαισθησίες γύρω από οποιοδήποτε εξ αποστάσεως πολιτικό κίνητρο για την επίθεση. Οι δημοσιογράφοι των *Sunday Times* ήταν προφανώς πολύ ενδελεχείς και ικανοί και συνέθεσαν μια εύλογη εξήγηση για το γιατί ο Παπαπέτρου μπορεί να ήθελε να βάλει τέλος στη ζωή του με τέτοιο τρόπο. Φαίνεται ότι ήσαν εξαιρετικά καλά ενημερωμένοι και δυστυχώς η θεωρία τους δεν μπορεί να συγκριθεί με την έκθεση της αστυνομίας. Φαίνονται τόσο καλά ενημερωμένοι που ο αναγνώστης μπορεί να κάνει εικασίες για το αν τους δόθηκαν πληροφορίες από, ή για λογαριασμό, των ανακριτών. Ο λόγος για να γίνει αυτό μπορεί να ήταν για να διασφαλιστεί ότι η ιστορία της ασφαλιστικής απάτης θα γινόταν αποδεκτή ως η αλήθεια, και ως εκ τούτου τελικά έριξε τη θεωρία του Γρίβα.

Θα ήταν μια παράξενη σύμπτωση και μια άγρια ειρωνεία εάν ο Στρατηγός Γρίβας, του οποίου η ζωή θεωρήθηκε ότι κινδύνευε δυνητικά από έναν πολιτικό αντίπαλο, είχε χάσει τη ζωή του επειδή απλώς ταξίδευε με ένα αεροσκάφος που καταστράφηκε σε μια βομβιστική επίθεση που έγινε από άλλο επιβάτη για ασφαλιστική απάτη.

Τα έγγραφα που σχετίζονται με την αστυνομική έρευνα και τη συμμετοχή του Βρετανικού Υπουργείου Εσωτερικών και του Βρετανικού Υπουργείου Εξωτερικών στον απόηχο της καταστροφής, δεν περιέχουν πληροφορίες που να υποστηρίζουν τον ισχυρισμό ότι ο Γρίβας σχεδίαζε να πετάξει με το CY284. Η μόνη σημαντική αναφορά είναι το μήνυμα προς τον John Veal από την MI5, που μεταδίδει τον ισχυρισμό του Special Branch της Κύπρου ότι ο Γρίβας δεν ταξίδεψε ποτέ εκείνη την ώρα της ημέρας. Το 2018, ο συγγραφέας ταξίδεψε στην Κύπρο για την παρουσίαση της πρώτης έκδοσης του *Bealine Charlie Oscar*. Δημόσια συνάντηση και συνέντευξη Τύπου διοργάνωσε στη Λεμεσό ο Κύπριος δημοσιογράφος και ραδιοφωνικός και τηλεοπτικός αναλυτής Χρήστος Ιακώβου. Σε αυτήν παραβρέθηκαν περίπου εβδομήντα δημοσιογράφοι, συγγενείς των θυμάτων, και άλλοι ενδιαφερόμενοι, μεταξύ των οποίων και πρώην μέλος της ΕΟΚΑ που είχε προφυλάξει τον Γρίβα κατά τη διάρκεια του αγώνος. Στο τέλος του συνεδρίου, ο γιος του Αβραάμ Σολωμού, ο οποίος ήταν οκτώ ημερών όταν σκοτώθηκε ο πατέρας του, είπε στη συνάντηση ότι ο πατέρας του είχε πράγματι παρευρεθεί στην Κυπριακή Πρεσβεία στην Αθήνα λίγο πριν επιβιβαστεί της πτήσης. Η οικογένειά του είχε ενημερωθεί ότι δόθηκαν δύο φάκελοι στον Σολωμού, που απευθύνονταν στον Πολύκαρπο Γιωρκάτζη και στον Πρόεδρο Μακάριο. Οι φάκελοι ήταν προφανώς πολύ μικροί για να περιέχουν μια βόμβα. Ο κ. Σολωμού πρόσθεσε, με θλίψη, ότι σε όλη του τη ζωή σήκωσε το βάρος να κατηγορείται ότι είναι γιος μαζικού δολοφόνου.

Ο συγγραφέας και δημοσιογράφος Νίκος Παπαναστασίου έχει κάνει ξεχωριστές έρευνες σε διάφορες χρονικές στιγμές και έχει δώσει περισσότερες λεπτομέρειες για το τι συνέβη στη συνέχεια.

Εκρηκτικός μηχανισμός, σε «ασφαλή» κατάσταση, μεταφέρθηκε με courier στην Κυπριακή Πρεσβεία στην Αθήνα. Πιστεύεται ότι ο courier ήταν ο Αβραάμ Σολωμού, ο οποίος δεν γνώριζε τίποτα για το περιεχόμενό του. Ο Σολωμού ταξίδευε με μια συνάδελφο, τη δεσποινίς Ιακωβίδου. Ο Σολωμού κλήθηκε πίσω στην Πρεσβεία το βράδυ της 11ης Οκτωβρίου και του είπαν να πάρει ένα πακέτο υπό διπλωματική κάλυψη στον Γιωρκάτζη. Τέτοιες δραστηριότητες ήταν μέρος της ρουτίνας των καθηκόντων του Σολωμού. Το πακέτο επρόκειτο να μεταφερθεί σε τσάντα καμπίνας. Στην οικογένεια του Αβραάμ Σολωμού λέχθηκε ότι η τσάντα καμπίνας που περιείχε τη βόμβα δόθηκε στον Σολωμού στην Κυπριακή Πρεσβεία[155]. Η βόμβα ήταν ένας πλήρως αυτοσχέδιος εκρηκτικός μηχανισμός με χρονόμετρο, ο οποίος είχε ρυθμιστεί λίγο πριν πακεταριστεί και παραδοθεί στο Σολωμού. Ο μηχανισμός είχε χρονομετρηθεί ώστε να εκραγεί στο βαθύτερο σημείο της Μεσογείου στη διαδρομή από Αθήνα προς Λευκωσία. Αναμενόταν ότι δεν θα υπήρχε κανένα ίχνος του αεροπλάνου, επομένως καμία πλοκή δεν μπορούσε να αποδειχθεί στη συνέχεια.

Το άτομο που φέρεται να παρέδωσε την τσάντα στον Σολωμού ονομάστηκε στον συγγραφέα ως ο Ντίνος Μιχαηλίδης, ο οποίος ως γνωστόν βρισκόταν στην Κυπριακή Πρεσβεία στην Αθήνα την ώρα της βομβιστικής επίθεσης. Δεν αναφέρθηκε αν ο Μιχαηλίδης γνώριζε ή όχι το περιεχόμενό του. Αργότερα ανέβηκε σε υψηλό αξίωμα, υπηρετώντας ως υπουργός Εσωτερικών υπό τους Προέδρους Κυπριανού και Κληρίδη. Ωστόσο, το 1999, ο Μιχαηλίδης παραιτήθηκε μετά από καταγγελίες για διαφθορά. Το 2015, ο Μιχαηλίδης και ο γιος του καταδικάστηκαν από δικαστήριο στην Αθήνα για διευκόλυνση πληρωμών στον πρώην υπουργό Άμυνας της Ελλάδας Άκη Τσοχατζόπουλο ως μίζες από μια συμφωνία για να αγοράσει η Ελλάδα ρωσικής κατασκευής αντιαεροπορικούς πυραύλους. Ο Μιχαηλίδης και ο γιος του καταδικάστηκαν σε δεκαπέντε χρόνια φυλάκιση, αλλά επετράπη στον Ντίνο Μιχαηλίδη να παραμείνει σε κατ' οίκον περιορισμό μέχρι το θάνατό του τον Απρίλιο του 2020[156]. Παρά τις προσπάθειες εκ μέρους του συγγραφέα να επικοινωνήσει με τον Μιχαηλίδη, αυτές ήταν ανεπιτυχείς και ο Μιχαηλίδης φαίνεται ότι πήρε το μυστικό της αληθινής ανάμειξης ή της αθωότητάς του στον τάφο του. Αυτές οι πληροφορίες διαβιβάστηκαν στις αρμόδιες αρχές, αλλά κατά τη στιγμή της σύνταξης δεν είναι γνωστό ποια, εάν κάποια, δράση ελήφθη.

Ο Σολωμού ταξίδεψε στο αεροδρόμιο της Αθήνας με όχημα της Κυπριακής Πρεσβείας και, στο αεροδρόμιο, διαπίστωσε ότι είχε φέρει κατά λάθος το αεροπορικό εισιτήριο της κυρίας Ιακωβίδου και όχι το δικό του. Αυτό είχε ως αποτέλεσμα την κάπως έντονη συζήτηση που αναφέρθηκε από το προσωπικό του check-in στο αεροδρόμιο της Αθήνας.

---

[155] *Οικογένεια Σολωμού στη Φανούλλα Αργυρού σε ανοιχτή συνάντηση στη Λεμεσό, Οκτώβριος 2018.*

[156] *Cyprus Mail, 7 Απριλίου 2020, ο πρώην υπουργός Εσωτερικών Ντίνος Μιχαηλίδης πεθαίνει σε ηλικία 83 ετών.*

Ο Γρίβας, στο μεταξύ, είχε ετοιμαστεί να ταξιδέψει στο αεροδρόμιο της Αθήνας και βρισκόταν στο αυτοκίνητό του και περίμενε τον οδηγό του. Τον κάλεσαν πίσω για να δεχτεί ένα τηλεφώνημα. Ο Νεόφυτος Σοφοκλέους, ο επιτελικός αξιωματικός του (στη Κύπρο) είχε αντιληφθεί αυτό που περιγράφεται ως «ύποπτη δραστηριότητα των ανδρών του Γιωρκάτζη». Λέχθηκε στον Γρίβα ότι έπρεπε να παραστεί σε επείγουσα συνάντηση με το ελληνικό στρατιωτικό προσωπικό και ότι θα έπρεπε να πάρει την πτήση της Ολυμπιακής Αεροπορίας αργότερα στις 12 Οκτωβρίου. Σύμφωνα με τον βιογράφο του Γρίβα, Λεωνίδα Λεωνίδου, πέρασε αρκετός καιρός πριν ο Γρίβας αντιληφθεί ότι είχε κρατηθεί για το CY284.

Ο Γρίβας γεννήθηκε το 1897 στην Κύπρο, φοιτώντας στο Παγκύπριο Γυμνάσιο. Το 1916 έφυγε από την Κύπρο μετακομίζοντας στην Ελλάδα. Παίρνοντας την υπηκοότητα της τελευταίας χώρας, γράφτηκε στη Στρατιωτική Ακαδημία Αθηνών. Μετά την ολοκλήρωση των στρατιωτικών του σπουδών, συμπεριλαμβανομένου του χρόνου στην École Militaire στο Παρίσι, ο Γρίβας εντάχθηκε στον Ελληνικό Στρατό ως υπολοχαγός. Ο ελληνοτουρκικός πόλεμος βρισκόταν σε εξέλιξη και τοποθετήθηκε κανονικά στη 10η Μεραρχία του Ελληνικού Στρατού, πολεμώντας στη σημερινή Τουρκία. Συμμετείχε στη Μάχη του Σαγγαρίου, το 1921. Ο Γρίβας παρασημοφορήθηκε για την ανδρεία του στη μάχη και προήχθη σε Υπολοχαγό. Ακολούθησαν περαιτέρω προαγωγές και το 1935 ο Γρίβας έγινε Ταγματάρχης.

Μετά το ξέσπασμα του Β' Παγκοσμίου Πολέμου, ο Γρίβας τοποθετήθηκε στο Αλβανικό Μέτωπο, υπηρετώντας ως Αρχηγός του Επιτελείου της 2ης Μεραρχίας. Όταν η Ελλάδα καταλήφθηκε από τις δυνάμεις του Άξονα, δημιούργησε και ηγήθηκε μιας μικρής αντάρτικης οργάνωσης, που αρχικά ονομαζόταν Στρατιωτική Οργάνωση Γρίβας και αργότερα γνωστή ως Επιχείρηση Χ, την οποία αποτελούσαν αξιωματικοί του Ελληνικού Στρατού. Η ομάδα, η οποία πέρα από τη μάχη κατά των κατακτητών ήταν αντι-κομμουνιστική, εστίασε τις επιχειρήσεις της σε περιοχές των προαστίων της Αθήνας και απέκτησε δύο έως τρεις χιλιάδες μέλη.

Το 1946 ο Γρίβας συνταξιοδοτήθηκε από τον Ελληνικό Στρατό με τον βαθμό του Συνταγματάρχη. Στην Αθήνα γνώρισε τον Αρχιεπίσκοπο Μακάριο Γ' ο οποίος του ζήτησε τελικά να ενώσουν τις δυνάμεις του και να προετοιμαστούν για ένοπλο αγώνα στην Κύπρο. Μετά από κάποιες μυστικές επισκέψεις στο νησί το 1954 και μυστικές αποστολές όπλων, η εξέγερση της ΕΟΚΑ ξεκίνησε την 1η Απριλίου 1955 για την Ένωση της Κύπρου με την Ελλάδα. Με τον Μακάριο να αποδέχεται την Ανεξαρτησία, ο Γρίβας έφυγε από το νησί το 1959.

Κατά την άποψη πολλών Κυπρίων, ο κύριος ύποπτος για μια τέτοια απόπειρα κατά της ζωής του Γρίβα είναι ο Πολύκαρπος Γιωρκάτζης, υπουργός Εσωτερικών στην κυβέρνηση Μακαρίου. Σε αυτόν τον ρόλο, πολλοί θεώρησαν ότι ο Γιωρκάτζης έστησε ένα τεράστιο δίκτυο πληροφοριών και έγινε διαβόητος χρησιμοποιώντας την αστυνομία ως τον «προσωπικό του στρατό».

Ο Γιωρκάτζης γεννήθηκε το 1932. Κατά τη διάρκεια της «Κυπριακής Έκτακτης Ανάγκης» ήταν ενεργό μέλος της ΕΟΚΑ, με το όνομα «*Λαέρτης*». Ανέβηκε σε βαθμίδα και έγινε διοικητής των επιχειρήσεων της ΕΟΚΑ στη Λευκωσία. Συνελήφθη από τους Βρετανούς σε πολλές περιπτώσεις και κατάφερε ο Γιωρκάτζης να δραπετεύσει σε πολλές περιπτώσεις, κερδίζοντας το παρατσούκλι «*Χουντίνι*». Αυτή η φαινομενική ικανότητα να δραπετεύει από την κράτηση όποτε τον αιχμαλώτιζαν θα μπορούσε εύκολα να γεννήσει την υποψία ότι ο Γιωρκάτζης ήταν πληροφοριοδότης των βρετανικών δυνάμεων. Όπως σε κάθε σύγκρουση, οι πληροφορίες και παρακολουθήσεις (information and intelligence) μεταβιβάζονταν από τη μια πλευρά στην άλλη από συμπαθούντες ή πληρωμένους πράκτορες. Αυτό ίσχυε και για την έκτακτη ανάγκη της Κύπρου. Πράγματι, ο Πέτρος Γεωργιάδης είχε αναφέρει στην επιστολή του από τη φυλακή προς τον Πρόεδρο της ΒΕΑ στις 9 Ιανουαρίου 1968 ότι ο ίδιος ο Γρίβας διηύθυνε μια «ομάδα εξοντώσεως προδοτών».

Το συμπέρασμα από τη συμβουλή του Υπουργείου Εξωτερικών στον ντετέκτιβ Επιθεωρητή Browne ήταν ότι είχαν ανησυχίες για το τι θα μπορούσε να αποκαλυφθεί εάν ο ντετέκτιβ άρχιζε να κάνει σε βάθος έρευνες στην πολιτική αρένα.

Σύμφωνα με ορισμένες πηγές, ο Γρίβας δεν ήταν η μόνη εξέχουσα προσωπικότητα που είχε αρχικά κρατηθεί στο CY284 στις 12 Οκτωβρίου 1967. Η κυπριακή εφημερίδα Φιλελεύθερος δημοσίευσε άρθρο την 1η Οκτωβρίου 2006, αναφέροντας ότι ο Μιχαλάκης Τριανταφυλλίδης, τότε Γενικός Εισαγγελέας και επικεφαλής του Ανωτάτου Δικαστηρίου της Κύπρου επρόκειτο να ταξιδέψει με το αεροσκάφος από την Αθήνα αλλά άλλαξε γνώμη και επέστρεψε στο νησί με πλοίο. Ο Γλαύκος Κληρίδης, τότε Πρόεδρος της Βουλής των Αντιπροσώπων και αργότερα Πρόεδρος της Κυπριακής Δημοκρατίας, επρόκειτο επίσης να πετάξει με BE/CY284 από το Λονδίνο, αλλά άλλαξε γνώμη λόγω κάποιων περαιτέρω εργασιών στην Αγγλία[157].

---

[157] *Ο Πολύβιος και ο Ρένος Γεωργίου, αδέρφια του επιβάτη Σωτήρη Γεωργίου, γνώριζαν καλά τον Κληρίδη και τον συνάντησαν πολλές φορές τα χρόνια μετά το δυστύχημα. Ο Κληρίδης γνώριζε ότι ο Σωτήρης είχε σκοτωθεί και συζήτησε την καταστροφή πολλές φορές. Σε καμία στιγμή ο Πολύβιος δεν θυμάται τον Κληρίδη να είπε ότι του είχαν κάνει κράτηση στην πτήση. (Ο Πολύβιος Γεωργίου σε συνομιλία με τον συγγραφέα, 2018).*

Μια κυπριακή πηγή, που επιθυμεί να διατηρήσει την ανωνυμία της, είπε στον συγγραφέα το 2018:

«Ο Γιωρκάτζης είχε πολλούς λόγους να θέλει να ξεφορτωθεί τον Γρίβα, καθώς ο Γρίβας συχνά εναντιωνόταν στην προσπάθεια αυτού του ανθρώπου να ελέγξει τις ένοπλες δυνάμεις της Κύπρου. Το γεγονός ότι οι δύο άλλοι κυβερνητικοί αξιωματούχοι, ο Τριανταφυλλίδης και ο Κληρίδης, έκλεισαν θέσεις σε αυτή την πτήση αλλά ακύρωσαν τα ταξίδια τους την τελευταία στιγμή υποδηλώνει ότι γνώριζαν για τη βόμβα και είχαν κάνει κράτηση μόνο στην πτήση για να εξασφαλίσουν ότι ο Γρίβας δεν θα υποψιαζόταν οτιδήποτε. Επίσης, τη βόμβα μετέφερε ως δέμα συνεργαζόμενος με το υπουργείο Εξωτερικών. Έπρεπε να πάει στη θέση που του είχαν ορίσει, να αφήσει την τσάντα του και μετά να βρει κάποια δικαιολογία να κατεβεί από το αεροπλάνο.

Κάποιες πηγές αναφέρουν ότι μόλις επιβιβάστηκε και συνειδητοποιώντας ότι ο Γρίβας δεν επέβαινε, αποφάσισε να ταξιδέψει για να μην δημιουργήσει υποψία και να ακινητοποιούσε το χρονόμετρο του εκρηκτικού μηχανισμού, αλλά απέτυχε, σκοτώνοντας τον εαυτό του και τους άλλους.

Άλλοι συγγραφείς έχουν προτείνει ότι η ελληνική χούντα ήταν πίσω από αυτό, αλλά εκείνη την εποχή δεν είχαν πραγματικά κίνητρα να το κάνουν, καθώς ο Γρίβας εκείνη την εποχή δεν ήταν εναντίον τους και θεωρήθηκε από τους Έλληνες πιο χρήσιμος για αυτούς ως 'εργαλείο'. Το τρελό είναι ότι αν διαβάσετε τις περισσότερες πηγές (αν και στα ελληνικά) η ιστορία είναι εμφανής, αλλά κανείς δεν την έχει αναγνωρίσει ως πλήρη πλοκή. Οι πολύπλοκες σχέσεις μεταξύ του Προέδρου Μακαρίου, του Στρατηγού Γρίβα, της ελληνικής χούντας και του Πολύκαρπου Γιωρκάτζη, παραμένουν ένα ευαίσθητο θέμα μεταξύ των Κυπρίων μέχρι σήμερα. Στον Γιωρκάτζη δεν άρεσε η ανεξαρτησία που ήθελε ο Γρίβας για τις στρατιωτικές δυνάμεις και μάλλον φοβόταν τη δημοτικότητά του».

Ο Νεόφυτος Σοφοκλέους, υπεύθυνος του γραφείου του Γρίβα, ήταν στενός συνεργάτης και έμπιστος του Στρατηγού. Ο κ. Σοφοκλέους είπε στον συγγραφέα, μέσω του Χρήστου Ιακώβου, ότι είχε κάνει προσωπικά τη κράτηση για τον Στρατηγό Γρίβα να ταξιδέψει με την πτήση CY284 από Αθήνα στη Λευκωσία την Πέμπτη 12 Οκτωβρίου 1967. Τηλεφώνησε στην Cyprus Airways για να ακυρώσει την κράτηση και επικοινώνησε με τον Στρατηγό Γρίβα να του πει την αλλαγή σχεδίου. Ο κ. Σοφοκλέους είπε ότι δεν γνώριζε άμεσα την απειλή για το CY284, νόμιζε ότι αυτή θα πραγματοποιείτο εναντίον του Γρίβα κατά ή μετά την άφιξή του στην Κύπρο. Για το λόγο αυτό, δεν ειδοποίησε την αεροπορική εταιρεία για την πιθανότητα επίθεσης.

«Ο Γιωρκάτζης μου ζήτησε να του αποκαλύψω τις κινήσεις του Γρίβα πριν την επίθεση στο αεροσκάφος, αλλά αρνήθηκα, καθώς ήξερα γιατί το ζητούσε ο Γιωρκάτζης. Η επίθεση (εναντίον του Γρίβα) δεν μπορούσε να γίνει στην Κύπρο. Μίλησα με τον κουνιάδο του Γρίβα και τον συμβούλεψα να μην επιβιβαστεί στο αεροσκάφος, καθώς ήξερα ότι ο Τύπος θα γνώριζε ότι ο Γρίβας ταξίδευε στην Κύπρο, οπότε θα το ήξερε και ο Γιωρκάτζης. Ο Αβραάμ Σολωμού (ο courier) απλά στάλθηκε από τον Γιωρκάτζη ως αρνί στη σφαγή, όπως και τα άλλα 65 άτομα στην πτήση. Ο Γιωρκάτζης και ο Μακάριος δεν μετάνιωσαν καθόλου για την επίθεση, δεν έριξαν βλέφαρο. Πήγαν ακόμη και στις κηδείες κάποιων από τα θύματα, όπως ο γιατρός Ιωαννίδης.

Ο Γιωρκάτζης ενεργούσε με εντολή του Μακαρίου, όπως και τις περισσότερες φορές. Είχε κάνει και διάφορες άλλες πράξεις για τον Μακάριο αλλά το πρόβλημα είναι ότι δεν υπάρχουν συγκεκριμένα στοιχεία. Ο Γιωρκάτζης είχε κάποιες ενοχοποιητικές ηχογραφήσεις του Μακαρίου, όπως υποψιάζομαι ότι είχαν και άλλα πρακτορεία. Αυτός είναι ο λόγος για τον οποίο οι φάκελοι (της Μητροπολιτικής Αστυνομίας) είναι σφραγισμένοι μέχρι το 2040. Πολλοί πολιτικοί, ορισμένοι σε πολύ υψηλό επίπεδο, και διάφοροι άλλοι άνθρωποι τα γνωρίζουν όλα αυτά, αλλά δεν υπάρχουν συγκεκριμένα στοιχεία μέχρι να ανοίξουν τα αρχεία. Κανείς δεν θέλει τώρα να ανακατέψει το παρελθόν. Η κυπριακή κυβέρνηση ανησυχεί για αποζημιώσεις και η βρετανική κυβέρνηση ανησυχεί για πολιτικούς λόγους».

Η εισήγηση ότι ο Πρόεδρος Μακάριος γνώριζε, ή έστω υποκίνησε, τον βομβαρδισμό του CY284 εγείρει πολύ σοβαρούς πολιτικούς προβληματισμούς. Θα ήταν αρκετά κακό για έναν εν ενεργεία υπουργό της κυβέρνησης να οργανώσει την καταστροφή ενός πολιτικού αεροσκάφους που μετέφερε, μεταξύ άλλων, υπηκόους της χώρας του. Το να δέχεται ή, χειρότερα, να κατευθύνει ο αρχηγός του κράτους αυτής της χώρας, μια τέτοια πράξη την επιδεινώνει ακόμα περισσότερο. Η σκόπιμη καταστροφή ενός αεροσκάφους που ανήκει στον αερομεταφορέα άλλης χώρας, που μεταφέρει υπηκόους τριών άλλων εθνών, θα θεωρείται σήμερα ισότιμη με πράξη πολέμου. Ο απόηχος του Λόκερμπι, που είδε τη Λιβύη να χαρακτηρίζεται ως κράτος παρία, είναι ένα παράδειγμα για δυστυχήματα τέτοιας εμβέλειας. Θα μπορούσε κανείς να καταλάβει γιατί το βρετανικό Υπουργείο Εξωτερικών θα έβλεπε την εμφάνιση αποδεικτικών στοιχείων «μιας πολιτικής διάστασης» να είναι γεμάτη κινδύνους.

Το ερώτημα γιατί οι υποτιθέμενοι πολιτικοί συνεργάτες του Γρίβα μπορεί να θέλουν να τον σκοτώσουν απαιτεί λεπτομερή εξήγηση. Ο Γρίβας, ο οποίος τελικά έλεγχε ακόμη την Ανώτατη Στρατιωτική Διοίκηση Άμυνας Κύπρου, βρισκόταν σε αντίθεση με τον Κύπριο πρόεδρο,

Αρχιεπίσκοπο Μακάριο Γ'. Εν τω μεταξύ, τον Μακάριο υποστήριζε (τότε) ο Πολύκαρπος Γιωρκάτζης, ο οποίος έλεγχε ήδη την αστυνομία και το Special Branch της Κύπρου. Ορισμένες ενέργειες κατά του τουρκοκυπριακού πληθυσμού είχαν κατευθυνθεί από τον Μακάριο, τις οποίες ο Γρίβας ήταν απρόθυμος να υποστηρίξει. Έχοντας λοιπόν διαβουλεύσεις στην Αθήνα με τον Έλληνα υπουργό Άμυνας και τους αρχηγούς του στρατού, ο Γρίβας σκόπευε να επιστρέψει στην Κύπρο και να κρατήσει μια τέτοια στάση αντίθετη με τα συμφέροντα του Γιωρκάτζη και του Μακαρίου.

Στο πλαίσιο των πολύπλοκων σχέσεων μεταξύ του Μακαρίου, του Γιωρκάτζη και του Γρίβα, γίνεται αρκετά αξιόπιστο ότι μπορούν να στραφούν ο ένας εναντίον του άλλου. Ο ερευνητής και συγγραφέας[158] Λεωνίδας Λεωνίδου προσέφερε το ακόλουθο σκεπτικό στον συγγραφέα το 2021:

• Μετά τις Συμφωνίες του Λονδίνου και της Ζυρίχης τον Φεβρουάριο του 1959, η Κύπρος έγινε ανεξάρτητη και στη συνέχεια ο Μακάριος εξελέγη Πρόεδρος. Με τον καιρό βολεύτηκε με την ανεξαρτησία της Κύπρου και με τον ρόλο του ως Προέδρου. Δεν επεδίωκε πλέον ενεργά την ένωση με την Ελλάδα. Ο Γρίβας, που παρέμενε ενθουσιώδης υπέρμαχος της Ένωσης, είχε επιστρέψει στην Ελλάδα, όπου προήχθη σε Στρατηγό.

• Το 1964, με τις αυξανόμενες διαμάχες μεταξύ της ελληνοκυπριακής και της τουρκοκυπριακής κοινότητας και οι απειλές της Τουρκίας για στρατιωτική εισβολή, ο Γρίβας επέστρεψε στην Κύπρο και οργάνωσε τις ελληνοκυπριακές ένοπλες δυνάμεις και ανέλαβε ως Ανώτατος Διοικητής τους. Πέρα από τη μεραρχία 900 Ελλήνων στρατιωτών που καθορίζεται από τις συμφωνίες της Ζυρίχης και του Λονδίνου, η ελληνική κυβέρνηση παρείχε επιπλέον 10.000 στρατιώτες (Ελληνική Μεραρχία) για να βοηθήσουν στην προστασία της ελληνοκυπριακής κοινότητας. Ο Μακάριος, εν τω μεταξύ, είχε διορίσει τον Γιωρκάτζη στη θέση του Υπουργού Εσωτερικών, η οποία περιελάμβανε τον έλεγχο της αστυνομίας. Ο Γιωρκάτζης, σύμφωνα με τους σχολιαστές, επιδίωξε επίσης τον έλεγχο των ενόπλων δυνάμεων για να του δώσουν πλήρη έλεγχο στην εξουσία, προς υποστήριξη του Μακαρίου.

• Μέχρι το 1967, ο Μακάριος πήρε για τα καλά τα ηνία της εξουσίας και θεωρήθηκε ότι τίποτα δεν συνέβαινε στην πολιτική ζωή του νησιού χωρίς τη ρήση του. Η σχέση του όμως με την Ελλάδα είχε επιδεινωθεί και

---

[158] *Λεωνίδας Λεωνίδου, Γιώργος Γρίβας Διγενής – Βιογραφία, Τόμ. III, σελ. 349–419 (2008).Ν.Β. αυτό το βιβλίο είναι στα ελληνικά.*

ο Γεώργιος Παπανδρέου, του οποίου η πολιτική καριέρα κορυφώθηκε σε τρεις περιόδους ως πρωθυπουργός της Ελλάδας, τελευταία το 1964/5, ήθελε τον Μακάριο να καθαιρείται. Αν και το βάρος του Γρίβα στην Ελλάδα αποδυναμώθηκε μετά το στρατιωτικό πραξικόπημα τον Απρίλιο του 1967 (ο Γρίβας ήταν αντίθετος με τους Συνταγματάρχες που είχαν καταλάβει την εξουσία), ο Μακάριος εξακολουθούσε να βλέπει τον Γρίβα ως απειλή. Ο Γρίβας, όμως, με την Εθνική Φρουρά και την Ελληνική Μεραρχία πίσω του, ήταν σε ισχυρή θέση.

• Ο Μακάριος ήθελε να αναλάβει σθεναρή δράση στην Κύπρο για να αποφύγει τη δημιουργία περαιτέρω τουρκοκυπριακών καντονιών (ζώνες υπό τουρκικό έλεγχο). Ο Γρίβας επέμενε ότι η αστυνομία έπρεπε να αναλάβει και ήτο αντίθετος στη χρήση των στρατιωτικών δυνάμεων κάτω από την διοίκησή του καθώς πίστευε ότι θα έπρεπε (οι στρατιωτικές δυνάμεις) να χρησιμοποιηθούν για την αντιμετώπιση εξωτερικών απειλών μόνο. Αυτό έκανε τον Γιωρκάτζη ακόμα πιο αποφασισμένο να αναλάβει την Εθνική Φρουρά.

• Ο Μακάριος αποφάσισε ότι ήταν η κατάλληλη στιγμή να απομακρύνει τον Γρίβα από τη σκηνή. Με τα στρατεύματα της Εθνοφρουράς και την Ελληνική Μεραρχία υπό τις διαταγές του Γρίβα, είναι πιθανό ότι θεώρησε ότι θα ήταν καλύτερο να εξαφανιστεί ο Γρίβας, αντί να τον δολοφονήσουν, καθώς αυτό θα έκανε τον Μακάριο τον κακό. Τα ταξιδιωτικά σχέδια του Γρίβα, λοιπόν, του έδωσαν την ευκαιρία να εμπλακεί σε ένα μυστηριώδες ατύχημα.

• Ούτε ο Μακάριος ούτε ο Γιωρκάτζης θα είχαν κανέναν ενδοιασμό να σκοτώσουν αθώους ανθρώπους για να πετύχουν τους σκοπούς τους.

• Είναι επομένως απολύτως αξιόπιστο ότι ο Μακάριος θα είχε εγκρίνει ή θα είχε δεχτεί μια επίθεση σε πολιτικό αεροσκάφος που πιστεύεται ότι μετέφερε τον Γρίβα. Ο Γιωρκάτζης θα είχε εκτελέσει τις οδηγίες του Μακαρίου χωρίς δεύτερη σκέψη.

Η αξιοπιστία του Γιωρκάτζη ως οργανωτή της πλοκής ενισχύεται από την υποτιθέμενη συμμετοχή του σε άλλες απόπειρες δολοφονίας εναντίον βασικών πολιτικών προσώπων. Το 1968 συνδέθηκε με αποτυχημένες δολοφονίες του Έλληνα πρωθυπουργού, καθώς βοήθησε τον Αλέκο Παναγούλη, Έλληνα πολιτικό αντίπαλο της χούντας, στην προσπάθειά του να δολοφονήσει τον ηγέτη της, Γεώργιο Παπαδόπουλο. Μετά την απόπειρα, το ελληνικό καθεστώς ανάγκασε τον Μακάριο να ζητήσει την παραίτηση του Γιωρκάτζη. Μετά την ουσιαστική απομάκρυνσή του από τη θέση του, ο Γιωρκάτζης έγινε ένας από τους κύριους πολιτικούς αντιπάλους του Προέδρου.

Στις 8 Μαρτίου 1970 ο Πρόεδρος Μακάριος σκόπευε να παραστεί στο ετήσιο μνημόσυνο ενός αγωνιστή της ΕΟΚΑ, του Γρηγόρη Αυξεντίου, που θα γινόταν στα βουνά του Μαχαιρά. Ο πρόεδρος θα ταξίδευε με ελικόπτερο και, καθώς απογειωνόταν από την Αρχιεπισκοπή στη Λευκωσία, ακούστηκαν πυροβολισμοί, προκαλώντας ζημιές στο ελικόπτερο και τραυματισμό του πιλότου. Παρόλα αυτά, ο πιλότος πραγματοποίησε επιτυχή αναγκαστική προσγείωση. Ο Μακάριος βοηθούμενος από περαστικούς κατάφερε να διαφύγει μεταφέροντας τον πιλότο στο Γενικό Νοσοκομείο Λευκωσίας. Η απόπειρα δολοφονίας είχε αποτύχει. Η ίδια πηγή που έδωσε στον συγγραφέα την αφήγηση για τον εντοπισμό του Γρίβα από τον Γιωρκάτζη είπε επίσης ότι είχε προσπαθήσει να προειδοποιήσει τον Μακάριο να μην ταξιδέψει στο μνημόσυνο του Αυξεντίου, αλλά αγνοήθηκε.

Ο Πρόεδρος σίγουρα πίστευε ότι ο Γιωρκάτζης είχε παίξει ρόλο σε αυτή την απόπειρα δολοφονίας. Καθώς έβγαινε από το κατεστραμμένο ελικόπτερο, ο Μακάριος είπε στο κόσμο : «*Ο Γιωρκάτζης το έκανε αυτό.*»[159] Ο Γιωρκάτζης, σύμφωνα με ορισμένες πηγές, προσπάθησε να φύγει από την Κύπρο και επιβιβάστηκε σε πτήση για τη Βηρυτό. Ωστόσο, η απόπειρα αναχώρησής του ανακαλύφθηκε και του δόθηκε εντολή να βγει από το αεροσκάφος. Υπάρχουν αντικρουόμενες και μη επιβεβαιωμένες μαρτυρίες για τις μηχανορραφίες που ακολούθησαν, αλλά δεν τελείωσαν καλά για τον Γιωρκάτζη. Μία εβδομάδα μετά την απόπειρα κατά της ζωής του Μακαρίου, ο Γιωρκάτζης πυροβολήθηκε και σκοτώθηκε σε μια απομακρυσμένη τοποθεσία κοντά στο χωριό Μια Μηλιά, έξω από τη Λευκωσία.

Ο Μακάριος έδωσε συνέντευξη σε γερμανική εφημερίδα, η οποία δημοσιεύτηκε στις 16 Απριλίου 1970. Το άρθρο αναφέρθηκε από Έλληνες συγγραφείς[160] το 2014 και το 2016. Ήταν η πρώτη φορά, προφανώς, που ο Μακάριος μίλησε για την απόπειρα θανάτωσης του. Ο Μακάριος ρωτήθηκε για μια ομάδα «τρομοκρατών», γνωστή σ'αυτόν (το Μακάριο) και στην κυβέρνηση. Δεν υπήρχε καμία διαβεβαίωση ότι βρίσκονταν υπό παρακολούθηση από την αστυνομία. Ο δημοσιογράφος ήθελε να μάθει εάν οι έξι ύποπτοι, που συνελήφθησαν μετά την απόπειρα κατά της ζωής του Μακαρίου, και ο ίδιος ο Γιωρκάτζης, ήταν μέλη αυτής της ομάδας.

Ο Μακάριος απάντησε:

---

[159] «*Υπό την απειλή των όπλων*». Περιοδικό Time. 30 Μαρτίου 1970.

[160] . *Ο Έλληνας ακαδημαϊκός (Λάρισας) Αυγουστίνος Αυγουστή παρέθεσε μια αφήγηση των συγγραφέων Π. Παπαδημήτρη και Α. Νεοφύτου σε ένα βιβλίο «Πολύκαρπος Γιωρκάτζης, Οι Τελευταίες Στιγμές του» (2014) Ο Ανδρέας Πολυκάρπου δημοσίευσε τις ίδιες πληροφορίες σε ένα άρθρο στο διαδίκτυο, με τίτλο «Το ιστορικό χρονικό της δολοφονίας του Πολύκαρπου Yiorkadjis ': https://www.offsite.com.cy/articles/kyria-themata/topika/83215-poioi-ithela-ton-polykarpo-giorkatzi-nekro-ti-gnorize-kai-poioi (2016).*

«Ενώ οι έρευνες της αστυνομίας συνεχίζονται, δεν νομίζω ότι είμαι σε θέση να απαντήσω λεπτομερώς στην ερώτησή σας. Περιορίζομαι λέγοντας μόνο ότι υπάρχουν στοιχεία που εμπλέκουν ορισμένα πρόσωπα σε σχέση με την απόπειρα εναντίον της ζωής μου και ότι ο πρώην υπουργός Γιωρκάτζης σχετιζόταν με αυτά τα άτομα και ότι ήταν αναμεμειγμένος στην οργάνωση της απόπειρας».

Ο Πολύκαρπος Γιωρκάτζης, σημείωσε το δημοσίευμα, είχε διακηρύξει την αθωότητά του στο σύντομο χρονικό διάστημα που μεσολάβησε από την επίθεση εναντίον του Μακαρίου και τον θάνατο του. Στην εφημερίδα της Αθήνας «ΒΗΜΑ» είχε δηλώσει ότι οι σύμβουλοι του Μακαρίου απλώς ασχολούνταν με το να του ρίχνουν λάσπη και ότι μέχρι τότε ήταν σίγουρος ότι κάποιοι ήθελαν να τον βγάλουν από τη μέση για δικά τους συμφέροντα.

Το άρθρο δημοσιεύτηκε την ίδια μέρα που έξι άτομα κατηγορήθηκαν για την απόπειρα κατά της ζωής του Μακαρίου. Μεταξύ των κατηγοριών ήταν ότι οι έξι από αυτούς, μεταξύ 1ης Σεπτεμβρίου 1969 και 8ης Μαρτίου 1970, συνωμότησαν στη Λευκωσία μαζί με τον αποθανόντα Π. Γιωρκάτζη και με άλλα γνωστά πρόσωπα στην εισαγγελική αρχή για την αλλαγή της κυβέρνησης με τη χρήση βίας, ή να επιδείξουν χρήση βίας και ότι συνωμότησαν μαζί με τον αποθανόντα Π. Γιωρκάτζη και άλλα πρόσωπα για να δολοφονήσουν τον Πρόεδρο Μακάριο.

Πιο πρόσφατο είναι ένα απόσπασμα[161] από άρθρο του Πανεπιστημιακού Ιστορικού Δρ. Πέτρου Παπαπολυβίου:

«...η δικαστική υπόθεση εκδικάστηκε μεταξύ Σεπτεμβρίου και Νοεμβρίου 1970. Οι επίδοξοι δολοφόνοι ανήκαν σε δύο εκ διαμέτρου αντίθετες ομάδες αντιπάλων του Αρχιεπισκόπου Μακαρίου:: Ένας «ιστορικός συμβιβασμός» ένωσε για την απόπειρα αφοσιωμένους φίλους του Πολύκαρπου Γιωρκάτζη, που ένοιωθαν παραγκωνισμένοι μετά την παραίτησή του, και άνδρες της σκληρής αντι-μακαριακής αντιπολίτευσης, που ήταν της άποψης ότι ο πρόεδρος της Κύπρου είχε εγκαταλείψει την πολιτική του υπέρ της ένωσης με την Ελλάδα. Για την απόπειρα τέσσερα άτομα κρίθηκαν ένοχα από το Κακουργιοδικείο Λευκωσίας. Το Δικαστήριο δέχθηκε ότι «φαίνεται εκ πρώτης όψεως ο Πολύκαρπος Γιωρκάτζης συμμετείχε στη συνωμοσία».

Ένας άλλος από τους κατηγορούμενους, ο Κώστας Ιωαννίδης... κρίθηκε αθώος λόγω έλλειψης επαρκών αποδεικτικών στοιχείων που θα έδιναν κ πρώτης όψεως υπόθεση εναντίον του...»

---

[161] .«Η απόπειρα δολοφονίας του Μακαρίου» του Δρ Πέτρου Παπαπολυβίου, δημοσίευση 4 Ιουνίου 2018 «Καθημερινή».

Τα βασικά άτομα ήταν άνδρες της εποχής τους. Ο Γρίβας ήταν στρατιώτης σταδιοδρομίας, ακόμα κι αν ο μεγαλύτερος αντίκτυπός του ήταν ως εξεγερμένος ή αγωνιστής της ελευθερίας, ανάλογα με την άποψή του καθενός. Δεν ήταν η πρώτη τέτοια φιγούρα που πολέμησε έναν απελευθερωτικό πόλεμο και πέτυχε αυτόν τον στόχο και μετά ξέφυγε από τη νέα κατεύθυνση της χώρας του με τους συναδέλφους του πολιτικούς. Αν, όπως υπονοείται, συμμετείχε στις απόπειρες δολοφονίας κατά του Μακαρίου και του Παπαδόπουλου, ο Γιωρκάτζης έδειξε ότι ήταν άνθρωπος ικανός για ακραία βία για πολιτικούς σκοπούς. Αν έβλεπε τον Γρίβα ως εμπόδιο που έπρεπε να ξεπεραστεί, το να τον σκοτώσει θα ήταν απλώς μια επιλογή τακτικής. Αν ενεργούσε με τις εντολές του Μακαρίου, θα είχε ελάχιστες τύψεις να εκτελέσει τις εντολές του.

Είναι ύψιστη ειρωνεία το γεγονός ότι, αφού φέρεται ότι συμμετείχε στις δύο προαναφερθείσες πλοκές, και εμπλεκόμενος, σύμφωνα με τις πληροφορίες που δόθηκαν στον συγγραφέα, στην απόπειρα κατά του Γρίβα, το μοναδικό πρόσωπο μεταξύ αυτών των εξεχόντων προσωπικοτήτων να έχει βίαιο τέλος ήταν ο ίδιος ο Γιωρκάτζης.

Το τελευταίο αίνιγμα σε όλη αυτή τη περιπέτεια καταστροφής του Charlie Oscar αφορά το ενδεχόμενο συγκάλυψης από το βρετανικό Υπουργείο Εξωτερικών, όπως αποδεικνύεται από τα έγγραφα και τις υποστηρικτικές πληροφορίες στα Εθνικά Αρχεία.

Η αλληλογραφία μεταξύ του Βρετανικού Υπουργείου Εξωτερικών και της Scotland Yard υποδηλώνει έντονα ότι οι Browne και Hill δεν είχαν σκοπό να βρουν στοιχεία ότι ο Γρίβας ήταν ο στόχος ή ότι ο Μακάριος ή ο Γιωρκάτζης ήταν οι δράστες. Εν μέρει, η επιδείνωση της πολιτικής κατάστασης θα είχε χειροτερέψει σημαντικά εάν ο Μακάριος απομακρυνόταν, παρά να τον επηρέαζαν.

Η Κύπρος είχε τεράστια στρατηγική αξία στον Ψυχρό Πόλεμο, λόγω της θέσης της στην Ανατολική Μεσόγειο. Ο Μακάριος, εκείνη την εποχή, έδειχνε σημάδια ότι πλησίαζε περισσότερο τη Σοβιετική Ένωση, και ακόμη και ο προβληματισμός κατά πόσο ήταν αναμεμειγμένος θα μπορούσε να είχε κάνει την κατάσταση χειρότερη.

Υπάρχουν περιστασιακά στοιχεία που υποδηλώνουν ότι ο Γιωρκάτζης ήταν, τουλάχιστον, τυχερός στις προηγούμενες επαφές του με τις βρετανικές δυνάμεις ασφαλείας. Αν ήταν πληροφοριοδότης στη Κατάσταση Έκτακτης Ανάγκης στην Κύπρο , δεν θα τον είχαν αφήσει μετά, ειδικά όταν κέρδιζε υψηλά πολιτικά αξιώματα.

Είναι πιθανό η καταστροφή του Charlie Oscar και ο θάνατος 66 αθώων ανθρώπων να θεωρήθηκε , πολύ λυπηρό γεγονός, αλλά ο κίνδυνος της εθνικής ασφάλειας χάνοντας την επιρροή στην Κύπρο δεν θα έφερνε κανέναν πίσω. Στη δεκαετία του '60, ένα νεύμα και ένα κλείσιμο του ματιού από το Υπουργείο Εξωτερικών σε έναν ανώτερο αξιωματικό της αστυνομίας θα ήταν αρκετό για να διασφαλιστεί ότι δεν θα έβγαιναν στο φως στοιχεία. Δεν ήταν προς το εθνικό συμφέρον να γίνει κάτι τέτοιο.

Συμπέρασμα

Είναι απίθανο να υπάρξουν ποτέ οριστικά στοιχεία για την ταυτότητα των δραστών και το κίνητρο της καταστροφής του Charlie Oscar και των επιβατών και του πληρώματος του. Τούτου λεχθέντος, πιστεύω ότι η πραγματική πορεία των γεγονότων είναι πολύ πιθανό να είναι όπως περιγράφεται στο προηγούμενο κεφάλαιο. Ο πληθυσμός της Κύπρου είναι μικρός, σε σύγκριση με πολλές άλλες χώρες, και δεμένος μέσα στις κοινότητές του. Πολλοί άνθρωποι στην Κύπρο, τον τελευταίο μισό αιώνα, έχουν συζητήσει μεταξύ τους για όσα συνέβησαν το απόγευμα της Τετάρτης 11 Οκτωβρίου 1967 και τα ξημερώματα της Πέμπτης 12 Οκτωβρίου.

Από τις διάφορες βρετανικές και κυπριακές αρχές, οι λίγοι που βγήκαν από το δυστύχημα και τα επακόλουθά του με πίστωση ήταν εκείνοι που συμμετείχαν στην επιχείρηση έρευνας και ανάκτησης και στη μετέπειτα έρευνα του ατυχήματος. Συγκεκριμένα, τα πληρώματα του Hastings βρήκαν τα συντρίμμια πολύ γρήγορα, επιτρέποντας την ανάκτηση των σορών των περισσότερων θυμάτων, μαζί με τα καλύμματα των καθισμάτων με τα ζωτικά τους στοιχεία. Η ομάδα της AIB των John Veal και Eric Newton επέβλεψε μια έρευνα που μέχρι σήμερα θεωρείται υποδειγματική. Ήταν ασυνήθιστα περίπλοκη και δεν άφηνε καμία πέτρα αγύριστη. Το έργο των παθολόγων, Ken Mason και Stan Tarlton, θεωρείται επίσης αριστοτεχνικό, ιδιαίτερα κάτω από τις πιο φρικτές συνθήκες.

Φαίνεται πολύ απίθανο ο Νίκος Παπαπέτρου να ανατίναξε τον εαυτό του, ή ένα άβουλο δικό του, για ασφαλιστικούς λόγους, παρά πως ο Αβραάμ Σολωμού ήταν ο «courier» που μετέφερε άθελά του τη βόμβα στο αεροπλάνο. Η βόμβα φάνηκε στους ερευνητές ως μια σχετικά εξελιγμένη συσκευή, που περιελάμβανε πλαστικό εκρηκτικό στρατιωτικής ποιότητας με πυροκροτητή άγνωστης προέλευσης. Το γεγονός ότι εξερράγη στο επίπεδο του δαπέδου, εν μέρει κάτω από ένα κάθισμα, θα δυσκόλευε τον Παπαπέτρου να την ενεργοποιήσει δια χειρός και ήταν λιγότερο πιθανό να βασιζόταν σε χρονόμετρο. Τον Οκτώβριο του 2018, η οικογένεια Σολωμού επιβεβαίωσε ότι τους είπαν ο Αβραάμ Σολωμού πράγματι πήγε στην Κυπριακή Πρεσβεία το βράδυ πριν από την πτήση και του έδωσαν δέματα για να πάρει μαζί του στη Λευκωσία στο CY284. Διάφορες ξεχωριστές πηγές ανέφεραν ότι του δόθηκε η βόμβα εκεί, εν αγνοία του. Ο Αβραάμ Σολωμού δεν ήταν δολοφόνος, ήταν και ο ίδιος ένα θύμα όπως και όλοι οι άλλοι στο αεροσκάφος.

Δόθηκε μεγάλη έμφαση καθ΄όλη την έρευνα ότι δεν υπήρχαν στοιχεία ότι ο Στρατηγός Γρίβας επρόκειτο να ταξιδέψει στο CY284. Για πρώτη φορά, υπάρχουν άμεσες ενδείξεις ότι, στην πραγματικότητα, ο Γρίβας είχε αρχικά κρατηθεί στην πτήση. Πράγματι, το πλήρωμα είχε ενημερωθεί την ημέρα πριν από την πτήση να τον περιμένει στο αεροπλάνο. Η απόλυτη απόδειξη είναι ότι ο Νεόφυτος Σοφοκλέους, υπεύθυνος του γραφείου του Γρίβα και έμπιστος του Στρατηγού, δήλωσε για αυτό το βιβλίο ότι είχε κάνει κράτηση προσωπικά για τον Γρίβα στο CY284 για τις 12 Οκτωβρίου 1967 και ότι είχε ακυρώσει την κράτηση αμέσως πριν την πτήση, όταν αντιλήφθηκε το έντονο ενδιαφέρον του Γιωρκάτζη για τα ταξιδιωτικά σχέδια του Γρίβα. Η αξιοπιστία του κ. Σοφοκλέους είναι αναμφισβήτητη. Ως 20χρονος αγωνιστής της ΕΟΚΑ το 1956 εμπλεκόταν σε σχέδιο ανατίναξης της κατοικίας του Κυβερνήτη της Κύπρου, Στρατάρχη Sir John Harding.

Η εμπλοκή του Γιωρκάτζη στην απόπειρα δολοφονίας του Γρίβα είχε υποστηριχθεί στο παρελθόν, και αυτό τώρα επιβεβαιώνεται από τον Νεόφυτο Σοφοκλέους. Ο Γιωρκάτζης αποδείχθηκε ικανός για μια τέτοια τραγικά βίαιη πράξη εναντίον ενός υποτιθέμενου αντιπάλου, εν τέλει με τη συμμετοχή του στην απόπειρα δολοφονίας κατά του Μακαρίου τρία χρόνια αργότερα. Λίγο πριν πεθάνει σε ένα μοναχικό σημείο έξω από τη Λευκωσία, ο Γιωρκάτζης είπε "*Τώρα όλα μπορούν να συμβούν. Για τον Μακάριο οι άνθρωποι είναι σαν τα λεμόνια: αφού τα στύψει μέχρι τη τελευταία σταγόνα τα πετάει.*» Ίσως, για τον Μακάριο στα τέλη του 1967, ο Γρίβας να είχε φανεί εξίσου περιττός.

Είναι απίθανο να μάθουμε ποτέ τον πραγματικό λόγο για τον οποίο το βρετανικό Υπουργείο Εξωτερικών ήταν τόσο πρόθυμο η έρευνα να αποφύγει στα συμπεράσματα της ότι υπήρχε πολιτικό κίνητρο. Η Κύπρος ήταν στρατηγικής σημασίας στο αποκορύφωμα του Ψυχρού Πολέμου και ο Μακάριος πιστευόταν, εκείνη την εποχή, ότι ήταν άβολα φιλικός με τη Σοβιετική Ένωση. Η εμπλοκή του Υπουργού Εσωτερικών ενός κυρίαρχου κράτους θα είχε προκαλέσει διπλωματική αναταραχή. Αν είχε αποδειχτεί ότι ο ίδιος ο Πρόεδρος είχε εμπλακεί, θα ήταν κόλαση να πληρωθεί. Το συμπέρασμα από τα έγγραφα υποδηλώνει παρέμβαση του βρετανικού κατεστημένου στην αστυνομική έρευνα. Υπήρχε μια πολύ καθαρή καθοδήγηση, από το Φόρεϊν Όφις μέσω του Βοηθού Επιθεωρητή Brodie, στους δύο ντετέκτιβς να απέφευγαν να μελετήσουν οποιεσδήποτε διασυνδέσεις με πολιτικά κίνητρα. Επομένως, δεν προκαλεί έκπληξη το γεγονός ότι ο John Macrae του Υπουργείου Εξωτερικών, έγραψε σε έναν συνάδελφό του ότι «*Σε γενικές γραμμές, η ασφαλιστική θεωρία φαίνεται η πιο πιθανή...*» Το εάν αυτό ήταν ευσεβής πόθος, αντί να προσπαθήσει ο Macrae να ρίξει ίχνη μακριά από οτιδήποτε απομακρυσμένη πολιτική ανάμιξη, δεν θα γίνει ποτέ γνωστό, αλλά φαίνεται ενδεικτικό αυτού που ήλπιζε το Foreign Office ότι θα ήταν το συμπέρασμα της αστυνομικής έρευνας.

Εάν ο Γιωρκάτζης ήταν πληροφοριοδότης των βρετανικών υπηρεσιών ασφαλείας κατά τη διάρκεια της Κυπριακής Έκτακτης Ανάγκης μια δεκαετία νωρίτερα, είναι πολύ απίθανο στη συνέχεια να είχε απορριφθεί ως πηγή. Ως υψηλόβαθμος πολιτικός, θα ήταν πράγματι πολύτιμος. Οι υπηρεσίες ασφαλείας θα είχαν επίσης ισχυρό έλεγχο πάνω του. Δεν θα ήθελε ο προηγούμενος ρόλος του να γίνει γνωστός σε κανέναν πολιτικό αντίπαλο, ειδικά αν κάποιος είχε πραγματικά μια «Ομάδα Εξολοθρευτών-Προδοτών», όπως πρότεινε ο Πέτρος Γεωργιάδης. Σύμφωνα με τον βρετανικό νόμο περί ελευθερίας της πληροφόρησης, υπάρχει απόλυτη εξαίρεση για τη δημοσιοποίηση στοιχείων τέτοιων πληροφοριοδοτών, για την προστασία των οικογενειών και των συνεργατών τους ακόμη και μετά το θάνατό τους. Προστατεύει φυσικά και τη φήμη του κράτους.

Η έρευνα της Μητροπολιτικής Αστυνομίας, σύμφωνα με τα σημερινά δεδομένα, ήταν θλιβερά ανεπαρκής και φαίνεται, στην καλύτερη περίπτωση, να ήταν επιφανειακή. Η προφανής κατανομή μόνο δύο ντετέκτιβ στην υπόθεση υποδηλώνει ότι η δύναμη θεώρησε την έρευνα ως πιθανή σπατάλη χρόνου και χρημάτων. Τα σχόλια του πρώην DC Dave O'Connell εντόπισαν την φαινομενικά χαλαρή στάση του ντετέκτιβ επικεφαλής επιθεωρητή Browne στην έρευνα για τη δολοφονία του Roy Tuthill αμέσως μετά την επιστροφή του Browne από την υπόθεση Charlie Oscar. Μια σημαντική ομάδα αξιωματικών φαίνεται να έχει εμπλακεί στη δολοφονία ενός μόνο παιδιού. Υπήρχαν τρία παιδιά, δύο από αυτά Βρετανοί, στο Charlie Oscar μαζί με όλους τους άλλους.

Ελλείψει πλήρους φακέλου εγκλήματος, δεν είναι δυνατό να εκτιμηθεί πόση προσπάθεια κατέβαλαν ο Μπράουν και ο συνάδελφός του στην έρευνά τους. Ο συγγραφέας ρώτησε όλες τις οικογένειες στην Κύπρο με τις οποίες μίλησε σε σχέση με αυτό το βιβλίο εάν γνώριζαν κάποια επαφή από τους ντετέκτιβ. κανείς δεν γνώριζε τέτοιες έρευνες.

Η έρευνα για την θηριωδία του Charlie Oscar έκλεισε όταν ο Βοηθός Επίτροπος Brodie είπε στον κ. Bampton του Υπουργείου Εσωτερικών: *«Έχει ληφθεί τώρα απάντηση από τον Διευθυντή της Δημόσιας Εισαγγελίας ότι «δεν μπορεί να αναληφθεί δράση για τα παρόντα στοιχεία».. Ελλείψει περαιτέρω αποδεικτικών στοιχείων, δεν νομίζω ότι ο Διευθυντής θα προβεί σε οποιαδήποτε ενέργεια στο μέλλον.»* Όπως αναφέρθηκε προηγουμένως, είναι απίθανο τα κλειστά αρχεία να περιέχουν τέτοια στοιχεία, αν και θα πρέπει να περιμένουμε για να μάθουμε μέχρι την 1η Ιανουαρίου 2067. Ωστόσο, υπάρχουν στοιχεία που προσκομίστηκαν από μάρτυρες, που δημοσιεύονται για πρώτη φορά σε αυτό το βιβλίο, ότι:

(i) Ο Στρατηγός Γρίβας έλαβε κράτηση για να πετάξει στο CY284 τις πρώτες πρωινές ώρες της 12ης Οκτωβρίου 1967.

(ii) Ο πολιτικός του αντίπαλος, Πολύκαρπος Γιωρκάτζης, παρακολουθούσε ενεργά τις κινήσεις του Γρίβα, μεταξύ των οποίων και η επικοινωνία με το γραφείο του Γρίβα λίγο πριν την πτήση.

(iii) Ο Γιωρκάτζης και ο Μακάριος εμπλέκονται σε μεγάλο βαθμό στην καταστροφή του Charlie Oscar, με σκοπό να σκοτώσουν τον Γρίβα.

(iv) Ο Γιωρκάτζης είχε την τάση να εμπλακεί σε περίπλοκες απόπειρες να σκοτώσει τους αντιπάλους του. Αργότερα ενεπλάκη σε άλλες δύο απόπειρες δολοφονίας, με την ισχυρότερη κατά του Μακαρίου τρία χρόνια αργότερα. Η πραγματικότητα μιας τέτοιας ενδοοικογενειακής βίας αποδείχθηκε όταν ο ίδιος ο Γιωρκάτζης πυροβολήθηκε και σκοτώθηκε λίγο μετά την απόπειρα κατά του Μακαρίου.

(v) Ένας βιώσιμος αυτοσχέδιος εκρηκτικός μηχανισμός (IED) συσκευάστηκε σε καμπίνα και δόθηκε από έναν άνδρα που λέγεται ότι ήταν ο Ντίνος Μιχαηλίδης στον Αβραάμ Σολωμού στην Κυπριακή Πρεσβεία στην Αθήνα. Ο Σολωμού ανέλαβε να πάρει την τσάντα στη Λευκωσία και του είπαν ότι πρέπει να πετάξει στο CY284. Δεν γνώριζε τίποτα για τη φύση του πακέτου.

(vi) Η οικογένεια Παπαπέτρου εξηγεί τις κινήσεις του Νίκου Παπαπέτρου τις ημέρες πριν από την πτήση του στο CY284 και διαψεύδει τους ισχυρισμούς που διέρρευσαν στον Τύπο το 1968.

Υπάρχουν ακόμη επιζώντες μάρτυρες που θα μπορούσαν, εάν τους ζητηθεί, να παράσχουν πολύ χρήσιμα και αξιόπιστα στοιχεία σε μια νέα αστυνομική έρευνα. Μόνο αυτό θα έκλεινε πραγματικά ένα καταστροφικό περιστατικό που αισθάνονται ακόμη βαθιά οι συγγενείς και οι φίλοι των 66 θυμάτων.

Αυτό το βιβλίο είναι διαθέσιμο στο κοινό από το 2018, οι βρετανικές υπηρεσίες ασφαλείας έχουν λάβει όλες τις σχετικές πληροφορίες και υπήρξε κάλυψη από τα μέσα ενημέρωσης των πληροφοριών που ήρθαν στο φως. Ο συγγραφέας επικοινώνησε με την οικογένεια Γιωρκάτζη για να τους προσφέρει την ευκαιρία να απαντήσουν, να διαψεύσουν τις πληροφορίες ή να ξεκαθαρίσουν τις δραστηριότητες του Πολύκαρπου Γιωρκάτζη. Έχουν απαντήσει ευγενικά, λέγοντας ότι δεν είναι σε θέση να παράσχουν οποιαδήποτε πληροφορία.

Κανείς δεν έχει αμφισβητήσει ακόμη τα συμπεράσματα που εκτίθενται σε αυτό το βιβλίο.

Η καταστροφή της πτήσης CY284 είναι μια ακόμη τραγωδία στη βασανισμένη ιστορία της Κύπρου. Φαίνεται πιθανότατα ότι έγινε από τον υπουργό Εσωτερικών Πολύκαρπο Γιωρκάτζη με εντολή του προέδρου Αρχιεπισκόπου Μακαρίου για να δολοφονήσει τον αρχηγό της Εθνικής Φρουράς στρατηγό Γρίβα. Το ότι φαίνεται να έχει κουκουλωθεί από το βρετανικό Υπουργείο Εξωτερικών, είτε για να κρατήσει τον Μακάριο μακριά από τη σοβιετική σφαίρα επιρροής, είτε για να προστατεύσει μια ισχυρή πηγή πληροφοριών με τον Γιωρκάτζη, ή ίσως και τα δύο, είναι ασυγχώρητο. Ακόμη και μισό αιώνα μετά από αυτή την άθλια πράξη, ο βομβαρδισμός της πτήσης CY284 εξακολουθεί να είναι η μεγαλύτερη επίσημη μη ανιχνευθείσα μαζική δολοφονία της Βρετανίας. προσπάθησε να αποφύγει οποιαδήποτε πολιτική σχέση στο θέμα , δεν θα γίνει ποτέ γνωστό, αλλά φαίνεται ενδεικτικό τι το Φόρεϊν Όφις ήλπιζε ότι θα ήταν το συμπέρασμα της αστυνομικής έρευνας.

Ευχαριστίες

Η έρευνα που απαιτείται για κάθε βιβλίο που ασχολείται με ένα περίπλοκο θέμα είναι αναπόφευκτα ένα τρομακτικό έργο. Το Bealine Charlie Oscar καλύπτει ορισμένους τομείς στους οποίους έχω κάποιες γνώσεις εργασίας. Η επαγγελματική μου ζωή ήταν στην εμπορική αεροπορία, στην αστυνόμευση και, τελευταία, στην αστυνομική αεροπορία. Ωστόσο, ήξερα ελάχιστα για τις περιπλοκές της έρευνας αεροπορικών δυστυχημάτων, πολύ λιγότερο για την έρευνα στον τομέα των εξοπλισμών και σχεδόν τίποτα για τις πολιτικές ίντριγκες της Ελλάδας και της Κύπρου τη δεκαετία του '50 και του '60. Το πιο σημαντικό είναι ότι δεν είχα σχεδόν καμία πληροφορία για τους ανθρώπους που βρίσκονται στην καρδιά αυτού του βιβλίου, τους επιβάτες και το πλήρωμα που έχασαν τη ζωή τους στο Charlie Oscar. Οι μόνες εξαιρέσεις ήταν δύο από τους πιλότους, ο Καπετάνιος Gordon Blackwood και ο Ανώτερος Πρώτος Αξιωματικός Denis Plamer.

Καθώς η έρευνά μου επεκτάθηκε στην Κύπρο, τόσο πριν όσο και μετά την έκδοση της πρώτης έκδοσης αυτού του βιβλίου, δύο πράγματα έγιναν ξεκάθαρα. Πρώτον, στη Κύπρο θυμούνται την ανατίναξη του CY284 σε πολύ μεγαλύτερο βαθμό από ό,τι στο Ηνωμένο Βασίλειο και, δεύτερον, εξακολουθεί να είναι ικανή να προσελκύει διαμάχες και έντονα συναισθήματα. Ποτέ δεν ήταν πρόθεσή μου να αναζωπυρώσω άσκοπα παλιές αναμνήσεις, αλλά έχω ακούσει πολλές απόψεις να εκφράζονται που ενισχύουν την ευαισθησία γύρω από το περιστατικό. Θα ήθελα να αναγνωρίσω το μεγάλο θάρρος που έδειξαν οι άνθρωποι που πιστεύουν ότι η αλήθεια πρέπει να ειπωθεί και ότι το βιβλίο μου θα τους βοηθήσει να το πετύχουν.

Ενδιαφέρομαι δια βίου για την τραγωδία, καθώς ο Gordon ήταν γείτονας, στενός φίλος των γονιών μου και συνάδελφος του πατέρα μου. Θυμάμαι επίσης τον Denis Palmer, τον οποίο οι γονείς μου γνώριζαν ως Τόνι, να επισκέπτεται το σπίτι μας. Πάντα πίστευα ότι το περιστατικό ήταν κλειστό και ξεχασμένο από όλους, εκτός από εκείνους που είχαν μακρινές αναμνήσεις από χαμένους φίλους και συγγενείς. Ο Καπετάνιος James Booth, ένας φίλος και συνάδελφός μου πιλότος, μου πρότεινε να δημοσιεύσω στο φόρουμ του Pprune, το οποίο έδωσε αμέσως ανταπόκριση. Ο ιστότοπος με συνέδεσε με τον Μιχαήλ Θωμαΐδη, του οποίου ο πατέρας βρισκόταν στην πτήση CY284, και τη Φανούλλα Αργυρού, μια Ελληνοκύπρια δημοσιογράφο με έδρα το Λονδίνο. Μαζί έχουν περάσει πολλά χρόνια προσπαθώντας να σημειώσουν πρόοδο στον προσδιορισμό του υπεύθυνου για την καταστροφή, και ήταν χαρά να ενώσω τις δυνάμεις μου μαζί τους. Η γνώση της Φανούλλας για τον εντοπισμό των σχετικών πληροφοριών και οι πολλές επαφές του Μιχαήλ στην Κύπρο, κατέστησαν πραγματικά δυνατό το βιβλίο. Ο Ρολάνδης Κωνσταντινίδης ήταν επίσης χρήσιμος στο να ξεκινήσω τον δρόμο για να ξετυλίξω τι είχε συμβεί στο CY284.

Πολλές από αυτές τις πληροφορίες φυλάσσονται στα Εθνικά Αρχεία του Λονδίνου, και είμαι υπόχρεος στη Φανούλλα για τον χρόνο και την υπομονή της που με βοήθησε να αποκτήσω πρόσβαση σε αυτά, και μάλιστα για τις επανειλημμένες επισκέψεις της για να συγκεντρώσει μικρές ποσότητες πρόσθετων πληροφοριών εκ μέρους μου. Είμαι υποχρεωμένος, αλλά και με ικανοποίηση, να αναγνωρίσω την πρόσβαση στις 2.500 περίπου σελίδες εγγράφων, που είναι διαθέσιμα για ανάγνωση, αντιγραφή και αναπαραγωγή σε αυτό το βιβλίο με την Ανοικτή Άδεια της Κυβέρνησης του HB V2.0.(UK Government's Open Licence V2.0).

Η επαφή με τον Michael (Μιχαήλ Θωμαΐδη) και την οικογένειά του με καθησύχασε ότι δεν άνοιγα ξανά παλιές πληγές δημοσιεύοντας αυτό το βιβλίο. Αντίθετα, ο Michael, και κάθε άλλο μέλος της οικογένειας (θυμάτων) με το οποίο έχω μιλήσει, εξακολουθεί να αισθάνεται τον πόνο της απώλειας τους, που επιδεινώνεται από την απουσία κλεισίματος και την προφανή έλλειψη επίσημου ενδιαφέροντος να προσδιορίσει μια για πάντα γιατί και από ποιον, οι αγαπημένοι τους σκοτώθηκαν. Θα ήθελα επίσης να εκφράσω την ευγνωμοσύνη μου στον Michael που πρόσφερε τις διευκολύνσεις για την υποστήριξη της επίσκεψής μου στην Κύπρο για να προωθήσω αυτό το βιβλίο και να συναντήσω όσες από τις οικογένειες μπόρεσαν να ενωθούν μαζί μας.

Είμαι ευγνώμων στην Jill Harper και την Elizabeth Carey-Hughes, τις κόρες του Gordon που μοιράστηκαν πληροφορίες σχετικά με την πρώιμη ζωή του πατέρα τους και που μου εμπιστεύτηκαν σπάνιες φωτογραφίες του Gordon και της Joyce. Ελπίζω ότι και αυτός θα είχε εγκρίνει το βιβλίο. Παρά τις καλύτερες προσπάθειές του, ο πατέρας μου δεν μπόρεσε να πείσει τον Gordon να αφήσει τον στόλο του Comet 4B και να αλλάξει στο στόλο των Trident. Όπως έλεγε στην οικογένειά του ο Gordon, θα πετούσε τον Κομήτη χωρίς αμοιβή αν το ήθελε η BEA, τέτοια ήταν η απόλαυση που αποκόμισε πετώντας το αεροσκάφος. Ομοίως, η σύζυγος του Mike Thomas , Sally, και η κόρη της Alison Whelan , έδωσαν ευγενικά πληροφορίες και φωτογραφίες.

Ο Λούις Λοΐζου, του οποίου ο αδερφός, Τζον, ήταν Ανώτερος Αεροσυνοδός στην πτήση, παρείχε πολλές λεπτομέρειες για τις πτήσεις της Cyprus Airways με Κομήτες και την ιστορία του Τζον και της κοπέλας του Josephine Coldicott. Η ανάμνησή του από τη νύχτα της 11ης προς 12η Οκτωβρίου 1967 είναι κατανοητά ξεκάθαρη και τον ευχαριστώ ειλικρινά που ήταν πρόθυμος να τη μοιραστεί με συγκλονιστικές λεπτομέρειες. Η ιστορία του δύσμοιρου ειδυλλίου του Τζον και της Josephine είναι μια τραγωδία από μόνη της.

Πολλοί άνθρωποι με βοήθησαν να συγκεντρώσω τις πληροφορίες για αυτό που έχει γίνει ένα αρκετά περίπλοκο συγγραφικό έργο. Μεμονωμένες φωτογραφίες αποδίδονται στο άτομο που τις προμηθεύει. Ειδικότερα, θα ήθελα να ευχαριστήσω το προσωπικό της *Cyprus Mail* για την παροχή φωτογραφιών αρχείου της κάλυψης των εφημερίδων τους και τον Χρύσανθο Χρυσάνθου, δημοσιογράφο της εφημερίδας *Φιλελεύθερος*, για την ίδια διευκόλυνση. Ο Simon Growcott κατέβαλε ιδιαίτερη προσπάθεια για μένα, αποκτώντας πρόσβαση στο τμήμα αποσκευών ενός από τα ελάχιστα άθικτα αεροσκάφη Comet 4 που υπάρχουν ακόμα, προκειμένου να λάβω λεπτομερείς φωτογραφίες των χειριστηρίων κάτω από το πάτωμα της καμπίνας επιβατών, κοντά στη συσκευή στο Charlie Oscar. Μια εικόνα ζωγραφίζει χίλιες λέξεις, ειδικά όταν πρόκειται για τεχνικά θέματα.

Ο Roger Aves ευγενικά έκανε κάποια έρευνα για μένα στο νησί του Καστελλόριζου. Αυτό με έφερε σε επαφή με τον Πανταζή Χούλη και τον Νίκο Μισομίκη, που μπόρεσαν να ρίξουν λίγο περισσότερο φως στην επιχείρηση περισυλλογής.

Οι φωτογραφίες προέρχονται από πολλές πηγές και είναι κυρίως από την εποχή του συμβάντος. Πολλές ήταν ψηφιακές εικόνες που δημιουργήθηκαν από παλιά πρωτότυπα ή έχουν σαρωθεί από αντίγραφα αντιγράφων. Ως αποτέλεσμα, υπάρχουν μερικές φωτογραφίες που δεν έχουν την ποιότητα που σχετίζεται με τις σύγχρονες εικόνες. Ωστόσο, στις περισσότερες περιπτώσεις η συνάφειά τους με το βιβλίο και η σπανιότητα εναλλακτικών επιλογών υπερτερεί της χαμηλής ανάλυσης της εικόνας. Είναι, όπως συχνά, μια ερώτηση για τον συγγραφέα «Είναι αυτή η εικόνα σχετικά χαμηλής ποιότητας καλύτερα από το τίποτα;» Είμαι πολύ ευγνώμων για κάθε ένα από αυτά. Όπου είναι δυνατόν, αποδίδονται στην πηγή που μου έδωσε την άδεια να τα χρησιμοποιήσω. Ένας αριθμός, ιδιαίτερα που σχετίζεται με πιο γενικό και συμφραζόμενο υλικό, δεν έχει αποδοθεί και προέρχεται από πολλές πηγές στο Διαδίκτυο. Καλώ τους αρχικούς ιδιοκτήτες να επικοινωνήσουν μαζί μου μέσω του εκδότη.

Οι τεχνικοί εμπειρογνώμονες για ένα ιστορικό αεροσκάφος όπως τον Κομήτη 4Β είναι δύσκολο να βρεθούν, αλλά ήμουν πολύ τυχερός που βρήκα τρεις άντρες που θα μπορούσαν να μου δώσουν συμβουλές, καθοδήγηση και να περάσουν με κριτική ματιά πολλές από τις σχετικές λεπτομέρειες, επαναφέροντάς με σε καλό δρόμο όταν η έλλειψη λεπτομερών γνώσεων κινδύνευε να με βγάλει εκτός τροχιάς. Είναι ο Graham M. Simons, συγγραφέας του *Comet! Το πρώτο Τζέτ αεροπλάνο στον κόσμο*, ο Καπετάνιος Simon Searle, πρώην της Dan Air, ο οποίος πέταξε την τελευταία εμπορική πτήση με Κομήτη, ο Καπετάνιος Bill Innes, ο συν-κυβερνήτης (co-pilot) του Κομήτη 4Β της ΒΕΑ, τον καιρό της απώλειας του Charlie Oscar. Ο Bill, ειδικότερα, έριξε σημαντικό φως στην κουλτούρα στη ΒΕΑ, και ειδικά στον στόλο του Κομήτη, όταν ορισμένες από αυτές τις πτυχές είχαν παρερμηνευθεί από άλλες πηγές. Ο

David Nicholas, , ο οποίος βρισκόταν σε υπηρεσία στο Κέντρο Ελέγχου Επιχειρήσεων ΒΕΑ στο Heathrow τη νύχτα της καταστροφής, παρείχε μια ολοκληρωμένη επισκόπηση του τρόπου με τον οποίο επέβλεπαν τη λειτουργία της αεροπορικής εταιρείας.

Το οριστικό έργο του Martin Painter, *The DH.106 Comet – An Illustrated History*, που δημοσιεύτηκε από την Air Britain το 2002, παρείχε ανεκτίμητες λεπτομέρειες για την ιστορία του Κομήτη. Είμαι ευγνώμων στον Martin και τον εκδότη του, την Air Britain, που μου επέτρεψαν να συγκεντρώσω τις πληροφορίες σχετικά με τις απώλειες του σκάφους το οποίο ελπίζω ότι θα βοηθήσει να καταρριφθεί ο διαρκής μύθος ότι ο Κομήτης ήταν μια παγίδα θανάτου. Οπωσδήποτε δεν ήταν.

Τον δαιδαλώδη κόσμο της κυπριακής πολιτικής της δεκαετίας του 1960 μου εξήγησε η Φανούλλα Αργυρού και είμαι επίσης ευγνώμων στους δημοσιογράφους Χρήστο Ιακώβου και Νίκο Παπαναστασίου για τη βοήθεια που μπόρεσαν να προσφέρουν. Μια εξαιρετική πηγή βασικών πληροφοριών για την «Κυπριακή Έκτακτη Ανάγκη» ήταν το ομώνυμο βιβλίο, γραμμένο από τον στρατιωτικό ιστορικό Nik Van Der Bijl. Είμαι ευγνώμων στον Νικ για τον χρόνο του κατά τη διάρκεια μιας μακράς τηλεφωνικής επικοινωνίας που συζητούσε τις δυνατότητες της ΕΟΚΑ στην καταστροφή αεροσκαφών και για την άδεια χρήσης πληροφοριών από το βιβλίο του.

Ο συγγραφέας και ερευνητής Λεωνίδας Λεωνίδου, ο οποίος έγραψε μια πολύ περιεκτική βιογραφία του Γεωργίου Γρίβα μεταξύ άλλων έργων, έπαιξε ανεκτίμητο ρόλο στην εξήγηση των περίπλοκων σχέσεων μεταξύ Γρίβα, Μακαρίου και Γιωρκάτζη. Οι πληροφορίες που έδωσε είναι πειστικές εξηγώντας γιατί αυτοί οι ηγέτες ενός κυρίαρχου κράτους δεν σκέφτηκαν τίποτα να καταστρέψουν ένα αεροπλάνο και να σκοτώσουν 66 αθώους ανθρώπους.

Επικοινώνησα με την οικογένεια του Πολύκαρπου Γιωρκάτζη, μέσω του γιου του Κωνσταντίνου Γιωρκάτζη, του σημερινού Δημάρχου Λευκωσίας, για να τους δώσω την ευκαιρία να σχολιάσουν τους ισχυρισμούς αυτού του βιβλίου. Ο κ. Γιωρκάτζης απάντησε ευγενικά ότι δεν είναι σε θέση να ρίξει φως στην υποτιθέμενη ανάμειξη του πατέρα του.

Ο γιος μου, William Hepworth, περνούσε ώρες φωτογραφίζοντας έγγραφα για μένα και γενικά ενεργώντας ως ο προσωπικός μου βοηθός . Όπως πάντα, ο ενθουσιασμός και η υποστήριξή του ήταν εξαιρετική, όπως και η υπομονή της συζύγου μου, της Mandy, της οποίας το κατώφλι της πλήξης ξεπερνιέται τακτικά μόλις αρχίσω να μιλάω για θέματα όπως αυτό, αλλά με υποστηρίζει δίχως δισταγμό.

Πάνω απ'όλα, δεν θα μπορούσα και δεν θα είχα ολοκληρώσει το έργο της παραγωγής αυτού του βιβλίου χωρίς την υποστήριξη των μελών της οικογένειας άλλων θυμάτων της πτήσης CY284. Ευχαριστώ ιδιαίτερα την Ελένη Κυριάκου (Ροδοσθένης Χρήστου και Νίκη Ροδοσθένου), τον

Ιωάννη Ιωαννίδη (Δρ. Γιώργο Ιωαννίδη), τον Γιώργο Δημητρίου και την Άντρια Σωτηρίου (Κατερίνα Λιασίδη), την οικογένεια Παπαπέτρου και τη Macha Miller and οικογένεια (η οικογένεια McComb) και τη Louise Fawcett, μέλος της οικογένειας των Jan και Guy Tasker. Ο Μάκης Εφραίμ, κουνιάδος της αεροσυνοδού Θέλμας Εφρέμη, εντάχθηκε μαζί μας και διοργάνωσε μια επίσκεψη στην υπέροχη ψαροταβέρνα του, Το Λάτσι, στη Λευκωσία. Η οικογένεια του Αβραάμ Σολωμού παραχώρησε χρήσιμες πληροφορίες, συμπεριλαμβανομένων των πληροφοριών που της δόθηκαν από τις κυπριακές αρχές μετά το περιστατικό. Ο Πολύβιος Γεωργίου ήταν επίσης πολύ χρήσιμος στην παροχή στοιχείων για τον αδελφό του, Σωτήρη. Ένα ιδιαίτερο ευχαριστώ στην Christine και τον Bob Marlborough, οι οποίοι βοήθησαν τόσο πολύ και που έπεισαν την British Airways να τιμήσουν τη μνήμη των θυμάτων.

Είναι σημαντικό να τονίσω ότι έχω εξετάσει όλες τις πληροφορίες που μου διαβιβάστηκαν ή ανακαλύφθηκαν από την έρευνα που πραγματοποίησα μαζί με άλλες. Πολλά από αυτά είναι αντικρουόμενα και έχω κάνει τις καλύτερες μου προσπάθειες για να ξεχωρίσω το σιτάρι από την ήρα. Ωστόσο, ακόμη και μετά από μισό αιώνα το περιστατικό με τον Charlie Oscar, το οποίο σε Ελλάδα και Κύπρο αναφέρεται και ως Η Καταστροφή του Καστελλόριζου, είναι πολύ αμφιλεγόμενο. Τα συμπεράσματά μου δεν γίνονται αποδεκτά από όλους, αλλά τα έχω κάνει καλόπιστα και με βάση την όσο το δυνατόν πιο αντικειμενική ερμηνεία των στοιχείων.

Ελπίζω ότι, παρουσιάζοντας τα αποδεικτικά στοιχεία με αναλογικό και μελετημένο τρόπο, μπορώ να βοηθήσω να έρθουν κοντά οι οικογένειες και οι φίλοι των θυμάτων. Με έχουν ευχαριστήσει για τις προσπάθειές μου εκείνοι με τους οποίους έχω έρθει σε επαφή. που τα κάνει όλα αξιόλογα. Εάν οι πληροφορίες ως προς το κίνητρο και τους δράστες είναι σωστές, και πιστεύω ότι οι πηγές μου είναι αξιόπιστες, μπορώ να καταλάβω γιατί επικρατεί σιωπή εδώ και μισό αιώνα από τα βρετανικά και κυπριακά κατεστημένα. Δεν θα με εξέπληττε αν συνεχιστεί αυτή η σιωπή. Αυτό δεν δικαιολογεί τη φαινομενική δαιμονοποίηση του Νίκου Παπαπέτρου, ο οποίος φαίνεται ότι έγινε σκόπιμα αποδιοπομπαίος τράγος για να αποσπάσει την προσοχή από τις απαίσιες πολιτικές μηχανορραφίες που είχαν ως αποτέλεσμα την κατάρριψη του CY284. Οι οικογένειες πάντα άξιζαν καλύτερα.

Τον Ιούνιο του 2021, η British Airways ανέθεσε και πλήρωσε για μια μόνιμη αναμνηστική πλακέτα για τα θύματα της πτήσης CY284, στο Memorial Garden στο παρεκκλήσι του St. George, στο αεροδρόμιο Heathrow. Είμαστε πολύ ευγνώμονες στον CEO της BA, Sean Doyle, επικεφαλής του Global PR Victoria Madden και την ομάδα της.

Η αναζήτηση, η οποία εκτείνεται σε τέσσερα έθνη, συνεχίζεται για όλους που έχασαν έναν φίλο ή συγγενή εκείνη τη φρικτή νύχτα πριν από μισό αιώνα. Θα ήθελα να επικοινωνήσω μαζί τους, κυρίως για να τους πω ότι τα αγαπημένα τους πρόσωπα δεν ξεχνιούνται. Μπορούν να επικοινωνήσουν μαζί μου μέσω της διεύθυνσης ηλεκτρονικού ταχυδρομείου του εκδότη μου, mtwpublications@gmail.com

Simon Hepworth, Ιούλιος 2022

About the Author - Σχετικά με τον Συγγραφέα

Simon Hepworth has spent his working life in aviation and policing. His father served in the Royal Navy's Fleet Air Arm and then joined British European Airways in 1961.

After gaining a degree in International Transport Management, Simon worked as a Technical Sales Engineer for British Aerospace, before moving into the airline industry with Orion Airways, operating charter flights to the Mediterranean. After developing his career in general aviation, including holding an Air Operator's Certificate for a commercial balloon rides company, he changed his career direction and joined the police service.

His policing experience included general duties, investigating a wide range of crimes, then setting up a policing team at a major regional airport in the UK. A spell in criminal and public order intelligence followed, after which he moved into police air support. He left the policing ranks in 2018, and now works as a civilian staff member in police aviation.

In his spare time, Simon has written and published a number of books, primarily covering RAF Bomber Command and the strategic bombing offensive against Germany in 1939-45. He is now working on a comprehensive study of British civil air accident investigations.

Married to Mandy, he lives in South Wales.

Ο Simon Hepworth έχει περάσει την επαγγελματική του ζωή στην αεροπορία και την αστυνόμευση. Ο πατέρας του υπηρέτησε στο Fleet Air Arm του Βασιλικού Ναυτικού και στη συνέχεια εντάχθηκε στην British European Airways το 1961.

Αφού απέκτησε πτυχίο στη Διοίκηση Διεθνών Μεταφορών, ο Simon εργάστηκε ως Τεχνικός Μηχανικός Πωλήσεων για τη British Aerospace, προτού μετακομίσει στον κλάδο των αεροπορικών εταιρειών με την Orion Airways, εκτελώντας πτήσεις τσάρτερ στη Μεσόγειο. Αφού ανέπτυξε τη σταδιοδρομία του στη γενική αεροπορία, συμπεριλαμβανομένης της κατοχής Πιστοποιητικού Αερομεταφορέα (Air Operator's Certificate) για μια εμπορική εταιρεία με αερόστατα, άλλαξε την κατεύθυνση της καριέρας του και εντάχθηκε στην αστυνομική υπηρεσία.

Η εμπειρία του στην αστυνόμευση περιελάμβανε γενικά καθήκοντα, διερεύνηση μεγάλου φάσματος εγκλημάτων και στη συνέχεια συγκρότηση ομάδας αστυνόμευσης σε μεγάλο περιφερειακό αεροδρόμιο στο Ηνωμένο Βασίλειο. Ακολούθως υπηρέτησε για ένα μικρό διάστημα στις πληροφορίες για την εγκληματική και δημόσια τάξη, μετά το οποίο πήγε στην αστυνομική εναέρια υποστήριξη. Έφυγε από τις τάξεις της αστυνομίας το 2018 και τώρα εργάζεται ως πολιτικός υπάλληλος στην αστυνομική αεροπορία.

Στον ελεύθερο χρόνο του, ο Simon έχει γράψει και δημοσιεύσει μια σειρά βιβλίων, που καλύπτουν κυρίως τη Διοίκηση των Βομβαρδιστικών της RAF και τη στρατηγική επίθεση βομβαρδισμών κατά της Γερμανίας το 1939-45. Τώρα εργάζεται σε μια ολοκληρωμένη μελέτη των βρετανικών ερευνών για πολιτικά αεροπορικά ατυχήματα.

Παντρεμένος με τη Mandy, ζει στη Νότια Ουαλία.

www.ingramcontent.com/pod-product-compliance
Lightning Source LLC
Chambersburg PA
CBHW050121170426
43197CB00011B/1663